The Waverley Novels

VOLUME SIXTEEN

QUENTIN DURWARD

BY
Sir WALTER SCOTT, Bart.

ILLUSTRATED

NEW YORK
P. F. COLLIER & SON
MCMII

List of Illustrations

VOLUME SIXTEEN

QUENTIN DURWARD

Quentin Durward...*Frontispiece*

Louis XI., King of France..

Charles the Bold, Duke of Burgundy..............................

" 'There lies my gage, in evidence of what I have said' "...............

" 'These news, fair cousin, have staggered your reason' "..............

QUENTIN DURWARD

QUENTIN DURWARD.

Quentin Durward, Frontis.

QUENTIN DURWARD.

La guerre est ma patrie,
 Mon harnois ma maison
 Et en toute saison
 Combattre c'est ma vie.

INTRODUCTION TO QUENTIN DURWARD.

The scene of this romance is laid in the 15th century, when the feudal system, which had been the sinews and nerves of national defence, and the spirit of chivalry, by which, as by a vivifying soul, that system was animated, began to be innovated upon and abandoned by those grosser characters who centred their sum of happiness in procuring the personal objects on which they had fixed their own exclusive attachment. The same egotism had indeed displayed itself even in more primitive ages; but it was now for the first time openly avowed as a professed principle of action. The spirit of chivalry had in it this point of excellence, that however overstrained and fantastic many of its doctrines may appear to us, they were all founded on generosity and self-denial, of which if the earth were deprived, it would be difficult to conceive the existence of virtue among the human race.

Among those who were the first to ridicule and abandon the self-denying principles in which the young knight was instructed, and to which he was so carefully trained up, Louis the Eleventh of France was the chief. That sovereign was of a character so purely selfish—so guiltless of entertaining any purpose unconnected with his ambition, covetousness, and desire of selfish enjoyment, that he almost seems an incarnation of the devil himself, permitted to do his utmost to corrupt our ideas of honour in its very source. Nor is it to be forgotten that Louis possessed to a great extent that caustic wit which can turn into ridicule all that a man does for any other person's advantage but his own, and was, therefore, peculiarly qualified to play the part of a cold-hearted and sneering fiend.

In this point of view, Goethe's conception of the character and reasoning of Mephistophiles, the tempting spirit in the singular play of *Faust*, appears to me more happy than that which has been formed by Byron, and even than the Satan of Milton. These last great authors have given to the Evil Principle something which elevates and dignifies his wickedness— a sustained and unconquerable resistance again Omnipotence itself, a lofty scorn of suffering compared with submission, and all those points of attraction in the Author of Evil which have induced Burns and others to consider him as the hero of the *Paradise Lost*. The great German poet has, on the contrary, rendered his seducing spirit a being who, otherwise totally unimpassioned, seems only to have existed for the purpose of increasing, by his persuasions and temptations, the mass of moral evil, and who calls forth by his seductions those slumbering passions which otherwise might have allowed the human being who was the object of the evil spirit's operations to pass the tenor of his life in tranquillity. For this purpose Mephistophiles is, like Louis XI., endowed with an acute and depreciating spirit of caustic wit, which is employed incessantly in undervaluing and vilifying all actions the consequences of which do not lead certainly and directly to self-gratification.

Even an author of works of mere amusement may be permitted to be serious for a moment, in order to reprobate all policy, whether of a public or private character, which rests its basis upon the principles of Machiavel or the practice of Louis XI.

The cruelties, the perjuries, the suspicions of this prince were rendered more detestable, rather than amended, by the gross and debasing superstition which he constantly practised. The devotion to the Heavenly saints, of which he made such a parade, was upon the miserable principle of some petty deputy in office, who endeavours to hide or atone for the malversations of which he is conscious, by liberal gifts to those whose duty it is to observe his conduct, and endeavours to support a system of fraud by an attempt to corrupt the incorruptible. In no other light can we regard his creating the Virgin Mary a countess and colonel of his guards, or the cunning that admitted to one or two peculiar forms of oaths the force of a binding obligation which he denied to all others, strictly preserving the secret, which mode of swearing he really accounted obligatory, as one of the most valuable of state mysteries.

To a total want of scruple, or, it would appear, of any sense whatever of moral obligation, Louis XI. added great natural firmness and sagacity of character, with a system of policy so highly refined, considering the times he lived in, that he sometimes overreached himself by giving way to its dictates.

Probably there is no portrait so dark as to be without its softer shades. He understood the interests of France, and faithfully pursued them so long as he could identify them with his own. He carried the country safe through the dangerous crisis of the war termed for "the public good"; in thus disuniting and dispersing this grand and dangerous alliance of the great crown vassals of France against the sovereign, a king of a less cautious and temporising character, and of a more bold and less crafty disposition, than Louis XI. would, in all probability, have failed. Louis had also some personal accomplishments not inconsistent with his public character. He was cheerful and witty in society; caressed his victim like the cat, which can fawn when about to deal the most bitter wound; and none was better able to sustain and extol the superiority of the coarse and selfish reasons by which he endeavoured to supply those nobler motives for exertion which his predecessors had derived from the high spirit of chivalry.

In fact that system was now becoming ancient, and had, even while in its perfection, something so overstrained and fantastic in its principles, as rendered it peculiarly the object of ridicule, whenever, like other old fashions, it began to fall out of repute, and the weapons of raillery could be employed against it, without exciting the disgust and horror with which they would have been rejected at an early period as a species of blasphemy. In the 14th century a tribe of scoffers had arisen who pretended to supply what was naturally useful in chivalry by other resources, and threw ridicule upon the extravagant and exclusive principles of honour and virtue which were openly treated as absurd, because, in fact, they were cast in a mould of perfection too lofty for the practice of fallible beings. If an ingenuous and high-spirited youth proposed to frame himself on his father's principles of honour, he was vulgarly derided as if he had brought to the field the good old knight's Durindarte or two-handed sword, ridiculous from its antique make and fashion, although its blade might be the Ebro's temper, and its ornaments of pure gold.

In like manner, the principles of chivalry were cast aside, and their aid supplied by baser stimulants. Instead of the high spirit which pressed every man forward in the defence of his country, Louis XI. substituted the exertions of the ever ready mercenary soldier, and persuaded his subjects, among whom the mercantile class began to make a figure, that it was better to leave to mercenaries the risks and labours of war, and to supply the crown with the means of paying them, than to peril themselves in defence of their own substance. The merchants were easily persuaded by this reasoning. The hour did not arrive, in the days of Louis XI., when the landed gentry and nobles could be in like manner excluded from the ranks of war; but the wily monarch commenced that system, which, acted upon by his successors, at length threw the whole military defence of the state into the hands of the crown.

He was equally forward in altering the principles which were wont to regulate the intercourse of the sexes. The doctrines of chivalry had established in theory, at least, a system in which Beauty was the governing and remunerating divinity, Valour her slave, who caught his courage from her eye, and gave his life for her slightest service. It is true, the system here, as in other branches, was stretched to fantastic extravagance, and cases of scandal not unfrequently arose. Still they were generally such as those mentioned by Burke, where frailty was deprived of half its guilt by being purified from all its grossness. In Louis XI.'s practice, it was far otherwise. He was a low voluptuary, seeking pleasure without sentiment, and despising the sex from whom he desired to obtain it; his mistresses were of inferior rank, as little to be compared with the elevated though faulty character of Agnes Sorel, as Louis was to his heroic father, who freed France from the threatening yoke of England. In like manner, by selecting his favourites and ministers from among the dregs of the people, Louis showed the slight regard which he paid to eminent station and high birth; and although this might be not only excusable but meritorious, where the monarch's fiat promoted obscure talent, or called forth modest worth, it was very different when the King made his favourite associates of such men as Tristan l'Hermite, the chief of his marshalsea or police; and it was evident that such a prince could no longer be, as his descendant Francis elegantly designed himself, "the first gentleman in his dominions."

Nor were Louis's sayings and actions, in private or public, of a kind which could redeem such gross offences against the character of a man of honour. His word, generally accounted the most sacred test of a man's character, and the least impeachment of which is a capital offence by the code of honour, was forfeited without scruple on the slightest occasion, and often accompanied by the perpetration of the most enormous crimes. If he broke his own personal and plighted faith, he did not treat that of the public with more ceremony. His sending an inferior person disguised as a herald to Edward IV. was in those days, when heralds were esteemed the sacred depositaries of public and national faith, a daring imposition, of which few save this unscrupulous prince would have been guilty.[1]

In short, the manners, sentiments, and actions of Louis XI. were such as were inconsistent with the principles of chivalry, and his caustic wit was sufficiently disposed to ridicule a system adopted on what he considered as the most absurd of all bases, since it was founded on the principle of devoting toil, talents, and time to the accomplishment of objects from which no personal advantage could, in the nature of things, be obtained.

It is more than probable that, in thus renouncing almost openly the ties of religion, honour, and morality, by which mankind at large feel themselves influenced, Louis sought to

[1] See Note 46.

obtain great advantages in his negotiations with parties who might esteem themselves bound, while he himself enjoyed liberty. He started from the goal, he might suppose, like the racer who has got rid of the the weights with which his competitors are still encumbered, and expects to succeed of course. But Providence seems always to unite the existence of peculiar danger with some circumstance which may put those exposed to the peril upon their guard. The constant suspicion attached to any public person who becomes badly eminent for breach of faith is to him what the rattle is to the poisonous serpent; and men come at last to calculate, not so much on what their antagonist says, as upon that which he is likely to do; a degree of mistrust which tends to counteract the intrigues of such a faithless character more than his freedom from the scruples of conscientious men can afford him advantage. The example of Louis XI. raised disgust and suspicion rather than a desire of imitation among other nations in Europe, and the circumstance of his outwitting more than one of his contemporaries operated to put others on their guard. Even the system of chivalry, though much less generally extended than heretofore, survived this profligate monarch's reign, who did so much to sully its lustre, and long after the death of Louis XI. it inspired the Knight without Fear and Reproach and the gallant Francis I.

Indeed, although the reign of Louis had been as successful in a political point of view as he himself could have desired, the spectacle of his death-bed might of itself be a warning-piece against the seduction of his example. Jealous of every one, but chiefly of his own son, he immured himself in his Castle of Plessis, entrusting his person exclusively to the doubtful faith of his Scottish mercenaries. He never stirred from his chamber, he admitted no one into it; and wearied Heaven and every saint with prayers, not for the forgiveness of his sins, but for the prolongation of his life. With a poverty of spirit totally inconsistent with his shrewd worldly sagacity, he importuned his physicians until they insulted as well as plundered him. In his extreme desire of life, he sent to Italy for supposed relics, and the yet more extraordinary importation of an ignorant crack-brained peasant, who, from laziness probably, had shut himself up in a cave, and renounced flesh, fish, eggs, or the produce of the dairy. This man, who did not possess the slightest tincture of letters, Louis reverenced as if he had been the Pope himself, and to gain his good-will founded two cloisters.

It was not the least singular circumstance of this course of superstition that bodily health and terrestrial felicity seemed to be his only objects. Making any mention of his sins when talking on the state of his health was strictly prohibited; and when at his command a priest recited a prayer to St. Eutropius, in which he recommended the King's welfare both in body and soul, Louis caused the two last words to be omitted, saying it was not prudent to importune the blessed saint by too many requests at once. Perhaps he thought by being silent on his crimes, he might suffer them to pass out of the recollection of the celestial patrons, whose aid he invoked for his body.

So great were the well-merited tortures of this tyrant's death-bed, that Philip des Comines enters into a regular comparison between them and the numerous cruelties inflicted on others by his order; and, considering both, comes to express an opinion, that the worldly pangs and agony suffered by Louis were such as might compensate the crimes he had committed, and that, after a reasonable quarantine in purgatory, he might in mercy be found duly qualified for the superior regions.

Fénelon also has left his testimony against this prince, whose mode of living and governing he has described in the following remarkable passage:

Pygmalion, tourmenté par une soif insatiable des richesses, se rend de plus en plus misérable et odieux à ses sujets. C'est un crime à Tyr que d'avoir de grands biens; l'avarice le rend défiant, soupçonneux, cruel; il persécute les riches, et il craint les pauvres.

C'est un crime encore plus grand à Tyr d'avoir de la vertu; car Pygmalion suppose que les bons ne peuvent souffrir ses injustices et ses infamies; la vertu le condamne; il s'aigrit et s'irrite contre elle. Tout l'agite, l'inquiète, le ronge; il a peur de son ombre; il ne dort ni nuit ni jour; les Dieux, pour le confondre, l'accablent de trésors dont il n'ose jouir. Ce qu'il cherche pour être heureux est précisément ce qui l'empêche de l'être. Il regrette tout ce qu'il donne ; il craint toujours de perdre ; il se tourmente pour gagner.

On ne le voit presque jamais ; il est seul, triste, abattu, au fond de son palais ; ses amis mêmes n'osent l'aborder, de peur de lui devenir suspects. Une garde terrible tient toujours des épées nues et des piques levées autour de sa maison. Trente chambres qui communiquent les unes aux autres, et dont chacune a une porte de fer avec six gros verroux, sont le lieu où il se renferme ; on ne sait jamais dans laquelle de ces chambres il couche ; et on assure qu'il ne couche jamais deux nuits de suite dans la même, de peur d'y être égorgé. Il ne connoît ni les doux plaisirs, ni l'amitié encore plus douce. Si on lui parle de chercher la joie, il sent qu'elle fuit loin de lui, et qu'elle refuse d'entrer dans son cœur. Ses yeux creux sont pleins d'un feu âpre et farouche ; ils sont sans cesse errans de tous cotés ; il prête l'oreille au moindre bruit, et se sent tout ému ; il est pâle, défait, et les noirs soucis sont peints sur son visage toujours ridé. Il se tait, il soupire, il tire de son cœur de profonds gémissemens, il ne peut cacher les remords qui déchirent ses entrailles. Les mets les plus exquis le dégoûtent. Ses enfans, loin d'être son espérance, sont le sujet de sa terreur : il en a fait ses plus dangereux ennemis. Il n'a eu toute sa vie aucun moment d'assuré : il ne se conserve qu'à force de répandre le sang de tous ceux qu'il craint. Insensé, qui ne voit pas que sa cruauté, à laquelle il se confie, le fera périr ! Quelqu'un de ses domestiques, aussi défiant que lui, se hâtera de délivrer le monde de ce monstre.

The instructive but appalling scene of this tyrant's sufferings was at length closed by death, 30th August 1483.

The selection of this remarkable person as the principal character in the romance—for it will be easily comprehended that the little love intrigue of Quentin is only employed as the means of bringing out the story—afforded considerable facilities to the Author. The whole of Europe was, during the 15th century, convulsed with dissensions from such various causes, that it would have required almost a dissertation to have brought the English reader with a mind perfectly alive and prepared to admit the possibility of the strange scenes to which he was introduced.

In Louis XI.'s time, extraordinary commotions existed throughout all Europe. England's civil wars were ended rather in appearance than reality by the short-lived ascendency of the house of York. Switzerland was asserting that freedom which was afterwards so bravely defended. In the Empire and in France the great vassals of the crown were endeavouring to emancipate themselves from its control, while Charles of Burgundy by main force, and Louis more artfully by indirect means, laboured to subject them to subservience to their respective sovereignties. Louis, while with one hand he circumvented and subdued his own rebellious vassals, laboured secretly with the other to aid and encourage the large trading towns of Flanders to rebel against the Duke of Burgundy, to which their wealth and irritability naturally disposed them. In the more woodland districts of Flanders, the Duke of Gueldres, and William de la Marck, called from his ferocity the Wild Boar of Ardennes, were throwing off the habits of knights and gentlemen, to practise the violences and brutalities of common bandits.

A hundred secret combinations existed in the different provinces of France and Flanders; numerous private emissaries of the restless Louis—Bohemians, pilgrims, beggars, or agents disguised as such—were everywhere spreading the discontent which it was his policy to maintain in the dominions of Burgundy.

Amidst so great an abundance of materials, it was difficult to select such as should be most intelligible and interesting to the reader; and the Author had to regret that, though he made liberal use of the power of departing from the reality of history, he felt by no means confident of having brought his story into a pleasing, compact, and sufficiently intelligible form. The mainspring of the plot is that which all who know the least of the feudal system can easily understand, though the facts are absolutely fictitious. The right of a feudal superior was in nothing more universally acknowledged than in his power to interfere in the marriage of a female vassal. This may appear to exist as a contradiction both of the civil and canon law, which declare that marriage shall be free, while the feudal or municipal jurisprudence, in case of a fief passing to a female, acknowledges an interest in the superior of the fief to dictate the choice of her companion in marriage. This is accounted for on the principle that the superior was, by his bounty, the original grantor of the fief, and is still interested that the marriage of the vassal shall place no one there who may be inimical to his liege lord. On the other hand, it might be reasonably pleaded that this right of dictating to the vassal, to a certain extent, in the choice of a husband is only competent to the superior from whom the fief is originally derived. There is therefore no violent improbability in a vassal of Burgundy flying to the protection of the King of France, to whom the Duke of Burgundy himself was vassal; nor is it a great stretch of probability to affirm, that Louis, unscrupulous as he was, should have formed the design of betraying the fugitive into some alliance which might prove inconvenient, if not dangerous, to his formidable kinsman and vassal of Burgundy.

I may add, that the romance of *Quentin Durward*, which acquired a popularity at home more extensive than some of its predecessors, found also unusual success on the continent,[1] where the historical allusions awakened more familiar ideas.

ABBOTSFORD, *1st December 1831.*

[1] [See Lockhart's *Life of Scott*, vol. vii. pp. 161-167.]

INTRODUCTION TO FIRST EDITION.[1]

And one who hath had losses—go to!
Much Ado About Nothing.

WHEN honest Dogberry sums up and recites all the claims which he had to respectability, and which, as he opined, ought to have exempted him from the injurious appellation conferred on him by Master Gentleman Conrade, it is remarkable that he lays not more emphasis even upon his double gown (a matter of some importance in a certain *ci-devant* capital which I wot of), or upon his being "a pretty piece of flesh as any in Messina," or even upon the conclusive argument of his being "a *rich* fellow enough," than upon his being one "*that hath had losses.*"

Indeed, I have always observed your children of prosperity, whether by way of hiding their full glow of splendour from those whom fortune has treated more harshly, or whether that to have risen in spite of calamity is as honourable to their fortune as it is to a fortress to have undergone a siege,—however this be, I have observed that such persons never fail to entertain you with an account of the damage they sustain by the hardness of the times. You seldom dine at a well-supplied table, but the intervals between the champagne, the burgundy, and the hock are filled, if your entertainer be a monied man, with the fall of interest and the difficulty of finding investments for cash, which is therefore lying idle on his hands; or, if he be a landed proprietor, with a woful detail of arrears and diminished rents. This hath its effects. The guests sigh and shake their heads in cadence with their landlord, look on the sideboard loaded with plate, sip once

[1] It is scarcely necessary to say, that all that follows is imaginary.

more the rich wines which flow around them in quick circulation, and think of the genuine benevolence, which, thus stinted of its means, still lavishes all that it yet possesses on hospitality, and, what is yet more flattering, on the wealth, which, undiminished by these losses, still continues, like the inexhaustible hoard of the generous Aboulcasem, to sustain, without impoverishment, such copious drains.

This querulous humour, however, hath its limits, like to the conning of grievances, which all valetudinarians know is a most fascinating pastime, so long as there is nothing to complain of but chronic complaints. But I never heard a man whose credit was actually verging to decay talk of the diminution of his funds; and my kind and intelligent physician assures me, that it is a rare thing with those afflicted with a good rousing fever, or any such active disorder, which

<blockquote>With mortal crisis doth pretend
His life to appropinque an end,</blockquote>

to make their agonies the subject of amusing conversation.

Having deeply considered all these things, I am no longer able to disguise from my readers that I am neither so unpopular nor so low in fortune as not to have my share in the distresses which at present afflict the monied and landed interest of these realms. Your authors who live upon a mutton chop may rejoice that it has fallen to threepence per pound, and, if they have children, gratulate themselves that the peck-loaf may be had for sixpence; but we who belong to the tribe which is ruined by peace and plenty—we who have lands and beeves, and sell what these poor gleaners must buy—we are driven to despair by the very events which would make all Grub Street illuminate its attics, if Grub Street could spare candle-ends for the purpose. I therefore put in my proud claim to share in the distresses which only affect the wealthy; and write myself down, with Dogberry, "a rich fellow enough," but still one "who hath had losses."

With the same generous spirit of emulation, I have had lately recourse to the universal remedy for the brief impecuniosity of which I complain—a brief residence in a southern climate, by which I have not only saved many cart-loads of coals, but have also had the pleasure to excite general sympathy for my decayed circumstances among those who, if my revenue had continued to be spent among them, would have cared little if I had been hanged. Thus, while I drink my *vin ordinaire*, my brewer finds the sale of his small-beer diminished—while I discuss my flask of *cinq francs*, my modicum of port hangs on my wine-merchant's hands—while my *côtelette à la Maintenon* is smoking on my plate, the mighty sirloin hangs on its peg in the shop of my blue-aproned friend in the village. Whatever, in short, I spend here is missed at home; and the few sous gained by the *garçon perruquier*, nay, the very crust I give to his little bare-bottomed, red-eyed poodle, are *autant de perdu* to my old friend the barber, and honest Trusty, the mastiff-dog in the yard. So that I have the happiness of knowing at every turn that my absence is both missed and moaned by those who would care little were I in my coffin, were they sure of the custom of my executors. From this charge of self-seeking and indifference, however, I solemnly except Trusty, the yard-dog, whose courtesies towards me, I have reason to think, were of a more disinterested character than those of any other person who assisted me to consume the bounty of the public.

Alas! the advantage of exciting such general sympathies at home cannot be secured without incurring considerable personal inconvenience. "If thou wishest me to weep, thou must first shed tears thyself," says Horace; and, truly, I could sometimes cry myself at the exchange I have made of the domestic comforts which custom had rendered necessaries for the foreign substitutes which caprice and love of change had rendered fashionable. I cannot but confess with shame, that my homebred stomach longs for the genuine steak, after the fashion of Dolly's, hot from the gridiron, brown without, and scarlet when the knife is applied; and that all the delicacies of Very's *carte*, with his thousand various orthographies of *bifticks de mouton*, do not supply the vacancy. Then my mother's son cannot learn to delight in thin potations; and, in these days when malt is had for nothing, I am convinced that a double "straick" of John Barleycorn must have converted "the poor domestic creature, small-beer," into a liquor twenty times more generous than the acid unsubstantial tipple which here bears the honoured name of wine, though, in substance and qualities, much similar to your Seine water. Their higher wines, indeed, are well enough—there is nothing to except against in their Château Margout, or Sillery; yet I cannot but remember the generous qualities of my sound old Oporto. Nay, down to the *garçon* and his poodle, though they are both amusing animals, and play ten thousand monkey tricks which are diverting enough, yet there was more sound humour in the wink with which our village Packwood used to communicate the news of the morning than all Antoine's gambols could have expressed in a week, and more of human and dog-like sympathy in the wag of old Trusty's tail than if his rival, Touton, had stood on his hind-legs for a twelvemonth.

These signs of repentance come perhaps a little late, and I own, for I must be entirely candid with my dear friend the public, that they have been somewhat matured by the perversion of my niece Christy to the ancient Popish faith by a certain whacking priest in our neighbourhood, and the marriage of my aunt Dorothy to a *demi-solde* captain of horse, a *ci-devant* member of the Legion of Honour, and who would, he assures us, have been a field-marshal by this time, had our old friend Bonaparte continued to live and to triumph. For the matter of Christy, I must own her head had been so fairly turned at Edinburgh with five routs a-night, that, though I somewhat distrusted the means and medium of her conversation, I was at the same time glad to see that she took a serious thought of any kind; besides, there was little loss in the matter, for the convent took her off my hands for a very reasonable pension. But aunt Dorothy's marriage on earth was a very different matter from Christian's celestial espousals. In the first place, there were two thousand three per cents as much lost to my family as if the sponge had been drawn over the national slate, for who the deuce could have thought aunt Dorothy would have married? Above all, who would have thought a woman of fifty years' experience would have married a French anatomy, his lower branch of limbs corresponding with the upper branch, as if one pair of half-extended compasses had been placed perpendicularly upon the top of another, while the space on which the hinges revolved quite sufficed to represent the body? All the rest was mustache, pelisse, and calico trowser. She might have commanded a polk of real Cossacks in 1815, for half the wealth which she surrendered to this military scarecrow. However, there is no more to be said upon the matter, especially as she had come the length of quoting Rousseau for sentiment; and so let that pass.

Having thus expectorated my bile against a land which is, notwithstanding, a very merry land, and which I cannot blame, because I sought it and it did not seek me, I come to the more immediate purpose of this Introduction, and which, my dearest public, if I do not reckon too much on the continuance of your favours (though, to say truth, consistency and uniformity of taste are scarce to be reckoned upon by those who court your good graces) may perhaps go far to make me amends for the loss and damage I have sustained by bringing aunt Dorothy to the country of thick calves, slender ankles, black mustachios, bodiless limbs (I assure you the fellow is, as my friend Lord L—— said, a complete giblet-pie, all legs and wings), and fine sentiments. If she had taken from the half-pay list a ranting Highlandman, ay, or a dashing son of Erin, I would never have mentioned the subject; but as the affair has happened, it is scarce possible not to resent such a gratuitous plundering of her own lawful heirs and executors. But "be hushed, my dark spirit!" and let us invite our dear public to a more pleasing theme to us, a more interesting one to others.

By dint of drinking acid tiff, as above mentioned, and smoking cigars, in which I am no novice, my public are to be informed that I gradually sipped and smoked myself into a certain degree of acquaintance with *un homme comme il faut*, one of the few fine old specimens of nobility who are still to be found in France, who, like mutilated statues of an antiquated and obsolete worship, still command a certain portion of awe and estimation in the eyes even of those by whom neither one nor other are voluntarily rendered.

On visiting the coffee-house of the village, I was at first struck with the singular dignity and gravity of this gentleman's manners, his sedulous attachment to shoes and stockings in contempt of half-boots and pantaloons, the *croix de St. Louis* at his button-hole, and a small white cockade in the loop of his old-fashioned *schakos*. There was something interesting in his whole appearance; and besides, his gravity among the lively group around him seemed like the shade of a tree in the glare of a sunny landscape, more interesting from its rarity. I made such advances towards acquaintance as the circumstances of the place and the manners of the country authorised—that is to say, I drew near him, smoked my cigar by calm and intermitted puffs, which were scarcely visible, and asked him those few questions which good-breeding everywhere, but more especially in France, permits strangers to put without hazarding the imputation of impertinence. The Marquis de Hautlieu, for such was his rank, was as short and sententious as French politeness permitted. He answered every question, but proposed nothing, and encouraged no farther inquiry.

The truth was, that, not very accessible to foreigners of any nation, or even to strangers among his own countrymen, the marquis was peculiarly shy towards the English. A remnant of ancient national prejudices might dictate this feeling; or it might arise from his idea that they are a haughty, purse-proud people, to whom rank, united with straitened circumstances, affords as much subject for scorn as for pity; or, finally, when he reflected on certain recent events, he might perhaps feel mortified as a Frenchman even for those successes which had restored his master to the throne and himself to a diminished property and dilapidated *château*. His dislike, however, never assumed a more active form than that of alienation from English society. When the affairs of strangers required the interposition of his influence in their behalf, it was uniformly granted with the courtesy of a French gentleman who knew what is due to himself and to national hospitality.

At length, by some chance, the marquis made the discovery that the new frequenter of his ordinary was a native of Scotland—a circumstance which told mightily in my favour. Some of his own ancestors, he informed me, had been of Scottish origin, and he believed his house had still some relations in what he was pleased to call the province of Hanguisse in that country. The connexion had been acknowledged early in the last century on both sides, and he had once almost determined during his exile (for it may be supposed that the marquis had joined the ranks of Condé, and shared all the misfortunes and distresses of emigration) to claim the acquaintance and protection of his Scottish friends. But after all, he said, he cared not to present himself before them in circumstances which could do them but small credit, and which they might think entailed some little burden, perhaps even some little disgrace; so that he thought it best to trust in Providence and do the best he could for his own support. What that was I never could learn; but I am sure it inferred nothing which could be discreditable to the excellent old man, who held fast his opinions and his loyalty, through good and bad repute, till time restored him, aged, indigent, and broken-spirited, to the country which he had left in the prime of youth and health, and sobered by age into patience, instead of that tone of high resentment which promised speedy vengeance upon those who expelled him. I might have laughed at some points of the marquis's character, at his prejudices particularly, both of birth and politics, if I had known him under more prosperous circumstances; but, situated as he was, even if they had not been fair and honest prejudices, turning on no base or interested motive, one must have respected him as we respect the confessor or the martyr of a religion which is not entirely our own.

By degrees we became good friends, drank our coffee, smoked our cigar, and took our *bavaroise* together, for more than six weeks, with little interruption from avocations on either side. Having with some difficulty got the key-note of his inquiries concerning Scotland, by a fortunate conjecture that the *province d'Hanguisse* could only be our shire of Angus, I was enabled to answer the most of his queries concerning his allies there in a manner more or less satisfactory, and was much surprised to find the marquis much better acquainted with the genealogy of some of the distinguished families in that country than I could possibly have expected.

On his part his satisfaction at our intercourse was so great that he at length wound himself to such a pitch of resolution as to invite me to dine at the Château de Hautlieu, well deserving the name, as occupying a commanding eminence on the banks of the Loire. This building lay about three miles from the town at which I had settled my temporary establishment; and when I first beheld it I could easily forgive the mortified feelings which the owner testified at receiving a guest in the asylum which he had formed out of the ruins of the palace of his fathers. He gradually, with much gaiety, which yet evidently covered a deeper feeling, prepared me for the sort of place I was about to visit; and for this he had full opportunity whilst he drove me in his little cabriolet, drawn by a large heavy Norman horse, towards the ancient building.

Its remains run along a beautiful terrace overhanging the river Loire, which had been formerly laid out with a succession of flights of steps, highly ornamented with statues, rockwork, and other artificial embellishments, descending from one terrace to another until the very verge of the river was attained. All this architectural decoration, with its accompanying parterres of rich flowers and exotic shrubs, had, many years since, given place to the more profitable scene of the vine-dresser's labours; yet the remains, too massive to be destroyed, are still visible, and, with the various artificial slopes and levels of the high bank, bear perfect evidence how actively art had been here employed to decorate nature.

Few of these scenes are now left in perfection; for the fickleness of fashion had accomplished in England the total change which devastation and popular fury have produced in the French pleasure-grounds. For my part, I am contented to subscribe to the opinion of the best qualified judge of our time,[1] who thinks we have carried to an extreme our taste for simplicity, and that the neighbourhood of a stately mansion

[1] See Price on the Picturesque. Note 1.

requires some more ornate embellishments than can be derived from the meagre accompaniments of grass and gravel. A highly romantic situation may be degraded, perhaps, by an attempt at such artificial ornaments; but then, in by far the greater number of sites, the intervention of more architectural decoration than is now in use seems necessary to redeem the naked tameness of a large house, placed by itself in the midst of a lawn, where it looks as much unconnected with all around as if it had walked out of town upon an airing.

How the taste came to change so suddenly and absolutely is rather a singular circumstance, unless we explain it on the same principle on which the three friends of the father in Molière's comedy recommend a cure for the melancholy of his daughter — that he should furnish her apartments, viz. with paintings, with tapestry, or with china, according to the different commodities in which each of them was a dealer. Tried by this scale, we may perhaps discover that, of old, the architect laid out the garden and the pleasure-grounds in the neighbourhood of the mansion, and, naturally enough, displayed his own art there in statues and vases, and paved terraces and flights of steps, with ornamented balustrades; while the gardener, subordinate in rank, endeavoured to make the vegetable kingdom correspond to the prevailing taste, and cut his evergreens into verdant walls, with towers and battlements, and his detached trees into a resemblance of statuary. But the wheel has since revolved, so as to place the landscape-gardener, as he is called, almost upon a level with the architect; and hence a liberal and somewhat violent use is made of spade and pick-axe, and a conversion of the ostentatious labours of the architect into a *ferme ornée*, as little different from the simplicity of nature, as displayed in the surrounding country, as the comforts of convenient and cleanly walks imperiously demanded in the vicinage of a gentleman's residence can possibly admit.

To return from this digression, which has given the marquis's cabriolet (its activity greatly retarded by the downward propensities of Jean Roast-Beef, which I suppose the Norman horse cursed as heartily as his countrymen of old time execrated the stolid obesity of a Saxon slave) time to ascend the hill by a winding causeway, now much broken, we came in sight of a long range of roofless buildings connected with the western extremity of the castle, which was totally ruinous. "I should apologise," he said, "to you, as an Englishman, for the taste of my ancestors, in connecting that row of stables with the architecture of the château. I know in your country it is usual to remove them to some distance; but my family had an hereditary pride in horses, and were fond of visiting them more frequently than would have been convenient if they had been kept at a greater distance. Before the Revolution I had thirty fine horses in that ruinous line of buildings."

This recollection of past magnificence escaped from him accidentally, for he was generally sparing in alluding to his former opulence. It was quietly said, without any affectation either of the importance attached to early wealth, or as demanding sympathy for its having passed away. It awakened unpleasing reflections, however, and we were both silent, till, from a partially repaired corner of what had been a porter's lodge, a lively French *paysanne*, with eyes as black as jet and as brilliant as diamonds, came out with a smile, which showed a set of teeth that duchesses might have envied, and took the reins of the little carriage.

"Madelon must be groom to-day," said the marquis, after graciously nodding in return for her deep reverence to Monsieur, "for her husband is gone to market; and for La Jeunesse, he is almost distracted with his various occupations. Madelon," he continued, as we walked forward under the entrance-arch, crowned with the mutilated armorial bearings of former lords, now half-obscured by moss and rye-grass, not to mention the vagrant branches of some unpruned shrubs— "Madelon was my wife's god-daughter, and was educated to be *fille-de-chambre* to my daughter."

This passing intimation, that he was a widowed husband and childless father, increased my respect for the unfortunate nobleman, to whom every particular attached to his present situation brought doubtless its own share of food for melancholy reflection. He proceeded, after the pause of an instant, with something of a gayer tone: "You will be entertained with my poor La Jeunesse," he said, "who, by the way, is ten years older than I am (the marquis is above sixty); he reminds me of the player in the *Roman Comique*, who acted a whole play in his own proper person: he insists on being *maître d'hôtel, maître de cuisine, valet-de-chambre,* a whole suite of attendants in his own poor individuality. He sometimes reminds me of a character in the *Bridle of Lammermore*, which you must have read, as it is the work of one of your *gens de lettres, qu'on appelle, je crois, le Chevalier Scott.*"[1]

"I presume you mean Sir Walter?"

"Yes—the same—the same," answered the marquis.

We were now led away from more painful recollections; for I had to put my French friend right in two particulars. In the first I prevailed with difficulty; for the marquis, though he disliked the English, yet, having been three months in London, piqued himself on understanding the most intricate difficulties of our language, and appealed to every dictionary, from Florio downwards, that *la bride* must mean "the bridle." Nay, so sceptical was he on this point of philology that, when I ventured to hint that there was nothing about a bridle in the whole story, he with great composure, and little knowing to whom he spoke, laid the whole blame of that inconsistency on the unfortunate author. I had next the common candour to inform my friend, upon grounds which no one could know so well as myself, that my distinguished literary countryman, of whom I shall always speak with the respect his talents deserve, was not responsible for the slight works which the humour of the public had too generously, as well as too rashly, ascribed to him. Surprised by the impulse of the moment, I might even have gone farther, and clenched the negative by positive evidence, owning to my entertainer that no one else could possibly have written these works, since I myself was the author, when I was saved from so rash a commitment of myself by the calm reply of the marquis, that he was glad to

---

[1] It is scarce necessary to remind the reader that this passage was published during the Author's incognito; and, as Lucio expresses it, spoken "according to the trick."

hear these sort of trifles were not written by a person of condition. "We read them," he said, "as we listen to the pleasantries of a comedian, or as our ancestors did to those of a professed family-jester, with a good deal of amusement, which, however, we should be sorry to derive from the mouth of one who has better claims to our society."

I was completely recalled to my constitutional caution by this declaration; and became so much afraid of committing myself, that I did not even venture to explain to my aristocratic friend that the gentleman whom he had named owed his advancement, for aught I had ever heard, to certain works of his, which may, without injury, be compared to romances in rhyme.

The truth is, that amongst some other unjust prejudices, at which I have already hinted, the marquis had contracted a horror, mingled with contempt, for almost every species of author-craft slighter than that which compounds a folio volume of law or of divinity, and looked upon the author of a romance, novel, fugitive poem, or periodical piece of criticism as men do on a venomous reptile, with fear at once and with loathing. The abuse of the press, he contended, especially in its lighter departments, had poisoned the whole morality of Europe, and was once more gradually regaining an influence which had been silenced amidst the voice of war. All writers, except those of the largest and heaviest calibre, he conceived to be devoted to this evil cause, from Rousseau and Voltaire down to Pigault le Brun and the author of the Scotch novels; and although he admitted he read them *pour passer le temps*, yet, like Pistol eating his leek, it was not without execrating the tendency, as he devoured the story, of the work with which he was engaged.

Observing this peculiarity, I backed out of the candid confession which my vanity had meditated, and engaged the marquis in farther remarks on the mansion of his ancestors. "There," he said, "was the theatre where my father used to procure an order for the special attendance of some of the principal actors of the Comédie Française, when the King and Madame Pompadour more than once visited him at this place;

yonder, more to the centre, was the baron's hall, where his feudal jurisdiction was exercised when criminals were to be tried by the seigneur or his bailiff; for we had, like your old Scottish nobles, the right of pit and gallows, or *fossa cum furca*, as the civilians terms it. Beneath that lies the question-chamber, or apartment for torture; and, truly, I am sorry a right so liable to abuse should have been lodged in the hands of any living creature. But," he added, with a feeling of dignity derived even from the atrocities which his ancestors had committed beneath the grated windows to which he pointed, "such is the effect of superstition that, to this day, the peasants dare not approach the dungeons, in which, it is said, the wrath of my ancestors had perpetrated, in former times, much cruelty."

As we approached the window, while I expressed some curiosity to see this abode of terror, there arose from its subterranean abyss a shrill shout of laughter, which we easily detected as produced by a group of playful children, who had made the neglected vaults a theatre for a joyous romp at Colin Maillard.

The marquis was somewhat disconcerted, and had recourse to his *tabatière*; but, recovering in a moment, observed these were Madelon's children, and familiar with the supposed terrors of the subterranean recesses. "Besides," he added, "to speak the truth, these poor children have been born after the period of supposed illumination, which dispelled our superstition and our religion at once; and this bids me to remind you, that this is a *jour maigre*. The *curé* of the parish is my only guest, besides yourself, and I would not voluntarily offend his opinions. Besides," he continued, more manfully, and throwing off his restraint, "adversity has taught me other thoughts on these subjects than those which prosperity dictated; and I thank God I am not ashamed to avow that I follow the observances of my church."

I hastened to answer, that, though they might differ from those of my own, I had every possible respect for the religious rules of every Christian community, sensible that we addressed the same Deity, on the same grand principle of salvation, though with different forms; which variety of worship, had it pleased the Almighty not to permit, our observances would have been as distinctly prescribed to us as they are laid down under the Mosaic law.

The marquis was no shaker of hands, but upon the present occasion he grasped mine and shook it kindly—the only mode of acquiescence in my sentiments which perhaps a zealous Catholic could or ought consistently to have given upon such an occasion.

This circumstance of explanation and remark, with others which arose out of the view of the extensive ruins, occupied us during two or three turns upon the long terrace, and a seat of about a quarter of an hour's duration in a vaulted pavilion of freestone, decorated with the marquis's armorial bearings, the roof of which, though disjointed in some of its groined arches, was still solid and entire. "Here," said he, resuming the tone of a former part of his conversation, "I love to sit, either at noon, when the alcove affords me shelter from the heat, or in the evening, when the sun's beams are dying on the broad face of the Loire—here, in the words of your great poet, whom, Frenchman as I am, I am more intimately acquainted with than most Englishmen, I love to rest myself,

"Showing the code of sweet and bitter fancy."

Against this various reading of a well-known passage in Shakspeare I took care to offer no protest; for I suspect Shakspeare would have suffered in the opinion of so delicate a judge as the marquis, had I proved his having written "chewing the cud," according to all other authorities. Besides, I had had enough of our former dispute, having been long convinced (though not till ten years after I had left Edinburgh College) that the pith of conversation does not consist in exhibiting your own superior knowledge on matters of small consequence, but in enlarging, improving, and correcting the information you possess by the authority of othres. I therefore let the marquis *show* his *code* at his pleasure, and was rewarded by his entering into a learned and well-informed disquisition on the florid style of architecture introduced into France during the 17th century. He pointed out its merits and its defects with considerable taste; and having touched on topics similar to those upon which I have formerly digressed, he made an appeal of a different kind in their favour, founded on the associations with which they were combined. "Who," he said, "would willingly destroy the terraces of the château of Sully, since we cannot tread them without recalling the image of that statesman, alike distinguished for severe integrity and for strong and unerring sagacity of mind? Were they an inch less broad, a ton's weight less massive, or were they deprived of their formality by the slightest inflections, could we suppose them to remain the scene of his patriotic musings? Would an ordinary root-house be a fit scene for the duke occupying an arm-chair and his duchess a *tabouret*, teaching from thence lessons of courage and fidelity to his sons, of modesty and submission to his daughters, of rigid morality to both; while the circle of young *noblesse* listened with ears attentive, and eyes modestly fixed on the ground, in a standing posture, neither replying nor sitting down without the express command of their prince and parent? No, monsieur," he said, with enthusiasm; "destroy the princely pavilion in which this edifying family-scene was represented, and you remove from the mind the vraisemblance, the veracity, of the whole representation. Or can your mind suppose this distinguished peer and patriot walking in a *jardin Anglois*? Why, you might as well fancy him dressed with a blue frock and white waistcoat, instead of his Henry Quatre coat and *chapeau-à-plumes*. Consider how he could have moved in the tortuous maze of what you have called a *ferme ornée*, with his usual attendants of two files of Swiss guards preceding and the same number following him. To recall his figure, with his beard, *haut-de-chausses à canon*, united to his doublet by ten thousand *aiguilettes* and knots of ribbon, you could not, supposing him in a modern *jardin Anglois*, distinguish the picture in your imagination from the sketch of some mad old man, who has adopted the humour of dressing like his great-great-grandfather, and whom a party of *gens-d'armes* were conducting to the *hôpital des fous*. But look on the long and magnificent terrace, if it yet exists, which the loyal and exalted Sully was wont to make the scene of his solitary walk twice a-day, while he pondered over the patriotic schemes which he nourished for advancing the glory of France, or, at a later and more sorrowful period of life, brooded over the memory of his murdered master and the fate of his distracted country; throw in that noble background of arcades, vases, images, urns, and whatever could express the vicinity of a ducal palace, and the landscape becomes consistent at once. The *factionnaires*, with their harquebusses ported, placed at the extremities of the long and level walk, intimate the presence of the feudal prince; while the same is more clearly shown by the guard of honour which precede and follow him, their halberds carried upright, their mien martial and stately, as if in the presence of an enemy, yet moved, as it were, with the same soul as their princely superior; teaching their steps to attend upon his, marching as he marches, halting as he halts, accommodating their pace even to the slight irregularities of pause and advance dictated by the fluctuations of his reverie, and wheeling with military precision before and behind him, who seems the centre and animating principle of their armed files, as the heart gives life and energy to the human body. Or, if you smile," added the marquis, looking doubtfully on my countenance, "at a promenade so inconsistent with the light freedom of modern manners, could you bring your mind to demolish that other terrace trod by the fascinating Marchioness de Sévigné, with which are united so many recollections connected with passages in her enchanting letters?"

A little tired of this disquisition, which the marquis certainly dwelt upon to exalt the natural beauties of his own terrace, which, dilapidated as it was, required no such formal recommendation, I informed my companion that I had just received from England a journal of a tour made in the south of France by a young Oxonian friend of mine, a poet, a draughtsman, and a scholar, in which he gives such an animated and interesting description of the Château Grignan, the dwelling of Madame de Sévigné's beloved daughter, and frequently the place of her own residence, that no one who ever read the book would be within forty miles of the same without going a pilgrimage to the spot. The marquis smiled, seemed very much pleased, and asked the title at length of the work in question; and writing down to my dictation, *An Itinerary of Provence and the Rhone, made during the year 1819*,[1] by John Hughes, A.M., of Oriel College, Oxford, observed, he could now purchase no books for the château, but would recommend that the *Itinéraire* should be commissioned for the library to which he was *abonné* in the neighbouring town. "And here," he said, "comes the curé, to save us farther disquisition; and I see La Jeunesse gliding round the old portico on the terrace, with the purpose of ringing the dinner-bell—a most unnecessary ceremony for assembling three persons, but which it would break the old man's heart to forego. Take no notice of him at present, as he wishes to perform the duties of the inferior departments incognito; when the bell has ceased to sound, he will blaze forth on us in the character of major-domo."

As the marquis spoke, we had advanced towards the eastern extremity of the château, which was the only part of the edifice that remained still habitable.

"The *Bande Noire*," said the marquis, "when they pulled the rest of the house to pieces, for the sake of the lead, timber, and other materials, have, in their ravages, done me the undesigned favour to reduce it to dimensions better fitting the circumstances of the owner. There is enough of the leaf left for the caterpillar to coil up his chrysalis in, and what needs he care though reptiles have devoured the rest of the bush?"

As he spoke thus, we reached the door, at which La Jeunesse appeared, with an air at once of prompt service and deep respect, and a countenance which, though puckered by a thousand wrinkles, was ready to answer the first good-natured word of his master with a smile, which showed his white set of teeth firm and fair, in despite of age and suffering. His clean silk stockings, washed till their tint had become yellowish, his cue tied with a rosette, the thin grey curl on either side of his lank cheek, the pearl-coloured coat, without a col-

[1] See Hughes's *Itinerary*. Note 2.

lar, the solitaire, the *jabot*, the ruffles at the wrist, and the *chapeau-bras*—all announced that La Jeunesse considered the arrival of a guest at the château as an unusual event, which was to be met with a corresponding display of magnificence and parade on his part.

As I looked at the faithful though fantastic follower of his master, who doubtless inherited his prejudices as well as his cast-clothes, I could not but own, in my own mind, the resemblance pointed out by the marquis betwixt him and my own Caleb, the trusty squire of the Master of Ravenswood. But a Frenchman, a Jack-of-all-trades by nature, can, with much more ease and suppleness, address himself to a variety of services, and suffice in his own person to discharge them all, than is possible for the formality and slowness of a Scottishman. Superior to Caleb in dexterity, though not in zeal, La Jeunesse seemed to multiply himself with the necessities of the occasion, and discharged his several tasks with such promptitude and assiduity, that farther attendance than his was neither missed nor wished for.

The dinner, in particular, was exquisite. The soup, although bearing the term of *maigre*, which Englishmen use in scorn, was most delicately flavoured, and the matelot of pike and eels reconciled me, though a Scottishman, to the latter. There was even a *petit plat* of *bouilli* for the heretic, so exquisitely dressed as to retain all the juices, and, at the same time, rendered so thoroughly tender, that nothing could be more delicate. The *potage*, with another small dish or two, was equally well arranged. But what the old *maître d'hôtel* valued himself upon as something superb, smiling with self-satisfaction, and in enjoyment of my surprise, as he placed it on the table, was an immense *assiettée* of spinage, not smoothed into a uniform surface, as by our uninaugurated cooks upon your side of the water, but swelling into hills and declining into vales, over which swept a gallant stag, pursued by a pack of hounds in full cry, and a noble field of horsemen with bugle-horns, and whips held upright, and brandished after the manner of broadswords—hounds, huntsman, and stag being all very artificially cut out of toasted bread. Enjoying the praises which I failed not to bestow on this *chef d'œuvre*, the old man acknowledged it had cost the best part of two days to bring it to perfection; and added, giving honour where honour was due, that an idea so brilliant was not entirely his own, but that Monsieur himself had taken the trouble to give him several valuable hints, and even condescended to assist in the execution of some of the most capital figures. The marquis blushed a little at this *éclaircissement*, which he might probably have wished to suppress, but acknowledged he had wished to surprise me with a scene from the popular poem of my country, *Miladi Lac*. I answered, that "So splendid a cortège much more resembled a *grand chasse* of Louis Quatorze than of a poor King of Scotland, and that the *paysage* was rather like Fontainebleau than the wilds of Callander." He bowed graciously in answer to this compliment, and acknowledged that recollections of the costume of the old French court, when in its splendour, might have misled his imagination—and so the conversation passed on to other matters.

Our dessert was exquisite: the cheese, the fruits, the salad, the olives, the *cerneaux*, and the delicious white wine, each in their way were *impayables;* and the good marquis, with an air of great satisfaction, observed, that his guest did sincere homage to their merits. "After all," he said, "and yet it is but confessing a foolish weakness—but, after all, I cannot but rejoice in feeling myself equal to offering a stranger a sort of hospitality which seems pleasing to him. Believe me, it is not entirely out of pride that we *pauvres revenants* live so very retired, and avoid the duties of hospitality. It is true, that too many of us wander about the halls of our fathers, rather like ghosts of their deceased proprietors than like living men restored to their own possessions; yet it is rather on your account, and to spare our own feelings, that we do not cultivate the society of our foreign visitors. We have an idea that your opulent nation is particularly attached to *faste* and to *grande chère*—to your ease and enjoyment of every kind; and the means of entertainment left to us are, in most cases, so limited, that we feel ourselves totally precluded from such expense and ostentation. No one wishes to offer his best where he has reason to think it will not give pleasure; and as many of you publish your journals, *monsieur le marquis* would not probably be much gratified by seeing the poor dinner which he was able to present to *milord Anglois* put upon permanent record."

I interrupted the marquis, that were I to wish an account of my entertainment published, it would be only in order to preserve the memory of the very best dinner I ever had eaten in my life. He bowed in return, and presumed that "I either differed much from the national taste, or the accounts of it were greatly exaggerated. He was particularly obliged to me for showing the value of the possessions which remained to him. The useful," he said, "had no doubt survived the sumptuous at Hautlieu as elsewhere. Grottoes, statues, curious conservatories of exotics, temple and tower, had gone to the ground; but the vineyard, the *potager*, the orchard, the *étang*, still existed"; and once more he expressed himself "happy to find that their combined productions could make what even a Briton accepted as a tolerable meal. I only hope," he continued, "that you will convince me your compliments are sincere by accepting the hospitality of the Château de Hautlieu as often as better engagements will permit during your stay in this neighbourhood."

I readily promised to accept an invitation offered with such grace as to make the guest appear the person conferring the obligation.

The conversation then changed to the history of the château and its vicinity—a subject which was strong ground to the marquis, though he was no great antiquary, and even no very profound historian, when other topics were discussed. The curé, however, chanced to be both, and withal a very conversable pleasing man, with an air of *prévenance* and ready civility of communication, which I have found a leading characteristic of the Catholic clergy, whether they are well-informed or otherwise. It was from him that I learned there still existed the remnant of a fine library in the Château de Hautlieu. The marquis shrugged his shoulders as the curé gave me this intimation, looked to the one side and the other, and displayed the same sort of petty embarrassment which he had been unable to suppress when La Jeunesse blabbed something of his interference with the arrangements of the *cuisine*. "I should be happy to show the books," he said, "but they are in such a wild condition, so dismantled, that I am ashamed to exhibit them to any one."

"Forgive me, my dear sir," said the curé, "you know you permitted the great English bibliomaniac, Dr. Dibdin, to consult your curious relics, and you know how highly he spoke of them."

"What could I do, my dear friend?" said the marquis; "the good doctor had heard some exaggerated account of these remnants of what was once a library; he had stationed himself in the *auberge* below, determined to carry his point or die under the walls. I even heard of his taking the altitude of the turret in order to provide scaling-ladders. You would not have had me reduce a respectable divine, though of another church, to such an act of desperation? I could not have answered it in conscience."

"But you know, besides, *monsieur le marquis*," continued the curé, "that Dr. Dibdin was so much grieved at the dilapidation your library had sustained, that he avowedly envied the powers of our church, so much did he long to launch an anathema at the heads of the perpetrators."

"His resentment was in proportion to his disappointment, I suppose," said our entertainer.

"Not so," said the curé; "for he was so enthusiastic on the value of what remains, that I am convinced nothing but your positive request to the contrary prevented the Château of Hautlieu occupying at least twenty pages in that splendid work of which he sent us a copy, and which will remain a lasting monument of his zeal and erudition."

"Dr. Dibdin is extremely polite," said the marquis; "and when we have had our coffee—here it comes—we will go to the turret; and I hope, as monsieur has not despised my poor fare, so he will pardon the state of my confused library, while I shall be equally happy if it can afford anything which can give him amusement. Indeed," he added, "were it otherwise, you, my good father, have every right over books which, without your intervention, would never have returned to the owner."

Although this additional act of courtesy was evidently wrested by the importunity of the curé from his reluctant friend, whose desire to conceal the nakedness of the land, and the extent of his losses, seemed always to struggle with his disposition to be obliging, I could not help accepting an offer which, in strict politeness, I ought perhaps to have refused. But then the remains of a collection of such curiosity as had given to our bibliomaniacal friend the desire of leading the forlorn hope in an escalade—it would have been a desperate act of self-denial to have declined an opportunity of seeing it. La Jeunesse brought coffee, such as we only taste on the continent, upon a salver, covered with a napkin, that it might be *censé* for silver, and *chasse-café* from Martinique on a small waiter, which was certainly so. Our repast thus finished, the marquis led me up an *escalier derobé* into a very large and well-proportioned saloon of nearly one hundred feet in length; but so waste and dilapidated, that I kept my eyes on the ground, lest my kind entertainer should feel himself called upon to apologise for tattered pictures and torn tapestry, and, worse than both, for casements that had yielded, in one or two instances, to the boisterous blast.

"We have contrived to make the turret something more habitable," said the marquis, as he moved hastily through this chamber of desolation. "This," he said, "was the picture gallery in former times, and in the boudoir beyond, which we now occupy as a book-closet, were preserved some curious cabinet paintings, whose small size required that they should be viewed closely."

As he spoke, he held aside a portion of the tapestry I have mentioned, and we entered the room of which he spoke.

It was octangular, corresponding to the external shape of the turret whose interior it occupied. Four of the sides had latticed windows, commanding each, from a different point, the most beautiful prospect over the majestic Loire and the adjacent country through which it winded; and the casements were filled with stained glass, through two of which streamed the lustre of the setting sun, showing a brilliant assemblage of religious emblems and armorial bearings, which it was scarcely possible to look at with an undazzled eye; but the other two windows, from which the sunbeams had passed away, could be closely examined, and plainly showed that the lattices were glazed with stained glass, which did not belong to them originally, but, as I afterwards learned, to the profaned and desecrated chapel of the castle. It had been the amusement of the marquis for several months to accomplish this *rifacimento*, with the assistance of the curate and the all-capable La Jeunesse; and though they had only patched together fragments, which were in many places very minute, yet the stained glass, till examined very closely, and with the eye of an antiquary, produced, on the whole, a very pleasing effect.

The sides of the apartment not occupied by the lattices were, except the space for the small door, fitted up with presses and shelves, some of walnut-tree, curiously carved, and brought to a dark colour by time, nearly resembling that of a ripe chestnut, and partly of common deal, employed to repair and supply the deficiencies occasioned by violence and devastation. On these shelves were deposited the wrecks, or rather the precious relics of, a most splendid library. The marquis's father had been a man of information, and his grandfather was famous, even in the court of Louis XIV., where literature was in some degree considered as the fashion, for the extent of his acquirements. Those two proprietors, opulent in their fortunes, and liberal in the indulgence of their taste, had made such additions to a curious old Gothic library, which had descended from their ancestors, that there were few collections in France which could be compared to that of Hautlieu. It had been completely dispersed, in consequence of an ill-judged attempt of the present marquis, in 1790, to defend his château against a revolutionary mob. Luckily, the curé, who, by his charitable and moderate conduct and his evangelical virtues, possessed much interest among the neighbouring peasantry, prevailed on many of them to buy, for the petty sum of a few sous, and sometimes at the vulgar rate of a glass of brandy, volumes which had cost large sums, but which were carried off in mere spite by the ruffians who pillaged the castle. He himself also had purchased as many of the books as his funds could possibly reach, and to his care it was owing that they were restored to the turret in which I found them. It was no wonder, therefore, that the good curé had some pride and pleasure in showing the collection to strangers.

In spite of odd volumes, imperfections, and all the other mortifications which an amateur encounters in looking through an ill-kept library, there were many articles in that of Hautlieu calculated, as Bayes says, "to elevate and surprise" the bibliomaniac. There were,

> The small rare volume, dark with tarnish'd gold,

as Dr. Ferriar feelingly sings—curiously and richly painted missals, manuscripts of 1380, 1320, and even earlier, and works in Gothic type, printed in the 15th and 16th centuries. But of these I intend to give a more detailed account should the marquis grant his permission.

In the mean time, it is sufficient to say that, delighted with the day I had spent at Hautlieu, I frequently repeated my visit, and that the key of the octangular tower was always at my command. In those hours, I became deeply enamoured of a part of French history, which, although most important to that of Europe at large, and illustrated by an inimitable old historian, I had never sufficiently studied. At the same time, to gratify the feelings of my excellent host, I occupied myself occasionally with some family memorials which had fortunately been preserved, and which contained some curious particulars respecting the connexion with Scotland, which first found me favour in the eyes of the Marquis de Hautlieu.

I pondered on these things, *more meo*, until my return to Britain, to beef and sea-coal fires—a change of residence which took place since I drew up these Gallic reminiscences. At length the result of my meditations took the form of which my readers, if not startled by this preface, will presently be enabled to judge. Should the public receive it with favour, I shall not regret having been for a short time an absentee.

QUENTIN DURWARD.

CHAPTER I.

THE CONTRAST.

> Look here upon this picture, and on this,
> The counterfeit presentment of two brothers.
> *Hamlet.*

THE latter part of the 15th century prepared a train of future events, that ended by raising France to that state of formidable power which has ever since been, from time to time, the principal object of jealousy to the other European nations. Before that period she had to struggle for her very existence with the English, already possessed of her fairest provinces; while the utmost exertions of her king, and the gallantry of her people, could scarcely protect the remainder from a foreign yoke. Nor was this her sole danger. The princes who possessed the grand fiefs of the crown, and, in particular, the Dukes of Burgundy and Bretagne, had come to wear their feudal bonds so lightly, that they had no scruples in lifting the standard against their liege and sovereign lord, the King of France, on the slightest pretence. When at peace, they reigned as absolute princes in their own provinces; and the house of Burgundy, possessed of the district so called, together with the fairest and richest part of Flanders, was itself so wealthy and so powerful as to yield nothing to the crown, either in splendour or in strength.

In imitation of the grand feudatories, each inferior vassal of the crown assumed as much independence as his distance from the sovereign power, the extent of his fief, or the strength of his château, enabled him to maintain; and these petty tyrants, no longer amenable to the exercise of the law, perpetrated with impunity the wildest excesses of fantastic oppression and cruelty. In Auvergne alone, a report was made of more than three hundred of these independent nobles, to whom incest, murder, and rapine were the most ordinary and familiar actions.

Besides these evils, another, springing out of the long-continued wars betwixt the French and English, added no small misery to this distracted kingdom. Numerous bodies of soldiers, collected into bands, under officers chosen by themselves from among the bravest and most successful adventurers, had been formed in various parts of France out of the refuse of all other countries. These hireling combatants sold their swords for a time to the best bidder; and, when such service was not to be had, they made war on their own account, seizing castles and towers, which they used as the places of their retreat, making prisoners and ransoming them, exacting tribute from the open villages and the country around them, and acquiring, by every species of rapine, the appropriate epithets of *tondeurs* and *écorcheurs*, that is, "clippers" and "flayers."

In the midst of the horrors and miseries arising from so distracted a state of public affairs, reckless and profuse expense distinguished the courts of the lesser nobles, as well as of the superior princes; and their dependents, in imitation, expended in rude but magnificent display the wealth which they extorted from the people. A tone of romantic and chivalrous gallantry, which, however, was often disgraced by unbounded license, characterised the intercourse between the sexes; and the language of knight-errantry was yet used, and its observances followed, though the pure spirit of honourable love and benevolent enterprise which it inculcates had ceased to qualify and atone for its extravagances. The jousts and tournaments, the entertainments and revels, which each petty court displayed, invited to France every wandering adventurer; and it was seldom that, when arrived there, he failed to employ his rash courage and headlong spirit of enterprise in actions for which his happier native country afforded no free stage.

At this period, and as if to save this fair realm from the various woes with which it was menaced, the tottering throne was ascended by Louis XI., whose character, evil as it was in itself, met, combated, and in a great degree neutralized, the mischiefs of the time—as poisons of opposing qualities are said, in ancient books of medicine, to have the power of counteracting each other.

Brave enough for every useful and political purpose, Louis had not a spark of that romantic valour, or of the pride generally associated with it, which fought on for the point of honour, when the point of utility had been long gained. Calm, crafty, and profoundly attentive to his own interest, he made every sacrifice, both of pride and passion, which could interfere with it. He was careful in disguising his real sentiments and purposes from all who approached him, and frequently used the expressions: "The king knew not how to reign who knew not how to dissemble; and that, for himself, if he thought his very cap knew his secrets, he would throw it into the fire." No man of his own or of any other time better understood how to avail himself of the frailties of others, and when to avoid giving any advantage by the untimely indulgence of his own.

He was by nature vindictive and cruel, even to the extent of finding pleasure in the frequent executions which he commanded. But, as no touch of mercy ever induced him to spare when he could with safety condemn, so no sentiment of vengeance ever stimulated him to a premature violence. He seldom sprung on his prey till it was fairly within his grasp, and till all hope of rescue was vain; and his movements were so studiously disguised, that his success was generally what first announced to the world the object he had been manœuvring to attain.

In like manner, the avarice of Louis gave way to apparent profusion, when it was necessary to bribe the favourite or minister of a rival prince for averting any impending attack, or to break up any alliance confederated against him. He was fond of license and pleasure; but neither beauty nor the chase, though both were ruling passions, ever withdrew him from the most regular attendance to public business and the affairs of his kingdom. His knowledge of mankind was profound, and he had sought it in the private walks of life, in which he often personally mingled; and, though naturally proud and haughty, he hesitated not, with an inattention to the arbitrary divisions of society which was then thought something portentously unnatural, to raise from the lowest rank men whom he employed on the most important duties, and knew so well how to choose them, that he was rarely disappointed in their qualities.

Yet there were contradictions in the character of this artful and able monarch; for human nature is rarely uniform. Himself the most false and insincere of mankind, some of the greatest errors of his life arose from too rash a confidence in the honour and integrity of others. When these errors took place, they seem to have arisen from an over-refined system of policy, which induced Louis to assume the appearance of undoubting confidence in those to whom it was his object to overreach; for, in his general conduct, he was as jealous and suspicious as any tyrant whoever breathed.

Two other points may be noticed to complete the sketch of this formidable character, by which he rose among the rude chivalrous sovereigns of the period to the rank of a keeper among wild beasts, who, by superior wisdom and policy, by distribution of food, and some discipline by blows, comes finally to predominate over those who, if unsubjected by his arts, would by main strength have torn him to pieces.

The first of these attributes was Louis's excessive superstition—a plague with which Heaven often afflicts those who refuse to listen to the dictates of religion. The remorse arising from his evil actions, Louis never endeavoured to appease by any relaxation in his Machiavellian stratagems, but laboured, in vain, to soothe and silence that painful feeling by superstitious observances, severe penance, and profuse gifts to the ecclesiastics. The second property, with which the first is sometimes found strangely united, was a disposition to low pleasures and obscure debauchery. The wisest, or at least the most crafty, sovereign of his time, he was fond of low life, and, being himself a man of wit, enjoyed the jests and repartees of social conversation more than could have been expected from other points of his character. He even mingled in the comic adventures of obscure intrigue, with a freedom little consistent with the habitual and guarded jealousy of his character; and he was so fond of this species of humble gallantry, that he caused a number of its gay and licentious anecdotes to be enrolled in a collection well known to book-collectors, in whose eyes (and the work is unfit for any other) the *right* edition is very precious.[1]

By means of this monarch's powerful and prudent, though most unamiable, character, it pleased Heaven, who works by the tempest as well as by the soft small rain, to restore to the great French nation the benefits of civil government, which, at the time of his accession, they had nearly lost.

Ere he succeeded to the crown, Louis had given evidence of his vices rather than of his talents. His first wife, Margaret of Scotland, was "done to death by slanderous tongues" in her husband's court, where, but for the encouragement of Louis himself, not a word would have been breathed against that amiable and injured princess. He had been an ungrateful and a rebellious son, at one time conspiring to seize his father's person, and at another levying open war against him. For the first offence, he was banished to his appanage of Dauphiné, which he governed with much sagacity; for the second, he was driven into absolute exile, and forced to throw himself on the mercy, and almost on the charity, of the Duke of Burgundy and his son, where he enjoyed hospitality, afterwards indifferently requited, until the death of his father in 1461.

In the very outset of his reign, Louis was almost overpowered by a league formed against him by the great vassals of France, with the Duke of Burgundy, or rather his son, the Count de Charalois, at its head. They levied a powerful army, blockaded Paris, fought a battle of doubtful issue under its very walls, and placed the French monarchy on the brink

[1] See Edition of *Cent Nouvelles*. Note 3.

of actual destruction. It usually happens in such cases that the more sagacious general of the two gains the real fruit, though perhaps not the martial fame, of the disputed field. Louis, who had shown great personal bravery during the battle of Montl'héry, was able, by his prudence, to avail himself of its undecided character, as if it had been a victory on his side. He temporised until the enemy had broken up their leaguer, and showed so much dexterity in sowing jealousies among those great powers, that their alliance "for the public weal," as they termed it, but in reality for the overthrow of all but the external appearance of the French monarchy, dissolved itself, and was never again renewed in a manner so formidable. From this period, Louis, relieved of all danger from England by the civil wars of York and Lancaster, was engaged for several years, like an unfeeling but able physician, in curing the wounds of the body politic, or rather in stopping, now by gentle remedies, now by the use of fire and steel, the progress of those mortal gangrenes with which it was then infected. The *brigandage* of the Free Companies, and the unpunished oppressions of the nobility, he laboured to lessen, since he could not actually stop them; and, by dint of unrelaxed attention, he gradually gained some addition to his own regal authority, or effected some diminution of those by whom it was counterbalanced.

Still the King of France was surrounded by doubt and danger. The members of the league "for public weal," though not in unison, were in existence, and, like a scotched snake, might re-unite and become dangerous again. But a worse danger was the increasing power of the Duke of Burgundy, then one of the greatest princes of Europe, and little diminished in rank by the very slight dependence of his duchy upon the crown of France.

Charles, surnamed the Bold, or rather the Audacious, for his courage was allied to rashness and frenzy, then wore the ducal coronet of Burgundy, which he burned to convert into a royal and independent regal crown. The character of this duke was in every respect the direct contrast to that of Louis XI.

The latter was calm, deliberate, and crafty, never prosecuting a desperate enterprise, and never abandoning one likely to be successful, however distant the prospect. The genius of the Duke was entirely different. He rushed on danger because he loved it, and on difficulties because he despised them. As Louis never sacrificed his interest to his passion, so Charles, on the other hand, never sacrificed his passion, or even his humour, to any other consideration. Notwithstanding the near relationship that existed between them, and the support which the Duke and his father had afforded to Louis in his exile when Dauphin, there was mutual contempt and hatred betwixt them. The Duke of Burgundy despised the cautious policy of the King, and imputed to the faintness of his courage, that he sought by leagues, purchases, and other indirect means those advantages which, in his place, the Duke would have snatched with an armed hand. He likewise hated the King, not only for the ingratitude he had manifested for former kindnesses, and for personal injuries and imputations which the ambassadors of Louis had cast upon him when his father was yet alive, but also, and especially, because of the support which he afforded in secret to the discontented citizens of Ghent, Liege, and other great towns in Flanders. These turbulent cities, jealous of their privileges and proud of their wealth, were frequently in a state of insurrection against their liege lords the Dukes of Burgundy, and never failed to find underhand countenance at the court of Louis, who embraced every opportunity of fomenting disturbance within the dominions of his overgrown vassal.

The contempt and hatred of the Duke were retaliated by Louis with equal energy, though he used a thicker veil to conceal his sentiments. It was impossible for a man of his profound sagacity not to despise the stubborn obstinacy which never resigned its purpose, however fatal perseverance might prove, and the headlong impetuosity which commenced its career without allowing a moment's consideration for the obstacles to be encountered. Yet the King hated Charles even more than he contemned him, and his scorn and hatred were the more intense that they were mingled with fear; for he knew that the onset of the mad bull, to whom he likened the Duke of Burgundy, must ever be formidable though the animal makes it with shut eyes. It was not alone the wealth of the Burgundian provinces, the discipline of the warlike inhabitants, and the mass of their crowded population, which the King dreaded, for the personal qualities of their leader had also much in them that was dangerous. The very soul of bravery, which he pushed to the very verge of rashness, and beyond it, profuse in expenditure, splendid in his court, his person, and his retinue, in all which he displayed the hereditary magnificence of the house of Burgundy, Charles the Bold drew into his service almost all the fiery spirits of the age whose tempers were congenial; and Louis saw too clearly what might be attempted and executed by such a train of resolute adventurers, following a leader of a character as ungovernable as their own.

There was yet another circumstance which increased the animosity of Louis towards his overgrown vassal: he owed him favours which he never meant to repay, and was under the frequent necessity of temporising with him, and even of enduring bursts of petulant insolence, injurious to the regal dignity, without being able to treat him otherwise than as his "fair cousin of Burgundy."

It was about the year 1468, when their feuds were at the highest, though a dubious and hollow truce, as frequently happened, existed for the time betwixt them, that the present narrative opens. The person first introduced on the stage will be found indeed to be of a rank and condition the illustration of whose character scarcely called for a dissertation on the relative position of two great princes; but the passions of the great, their quarrels, and their reconciliations, involve the fortunes of all who approach them; and it will be found, on proceeding farther in our story, that this preliminary chapter is necessary for comprehending the history of the individual whose adventures we are about to relate.

CHAPTER II.

THE WANDERER.

Why then the world is my oyster, which I with sword will open.
Ancient Pistol.

It was upon a delicious summer morning, before the sun had assumed its scorching power, and while the dews yet cooled and perfumed the air, that a youth, coming from the northeastward, approached the ford of a small river, or rather a large brook, tributary to the Cher, near to the royal Castle of Plessis-lès-Tours, whose dark and multiplied battlements rose in the background over the extensive forest with which they were surrounded. These woodlands comprised a noble chase, or royal park, fenced by an inclosure, termed, in the Latin of the middle ages, *plexitium*, which gives the name of Plessis to so many villages in France. The castle and village of which we particularly speak was called Plessis-lès-Tours, to distinguish it from others, and was built about two miles to the southward of the fair town of that name, the capital of ancient Touraine, whose rich plain has been termed the Garden of France.

On the bank of the above-mentioned brook, opposite to that which the traveller was approaching, two men, who appeared in deep conversation, seemed, from time to time, to watch his motions; for, as their station was much more elevated, they could remark him at considerable distance.

The age of the young traveller might be about nineteen, or betwixt that and twenty, and his face and person, which were very prepossessing, did not, however, belong to the country in which he was now a sojourner. His short grey cloak and hose were rather of Flemish than of French fashion, while the smart blue bonnet, with a single sprig of holly and an eagle's feather, was already recognised as the Scottish head-gear. His dress was very neat, and arranged with the precision of a youth conscious of possessing a fine person. He had at his back a satchel, which seemed to contain a few necessaries, a hawking gauntlet on his left hand, though he carried no bird, and in his right a stout hunter's pole. Over his left shoulder hung an embroidered scarf which sustained a small pouch of scarlet velvet, such as was then used by fowlers of distinction to carry their hawk's food, and other matters belonging to that much admired sport. This was crossed by another shoulder-belt, to which was hung a hunting-knife, or *couteau de chasse*. Instead of the boots of the period, he wore buskins of half-dressed deer's-skin.

Although his form had not yet attained its full strength, he was tall and active, and the lightness of the step with which he advanced showed that his pedestrian mode of travelling was pleasure rather than pain to him. His complexion was fair, in spite of a general shade of darker hue, with which the foreign sun, or perhaps constant exposure to the atmosphere in his own country, had in some degree embrowned it.

His features, without being quite regular, were frank, open, and pleasing. A half smile, which seemed to arise from a happy exuberance of animal spirits, showed, now and then, that his teeth were well set, and as pure as ivory; whilst his bright blue eyes, with a corresponding gaiety, had an appropriate glance for every object which it encountered, expressing good-humour, lightness of heart, and determined resolution.

He received and returned the salutation of the few travellers who frequented the road in those dangerous times with the action which suited each. The strolling spearman, half soldier, half brigand, measured the youth with his eye, as if balancing the prospect of booty with the chance of desperate resistance; and read such indications of the latter in the fearless glance of the passenger, that he changed his ruffian purpose for a surly "Good morrow, comrade," which the young Scot answered with as martial, though less sullen, tone. The wandering pilgrim or the begging-friar answered his reverend greeting with a paternal benedicite; and the dark-eyed peasant girl looked after him for many a step after they had passed each other, and interchanged a laughing "good morrow." In short, there was an attraction about his whole appearance not easily escaping attention, and which was derived from the

Louis XI., King of France.

Quentin Durward, Chap. i., p. 43.

combination of fearless frankness and good-humour with sprightly looks and a handsome face and person. It seemed, too, as if his whole demeanour bespoke one who was entering on life with no apprehension of the evils with which it is beset, and small means for struggling with its hardships, except a lively spirit and a courageous disposition; and it is with such tempers that youth most readily sympathises, and for whom chiefly age and experience feel affectionate and pitying interest.

The youth whom we have described had been long visible to the two persons who loitered on the opposite side of the small river which divided him from the park and the castle; but as he descended the rugged bank to the water's edge, with the light step of a roe which visits the fountain, the younger of the two said to the other: "It is our man—it is the Bohemian! If he attempts to cross the ford, he is a lost man: the water is up, and the ford impassable."

"Let him make that discovery himself, gossip," said the elder personage; "it may, perchance, save a rope, and break a proverb."

"I judge him by the blue cap," said the other, "for I cannot see his face. Hark, sir; he hallooes to know whether the water is deep."

"Nothing like experience in this world," answered the other: "let him try."

The young man, in the mean while, receiving no hint to the contrary, and taking the silence of those to whom he applied as an encouragement to proceed, entered the stream without farther hesitation than the delay necessary to take off his buskins. The elder person, at the same moment, hallooed to him to beware, adding, in a lower tone, to his companion: "*Mortdieu*, gossip, you have made another mistake: this is not the Bohemian chatterer."

But the intimation to the youth came too late. He either did not hear or could not profit by it, being already in the deep stream. To one less alert and practised in the exercise of swimming, death had been certain, for the brook was both deep and strong.

"By St. Anne! but he is a proper youth," said the elder man. "Run, gossip, and help your blunder by giving him aid, if thou canst. He belongs to thine own troop; if old saws speak truth, water will not drown him."

Indeed, the young traveller swam so strongly, and buffeted the waves so well, that, notwithstanding the strength of the current, he was carried but a little way down from the ordinary landing-place.

By this time the younger of the two strangers was hurrying down to the shore to render assistance, while the other followed him at a graver pace, saying to himself as he approached: "I knew water would never drown that young fellow. By my halidome, he is ashore, and grasps his pole! If I make not the more haste, he will beat my gossip for the only charitable action which I ever saw him perform, or attempt to perform, in the whole course of his life."

There was some reason to augur such a conclusion of the adventure, for the bonny Scot had already accosted the younger Samaritan, who was hastening to his assistance, with these ireful words: "Discourteous dog! why did you not answer when I called to know if the passage was fit to be attempted? May the foul fiend catch me, but I will teach you the respect due to strangers on the next occasion!"

This was accompanied with that significant flourish with his pole which is called *le moulinet*, because the artist, holding it in the middle, brandishes the two ends in every direction, like the sails of a windmill in motion. His opponent, seeing himself thus menaced, laid hand upon his sword, for he was one of those who on all occasions are more ready for action than for speech; but his more considerate comrade, who came up, commanded him to forbear, and, turning to the young man, accused him in turn of precipitation in plunging into the swollen ford, and of intemperate violence in quarrelling with a man who was hastening to his assistance.

The young man, on hearing himself thus reproved by a man of advanced age and respectable appearance, immediately lowered his weapon, and said: "He would be sorry if he had done them injustice; but, in reality, it appeared to him as if they had suffered him to put his life in peril for want of a word of timely warning, which could be the part neither of honest men nor of good Christians, far less of respectable burgesses, such as they seemed to be."

"Fair son," said the elder person, "you seem, from your accent and complexion, a stranger; and you should recollect your dialect is not so easily comprehended by us as perhaps it may be uttered by you."

"Well, father," answered the youth, "I do not care much about the ducking I have had, and I will readily forgive your being partly the cause, provided you will direct me to some place where I can have my clothes dried; for it is my only suit, and I must keep it somewhat decent."

"For whom do you take us, fair son?" said the elder stranger, in answer to this question.

"For substantial burgesses, unquestionably," said the youth; "or, hold—you, master, may be a money-broker or a corn-merchant, and this man a butcher or grazier."

"You have hit our capacities rarely," said the elder, smiling. "My business is indeed to trade in as much money as I can; and my gossip's dealings are somewhat of kin to the butcher's. As to your accommodation, we will try to serve you; but I must first know who you are, and whither you are going; for, in these times, the roads are filled with travellers on foot and horseback who have anything in their head but honesty and the fear of God."

The young man cast another keen and penetrating glance on him who spoke, and on his silent companion, as if doubtful whether they, on their part, merited the confidence they demanded; and the result of his observation was as follows.

The eldest and most remarkable of these men, in dress and appearance, resembled the merchant or shopkeeper of the period. His jerkin, hose, and cloak were of a dark uniform colour, but worn so threadbare that the acute young Scot conceived that the wearer must be either very rich or very poor, probably the former. The fashion of the dress was close and short—a kind of garments which were not then held decorous among gentry, or even the superior class of citizens, who generally wore loose gowns which descended below the middle of the leg.

The expression of this man's countenance was partly attractive and partly forbidding. His strong features, sunk cheeks, and hollow eyes had, nevertheless, an expression of shrewdness and humour congenial to the character of the young adventurer. But then, those same sunken eyes, from under the shroud of thick black eyebrows, had something in them that was at once commanding and sinister. Perhaps this effect was increased by the low fur cap, much depressed on the forehead, and adding to the shade from under which those eyes peered out; but it is certain that the young stranger had some difficulty to reconcile his looks with the meanness of his appearance in other respects. His cap, in particular, in which all men of any quality displayed either a brooch of gold or of silver, was ornamented with a paltry image of the Virgin, in lead, such as the poorer sort of pilgrims bring from Loretto.

His comrade was a stout-formed, middle-sized man, more than ten years younger than his companion, with a down-looking visage and a very ominous smile, when by chance he gave way to that impulse, which was never, except in reply to certain secret signs that seemed to pass between him and the elder stranger. This man was armed with a sword and dagger; and, underneath his plain habit, the Scotsman observed that he concealed a *jazeran*, or flexible shirt of linked mail, which, as being often worn by those, even of peaceful professions, who were called upon at that perilous period to be frequently abroad, confirmed the young man in his conjecture that the wearer was by profession a butcher, grazier, or something of that description, called upon to be much abroad.

The young stranger, comprehending in one glance the result of the observation which has taken us some time to express, answered, after a moment's pause: "I am ignorant whom I may have the honour to address," making a slight reverence at the same time; "but I am indifferent who knows that I am a cadet of Scotland, and that I come to seek my fortune in France, or elsewhere, after the custom of my countrymen."

"*Pasques-dieu!* and a gallant custom it is," said the elder stranger. "You seem a fine young springald, and at the right age to prosper, whether among men or women. What say you? I am a merchant, and want a lad to assist in my traffic. I suppose you are too much a gentleman to assist in such mechanical drudgery?"

"Fair sir," said the youth, "if your offer be seriously made, of which I have my doubts, I am bound to thank you for it, and I thank you accordingly; but I fear I should be altogether unfit for your service."

"What!" said the senior, "I warrant thou knowest better how to draw the bow than how to draw a bill of charges—canst handle a broadsword better than a pen—ha!"

"I am, master," answered the young Scot, "a braeman, and therefore, as we say, a bowman. But besides that, I have been in a convent, where the good fathers taught me to read and write, and even to cipher."

"*Pasques-dieu!* that is too magnificent," said the merchant. "By our Lady of Embrun, thou art a prodigy, man!"

"Rest you merry, fair master," said the youth, who was much pleased with his new acquaintance's jocularity, "I must go dry myself, instead of standing dripping here, answering questions."

The merchant only laughed louder as he spoke, and answered, "*Pasques-dieu!* the proverb never fails—*fier comme un Écossois;* but come, youngster, you are of a country I have a regard for, having traded in Scotland in my time—an honest poor set of folks they are; and, if you will come with us to the village, I will bestow on you a cup of burnt sack and a warm breakfast, to atone for your drenching. But, *tête-bleau!* what do you with a hunting-glove on your hand? Know you not there is no hawking permitted in a royal chase?"

"I was taught that lesson," answered the youth, "by a rascally forester of the Duke of Burgundy. I did but fly the falcon I had brought with me from Scotland, and that I reckoned on for bringing me into some note, at a heron near Péronne, and the rascally *schelm* shot my bird with an arrow."

"What did you do?" said the merchant.

"Beat him," said the youngster, brandishing his staff, "as

near to death as one Christian man should belabour another. I wanted not to have his blood to answer for."

"Know you," said the burgess, "that, had you fallen into the Duke of Burgundy's hands, he would have hung you up like a chestnut?"

"Ay, I am told he is as prompt as the King of France for that sort of work. But, as this happened near Péronne, I made a leap over the frontiers, and laughed at him. If he had not been so hasty, I might perhaps have taken service with him."

"He will have a heavy miss of such a paladin as you are, if the truce should break off," said the merchant, and threw a look at his own companion, who answered him with one of the downcast lowering smiles, which gleamed along his countenance, enlivening it as a passing meteor enlivens a winter sky.

The young Scot suddenly stopped, pulled his bonnet over his right eyebrow, as one that would not be ridiculed, and said firmly: "My masters, and especially you, sir, the elder, and who should be the wiser, you will find, I presume, no sound or safe jesting at my expense. I do not altogether like the tone of your conversation. I can take a jest with any man, and a rebuke, too, from my elder, and say 'Thank you, sir,' if I know it to be deserved; but I do not like being borne in hand as if I were a child, when, God wot, I find myself man enough to belabour you both, if you provoke me too far."

The eldest man seemed like to choke with laughter at the lad's demeanour; his companion's hand stole to his swordhilt, which the youth observing dealt him a blow across the wrist, which made him incapable of grasping it; while his companion's mirth was only increased by the incident. "Hold—hold," he cried, "most doughty Scot, even for thine own dear country's sake; and you, gossip, forbear your menacing look. *Pasques-dieu!* let us be just traders, and set off the wetting against the knock on the wrist, which was given with so much grace and alacrity. And hark ye, my young friend," he said to the young man with a grave sternness which, in spite of all the youth could do, damped and overawed him, "no more violence. I am no fit object for it, and my gossip, as you may see, has had enough of it. Let me know your name."

"I can answer a civil question civilly," said the youth; "and will pay fitting respect to your age, if you do not urge my patience with mockery. Since I have been here in France and Flanders, men have called me, in their fantasy, the Varlet with the Velvet Pouch, because of this hawk purse which I carry by my side; but my true name, when at home, is Quentin Durward."

"Durward!" said the querist; "is it a gentleman's name?"

"By fifteen descents in our family," said the young man. "and that makes me reluctant to follow any other trade than arms."

"A true Scot! Plenty of blood, plenty of pride, and right great scarcity of ducats, I warrant thee. Well, gossip," he said to his companion, "go before us, and tell them to have some breakfast ready yonder at the Mulberry Grove; for this youth will do as much honour to it as a starved mouse to a housewife's cheese. And for the Bohemian—hark in thy ear——"

His comrade answered by a gloomy but intelligent smile, and set forward at a round pace, while the elder man continued, addressing young Durward: "You and I will walk leisurely forward together, and we may take a mass at St. Hubert's chapel in our way through the forest; for it is not good to think of our fleshly before our spiritual wants."

Durward, as a good Catholic, had nothing to object against this proposal, although he might probably have been desirous, in the first place, to have dried his clothes and refreshed himself. Meanwhile, they soon lost sight of their downward-looking companion, but continued to follow the same path which he had taken, until it led them into a wood of tall trees, mixed with thickets and brushwood, traversed by long avenues, through which were seen, as through a vista, the deer trotting in little herds with a degree of security which argued their consciousness of being completely protected.

"You asked me if I were a good bowman," said the young

Scot. "Give me a bow and a brace of shafts, and you shall have a piece of venison in a moment."

"*Pasques-dieu!* my young friend," said his companion, "take care of that; my gossip yonder hath a special eye to the deer; they are under his charge, and he is a strict keeper."

"He hath more the air of a butcher than of a gay forester," answered Durward. "I cannot think yon hang-dog look of his belongs to any one who knows the gentle rules of woodcraft."

"Ah, my young friend," answered his companion, "my gossip hath somewhat an ugly favour to look upon at the first; but those who become acquainted with him never are known to complain of him."

Quentin Durward found something singularly and disagreeably significant in the tone with which this was spoken; and, looking suddenly at the speaker, thought he saw in his countenance, in the slight smile that curled his upper lip, and the accompanying twinkle of his keen dark eye, something to justify his unpleasing surprise. "I have heard of robbers," he thought to himself, "and of wily cheats and cut-throats; what if yonder fellow be a murderer, and this old rascal his decoy-duck? I will be on my guard; they will get little by me but good Scottish knocks."

While he was thus reflecting, they came to a glade, where the large forest trees were more widely separated from each other, and where the ground beneath, cleared of underwood and bushes, was clothed with a carpet of the softest and most lovely verdure, which, screened from the scorching heat of the sun, was here more beautifully tender than it is usually to be seen in France. The trees in this secluded spot were chiefly beeches and elms of huge magnitude, which rose like great hills of leaves into the air. Amidst these magnificent sons of the earth, there peeped out, in the most open spot of the glade, a lowly chapel, near which trickled a small rivulet. Its architecture was of the rudest and most simple kind; and there was a very small lodge beside it, for the accommodation of a hermit or solitary priest, who remained there for regularly discharging the duty of the altar. In a small niche, over the arched doorway, stood a stone image of St. Hubert,[1] with the bugle-horn around his neck and a leash of greyhounds at his feet. The situation of the chapel in the midst of a park or chase so richly stocked with game made the dedication to the sainted huntsman peculiarly appropriate.

Towards this little devotional structure the old man directed his steps, followed by young Durward; and, as they approached, the priest, dressed in his sacerdotal garments, made his appearance, in the act of proceeding from his cell to the chapel, for the discharge, doubtless, of his holy office. Durward bowed his body reverently to the priest, as the respect due to his sacred office demanded; whilst his companion, with an appearance of still more deep devotion, kneeled on one knee to receive the holy man's blessing, and then followed him into church, with a step and manner expressive of the most heartfelt contrition and humility.

The inside of the chapel was adorned in a manner adapted to the occupation of the patron saint while on earth. The richest furs of such animals as are made the objects of the chase in different countries supplied the place of tapestry and hangings around the altar and elsewhere, and the characteristic emblazonments of bugles, bows, quivers, and other emblems of hunting, surrounded the walls, and were mingled with the heads of deer, wolves, and other animals considered beasts of sport. The whole adornments took an appropriate and silvan character; and the mass itself, being considerably shortened, proved to be of that sort which is called a "hunting-mass," because in use before the noble and powerful, who, while assisting at the solemnity, are usually impatient to commence their favourite sport.

Yet, during this brief ceremony, Durward's companion seemed to pay the most rigid and scrupulous attention; while Durward, not quite so much occupied with religious thoughts, could not forbear blaming himself in his own mind for having entertained suspicions derogatory to the character of so good and so humble a man. Far from now holding him as a com-

[1] See Note 4.

panion and accomplice of robbers, he had much to do to forbear regarding him as a saint-like personage.

When mass was ended, they retired together from the chapel, and the elder said to his young comrade: "It is but a short walk from hence to the village; you may now break your fast with an unprejudiced conscience; follow me."

Turning to the right, and proceeding along a path which seemed gradually to ascend, he recommended to his companion by no means to quit the track, but, on the contrary, to keep the middle of it as nearly as he could. Durward could not help asking the cause of this precaution.

"You are now near the court, young man," answered his guide; "and, *Pasques-dieu!* there is some difference betwixt walking in this region and your own heathy hills. Every yard of this ground, excepting the path which we now occupy, is rendered dangerous, and wellnigh impracticable, by snares and traps, armed with scythe-blades, which shred off the unwary passenger's limb as sheerly as a hedge-bill lops a hawthorn-spring, and calthrops that would pierce your foot through, and pitfalls deep enough to bury you in them for ever; for you are now within the precincts of the royal demesne, and we shall presently see the front of the château."

"Were I the King of France," said the young man, "I would not take so much trouble with traps and gins, but would try instead to govern so well that no man should dare to come near my dwelling with a bad intent; and for those who came there in peace and good-will, why, the more of them the merrier we should be."

His companion looked round affecting an alarmed gaze, and said: "Hush—hush, Sir Varlet with the Velvet Pouch! for I forgot to tell you that one great danger of these precincts is that the very leaves of the trees are like so many ears, which carry all which is spoken to the King's own cabinet."

"I care little for that," answered Quentin Durward; "I bear a Scottish tongue in my head bold enough to speak my mind to King Louis's face, God bless him! and for the ears you talk of, if I could see them growing on a human head, I would crop them out of it with my wood-knife."

CHAPTER III.

THE CASTLE.

Full in the midst a mighty pile arose,
Where iron-grated gates their strength oppose
To each invading step, and, strong and steep,
The battled walls arose, the fosse sunk deep.
Slow round the fortress rolled the sluggish stream,
And high in middle air the warder's turrets gleam.
Anonymous.

WHILE Durward and his new acquaintance thus spoke, they came in sight of the whole front of the Castle of Plessis-lès-Tours, which, even in those dangerous times, when the great found themselves obliged to reside within places of fortified strength, was distinguished for the extreme and jealous care with which it was watched and defended.

From the verge of the wood where young Durward halted with his companion, in order to take a view of this royal residence, extended, or rather arose, though by a very gentle elevation, an open esplanade, devoid of trees and bushes of every description, excepting one gigantic and half-withered old oak. This space was left open, according to the rules of fortification in all ages, in order that an enemy might not approach the walls under cover, or unobserved from the battlements; and beyond it arose the castle itself.

There were three external walls, battlemented and turreted from space to space, and at each angle, the second inclosure rising higher than the first, and being built so as to command the exterior defence in case it was won by the enemy; and being again, in the same manner, itself commanded by the third and innermost barrier. Around the external wall, as the Frenchman informed his young companion (for, as they stood lower than the foundation of the walls, he could not see it), was sunk a ditch of about twenty feet in depth, supplied with water by a damhead on the river Cher, or rather on one of its tributary branches. In front of the second inclosure, he said, there ran another fosse; and a third, both of the same unusual dimensions, was led between the second and the innermost inclosure. The verge, both of the outer and inner circuit of this triple moat, was strongly fenced with palisades of iron, serving the purpose of what are called *chevaux-de-frise* in modern fortification, the top of each pale being divided into a cluster of sharp spikes, which seemed to render any attempt to climb over an act of self-destruction.

From within the innermost inclosure arose the castle itself, containing buildings of different periods, crowded around and united with the ancient and grim-looking donjon-keep, which was older than any of them, and which rose, like a black Ethiopian giant, high into the air, while the absence of any windows larger than shot-holes, irregularly disposed for defence, gave the spectator the same unpleasant feeling which we experience on looking at a blind man. The other buildings seemed scarcely better adapted for the purposes of comfort, for the windows opened to an inner and inclosed court-yard; so that the whole external front looked much more like that of a prison than a palace. The reigning king had even increased this effect; for, desirous that the additions which he himself had made to the fortifications should be of a character not easily distinguished from the original building (for, like many jealous persons, he loved not that his suspicions should be observed), the darkest-coloured brick and freestone were employed, and soot mingled with the lime, so as to give the whole castle the same uniform tinge of extreme and rude antiquity.

This formidable place had but one entrance, at least Durward saw none along the spacious front except where, in the centre of the first and outward boundary, arose two strong towers, the usual defences of a gateway; and he could observe their ordinary accompaniments, portcullis and drawbridge, of which the first was lowered and the last raised. Similar entrance-towers were visible on the second and third bounding wall, but not in the same line with those on the outward circuit; because the passage did not cut right through the whole three inclosures at the same point, but, on the contrary, those who entered had to proceed nearly thirty yards betwixt the first and second wall, exposed, if their purpose were hostile, to missiles from both; and again, when the second boundary was passed, they must make a similar digression from the straight line, in order to attain the portal of the third and innermost inclosure; so that before gaining the outer court, which ran along the front of the building, two narrow and dangerous defiles were to be traversed under a flanking discharge of artillery, and three gates, defended in the strongest manner known to the age, were to be successively forced.

Coming from a country alike desolated by foreign war and internal feuds—a country, too, whose unequal and mountainous surface, abounding in precipices and torrents, affords so many situations of strength—young Durward was sufficiently acquainted with all the various contrivances by which men, in that stern age, endeavoured to secure their dwellings; but he frankly owned to his companion that he did not think it had been in the power of art to do so much for defence, where nature had done so little; for the situation, as we have hinted, was merely the summit of a gentle elevation ascending upwards from the place where they were standing.

To enhance his surprise, his companion told him that the environs of the castle, except the single winding path by which the portal might be safely approached, were, like the thickets through which they had passed, surrounded with every species of hidden pitfall, snare, and gin, to entrap the wretch who should venture thither without a guide; that upon the walls were constructed certain cradles of iron, called "swallows' nests," from which the sentinels who were regularly posted there could, without being exposed to any risk, take deliberate aim at any who should attempt to enter without the proper signal or password of the day; and that the archers of the Royal Guard performed that duty day and night, for which they received high pay, rich clothing, and much honour and profit at the hands of King Louis. "And now tell me, young man," he continued, "did you ever see so strong a fortress, and do you think there are men bold enough to storm it?"

The young man looked long and fixedly on the place, the

sight of which interested him so much that he had forgotten, in the eagerness of youthful curiosity, the wetness of his dress. His eye glanced, and his colour mounted to his cheek like that of a daring man who meditates an honourable action, as he replied: "It is a strong castle, and strongly guarded; but there is no impossibility to brave men."

"Are there any in your country who could do such a feat?" said the elder, rather scornfully.

"I will not affirm that," answered the youth; "but there are thousands that, in a good cause, would attempt as bold a deed."

"Umph!" said the senior, "perhaps you are yourself such a gallant?"

"I should sin if I were to boast where there is no danger," answered young Durward; "but my father has done as bold an act, and I trust I am no bastard."

"Well," said his companion, smiling, "you might meet your match, and your kindred withal, in the attempt; for the Scottish Archers of King Louis's Life Guards stand sentinels on yonder walls—three hundred gentlemen of the best blood in your country."

"And were I King Louis," said the youth, in reply, "I would trust my safety to the faith of the three hundred Scottish gentlemen, throwing down my bounding walls to fill up the moat, call in my noble peers and paladins, and live as became me, amid breaking of lances in gallant tournaments, and feasting of days with nobles and dancing of nights with ladies, and have no more fear of a foe than I have of a fly."

His companion again smiled, and turning his back on the castle, which, he observed, they had approached a little too nearly, he led the way again into the wood, by a more broad and beaten path than they had yet trodden. "This," he said, "leads us to the village of Plessis, as it is called, where you, as a stranger, will find reasonable and honest accommodation. About two miles onward lies the fine city of Tours, which gives name to this rich and beautiful earldom. But the village of Plessis, or Plessis of the Park, as it is sometimes called, from its vicinity to the royal residence, and the chase with which it is encircled, will yield you nearer, and as convenient, hospitality."

"I thank you, kind master, for your information," said the Scot; "but my stay will be so short here that, if I fail not in a morsel of meat and a drink of something better than water, my necessities in Plessis, be it of the park or the pool, will be amply satisfied."

"Nay," answered his companion, "I thought you had some friend to see in this quarter."

"And so I have—my mother's own brother," answered Durward; "and as pretty a man, before he left the braes of Angus, as ever planted brogue on heather."

"What is his name?" said the senior. "We will inquire him out for you; for it is not safe for you to go up to the castle, where you might be taken for a spy."

"Now, by my father's hand!" said the youth, "I taken for a spy! By Heaven, he shall brook cold iron that brands me with such a charge! But for my uncle's name, I care not who knows it—it is Lesly—Lesly, an honest and noble name!"

"And so it is, I doubt not," said the old man; "but there are three of the name in the Scottish Guard."

"My uncle's name is Ludovic Lesly," said the young man.

"Of the three Leslies," answered the merchant, "two are called Ludovic."

"They call my kinsman Ludovic with the Scar," said Quentin. "Our family names are so common in a Scottish house, that, where there is no land in the case, we always give a 'to-name.'"

"A *nom de guerre*, I suppose you to mean," answered his companion; "and the man you speak of, we, I think, call *Le Balafré*, from that scar on his face—a proper man and a good soldier. I wish I may be able to help you to an interview with him, for he belongs to a set of gentlemen whose duty is strict, and who do not often come out of garrison, unless in the immediate attendance on the King's person. And now, young man, answer me one question. I will wager you are desirous to take service with your uncle in the Scottish Guard. It is a great thing, if you propose so; especially as you are very young, and some years' experience is necessary for the high office which you aim at."

"Perhaps I may have thought on some such thing," said Durward, carelessly; "but if I did, the fancy is off."

"How so, young man?" said the Frenchman, something sternly. "Do you speak thus of a charge which the most noble of your countrymen feel themselves emulous to be admitted to?"

"I wish them joy of it," said Quentin, composedly. "To speak plain, I should have liked the service of the French king full well, only, dress me as fine and feed me as high as you will, I love the open air better than being shut up in a cage or a swallow's nest yonder, as you call these same grated pepper-boxes. Besides," he added, in a lower voice, "to speak truth, I love not the castle when the covin-tree [1] bears such acorns as I see yonder."

"I guess what you mean," said the Frenchman; "but speak yet more plainly."

"To speak more plainly, then," said the youth, "there grows a fair oak some flight-shot or so from yonder castle; and on that oak hangs a man in a grey jerkin, such as this which I wear."

"Ay and indeed!" said the man of France. "*Pasques-dieu!* what it is to have youthful eyes! Why, I did see something, but only took it for a raven among the branches. But the sight is no way strange, young man; when the summer fades into autumn, and moonlight nights are long, and roads become unsafe, you will see a cluster of ten, ay, of twenty such acorns, hanging on that old doddered oak. But what then? they are so many banners displayed to scare knaves; and for each rogue that hangs there, an honest man may reckon that there is a thief, a traitor, robber on the highway, a *pilleur* and oppressor of the people, the fewer in France. These, young man, are signs of our sovereign's justice."

"I would have hung them farther from my palace, though, were I King Louis," said the youth. "In my country, we hang up dead corbies where living corbies haunt, but not in

[1] See Note 5.

our gardens or pigeon-houses. The very scent of the carrion—faugh—reached my nostrils at the distance where we stood."

"If you live to be an honest and loyal servant of your prince, my good youth," answered the Frenchman, "you will know there is no perfume to match the scent of a dead traitor."

"I shall never wish to live till I lose the scent of my nostrils or the sight of my eyes," said the Scot. "Show me a living traitor, and here are my hand and my weapon; but when life is out, hatred should not live longer. But here, I fancy, we come upon the village; where I hope to show you that neither ducking nor disgust have spoiled mine appetite for my breakfast. So my good friend, to the hostelry, with all the speed you may. Yet, ere I accept of your hospitality, let me know by what name to call you."

"Men call me Maître Pierre," answered his companion. "I deal in no titles. A plain man, that can live on mine own good—that is my designation."

"So be it, Maître Pierre," said Quentin, "and I am happy my good chance has thrown us together; for I want a word of seasonable advice, and can be thankful for it."

While they spoke thus, the tower of the church and a tall wooden crucifix, rising above the trees, showed that they were at the entrance of the village.

But Maître Pierre, deflecting a little from the road, which had now joined an open and public causeway, said to his companion, that the inn to which he intended to introduce him stood somewhat secluded, and received only the better sort of travellers.

"If you mean those who travel with the better-filled purses," answered the Scot, "I am none of the number, and will rather stand my chance of your flayers on the highway than of your flayers in the hostelry!"

"*Pasques-dieu!*" said his guide, "how cautious your countrymen of Scotland are! An Englishman, now, throws himself headlong into a travern, eats and drinks of the best, and never thinks of the reckoning till his belly is full. But you forget, Master Quentin, since Quentin is your name—you forget I owe you a breakfast for the wetting which my mistake procured you. It is the penance of my offence towards you."

"In truth," said the light-hearted young man, "I had forgot wetting, offence, and penance, and all. I have walked my clothes dry, or nearly so; but I will not refuse your offer in kindness, for my dinner yesterday was a light one, and supper I had none. You seem an old and respectable burgess, and I see no reason why I should not accept your courtesy."

The Frenchman smiled aside, for he saw plainly that the youth, while he was probably half-famished, had yet some difficulty to reconcile himself to the thoughts of feeding at a stranger's cost, and was endeavouring to subdue his inward pride by the reflection that, in such slight obligations, the acceptor performed as complacent a part as he by whom the courtesy was offered.

In the mean while, they descended a narrow lane, overshadowed by tall elms, at the bottom of which a gateway admitted them into the courtyard of an inn of unusual magnitude, calculated for the accommodation of the nobles and suitors who had business at the neighbouring castle, where very seldom, and only when such hospitality was altogether unavoidable, did Louis XI. permit any of his court to have apartments. A scutcheon, bearing the *fleur-de-lys*, hung over the principal door of the large irregular building; but there was about the yard and the offices little or none of the bustle which in those days, when attendants were maintained both in public and in private houses, marked that business was alive and custom plenty. It seemed as if the stern and unsocial character of the royal mansion in the neighbourhood had communicated a portion of its solemn and terrific gloom even to a place designed, according to universal custom elsewhere, for the temple of social indulgence, merry society, and good cheer.

Maître Pierre, without calling any one, and even without approaching the principal entrance, lifted the latch of a side door, and led the way into a large room, where a fagot was blazing on the hearth, and arrangements made for a substantial breakfast.

"My gossip has been careful," said the Frenchman to the Scot. "You must be cold, and I have commanded a fire; you must be hungry, and you shall have breakfast presently."

He whistled, and the landlord entered; answered Maître Pierre's "*bon jour*" with a reverence; but in no respect showed any part of the prating humour properly belonging to a French publican of all ages.

"I expected a gentleman," said Maître Pierre, "to order breakfast. Hath he done so?"

In answer, the landlord only bowed; and while he continued to bring, and arrange upon the table, the various articles of a comfortable meal, omitted to extol their merits by a single word. And yet the breakfast merited such eulogiums as French hosts are wont to confer upon their regales, as the reader will be informed in the next chapter.

CHAPTER IV.

THE DÉJEUNER.

Sacred heaven! what masticators! what bread!
Yorick's Travels.

WE left our young stranger in France situated more comfortably than he had found himself since entering the territories of the ancient Gauls. The breakfast, as we hinted in the conclusion of the last chapter, was admirable. There was a *pâté de Périgord*, over which a gastronome would have wished to live and die, like Homer's lotus-eaters, forgetful of kin, native country, and all social obligations whatever. Its vast walls of magnificent crust seemed raised like the bulwarks of some rich metropolitan city, an emblem of the wealth which they are designed to protect. There was a delicate ragout, with just that *petite pointe de l'ail* which Gascons love and Scottishmen do not hate. There was, besides, a delicate ham, which had once supported a noble wild boar in the neighbouring wood of Mountrichart. There was the most exquisite white bread made into little round loaves called *boules* (whence the bakers took their French name of *boulangers*), of which the crust was so inviting that, even with water alone, it would have been a delicacy. But the water was not alone, for there was a flask of leather called *bottrine*, which contained about a quart of exquisite *vin de Beaulne*. So many good things might have created appetite under the ribs of death. What effect, then, must they have produced upon a youngster of scarce twenty, who (for the truth must be told) had eaten little for the two last days, save the scarcely ripe fruit which chance afforded him an opportunity of plucking, and a very moderate portion of barley-bread? He threw himself upon the ragout, and the plate was presently vacant; he attacked the mighty pasty, marched deep into the bowels of the land, and, seasoning his enormous meal with an occasional cup of wine, returned to the charge again and again, to the astonishment of mine host and the amusement of Maître Pierre.

The latter, indeed, probably because he found himself the author of a kinder action than he had thought of, seemed delighted with the appetite of the young Scot; and when, at length, he observed that his exertions began to languish, endeavoured to stimulate him to new efforts, by ordering confections, *darioles*, and any other light dainties he could think of, to entice the youth to continue his meal. While thus engaged, Maître Pierre's countenance expressed a kind of good-humour almost amounting to benevolence, which appeared remote from its ordinary sharp, caustic, and severe character. The aged almost always sympathise with the enjoyments of youth, and with its exertions of every kind, when the mind of the spectator rests on its natural poise, and is not disturbed by inward envy or idle emulation.

Quentin Durward also, while thus agreeably employed, could do no otherwise than discover that the countenance of his entertainer, which he had at first found so unprepossessing, mended when it was seen under the influence of the *vin de Beaulne*, and there was kindness in the tone with which he reproached Maître Pierre, that he amused himself with laughing at his appetite, without eating anything himself.

"I am doing penance," said Maître Pierre, "and may not

eat anything before noon, save some comfiture and a cup of water. Bid yonder lady," he added, turning to the innkeeper, "bring them hither to me."

The innkeeper left the room, and Maître Pierre proceeded: "Well, have I kept faith with you concerning the breakfast I promised you?"

"The best meal I have eaten," said the youth, "since I left Glen Houlakin."

"Glen—what?" demanded Maître Pierre; "are you going to raise the devil, that you use such long-tailed words?"

"Glen Houlakin," answered Quentin, good-humouredly, "which is to say the Glen of the Midges, is the name of our ancient patrimony, my good sir. You have bought the right to laugh at the sound, if you please."

"I have not the least intention to offend," said the old man; "but I was about to say, since you like your present meal so well, that the Scottish Archers of the Guard eat as good a one, or a better, every day."

"No wonder," said Durward, "for if they be shut up in the swallows' nests all night, they must needs have a curious appetite in the morning."

"And plenty to gratify it upon," said Maître Pierre. "They need not, like the Burgundians, chouse a bare back, that they may have a full belly: they dress like counts, and feast like abbots."

"It is well for them," said Durward.

"And wherefore will you not take service here, young man? Your uncle might, I dare say, have you placed on the file when there should a vacancy occur. And, hark in your ear, I myself have some little interest, and might be of some use to you. You can ride, I presume, as well as draw the bow?"

"Our race are as good horsemen as ever put a plated shoe into a steel stirrup; and I know not but I might accept of your kind offer. Yet, look you, food and raiment are needful things, but, in my case, men think of honour, and advancement, and brave deeds of arms. Your King Louis—God bless him! for he is a friend and ally of Scotland—but he lies here in this castle, or only rides about from one fortified town to another; and gains cities and provinces by politic embassies, and not in fair fighting. Now, for me, I am of the Douglasses' mind, who always kept the fields, because they loved better to hear the lark sing than the mouse squeak."

"Young man," said Maître Pierre, "do not judge too harshly of the actions of sovereigns. Louis seeks to spare the blood of his subjects, and cares not for his own. He showed himself a man of courage at Montl'héry."

"Ay, but that was some dozen years ago or more," answered the youth. "I should like to follow a master that would keep his honour as bright as his shield, and always venture foremost in the very throng of the battle."

"Why did you not tarry at Brussels, then," said Maître Pierre, "with the Duke of Burgundy? He would put you in the way to have your bones broken every day; and rather than fail, would do the job for you himself, especially if he heard that you had beaten his forester."

"Very true," said Quentin; "my unhappy chance has shut that door against me."

"Nay, there are plenty of dare-devils abroad, with whom mad youngsters may find service," said his adviser. "What think you, for example, of William de la Marck?"

"What!" exclaimed Durward, "serve Him with the Beard —serve the Wild Boar of Ardennes—a captain of pillagers and murderers, who would take a man's life for the value of his gaberdine, and who slays priests and pilgrims as if they were so many lance-knights and men-at-arms? It would be a blot on my father's scutcheon for ever."

"Well, my young hot-blood," replied Maître Pierre, "if you hold the *Sanglier* too unscrupulous, wherefore not follow the young Duke of Gueldres?"[1]

"Follow the foul fiend as soon," said Quentin. "Hark in your ear—he is a burden too heavy for earth to carry: hell gapes for him. Men say that he keeps his own father imprisoned, and that he has even struck him. Can you believe it?"

Maître Pierre seemed somewhat disconcerted with the naïve horror with which the young Scotsman spoke of filial ingrati-

[1] See Note 6.

tude, and he answered: "You know not, young man, how short a while the relations of blood subsist among those of elevated rank"; then changed the tone of feeling in which he had begun to speak, and added gaily: "Besides, if the duke has beaten his father, I warrant you his father hath beaten him of old, so it is but a clearing of scores."

"I marvel to hear you speak thus," said the Scot, colouring with indignation; "grey hairs such as yours ought to have fitter subjects for jesting. If the old duke did beat his son in childhood, he beat him not enough; for better he had died under the rod than have lived to make the Christian world ashamed that such a monster had ever been baptized."

"At this rate," said Maître Pierre, "as you weigh the characters of each prince and leader, I think you had better become a captain yourself; for where will one so wise find a chieftain fit to command him?"

"You laugh at me, Maître Pierre," said the youth, good-humouredly, "and perhaps you are right; but you have not named a man who is a gallant leader, and keeps a brave party up here, under whom a man might seek service well enough."

"I cannot guess whom you mean."

"Why, he that hangs like Mahomet's coffin—a curse be upon Mahomet!—between the two loadstones; he that no man can call either French or Burgundian, but who knows to hold the balance between them both, and makes both of them fear and serve him, for as great princes as they be."

"I cannot guess whom you mean," said Maître Pierre, thoughtfully.

"Why, whom should I mean but the noble Louis de Luxembourg, Count of St. Paul, the High Constable of France?[1] Yonder he makes his place good, with his gallant little army, holding his head as high as either King Louis or Duke Charles, and balancing between them, like the boy who stands on the midst of a plank, while two others are swinging on the opposite ends."

"He is in danger of the worst fall of the three," said Maître

[1] See Note 7.

Pierre. "And hark ye, my young friend, you who hold pillaging such a crime, do you know that your politic Count of St. Paul was the first who set the example of burning the country during the time of war, and that, before the shameful devastation which he committed, open towns and villages, which made no resistance, were spared on all sides?"

"Nay, faith," said Durward, "if that be the case, I shall begin to think no one of these great men is much better than another, and that a choice among them is but like choosing a tree to be hung upon. But this Count de St. Paul, this Constable, hath possessed himself by clean conveyance of the town which takes its name from my honoured saint and patron, St. Quentin[1] (here he crossed himself), and methinks, were I dwelling there, my holy patron would keep some lookout for me; he has not so many named after him as your more popular saints; and yet he must have forgotten me, poor Quentin Durward, his spiritual god-son, since he lets me go one day without food, and leaves me the next morning to the harbourage of St. Julian, and the chance courtesy of a stranger, purchased by a ducking in the renowned river Cher, or one of its tributaries."

"Blaspheme not the saints, my young friend," said Maître Pierre. "St. Julian is the faithful patron of travellers; and, peradventure, the blessed St. Quentin hath done more and better for thee than thou art aware of."

As he spoke, the door opened, and a girl, rather above than under fifteen years old, entered with a platter, covered with damask, on which was placed a small saucer of the dried plums which have always added to the reputation of Tours, and a cup of the curiously chased plate which the goldsmiths of that city were anciently famous for executing with a delicacy of workmanship that distinguished them from the other cities of France, and even excelled the skill of the metropolis. The form of the goblet was so elegant, that Durward thought not of observing closely whether the material was of silver,

---

[1] It was by his possession of this town of St. Quentin that the Constable was able to carry on those political intrigues which finally cost him so dear.

or, like what had been placed before himself, of a baser metal, but so well burnished as to resemble the richer ore.

But the sight of the young person by whom this service was executed attracted Durward's attention far more than the petty minutiæ of the duty which she performed.

He speedily made the discovery that a quantity of long black tresses, which, in the maiden fashion of his own country, were unadorned by any ornament, except a single chaplet lightly woven out of ivy leaves, formed a veil around a countenance which, in its regular features, dark eyes, and pensive expression, resembled that of Melpomene, though there was a faint glow on the cheek, and an intelligence on the lips and in the eye, which made it seem that gaiety was not foreign to a countenance so expressive, although it might not be its most habitual expression. Quentin even thought he could discern that depressing circumstances were the cause why a countenance so young and so lovely was graver than belongs to early beauty; and as the romantic imagination of youth is rapid in drawing conclusions from slight premises, he was pleased to infer, from what follows, that the fate of this beautiful vision was wrapped in silence and mystery.

"How now, Jacqueline!" said Maître Pierre, when she entered the apartment. "Wherefore this? Did I not desire that Dame Perette should bring what I wanted? *Pasquesdieu!* Is she, or does she think herself, too good to serve me?"

"My kinswoman is ill at ease," answered Jacqueline, in a hurried yet humble tone—"ill at ease, and keeps her chamber."

"She keeps it *alone*, I hope?" replied Maître Pierre with some emphasis. "I am *vieux routier*, and none of those upon whom feigned disorders pass for apologies."

Jacqueline turned pale, and even tottered, at the answer of Maître Pierre; for it must be owned that his voice and looks, at all times harsh, caustic, and unpleasing, had, when he expressed anger or suspicion, an effect both sinister and alarming.

The mountain chivalry of Quentin Durward was instantly awakened, and he hastened to approach Jacqueline and relieve her of the burden she bore, and which she passively resigned to him, while with a timid and anxious look she watched the countenance of the angry burgess. It was not in nature to resist the piercing and pity-craving expression of her looks, and Maître Pierre proceeded, not merely with an air of diminished displeasure, but with as much gentleness as he could assume in countenance and manner: "I blame not thee, Jacqueline, and thou art too young to be—what it is pity to think thou must be one day—a false and treacherous thing, like the rest of thy giddy sex.[1] No man ever lived to man's estate but he had the opportunity to know you all. Here is a Scottish cavalier will tell you the same."

Jacqueline looked for an instant on the young stranger, as if to obey Maître Pierre, but the glance, momentary as it was, appeared to Durward a pathetic appeal to him for support and sympathy; and with the promptitude dictated by the feelings of youth, and the romantic veneration for the female sex inspired by his education, he answered, hastily: "That he would throw down his gage to any antagonist, of equal rank and equal age, who should presume to say such a countenance as that which he now looked upon could be animated by other than the purest and the truest mind."

The young woman grew deadly pale, and cast an apprehensive glance upon Maître Pierre, in whom the bravado of the young gallant seemed only to excite laughter, more scornful than applausive. Quentin, whose second thoughts generally corrected the first, though sometimes after they had found utterance, blushed deeply at having uttered what might be construed into an empty boast, in presence of an old man of a peaceful profession; and, as a sort of just and appropriate penance, resolved patiently to submit to the ridicule which he had incurred. He offered the cup and trencher to Maître Pierre with a blush in his cheek, and a humiliation of countenance which endeavoured to disguise itself under an embarrassed smile.

[1] It was a part of Louis's very unamiable character, and not the best part of it, that he entertained a great contempt for the understanding, and not less for the character, of the fair sex.

"You are a foolish young man," said Maître Pierre, "and know as little of women as of princes, whose hearts," he said, crossing himself devoutly, "God keeps in His right hand."

"And who keeps those of the women, then?" said Quentin, resolved, if he could help it, not to be borne down by the assumed superiority of this extraordinary old man, whose lofty and careless manner possessed an influence over him of which he felt ashamed.

"I am afraid you must ask of them in another quarter," said Maître Pierre, composedly.

Quentin was again rebuffed, but not utterly disconcerted. "Surely," he said to himself, "I do not pay this same burgess of Tours all the deference which I yield him on account of the miserable obligation of a breakfast, though it was a right good and substantial meal. Dogs and hawks are attached by feeding only; man must have kindness, if you would bind him with cords of affection and obligation. But he is an extraordinary person; and that beautiful emanation that is even now vanishing—surely a thing so fair belongs not to this mean place, belongs not even to the money-gathering merchant himself, though he seems to exert authority over her, as doubtless he does over all whom chance brings within his little circle. It is wonderful what ideas of consequence these Flemings and Frenchmen attach to wealth, so much more than wealth deserves, that I suppose this old merchant thinks the civility I pay to his age is given to his money—I, a Scottish gentleman of blood and coat-armour, and he a mechanic of Tours!"

Such were the thoughts which hastily traversed the mind of young Durward; while Maître Pierre said, with a smile, and at the same time patting Jacqueline's head, from which hung down her long tresses: "This young man will serve me, Jacqueline; thou mayst withdraw. I will tell thy negligent kinswoman she does ill to expose thee to be gazed on unnecessarily."

"It was only to wait on you," said the maiden. "I trust you will not be displeased with my kinswoman, since——"

"*Pasques-dieu!*" said the merchant, interrupting her, but not harshly, "do you bandy words with me, you brat, or stay you to gaze upon the youngster here? Begone; he is noble, and his services will suffice me."

Jacqueline vanished; and so much was Quentin Durward interested in her sudden disappearance, that it broke his previous thread of reflection, and he complied mechanically, when Maître Pierre said, in the tone of one accustomed to be obeyed, as he threw himself carelessly upon a large easy-chair, "Place that tray beside me."

The merchant then let his dark eyebrows sink over his keen eyes, so that the last became scarce visible, or but shot forth occasionally a quick and vivid ray, like those of the sun setting behind a dark cloud, through which its beams are occasionally darted, but singly, and for an instant.

"That is a beautiful creature," said the old man at last, raising his head, and looking steadily and firmly at Quentin, when he put the question—"a lovely girl to be the servant of an *auberge?* She might grace the board of an honest burgess; but 'tis a vile education, a base origin."

It sometimes happens that a chance shot will demolish a noble castle in the air, and the architect on such occasions entertains little good-will towards him who fires it, although the damage on the offender's part may be wholly unintentional. Quentin was disconcerted, and was disposed to be angry, he himself knew not why, with this old man for acquainting him that this beautiful creature was neither more nor less than what her occupation announced—the servant of the *auberge*—an upper servant, indeed, and probably a niece of the landlord, or such-like; but still a domestic, and obliged to comply with the humour of the customers, and particularly of Maître Pierre, who probably had sufficiency of whims, and was rich enough to ensure their being attended to.

The thought, the lingering thought, again returned on him, that he ought to make the old gentleman understand the difference betwixt their conditions, and call on him to mark that, how rich soever he might be, his wealth put him on no level with a Durward of Glen Houlakin. Yet, whenever he looked on Maître Pierre's countenance with such a purpose, there was, notwithstanding the downcast look, pinched features, and mean and miserly dress, something which prevented the young man from asserting the superiority over the merchant which he conceived himself to possess. On the contrary, the oftener and more fixedly Quentin looked at him, the stronger became his curiosity to know who or what this man actually was; and he set him down internally for at least a syndic or high magistrate of Tours, or one who was, in some way or other, in the full habit of exacting and receiving deference.

Meantime, the merchant seemed again sunk into a reverie, from which he raised himself only to make the sign of the cross devoutly, and to eat some of the dried fruit, with a morsel of biscuit. He then signed to Quentin to give him the cup, adding, however, by way of question, as he presented it: "You are noble, you say?"

"I surely am," replied the Scot, "if fifteen descents can make me so. So I told you before. But do not constrain yourself on that account, Maître Pierre: I have always been taught it is the duty of the young to assist the more aged."

"An excellent maxim," said the merchant, availing himself of the youth's assistance in handing the cup, and filling it from a ewer which seemed of the same materials with the goblet, without any of those scruples in point of propriety which perhaps Quentin had expected to excite.

"The devil take the ease and familiarity of this old merchanical burgher," said Durward once more to himself; "he uses the attendance of a noble Scottish gentleman with as little ceremony as I would that of a gillie from Glen Isla."

The merchant, in the mean while, having finished his cup of water, said to his companion: "From the zeal with which you seemed to relish the *vin de Beaulne*, I fancy you would not care much to pledge me in this elemental liquor. But I have an elixir about me which can convert even the rock water into the richest wines of France."

As he spoke, he took a large purse from his bosom, made of the fur of the sea-otter, and streamed a shower of small silver pieces into the goblet, until the cup, which was but a small one, was more than half full.

"You have reason to be more thankful, young man," said

Maître Pierre, "both to your patron St. Quentin and to St. Julian than you seemed to be but now. I would advise you to bestow alms in their name. Remain in this hostelry until you see your kinsman, Le Balafré, who will be relieved from guard in the afternoon. I will cause him to be acquainted that he may find you here, for I have business in the castle."

Quentin Durward would have said something to have excused himself from accepting the profuse liberality of his new friend; but Maître Pierre, bending his dark brows and erecting his stooping figure into an attitude of more dignity than he had yet seen him assume, said, in a tone of authority: "No reply, young man, but do what you are commanded."

With these words, he left the apartment, making a sign, as he departed, that Quentin must not follow him.

The young Scotsman stood astounded, and knew not what to think of the matter. His first most natural, though perhaps not most dignified, impulse drove him to peep into the silver goblet, which assuredly was more than half full of silver pieces, to the number of several scores, of which perhaps Quentin had never called twenty his own at one time during the course of his whole life. But could he reconcile it to his dignity as a gentleman to accept the money of this wealthy plebeian? This was a trying question; for though he had secured a good breakfast, it was no great reserve upon which to travel either back to Dijon, in case he chose to hazard the wrath, and enter the service, of the Duke of Burgundy, or to St. Quentin, if he fixed on that of the Constable St. Paul; for to one of those powers, if not to the King of France, he was determined to offer his services. He perhaps took the wisest resolution in the circumstances, in resolving to be guided by the advice of his uncle; and, in the mean time, he put the money into his velvet hawking-pouch, and called for the landlord of the house, in order to restore the silver cup—resolving, at the same time, to ask him some questions about this liberal and authoritative merchant.

The man of the house appeared presently; and, if not more communicative, was at least more loquacious, than he had been formerly. He positively declined to take back the silver cup. "It was none of his," he said, "but Maître Pierre's, who had bestowed it on his guest. He had, indeed, four silver *hanaps* of his own, which had been left him by his grandmother, of happy memory, but no more like the beautiful carving of that in his guest's hand than a peach was like a turnip: that was one of the famous cups of Tours, wrought by Martin Dominique, an artist who might brag all Paris."

"And, pray, who is this Maître Pierre," said Durward, interrupting him, "who confers such valuable gifts on strangers?"

"Who is Maître Pierre?" said the host, dropping the words as slowly from his mouth as if he had been distilling them.

"Ay," said Durward, hastily and peremptorily, "who is this Maître Pierre, and why does he throw about his bounties in this fashion? And who is the butcherly-looking fellow whom he sent forward to order breakfast?"

"Why, fair sir, as to who Maître Pierre is, you should have asked the question of himself; and for the gentleman who ordered breakfast to be made ready, may God keep us from his closer acquaintance!"

"There is something mysterious in all this," said the young Scot. "This Maître Pierre tells me he is a merchant."

"And if he told you so," said the innkeeper, "surely he is a merchant."

"What commodities does he deal in?"

"Oh, many a fair matter of traffic," said the host; "and especially he has set up silk manufactories here, which match those rich bales that the Venetians bring from India and Cathay. You might see the rows of mulberry-trees as you came hither, all planted by Maître Pierre's commands, to feed the silk-worms."

"And that young person who brought in the confections, who is she, my good friend?" said the guest.

"My lodger, sir, with her guardian, some sort of aunt or kinswoman, as I think," replied the innkeeper.

"And do you usually employ your guests in waiting on each other?" said Durward; "for I observed that Maître Pierre would take nothing from your hand or that of your attendant."

"Rich men may have their fancies, for they can pay for them," said the landlord; "this is not the first time that Maître Pierre has found the true way to make gentlefolks serve at his beck."

The young Scotsman felt somewhat offended at the insinuation; but, disguising his resentment, he asked whether he could be accommodated with an apartment at this place for a day, and perhaps longer.

"Certainly," the innkeeper replied; "for whatever time he was pleased to command it."

"Could he be permitted," he asked, "to pay his respects to the ladies, whose fellow-lodger he was about to become?"

The innkeeper was uncertain. "They went not abroad," he said, "and received no one at home."

"With the exception, I presume, of Maître Pierre?" said Durward.

"I am not at liberty to name any exceptions," answered the man, firmly but respectfully.

Quentin, who carried the notions of his own importance pretty high, considering how destitute he was of means to support them, being somewhat mortified by the innkeeper's reply, did not hesitate to avail himself of a practice common enough in that age. "Carry to the ladies," he said, "a flask of *Auvernat*, with my humble duty; and say, that Quentin Durward, of the house of Glen Houlakin, a Scottish cavalier of honour, and now their fellow-lodger, desires the permission to dedicate his homage to them in a personal interview."

The messenger departed, and returned, almost instantly, with the thanks of the ladies, who declined the proffered refreshment, and with their acknowledgments to the Scottish cavalier, regretted that, residing there in privacy, they could not receive his visit.

Quentin bit his lip, took a cup of the rejected *Auvernat*, which the host had placed on the table. "By the mass, but this is a strange country," said he to himself, "where merchants and mechanics exercise the manners and munificence of nobles, and little travelling damsels, who hold their court in a *cabaret*, keep their state like disguised princesses! I will

Charles the Bold, Duke of Burgundy.

Quentin Durward, Chap. i., p. 47.

see that black-browed maiden again, or it will go hard, however"; and having formed this prudent resolution, he demanded to be conducted to the apartment which he was to call his own.

The landlord presently ushered him up a turret staircase, and from thence along a gallery, with many doors opening from it, like those of cells in a convent—a resemblance which our young hero, who recollected, with much *ennui*, an early specimen of a monastic life, was far from admiring. The host paused at the very end of the gallery, selected a key from the large bunch which he carried at his girdle, opened the door, and showed his guest the interior of a turret-chamber, small, indeed, but which, being clean and solitary, and having the pallet bed and the few articles of furniture in unusually good order, seemed, on the whole, a little palace.

"I hope you will find your dwelling agreeable here, fair sir," said the landlord. "I am bound to pleasure every friend of Maître Pierre."

"O happy ducking!" exclaimed Quentin Durward, cutting a caper on the floor so soon as his host had retired. "Never came good luck in a better or a wetter form. I have been fairly deluged by my good fortune."

As he thus spoke, he stepped towards the little window, which, as the turret projected considerably from the principal line of the building, not only commanded a very pretty garden of some extent, belonging to the inn, but overlooked beyond its boundary a pleasant grove of those very mulberry-trees which Maître Pierre was said to have planted for the support of the silk-worm. Besides, turning the eye from those more remote objects, and looking straight along the wall, the turret of Quentin was opposite to another turret, and the little window at which he stood commanded a similar little window in a corresponding projection of the building. Now, it would be difficult for a man twenty years older than Quentin to say why this locality interested him more than either the pleasant garden or the grove of mulberry-trees; for, alas! eyes which have been used for forty years and upwards look with indifference on little turret-windows, though the lattice be half open to admit the air, while the shutter is half closed to exclude the sun, or perhaps a too curious eye—nay, even though there hang on the one side of the casement a lute, partly mantled by a light veil of sea-green silk. But, at Durward's happy age, such "accidents," as a painter would call them, form sufficient foundation for a hundred airy visions and mysterious conjectures, at recollection of which the full-grown man smiles while he sighs, and sighs while he smiles.

As it may be supposed that our friend Quentin wished to learn a little more of his fair neighbour, the owner of the lute and veil—as it may be supposed he was at least interested to know whether she might not prove the same whom he had seen in humble attendance on Maître Pierre, it must of course be understood that he did not produce a broad staring visage and person in full front of his own casement. Durward knew better the art of bird-catching; and it was to his keeping his person skilfully withdrawn on one side of his window, while he peeped through the lattice, that he owed the pleasure of seeing a white, round, beautiful arm take down the instrument, and that his ears had presently after their share in the reward of his dexterous management.

The maid of the little turret, of the veil, and of the lute sung exactly such an air as we are accustomed to suppose flowed from the lips of the high-born dames of chivalry, when the knights and troubadours listened and languished. The words had neither so much sense, wit, or fancy as to withdraw the attention from the music, nor the music so much of art as to drown all feeling of the words. The one seemed fitted to the other; and if the song had been recited without the notes, or the air played without the words, neither would have been worth noting. It is, therefore, scarcely fair to put upon record lines intended not to be said or read, but only to be sung. But such scraps of old poetry have always had a sort of fascination for us; and as the tune is lost for ever, unless Bishop happens to find the notes, or some lark teaches Stephens[1] to warble the air, we will risk our credit, and the taste of the Lady of the Lute, by preserving the verses, simple and even rude as they are.

[1] See Note 8.

"Ah! County Guy, the hour is nigh,
 The sun has left the lea,
The orange flower perfumes the bower,
 The breeze is on the sea.
The lark, his lay who thrill'd all day,
 Sits hush'd his partner nigh;
Breeze, bird, and flower, confess the hour,
 But where is County Guy?

"The village maid steals through the shade,
 Her shepherd's suit to hear;
To beauty shy, by lattice high,
 Sings high-born cavalier.
The star of Love, all stars above,
 Now reigns o'er earth and sky;
And high and low the influence know—
 But where is County Guy?"

Whatever the reader may think of this simple ditty, it had a powerful effect on Quentin, when married to heavenly airs, and sung by a sweet and melting voice, the notes mingling with the gentle breezes which wafted perfumes from the garden, and the figure of the songstress being so partially and obscurely visible as threw a veil of mysterious fascination over the whole.

At the close of the air, the listener could not help showing himself more boldly than he had yet done, in a rash attempt to see more than he had yet been able to discover. The music instantly ceased, the casement was closed, and a dark curtain, dropped on the inside, put a stop to all farther observation on the part of the neighbour in the next turret.

Durward was mortified and surprised at the consequence of his precipitance, but comforted himself with the hope that the Lady of the Lute could neither easily forego the practice of an instrument which seemed so familiar to her, nor cruelly resolve to renounce the pleasures of fresh air and an open window, for the churlish purpose of preserving for her own exclusive ear the sweet sounds which she created. There came, perhaps, a little feeling of personal vanity to mingle with these consolatory reflections. If, as he shrewdly suspected, there was a beautiful, dark-tressed damsel inhabitant of the one turret, he could not but be conscious that a handsome, young, roving, bright-locked gallant, a cavalier of fortune, was the tenant of the other; and romances, those prudent instructors, had taught his youth that if damsels were shy, they were yet neither void of interest nor of curiosity in their neighbour's affairs.

Whilst Quentin was engaged in these sage reflections, a sort of attendant or chamberlain of the inn informed him that a cavalier desired to speak with him below.

CHAPTER V.

THE MAN-AT-ARMS.

> Full of strange oaths, and bearded like the pard,
> Seeking the bubble reputation even in the cannon's mouth.
> *As You Like It.*

THE cavalier who awaited Quentin Durward's descent into the apartment where he had breakfasted was one of those of whom Louis XI. had long since said, that they held in their hands the fortune of France, as to them were entrusted the direct custody and protection of the royal person.

Charles the Sixth had instituted this celebrated body, the Archers, as they were called, of the Scottish Body-Guard, with better reason than can generally be alleged for establishing round the throne a guard of foreign and mercenary troops. The divisions which tore from his side more than half of France, together with the wavering and uncertain faith of the nobility who yet acknowledged his cause, rendered it impolitic and unsafe to commit his personal safety to their keeping. The Scottish nation was the hereditary enemy of the English, and the ancient, and, as it seemed, the natural, allies of France. They were poor, courageous, faithful; their ranks were sure to be supplied from the superabundant population of their own country, than which none in Europe sent forth more or bolder adventurers. Their high claims of descent, too, gave them a good title to approach the person of a monarch more closely than other troops, while the comparative smallness of their numbers prevented the possibility of their mutinying, and becoming masters where they ought to be servants.

On the other hand, the French monarchs made it their policy to conciliate the affections of this select band of foreigners, by allowing them honorary privileges and ample pay, which last most of them disposed of with military profusion in supporting their supposed rank. Each of them ranked as a gentleman in place and honour; and their near approach to the king's person gave them dignity in their own eyes, as well as importance in those of the nation of France. They were sumptuously armed, equipped, and mounted; and each was entitled to allowance for a squire, a valet, a page, and two yeomen, one of whom was termed *coutelier*, from the large knife which he wore to despatch those whom in the *mêlée* his master had thrown to the ground. With these followers, and a corresponding equipage, an archer of the Scottish Guard was a person of quality and importance; and vacancies being generally filled up by those who had been trained in the service as pages or valets, the cadets of the best Scottish families were often sent to serve under some friend and relation in those capacities, until a chance of preferment should occur.

The coutelier and his companion, not being noble or capable of this promotion, were recruited from persons of inferior quality; but as their pay and appointments were excellent, their masters were easily able to select from among their wandering countrymen the strongest and most courageous to wait upon them in these capacities.

Ludovic Lesly, or, as we shall more frequently call him, Le Balafré, by which name he was generally known in France, was upwards of six feet high, robust, strongly compacted in person, and hard-favoured in countenance, which latter attribute was much increased by a large and ghastly scar, which, beginning on his forehead, and narrowly missing his right eye, had laid bare the cheek-bone, and descended from thence almost to the tip of his ear, exhibiting a deep seam, which was sometimes scarlet, sometimes purple, sometimes blue, and sometimes approaching to black; but always hideous, because at variance with the complexion of the face in whatever state it chanced to be, whether agitated or still, flushed with unusual passion, or in its ordinary state of weather-beaten and sunburnt swarthiness.

His dress and arms were splendid. He wore his national bonnet, crested with a tuft of feathers, and with a Virgin Mary of massive silver for a brooch. These brooches had been presented to the Scottish Guard, in consequence of the King, in one of his fits of superstitious piety, having devoted the swords of his guard to the service of the Holy Virgin, and, as some say, carried the matter so far as to draw out a commission to Our Lady as their captain-general. The archer's gorget, arm-pieces, and gauntlets were of the finest steel, curiously inlaid with silver, and his hauberk, or shirt of mail, was as clear and bright as the frostwork of a winter morning upon fern or brier. He wore a loose surcoat, or cassock, of rich blue velvet, open at the sides like that of a herald, with a large white St. Andrew's cross of embroidered silver bisecting it both before and behind; his knees and legs were protected by hose of mail and shoes of steel; a broad strong poniard, called the "mercy of God," hung by his right side; the baldric for his two-handed sword, richly embroidered, hung upon his left shoulder; but, for convenience, he at present carried in his hand that unwieldy weapon, which the rules of his service forbade him to lay aside.

Quentin Durward, though, like the Scottish youth of the period, he had been early taught to look upon arms and war, thought he had never seen a more martial-looking, or more completely equipped and accomplished, man-at-arms than now saluted him in the person of his mother's brother, called Ludovic with the Scar, or Le Balafré; yet he could not but shrink a little from the grim expression of his countenance, while, with its rough mustachios, he brushed first the one and then the other cheek of his kinsman, welcomed his nephew to France, and in the same breath, asked what news from Scotland.

"Little good tidings, dear uncle," replied young Durward; "but I am glad that you know me so readily."

"I would have known thee, boy, in the *landes* of Bordeaux,

had I met thee marching there like a crane on a pair of stilts.[1] But sit thee down—sit thee down; if there is sorrow to hear of, we will have wine to make us bear it. Ho! old Pinch-Measure, our good host, bring us of thy best, and that in an instant."

The well-known sound of the Scottish French was as familiar in the taverns near Plessis as that of the Swiss French in the modern *guinguettes* of Paris; and promptly—ay, with the promptitude of fear and precipitation—was it heard and obeyed. A flagon of champagne stood before them, of which the elder took a draught, while the nephew helped himself only to a moderate sip, to acknowledge his uncle's courtesy, saying, in excuse, that he had already drunk wine that morning.

"That had been a rare good apology in the mouth of thy sister, fair nephew," said Le Balafré; "you must fear the wine-pot less, if you would wear beard on your face, and write yourself soldier. But come—come, unbuckle your Scottish mail-bag—give us the news of Glen Houlakin. How doth my sister?"

"Dead, fair uncle," answered Quentin, sorrowfully.

"Dead!" echoed his uncle with a tone rather marked by wonder than sympathy; "why, she was five years younger than I, and I was never better in my life. Dead! the thing is impossible. I have never had so much as a headache, unless after revelling out my two or three days' furlough with the brethren of the joyous science; and my poor sister is dead! And your father, fair nephew, hath he married again?"

And ere the youth could reply, he read the answer in his surprise at the question, and said: "What! no? I would have sworn that Allan Durward was no man to live without a wife. He loved to have his house in order, loved to look on a pretty woman too, and was somewhat strict in life withal; matrimony did all this for him. Now, I care little about these comforts; and I can look on a pretty woman without thinking on the sacrament of wedlock; I am scarce holy enough for that."

See Use of Stilts. Note 9.

"Alas! dear uncle, my mother was left a widow a year since, when Glen Houlakin was harried by the Ogilvies. My father, and my two uncles, and my two elder brothers, and seven of my kinsmen, and the harper, and the tasker, and some six more of our people, were killed in defending the castle; and there is not a burning hearth or a standing stone in all Glen Houlakin."

"Cross of St. Andrew!" said Le Balafré; "that is what I call an onslaught! Ay, these Ogilvies were ever but sorry neighbours to Glen Houlakin; an evil chance it was, but fate of war—fate of war. When did this mishap befall, fair nephew?" With that he took a deep draught of wine, and shook his head with much solemnity when his kinsman replied that his family had been destroyed upon the festival of St. Jude last bye-past.

"Look ye there," said the soldier, "I said it was all chance. On that very day I and twenty of my comrades carried the Castle of Roche-Noir by storm, from Amaury Bras-de-Fer, a captain of free lances, whom you must have heard of. I killed him on his own threshold, and gained as much gold as made this fair chain, which was once twice as long as it now is; and that minds me to send part of it on an holy errand. Here, Andrew—Andrew!"

Andrew, his yeoman, entered, dressed like the archer himself in the general equipment, but without the armour for the limbs; that of the body more coarsely manufactured; his cap without a plume, and his cassock made of serge, or ordinary cloth, instead of rich velvet. Untwining his gold chain from his neck, Balafré twisted off, with his firm and strong-set teeth, about four inches from the one end of it, and said to his attendant: "Here, Andrew, carry this to my gossip, jolly Father Boniface, the monk of St. Martin's; greet him well from me, by the same token that he could not say 'God save ye' when we last parted at midnight. Tell my gossip that my brother and sister, and some others of my house, are all dead and gone, and I pray him to say masses for their souls as far as the value of these links will carry him, and to do on trust what else may be necessary to free them from purgatory.

And hark ye, as they were just-living people, and free from all heresy, it may be that they are wellnigh out of limbo already, so that a little matter may have them free of the fetlocks; and in that case, look ye, ye will say I desire to take out the balance of the gold in curses upon a generation called the Ogilvies of Angusshire, in what way soever the church may best come at them. You understand all this, Andrew?"

The coutelier nodded.

"Then look that none of the links find their way to the wine-house ere the monk touches them; for if it so chance, thou shalt taste of saddle-girth and stirrup-leather, till thou art as raw as St. Bartholomew. Yet hold, I see thy eye has fixed on the wine measure, and thou shalt not go without tasting."

So saying, he filled him a brimful cup, which the coutelier drank off, and retired to do his patron's commission.

"And now, fair nephew, let us hear what was your own fortune in this unhappy matter."

"I fought it out among those who were older and stouter than I was, till we were all brought down," said Durward, "and I received a cruel wound."

"Not a worse slash than I received ten years since myself," said Le Balafré. "Look at this now, my fair nephew," tracing the dark crimson gash which was imprinted on his face. "An Ogilvie's sword never ploughed so deep a furrow."

"They ploughed deep enough," answered Quentin, sadly; "but they were tired at last, and my mother's entreaties procured mercy for me, when I was found to retain some spark of life; but although a learned monk of Aberbrothock, who chanced to be our guest at the fatal time, and narrowly escaped being killed in the fray, was permitted to bind my wounds, and finally to remove me to a place of safety, it was only on promise, given both by my mother and him, that I should become a monk."

"A monk!" exclaimed the uncle—"Holy St. Andrew! that is what never befell me. No one, from my childhood upwards, ever so much as dreamed of making me a monk. And yet I wonder when I think of it; for you will allow that, bating the reading and writing, which I could never learn; and the psalmody, which I could never endure; and the dress, which is that of a mad beggar—Our Lady forgive me! (here he crossed himself); and their fasts, which do not suit my appetite, I would have made every whit as good a monk as my little gossip at St. Martin's yonder. But I know not why, none ever proposed the station to me. Oh so, fair nephew, you were to be a monk, then; and wherefore, I pray you?"

"That my father's house might be ended, either in the cloister or in the tomb," answered Quentin, with deep feeling.

"I see," answered his uncle—"I comprehend. Cunning rogues—very cunning! They might have been cheated, though; for, look ye, fair nephew, I myself remember the canon Robersart who had taken the vows, and afterwards broke out of cloister, and became a captain of Free Companions. He had a mistress, the prettiest wench I ever saw, and three as beautiful children. There is no trusting monks, fair nephew,—no trusting them: they may become soldiers and fathers when you least expect it; but on with your tale."

"I have little more to tell," said Durward, "except that, considering my poor mother to be in some degree a pledge for me, I was induced to take upon me the dress of a novice, and conformed to the cloister rules, and even learned to read and write."

"To read and write!" exclaimed Le Balafré, who was one of that sort of people who think all knowledge is miraculous which chances to exceed their own. "To write, say'st thou, and to read! I cannot believe it: never Durward could write his name that ever I heard of, nor Lesly either. I can answer for one of them: I can no more write than I can fly. Now, in St. Louis's name, how did they teach it you?"

"It was troublesome at first," said Durward, "but became more easy by use; and I was weak with my wounds and loss of blood, and desirous to gratify my preserver, Father Peter, and so I was the more easily kept to my task. But after several months' languishing, my good kind mother died, and as my health was now fully restored, I communicated to my benefactor, who was also sub-prior of the convent, my reluctance to take the vows; and it was agreed between us, since my vocation lay not to the cloister, that I should be sent out into the world to seek my fortune, and that, to save the sub-prior from the anger of the Ogilvies, my departure should have the appearance of flight; and to colour it, I brought off the abbot's hawk with me. But I was regularly dismissed, as will appear from the hand and seal of the abbot himself."

"That is right—that is well," said his uncle. "Our king cares little what other theft thou mayst have made, but hath a horror at anything like a breach of the cloister. And, I warrant thee, thou hadst no great treasure to bear thy charges?"

"Only a few pieces of silver," said the youth; "for to you, fair uncle, I must make a free confession."

"Alas!" replied Le Balafré, "that is hard. Now, though I am never a hoarder of my pay, because it doth ill to bear a charge about one in these perilous times, yet I always have —and I would advise you to follow my example—some odd gold chain, or bracelet, or carcanet, that serves for the ornament of my person, and can at need spare a superfluous link or two, or it may be a superfluous stone, for sale, that can answer any immediate purpose. But you may ask, fair kinsman, how you are to come by such toys as this?" (he shook his chain with complacent triumph). They hang not on every bush; they grow not in the fields like the daffodils with whose stalks children make knights' collars. What then? you may get such where I got this, in the service of the good King of France, where there is always wealth to be found, if a man has but the heart to seek it, at the risk of a little life or so."

"I understand," said Quentin, evading a decision to which he felt himself as yet scarcely competent, "that the Duke of Burgundy keeps a more noble state than the King of France, and that there is more honour to be won under his banners, that good blows are struck there, and deeds of arms done; while the Most Christian King, they say, gains his victories by his ambassadors' tongues."

"You speak like a foolish boy, fair nephew," answered he with the scar; "and yet, I bethink me, when I came hither I was nearly as simple: I could never think of a king but what I supposed him either sitting under the high deas and feasting amid his high vassals and paladins, eating *blancmanger*, with a great gold crown upon his head, or else charging at the head of his troops like Charlemagne in the romaunts, or like Robert Bruce or William Wallace in our own true histories, such as Barbour and the Minstrel. Hark in thine ear, man—it is all moonshine in the water. Policy—policy does it all. But what is policy, you will say? It is an art this French king of ours has found out, to fight with other men's swords, and to wage his soldiers out of other men's purses. Ah! it is the wisest prince that ever put purple on his back; and yet he weareth not much of that neither: I see him often go plainer than I would think befitted me to do."

"But you meet not my exception, fair uncle," answered young Durward; "I would serve, since serve I must in a foreign land, somewhere where a brave deed, were it my hap to do one, might work me a name."

"I understand you, my fair nephew," said the royal man-at-arms—"I understand you passing well; but you are unripe in these matters. The Duke of Burgundy is a hot-brained, impetuous, pudding-headed, iron-ribbed dare-all. He charges at the head of his nobles and native knights, his liegemen of Artois and Hainault; think you, if you were there, or if I were there myself, that we could be much farther forward than the Duke and all his brave nobles of his own land? If we were not up with them, we had a chance to be turned on the provost-marshal's hands for being slow in making to; if we were abreast of them, all would be called well, and we might be thought to have deserved our pay; and grant that I was a spear's-length or so in the front, which is both difficult and dangerous in such a *mêlée* where all do their best, why my lord duke says, in his Flemish tongue, when he sees a good blow struck, 'Ha! *gut getroffen!* a good lance—a brave Scot; give him a florin to drink our health'; but neither rank, nor lands, nor treasures come to the stranger in such a service: all goes to the children of the soil."

"And where should it go, in Heaven's name, fair uncle?" demanded young Durward.

"To him that protects the children of the soil," said Balafré, drawing up his gigantic height. "Thus says King Louis: 'My good French peasant—mine honest Jacques Bonhomme—get you to your tools, your plough and your harrow, your pruning-knife and your hoe; here is my gallant Scot that will fight for you, and you shall only have the trouble to pay him. And you, my most serene duke, my illustrious count, and my most mighty marquis, e'en rein up your fiery courage till it is wanted, for it is apt to start out of the course, and to hurt its master; here are my companies of ordnance—here are my French Guards—here are, above all, my Scottish Archers, and mine honest Ludovic with the Scar, who will fight, as well or better than you, with all that undisciplined valour which, in your fathers' time, lost Cressy and Azincour.' Now, see you not in which of these states a cavalier of fortune holds the highest rank, and must come to the highest honour?"

"I think I understand you, fair uncle," answered the nephew; "but, in my mind, honour cannot be won where there is no risk. Sure, this is—I pray you pardon me—an easy and almost slothful life, to mount guard round an elderly man whom no one thinks of harming, to spend summer day and winter night up in yonder battlements, and shut up all the while in iron cages, for fear you should desert your posts; uncle—uncle, it is but the hawk upon his perch, who is never carried out to the fields!"

"Now, by St. Martin of Tours, the boy has some spirit—a right touch of the Lesly in him—much like myself, though always with a little more folly in it! Hark ye, youth—long live the King of France!—scarce a day but there is some commission in hand, by which some of his followers may win both coin and credit. Think not that the bravest and most dangerous deeds are done by daylight. I could tell you of some, as scaling castles, making prisoners, and the like, where one who shall be nameless hath run higher risk, and gained greater favour, than any desperado in the train of desperate Charles of Burgundy. And if it please his Majesty to remain behind and in the background while such things are doing, he hath the more leisure of spirit to admire, and the more liberality of hand to reward, the adventurers, whose dangers, perhaps, and whose feats of arms, he can better judge of than if he had personally shared them. Oh, 'tis a sagacious and most politic monarch!"

His nephew paused, and then said, in a low but impressive tone of voice: "The good Father Peter used often to teach me there might be much danger in deeds by which little glory was acquired. I need not say to you, fair uncle, that I do in course suppose that these secret commissions must needs be honourable."

"For whom or for what take you me, fair nephew?" said Balafré, somewhat sternly; "I have not been trained, indeed, in the cloister, neither can I write nor read. But I am your mother's brother: I am a loyal Lesly. Think you that I am like to recommend to you anything unworthy? The best knight in France, Du Guesclin himself, if he were alive again, might be proud to number my deeds among his achievements."

"I cannot doubt your warranty, fair uncle," said the youth; "you are the only adviser my mishap has left me. But is it true, as fame says, that this king keeps a meagre court here at his Castle of Plessis? No repair of nobles or courtiers, none of his grand feudatories in attendance, none of the high officers of the crown; half solitary sports, shared only with the menials of his household; secret councils, to which only low and obscure men are invited; rank and nobility depressed, and men raised from the lowest origin to the kingly favour— all this seems unregulated, resembles not the manners of his father, the noble Charles, who tore from the fangs of the English lion this more than half-conquered kingdom of France."

"You speak like a giddy child," said Le Balafré; "and even as a child, you harp over the same notes on a new string. Look you: if the King employs Oliver Dain, his barber, to do what Oliver can do better than any peer of them all, is not the kingdom the gainer? If he bids his stout provost-marshal, Tristan, arrest such or such a seditious burgher, take off such or such a turbulent noble, the deed is done and no more of it; when, were the commission given to a duke or peer of France, he might perchance send the King back a defiance in exchange. If, again, the King pleases to give to plain Ludovic le Balafré a commission which he will execute, instead of employing the high constable, who would perhaps betray it, doth it not show wisdom? Above all, doth not a monarch of such conditions best suit cavaliers of fortune, who must go where their services are most highly prized and most frequently in demand? No—no, child, I tell thee Louis knows how to choose his confidants, and what to charge them with, suiting, as they say, the burden to each man's back. He is not like the King of Castile, who choked of thirst because the great butler was not beside to hand his cup. But hark to the bell of St. Martin's! I must hasten back to the castle. Farewell; make much of yourself, and at eight to-morrow morning present yourself before the drawbridge, and ask the sentinel for me. Take heed you step not off the straight and beaten path in approaching the portal! There are such traps and snap-haunches as may cost you a limb, which you will sorely miss. You shall see the King, and learn to judge him for yourself. Farewell.

So saying, Balafré hastily departed, forgetting, in his hurry, to pay for the wine he had called for—a shortness of memory incidental to persons of his description, and which his host, overawed, perhaps, by the nodding bonnet and ponderous two-handed sword, did not presume to use any efforts for correcting.

It might have been expected that, when left alone, Durward would have again betaken himself to his turret, in order to watch for the repetition of those delicious sounds which had soothed his morning reverie. But that was a chapter of romance, and his uncle's conversation had opened to him a page of the real history of life. It was no pleasing one, and for the present the recollections and reflections which it excited were qualified to overpower other thoughts, and especially all of a light and soothing nature.

Quentin resorted to a solitary walk along the banks of the rapid Cher, having previously inquired of his landlord for one which he might traverse without fear of disagreeable interruption from snares and pitfalls, and there endeavoured to compose his turmoiled and scattered thoughts, and consider his future motions, upon which his meeting with his uncle had thrown some dubiety.

CHAPTER VI.

THE BOHEMIANS.

> Sae rantingly, sae wantonly
> Sae dauntingly gaed he,
> He play'd a spring and danced a round
> Beneath the gallows-tree!
> *Old Song.*

THE manner in which Quentin Durward had been educated was not of a kind to soften the heart, or perhaps to improve the moral feelings. He, with the rest of his family, had been trained to the chase as an amusement, and taught to consider war as their only serious occupation, and that it was the great duty of their lives stubbornly to endure, and fiercely to retaliate, the attacks of their feudal enemies, by whom their race had been at last almost annihilated. And yet there mixed with these feuds a spirit of rude chivalry, and even courtesy, which softened their rigour; so that revenge, their only justice, was still prosecuted with some regard to humanity and generosity. The lessons of the worthy old monk, better attended to, perhaps, during a long illness and adversity than they might have been in health and success, had given young Durward still farther insight into the duties of humanity towards others; and, considering the ignorance of the period, the general prejudices entertained in favour of a military life, and the manner in which he himself had been bred, the youth was disposed to feel more accurately the moral duties incumbent on his station than was usual at the time.

He reflected on his interview with his uncle with a sense of embarrassment and disappointment. His hopes had been high; for although intercourse by letters was out of the question, yet a pilgrim, or an adventurous trafficker, or a crippled soldier, sometimes brought Lesly's name to Glen Houlakin, and all united in praising his undaunted courage, and his success in many petty enterprises which his master had entrusted to him. Quentin's imagination had filled up the sketch in his own way, and assimilated his successful and adventurous uncle (whose exploits probably lost nothing in the telling) to some of the champions and knights-errant of whom minstrels sang, and who won crowns and king's daughters by dint of sword and lance. He was now compelled to rank his kinsman greatly lower in the scale of chivalry; but, blinded by the high respect paid to parents and those who approach that character, moved by every early prejudice in his favour, inexperienced besides, and passionately attached to his mother's memory, he saw not, in the only brother of that dear relation, the character he truly held, which was that of an ordinary mercenary soldier, neither much worse nor greatly better than many of the same profession whose presence added to the distracted state of France.

Without being wantonly cruel, Le Balafré was, from habit, indifferent to human life and human suffering; he was profoundly ignorant, greedy of booty, unscrupulous how he acquired it, and profuse in expending it on the gratification of his passions. The habit of attending exclusively to his own wants and interests had converted him into one of the most selfish animals in the world; so that he was seldom able, as the reader may have remarked, to proceed far in any subject without considering how it applied to himself, or, as it is called, making the case his own, though not upon feelings connected with the golden rule, but such as were very different. To this must be added, that the narrow round of his duties and his pleasures had gradually circumscribed his thoughts, hopes, and wishes, and quenched in a great measure the wild spirit of honour, and desire of distinction in arms, by which his youth had been once animated. Balafré was, in short, a keen soldier, hardened, selfish, and narrow-minded; active and bold in the discharge of his duty, but acknowledging few objects beyond it, except the formal observance of a careless devotion, relieved by an occasional debauch with brother Boniface, his comrade and confessor. Had his genius been of a more extended character, he would probably have been promoted to some important command, for the King, who knew every soldier of his body-guard personally, reposed much confidence in Balafré's courage and fidelity; and, besides, the Scot had either wisdom or cunning enough perfectly to understand, and ably to humour, the peculiarities of that sovereign. Still, however, his capacity was too much limited to admit of his rising to higher rank, and though smiled on and favoured by Louis on many occasions, Balafré continued a mere Life-Guardsman, or Scottish Archer.

Without seeing the full scope of his uncle's character, Quentin felt shocked at his indifference to the disastrous extirpation of his brother-in-law's whole family, and could not help being surprised, moreover, that so near a relative had not offered him the assistance of his purse, which, but for the generosity of Maître Pierre, he would have been under the necessity of directly craving from him. He wronged his uncle, however, in supposing that this want of attention to his probable necessities was owing to avarice. Not precisely needing money himself at that moment, it had not occurred to Balafré that his nephew might be in exigencies; otherwise, he held a near kinsman so much a part of himself, that he would have provided for the weal of the living nephew, as he endeavoured to do for that of his deceased sister and her husband. But, whatever was the motive, the neglect was very unsatisfactory to young Durward, and he wished more than once he had taken service with the Duke of Burgundy before he quarrelled with his forester. "Whatever had then become of me," he thought to himself, "I should always have been able to keep up my spirits with the reflection that I had, in case of the worst, a stout back-friend in this uncle of mine.

But now I have seen him, and, woe worth him! there has been more help in a mere mechanical stranger than I have found in my own mother's brother, my countryman and a cavalier. One would think the slash, that has carved all comeliness out of his face, had let at the same time every drop of gentle blood out of his body."

Durward now regretted he had not had an opportunity to mention Maître Pierre to Le Balafré, in the hope of obtaining some farther account of that personage; but his uncle's questions had followed fast on each other, and the summons of the great bell of St. Martin of Tours had broken off their conference rather suddenly. "That old man," he thought to himself, "was crabbed and dogged in appearance, sharp and scornful in language, but generous and liberal in his actions; and such a stranger is worth a cold kinsman. What says our old Scottish proverb? 'Better kind fremit, than fremit kindred.'¹ I will find out that man, which, methinks, should be no difficult task, since he is so wealthy as mine host bespeaks him. He will give me good advice for my governance at least; and if he goes to strange countries, as many such do, I know not but his may be as adventurous a service as that of those guards of Louis."

As Quentin framed this thought, a whisper from those recesses of the heart in which lies much that the owner does not know of, or will not acknowledge willingly, suggested that, perchance, the lady of the turret, she of the veil and lute, might share that adventurous journey.

As the Scottish youth made these reflections, he met two grave-looking men, apparently citizens of Tours, whom, doffing his cap with the reverence due from youth to age, he respectfully asked to direct him to the house of Maître Pierre.

"The house of whom, my fair son?" said one of the passengers.

"Of Maître Pierre, the great silk merchant, who planted all the mulberry-trees in the park yonder," said Durward.

"Young man," said one of them who was nearest to him, "you have taken up an idle trade a little too early."

¹ See Note 10.

"And have chosen wrong subjects to practise your fooleries upon," said the farther one, still more gruffly. "The syndic of Tours is not accustomed to be thus talked to by strolling jesters from foreign parts."

Quentin was so much surprised at the causeless offence which these two decent-looking persons had taken at a very simple and civil question, that he forgot to be angry at the rudeness of their reply, and stood staring after them as they walked on with amended pace, often looking back at him, as if they were desirous to get as soon as possible out of his reach.

He next met a party of vine-dressers, and addressed to them the same question; and, in reply, they demanded to know whether he wanted Maître Pierre the schoolmaster, or Maître Pierre the carpenter, or Maître Pierre the beadle, or half a dozen of Maître Pierres besides. When none of these corresponded with the description of the person after whom he inquired, the peasants accused him of jesting with them impertinently, and threatened to fall upon him and beat him, in guerdon of his raillery. The oldest amongst them, who had some influence over the rest, prevailed on them to desist from violence.

"You see by his speech and his fool's cap," said he, "that he is one of the foreign mountebanks who are come into the country, and whom some call magicians and soothsayers, and some jugglers, and the like, and there is no knowing what tricks they have amongst them. I have heard of such a one paying a laird to eat his bellyful of grapes in a poor man's vineyard; and he ate as many as would have loaded a wain, and never undid a button of his jerkin; and so let him pass quietly, and keep his way, as we will keep ours. And you, friend, if you would shun worse, walk quietly on, in the name of God, our Lady of Marmoutier, and St. Martin of Tours, and trouble us no more about your Maître Pierre, which may be another name for the devil, for aught we know."

The Scot, finding himself much the weaker party, judged it his wisest course to walk on without reply; but the peasants, who at first shrunk from him in horror at his supposed talents for sorcery and grape-devouring, took heart of grace as he got to a distance, and having uttered a few cries and curses, finally gave them emphasis with a shower of stones, although at such a distance as to do little or no harm to the object of their displeasure. Quentin, as he pursued his walk, began to think, in his turn, either that he himself lay under a spell or that the people of Touraine were the most stupid, brutal, and inhospitable of the French peasants. The next incident which came under his observation did not tend to diminish this opinion.

On a slight eminence rising above the rapid and beautiful Cher, in the direct line of his path, two or three large chestnut trees were so happily placed as to form a distinguished and remarkable group; and beside them stood three or four peasants, motionless, with their eyes turned upwards, and fixed, apparently, upon some object amongst the branches of the tree next to them. The meditations of youth are seldom so profound as not to yield to the slightest impulse of curiosity, as easily as the lightest pebble, dropped casually from the hand, breaks the surface of a limpid pool. Quentin hastened his pace, and ran lightly up the rising ground, time enough to witness the ghastly spectacle which attracted the notice of these gazers—which was nothing less than the body of a man, convulsed by the last agony, suspended on one of the branches.

"Why do you not cut him down?" said the young Scot, whose hand was as ready to assist affliction as to maintain his own honour when he deemed it assailed.

One of the peasants, turning on him an eye from which fear had banished all expression but its own, and a face as pale as clay, pointed to a mark cut upon the bark of the tree, having the same rude resemblance to a *fleur-de-lys* which certain talismanic scratches, well known to our revenue officers, bear to a broad arrow. Neither understanding nor heeding the import of this symbol, young Durward sprung lightly as the ounce up into the tree, drew from his pouch that most necessary implement of a Highlander or woodsman, the trusty *skene dhu*,[1] and calling to those below to receive the body on

[1] See Note 11.

their hands, cut the rope asunder in less than a minute after he had perceived the exigency.

But his humanity was ill seconded by the bystanders. So far from rendering Durward any assistance they seemed terrified at the audacity of his action, and took to flight with one consent, as if they feared their merely looking on might have been construed into accession to his daring deed. The body, unsupported from beneath, fell heavily to earth, in such a manner that Quentin, who presently afterwards jumped down, had the mortification to see that the last sparks of life were extinguished. He gave not up his charitable purpose, however, without farther efforts. He freed the wretched man's neck from the fatal noose, undid the doublet, threw water on the face, and practised the other ordinary remedies restored to for recalling suspended animation.

While he was thus humanely engaged, a wild clamour of tongues, speaking a language which he knew not, arose around him; and he had scarcely time to observe that he was surrounded by several men and women of a singular and foreign appearance, when he found himself roughly seized by both arms, while a naked knife at the same moment was offered to his throat.

"Pale slave of Eblis!" said a man, in imperfect French, "are you robbing him you have murdered? But we have you, and you shall abye it."

There were knives drawn on every side of him as these words were spoken, and the grim and distorted countenances which glared on him were like those of wolves rushing on heir prey.

Still the young Scot's courage and presence of mind bore him out. "What mean ye, my masters?" he said. "If that be your friend's body, I have just now cut him down in pure charity, and you will do better to try to recover his life than to misuse an innocent stranger to whom he owes his chance of escape."

The women had by this time taken possession of the dead body, and continued the attemps to recover animation which Durward had been making use of, though with the like bad success; so that, desisting from their fruitless efforts, they seemed to abandon themselves to all the Oriental expressions of grief; the women making a piteous wailing, and tearing their long black hair, while the men seemed to rend their garments and to sprinkle dust upon their heads. They gradually became so much engaged in their mourning rites, that they bestowed no longer any attentions on Durward, of whose innocence they were probably satisfied from circumstances. It would certainly have been his wisest plan to have left these wild people to their own courses, but he had been bred in almost reckless contempt of danger, and felt all the eagerness of youthful curiosity.

The singular assemblage,[1] both male and female, wore turbans and caps, more similar, in general appearance, to his own bonnet than to the hats commonly worn in France. Several of the men had curled black beards, and the complexion of all was nearly as dark as that of Africans. One or two, who seemed their chiefs, had some tawdry ornaments of silver about their necks and in their ears, and wore showy scarfs of yellow, or scarlet, or light green; but their legs and arms were bare, and the whole troop seemed wretched and squalid in appearance. There were no weapons among them that Durward saw, except the long knives with which they had lately menaced him, and one short crooked sabre, or Moorish sword, which was worn by an active-looking young man, who often laid his hand upon the hilt, while he surpassed the rest of the party in his extravagant expressions of grief, and seemed to mingle with them threats of vengeance.

The disordered and yelling group were so different in appearance from any beings whom Quentin had yet seen, that he was on the point of concluding them to be a party of Saracens, of those "heathen hounds" who were the opponents of gentle knights and Christian monarchs in all the romances which he had heard or read, and was about to withdraw himself from a neighbourhood so perilous, when a galloping of horse was heard, and the supposed Saracens, who had raised

See Gipsies or Bohemians. Note 12.

by this time the body of their comrade upon their shoulders, were at once charged by a party of French soldiers.

This sudden apparition changed the measured wailing of the mourners into irregular shrieks of terror. The body was thrown to the ground in an instant, and those who were around it showed the utmost and most dexterous activity in escaping, under the bellies as it were of the horses, from the point of the lances which were levelled at them with exclamations of "Down with the accursed heathen thieves—take and kill—bind them like beasts—spear them like wolves!"

These cries were accompanied with corresponding acts of violence; but such was the alertness of the fugitives, the ground being rendered unfavourable to the horsemen by thickets and bushes, that only two were struck down and made prisoners, one of whom was the young fellow with the sword, who had previously offered some resistance. Quentin, whom fortune seemed at this period to have chosen for the butt of her shaft, was at the same time seized by the soldiers, and his arms, in spite of his remonstrances, bound down with a cord; those who apprehended him showing a readiness and despatch in the operation which proved them to be no novices in matters of police.

Looking anxiously to the leader of the horsemen, from whom he hoped to obtain liberty, Quentin knew not exactly whether to be pleased or alarmed upon recognising in him the down-looking and silent companion of Maître Pierre. True, whatever crime these strangers might be accused of, this officer might know, from the history of the morning, that he, Durward, had no connexion with them whatever; but it was a more difficult question whether this sullen man would be either a favourable judge or a willing witness in his behalf, and he felt doubtful whether he would mend his condition by making any direct application to him.

But there was little leisure for hesitation. "Trois-Eschelles and Petit-André," said the down-looking officer to two of his band, "these same trees stand here quite convenient. I will teach these misbelieving, thieving sorcerers to interfere with the King's justice, when it has visited any of their accursed race. Dismount, my children, and do your office briskly."

Trois-Eschelles and Petit-André were in an instant on foot, and Quentin observed that they had each, at the crupper and pommel of his saddle, a coil or two of ropes, which they hastily undid, and showed that, in fact, each coil formed a halter, with the fatal noose adjusted, ready for execution. The blood ran cold in Quentin's veins when he saw three cords selected, and perceived that it was proposed to put one around his own neck. He called on the officer loudly, reminded him of their meeting that morning, claimed the right of a free-born Scotsman, in a friendly and allied country, and denied any knowledge of the persons along with whom he was seized, or of their misdeeds.

The officer whom Durward thus addressed scarce deigned to look at him while he was speaking, and took no notice whatever of the claim he preferred to prior acquaintance. He barely turned to one or two of the peasants who were now come forward, either to volunteer their evidence against the prisoners or out of curiosity, and said gruffly, "Was yonder young fellow with the vagabonds?"

"That he was, sir, and it please your noble provostship," answered one of the clowns; "he was the very first blasphemously to cut down the rascal whom his Majesty's justice most deservedly hung up, as we told your worship."

"I'll swear by God and St. Martin of Tours to have seen him with their gang," said another, "when they pillaged our *métairie*."

"Nay, but father," said a boy, "yonder heathen was black, and this youth is fair; yonder one had short curled hair, and this hath long fair locks."

"Ay, child," said the peasant, "and perhaps you will say yonder one had a green coat and this a grey jerkin. But his worship, the provost, knows that they can change their complexions as easily as their jerkins, so that I am still minded he was the same."

"It is enough that you have seen him intermeddle with the course of the King's justice, by attempting to recover an executed traitor," said the officer. "Trois-Eschelles and Petit-André, despatch."

"Stay, seignoir officer!" exclaimed the youth, in mortal agony—"hear me speak—let men not die guiltlessly; my blood will be required of you by my countrymen in this world, and by Heaven's justice in that which is to follow."

"I will answer for my actions in both," said the provost, coldly, and made a sign with his left hand to the executioners; then, with a smile of triumphant malice, touched with his forefinger his right arm, which hung suspended in a scarf, disabled probably by the blow which Durward had dealt him that morning.

"Miserable vindictive wretch!" answered Quentin, persuaded by that action that private revenge was the sole motive of this man's rigour, and that no mercy whatever was to be expected from him. "The poor youth raves," said the functionary; "speak a word of comfort to him ere he make his transit, Trois-Eschelles; thou art a comfortable man in such cases, when a confessor is not to be had. Give him one minute of ghostly advice, and despatch matters in the next. I must proceed on the rounds. Soldiers, follow me!"

The provost rode on, followed by his guard, excepting two or three who were left to assist in the execution. The unhappy youth cast after him an eye almost darkened by despair, and thought he heard, in every tramp of his horse's retreating hoofs, the last slight chance of his safety vanish. He looked around him in agony, and was surprised, even in that moment, to see the stoical indifference of his fellow-prisoners. They had previously testified every sign of fear, and made every effort to escape; but now, when secured, and destined apparently to inevitable death, they awaited its arrival with the utmost composure. The scene of fate before them gave, perhaps, a more yellow tinge to their swarthy cheeks; but it neither agitated their features nor quenched the stubborn haughtiness of their eye. They seemed like foxes, which, after all their wiles and artful attempts at escape are exhausted, die with a silent and sullen fortitude, which wolves and bears, the fiercer objects of the chase, do not exhibit.

They were undaunted by the conduct of the fatal executioners, who went about their work with more deliberation than their master had recommended, and which probably arose from their having acquired by habit a kind of pleasure in the discharge of their horrid office. We pause an instant to describe them, because under a tyranny, whether despotic or popular, the character of the hangman becomes a subject of grave importance.

These functionaries were essentially different in their appearance and manners. Louis used to call them Democritus and Heraclitus, and their master, the provost, termed them *Jean qui pleure* and *Jean qui rit*.

Trois-Eschelles was a tall, thin, ghastly man, with a peculiar gravity of visage, and a large rosary round his neck, the use of which he was accustomed piously to offer to those sufferers on whom he did his duty. He had one or two Latin texts continually in his mouth on the nothingness and vanity of human life; and, had it been regular to have enjoyed such a plurality, he might have held the office of confessor to the jail *in commendam* with that of executioner. Petit-André, on the contrary, was a joyous-looking, round, active little fellow, who rolled about in execution of his duty as if it were the most diverting occupation in the world. He seemed to have a sort of fond affection for his victims, and always spoke of them in kindly and affectionate terms. They were his poor honest fellows, his pretty dears, his gossips, his good old fathers, as their age or sex might be; and as Trois-Eschelles endeavoured to inspire them with a philosophical or religious regard to futurity, Petit-André seldom failed to refresh them with a jest or two, as if to induce them to pass from life as something that was ludicrous, contemptible, and not worthy of serious consideration.

I cannot tell why or wherefore it was, but these two excellent persons, notwithstanding the variety of their talents and the rare occurrence of such among persons of their profession, were both more utterly detested than, perhaps, any creatures of their kind, whether before or since; and the only doubt of those who knew aught of them was, whether the grave and pathetic Trois-Eschelles or the frisky, comic, alert Petit-André[1] was the object of the greatest fear or of the deepest execration. It is certain they bore the palm in both particulars over every hangman in France, unless it were perhaps their master, Tristan l'Hermite, the renowned provost-marshal, or *his* master, Louis XI.

It must not be supposed that these reflections were of Quentin Durward's making. Life, death, time, and eternity were swimming before his eyes—a stunning and overwhelming prospect, from which human nature recoiled in its weakness, though human pride would fain have borne up. He addressed himself to the God of his fathers; and when he did so, the little rude and unroofed chapel, which now held almost all his race but himself, rushed on his recollection. "Our feudal enemies gave my kindred graves in our own land," he thought, "but I must feed the ravens and kites of a foreign land, like an excommunicated felon!" The tears gushed involuntarily from his eyes. Trois-Eschelles, touching one shoulder, gravely congratulated him on his Heavenly disposition for death, and pathetically exclaiming, "*Beati qui in Domino moriuntur,*" remarked the soul was happy that left the body while the tear was in the eye. Petit-André, slapping the other shoulder, called out: "Courage, my fair son! since you must begin the dance, let the ball open gaily, for all the rebecs are in tune," twitching the halter at the same time, to give point to his joke. As the youth turned his dismayed looks first on one and then on the other, they made their meaning plainer by gently urging him forward to the fatal tree, and bidding him be of good courage, for it would be over in a moment.

In this fatal predicament, the youth cast a distracted look around him. "Is there any good Christian who hears me," he said, "that will tell Ludovic Lesly of the Scottish Guard, called in this country Le Balafré, that his nephew is here basely murdered?"

The words were spoken in good time, for an archer of the Scottish Guard, attracted by the preparations for the execu-

[1] See Note 13.

tion, was standing by, with one or two other chance passengers, to witness what was passing.

"Take heed what you do," he said to the executioners; "if this young man be of Scottish birth, I will not permit him to have foul play."

"Heaven forbid, sir cavalier," said Trois-Eschelles; "but we must obey our orders," drawing Durward forward by one arm.

"The shortest play is ever the fairest," said Petit-André, pulling him onward by the other.

But Quentin had heard words of comfort, and, exerting his strength, he suddenly shook off both the finishers of the law, and, with his arms still bound, ran to the Scottish archer. "Stand by me, countryman," he said in his own language, "for the love of Scotland and St. Andrew! I am innocent—I am your own native landsman. Stand by me, as you shall answer at the last day!"

"By St. Andrew! they shall make at you through me," said the archer, and unsheathed his sword.

"Cut my bonds, countryman," said Quentin, "and I will do something for myself."

This was done with a touch of the archer's weapon; and the liberated captive, springing suddenly on one of the provost's guard, wrested from him a halberd with which he was armed. "And now," he said, "come on, if you dare!"

The two officers whispered together.

"Ride thou after the provost-marshal," said Trois-Eschelies, "and I will detain them here, if I can. Soldiers of the provost's guard, stand to your arms."

Petit-André mounted his horse and left the field, and the other marshals-men in attendance drew together so hastily at the command of Trois-Eschelles, that they suffered the other two prisoners to make their escape during the confusion. Perhaps they were not very anxious to detain them; for they had of late been sated with the blood of such wretches, and, like other ferocious animals, were, through long slaughter, become tired of carnage. But the pretext was, that they thought themselves immediately called upon to attend to the safety of Trois-Eschelles; for there was a jealousy which occasionally led to open quarrels betwixt the Scottish Archers and the marshal's guards, who executed the orders of their provost.

"We are strong enough to beat the proud Scots twice over, if it be your pleasure," said one of these soldiers to Trois-Eschelles.

But that cautious official made a sign to him to remain quiet, and addressed the Scottish archer with great civility. "Surely, sir, this is a great insult to the provost-marshal, that you should presume to interfere with the course of the King's justice, duly and lawfully committed to his charge; and it is no act of justice to me, who am in lawful possession of my criminal. Neither is it a well-meant kindness to the youth himself, seeing that fifty opportunities of hanging him may occur, without his being found in so happy a state of preparation as he was before your ill-advised interference."

"If my young countryman," said the Scot, smiling, "be of opinion I have done him an injury, I will return him to your charge without a word more dispute."

"No, no!—for the love of Heaven, no!" exclaimed Quentin. "I would rather you swept my head off with your long sword; it would better become my birth than to die by the hands of such a foul churl."

"Hear how he revileth!" said the finisher of the law. "Alas! how soon our best resolutions pass away! He was in a blessed frame for departure but now, and in two minutes he has become a contemner of authorities."

"Tell me at once," said the archer, "what has this young man done?"

"Interfered," answered Trois-Eschelles, with some earnestness, "to take down the dead body of a criminal, when the *fleur-de-lys* was marked on the tree where he was hung with my own proper hand."

"How is this, young man?" said the archer; "how came you to have committed such an offence?"

"As I desire your protection," answered Durward, "I will tell you the truth as if I were at confession. I saw a man struggling on the tree, and I went to cut him down out of mere humanity. I thought neither of *fleur-de-lys* nor of clove-gilliflower, and had no more idea of offending the King of France than our father the Pope."

"What a murrain had you to do with the dead body, then?" said the archer. "You'll see them hanging, in the rear of this gentleman, like grapes on every tree, and you will have enough to do in this country if you go a-gleaning after the hangman. However, I will not quit a countryman's cause if I can help it. Hark ye, master marshals-man, you see this is entirely a mistake. You should have some compassion on so young a traveller. In our country at home he has not been accustomed to see such active proceedings as yours and your master's."

"Not for want of need of them, seignior archer," said Petit-André, who returned at this moment. "Stand fast, Trois-Eschelles, for here comes the provost-marshal; we shall presently see how he will relish having his work taken out of his hand before it is finished."

"And in good time," said the archer, "here come some of my comrades."

Accordingly, as the Provost Tristan rode up with his patrol on one side of the little hill which was the scene of the altercation, four or five Scottish Archers came as hastily up on the other, and at their head the Balafré himself.

Upon this urgency, Lesly showed none of that indifference towards his nephew of which Quentin had in his heart accused him; for he no sooner saw his comrade and Durward standing upon their defence than he exclaimed: "Cunningham, I thank thee. Gentlemen—comrades, lend me your aid. It is a young Scottish gentleman—my nephew. Lindesay—Guthrie—Tyrie, draw and strike in!"

There was now every prospect of a desperate scuffle between the parties, who were not so disproportioned in numbers but that the better arms of the Scottish cavaliers gave them an equal chance of victory. But the provost-marshal, either doubting the issue of the conflict or aware that it would be disagreeable to the King, made a sign to his followers to forbear from violence, while he demanded of Balafré, who now put himself forward as the head of the other party: "What he, a cavalier of the King's Body-Guard, purposed by opposing the execution of a criminal?"

"I deny that I do so," answered the Balafré. "St. Martin! there is, I think, some difference between the execution of a criminal and the slaughter of my own nephew?"

"Your nephew may be a criminal as well as another, seignior," said the provost-marshal; "and every stranger in France is amenable to the laws of France."

"Yes, but we have privileges, we Scottish Archers," said Balafré; "have we not, comrades?"

"Yes—yes," they all exclaimed together. "Privileges—privileges! Long live King Louis—long live the bold Balafré—long live the Scottish Guard—and death to all who would infringe our privileges?"

"Take reason with you, gentlemen cavaliers," said the provost-marshal; "consider my commission."

"We will have no reason at your hand," said Cunningham; "our own officers shall do us reason. We will be judged by the King's grace, or by our own captain, now that the Lord High Constable is not in presence."

"And we will be hanged by none," said Lindesay, "but Sandie Wilson, the auld marshals-man of our ain body."

"It would be a positive cheating of Sandie, who is as honest a man as ever tied noose upon hemp, did we give way to any other proceeding," said the Balafré. "Were I to be hanged myself, no other should tie tippet about my craig."

"But hear ye," said the provost-marshal, "this young fellow belongs not to you, and cannot share what you call your privileges."

"What we *call* our privileges all shall admit to be such," said Cunningham.

"We will not hear them questioned!" was the universal cry of the archers.

"Ye are mad, my masters," said Tristan l'Hermite. "No one disputes your privileges; but this youth is not one of you."

"He is *my* nephew," said the Balafré, with a triumphant air.

"But no Archer of the Guard, I think," retorted Tristan l'Hermite.

The archers looked on each other in some uncertainty.

"Stand to it yet, comrade," whispered Cunningham to Balafré. "Say he is engaged with us."

"St. Martin! you say well, fair countryman," answered Lesly; and, raising his voice, swore that he had that day enrolled his kinsman as one of his own retinue.

This declaration was a decisive argument.

"It is well, gentlemen," said the Provost Tristan, who was aware of the King's nervous apprehension of disaffection creeping in among his Guards. "You know, as you say, your privileges, and it is not my duty to have brawls with the King's Guards, if it is to be avoided. But I will report this matter for the King's own decision; and I would have you to be aware that, in doing so, I act more mildly than perhaps my duty warrants me."

So saying he put his troop into motion, while the archers, remaining on the spot, held a hasty consultation what was next to be done.

"We must report the matter to Lord Crawford, our captain, in the first place, and have the young fellow's name put on the roll."

"But, gentlemen, and my worthy friends and preservers," said Quentin, with some hesitation, "I have not yet determined whether to take service with you or no."

"Then settle in your own mind," said his uncle, "whether you choose to do so or be hanged; for I promise you that, nephew of mine as you are, I see no other chance of your 'scaping the gallows."

This was an unanswerable argument, and reduced Quentin at once to acquiesce in what he might have otherwise considered as no very agreeable proposal; but the recent escape from the halter, which had been actually around his neck, would probably have reconciled him to a worse alternative than was proposed.

"He must go home with us to our *caserne*," said Cunningham; "there is no safety for him out of our bounds, whilst these man-hunters are prowling about."

"May I not then abide for this night at the hostelry where I breakfasted, fair uncle?" said the youth, thinking, perhaps, like many a new recruit, that even a single night of freedom was something gained.

"Yes, fair nephew," answered his uncle, ironically, "that we may have the pleasure of fishing you out of some canal or moat, or perhaps out of a loop of the Loire, knit up in a sack, for the greater convenience of swimming, for that is like to be the end on't. The provost-marshal smiled on us when we parted, continued he, addressing Cunningham, "and that is a sign his thoughts were dangerous."

"I care not for his danger," said Cunningham; "such game as we are beyond his bird-bolts. But I would have thee tell the whole to the Devil's Oliver, who is always a good friend to the Scottish Guard, and will see Father Louis before the provost can, for he is to shave him to-morrow."

"But hark you," said Balafré, "it is ill going to Oliver empty-handed, and I am as bare as the birch in December."

"So are we all," said Cunningham; "Oliver must not scruple to take our Scottish words for once. We will make up something handsome among us against the next pay-day; and if *he* expects to share, let me tell you, the pay-day will come about all the sooner."

"And now for the château," said Balafré; "and my nephew shall tell us by the way how he brought the provost-marshal on his shoulders, that we may know how to frame our report both to Crawford and Oliver."

CHAPTER VII.

THE ENROLMENT.

> *Justice of Peace.* Here, hand me down the statute—
> read the articles—
> Swear, kiss the book—subscribe, and be a hero;
> Drawing a portion from the public stock
> For deeds of valour to be done hereafter—
> Sixpence per day, subsistence and arrears.
> *The Recruiting Officer.*

An attendant upon the archers having been dismounted, Quentin Durward was accommodated with his horse, and, in company of his martial countrymen, rode at a round pace towards the Castle of Plessis, about to become, although on his own part involuntarily, an inhabitant of that gloomy fortress, the outside of which had, that morning, struck him with so much surprise.

In the mean while, in answer to his uncle's repeated interrogations, he gave him an exact account of the accident which had that morning brought him into so much danger. Although he himself saw nothing in his narrative save what was affecting, he found it was received with much laughter by his escort.

"And yet it is no good jest either," said his uncle, "for what, in the devil's name, could lead the senseless boy to meddle with the body of a cursed misbelieving Jewish Moorish pagan?"

"Had he quarrelled with the marshals-men about a pretty wench, as Michael of Moffat did, there had been more sense in it," said Cunningham.

"But I think it touches our honour, that Tristan and his people pretend to confound our Scottish bonnets with these pilfering vagabonds' *tocques* and *turbands,* as they call them," said Lindesay. "If they have not eyes to see the difference, they must be taught by rule of hand. But it's my belief, Tristan but pretends to mistake, that he may snap up the kindly Scots that come over to see their kinsfolks."

"May I ask, kinsman," said Quentin, "what sort of people these are of whom you speak?"

"In truth you may ask," said his uncle, "but I know not, fair nephew, who is able to answer you. Not I, I am sure, although I know, it may be, as much as other people; but they have appeared in this land within a year or two, just as a flight of locusts might do."

"Ay," said Lindesay, "and Jacques Bonhomme—that is our name for the peasant, young man—you will learn our way of talk in time—honest Jacques, I say, cares little what wind either brings them or the locusts, so he but knows any gale that would carry them away again."

"Do they do so much evil?" asked the young man.

"Evil! why, boy, they are heathens, or Jews, or Mahommedans at the least, and neither worship Our Lady nor the saints (crossing himself), and steal what they can lay hands on, and sing, and tell fortunes," added Cunningham.

"And they say there are some goodly wenches amongst these women," said Guthrie; "but Cunningham knows that best."

"How, brother!" said Cunningham; "I trust ye mean me no reproach?"

"I am sure I said ye none," answered Guthrie.

"I will be judged by the company," said Cunningham. "Ye said as much as that I, a Scottish gentleman, and living within pale of holy church, had a fair friend among these offscourings of heathenesse."

"Nay—nay," said Balafré, "he did but jest. We will have no quarrels among comrades."

"We must have no such jesting then," said Cunningham, murmuring as if he had been speaking to his own beard.

"Be there such vagabonds in other lands than France?" said Lindesay.

"Ay, in good sooth, are there: tribes of them have appeared in Germany, and in Spain, and in England," answered Balafré. "By the blessing of good St. Andrew, Scotland is free of them yet."

"Scotland," said Cunningham, "is too cold a country for locusts, and too poor a country for thieves."

"Or perhaps, John Highlander will suffer no thieves to thrive there but his own," said Guthrie.

"I let you all know," said Balafré, "that I come from the braes of Angus, and have gentle Highland kin in Glen Isla, and I will not have the Highlanders slandered."

"You will not deny that they are cattle-lifters?" said Guthrie.

"To drive a spreagh or so is no thievery," said Balafré, "and that I will maintain when and how you dare."

"For shame, comrade," said Cunningham, "who quarrels now? The young man should not see such mad misconstruction. Come, here we are at the château. I will bestow a runlet of wine to have a rouse in friendship, and drink to Scotland, Highland and Lowland both, if you will meet me at dinner at my quarters."

"Agreed—agreed," said Balafré; "and I will bestow another, to wash away unkindness, and to drink a health to my nephew on his first entrance to our corps."

At their approach, the wicket was opened and the drawbridge fell. One by one they entered; but when Quentin appeared, the sentinels crossed their pikes, and commanded him to stand, while bows were bent, and harquebusses aimed at him from the walls—a rigour of vigilance used notwithstanding that the young stranger came in company of a party of the garrison, nay of the very body which furnished the sentinels who were then upon duty.

Le Balafré, who had remained by his nephew's side on purpose, gave the necessary explanations, and, after some considerable hesitation and delay, the youth was conveyed under a strong guard to the Lord Crawford's apartment.

This Scottish nobleman was one of the last relics of the gallant band of Scottish lords and knights who had so long and so truly served Charles VI. in those bloody wars which decided the independence of the French crown and the expulsion of the English. He had fought, when a boy, abreast with Douglas and with Buchan, had ridden beneath the banner of the Maid of Arc, and was perhaps one of the last of those associates of Scottish chivalry who had so willingly drawn their swords for the *fleur-de-lys* against their " auld enemies of England." Changes which had taken place in the Scottish kingdom, and perhaps his having become habituated to French climate and manners, had induced the old baron to resign all thoughts of returning to his native country, the rather that the high office which he held in the household of Louis, and his own frank and loyal character, had gained a considerable ascendency over the King, who, though in general no ready believer in human virtue or honour, trusted and confided in those of the Lord Crawford, and allowed him the greater influence, because he was never known to interfere excepting in matters which concerned his charge.

Balafré and Cunningham followed Durward and the guard to the apartment of their officer, by whose dignified appearance, as well as with the respect paid to him by these proud soldiers, who seemed to respect no one else, the young man was much and strongly impressed.

Lord Crawford was tall, and through advanced age had become gaunt and thin; yet retaining in his sinews the strength, at least, if not the elasticity, of youth, he was able to endure the weight of his armour during a march as well as the youngest man who rode in his band. He was hard-favoured, with a scarred and weather-beaten countenance, and an eye that had looked upon death as his playfellow in thirty pitched battles, but which nevertheless expressed a calm contempt of danger, rather than the ferocious courage of a mercenary soldier. His tall, erect figure was at present wrapped in a loose chamber-gown, secured around him by his buff belt, in which was suspended his richly-hilted poniard. He had round his neck the collar and badge of the order of St. Michael. He sat upon a couch covered with deer's hide, and with spectacles on his nose (then a recent invention) was labouring to read a huge manuscript, called the *Rosier de la Guerre*—a code of military and civil policy which Louis had compiled for the benefit of his son the Dauphin, and upon which he was desirous to have the opinion of the experienced Scottish warrior.

Lord Crawford laid his book somewhat peevishly aside upon the entrance of these unexpected visitors, and demanded, in his broad national dialect, "What, in the foul fiend's name, they lacked now?"

Le Balafré, with more respect than perhaps he would have shown to Louis himself, stated at full length the circumstances in which his nephew was placed, and humbly requested his lordship's protection. Lord Crawford listened very attentively. He could not but smile at the simplicity with which the youth had interfered in behalf of the hanged criminal, but he shook his head at the account which he received of the ruffle betwixt the Scottish Archers and the provost-marshal's guard.[1]

"How often," he said, "will you bring me such ill-winded pirns to ravel out? How often must I tell you, especially both you, Ludovic Lesly, and you, Archie Cunningham, that the foreign soldier should bear himself modestly and decorously towards the people of the country, if you would not have the whole dogs of the town at your heels? However, if you must have a bargain,[2] I would rather it were with that loon of a provost than any one else; and I blame you less for this onslaught than for other frays that you have made, Ludovic, for it was but natural and kindlike to help your young kinsman. This simple bairn must come to no skaith neither; so give me the roll of the company yonder down from the shelf, and we will even add his name to the troop, that he may enjoy the privileges."

"May it please your lordship," said Durward——

"Is the lad crazed!" exclaimed his uncle. "Would you speak to his lordship without a question asked?"

"Patience, Ludovic," said Lord Crawford, "and let us hear what the bairn has to say."

"Only this, if it may please your lordship," replied Quentin, "that I told my uncle formerly I had some doubts about entering this service. I have now to say that they are entirely removed, since I have seen the noble and experienced commander under whom I am to serve; for there is authority in your look."

"Weel said, my bairn," said the old lord, not insensible to the compliment; "we have had some experience, had God

[1] See Quarrels of Scottish Archers. Note 14. [2] A quarrel, videlicet.

sent us grace to improve by it, both in service and in command. There you stand, Quentin, in our honourable corps of Scottish Body-Guards, as esquire to your uncle, and serving under his lance. I trust you will do well, for you should be a right man-at-arms, if all be good that is upcome,[1] and you are come of a gentle kindred. Ludovic, you will see that your kinsman follow his exercise diligently, for we will have spears-breaking one of these days."

"By my hilts, and I am glad of it, my lord; this peace makes cowards of us all. I myself feel a sort of decay of spirit, closed up in this cursed dungeon of a castle."

"Well, a bird whistled in my ear," continued Lord Crawford, "that the old banner will be soon dancing in the field again."

"I will drink a cup the deeper this evening to that very tune," said Balafré.

"Thou wilt drink to any tune," said Lord Crawford; "and I fear me, Ludovic, you will drink a bitter browst of your own brewing one day."

Lesly, a little abashed, replied: "That it had not been his wont for many a day; but his lordship knew the use of the company to have a carouse to the health of a new comrade."

"True," said the old leader, "I had forgot the occasion. I will send a few stoups of wine to assist your carouse; but let it be over by sunset. And, hark ye—let the soldiers for duty be carefully pricked off; and see that none of them be more or less partakers of your debauch."

"Your lordship shall be lawfully obeyed," said Ludovic; "and your health duly remembered."

"Perhaps," said Lord Crawford, "I may look in myself upon your mirth, just to see that all is carried decently."

"Your lordship shall be most dearly welcome," said Ludovic; and the whole party retreated in high spirits to prepare for their military banquet, to which Lesly invited about a score of his comrades, who were pretty much in the habit of making their mess together.

A soldier's festival is generally a very extempore affair,

[1] That is, if your courage corresponds with your personal appearance.

providing there is enough of meat and drink to be had; but on the present occasion Ludovic bustled about to procure some better wine than ordinary, observing, that the "old lord was the surest gear in their aught, and that, while he preached sobriety to them, he himself, after drinking at the royal table as much wine as he could honestly come by, never omitted any creditable opportunity to fill up the evening over the wine-pot. So you must prepare, comrades," he said, to "hear the old histories of the battles of Vernoil and Beaugé."[1]

The Gothic apartment in which they generally met was, therefore, hastily put into the best order: their grooms were despatched to collect green rushes to spread upon the floor; and banners, under which the Scottish Guard had marched to battle, or which they had taken from the enemies' ranks, were displayed, by way of tapestry, over the table, and around the walls of the chamber.

The next point was to invest the young recruit as hastily as possible with the dress and appropriate arms of the Guard, that he might appear in every respect the sharer of its important privileges, in virtue of which, and by the support of his countrymen, he might freely brave the power and the displeasure of the provost-marshal, although the one was known to be as formidable as the other was unrelenting.

The banquet was joyous in the highest degree; and the guests gave vent to the whole current of their national partiality on receiving into their ranks a recruit from their beloved fatherland. Old Scottish songs were sung, old tales of Scottish heroes told; the achievements of their fathers, and the scenes in which they were wrought, were recalled to mind; and for a time the rich plains of Touraine seemed converted into the mountainous and sterile regions of Caledonia.

When their enthusiasm was at high flood, and each was endeavouring to say something to enhance the dear remembrance of Scotland, it received a new impulse from the arrival of Lord Crawford, who, as Le Balafré had well prophesied, sat as it were on thorns at the royal board until an opportunity occurred of making his escape to the revelry of his own

[1] See Scottish Auxiliaries. Note 15.

countrymen. A chair of state had been reserved for him at the upper end of the table; for, according to the manners of the age, and the constitution of that body, although their leader and commander under the King and High Constable, the members of the corps, as we should now say, the privates, being all ranked as noble by birth, their captain sat with them at the same table without impropriety, and might mingle when he chose in their festivity, without derogation from his dignity as commander.

At present, however, Lord Crawford declined occupying the seat prepared for him, and bidding them "hold themselves merry," stood looking on the revel with a countenance which seemed greatly to enjoy it.

"Let him alone," whispered Cunningham to Lindesay, as the latter offered the wine to their noble captain—"let him alone —hurry no man's cattle—let him take it of his own accord."

In fact, the old lord, who at first smiled, shook his head, and placed the untasted wine-cup before him, began presently, as if it were in absence of mind, to sip a little of the contents, and, in doing so, fortunately recollected that it would be ill-luck did he not drink a draught to the health of the gallant lad who had joined them this day. The pledge was filled and answered, as may be well supposed, with many a joyous shout, when the old leader proceeded to acquaint them that he had possessed Master Oliver with an account of what had passed that day. "And as," he said, "the scraper of chins hath no great love for the stretcher of throats, he has joined me in obtaining from the King an order commanding the provost to suspend all proceedings, under whatever pretence, against Quentin Durward, and to respect, on all occasion, the privileges of the Scottish Guard."

Another shout broke forth, the cups were again filled till the wine sparkled on the brim, and there was an acclaim to the health of the noble Lord Crawford, the brave conservator of the privileges and rights of his countrymen. The good old lord could not but in courtesy do reason to this pledge also, and gliding into the ready chair, as it were without reflecting what he was doing, he caused Quentin to come up beside him, and assailed him with many more questions concerning the state of Scotland, and the great families there, than he was well able to answer; while ever and anon, in the course of his queries, the good lord kissed the wine-cup by way of parenthesis, remarking, that sociality became Scottish gentlemen, but that young men like Quentin ought to practise it cautiously, lest it might degenerate into excess; upon which occasion he uttered many excellent things, until his own tongue, although employed in the praises of temperance, began to articulate something thicker than usual. It was now that, while the military ardour of the company augmented with each flagon which they emptied, Cunningham called on them to drink the speedy hoisting of the *Oriflamme*, the royal banner of France.

"And a breeze of Burgundy to fan it!" echoed Lindesay.

"With all the soul that is left in this worn body do I accept the pledge, bairns," echoed Lord Crawford; "and as old as I am, I trust I may see it flutter yet. Hark ye, my mates (for wine had made him something communicative), ye are all true servants to the French crown, and wherefore should ye not know there is an envoy come from Duke Charles of Burgundy, with a message of an angry favour."

"I saw the Count of Crèvecœur's equipage, horses and retinue," said another of the guests, "down at the inn yonder, at the Mulberry Grove. They say the King will not admit him into the castle."

"Now, Heaven send him an ungracious answer!" said Guthrie; "but what is it he complains of?"

"A world of grievances upon the frontier," said Lord Crawford; "and latterly, that the King hath received under his protection a lady of his land, a young countess, who hath fled from Dijon because, being a ward of the Duke, he would have her marry his favourite, Campo-basso."

"And hath she actually come hither alone, my lord?" said Lindesay.

"Nay, not altogether alone, but with the old countess, her kinswoman, who hath yielded to her cousin's wishes in this matter."

"And will the King," said Cunningham, "he being the Duke's feudal sovereign, interfere between the Duke and his ward, over whom Charles hath the same right which, were he himself dead, the King would have over the heiress of Burgundy?"

"The King will be ruled, as he is wont, by rules of policy; and you know," continued Crawford, "that he hath not publicly received these ladies, nor placed them under the protection of his daughters, the Lady of Beaujeau or the Princess Joan, so, doubtless, he will be guided by circumstances. He is our master; but it is no treason to say, he will chase with the hounds and run with the hare with any prince in Christendom."

"But the Duke of Burgundy understands no such doubling," said Cunningham.

"No," answered the old lord; "and, therefore, it is likely to make work between them."

"Well—St. Andrew further the fray!" said Le Balafré. "I had it foretold me ten, ay, twenty years since, that I was to make the fortune of my house by marriage. Who knows what may happen, if once we come to flight for honours and ladies' love, as they do in the old romaunts?"

"*Thou* name ladies' love, with such a trench in thy visage!" said Guthrie.

"As well not love at all, as love a Bohemian woman of heathenesse," retorted Le Balafré.

"Hold there, comrades," said Lord Crawford: "no tilting with sharp weapons, no jesting with keen scoffs—friends all. And for the lady, she is too wealthy to fall to a poor Scottish lord, or I would put in my own claim, fourscore years and all, or not very far from it. But here is her health, nevertheless, for they say she is a lamp of beauty."

"I think I saw her," said another soldier, "when I was upon guard this morning at the inner barrier; but she was more like a dark lantern than a lamp, for she and another were brought into the château in close litters."

"Shame!—shame! Arnot!" said Lord Crawford; "a soldier on duty should say nought of what he sees. Besides," he added after a pause, his own curiosity prevailing over the show of discipline which he had thought it necessary to exert, "why should these litters contain this very same Countess Isabelle de Croye?"

"Nay, my lord," replied Arnot, "I know nothing of it save this, that my coutelier was airing my horses in the road to the village, and fell in with Doguin the muleteer who brought back the litters to the inn, for they belong to the fellow of the Mulberry Grove yonder—he of the Fleur-de-Lys, I mean—and so Doguin asked Saunders Steed to take a cup of wine, as they were acquainted, which he was no doubt willing enough to do——"

"No doubt—no doubt," said the old lord; "it is a thing I wish were corrected among you, gentlemen; but all your grooms and couteliers, and jackmen, as we should call them in Scotland, are but too ready to take a cup of wine with any one. It is a thing perilous in war, and must be amended. But, Andrew Arnot, this is a long tale of yours, and we will cut it with a drink, as the Highlander says, *Skeoch doch nan skial*[1] —and that's good Gaelic. Here is to the Countess Isabelle of Croye, and a better husband to her than Campo-basso, who is a base Italian cullion! And now, Andrew Arnot, what said the muleteer to this yeoman of thine?"

"Why, he told him in secrecy, if it please your lordship," continued Arnot, "that these two ladies whom he had presently before convoyed up to the castle in the close litters were great ladies, who had been living in secret at his master's house for some days, and that the King had visited them more than once very privately, and had done them great honour; and that they had fled up to the castle as, he believed, for fear of the Count de Crèvecœur, the Duke of Burgundy's ambassador, whose approach was just announced by an advanced courier."

"Ay, Andrew, come you there to me?" said Guthrie; "then I will be sworn it was the countess whose voice I heard singing to the lute, as I came even now through the inner

[1] "Cut a tale with a drink," an expression used when a man preaches over his liquor, as *bon vivants* say in England.

court. The sound came from the bay-windows of the Dauphin's Tower; and such melody was there as no one ever heard before in the Castle of Plessis of the Park. By my faith, I thought it was the music of the fairy Melusina's making. There I stood, though I knew your board was covered and that you were all impatient—there I stood, like——"

"Like an ass, Johnny Guthrie," said his commander;" thy long nose smelling the dinner, thy long ears hearing the music, and thy short discretion not enabling thee to decide which of them thou didst prefer. Hark! is that the cathedral bell tolling to vespers? Sure it cannot be that time yet." The mad old sexton has toll'd evensong an hour too soon."

"In faith, the bell rings but too justly the hour," said Cunningham; "yonder the sun is sinking on the west side of the fair plain."

"Ay," said the Lord Crawford, "is it even so? Well, lads, we must live within compass. Fair and soft goes far—slow fire make sweet malt—to be merry and wise is a sound proverb. One other rouse to the weal of old Scotland, and then each man to his duty."

The parting-cup was emptied, and the guests dismissed; the stately old baron taking the Balafré's arm, under pretence of giving him some instructions concerning his nephew, but, perhaps, in reality, lest his own lofty pace should seem in the public eye less steady than became his rank and high command. A serious countenance did he bear as he passed through the two courts which separated his lodgings from the festal chamber, and solemn as the gravity of a hogshead was the farewell caution with which he prayed Ludovic to attend his nephew's motions, especially in the matters of wenches and wine-cups.

Meanwhile, not a word that was spoken concerning the beautiful Countess Isabelle had escaped the young Durward, who, conducted into a small cabin, which he was to share with his uncle's page, made his new and lowly abode the scene of much high musing. The reader will easily imagine that the young soldier should build a fine romance on such a foundation as the supposed, or rather the assumed, identification of the maiden of the turret, to whose lay he had listened with so much interest, and the fair cup-bearer of Maître Pierre, with a fugitive countess of rank and wealth, flying from the pursuit of a hated lover, the favourite of an oppressive guardian, who abused his feudal power. There was an interlude in Quentin's vision concerning Maître Pierre, who seemed to exercise such authority even over the formidable officer from whose hands he had that day, with much difficulty, made his escape. At length the youth's reveries, which had been respected by little Will Harper, the companion of his cell, were broken in upon by the return of his uncle, who commanded Quentin to bed, that he might arise betimes in the morning, and attend him to his Majesty's antechamber, to which he was called by his hour of duty, along with five of his comrades.

CHAPTER VIII.

THE ENVOY.

Be thou as lightning in the eyes of France;
For ere thou canst report I will be there,
The thunder of my cannon shall be heard.
So, hence! Be thou the trumpet of our wrath.
King John.

HAD sloth been a temptation by which Durward was easily beset, the noise with which the *caserne* of the guards resounded after the first toll of primes had certainly banished the siren from his couch; but the discipline of his father's tower and of the convent of Aberbrothock had taught him to start with the dawn; and he did on his clothes gaily, amid the sounding of bugles and the clash of armour, which announced the change of the vigilant guards—some of whom were returning to barracks after their nightly duty, whilst some were marching out to that of the morning; and others, again, amongst whom was his uncle, were arming for immediate attendance upon the person of Louis. Quentin Durward soon put on, with the feelings of so young a man on such an occasion, the splendid dress and arms appertaining to his new situation; and his uncle, who looked with great accuracy and interest to see that he was completely fitted out in every respect, did not conceal his satisfaction at the improvement which had been thus made in his nephew's appearance. "If thou dost prove as faithful and bold as thou art well-favoured, I shall have in thee one of the handsomest and best esquires in the Guard, which cannot but be an honour to thy mother's family. Follow me to the presence-chamber; and see thou keep close at my shoulder."

So saying, he took up a partizan, large, weighty, and beautifully inlaid and ornamented, and directing his nephew to assume a lighter weapon of a similar description, they proceeded to the inner court of the palace, where their comrades, who were to form the guard of the interior apartments, were already drawn up and under arms—the squires each standing behind their masters, to whom they thus formed a second rank. Here were also in attendance many yeomen-prickers, with gallant horses and noble dogs, on which Quentin looked with such inquisitive delight that his uncle was obliged more than once to remind him that the animals were not there for his private amusement, but for the King's, who had a strong passion for the chase, one of the few inclinations which he indulged, even when coming in competition with his course of policy; being so strict a protector of the game in the royal forests, that it was currently said you might kill a man with greater impunity than a stag.

On a signal given, the guards were put into motion by the command of Le Balafré, who acted as officer upon the occasion; and, after some minutiæ of word and signal, which all served to show the extreme and punctilious jealousy with which their duty was performed, they marched into the hall of audience where the King was immediately expected.

New as Quentin was to scenes of splendour, the effect of that which was now before him rather disappointed the expectations which he had formed of the brilliancy of a court. There were household officers, indeed, richly attired, there were guards gallantly armed, and there were domestics of various degrees; but he saw none of the ancient counsellors of the kingdom, none of the high officers of the crown; heard none of the names which in those days sounded an alarm to chivalry; saw none either of those generals or leaders who, possessed of the full prime of manhood, were the strength of France, or of the more youthful and fiery nobles, those early aspirants after honour, who were her pride. The jealous habits, the reserved manners, the deep and artful policy of the King, had estranged this splendid circle from the throne, and they were only called around it upon certain stated and formal occasions, when they went reluctantly, and returned joyfully, as the animals in the fable are supposed to have approached and left the den of the lion.

The very few persons who seemed to be there in the character of counsellors were mean-looking men, whose countenances sometimes expressed sagacity, but whose manners showed they were called into a sphere for which their previous education and habits had qualified them but indifferently. One or two persons, however, did appear to Durward to possess a more noble mien, and the strictness of the present duty was not such as to prevent his uncle communicating the names of those whom he thus distinguished.

With the Lord Crawford, who was in attendance, dressed in the rich habit of his office, and holding a leading staff of silver in his hand, Quentin, as well as the reader, was already acquainted. Among others who seemed of quality, the most remarkable was the Count de Dunois, the son of that celebrated Dunois, known by the name of the Bastard of Orleans, who, fighting under the banner of Jeanne d'Arc, acted such a distinguished part in liberating France from the English yoke. His son well supported the high renown which had descended to him from such an honoured source; and, notwithstanding his connexion with the royal family, and his hereditary popularity both with the nobles and the people, Dunois had, upon all occasions, manifested such an open, frank loyalty of character that he seemed to have escaped all suspicion, even on the part of the jealous Louis, who loved to see him near his person, and sometimes even called him to his councils. Although accounted complete in all the exercises of chivalry, and possessed of much of the character of what was then termed a perfect knight, the person of the count was far from being a model of romantic beauty. He was under the common size, though very strongly built, and his legs rather curved outwards into that make which more convenient for horseback than elegant in a pedestrian. His shoulders were broad, his hair black, his complexion swarthy, his arms remarkably long and nervous. The features of his countenance were irregular, even to ugliness; yet, after all, there was an air of conscious worth and nobility about the Count de Dunois which stamped, at the first glance, the character of the high-born nobleman and the undaunted soldier. His mien was bold and upright, his step free and manly, and the harshness of his countenance was dignified by a glance like an eagle and a frown like a lion. His dress was a hunting-suit, rather sumptuous than gay, and he acted on most occasions as Grand Huntsman, though we are not inclined to believe that he actually held the office.

Upon the arm of his relation Dunois, walking with a step so slow and melancholy that he seemed to rest on his kinsman and supporter, came Louis Duke of Orleans, the first prince of the blood royal (afterwards King, by the name of Louis XII.), and to whom the guards and attendants rendered their homage as such. The jealousy-watched object of Louis's suspicions, this prince, who, failing the King's offspring, was heir to the kingdom, was not suffered to absent himself from court, and, while residing there, was alike denied employment and countenance. The dejection which his degraded and almost captive state naturally impressed on the deportment of this unfortunate prince was at this moment greatly increased by his consciousness that the King meditated, with respect to him, one of the most cruel and unjust actions which a tyrant could commit, by compelling him to give his hand to the Princess Joan of France, the younger daughter of Louis, to whom he had been contracted in infancy, but whose deformed person rendered the insisting upon such an agreement an act of abominable rigour.[1]

The exterior of this unhappy prince was in no respect dis-

[1] See Note 19.

tinguished by personal advantages; and in mind he was of a
gentle, mild, and beneficent disposition, qualities which were
visible even through the veil of extreme dejection with which
his natural character was at present obscured. Quentin observed that the duke studiously avoided even looking at the
Royal Guards, and when he returned their salute, that he kept
his eyes bent on the ground, as if he feared the King's jealousy might have construed that gesture of ordinary courtesy
as arising from the purpose of establishing a separate and
personal interest among them.

Very different was the conduct of the proud cardinal and
prelate, John of Balue, the favourite minister of Louis for the
time, whose rise and character bore as close a resemblance to
that of Wolsey as the difference betwixt the crafty and politic
Louis and the headlong and rash Henry VIII. of England
would permit. The former had raised his minister from the
lowest rank to the dignity, or at least to the emoluments, of
Grand Almoner of France, loaded him with benefices, and
obtained for him the hat of a cardinal; and although he was
too cautious to repose in the ambitious Balue the unbounded
power and trust which Henry placed in Wolsey, yet he was
more influenced by him than by any other of his avowed counsellors. The cardinal, accordingly, had not escaped the error
incidental to those who are suddenly raised to power from an
obscure situation, for he entertained a strong persuasion, dazzled doubtless by the suddenness of his elevation, that his
capacity was equal to intermeddling with affairs of every
kind, even those most foreign to his profession and studies.
Tall and ungainly in his person, he affected gallantry and admiration of the fair sex, although his manners rendered his
pretensions absurd, and his profession marked them as inde-
corous. Some male or female flatterer had, in evil hour, possessed him with the idea that there was much beauty of con-
tour in a pair of huge, substantial legs, which he had derived
from his father, a carman of Limoges, or, according to other
authorities, a miller of Verdun; and with this idea he had
become so infatuated, that he always had his cardinal's robes
a little looped up on one side, that the sturdy proportion of

his limbs might not escape observation. As he swept through the stately apartment in his crimson dress and rich cope, he stopped repeatedly to look at the arms and appointments of the cavaliers on guard, asked them several questions in an authoritative tone, and took upon him to censure some of them for what he termed irregularities of discipline, in language to which these experienced soldiers dared no reply, although it was plain they listened to it with impatience and with contempt.

"Is the King aware," said Dunois to the cardinal, "that the Burgundian envoy is peremptory in demanding an audience?"

"He is," answered the cardinal; "and here, as I think, comes the all-sufficient Oliver Dain [1] to let us know the royal pleasure."

As he spoke, a remarkable person, who then divided the favour of Louis with the proud cardinal himself, entered from the inner apartment, but without any of that important and consequential demeanour which marked the full-blown dignity of the churchman. On the contrary, this was a little, pale, meagre man, whose black silk jerkin and hose, without either coat, cloak, or cassock, formed a dress ill qualified to set off to advantage a very ordinary person. He carried a silver basin in his hand, and a napkin flung over his arm indicated his menial capacity. His visage was penetrating and quick, although he endeavoured to vanish such expression from his features, by keeping his eyes fixed on the ground, while, with the stealthy and quiet pace of a cat, he seemed modestly rather to glide than to walk through the apartment. But, though modesty may easily obscure worth, it cannot hide court favour; and all attempts to steal unperceived through the presence-chamber were vain on the part of one known to have such possession of the King's ear as had been attained by his celebrated barber and groom of the chamber, Oliver le Dain, called sometimes Oliver le Mauvais, and sometimes Oliver le Diable— epithets derived from the unscrupulous cunning with which he assisted in the execution of the schemes of his master's tortuous

[1] See Note 16.

policy. At present he spoke earnestly for a few moments with the Count de Dunois, who instantly left the chamber, while the tonsor glided quietly back towards the royal apartment whence he had issued, every one giving place to him; which civility he only acknowledged by the most humble inclination of the body, excepting in a very few instances, where he made one or two persons the subject of envy to all the other courtiers by whispering a single word in their ear; and at the same time muttering something of the duties of his place, he escaped from their replies, as well as from the eager solicitations of those who wished to attract his notice. Ludovic Lesly had the good fortune to be one of the individuals who, on the present occasion, was favoured by Oliver with a single word, to assure him that his matter was fortunately terminated.

Presently afterwards, he had another proof of the same agreeable tidings; for Quentin's old acquaintance, Tristan l'Hermite, the provost-marshal of the royal household, entered the apartment, and came straight to the place where Le Balafré was posted. This formidable officer's uniform, which was very rich, had only the effect of making his sinister countenance and bad mien more strikingly remarkable, and the tone which he meant for conciliatory was like nothing so much as the growling of a bear. The import of his words, however, was more amicable than the voice in which they were pronounced. He regretted the mistake which had fallen between them on the preceding day, and observed it was owing to the Sieur Le Balafré's nephew not wearing the uniform of his corps, or announcing himself as belonging to it, which had led him into the error for which he now asked forgiveness.

Ludovic Lesly made the necessary reply, and as soon as Tristan had turned away, observed to his nephew that they had now the distinction of having a mortal enemy from henceforward in the person of this dreaded officer. "But we are above his *volée:* a soldier," said he, "who does his duty may laugh at the provost-marshal."

Quentin could not help being of his uncle's opinion, for, as Tristan parted from them, it was with the look of angry defiance which the bear casts upon the hunter whose spear has wounded him. Indeed, even when less strongly moved, the sullen eye of this official expressed a malevolence of purpose which made men shudder to meet his glance; and the thrill of the young Scot was the deeper and more abhorrent, that he seemed to himself still to feel on his shoulders the grasp of the two death-doing functionaries of this fatal officer.

Meanwhile, Oliver, after he had prowled around the room in the stealthy manner which we have endeavoured to describe—all, even the highest officers, making way for him, and loading him with their ceremonious attentions, which his modesty seemed desirous to avoid—again entered the inner apartment, the doors of which were presently thrown open, and King Louis entered the presence-chamber.

Quentin, like all others, turned his eyes upon him; and started so suddenly that he almost dropt his weapon, when he recognised in the King of France that silk-merchant, Maître Pierre, who had been the companion of his morning walk. Singular suspicions respecting the real rank of this person had at different times crossed his thought; but this, the proved reality, was wilder than his wildest conjecture.

The stern look of his uncle, offended at this breach of the decorum of his office, recalled him to himself; but not a little was he astonished when the King, whose quick eye had at once discovered him, walked straight to the place where he was posted, without taking notice of any one else. "So," he said, "young man, I am told you have been brawling on your first arrival in Touraine; but I pardon you, as it was chiefly the fault of a foolish old merchant, who thought your Caledonian blood required to be heated in the morning with *vin de Beaulne*. If I can find him, I will make him an example to those who debauch my Guards. Balafré," he added, speaking to Lesly, "your kinsman is a fair youth, though a fiery. We love to cherish such spirits, and mean to make more than ever we did of the brave men who are around us. Let the year, day, hour, and minute of your nephew's birth be written down and given to Oliver Dain."

Le Balafré bowed to the ground and reassumed his erect military position, as one who would show by his demeanour his promptitude to act in the King's quarrel or defence. Quentin, in the mean time, recovered from his first surprise, studied the King's appearance more attentively, and was surprised to find how differently he now construed his deportment and features than he had done at their first interview.

These were not much changed in exterior, for Louis, always a scorner of outward show, wore, on the present occasion, an old dark-blue hunting-dress, not much better than the plain burgher-suit of the preceding day, and garnished with a huge rosary of ebony, which had been sent to him by no less a personage than the Grand Seignior, with an attestation that it had been used by a Coptic hermit on Mount Lebanon, a personage of profound sanctity. And instead of his cap with a single image, he now wore a hat the band of which was garnished with at least a dozen of little paltry figures of saints stamped in lead. But those eyes which, according to Quentin's former impression, only twinkled with the love of gain, had, now that they were known to be the property of an able and powerful monarch, a piercing and majestic glance; and those wrinkles on the brow, which he had supposed were formed during a long series of petty schemes of commerce, seemed now the furrows which sagacity had worn while toiling in meditation upon the fate of nations.

Presently after the King's appearance, the Princesses of France, with the ladies of their suite, entered the apartment, With the eldest, afterwards married to Peter of Bourbon, and known in French history by the name of the Lady of Beaujeau, our story has but little to do. She was tall, and rather handsome, possessed eloquence, talent, and much of her father's sagacity, who reposed great confidence in her, and loved her as well perhaps as he loved any one.

The younger sister, the unfortunate Joan, the destined bride of the Duke of Orleans, advanced timidly by the side of her sister, conscious of a total want of those external qualities which women are most desirous of possessing, or being thought to possess. She was pale, thin, and sickly in her complexion; her shape visibly bent to one side, and her gait so unequal that she might be called lame. A fine set of teeth, and eyes which were expressive of melancholy, softness, and resignation, with a quantity of light brown locks, were the only redeeming points which flattery itself could have dared to number to counteract the general homeliness of her face and figure. To complete the picture, it was easy to remark, from the Princess's negligence in dress and the timidity of her manner, that she had an unusual and distressing consciousness of her own plainness of appearance, and did not dare to make any of those attempts to mend by manners or by art what nature had left amiss, or in any other way to exert a power of pleasing. The King, who loved her not, stepped hastily to her as she entered. "How now!" he said, " our world-contemning daughter. Are you robed for a hunting-party or for the convent this morning. Speak—answer."

"For which your Highness pleases, sire," said the Princess, scarce raising her voice above her breath.

"Ay, doubtless you would persuade me it is your desire to quit the court, Joan, and renounce the world and its vanities. Ha! maiden, wouldst thou have it thought that we, the first-born of holy church, would refuse our daughter to Heaven? Our Lady and St. Martin forbid we should refuse the offering, were it worthy of the altar, or were thy vocation in truth thitherward!"

So saying, the King crossed himself devoutly, looking, in the mean time, as appeared to Quentin, very like a cunning vassal, who was depreciating the merit of something which he was desirous to keep to himself, in order that he might stand excused for not offering it to his chief or superior. "Dares he thus play the hypocrite with Heaven," thought Durward, "and sport with God and the saints, as he may safely do with men, who dare not search his nature too closely?"

Louis meantime resumed, after a moment's mental devotion: "No, fair daughter, I and another know your real mind better. Ha! fair cousin of Orleans, do we not? Approach, fair sir, and lead this devoted vestal of ours to her horse."

Orleans started when the King spoke, and hastened to obey him; but with such precipitation of step and confusion that

Louis called out: "Nay, cousin, rein your gallantry, and look before you. Why, what a headlong matter a gallant's haste is on some occasions! You had wellnigh taken Anne's hand instead of her sister's. Sir, must I give Joan's to you myself?"

The unhappy prince looked up, and shuddered like a child, when forced to touch something at which it has instinctive horror; then making an effort, took the hand which the Princess neither gave nor yet withheld. As they stood, her cold damp fingers inclosed in his trembling hand, with their eyes looking on the ground, it would have been difficult to say which of these two youthful beings was rendered more utterly miserable—the duke, who felt himself fettered to the object of his aversion by bonds which he durst not tear asunder, or the unfortunate young woman, who too plainly saw that she was an object of abhorrence to him to gain whose kindness she would willingly have died.

"And how to horse, gentlemen and ladies. We will ourselves lead forth our daughter of Beaujeau," said the King; "and God's blessing and St. Hubert's be on our morning sport!"

"I am, I fear, doomed to interrupt it, sire," said the Count de Dunois—"the Burgundian envoy is before the gates of the castle, and demands an audience."

"*Demands* an audience, Dunois!" replied the King. "Did you not answer him, as we sent you word by Oliver, that we were not at leisure to see him to-day; and that to-morrow was the festival of St. Martin, which, please Heaven, we would disturb by no earthly thoughts; and that on the succeeding day we were designed for Amboise; but that we would not fail to appoint him as early an audience, when we returned, as our pressing affairs would permit?"

"All this I said," answered Dunois; "but yet, sire——"

"*Pasques-dieu!* man, what is it that thus sticks in thy throat?" said the King. "This Burgundian's terms must have been hard of digestion."

"Had not my duty, your Grace's commands, and his character as an envoy restrained me," said Dunois, "he should have tried to digest them himself, for, by our Lady of Orleans, I had more mind to have made him eat his own words than to have brought them to your Majesty."

"Body of me, Dunois," said King, "it is strange that thou, one of the most impatient fellows alive, shouldst have so little sympathy with the like infirmity in our blunt and fiery cousin, Charles of Burgundy. Why, man, I mind his blustering messages no more than the towers of this castle regard the whistling of the northeast wind, which comes from Flanders, as well as this brawling envoy."

"Know then, sire," replied Dunois, "that the Count of Crèvecœur tarries below, with his retinue of pursuivants and trumpets, and says that, since your Majesty refused him the audience which his master instructed him to demand, upon matters of most pressing concern, he will remain there till midnight, and accost your Majesty at whatever hour you are pleased to issue from your castle, whether for business, exercise, or devotion; and that no consideration, except the use of absolute force, shall compel him to desist from this resolution."

"He is a fool," said the King, with much composure. "Does the hot-headed Hainaulter think it any penance for a man of sense to remain for twenty-four hours quiet within the walls of his castle, when he hath the affairs of a kingdom to occupy him? These impatient coxcombs think that all men, like themselves, are miserable, save when in saddle and stirrup. Let the dogs be put up and well looked to, gentle Dunois. We will hold council to-day, instead of hunting."

"My liege," answered Dunois, "you will not thus rid yourself of Crèvecœur; for his master's instructions are, that, if he hath not this audience which he demands, he shall nail his gauntlet to the palisades before the castle, in token of mortal defiance on the part of his master, shall renounce the Duke's fealty to France, and declare instant war."

"Ay," said Louis, without any perceptible alteration of voice, but frowning until his piercing dark eyes became almost invisible under his shaggy eyebrows, "is it even so?— will our ancient vassal prove so masterful—our dear cousin treat us thus unkindly? Nay then, Dunois, we must unfold the *Oriflamme,* and cry '*Denis Montjoye!*'"

"Marry and amen, and in a most happy hour!" said the martial Dunois; and the guards in the hall, unable to resist the same impulse, stirred each upon his post, so as to produce a low but distinct sound of clashing arms. The King cast his eye proudly round, and for a moment thought and looked like his heroic father.

But the excitement of the moment presently gave way to the host of political considerations which, at that conjuncture, rendered an open breach with Burgundy so peculiarly perilous. Edward IV., a brave and victorious king, who had in his own person fought thirty battles, was now established on the throne of England, was brother to the Duchess of Burgundy, and, it might well be supposed, waited but a rupture between his near connexion and Louis to carry into France, through the ever-open gate of Calais, those arms which had been triumphant in the English civil wars, and to obliterate the recollection of internal dissensions by that most popular of all occupations amongst the English, an invasion of France. To this consideration was added the uncertain faith of the Duke of Bretagne and other weighty subjects of reflection. So that, after a deep pause, when Louis again spoke, although in the same tone, it was with an altered spirit. "But God forbid," he said, "that aught less than necessity should make us, the Most Christian King, give cause to the effusion of Christian blood, if anything short of dishonour may avert such a calamity. We tender our subjects' safety dearer than the ruffle which our own dignity may receive from the rude breath of a malapert ambassador, who hath perhaps exceeded the errand with which he was charged. Admit the envoy of Burgundy to our presence."

"*Beati pacifici,*" said the Cardinal Balue.

"True; and your eminence knoweth that they who humble themselves shall be exalted," added the King.

The cardinal spoke an "Amen," to which few assented; for even the pale cheek of Orleans kindled with shame, and Balafré suppressed his feelings so little as to let the butt-end of his partizan fall heavily on the floor—a movement of impatience for which he underwent a bitter reproof from the cardinal, with a lecture on the mode of handling his arms when in presence of the sovereign. The King himself seemed unusually embarrassed at the silence around him. "You are pensive, Dunois," he said. "You disapprove of our giving way to this hot-headed envoy."

"By no means," said Dunois; "I meddle not with matters beyond my sphere. I was but thinking of asking a boon of your Majesty."

"A boon, Dunois—what is it? You are an unfrequent suitor, and may count on our favour."

"I would, then, your Majesty would send me to Évreux to regulate the clergy," said Dunois, with military frankness.

"That were indeed beyond thy sphere," replied the King, smiling.

"I might order priests as well," replied the count, "as my Lord Bishop of Évreux, or my lord cardinal, if he likes the title better, can exercise the soldiers of your Majesty's Guard."

The King smiled again, and more mysteriously, while he whispered Dunois: "The time may come when you and I will regulate the priests together. But this is for the present a good conceited animal of a bishop. Ah, Dunois! Rome—Rome puts him and other burdens upon us. But patience, cousin, and shuffle the cards, till our hand is a stronger one."[1]

The flourish of trumpets in the courtyard now announced the arrival of the Burgundian nobleman. All in the presence-chamber made haste to arrange themselves according to their proper places of precedence, the King and his daughters remaining in the centre of the assembly.

The Count of Crèvecœur, a renowned and undaunted warrior, entered the apartment; and, contrary to the usage among the envoys of friendly powers, he appeared all armed, excepting his head, in a gorgeous suit of the most superb Milan armour, made of steel, inlaid and embossed with gold, which was wrought into the fantastic taste called the arabesque.

See Card-Playing. Note 17.

Around his neck, and over his polished cuirass, hung his master's order of the Golden Fleece,[1] one of the most honoured associations of chivalry then known in Christendom. A handsome page bore his helmet behind him; a herald preceded him, bearing his letters of credence, which he offered on his knee to the King; while the ambassador himself paused in the midst of the hall, as if to give all present time to admire his lofty look, commanding stature, and undaunted composure of countenance and manner. The rest of his attendants waited in the ante-chamber, or courtyard.

"Approach, Seignior Count de Crèvecœur," said Louis, after a moment's glance at his commission; "we need not our cousin's letters of credence either to introduce to us a a warrior so well known or to assure us of your highly deserved credit with your master. We trust that your fair partner, who shares some of our ancestral blood, is in good health. Had you brought her in your hand, seignior count, we might have thought you wore your armour, on this unwonted occasion, to maintain the superiority of her charms against the amorous chivalry of France. As it is, we cannot guess the reason of this complete panoply."

"Sire," replied the ambassador, "the Count of Crèvecœur must lament his misfortune, and entreat your forgiveness, that he cannot, on this occasion, reply with such humble deference as is due to the royal courtesy with which your Majesty has honoured him. But, although it is only the voice of Philip Crèvecœur de Cordès which speaks, the words which he utters must be those of his gracious lord and sovereign the Duke of Burgundy."

"And what has Crèvecœur to say in the words of Burgundy?" said Louis, with an assumption of sufficient dignity. "Yet hold—remember, that in this presence Philip Crèvecœur de Cordès speaks to him who is his sovereign's sovereign."

Crèvecœur bowed, and then spoke aloud: "King of France, the mighty Duke of Burgundy once more sends you a written schedule of the wrongs and oppressions committed on his frontiers by your Majesty's garrisons and officers; and the

---

[1] See Note 18.

first point of inquiry is, whether it is your Majesty's purpose to make him amends for these injuries?"

The King, looking slightly at the memorial which the herald delivered to him upon his knee, said: "These matters have been already long before our council. Of the injuries complained of, some are in requital of those sustained by my subjects, some are affirmed without any proof, some have been retaliated by the Duke's garrisons and soldiers; and if there remain any which fall under none of those predicaments, we are not, as a Christian prince, averse to make satisfaction for wrongs actually sustained by our neighbour, though committed not only without our countenance but against our express order."

"I will convey your Majesty's answer," said the ambassador, "to my most gracious master; yet, let me say that, as it is in no degree different from the evasive replies which have already been returned to his just complaints, I cannot hope that it will afford the means of re-establishing peace and friendship betwixt France and Burgundy."

"Be that at God's pleasure," said the King. "It is not for dread of thy master's arms, but for the sake of peace only, that I return so temperate an answer to his injurious reproaches. Proceed with thine errand."

"My master's next demand," said the ambassador, "is, that your Majesty will cease your secret and underhand dealings with his towns of Ghent, Liege, and Malines. He requests that your Majesty will recall the secret agents by whose means the discontents of his good citizens of Flanders are inflamed; and dismiss from your Majesty's dominions, or rather deliver up to the condign punishment of their liege lord, those traitorous fugitives who, having fled from the scene of their machinations, have found too ready a refuge in Paris, Orleans, Tours, and other French cities."

"Say to the Duke of Burgundy," replied the King, "that I know of no such indirect practices as those with which he injuriously charges me; that my subjects of France have frequent intercourse with the good cities of Flanders, for the purpose of mutual benefit by free traffic, which it would be as much contrary to the Duke's interest as mine to interrupt; and that many Flemings have residence in my kingdom, and enjoy the protection of my laws, for the same purpose; but none, to our knowledge, for those of treason or mutiny against the Duke. Proceed with your message; you have heard my answer."

"As formerly, sire, with pain," replied the Count of Crèvecœur; "it not being of that direct or explicit nature which the Duke, my master, will accept, in atonement for a long train of secret machinations, not the less certain though now disavowed by your Majesty. But I proceed with my message. The Duke of Burgundy further requires the King of France to send back to his dominions without delay, and under a secure safeguard, the persons of Isabelle Countess of Croye, and of her relation and guardian the Countess Hameline, of the same family, in respect the said Countess Isabelle, being, by the law of the country and the feudal tenure of her estates, the ward of the said Duke of Burgundy, hath fled from his dominions, and from the charge which he, as a careful guardian, was willing to extend over her, and is here maintained in secret by the King of France, and by him fortified in her contumacy to the Duke, her natural lord and guardian, contrary to the laws of God and man, as they ever have been acknowledged in civilised Europe. Once more I pause for your Majesty's reply."

"You did well, Count de Crèvecœur," said Louis, scornfully, "to begin your embassy at an early hour; for if it be your purpose to call on me to account for the flight of every vassal whom your master's heady passion may have driven from his dominions, the bead-roll may last till sunset. Who can affirm that these ladies are in my dominions? Who can presume to say, if it be so, that I have either countenanced their flight hither or have received them with offers of protection? Nay, who is it will assert that, if they are in France, their place of retirement is within my knowledge?"

"Sire," said Crèvecœur, "may it please your Majesty, I *was* provided with a witness on this subject—one who beheld these fugitive ladies in the inn called the Fleur-de-Lys, not far from this castle; one who saw your Majesty in their company, though under the unworthy disguise of a burgess of Tours; one who received from them, in your royal presence, messages and letters to their friends in Flanders—all which he conveyed to the hand and ear of the Duke of Burgundy."

"Bring him forward," said the King; "place the man before my face who dares maintain these palpable falsehoods."

"You speak in triumph, sire; for you are well aware that this witness no longer exists. When he lived, he was called Zamet Maugrabin, by birth none of those Bohemian wanderers. He was yesterday, as I have learned, executed by a party of your Majesty's provost-marshal, to prevent, doubtless, his standing here to verify what he said of this matter to the Duke of Burgundy, in presence of his council, and of me, Philip Crèvecœur de Cordès."

"Now, by our Lady of Embrun!" said the King, "so gross are these accusations, and so free of consciousness am I of aught that approaches them, that, by the honour of a king, I laugh rather than am wroth at them. My provost-guard daily put to death, as is their duty, thieves and vagabonds; and is my crown to be slandered with whatever these thieves and vagabonds may have said to our hot cousin of Burgundy and his wise counsellors? I pray you, tell my kind cousin, if he loves such companions, he had best keep them in his own estates; for here they are like to meet short shrift and a tight cord."

"My master needs no such subjects, sir king," answered the count, in a tone more disrespectful than he had yet permitted himself to make use of; "for the noble Duke uses not to inquire of witches, wandering Egyptians, or others upon the destiny and fate of his neighbours and allies."

"We have had patience enough and to spare," said the King, interrupting him; "and since thy sole errand here seems to be for the purpose of insult, we will send some one in our name to the Duke of Burgundy—convinced, in thus demeaning thyself towards us, thou hast exceeded thy commission, whatever that may have been."

"On the contrary," said Crèvecœur, "I have not yet ac-

"'There lies my gage, in evidence of what I have said.'"

Quentin Durward, Chap. viii., p. 147.

quitted myself of it. Hearken, Louis of Valois, King of France. Hearken, nobles and gentlemen who may be present. Hearken, all good and true men. And thou, Toison d'Or," addressing the herald, "make proclamation after me. I, Philip Crèvecœur of Cordès, Count of the Empire, and Knight of the honourable and princely Order of the Golden Fleece, in the name of the most puissant Lord and Prince, Charles, by the grace of God, Duke of Burgundy and Lotharingia, of Brabant and Limbourg, of Luxembourg and of Gueldres, Earl of Flanders and of Artois, Count Palatine of Hainault, of Holland, Zealand, Namur, and Zutphen, Marquis of the Holy Empire, Lord of Friezeland, Salines, and Malines, do give you, Louis, King of France, openly to know, that, you having refused to remedy the various griefs, wrongs, and offences done and wrought by you, or by and through your aid, suggestion, and instigation, against the said Duke and his loving subjects, he, by my mouth, renounces all allegiance and fealty towards your crown and dignity, pronounces you false and faithless, and defies you as a prince and as a man. There lies my gage, in evidence of what I have said."

So saying, he plucked the gauntlet off his right hand and flung it down on the floor of the hall.

Until this last climax of audacity, there had been a deep silence in the royal apartment during the extraordinary scene; but no sooner had the clash of the gauntlet, when cast down, been echoed by the deep voice of Toison d'Or, the Burgundian herald, with the ejaculation, "Vive Bourgogne!" than there was a general tumult. While Dunois, Orleans, old Lord Crawford, and one or two others, whose rank authorised their interference, contended which should lift up the gauntlet, the others in the hall exclaimed: "Strike him down! Cut him to pieces! Comes he here to insult the King of France in his own palace?"

But the King appeased the tumult by exclaiming, in a voice like thunder, which overawed and silenced every other sound: "Silence, my lieges! lay not a hand on the man, not a finger on the gage. And you, sir count, of what is your life composed or how is it warranted, that you thus place it on the cast of a die so perilous? Or is your duke made of a different metal from other princes, since he thus asserts his pretended quarrel in a manner so unusual?"

"He is indeed framed of a different and more noble metal than the other princes of Europe," said the undaunted Count of Crèvecœur; "for, when not one of them dared to give shelter to you—to *you*, I say, King Louis—when you were yet only Dauphin, an exile from France, and pursued by the whole bitterness of your father's revenge and all the power of his kingdom, you were received and protected like a brother by my noble master, whose generosity of disposition you have so grossly misused. Farewell, sire, my mission is discharged."

So saying, the Count de Crèvecœur left the apartment abruptly, and without farther leave-taking.

"After him—after him—take up the gauntlet and after him!" said the King. "I mean not you, Dunois, nor you, my Lord of Crawford, who, methinks, may be too old for such hot frays; nor you, cousin of Orleans, who are too young for them. My lord cardinal—my Lord Bishop of Auxerre—it is your holy office to make peace among princes; do you lift the gauntlet, and remonstrate with Count Crèvecœur on the sin he has committed, in thus insulting a great monarch in his own court, and forcing us to bring the miseries of war upon his kingdom and that of his neighbour."

Upon this direct personal appeal, the Cardinal Balue proceeded to lift the gauntlet, with such precaution as one would touch an adder—so great was apparently his aversion to this symbol of war—and presently left the royal apartment to hasten after the challenger.

Louis paused and looked round the circle of his courtiers, most of whom, except such as we have already distinguished, being men of low birth, and raised to their rank in the King's household for other gifts than courage or feats of arms, looked pale on each other, and had obviously received an unpleasant impression from the scene which had been just acted. Louis gazed on them with contempt, and then said aloud: "Although the Count of Crèvecœur be presumptuous and overweening, it must be confessed that in him the Duke of Burgundy hath as bold a servant as ever bore message for a prince. I would I knew where to find as faithful an envoy to carry back my answer."

"You do your French nobles injustice, sire," said Dunois; "not one of them but would carry a defiance to Burgundy on the point of his sword."

"And, sire," said old Crawford, "you wrong also the Scottish gentlemen who serve you. I, or any of my followers, being of meet rank, would not hesitate a moment to call yonder proud count to a reckoning; my own arm is yet strong enough for the purpose, if I have but your Majesty's permission."

"But your Majesty," continued Dunois, "will employ us in no service through which we may win honour to ourselves, to your Majesty, or to France."

"Say, rather," said the King, "that I will not give way, Dunois, to the headlong impetuosity which, on some punctilio of chivalry, would wreck yourselves, the throne, France, and all. There is not one of you who knows not how precious every hour of peace is at this moment, when so necessary to heal the wounds of a distracted country; yet there is not one of you who would not rush into war on account of the tale of a wandering gipsy, or of some errant damsel, whose reputation, perhaps, is scarce higher. Here comes the cardinal, and we trust with more pacific tidings. How now, my lord—have you brought the count to reason and to temper?"

"Sire," said Balue, "my task hath been difficult. I put it to yonder proud count, how he dared to use towards your Majesty the presumptuous reproach with which his audience had broken up, and which must be understood as proceeding, not from his master, but from his own insolence, and as placing him therefore in your Majesty's discretion, for what penalty you might think proper."

"You said right," replied the King; "and what was his answer?"

"The count," continued the cardinal, "had at that moment his foot in the stirrup, ready to mount; and, on hearing my expostulation, he turned his head without altering his position. 'Had I,' said he, 'been fifty leagues distant, and had heard by report that a question vituperative of my prince had been asked by the King of France, I had, even at that distance, instantly mounted, and returned to disburden my mind of the answer which I gave him but now.'"

"I said, sirs," said the King, turning around, without any show of angry emotion, "that in the Count Philip of Crèvecœur our cousin the Duke possesses as worthy a servant as ever rode at a prince's right hand. But you prevailed with him to stay?"

"To stay for twenty-four hours; and in the mean while to receive again his gage of defiance," said the cardinal: "he has dismounted at the Fleur-de-Lys."

"See that he be nobly attended and cared for at our charges," said the King; "such a servant is a jewel in a prince's crown. Twenty-four hours!" he added, muttering to himself, and, looking as if he were stretching his eyes to see into futurity—"twenty-four hours! 'tis of the shortest. Yet twenty-four hours, ably and skilfully employed, may be worth a year in the hand of indolent or incapable agents. Well. To the forest—to the forest, my gallant lords! Orleans, my fair kinsman, lay aside that modesty, though it becomes you; mind not my Joan's coyness. The Loire may as soon avoid mingling with the Cher as she from favouring your suit, or you from preferring it," he added, as the unhappy prince moved slowly on after his betrothed bride. "And now for your boar-spears, gentlemen; for Allegre, my pricker, hath harboured one that will try both dog and man. Dunois, lend me your spear; take mine, it is too weighty for me; but when did *you* complain of such a fault in your lance? To horse— to horse, gentlemen."

And all the chase rode on.

CHAPTER IX.

THE BOAR-HUNT.

> I will converse with unrespective boys
> And iron-witted fools. None are for me
> That look into me with suspicious eyes.
> *King Richard.*

ALL the experience which the cardinal had been able to collect of his master's disposition did not, upon the present occasion, prevent his falling into a great error of policy. His vanity induced him to think that he had been more successful in prevailing upon the Count of Crèvecœur to remain at Tours than any other moderator whom the King might have employed would, in all probability, have been. And as he was well aware of the importance which Louis attached to the postponement of a war with the Duke of Burgundy, he could not help showing that he conceived himself to have rendered the King great and acceptable service. He pressed nearer to the King's person than he was wont to do, and endeavoured to engage him in conversation on the events of the morning.

This was injudicious in more respects than one; for princes love not to see their subjects approach them with an air conscious of deserving, and thereby seeming desirous to extort, acknowledgment and recompense for their services; and Louis, the most jealous monarch that ever lived, was peculiarly averse and inaccessible to any one who seemed either to presume upon service rendered or to pry into his secrets.

Yet, hurried away, as the most cautious sometimes are, by the self-satisfied humour of the moment, the cardinal continued to ride on the King's right hand, turning the discourse, whenever it was possible, upon Crèvecœur and his embassy; which, although it might be the matter at that moment most in the King's thoughts, was nevertheless precisely that which he was least willing to converse on. At length Louis, who had listened to him with attention, yet without having returned any answer which could tend to prolong the conversation, signed to Dunois, who rode at no great distance, to come upon the other side of his horse.

"We came hither for sport and exercise," said he, "but the reverend father here would have us hold a council of state."

"I hope your Highness will excuse my assistance," said Dunois; "I am born to fight the battles of France, and have heart and hand for that, but I have no head for her councils."

"My lord cardinal hath a head turned for nothing else, Dunois," answered Louis; "he hath confessed Crèvecœur at the castle gate, and he hath communicated to us his whole shrift. Said you not the *whole?*" he continued, with an emphasis on the word, and a glance at the cardinal, which shot from betwixt his long dark eyelashes, as a dagger gleams when it leaves the scabbard.

The cardinal trembled, as, endeavouring to reply to the King's jest, he said: "That though his order were obliged to conceal the secrets of their penitents in general, there was no *sigillum confessionis* which could not be melted at his Majesty's breath."

"And as his Eminence," said the King, "is ready to communicate the secrets of others to us, he naturally expects that we should be equally communicative to him; and, in order to get upon this reciprocal footing, he is very reasonably desirous to know if these two Ladies of Croye be actually in our territories. We are sorry we cannot indulge his curiosity, not ourselves knowing in what precise place errant damsels, disguised princesses, distressed countesses, may lie leaguer within our dominions, which are, we thank God and our Lady of Embrun, rather too extensive for us to answer easily his Eminence's most reasonable inquiries. But supposing they were with us, what say you, Dunois, to our cousin's peremptory demand?"

"I will answer you, my liege, if you will tell me in sincerity whether you want war or peace," replied Dunois, with a frankness which, while it arose out of his own native openness and intrepidity of character, made him from time to time a considerable favourite with Louis, who, like all astucious persons, was as desirous of looking into the hearts of others as of concealing his own.

"By my halidome," said he, "I should be as well contented as thyself, Dunois, to tell thee my purpose, did I myself but know it exactly. But say I declared for war, what should I do with this beautiful and wealthy young heiress, supposing her to be in my dominions?"

"Bestow her in marriage on one of your own gallant followers, who has a heart to love and an arm to protect her," said Dunois.

"Upon thyself, ha?" said the King. "*Pasques-dieu!* thou art more politic than I took thee for, with all thy bluntness."

"Nay, sire," answered Dunois, "I am aught except politic. By our Lady of Orleans, I come to the point at once, as I ride my horse at the ring. Your Majesty owes the house of Orleans at least one happy marriage."

"And I will pay it, count—*Pasques-dieu*, I will pay it! See you not yonder fair couple?" The King pointed to the unhappy Duke of Orleans and the Princess, who, neither daring to remain at a greater distance from the King nor in his sight appear separate from each other, were riding side by side, yet with an interval of two or three yards betwixt them—a space which timidity on the one side and aversion on the other prevented them from diminishing, while neither dared to increase it.

Dunois looked in the direction of the King's signal, and as the situation of his unfortunate relative and the destined bride reminded him of nothing so much as of two dogs, which, forcibly linked together, remain nevertheless as widely separated as the length of their collars will permit, he could not help shaking his head, though he ventured not on any other reply to the hypocritical tyrant. Louis seemed to guess his thoughts."

"It will be a peaceful and quiet household they will keep—not much disturbed with children, I should augur.[1] But these are not always a blessing."

It was, perhaps, the recollection of his own filial ingrati-

---

[1] See Louis and his Daughter. Note 19.

tude that made the King pause as he uttered the last reflection, and which converted the sneer that trembled on his lip into something resembling an expression of contrition. But he instantly proceeded in another tone.

"Frankly, my Dunois, much as I revere the holy sacrament of matrimony (here he crossed himself), I would rather the house of Orleans raised for me such gallant soldiers as thy father and thyself, who share the blood-royal of France without claiming its rights, than that the country should be torn to pieces, like to England, by wars arising from the rivalry of legitimate candidates for the crown. The lion should never have more than one cub."

Dunois sighed and was silent, conscious that contradicting his arbitrary sovereign might well hurt his kinsman's interests, but could do him no service; yet he could not forbear adding, in the next moment:

"Since your Majesty has alluded to the birth of my father, I must needs own that, setting the frailty of his parents on one side, he might be termed happier, and more fortunate, as the son of lawless love than of conjugal hatred."

"Thou art a scandalous fellow, Dunois, to speak thus of holy wedlock," answered Louis, jestingly. "But to the devil with the discourse, for the boar is unharboured. Lay on the dogs, in the name of the holy St. Hubert! Ha! ha! tra-la-la-lira-la!" And the King's horn rung merrily through the woods as he pushed forward on the chase, followed by two or three of his guards, amongst whom was our friend Quentin Durward. And here it was remarkable that, even in the keen prosecution of his favourite sport, the King, in indulgence of his caustic disposition, found leisure to amuse himself by tormenting Cardinal Balue.

It was one of that able statesman's weaknesses, as we have elsewhere hinted, to suppose himself, though of low rank and limited education, qualified to play the courtier and the man of gallantry. He did not, indeed, actually enter the lists of chivalrous combat, like Becket, or levy soldiers like Wolsey. But gallantry, in which they also were proficient, was his professed pursuit; and he likewise affected great fondness for the martial amusement of the chase. Yet, however well he might succeed with certain ladies, to whom his power, his wealth, and his influence as a statesman might atone for deficiencies in appearance and manners, the gallant horses, which he purchased at almost any price, were totally insensible to the dignity of carrying a cardinal, and paid no more respect to him than they would have done to his father, the carter, miller, or tailor, whom he rivalled in horsemanship. The King knew this, and, by alternately exciting and checking his own horse, he brought that of the cardinal, whom he kept close by his side, into such a state of mutiny against his rider that it became apparent they must soon part company; and then, in the midst of its starting, bolting, rearing, and lashing out alternately, the royal tormentor rendered the rider miserable, by questioning him upon many affairs of importance, and hinting his purpose to take that opportunity of communicating to him some of those secrets of state which the cardinal had but a little while before seemed so anxious to learn.[1]

A more awkward situation could hardly be imagined than that of a privy-councillor forced to listen to and reply to his sovereign while each fresh gambade of his unmanageable horse placed him in a new and more precarious attitude—his violet robe flying loose in every direction, and nothing securing him from an instant and perilous fall save the depth of the saddle, and its height before and behind. Dunois laughed without restraint; while the King, who had a private mode of enjoying his jest inwardly, without laughing aloud, mildly rebuked his minister on his eager passion for the chase, which would not permit him to dedicate a few moments to business. "I will no longer be your hinderance to a course," continued he, addressing the terrified cardinal, and giving his own horse the rein at the same time.

Before Balue could utter a word by way of answer or apology, his horse, seizing the bit with his teeth, went forth at an uncontrollable gallop, soon leaving behind the King and Dunois, who followed at a more regulated pace, enjoying the statesman's distressed predicament. If any of our readers

[1] See Balue's Horsemanship. Note 20.

has chanced to be run away with in his time, as we ourselves have in ours, he will have a full sense at once of the pain, peril, and absurdity of the situation. Those four limbs of the quadruped, which, no way under the rider's control, nor sometimes under that of the creature they more properly belong to, fly at such a rate as if the hindermost meant to overtake the foremost; those clinging legs of the biped which we so often wish safely planted on the green sward, but which now only augment our distress by pressing the animal's sides; the hands which have forsaken the bridle for the mane; the body which, instead of sitting upright on the centre of gravity, as old Angelo used to recommend, or stooping forward like a jockey's at Newmarket, lies, rather than hangs, crouched upon the back of the animal, with no better chance of saving itself than a sack of corn—combine to make a picture more than sufficiently ludicrous to spectators, however uncomfortable to the exhibiter. But add to this some singularity of dress or appearance on the part of the unhappy cavalier—a robe of office, a splendid uniform, or any other peculiarity of costume—and let the scene of action be a race-course, a review, a procession, or any other place of concourse and public display, and if the poor wight would escape being the object of a shout of inextinguishable laughter, he must contrive to break a limb or two, or, which will be more effectual, to be killed on the spot; for on no slighter condition will his fall excite anything like serious sympathy. On the present occasion, the short violet-coloured gown of the cardinal, which he used as a riding-dress (having changed his long robes before he left the castle), his scarlet stockings and scarlet hat, with the long strings hanging down, together with his utter helplessness, gave infinite zest to his exhibition of horsemanship.

The horse, having taken matters entirely into his own hand, flew rather than galloped up a long green avenue, overtook the pack in hard pursuit of the boar, and then, having overturned one or two yeomen-prickers, who little expected to be charged in the rear, having ridden down several dogs, and greatly confused the chase, animated by the clamorous expostulations and threats of the huntsman, carried the terrified cardinal past the formidable animal itself, which was rushing on at a speedy trot, furious and embossed with the foam which he churned around his tusks. Balue, on beholding himself so near the boar, set up a dreadful cry for help, which, or perhaps the sight of the boar, produced such an effect on his horse, that the animal interrupted its headlong career by suddenly springing to one side; so that the cardinal, who had long kept his seat only because the motion was straight forward, now fell heavily to the ground. The conclusion of Balue's chase took place so near the boar that, had not the animal been at that moment too much engaged about his own affairs, the vicinity might have proved as fatal to the cardinal as it is said to have done to Favila, king of the Visigoths, of Spain. The powerful churchman got off, however, for the fright, and, crawling as hastily as he could out of the way of hounds and huntsmen, saw the whole chase sweep by him without affording him assistance; for hunters in those days were as little moved by sympathy for such misfortunes as they are in our own.

The King, as he passed, said to Dunois: "Yonder lies his Eminence low enough; he is no great huntsman, though for a fisher, when a secret is to be caught, he may match St. Peter himself. He has, however, for once, I think, met with his match."

The cardinal did not hear the words, but the scornful look with which they were spoken led him to suspect their general import. The devil is said to seize such opportunities of temptation as was now afforded by the passions of Balue, bitterly moved as they had been by the scorn of the King. The momentary fright was over so soon as he had assured himself that his fall was harmless; but mortified vanity, and resentment against his sovereign, had a much longer influence on his feelings.

After all the chase had passed him, a single cavalier, who seemed rather to be a spectator than a partaker of the sport, rode up with one or two attendants, and expressed no small surprise to find the cardinal upon the ground, without a horse or attendants, and in such a plight as plainly showed the nature of the accident which had placed him there. To dismount and offer his assistance in this predicament, to cause one of his attendants resign a staid and quiet palfrey for the cardinal's use, to express his surprise at the customs of the French court, which thus permitted them to abandon to the dangers of the chase, and forsake in his need, their wisest statesman, were the natural modes of assistance and consolation which so strange a rencontre supplied to Crèvecœur; for it was the Burgundian ambassador who came to the assistance of the fallen cardinal.

He found the minister in a lucky time and humour for essaying some of those practices on his fidelity to which it is well known that Balue had the criminal weakness to listen. Already in the morning, as the jealous temper of Louis had suggested, more had passed betwixt them than the cardinal durst have reported to his master. But although he had listened with gratified ears to the high value which, he was assured by Crèvecœur, the Duke of Burgundy placed upon his person and talents, and not without a feeling of temptation, when the count hinted at the munificence of his master's disposition, and the rich benefices of Flanders, it was not until the accident, as we have related, had highly irritated him, that, stung with wounded vanity, he resolved, in a fatal hour, to show Louis XI. that no enemy can be so dangerous as an offended friend and confidant.

On the present occasion, he hastily requested Crèvecœur to separate from him, lest they should be observed, but appointed him a meeting for the evening in the abbey of St. Martin's at Tours, after vesper service, and that in a tone which assured the Burgundian that his master had obtained an advantage hardly to have been hoped for, except in such a moment of exasperation.

In the mean while, Louis, who, though the most politic prince of his time, upon this, as on other occasions, had suffered his passions to interfere with his prudence, followed contentedly the chase of the wild boar, which was now come to an interesting point. It had so happened that a sounder (*i.e.*, in the language of the period, a boar of only two years old) had crossed the track of the proper object of the chase, and withdrawn in pursuit of him all the dogs, except two or three couple of old stanch hounds, and the greater part of the huntsmen. The King saw, with internal glee, Dunois, as well as others, follow upon this false scent, and enjoyed in secret the thought of triumphing over that accomplished knight in the art of venerie, which was then thought almost as glorious as war. Louis was well mounted, and followed close on the hounds; so that, when the original boar turned to bay in a marshy piece of ground, there was no one near him but the King himself.

Louis showed all the bravery and expertness of an experienced huntsman; for, unheeding the danger, he rode up to the tremendous animal, which was defending itself with fury against the dogs, and struck him with his boar-spear; yet, as the horse shied from the boar, the blow was not so effectual as either to kill or disable him. No effort could prevail on the horse to charge a second time; so that the King, dismounting, advanced on foot against the furious animal, holding naked in his hand one of those short, sharp, straight, and pointed swords which huntsmen used for such encounters. The boar instantly quitted the dogs to rush on his human enemy, while the King, taking his station, and posting himself firmly, presented the sword, with the purpose of aiming it at the boar's throat, or rather chest, within the collar-bone; in which case, the weight of the beast, and the impetuosity of its career, would have served to accelerate its own destruction. But, owing to the wetness of the ground, the King's foot slipped, just as this delicate and perilous manœuvre ought to have been accomplished, so that the point of the sword, encountering the cuirass of bristles on the outside of the creature's shoulder, glanced off without making any impression, and Louis fell flat on the ground. This was so far fortunate for the monarch, because the animal, owing to the King's fall, missed his blow in his turn, and in passing only rent with his tusk the King's short hunting-cloak, instead of ripping up his thigh. But when, after running a little ahead in the fury of his course, the boar turned to repeat his attack on the King at the moment when he was rising, the life of Louis was in imminent danger. At this critical moment, Quentin Durward, who had been thrown out in the chase by the slowness of his horse, but who, nevertheless, had luckily distinguished and followed the blast of the King's horn, rode up and transfixed the animal with his spear.

The King, who had by this time recovered his feet, came in turn to Durward's assistance, and cut the animal's throat with his sword. Before speaking a word to Quentin, he measured the huge creature not only by paces, but even by feet; then wiped the sweat from his brow and the blood from his hands; then took off his hunting-cap, hung it on a bush, and devoutly made his orisons to the little leaden images which it contained; and at length, looking upon Durward, said to him: "Is it thou, my young Scot? Thou hast begun thy woodcraft well, and Maître Pierre owes thee as good entertainment as he gave thee at the Fleur-de-Lys yonder. Why dost thou not speak? Thou hast lost thy forwardness and fire, methinks, at the court, where others find both."

Quentin, as shrewd a youth as ever Scottish breeze breathed caution into, had imbibed more awe than confidence towards his dangerous master, and was far too wise to embrace the perilous permission of familiarity which he seemed thus invited to use. He answered in very few and well-chosen words, that if he ventured to address his Majesty at all, it could be but to crave pardon for the rustic boldness with which he had conducted himself when ignorant of his high rank.

"Tush! man," said the King; "I forgive thy sauciness for thy spirit and shrewdness. I admired how near thou didst hit upon my gossip Tristan's occupation. You have nearly tasted of his handiwork since, as I am given to understand. I bid thee beware of him: he is a merchant who deals in rough bracelets and tight necklaces. Help me to my horse. I like thee, and will do thee good. Build on no man's favour but mine—not even on thine uncle's or Lord Crawford's; and say nothing of thy timely aid in this matter of the boar, for if a man makes boast that he has served a king in such a pinch, he must take the braggart honour for its own recompense."

The King then winded his horn, which brought up Dunois and several attendants, whose compliments he received on the slaughter of such a noble animal, without scrupling to appropriate a much greater share of merit than actually belonged to him; for he mentioned Durward's assistance as slightly as a sportsman of rank, who, in boasting of the number of birds which he has bagged, does not always dilate upon the presence and assistance of the gamekeeper. He then ordered Dunois to see that the boar's carcass was sent to the brotherhood of St. Martin, at Tours, to mend their fare on holydays, and that they might remember the King in their private devotions.

"And," said Louis, "who hath seen his Eminence my lord cardinal? Methinks it were but poor courtesy, and cold regard to holy church, to leave him afoot here in the forest."

"May it please you, sire," said Quentin, when he saw that all were silent, "I saw his lordship the cardinal accommodated with a horse, on which he left the forest."

"Heaven cares for its own," replied the King. "Set forward to the castle, my lords; we'll hunt no more this morning. You, sir squire," addressing Quentin, "reach me my wood-knife; it has dropped from the sheath beside the quarry there. Ride on, Dunois; I follow instantly."

Louis, whose lightest motions were often conducted like stratagems, thus gained an opportunity to ask Quentin privately: "My bonny Scot, thou hast an eye, I see. Canst thou tell me who helped the cardinal to a palfrey? Some stranger, I should suppose; for, as *I* passed without stopping, the courtiers would likely be in no hurry to do him such a timely good turn."

"I saw those who aided his Eminence but an instant, sire," said Quentin; "it was only a hasty glance, for I had been unluckily thrown out, and was riding fast, to be in my place; but I think it was the ambassador of Burgundy and his people."

"Ha!" said Louis. "Well, be it so; France will match them yet."

There was nothing more remarkable happened, and the King, with his retinue, returned to the castle.

CHAPTER X.

THE SENTINEL.

<blockquote>
Where should this music be? i' the air, or the earth?
The Tempest.

I was all ear,
And took in strains that might create a soul
Under the ribs of death.
Comus.
</blockquote>

Quentin had hardly reached his little cabin, in order to make some necessary changes in his dress, when his worthy relative required to know the full particulars of all that had befallen him at the hunt.

The youth, who could not help thinking that his uncle's hand was probably more powerful than his understanding, took care, in his reply, to leave the King in full possession of the victory which he had seemed desirous to appropriate. Le Balafré's reply was a boast of how much better he himself would have behaved in the like circumstances, and it was mixed with a gentle censure of his nephew's slackness, in not making in to the King's assistance, when he might be in imminent peril. The youth had prudence, in answer, to abstain from all farther vindication of his own conduct, except that, according to the rules of woodcraft, he held it ungentle to interfere with the game attacked by another hunter, unless he was specially called upon for his assistance. This discussion was scarcely ended, when occasion was afforded Quentin to congratulate himself for observing some reserve towards his kinsman. A low tap at the door announced a visitor; it was presently opened, and Oliver Dain, or Mauvais, or Diable, for by all these names he was known, entered the apartment.

This able but most unprincipled man has been already described, in so far as his exterior is concerned. The aptest resemblance of his motions and manners might perhaps be to those of the domestic cat, which, while couching in seeming slumber, or gliding through the apartment with slow, stealthy, and timid steps, is now engaged in watching the hole of some unfortunate mouse, now in rubbing herself with apparent confidence and fondness against those by whom she desires to be caressed, and, presently after, is flying upon her prey, or scratching, perhaps, the very object of her former cajolements.

He entered with stooping shoulders, a humble and modest look, and threw such a degree of civility into his address to the Seignior Balafré that no one, who saw the interview, could have avoided concluding that he came to ask a boon of the Scottish Archer. He congratulated Lesly on the excellent conduct of his young kinsman in the chase that day, which, he observed, had attracted the King's particular attention. He here paused for a reply; and with his eyes fixed on the ground, save just when once or twice they stole upwards to take a side glance at Quentin, he heard Balafré observe: "That his Majesty had been unlucky in not having himself by his side instead of his nephew, as he would questionless have made in and speared the brute, a matter which he understood Quentin had left upon his Majesty's royal hands, so far as he could learn the story. But it will be a lesson to his Majesty," he said, "while he lives, to mount a man of my inches on a better horse; for how could my great hill of a Flemish dray-horse keep up with his Majesty's Norman runner? I am sure I spurred till his sides were furrowed. It is ill considered, Master Oliver, and you must represent it to his Majesty."

Master Oliver only replied to this observation by turning towards the bold bluff speaker one of those slow, dubious glances which, accompanied by a slight motion of the hand and a gentle depression of the head to one side, may be either interpreted as a mute assent to what is said or as a cautious deprecation of farther prosecution of the subject. It was a keener, more scrutinising glance which he bent on the youth, as he said, with an ambiguous smile: "So, young man, is it the wont of Scotland to suffer your princes to be endangered for the lack of aid, in such emergencies as this of to-day?"

"It is our custom," answered Quentin, determined to throw no farther light on the subject, "not to encumber them with assistance in honourable pastimes, when they can aid themselves without it. We hold that a prince in a hunting-field must take his chance with others, and that he comes there for the very purpose. What were woodcraft without fatigue and without danger?"

"You hear the silly boy," said his uncle; "that is always the way with him: he hath an answer or a reason ready to be rendered to every one. I wonder whence he hath caught the gift; I never could give a reason for anything I have ever done in my life, except for eating when I was a-hungry, calling the muster-roll, and such points of duty as the like."

"And pray, worthy seignior," said the royal tonsor, looking at him from under his eyelids, "what might your reason be for calling the muster-roll on such occasions?"

"Because the captain commanded me," said Le Balafré. "By St. Giles, I know no other reason! If he had commanded Tyrie or Cunningham, they must have done the same."

"A most military final cause!" said Oliver. "But, Seignior Le Balafré, you will be glad, doubtless, to learn that his Majesty is so far from being displeased with your nephew's conduct, that he hath selected him to execute a piece of duty this afternoon."

"Selected *him?*" said Balafré, in great surprise. "Selected *me,* I suppose you mean?"

"I mean precisely as I speak," replied the barber, in a mild but decided tone: "the King hath a commission with which to entrust your nephew."

"Why, wherefore, and for what reason?" said Balafré. "Why doth he choose the boy, and not me?"

"I can go no farther back than your own ultimate cause, Seignior Le Balafré: such are his Majesty's commands. But," said he, "if I might use the presumption to form a conjecture, it may be his Majesty hath work to do fitter for a youth like your nephew than for an experienced warrior like yourself, Seignior Balafré. Wherefore, young gentleman, get your weapons and follow me. Bring with you a harquebuss, for you are to mount sentinel."

"Sentinel!" said the uncle; "are you sure you are right,

Master Oliver? The inner guards of the castle have ever been mounted by those only who have, like me, served twelve years in our honourable body."

"I am quite certain of his Majesty's pleasure," said Oliver, "and must no longer delay executing it."

"But," said Le Balafré, "my nephew is not even a free archer, being only an esquire, serving under my lance."

"Pardon me," answered Oliver, "the King sent for the register not half an hour since, and enrolled him among the Guard. Have the goodness to assist to put your nephew in order for the service."

Balafré, who had no ill-nature, or even much jealousy, in his disposition, hastily set about adjusting his nephew's dress, and giving him directions for his conduct under arms, but was unable to refrain from larding them with interjections of surprise at such luck chancing to fall upon the young man so early.

"It had never taken place before in the Scottish Guard," he said, "not even in his own instance. But doubtless his service must be to mount guard over the popinjays and Indian peacocks which the Venetian ambassador had lately presented to the King—it could be nothing else; and such duty being only fit for a beardless boy (here he twirled his own grim mustachios), he was glad the lot had fallen on his fair nephew."

Quick and sharp of wit, as well as ardent in fancy, Quentin saw visions of higher importance in this early summons to the royal presence, and his heart beat high at the anticipation of rising into speedy distinction. He determined carefully to watch the manners and language of his conductor, which he suspected must, in some cases at least, be interpreted by contraries, as soothsayers are said to discover the interpretation of dreams. He could not but hug himself on having observed strict secrecy on the events of the chase, and then formed a resolution which, for so young a person, had much prudence in it, that, while he breathed the air of this secluded and mysterious court, he would keep his thoughts locked in his bosom, and his tongue under the most careful regulation.

His equipment was soon complete, and with his harquebuss

on his shoulder (for though they retained the name of archers, the Scottish Guard very early substituted firearms for the long bow, in the use of which their nation never excelled), he followed Master Oliver out of the barrack.

His uncle looked long after him with a countenance in which wonder was blended with curiosity; and though neither envy nor the malignant feelings which it engenders entered into his honest meditation, there was yet a sense of wounded or diminished self-importance which mingled with the pleasure excited by his nephew's favourable commencement of service.

He shook his head gravely, opened a privy cupboard, took out a large *bottrine* of stout old wine, shook it to examine how low the contents had ebbed, filled and drank a hearty cup; then took his seat, half-reclining, on the great oaken settle, and having once again slowly shaken his head, received so much apparent benefit from the oscillation, that, like the toy called a mandarin, he continued the motion until he dropped into a slumber, from which he was first roused by the signal to dinner.

When Quentin Durward left his uncle to these sublime meditations, he followed his conductor, Master Oliver, who, without crossing any of the principal courts, led him partly through private passages exposed to the open air, but chiefly through a maze of stairs, vaults, and galleries, communicating with each other by secret doors and at unexpected points, into a large and spacious latticed gallery, which, from its breadth, might have been almost termed a hall, hung with tapestry more ancient than beautiful, and with a very few of the hard, cold, ghastly-looking pictures belonging to the first dawn of the arts, which preceded their splendid sunrise. These were designed to represent the paladins of Charlemagne, who made such a distinguished figure in the romantic history of France; and as the gigantic form of the celebrated Orlando constituted the most prominent figure, the apartment acquired from him the title of Roland's Hall, or Roland's Gallery.[1]

[1] See Louis XI. and Charlemagne. Note 21.

"You will keep watch here," said Oliver, in a low whisper, as if the hard delineations of monarchs and warriors around could have been offended at the elevation of his voice, or as if he had feared to awaken the echoes that lurked among the groined vaults and Gothic drop-work on the ceiling of this huge and dreary apartment.

"What are the orders and signs of my watch?" answered Quentin, in the same suppressed tone.

"Is your harquebuss loaded?" replied Oliver, without answering his query.

"That," answered Quentin, "is soon done"; and proceeded to charge his weapon, and to light the slow-match, by which when necessary it was discharged, at the embers of a wood fire, which was expiring in the huge hall chimney—a chimney itself so large that it might have been called a Gothic closet or chapel appertaining to the hall.

When this was performed, Oliver told him that he was ignorant of one of the high privileges of his own corps, which only received orders from the King in person, or the High Constable of France, in lieu of their own officers. "You are placed here by his Majesty's command, young man," added Oliver, "and you will not be long here without knowing wherefore you are summoned. Meantime, you walk extends along this gallery. You are permitted to stand still while you list, but on no account to sit down or quit your weapon. You are not to sing aloud or whistle upon any account; but you may, if you list, mutter some of the church's prayers, or what else you list that has no offence in it, in a low voice. Farewell, and keep good watch."

"Good watch!" thought the youthful soldier, as his guide stole away from him with that noiseless, gliding step which was peculiar to him, and vanished through a side door behind the arras—"good watch! but upon whom, and against whom? for what, save bats or rats, are there here to contend with, unless these grim old representatives of humanity should start into life for the disturbance of my guard? Well, it is my duty, I suppose, and I must perform it."

With the vigorous purpose of discharging his duty, even to

the very rigour, he tried to while away the time with some of the pious hymns which he had learned in the convent in which he had found shelter after the death of his father—allowing in his own mind that, but for the change of a novice's frock for the rich military dress which he now wore, his soldierly walk in the royal gallery of France resembled greatly those of which he had tired excessively in the cloistered seclusion of Aberbrothock.

Presently, as if to convince himself he now belonged not to the cell but to the world, he chanted to himself, but in such a tone as not to exceed the license given to him, some of the ancient rude ballads which the old family harper had taught him, of the defeat of the Danes at Aberlemmo and Forres, the murder of King Duffus at Forfar, and other pithy sonnets and lays, which appertained to the history of his distant native country, and particularly of the district to which he belonged. This wore away a considerable space of time, and it was now more than two hours past noon, when Quentin was reminded by his appetite that the good fathers of Aberbrothock, however strict in demanding his attendance upon the hours of devotion, were no less punctual in summoning him to those of refection; whereas here, in the interior of a royal palace, after a morning spent in exercise and a noon exhausted in duty, no man seemed to consider it as a natural consequence that he must be impatient for his dinner.

There are, however, charms in sweet sounds which can lull to rest even the natural feelings of impatience by which Quentin was now visited. At the opposite extremities of the long hall or gallery were two large doors, ornamented with heavy architraves, probably opening into different suites of apartments, to which the gallery served as a medium of mutual communication. As the sentinel directed his solitary walk betwixt these two entrances, which formed the boundary of his duty, he was startled by a strain of music, which was suddenly waked near one of those doors, and which, at least in his imagination, was a combination of the same lute and voice by which he had been enchanted on the preceding day. All the dreams of yesterday morning, so much weakened by the agitating circumstances which he had since undergone, again rose more vivid from their slumber, and, planted on the spot where his ear could most conveniently drink in the sounds, Quentin remained, with his harquebuss shouldered, his mouth half open, eye, ear, and soul directed to the spot, rather the picture of a sentinel than a living form—without any other idea than that of catching, if possible, each passing sound of the dulcet melody.

These delightful sounds were but partially heard: they languished, lingered, ceased entirely, and were from time to time renewed after uncertain intervals. But, besides that music, like beauty, is often most delightful, or at least most interesting to the imagination, when its charms are but partially displayed, and the imagination is left to fill up what is from distance but imperfectly detailed, Quentin had matter enough to fill up his reverie during the intervals of fascination. He could not doubt, from the report of his uncle's comrades and the scene which had passed in the presence-chamber that morning, that the siren who thus delighted his ears was not, as he had profanely supposed, the daughter or kinswoman of a base *cabaretier*, but the same disguised and distressed countess for whose cause kings and princes were now about to buckle on armour and put lance in rest. A hundred wild dreams, such as romantic and adventurous youth readily nourished in a romantic and adventurous age, chased from his eyes the bodily presentment of the actual scene, and substituted their own bewildering delusions, when at once, and rudely, they were banished by a rough grasp laid upon his weapon, and a harsh voice which exclaimed, close to his ear, "Ha! *Pasques-dieu*, sir squire, methinks you keep sleepy ward here!"

The voice was the tuneless, yet impressive and ironical, tone of Maître Pierre, and Quentin, suddenly recalled to himself, saw, with shame and fear, that he had, in his reverie, permitted Louis himself—entering probably by some secret door, and gliding along by the wall or behind the tapestry—to approach him so nearly as almost to master his weapon.

The first impulse of his surprise was to free his harquebuss by a violent exertion, which made the King stagger backward into the hall. His next apprehension was, that in obeying the animal instinct, as it may be termed, which prompts a brave man to resist an attempt to disarm him, he had aggravated, by a personal struggle with the King, the displeasure produced by the negligence with which he had performed his duty upon guard; and, under this impression, he recovered his harquebuss without almost knowing what he did, and, having again shouldered it, stood motionless before the monarch, whom he had reason to conclude he had mortally offended.

Louis, whose tyrannical disposition was less founded on natural ferocity or cruelty of temper than on cold-blooded policy and jealous suspicion, had, nevertheless, a share of that caustic severity which would have made him a despot in private conversation, and always seemed to enjoy the pain which he inflicted on occasions like the present. But he did not push his triumph far, and contented himself with saying: "Thy service of the morning hath already overpaid some negligence in so young a soldier. Hast thou dined?"

Quentin, who rather looked to be sent to the provost-marshal than greeted with such a compliment, answered humbly in the negative.

"Poor lad," said Louis, in a softer tone than he usually spoke in, "hunger hath made him drowsy. I know thine appetite is a wolf," he continued, "and I will save thee from one wild beast as thou didst me from another. Thou hast been prudent too in that matter, and I thank thee for it. Canst thou yet hold out an hour without food?"

"Four-and-twenty, sire," replied Durward, "or I were no true Scot."

"I would not for another kingdom be the pasty which should encounter thee after such a vigil," said the King; "but the question now is, not of thy dinner but of my own. I admit to my table this day, and in strict privacy, the Cardinal Balue and this Burgundian—this Count de Crèvecœur, and something may chance: the devil is most busy when foes meet on terms of truce."

He stopped, and remained silent, with a deep and gloomy

look. As the King was in no haste to proceed, Quentin at length ventured to ask what his duty was to be in these circumstances.

"To keep watch at the beauffet, with thy loaded weapon," said Louis; "and if there is treason, to shoot the traitor dead."

"Treason, sire! and in this guarded castle!" exclaimed Durward.

"You think it impossible," said the King, not offended, it would seem, by his frankness; "but our history has shown that treason can creep into an auger-hole. Treason excluded by guards! O thou silly boy! *Quis custodiat ipsos custodes*—who shall exclude the treason of those very warders?"

"Their Scottish honour," answered Durward, boldly.

"True—most right, thou pleasest me," said the King, cheerfully; "the Scottish honour was ever true, and I trust it accordingly. But treason!"—here he relapsed into his former gloomy mood, and traversed the apartment with unequal steps—"she sits at our feasts, she sparkles in our bowls, she wears the beard of our counsellors, the smiles of our courtiers, the crazy laugh of our jesters—above all, she lies hid under the friendly air of a reconciled enemy. Louis of Orleans trusted John of Burgundy: he was murdered in the Rue Barbette. John of Burgundy trusted the faction of Orleans: he was murdered on the bridge of Montereau. I will trust no one—no one. Hark ye; I will keep my eye on that insolent count; ay, and on the churchman too, whom I hold not too faithful. When I say, '*Écosse, en avant*,' shoot Crèvecœur dead on the spot."

"It is my duty," said Quentin, "your Majesty's life being endangered."

"Certainly—I mean it no otherwise," said the King. "What should I get by slaying this insolent soldier? Were it the Constable St. Paul indeed——" Here he paused, as if he thought he had said a word too much, but resumed, laughing—"There's our brother-in-law, James of Scotland—your own James, Quentin—poniarded the Douglas' when on a hospitable visit, within his own royal castle of Skirling."

See Murder of Douglas. Note 22.

"Of Stirling," said Quentin, "and so please your Highness. It was a deed of which came little good."

"Stirling call you the castle?" said the King, overlooking the latter part of Quentin's speech. "Well, let it be Stirling; the name is nothing to the purpose. But I meditate no injury to these men—none. It would serve me nothing. They may not purpose equally fair by me. I rely on thy harquebuss."

"I shall be prompt at the signal," said Quentin; "but yet——"

"You hesitate," said the King. "Speak out; I give thee full leave. From such as thou art, hints may be caught that are right valuable."

"I would only presume to say," replied Quentin, "that your Majesty having occasion to distrust this Burgundian, I marvel that you suffer him to approach so near your person, and that in privacy."

"Oh content you, sir squire," said the King. "There are some dangers which, when they are braved, disappear, and which yet, when there is an obvious and apparent dread of them displayed, become certain and inevitable. When I walk boldly up to a surly mastiff and caress him, it is ten to one I soothe him to good temper; if I show fear of him, he flies on me and rends me. I will be thus frank with thee. It concerns me nearly that this man returns not to his headlong master in a resentful humour. I run my risk, therefore. I have never shunned to expose my life for the weal of my kingdom. Follow me."

Louis led his young Life Guardsman, for whom he seemed to have taken a special favour, through the side door by which he had himself entered, saying, as he showed it him: "He who would thrive at court must know the private wickets and concealed staircases—ay, and the traps and pitfalls of the palace, as well as the principal entrances, folding-doors, and portals."

After several turns and passages, the King entered a small vaulted room, where a table was prepared for dinner with three covers. The whole furniture and arrangements of the room were plain almost to meanness. A beauffet, or folding and movable cupboard, held a few pieces of gold and silver plate, and was the only article in the chamber which had, in the slightest degree, the appearance of royalty. Behind this cupboard, and completely hidden by it, was the post which Louis assigned to Quentin Durward; and after having ascertained, by going to different parts of the room, that he was invisible from all quarters, he gave him his last charge: "Remember the word, '*Écosse, en avant*'; and so soon as ever I utter these sounds, throw down the screen—spare not for cup or goblet, and be sure thou take good aim at Crèvecœur. If thy piece fail, cling to him, and use thy knife. Oliver and I can deal with the cardinal."

Having thus spoken, he whistled aloud, and summoned into the apartment Oliver, who was premier valet of the chamber as well as barber, and who, in fact, performed all offices immediately connected with the King's person, and who now appeared, attended by two old men, who were the only assistants or waiters at the royal table. So soon as the King had taken his place, the visitors were admitted; and Quentin, though himself unseen, was so situated as to remark all the particulars of the interview.

The King welcomed his visitors with a degree of cordiality which Quentin had the utmost difficulty to reconcile with the directions which he had previously received, and the purpose for which he stood behind the beauffet with his deadly weapon in readiness. Not only did Louis appear totally free from apprehension of any kind, but one would have supposed that those visitors whom he had done the high honour to admit to his table were the very persons in whom he could most unreservedly confide, and whom he was most willing to honour. Nothing could be more dignified, and at the same time more courteous, than his demeanour. While all around him, including even his own dress, was far beneath the splendour which the petty princes of the kingdom displayed in their festivities, his own language and manners were those of a mighty sovereign in his most condescending mood. Quentin was tempted to suppose either that the whole of his previous conversation with Louis had been a dream, or that the dutiful demeanour of the cardinal, and the frank, open, and gallant bearing of the Burgundian noble, had entirely erased the King's suspicion.

But whilst the guests, in obedience to the King, were in the act of placing themselves at the table, his Majesty darted one keen glance on them, and then instantly directed his look to Quentin's post. This was done in an instant; but the glance conveyed so much doubt and hatred towards his guests, such a peremptory injunction on Quentin to be watchful in attendance and prompt in execution, that no room was left for doubting that the sentiments of Louis continued unaltered, and his apprehensions unabated. He was, therefore, more than ever astonished at the deep veil under which that monarch was able to conceal the movements of his jealous disposition.

Appearing to have entirely forgotten the language which Crèvecœur had held towards him in the face of his court, the King conversed with him of old times, of events which had occurred during his own exile in the territories of Burgundy, and inquired respecting all the nobles with whom he had been then familiar, as if that period had indeed been the happiest of his life, and as if he retained towards all who had contributed to soften the term of his exile the kindest and most graceful sentiments.

"To an ambassador of another nation," he said, "I would have thrown something of state into our reception; but to an old friend, who often shared my board at the Castle of Genappes,[1] I wished to show myself, as I love best to live, old Louis of Valois, as simple and plain as any of his Parisian *badauds*. But I directed them to make some better cheer than ordinary for you, sir count, for I know your Burgundian proverb, '*Mieux vault bon repas que bel habit*'; and therefore I bid them have some care of our table. For our wine, you know well it is the subject of an old emulation betwixt France and Burgundy, which we will presently reconcile; for I will

---

[1] During his residence in Burgundy, in his father's lifetime, Genappes was the usual abode of Louis. This period of exile is often alluded to in the novel.

drink to you in Burgundy, and you, sir count, shall pledge me in champagne. Here, Oliver, let me have a cup of *vin d'Auxerre*"; and he hummed gaily a song then well known—

"Auxerre est la boisson des rois."

Here, sir count, I drink to the health of the noble Duke of Burgundy, our kind and loving cousin. Oliver, replenish yon golden cup with *vin de Rheims,* and give it to the count on your knee; he represents our loving brother. My lord cardinal, we will ourself fill your cup."

"You have already, sire, even to overflowing," said the cardinal, with the lowly mien of a favourite towards an indulgent master.

"Because we know that your Eminence can carry it with a steady hand," said Louis. "But which side do you espouse in the great controversy—Sillery or Auxerre—France or Burgundy?"

"I will stand neutral, sire," said the cardinal, "and replenish my cup with Auvernat."

"A neutral has a perilous part to sustain," said the King; but as he observed the cardinal colour somewhat, he glided from the subject, and added: "But you prefer the Auvernat, because it is so noble a wine it endures not water. You, sir count, hesitate to empty your cup. I trust you have found no national bitterness at the bottom."

"I would, sir," said the Count de Crèvecœur, "that all national quarrels could be as pleasantly ended as the rivalry betwixt our vineyards."

"With time, sir count," answered the King—"with time— such time as you have taken to your draught of champagne. And now that it is finished, favour me by putting the goblet in your bosom, and keeping it as a pledge of our regard. It is not to every one that we would part with it. It belonged of yore to that terror of France, Henry V. of England, and was taken when Rouen was reduced, and those islanders expelled from Normandy by the joint arms of France and Burgundy. It cannot be better bestowed than on a noble and valiant Burgundian, who well knows that on the union of these two nations depends the continuance of the freedom of the Continent from the English yoke."

The count made a suitable answer, and Louis gave unrestrained way to the satirical gaiety of disposition which sometimes enlivened the darker shades of his character. Leading, of course, the conversation, his remarks, always shrewd and caustic, and often actually witty, were seldom good-natured, and the anecdotes with which he illustrated them were often more humorous than delicate; but in no one word, syllable, or letter did he betray the state of mind of one who, apprehensive of assassination, hath in his apartment an armed soldier, with his piece loaded, in order to prevent or anticipate an attack on his person.

The Count of Crèvecœur gave frankly into the King's humour; while the smooth churchman laughed at every jest, and enhanced every ludicrous idea, without exhibiting any shame at expressions which made the rustic young Scot blush even in his place of concealment.[1] In about an hour and a half the tables were drawn; and the King, taking courteous leave of his guests, gave the signal that it was his desire to be alone.

So soon as all, even Oliver, had retired, he called Quentin from his place of concealment; but with a voice so faint, that the youth could scarce believe it to be the same which had so lately given animation to the jest and zest to the tale. As he approached, he saw an equal change in his countenance. The light of assumed vivacity had left the King's eyes, the smile had deserted his face, and he exhibited all the fatigue of a celebrated actor, when he has finished the exhausting representation of some favourite character in which, while upon the stage, he had displayed the utmost vivacity.

"Thy watch is not yet over," said he to Quentin. "Refresh thyself for an instant—yonder table affords the means—I will then instruct thee in thy farther duty. Meanwhile, it is ill talking between a full man and a fasting."

He threw himself back on his seat, covered his brow with his hand, and was silent.

[1] See Louis's Humour. Note 23.

CHAPTER XI.

THE HALL OF ROLAND.

> Painters show Cupid blind. Hath Hymen eyes?
> Or is his sight warp'd by those spectacles
> Which parents, guardians, and advisers lend him,
> That he may look through them on lands and mansions,
> On jewels, gold, and all such rich dotations,
> And see their value ten times magnified?
> Methinks 'twill brook a question.
> *The Miseries of Enforced Marriage.*

Louis the XI. of France, though the sovereign in Europe who was fondest and most jealous of power, desired only its substantial enjoyment; and though he knew well enough, and at times exacted strictly, the observances due to his rank, was in general singularly careless of show.

In a prince of sounder moral qualities, the familiarity with which he invited subjects to his board—nay, occasionally sat at theirs—must have been highly popular; and even such as he was, the King's homeliness of manners atoned for many of his vices with that class of his subjects who were not particularly exposed to the consequences of his suspicion and jealousy. The *tiers état*, or commons, of France, who rose to more opulence and consequence under the reign of this sagacious prince, respected his person, though they loved him not; and it was resting on their support that he was enabled to make his party good against the hatred of the nobles, who conceived that he diminished the honour of the French crown, and obscured their own splendid privileges, by that very neglect of form which gratified the citizens and commons.

With patience, which most other princes would have considered as degrading, and not without a sense of amusement, the monarch of France waited till his Life Guardsman had satisfied the keenness of a youthful appetite. It may be supposed, however, that Quentin had too much sense and prudence to put the royal patience to a long or tedious proof; and indeed he was repeatedly desirous to break off his repast ere

Louis would permit him. "I see it in thine eye," he said, good-naturedly, "that thy courage is not half abated. Go on—God and St. Denis!—charge again. I tell thee that meat and mass (crossing himself) never hindered the work of a good Christian man. Take a cup of wine; but mind thou be cautious of the wine-pot; it is the vice of thy countrymen as well as of the English, who, lacking that folly, are the choicest soldiers ever wore armour. And now wash speedily; forget not thy benedicite, and follow me."

Quentin obeyed, and, conducted by a different, but as maze-like an approach as he had formerly passed, he followed Louis into the Hall of Roland.

"Take notice," said the King, imperatively, "thou hast never left this post—let that be thine answer to thy kinsman and comrades; and, hark thee, to bind the recollection on thy memory, I give thee this gold chain (flinging on his arm one of considerable value). If I go not brave myself, those whom I trust have ever the means to ruffle it with the best. But, when such chains as these bind not the tongue from wagging too freely, my gossip, L'Hermite, hath an amulet for the throat, which never fails to work a certain cure. And now attend. No man, save Oliver or I myself, enters here this evening; but ladies will come hither, perhaps from the one extremity of the hall, perhaps from the other, perhaps one from each. You may answer if they address you, but, being on duty, your answer must be brief; and you must neither address them in your turn nor engage in any prolonged discourse. But hearken to what they say. Thine ears, as well as thy hands, are mine: I have bought thee, body and soul. Therefore, if thou hearest aught of their conversation, thou must retain it in memory until it is communicated to me, and then forget it. And, now I think better on it, it will be best that thou pass for a Scottish recruit, who hath come straight down from his mountains, and hath not yet acquired our most Christian language. Right. So, if they speak to thee, thou wilt *not* answer; this will free you from embarrassment, and lead them to converse without regard to your presence. You understand me. Farewell. Be wary, and thou hast a friend."

The King had scarce spoken these words ere he disappeared behind the arras, leaving Quentin to meditate on what he had seen and heard. The youth was in one of those situations from which it is pleasanter to look forward than to look back; for the reflection that he had been planted like a marksman in a thicket who watches for a stag, to take the life of the noble Count of Crèvecœur, had in it nothing ennobling. It was very true, that the King's measures seemed on this occasion merely cautionary and defensive; but how did the youth know but he might be soon commanded on some offensive operation of the same kind? This would be an unpleasant crisis, since it was plain, from the character of his master, that there would be destruction in refusing, while his honour told him there would be disgrace in complying. He turned his thoughts from this subject of reflection, with the sage consolation so often adopted by youth when prospective dangers intrude themselves on their mind, that it was time enough to think what was to be done when the emergence actually arrived, and that sufficient for the day was the evil thereof.

Quentin made use of this sedative reflection the more easily, that the last commands of the King had given him something more agreeable to think of than his own condition. The lady of the lute was certainly one of those to whom his attention was to be dedicated; and well in his mind did he promise to obey one part of the King's mandate, and listen with diligence to every word that might drop from her lips, that he might know if the magic of her conversation equalled that of her music. But with as much sincerity did he swear to himself, that no part of her discourse should be reported by him to the King which might affect the fair speaker otherwise than favourably.

Meantime, there was no fear of his again slumbering on his post. Each passing breath of wind which, finding its way through the open lattice, waved the old arras, sounded like the approach of the fair object of his expectation. He felt, in short, all that mysterious anxiety and eagerness of expectation which is always the companion of love, and sometimes hath a considerable share in creating it.

At length, a door actually creaked and jingled, for the doors even of palaces did not in the 15th century turn on their hinges so noiseless as ours; but, alas! it was not at that end of the hall from which the lute had been heard. It opened, however, and a female figure entered, followed by two others, whom she directed by a sign to remain without, while she herself came forward into the hall. By her imperfect and unequal gait, which showed to peculiar disadvantage as she traversed this long gallery, Quentin at one recognised the Princess Joan, and, with the respect which became his situation, drew himself up in a fitting attitude of silent vigilance, and lowered his weapon to her as she passed. She acknowledged the courtesy by a gracious inclination of her head, and he had an opportunity of seeing her countenance more distinctly than he had in the morning.

There was little in the features of this ill-fated princess to atone for the misfortune of her shape and gait. Her face was, indeed, by no means disagreeable in itself, though destitute of beauty; and there was a meek expression of suffering patience in her large blue eyes, which were commonly fixed upon the ground. But, besides that she was extremely pallid in complexion, her skin had the yellowish, discoloured tinge which accompanies habitual bad health; and though her teeth were white and regular, her lips were thin and pale. The Princess had a profusion of flaxen hair, but it was so light-coloured as to be almost of a bluish tinge; and her tirewoman, who doubtless considered the luxuriance of her mistress's tresses as a beauty, had not greatly improved matters by arranging them in curls around her pale countenance, to which they added an expression almost corpse-like and unearthly. To make matters still worse, she had chosen a vest or cymar of a pale green silk, which gave her, on the whole, a ghastly and even spectral appearance.

While Quentin followed this singular apparition with eyes in which curiosity was blended with compassion, for every look and motion of the Princess seemed to call for the latter feeling, two ladies entered from the upper end of the apartment.

One of these was the young person who, upon Louis's summons, had served him with fruit, while Quentin made his memorable breakfast at the Fleur-de-Lys. Invested now with all the mysterious dignity belonging to the nymph of the veil and lute, and proved, besides, at least in Quentin's estimation, to be the high-born heiress of a rich earldom, her beauty made ten times the impression upon him which it had done when he beheld in her one whom he deemed the daughter of a paltry innkeeper, in attendance upon a rich and humorous old burgher. He now wondered what fascination could ever have concealed from him her real character. Yet her dress was nearly as simple as before, being a suit of deep mourning, without any ornaments. Her headdress was but a veil of crape, which was entirely thrown back, so as to leave her face uncovered; and it was only Quentin's knowledge of her actual rank which gave in his estimation new elegance to her beautiful shape, a dignity to her step which had before remained unnoticed, and to her regular features, brilliant complexion, and dazzling eyes an air of conscious nobleness that enhanced their beauty.

Had death been the penalty, Durward must needs have rendered to this beauty and her companion the same homage which he had just paid to the royalty of the Princess. They received it as those who were accustomed to the deference of inferiors, and returned it with courtesy; but he thought—perhaps it was but a youthful vision—that the young lady coloured slightly, kept her eyes on the ground, and seemed embarrassed, though in a trifling degree, as she returned his military salutation. This must have been owing to her recollection of the audacious stranger in the neighbouring turret at the Fleur-de-Lys; but did that discomposure express displeasure? This question he had no means to determine.

The companion of the youthful countess, dressed like herself simply, and in deep mourning, was at the age when women are apt to cling most closely to that reputation for beauty which has for years been diminishing. She had still remains enough to show what the power of her charms must once have been, and, remembering past triumphs, it was evident from her manner that she had not relinquished the pretensions to future conquests. She was tall and graceful, though somewhat haughty in her deportment, and returned the salute of Quentin with a smile of gracious condescension, whispering, the next instant, something into her companion's ear, who turned towards the soldier, as if to comply with some hint from the elder lady, but answered, nevertheless, without raising her eyes. Quentin could not help suspecting that the observation called on the young lady to notice his own good mien; and he was (I do not know why) pleased with the idea that the party referred to did not choose to look at him in order to verify with their own eyes the truth of the observation. Probably he thought there was already a sort of mysterious connexion beginning to exist between them, which gave importance to the slightest trifle.

This reflection was momentary, for he was instantly wrapped up in attention to the meeting of the Princess Joan with these stranger ladies. She had stood still upon their entrance, in order to receive them, conscious, perhaps, that motion did not become her well; and as she was somewhat embarrassed in receiving and repaying their compliments, the elder stranger, ignorant of the rank of the party whom she addressed, was led to pay her salutation in a manner rather as if she conferred than received an honour through the interview.

"I rejoice, madam," she said, with a smile, which was meant to express condescension at once and encouragement, "that we are at length permitted the society of such a respectable person of our own sex as you appear to be. I must say that my niece and I have had but little for which to thank the hospitality of King Louis. Nay, niece, never pluck my sleeve. I am sure I read in the looks of this young lady sympathy for our situation. Since we came hither, fair madam, we have been used little better than mere prisoners; and after a thousand invitations to throw our cause and our persons under the protection of France, the Most Christian King has afforded us at first but a base inn for our residence, and now a corner of this moth-eaten palace, out of which we are only permitted to creep towards sunset, as if we were bats or owls, whose appearance in the sunshine is to be held matter of ill omen."

"I am sorry," said the Princess, faltering with the awkward embarrassment of the interview, "that we have been unable, hitherto, to receive you according to your deserts. Your niece, I trust, is better satisfied?"

"Much—much better than I can express," answered the youthful countess. "I sought but safety, and I have found solitude and secrecy besides. The seclusion of our former residence, and the still greater solitude of that now assigned to us, augment, in my eye, the favour which the King vouchsafed to us unfortunate fugitives."

"Silence, my silly cousin," said the elder lady, "and let us speak according to our conscience, since at last we are alone with one of our own sex—I say alone, for that handsome young soldier is a mere statue, since he seems not to have the use of his limbs, and I am given to understand he wants that of his tongue, at least in civilised language—I say, since no one but this lady can understand us, I must own there is nothing I have regretted equal to taking this French journey. I looked for a splendid reception, tournaments, carousals, pageants, and festivals; and instead of which, all has been seclusion and obscurity! and the best society whom the King introduced to us was a Bohemian vagabond, by whose agency he directed us to correspond with our friends in Flanders. Perhaps," said the lady, "it is his politic intention to mew us up here until our lives' end, that he may seize on our estates, after the extinction of the ancient house of Croye. The Duke of Burgundy was not so cruel: he offered my niece a husband, though he was a bad one."

"I should have thought the veil preferable to an evil husband," said the Princess, with difficulty finding opportunity to interpose a word.

"One would at least wish to have the choice, madam," replied the voluble dame. "It is, Heaven knows, on account of my niece that I speak; for myself, I have long laid aside thoughts of changing my condition. I see you smile, but, by my halidome, it is true; yet that is no excuse for the King, whose conduct, like his person, hath more resemblance to that of old Michaud, the money-changer of Ghent, than to the successor of Charlemagne."

"Hold!" said the Princess, with some asperity in her tone; "remember you speak of my father."

"Of your father!" replied the Burgundian lady in surprise.

"Of my father," repeated the Princess, with dignity. "I am Joan of France. But fear not, madam," she continued, in the gentle accent which was natural to her, "you designed no offence, and I have taken none. Command my influence to render your exile and that of this interesting young person more supportable. Alas! it is but little I have in my power; but it is willingly offered."

Deep and submissive was the reverence with which the Countess Hameline de Croye, so was the elder lady called, received the obliging offer of the Princess's protection. She had been long the inhabitant of courts, was mistress of the manners which are there acquired, and held firmly the established rule of courtiers of all ages, who, although their usual private conversation turns upon the vices and follies of their patrons, and on the injuries and neglect which they themselves have sustained, never suffer such hints to drop from them in the presence of the sovereign or those of his family. The lady was, therefore, scandalised to the last degree at the mistake which had induced her to speak so indecorously in presence of the daughter of Louis. She would have exhausted herself in expressing regret and making apologies had she not been put to silence and restored to equanimity by the Princess, who requested in the most gentle manner, yet which, from a daughter of France, had the weight of a command, that no more might be said in the way either of excuse or of explanation.

The Princess Joan then took her own chair with a dignity which became her, and compelled the two strangers to sit, one on either hand, to which the younger consented with unfeigned and respectful diffidence, and the elder with an affectation of deep humility and deference, which was intended for such. They spoke together, but in such a low tone that the sentinel could not overhear their discourse, and only remarked, that the Princess seemed to bestow much of her regard on the younger and more interesting lady; and that the Countess Hameline, though speaking a great deal more, attracted less of the Princess's attention by her full flow of conversation and compliment than did her kinswoman by her brief and modest replies to what was addressed to her.

The conversation of the ladies had now lasted a quarter of an hour, when the door at the lower end of the hall opened, and a man entered shrouded in a riding-cloak. Mindful of the King's injunction, and determined not to be a second time caught slumbering, Quentin instantly moved towards the intruder, and, interposing between him and the ladies, requested him to retire instantly.

"By whose command?" said the stranger, in a tone of contemptuous surprise.

"By that of the King," said Quentin, firmly, "which I am placed here to enforce."

"Not against Louis of Orleans," said the duke, dropping his cloak.

The young man hesitated a moment; but how enforce his orders against the first prince of the blood, about to be allied, as the report now generally went, with the King's own family.

"You Highness," he said, "is too great that your pleasure should be withstood by me. I trust your Highness will bear me witness that I have done the duty of my post, so far as your will permitted."

"Go to—you shall have no blame, young soldier," said Orleans; and passing forward, paid his compliments to the Princess with that air of constraint which always marked his courtesy when addressing her.

"He had been dining," he said, "with Dunois, and understanding there was society in Roland's Gallery, he had ventured on the freedom of adding one to the number."

The colour which mounted into the pale cheek of the unfortunate Joan, and which for the moment spread something of beauty over her features, evinced that this addition to the company was anything but indifferent to her. She hastened to present the Prince to the two Ladies of Croye, who received him with the respect due to his eminent rank; and the Princess, pointing to a chair, requested him to join their conversation party.

The duke declined the freedom of assuming a seat in such society; but taking a cushion from one of the settles, he laid it at the feet of the beautiful young Countess of Croye, and so seated himself that, without appearing to neglect the Princess, he was enabled to bestow the greater share of his attention on her lovely neighbour.

At first, it seemed as if this arrangement rather pleased than offended his destined bride. She encouraged the duke in his gallantries towards the fair stranger, and seemed to regard them as complimentary to herself. But the Duke of Orleans, though accustomed to subject his mind to the stern yoke of his uncle when in the King's presence, had enough of princely nature to induce him to follow his own inclinations whenever that restraint was withdrawn; and his high rank giving him a right to overstep the ordinary ceremonies and advance at once to familiarity, his praises of the Countess Isabelle's beauty became so energetic, and flowed with such unrestrained freedom, owing perhaps to his having drunk a little more wine than usual, for Dunois was no enemy to the worship of Bacchus, that at length he seemed almost impassioned, and the presence of the Princess appeared wellnigh forgotten.

The tone of compliment which he indulged was grateful only to one individual in the circle; for the Countess Hameline already anticipated the dignity of an alliance with the first prince of the blood, by means of her whose birth, beauty, and large possessions rendered such an ambitious consummation by no means impossible, even in the eyes of a less sanguine projector, could the views of Louis XI. have been left out of the calculation of chances. The younger countess listened to the count's gallantries with anxiety and embarrassment, and ever and anon turned an entreating look towards the Princess, as if requesting her to come to her relief. But the wounded feelings and the timidity of Joan of France rendered her incapable of an effort to make the conversation more general; and at length, excepting a few interjectional civilities of the Lady Hameline, it was maintained almost exclusively by the Duke himself, though at the expense of the younger Countess of Croye, whose beauty formed the theme of the high-flown eloquence.

Nor must I forget there was a third person, the unregarded sentinel, who saw his fair visions melt away like wax before the sun, as the Duke persevered in the warm tenor of his passionate discourse. At length the Countess Isabelle de Croye made a determined effort to cut short what was becoming intolerably disagreeable to her, especially from the pain to which the conduct of the duke was apparently subjecting the Princess.

Addressing the latter, she said, modestly, but with some firmness, that the first boon she had to claim from her promised protection was: "That her Highness would undertake to convince the Duke of Orleans that the ladies of Burgundy, though inferior in wit and manners to those of France, were not such absolute fools as to be pleased with no other conversation than that of extravagant compliment."

"I grieve, lady," said the duke, preventing the Princess's answer, "that you will satirise, in the same sentence, the beauty of the dames of Burgundy and the sincerity of the knights of France. If we are hasty and extravagant in the expression of our admiration, it is because we love as we fight, without letting cold deliberation come into our bosoms, and surrender to the fair with the same rapidity with which we defeat the valiant."

"The beauty of our countrywomen," said the young countess, with more of reproof than she had yet ventured to use towards the high-born suitor, "is as unfit to claim such triumphs as the valour of the men of Burgundy is incapable of yielding them."

"I respect your patriotism, countess," said the duke; "and the last branch of your theme shall not be impugned by me till a Burgundian knight shall offer to sustain it with lance in rest. But for the injustice which you have done to the charms which your land produces, I appeal from yourself to yourself.

Look there," he said, pointing to a large mirror, the gift of the Venetian republic, and then of the highest rarity and value, "and tell me, as you look, what is the heart that can resist the charms there represented?"

The Princess, unable to sustain any longer the neglect of her lover, here sunk backwards on her chair with a sigh, which at once recalled the duke from the land of romance, and induced the Lady Hameline to ask whether her Highness found herself ill.

"A sudden pain shot through my forehead," said the Princess, attempting to smile; "but I shall be presently better."

Her increasing paleness contradicted her words, and induced the Lady Hameline to call for assistance, as the Princess was about to faint.

The duke, biting his lip and cursing the folly which could not keep guard over his tongue, ran to summon the Princess's attendants, who were in the next chamber; and when they came hastily with the usual remedies, he could not but, as a cavalier and gentleman, give his assistance to support and to recover her. His voice, rendered almost tender by pity and self-reproach, was the most powerful means of recalling her to herself, and just as the swoon was passing away the King himself entered the apartment.

CHAPTER XII.

THE POLITICIAN.

This is a lecturer so skill'd in policy,
That (no disparagement to Satan's cunning)
He well might read a lesson to the devil,
And teach the old seducer new temptations.
Old Play.

As Louis entered the gallery, he bent his brows in the manner we have formerly described as peculiar to him, and sent, from under his gathered and gloomy eyebrows, a keen look on all around; in darting which, as Quentin afterwards declared, his eyes seemed to turn so small, so fierce, and so piercing, as to resemble those of an aroused adder looking through the bush of heath in which he lies coiled.

When, by this momentary and sharpened glance, the King had reconnoitred the cause of the bustle which was in the apartment, his first address was to the Duke of Orleans.

"You here, my fair cousin?" he said; and turning to Quentin, added sternly, "Had you not charge?"

"Forgive the young man sire," said the duke; "he did not neglect his duty; but I was informed that the Princess was in this gallery."

"And I warrant you would not be withstood when you came hither to pay your court," said the King, whose detestable hypocrisy persisted in representing the duke as participating in a passion which was felt only on the side of his unhappy daughter; "and it is thus you debauch the sentinels of my Guard, young man? But what cannot be pardoned to a gallant who only lives *par amours!*"

The Duke of Orleans raised his head, as if about to reply in some manner which might correct the opinion conveyed in the King's observation; but the instinctive reverence, not to say fear, of Louis, in which he had been bred from childhood, chained up his voice.

"And Joan hath been ill?" said the King. "But do not be grieved, Louis, it will soon pass away; lend her your arm to her apartment, while I will conduct these strange ladies to theirs."

The order was given in a tone which amounted to a command, and Orleans accordingly made his exit with the Princess to one extremity of the gallery, while the King, ungloving his right hand, courteously handed the Countess Isabelle and her kinswoman to their apartment, which opened from the other. He bowed profoundly as they entered, and remained standing on the threshold for a minute after they had disappeared; then, with great composure, shut the door by which they had retired, and turning the huge key, took it from the lock and put it into his girdle—an appendage which gave him still more perfectly the air of some old miser, who cannot journey in comfort unless he bear with him the key of his treasure closet.

With slow and pensive step, and eyes fixed on the ground, Louis now paced towards Quentin Durward, who, expecting his share of the royal displeasure, viewed his approach with no little anxiety.

"Thou hast done wrong," said the King, raising his eyes, and fixing them firmly on him when he had come within a yard of him—"thou hast done foul wrong, and deservest to die. Speak not a word in defence! What hadst thou to do with dukes or princesses? what with *any* thing but my order?"

"So please your Majesty," said the young soldier, "what could I do?"

"What couldst thou do when thy post was forcibly passed?" answered the King, scornfully. "What is the use of that weapon on thy shoulder? Thou shouldst have levelled thy piece, and if the presumptuous rebel did not retire on the instant, he should have died within this very hall! Go—pass into these farther apartments. In the first thou wilt find a large staircase, which leads to the inner bailey; there thou wilt find Oliver Dain. Send him to me; do thou begone to thy quarters. As thou dost value thy life, be not so loose of thy tongue as thou hast been this day slack of thy hand."

Well pleased to escape so easily, yet with a soul which revolted at the cold-blooded cruelty which the King seemed to require from him in the execution of his duty, Durward took the road indicated, hastened downstairs, and communicated the royal pleasure to Oliver, who was waiting in the court beneath. The wily tonsor bowed, sighed, and smiled, as, with a voice even softer than ordinary, he wished the youth a good evening; and they parted, Quentin to his quarters, and Oliver to attend the King.

In this place, the Memoirs which we have chiefly followed in compiling this true history were unhappily defective; for, founded chiefly on information supplied by Quentin, they do not convey the purport of the dialogue which, in his absence, took place between the King and his secret counsellor. Fortunately, the library of Hautlieu contains a manuscript copy of the *Chronique Scandaleuse* of Jean de Troyes, much more full than that which has been printed; to which are added several curious memoranda, which we incline to think must have been written down by Oliver himself after the death of his master, and before he had the happiness to be rewarded with the halter which he had so long merited. From this we have been able to extract a very full account of the obscure favourite's conversation with Louis upon the present occasion, which throws a light upon the policy of that prince which we might otherwise have sought for in vain.

When the favourite attendant entered the Gallery of Roland, he found the King pensively seated upon a chair which his daughter had left some minutes before. Well acquainted with his temper, he glided on with his noiseless step until he had just crossed the line of the King's sight, so as to make him aware of his presence, then shrank modestly backward and out of sight, until he should be summoned to speak or to listen. The monarch's first address was an unpleasant one: "So, Oliver, your fine schemes are melting like snow before the south wind! I pray to our Lady of Embrun that they resemble not the ice-heaps of which the Switzer churls tell such stories, and come rushing down upon our heads."

"I have heard with concern that all is not well, sire," answered Oliver.

"Not well!" exclaimed the King, rising and hastily marching up and down the gallery. "All is ill, man, and as ill nearly as possible; so much for thy fond romantic advice that I, of all men, should become a protector of distressed damsels! I tell thee Burgundy is arming, and on the eve of closing an alliance with England. And Edward, who hath his hands idle at home, will pour his thousands upon us through that unhappy gate of Calais. Singly, I might cajole or defy them; but united—united, and with the discontent and treachery of that villain St. Paul! All thy fault, Oliver, who counselled me to receive the women, and to use the services of the damned Bohemian to carry messages to their vassals."

"My liege," said Oliver, "you know my reasons. The

countess's domains lie between the frontiers of Burgundy and Flanders, her castle is almost impregnable, her rights over neighbouring estates are such as, if well supported, cannot but give much annoyance to Burgundy, were the lady but wedded to one who should be friendly to France."

"It is—it *is* a tempting bait," said the King; "and could we have concealed her being here, we might have arranged such a marriage for this rich heiress as would have highly profited France. But that cursed Bohemian, how couldst thou recommend such a heathen hound for a commission which required trust?"

"Please you," said Oliver, "to remember it was your Majesty's self who trusted him too far—much farther than I recommended. He would have borne a letter trustily enough to the countess's kinsman, telling him to hold out her castle, and promising speedy relief; but your Highness must needs put his prophetic powers to the test; and thus he became possessed of secrets which were worth betraying to Duke Charles."

"I am ashamed—I am ashamed," said Louis. "And yet, Oliver, they say that these heathen people are descended from the sage Chaldeans, who did read the mysteries of the stars in the plains of Shinar."

Well aware that his master, with all his acuteness and sagacity, was but the more prone to be deceived by soothsayers, astrologers, diviners, and all that race of pretenders to occult science, and that he even conceived himself to have some skill in these arts, Oliver dared to press this point no farther; and only observed that the Bohemian had been a bad prophet on his own account, else he would have avoided returning to Tours, and saved himself from the gallows he had merited.

"It often happens that those who are gifted with prophetic knowledge," answered Louis, with much gravity, "have not the power of foreseeing those events in which they themselves are personally interested."

"Under your Majesty's favour," replied the confidant, "that seems as if a man could not see his own hand by means of the candle which he holds, and which shows him every other object in the apartment."

"He cannot see his own features by the light which shows the faces of others," replied Louis; "and that is the more faithful illustration of the case. But this is foreign to my purpose at present. The Bohemian hath had his reward, and peace be with him. But these ladies—not only does Burgundy threaten us with war for harbouring them, but their presence is like to interfere with my projects in my own family. My simple cousin of Orleans hath barely seen this damsel, and I venture to prophesy that the sight of her is like to make him less pliable in the matter of his alliance with Joan."

"Your Majesty," answered the counsellor, "may send the Ladies of Croye back to Burgundy, and so make your peace with the Duke. Many might murmur at this as dishonourable; but if necessity demands the sacrifice——"

"If profit demanded the sacrifice, Oliver, the sacrifice should be made without hesitation," answered the King. "I am an old experienced salmon, and use not to gulp the angler's hook because it is busked up with a feather called honour. But what is worse than a lack of honour, there were, in returning those ladies to Burgundy, a forfeiture of those views of advantage which moved us to give them an asylum. It were heartbreaking to renounce the opportunity of planting a friend to ourselves and an enemy to Burgundy in the very centre of his dominions, and so near to the discontented cities of Flanders. Oliver, I cannot relinquish the advantages which our scheme of marrying the maiden to a friend of our own house seems to hold out to us."

"Your Majesty," said Oliver, after a moment's thought, "might confer her hand on some right trusty friend, who would take all blame on himself, and serve your Majesty secretly, while in public you might disown him."

"And where am I to find such a friend?" said Louis. "Were I to bestow her upon any one of our mutinous and ill-ruled nobles, would it not be rendering him independent? and hath it not been my policy for years to prevent them from becoming so? Dunois indeed—him, and him only, I might perchance trust. He would fight for the crown of

France, whatever were his condition. But honours and wealth change men's natures. Even Dunois I will not trust."

"Your Majesty may find others," said Oliver, in his smoothest manner, and in a tone more insinuating than that which he usually employed in conversing with the King, who permitted him considerable freedom: "men dependent entirely on your own grace and favour, and who could no more exist without your countenance than without sun or air, men rather of head than of action, men who——"

"Men who resemble thyself, ha!" said King Louis. "No, Oliver, by my faith that arrow was too rashly shot! What! because I indulge thee with my confidence, and let thee, in reward, poll my lieges a little now and then, dost thou think it makes thee fit to be the husband of that beautiful vision, and a count of the highest class to the boot?—thee, thee, I say, low-born and lower-bred, whose wisdom is at best a sort of cunning, and whose courage is more than doubtful?"

"Your Majesty imputes to me a presumption of which I am not guilty, in supposing me to aspire so highly," said Oliver.

"I am glad to hear it, man," replied the King; "and truly, I hold your judgment the healthier that you disown such a reverie. But methinks thy speech sounded strangely in that key. Well, to return. I dare not wed this beauty to one of my subjects; I dare not return her to Burgundy; I dare not transmit her to England or to Germany, where she is likely to become the prize of some one more apt to unite with Burgundy than with France, and who would be more ready to discourage the honest malcontents in Ghent and Liege than to yield them that wholesome countenance which might always find Charles the Hardy enough to exercise his valour on, without stirring from his own domains—and they were in so ripe a humour for insurrection, the men of Liege in especial, that they alone, well heated and supported, would find my fair cousin work for more than a twelvemonth; and backed by a warlike Count of Croye—— Oh, Oliver! the plan is too hopeful to be resigned without a struggle. Cannot thy fertile brain devise some scheme?"

Oliver paused for a long time; then at last replied, "What

if a bridal could be accomplished betwixt Isabelle of Croye and young Adolphus, the Duke of Gueldres?"

"What!" said the King, in astonishment; "sacrifice her, and she, too, so lovely a creature, to the furious wretch who deposed, imprisoned, and has often threatened to murder, his own father! No, Oliver—no, that were too unutterably cruel even for you and me, who look so steadfastly to our excellent end, the peace and welfare of France, and respect so little the means by which it is attained. Besides, he lies distant from us, and is detested by the people of Ghent and Liege. No—no, I will none of Adolphus of Gueldres; think on some one else."

"My invention is exhausted, sire," said the counsellor; "I can remember no one who, as husband to the Countess of Croye, would be likely to answer your Majesty's views. He must unite such various qualities—a friend to your Majesty, an enemy to Burgundy, of policy enough to conciliate the Gauntois and Liegeois, and of valour sufficient to defend his little dominions against the power of Duke Charles; of noble birth besides—that your Highness insists upon; and of excellent and most virtuous character, to the boot of all."

"Nay, Oliver," said the King, "I leaned not so much—that is, so *very* much, on character; but methinks Isabelle's bridegroom should be something less publicly and generally abhorred than Adolphus of Gueldres. For example, since I myself must suggest some one, why not William de la Marck?"

"On my halidome, sire," said Oliver, "I cannot complain of your demanding too high a standard of moral excellence in the happy man, if the Wild Boar of Ardennes can serve your turn. De la Marck! why, he is the most notorious robber and murderer on all the frontiers, excommunicated by the Pope for a thousand crimes."

"We will have him released from the sentence, friend Oliver; holy church is merciful."

"Almost an outlaw," continued Oliver, "and under the ban of the Empire, by an ordinance of the Chamber at Ratisbon."

"We will have the ban taken off, friend Oliver," continued
G—Vol. 16

the King in the same tone; "the Imperial Chamber will hear reason."

"And admitting him to be of noble birth," said Oliver, "he hath the manners, the face, and the outward form, as well as the heart, of a Flemish butcher. She will never accept of him."

"His mode of wooing, if I mistake not," said Louis, "will render it difficult for her to make a choice."

"I was far wrong, indeed, when I taxed your Majesty with being over scrupulous," said the counsellor. "On my life, the crimes of Adolphus are but virtues to those of De la Marck! And then how is he to meet with his bride? Your Majesty knows he dare not stir far from his own Forest of Ardennes."

"That must be cared for," said the King; "and, in the first place, the two ladies must be acquainted privately that they can be no longer maintained at this court, except at the expense of a war between France and Burgundy, and that, unwilling to deliver them up to my fair cousin of Burgundy, I am desirous they should secretly depart from my dominions."

"They will demand to be conveyed to England," said Oliver; "and we shall have her return to Flanders with an island lord, having a round fair face, long brown hair, and three thousand archers at his back."

"No—no," replied the King; "we dare not—you understand me—so far offend our fair cousin of Burgundy as to let her pass to England. It would bring his displeasure as certainly as our maintaining her here. No—no, to the safety of the church alone we will venture to commit her; and the utmost we can do is to connive at the Ladies Hameline and Isabelle de Croye departing in disguise, and with a small retinue, to take refuge with the Bishop of Liege, who will place the fair Isabelle for the time under the safeguard of a convent."

"And if that convent protect her from William de la Marck, when he knows of your Majesty's favourable intentions, I have mistaken the man."

"Why, yes," answered the King, "thanks to our secret supplies of money, De la Marck hath together a handsome handful of as unscrupulous soldiery as ever were outlawed, with which he contrives to maintain himself among the woods, in such a condition as makes him formidable both to the Duke of Burgundy and the Bishop of Liege. He lacks nothing but some territory which he may call his own; and this being so fair an opportunity to establish himself by marriage, I think that, *Pasques-dieu!* he will find means to win and wed, without more than a hint on our part. The Duke of Burgundy will then have such a thorn in his side as no lancet of our time will easily cut out from his flesh. The Boar of Ardennes, whom he has already outlawed, strengthened by the possession of that fair lady's lands, castles, and seigniory, with the discontented Liegeois to boot, who, by my faith, will not be in that case unwilling to choose him for their captain and leader—let Charles then think of wars with France when he will, or rather let him bless his stars if she war not with him. How dost thou like the scheme, Oliver, ha?"

"Rarely," said Oliver, "save and except the doom which confers that lady on the Wild Boar of Ardennes. By my halidome, saving in a little outward show of gallantry, Tristan, the provost-marshal, were the more proper bridegroom of the two."

"Anon thou didst propose Master Oliver, the barber," said Louis; "but friend Oliver and gossip Tristan, though excellent men in the way of counsel and execution, are not the stuff that men make counts of. Know you not that the burghers of Flanders value birth in other men, precisely because they have it not themselves? A plebeian mob ever desire an aristocratic leader. Yonder Ked, or Cade, or—how called they him?—in England, was fain to lure his rascal rout after him by pretending to the blood of the Mortimers. William de la Marck comes of the blood of the princes of Sedan, as noble as mine own. And now to business. I must determine the Ladies of Croye to a speedy and secret flight, under sure guidance. This will be easily done: we have but to hint the alternative of surrendering them to Burgundy.

Thou must find means to let William de la Marck know of their motions, and let him choose his own time and place to push his suit. I know a fit person to travel with them."

"May I ask to whom your Majesty commits such an important charge?" asked the tonsor.

"To a foreigner, be sure," replied the King, "one who has neither kin nor interest in France, to interfere with the execution of my pleasure; and who knows too little of the country and its factions to suspect more of my purpose than I choose to tell him—in a word, I design to employ the young Scot who sent you hither but now."

Oliver paused in a manner which seemed to imply a doubt of the prudence of the choice, and then added: "Your Majesty has reposed confidence in that stranger boy earlier than is your wont."

"I have my reasons," answered the King. "Thou knowest (and he crossed himself) my devotion for the blessed St. Julian. I had been saying my orisons to that holy saint late in the night before last, wherein, as he is known to be the guardian of travellers, I made it my humble petition that he would augment my household with such wandering foreigners as might best establish throughout our kingdom unlimited devotion to our will; and I vowed to the good saint in guerdon that I would, in his name, receive, and relieve, and maintain them."

"And did St. Julian," said Oliver, "send your Majesty this long-legged importation from Scotland in answer to your prayers?"

Although the barber, who well knew that his master had superstition in a large proportion to his want of religion, and that on such topics nothing was more easy than to offend him —although, I say, he knew the royal weakness, and therefore carefully put the preceding question in the softest and most simple tone of voice, Louis felt the innuendo which it contained, and regarded the speaker with high displeasure.

"Sirrah," he said, "thou art well called Oliver the Devil, who darest thus to sport at once with thy master and with the blessed saints. I tell thee, wert thou one grain less necessary to me, I would have thee hung up on yonder oak before the castle, as an example to all who scoff at things holy! Know, thou infidel slave, that mine eyes were no sooner closed than the blessed St. Julian was visible to me, leading a young man, whom he presented to me, saying, that his fortune should be to escape the sword, the cord, the river, and to bring good fortune to the side which he should espouse, and to the adventures in which he should be engaged. I walked out on the succeeding morning, and I met this youth, whose image I had seen in my dream. In his own country he hath escaped the sword, amid the massacre of his whole family, and here, within the brief compass of two days, he hath been strangely rescued from drowning and from the gallows, and hath already, on a particular occasion, as I but lately hinted to thee, been of the most material service to me. I receive him as sent hither by St. Julian, to serve me in the most difficult, the most dangerous, and even the most desperate services."

The King, as he thus expressed himself, doffed his hat, and selecting from the numerous little leaden figures with which the hat-band was garnished that which represented St. Julian, he placed it on the table, as was often his wont when some peculiar feeling of hope, or perhaps of remorse, happened to thrill across his mind, and, kneeling down before it, muttered, with an appearance of profound devotion, "*Sancte Juliane, adsis precibus nostris! Ora—ora pro nobis!*"

This was one of those ague fits of superstitious devotion which often seized on Louis in such extraordinary times and places that they gave one of the most sagacious monarchs who ever reigned the appearance of a madman, or at least of one whose mind was shaken by some deep consciousness of guilt.

While he was thus employed, his favourite looked at him with an expression of sarcastic contempt, which he scarce attempted to disguise. Indeed, it was one of this man's peculiarities that, in his whole intercourse with his master, he laid aside that fondling, purring affectation of officiousness and humility which distinguished his conduct to others; and if he still bore some resemblance to a cat, it was when the animal is on its guard—watchful, animated, and alert for sudden exertion. The cause of this change was probably Oliver's consciousness that his master was himself too profound a hypocrite not to see through the hypocrisy of others.

"The features of this youth, then, if I may presume to speak," said Oliver, "resemble those of him whom your dream exhibited?"

"Closely and intimately," said the King, whose imagination, like that of superstitious people in general, readily imposed upon itself. "I have had his horoscope cast, besides, by Galeotti Martivalle, and I have plainly learned, through his art and mine own observation, that, in many respects, this unfriended youth has his destiny under the same constellation with mine."

Whatever Oliver might think of the causes thus boldly assigned for the preference of an inexperienced stripling, he dared make no farther objections, well knowing that Louis, who, while residing in exile, had bestowed much of his attention on the supposed science of judicial astrology, would listen to no raillery of any kind which impeached his skill. He therefore only replied, that "He trusted the youth would prove faithful in the discharge of a task so delicate."

"We will take care he hath no opportunity to be otherwise," said Louis; "for he shall be privy to nothing save that he is sent to escort the Ladies of Croye to the residence of the Bishop of Liege. Of the probable interference of William de la Marck he shall know as little as they themselves. None shall know that secret but the guide; and Tristan or thou must find one fit for our purpose."

"But in that case," said Oliver, "judging of him from his country and his appearance, the young man is like to stand to his arms so soon as the Wild Boar comes on them, and may not come off so easily from the tusks as he did this morning."

"If they rend his heart-strings," said Louis, composedly, "St. Julian, blessed be his name! can send me another in his stead. It skills as little that the messenger is slain after his duty is executed as that the flask is broken when the wine is drunk out. Meanwhile, we must expedite the ladies' departure, and then persuade the Count de Crèvecœur that it has taken place without our connivance, we having been desirous to restore them to the custody of our fair cousin, which their sudden departure has unhappily prevented."

"The count is perhaps too wise, and his master too prejudiced, to believe it."

"Holy Mother!" said Louis, "what unbelief would that be in Christian men! But, Oliver, they *shall* believe us. We will throw into our whole conduct towards our fair cousin, Duke Charles, such thorough and unlimited confidence that, not to believe we have been sincere with him in every respect, he must be worse than an infidel. I tell thee, so convinced am I that I could make Charles of Burgundy think of me in every respect as I would have him, that, were it necessary for silencing his doubts, I would ride unarmed, and on a palfrey, to visit him in his tent, with no better guard about me than thine own simple person, friend Oliver."

"And I," said Oliver, "though I pique not myself upon managing steel in any other shape than that of a razor, would rather charge a Swiss battalion of pikes than I would accompany your Highness upon such a visit of friendship to Charles of Burgundy, when he hath so many grounds to be well assured that there is enmity in your Majesty's bosom against him."

"Thou art a fool, Oliver," said the King, "with all thy pretensions to wisdom, and art not aware that deep policy must often assume the appearance of the most extreme simplicity, as courage occasionally shrouds itself under the show of modest timidity. Were it needful, full surely would I do what I have said—the saints always blessing our purpose, and the heavenly constellations bringing round, in their course, a proper conjuncture for such an exploit."

In these words did King Louis XI. give the first hint of the extraordinary resolution which he afterwards adopted in order to dupe his great rival, the subsequent execution of which had very nearly proved his own ruin.

He parted with his counsellor, and presently afterwards went to the apartment of the Ladies of Croye. Few persuasions beyond his mere license would have been necessary to determine their retreat from the court of France, upon the first hint that they might not be eventually protected against the Duke of Burgundy; but it was not so easy to induce them to choose Liege for the place of their retreat. They entreated and requested to be transferred to Bretagne or Calais, where, under protection of the Duke of Bretagne, or King of England, they might remain in a state of safety until the sovereign of Burgundy should relent in his rigorous purpose towards them. But neither of these places of safety at all suited the plans of Louis, and he was at last successful in inducing them to adopt that which did coincide with them.

The power of the Bishop of Liege for their defence was not to be questioned, since his ecclesiastical dignity gave him the means of protecting the fugitives against all Christian princes; while, on the other hand, his secular forces, if not numerous, seemed at least sufficient to defend his person and all under his protection from any sudden violence. The difficulty was to reach the little court of the bishop in safety; but for this Louis promised to provide, by spreading a report that the Ladies of Croye had escaped from Tours by night, under fear of being delivered up to the Burgundian envoy, and had taken their flight towards Bretagne. He also promised them the attendance of a small but faithful retinue, and letters to the commanders of such towns and fortresses as they might pass, with instructions to use every means for protecting and assisting them in their journey.

The Ladies of Croye, although internally resenting the ungenerous and discourteous manner in which Louis thus deprived them of the promised asylum in his court, were so far from objecting to the hasty departure which he proposed, that they even anticipated his project by entreating to be permitted to set forward that same night. The Lady Hameline was already tired of a place where there were neither admiring courtiers nor festivities to be witnessed; and the Lady Isabelle thought she had seen enough to conclude that, were the temptation to become a little stronger, Louis XI., not satisfied with expelling them from his court, would not hesitate to deliver her up to her irritated suzerain, the Duke of Burgundy.

Lastly, Louis himself readily acquiesced in their hasty departure, anxious to preserve peace with Duke Charles, and alarmed lest the beauty of Isabelle should interfere with and impede the favourite plan which he had formed for bestowing the hand of his daughter Joan upon his cousin of Orleans.

CHAPTER XIII.

THE JOURNEY.

> Talk not of kings—I scorn the poor comparison;
> I am a SAGE, and can command the elements,
> At least men think I can; and on that thought
> I found unbounded empire.
> *Albumazar.*

OCCUPATION and adventure might be said to crowd upon the young Scottishman with the force of a spring-tide; for he was speedily summoned to the apartment of his captain, the Lord Crawford, where, to his astonishment, he again beheld the King. After a few words respecting the honour and trust which were about to be reposed in him, which made Quentin internally afraid that they were again about to propose to him such a watch as he had kept upon the Count of Crèvecœur, or perhaps some duty still more repugnant to his feelings, he was not relieved merely, but delighted, with hearing that he was selected, with the assistance of four others under his command, one of whom was a guide, to escort the Ladies of Croye to the little court of their relative, the Bishop of Liege, in the safest and most commodious, and at the same time in the most secret, manner possible. A scroll was given him, in which were set down directions for his guidance, for the places of halt (generally chosen in obscure villages, solitary monasteries, and situations remote from towns), and for the general precautions which he was to attend to, especially on approaching the frontier of Burgundy. He was sufficiently supplied with instructions what he ought to say and do to sustain the personage of the *maître d'hôtel* of two English ladies of rank, who had been on a pilgrimage to St. Martin of Tours, and were about to visit the holy city of Cologne, and worship the relics of the sage Eastern monarchs who came to adore the nativity of Bethlehem; for under that character the Ladies of Croye were to journey.

Without having any defined notions of the cause of his delight, Quentin Durward's heart leapt for joy at the idea of approaching thus nearly to the person of the beauty of the turret, and in a situation which entitled him to her confidence, since her protection was in so great degree entrusted to his conduct and courage. He felt no doubt in his own mind that he should be her successful guide through the hazards of her pilgrimage. Youth seldom thinks of dangers; and bred up free, and fearless, and self-confiding, Quentin, in particular, only thought of them to defy them. He longed to be exempted from the restraint of the royal presence, that he might indulge the secret glee with which such unexpected tidings filled him, and which prompted him to bursts of delight which would have been totally unfitting for that society.

But Louis had not yet done with him. That cautious monarch had to consult a counsellor of a different stamp from Oliver de Diable, and who was supposed to derive his skill from the superior and astral intelligences, as men, judging from their fruits, were apt to think the counsels of Oliver sprung from the devil himself.

Louis therefore led the way, followed by the impatient Quentin, to a separate tower of the Castle of Plessis, in which was installed, in no small ease and splendour, the celebrated astrologer, poet, and philosopher, Galeotti Marti, or Martius, or Martivalle,[1] a native of Narni, in Italy, the author of the famous treatise, *De Vulgo Incognitis*,[2] and the subject of his age's admiration, and of the panegyrics of Paulus Jovius. He had long flourished at the court of the celebrated Matthias Corvinus, king of Hungary, from whom he was in some measure decoyed by Louis, who grudged the Hungarian monarch

---

[1] See Note 24.
[2] Concerning Things Unknown to the Generality of Mankind.

the society and the counsels of a sage accounted so skilful in reading the decrees of Heaven.

Martivalle was none of those ascetic, withered, pale professors of mystic learning of those days, who bleared their eyes over the midnight furnace, and macerated their bodies by outwatching the polar bear. He indulged in all courtly pleasures, and, until he grew corpulent, had excelled in all martial sorts and gymnastic exercises, as well as in the use of arms; insomuch, that Janus Pannonius has left a Latin epigram, upon a wrestling-match betwixt Galeotti and a renowned champion of that art, in the presence of the Hungarian king and court, in which the astrologer was completely victorious.

The apartments of this courtly and martial sage were far more splendidly furnished than any which Quentin had yet seen in the royal palace; and the carving and ornamented woodwork of his library, as well as the magnificence displayed in the tapestries, showed the elegant taste of the learned Italian. Out of his study one door opened to his sleeping-apartment, another led to the turret which served as his observatory. A large oaken table, in the midst of the chamber, was covered with a rich Turkey carpet, the spoils of the tent of a pacha after the great battle of Jaiza, where the astrologer had fought abreast with the valiant champion of Christendom, Matthias Corvinus. On the table lay a variety of mathematical and astrological instruments, all of the most rich materials and curious workmanship. His astrolabe of silver was the gift of the Emperor of Germany, and his Jacob's staff of ebony, jointed with gold and curiously inlaid, was a mark of esteem from the reigning Pope.

There were various other miscellaneous articles disposed on the table, or hanging around the walls; amongst others, two complete suits of armour, one of mail, the other of plate, both of which, from their great size, seemed to call the gigantic astrologer their owner, a Spanish toledo, a Scottish broadsword, a Turkish scimitar, with bows, quivers, and other warlike weapons, musical instruments of several different kinds, a silver crucifix, a sepulchral antique vase, and several of the little brazen Penates of the ancient heathens, with other curious nondescript articles, some of which, in the superstitious opinions of that period, seemed to be designed for magical purposes. The library of this singular character was of the same miscellaneous description with his other effects. Curious manuscripts of classical antiquity lay mingled with the voluminous labours of Christian divines, and of those painstaking sages who professed the chemical science, and proffered to guide their students into the most secret recesses of nature by means of the Hermetical philosophy. Some were written in the Eastern character, and others concealed their sense or nonsense under the veil of hieroglyphics and cabalistic characters. The whole apartment, and its furniture of every kind, formed a scene very impressive on the fancy, considering the general belief then indisputably entertained concerning the truth of the occult sciences; and that effect was increased by the manners and appearance of the individual himself, who, seated in a huge chair, was employed in curiously examining a specimen, just issued from the Frankfort press, of the newly invented art of printing.[1]

Galeotti Martivalle was a tall, bulky, yet stately man, considerably past his prime, and whose youthful habits of exercise, though still occasionally resumed, had not been able to contend with his natural tendency to corpulence, increased by sedentary study and indulgence in the pleasures of the table. His features, though rather overgrown, were dignified and noble, and a santon might have envied the dark and downward sweep of his long-descending beard. His dress was a chamber-robe of the richest Genoa velvet, with ample sleeves, clasped with frogs of gold, and lined with sables. It was fastened round his middle by a broad belt of virgin parchment, round which were represented in crimson characters the signs of the zodiac. He rose and bowed to the King, yet with the air of one to whom such exalted society was familiar, and who was not at all likely, even in the royal presence, to compromise the dignity then especially affected by the pursuers of science.

[1] See Invention of Printing. Note 25.

"You are engaged, father," said the King, "and, as I think, with this new-fashioned art of multiplying manuscripts by the intervention of machinery. Can things of such mechanical and terrestrial import interest the thoughts of one before whom Heaven has unrolled her own celestial volumes?"

"My brother," replied Martivalle—"for so the tenant of this cell must term even the King of France when he deigns to visit him as a disciple—believe me that, in considering the consequences of this invention, I read with as certain augury as by any combination of the heavenly bodies the most awful and portentous changes. When I reflect with what slow and limited supplies the stream of science hath hitherto descended to us, how difficult to be obtained by those most ardent in its search, how certain to be neglected by all who regard their ease, how liable to be diverted, or altogether dried up, by the invasions of barbarism—can I look forward without wonder and astonishment to the lot of a succeeding generation, on whom knowledge will descend like the first and second rain, uninterrupted, unabated, unbounded, fertilising some grounds and overflowing others, changing the whole form of social life, establishing and overthrowing religions, erecting and destroying kingdoms——"

"Hold, Galeotti," said Louis—"shall these changes come in our time?"

"No, my royal brother," replied Martivalle; "this invention may be likened to a young tree which is now newly planted, but shall, in succeeding generations, bear fruit as fatal, yet as precious, as that of the Garden of Eden—the knowledge, namely, of good and evil."

Louis answered, after a moment's pause: "Let futurity look to what concerns them; we are men of this age, and to this age we will confine our care. Sufficient for the day is the evil thereof. Tell me, hast thou proceeded farther in the horoscope which I sent to thee, and of which you made me some report? I have brought the party hither, that you may use palmistry, or chiromancy, if such is your pleasure. The matter is pressing."

The bulky sage arose from his seat, and, approaching the young soldier, fixed on him his keen large dark eyes, as if he were in the act of internally spelling and dissecting every lineament and feature. Blushing and borne down by this close examination on the part of one whose expression was so reverent at once and commanding, Quentin bent his eyes on the ground, and did not again raise them till in the act of obeying the sonorous command of the astrologer: "Look up and be not afraid, but hold forth thy hand."

When Martivalle had inspected his palm, according to the form of the mystic arts which he practised, he led the King some steps aside. "My royal brother," he said, "the physiognomy of this youth, together with the lines impressed on his hand, confirm, in a wonderful degree, the report which I founded on his horoscope, as well as that judgment which your own proficiency in our sublime arts induced you at once to form of him. All promises that this youth will be brave and fortunate."

"And faithful?" said the King; "for valour and fortune square not always with fidelity."

"And faithful also," said the astrologer; "for there is manly firmness in look and eye, and his *linea vitæ* is deeply marked and clear, which indicates a true and upright adherence to those who do benefit or lodge trust in him. But yet——"

"But what?" said the King. "Father Galeotti, wherefore do you now pause?"

"The ears of kings," said the sage, "are like the palates of those dainty patients which are unable to endure the bitterness of the drugs necessary for their recovery."

"My ears and my palate have no such niceness," said Louis; "let me hear what is useful counsel, and swallow what is wholesome medicine. I quarrel not with the rudeness of the one or the harsh taste of the other. I have not been cockered in wantonness or indulgence. My youth was one of exile and suffering. My ears are used to harsh counsel, and take no offence at it."

"Then plainly, sire," replied Galeotti, "if you have aught

in your purposed commission which—which, in short, may startle a scrupulous conscience—entrust it not to this youth—at least, not till a few years' exercise in your service has made him as unscrupulous as others."

"And is this what you hesitated to speak, my good Galeotti? and didst thou think thy speaking it would offend me?" said the King. "Alack, I know that thou art well sensible that the path of royal policy cannot be always squared, as that of private life ought invariably to be, by the abstract maxims of religion and of morality. Wherefore do we, the princes of the earth, found churches and monasteries, make pilgrimages, undergo penances, and perform devotions, with which others may dispense, unless it be because the benefit of the public, and the welfare of our kingdoms, force us upon measures which grieve our consciences as Christians? But Heaven has mercy, the church an unbounded stock of merits, and the intercession of Our Lady of Embrun and the blessed saints is urgent, everlasting, and omnipotent." He laid his hat on the table, and devoutly kneeling before the images stuck into the hatband, repeated, in an earnest tone: "*Sancte Huberte, Sancte Juliane, Sancte Martine, Sancta Rosalia, Sancti quotquot adestis, orate pro me peccatore!*" He then smote his breast, arose, resumed his hat, and continued: "Be assured, good father, that, whatever there may be in our commission of the nature at which you have hinted, the execution shall not be entrusted to this youth, nor shall he be privy to such part of our purpose."

"In this," said the astrologer, "you, my royal brother, will walk wisely. Something may be apprehended likewise from the rashness of this your young commissioner—a failing inherent in those of sanguine complexion. But I hold that, by the rules of art, this chance is not be weighed against the other properties discovered from his horoscope and otherwise."

"Will this next midnight be a propitious hour in which to commence a perilous journey?" said the King. "See, here is your ephemerides; you see the position of the moon in regard to Saturn and the ascendence of Jupiter. That should argue, methinks, in submission to your better art, success to him who sends forth the expedition at such an hour."

"To him who *sends forth* the expedition," said the astrologer, after a pause, "this conjunction doth indeed promise success; but methinks that Saturn, being combust, threatens danger and infortune to the party *sent;* whence I infer that the errand may be perilous, or even fatal, to those who are to journey. Violence and captivity, methinks, are intimated in that adverse conjunction."

"Violence and captivity to those who are sent," answered the King, "but success to the wishes of the sender. Runs it not thus, my learned father?"

"Even so," replied the astrologer.

The King paused, without giving any further indication how far this presaging speech (probably hazarded by the astrologer from his conjecture that the commission related to some dangerous purpose) squared with his real object, which, as the reader is aware, was to betray the Countess Isabelle of Croye into the hands of William de la Marck, a nobleman indeed of high birth, but degraded by his crimes into a leader of banditti, distinguished for his turbulent disposition and ferocious bravery.

The King then pulled forth a paper from his pocket, and, ere he gave it to Martivalle, said, in a tone which resembled that of an apology: "Learned Galeotti, be not surprised that, possessing in you an oracular treasure superior to that lodged in the breast of any now alive, not excepting the great Nostradamus himself, I am desirous frequently to avail myself of your skill in those doubts and difficulties which beset every prince who hath to contend with rebellion within his land and with external enemies, both powerful and inveterate."

"When I was honoured with your request, sire," said the philosopher, "and abandoned the court of Buda for that of Plessis, it was with the resolution to place at the command of my royal patron whatever my art had that might be of service to him."

"Enough, good Martivalle—I pray thee attend to the import of this question." He proceeded to read from the paper in his hand: "A person having on hand a weighty controversy, which is like to draw to debate either by law or by force of arms, is desirous, for the present, to seek accommodation by a personal interview with his antagonist. He desires to know what day will be propitious for the execution of such a purpose; also what is likely to be the success of such a negotiation, and whether his adversary will be moved to answer the confidence thus reposed in him with gratitude and kindness, or may rather be likely to abuse the opportunity and advantage which such meeting may afford him?"

"It is an important question," said Martinvalle, when the King had done reading, "and requires that I should set a planetary figure, and give it instant and deep consideration."

"Let it be so, my good father in the sciences, and thou shalt know what it is to oblige a King of France. We are determined, if the constellations forbid not—and our own humble art leads us to think that they approve our purpose— to hazard something, even in our own person, to stop these anti-Christian wars."

"May the saints forward your Majesty's pious intent," said the astrologer, "and guard your sacred person!"

"Thanks, learned father. Here is something, the while, to enlarge your curious library."

He placed under one of the volumes a small purse of gold; for, economical even in his superstitions, Louis conceived the astrologer sufficiently bound to his service by the pensions he had assigned him, and thought himself entitled to the use of his skill at a moderate rate, even upon great exigencies.

Louis, having thus, in legal phrase, added a refreshing fee to his general retainer, turned from him to address Durward. "Follow me," he said, "my bonny Scot, as one chosen by destiny and a monarch to accomplish a bold adventure. All must be got ready that thou mayst put foot in stirrup the very instant the bell of St. Martin's tolls twelve. One minute sooner, one minute later, were to forfeit the favourable aspect of the constellations which smile on your adventure."

Thus saying, the King left the apartment, followed by his young Guardsman; and no sooner were they gone than the astrologer gave way to very different feelings from those which seemed to animate him during the royal presence.

"The niggardly slave!" he said, weighing the purse in his hand, for, being a man of unbounded expense, he had almost constant occasion for money—"the base, sordid scullion! A coxswain's wife would give more to know that her husband had crossed the narrow seas in safety. *He* acquire any tincture of human letters! yes, when prowling foxes and yelling wolves become musicians. *He* read the glorious blazoning of the firmament! ay, when sordid moles shall become lynxes. *Post tot promissa*—after so many promises made, to entice me from the court of the magnificent Matthias, where Hun and Turk, Christian and infidel, the Czar of Muscovia and the Cham of Tartary themselves, contended to load me with gifts, doth he think I am to abide in this old castle, like a bullfinch in a cage, fain to sing as oft as he chooses to whistle, and all for seed and water? Not so—*aut inveniam viam, aut faciam:* I will discover or contrive a remedy. The Cardinal Balue is politic and liberal; this query shall to him, and it shall be his Eminence's own fault if the stars speak not as he would have them."

He again took the despised guerdon and weighed it in his hand. "It may be," he said, "there is some jewel or pearl of price concealed in this paltry case. I have heard he can be liberal even to lavishness when it suits his caprice or interest."

He emptied the purse, which contained neither more nor less than ten gold pieces. The indignation of the astrologer was extreme. "Thinks he that for such paltry rate of hire I will practise that celestial science which I have studied with the Armenian abbot of Istrohaff, who had not seen the sun for forty years; with the Greek Dubravius, who is said to have raised the dead, and have even visited the Scheik Ebn Hali in his cave in the deserts of Thebais? No, by Heaven! he that contemns art shall perish through his own ignorance. Ten pieces! a pittance which I am half ashamed to offer to Toinette, to buy her new breast-laces."

So saying, the indignant sage nevertheless plunged the contemned pieces of gold into a large pouch which he wore at his girdle, which Toinette and other abettors of lavish expense generally contrived to empty fully faster than the philosopher, with all his art, could find the means of filling.

CHAPTER XIV.

THE JOURNEY.

> I see thee yet, fair France: thou favour'd land
> Of art and nature, thou art still before me;
> Thy sons, to whom their labour is a sport,
> So well thy grateful soil returns its tribute;
> Thy sun-burnt daughters, with their laughing eyes
> And glossy raven-locks. But, favour'd France,
> Thou hast had many a tale of woe to tell,
> In ancient times as now.
> *Anonymous.*

AVOIDING all conversation with any one, for such was his charge, Quentin Durward proceeded hastily to array himself in a strong but plain cuirass, with thigh and arm pieces, and placed on his head a good steel cap without any visor. To these was added a handsome cassock of shamois leather, finely dressed, and laced down the seams with some embroidery, such as might become a superior officer in a noble household.

These were brought to his apartment by Oliver, who, with his quiet, insinuating smile and manner, acquainted him that his uncle had been summoned to mount guard purposely that he might make no inquiries concerning these mysterious movements.

"Your excuse will be made to your kinsman," said Oliver, smiling again; "and, my dearest son, when you return safe from the execution of this pleasing trust, I doubt not you will be found worthy of such promotion as will dispense with you accounting for your motions to any one, while it will place you at the head of those who must render an account of theirs to you."

So spoke Oliver le Diable, calculating, probably, in his own mind the great chance there was that the poor youth whose hand he squeezed affectionately as he spoke must necessarily encounter death or captivity in the commission entrusted to his charge. He added to his fair words a small purse of gold, to defray necessary expenses on the road, as a gratuity on the King's part.

At a few minutes before twelve at midnight, Quentin, according to his directions, proceeded to the second courtyard, and paused under the Dauphin's Tower, which, as the reader knows, was assigned for the temporary residence of the Countesses of Croye. He found, at this place of rendezvous, the men and horses appointed to compose the retinue, leading two sumpter mules already loaded with baggage, and holding three palfreys for the two countesses and a faithful waiting-woman, with a stately war-horse for himself, whose steel-plated saddle glanced in the pale moonlight. Not a word of recognition was spoken on either side. The men sat still in their saddles, as if they were motionless; and by the same imperfect light Quentin saw with pleasure that they were all armed, and held long lances in their hands. They were only three in number; but one of them whispered to Quentin, in a strong Gascon accent, that their guide was to join them beyond Tours.

Meantime, lights glanced to and fro at the lattices of the tower, as if there was bustle and preparation among its inhabitants. At length, a small door, which led from the bottom of the tower to the court, was unclosed, and three females came forth, attended by a man wrapped in a cloak. They mounted in silence the palfreys which stood prepared for them, while their attendant on foot led the way and gave the passwords and signals to the watchful guards, whose posts they passed in succession. Thus they at length reached the exterior of these formidable barriers. Here the man on foot, who had hitherto acted as their guide, paused, and spoke low and earnestly to the two foremost females.

"May Heaven bless you, sire," said a voice which thrilled upon Quentin Durward's ear, "and forgive you, even if your purposes be more interested than your words express! To be placed in safety under the protection of the good Bishop of Liege is the utmost extent of my desire."

The person whom she thus addressed muttered an inaudible answer, and retreated back through the barrier-gate, while Quentin thought that, by the moon-glimpse, he recognised in him the King himself, whose anxiety for the departure of his guests had probably induced him to give his presence, in case scruples should arise on their part or difficulties on that of the guards of the castle.

When the riders were beyond the castle, it was necessary for some time to ride with great precaution, in order to avoid the pitfalls, snares, and similar contrivances which were placed for the annoyance of strangers. The Gascon was, however, completely possessed of the clue to this labyrinth, and in a quarter of an hour's riding they found themselves beyond the limits of Plessis le Parc, and not far distant from the city of Tours.

The moon, which had now extricated herself from the clouds through which she was formerly wading, shed a full sea of glorious light upon a landscape equally glorious. They saw the princely Loire rolling his majestic tide through the richest plain in France, and sweeping along between banks ornamented with towers and terraces, and with olives and vineyards. They saw the walls of the city of Tours, the ancient capital of Touraine, raising their portal towers and embattlements white in the moonlight, while from within their circle rose the immense Gothic mass which the devotion of the sainted Bishop Perpetuus erected as early as the 5th century, and which the zeal of Charlemagne and his successors had enlarged with such architectural splendour as rendered it the most magnificent church in France. The towers of the church of St. Gatien were also visible, and the gloomy strength of the castle, which was said to have been, in ancient times, the residence of the Emperor Valentinian.

Even the circumstances in which he was placed, though of a nature so engrossing, did not prevent the wonder and delight with which the young Scottishman, accustomed to the waste though impressive landscape of his own mountains, and the poverty even of his country's most stately scenery, looked on a scene which art and nature seemed to have vied in adorning with their richest splendour. But he was recalled to the business of the moment by the voice of the elder lady, pitched at least an octave higher than those soft tones which bid adieu to King Louis, demanding to speak with the leader of the band. Spurring his horse forward, Quentin respectfully presented himself to the ladies in that capacity, and thus underwent the interrogatories of the Lady Hameline.

"What was his name, and what his degree?"

He told both.

"Was he perfectly acquainted with the road?"

"He could not," he replied, "pretend to much knowledge of the route, but he was furnished with full instructions, and he was, at their first resting-place, to be provided with a guide in all respects competent to the task of directing their farther journey; meanwhile, a horseman who had just joined them, and made the number of their guard four, was to be their guide for the first stage."

"And wherefore were you selected for such a duty, young gentleman?" said the lady. "I am told you are the same youth who was lately upon guard in the gallery in which we met the Princess of France. You seem young and inexperienced for such a charge; a stranger, too, in France, and speaking the language as a foreigner."

"I am bound to obey the commands of the King, madam, but am not qualified to reason on them," answered the young soldier.

"Are you of noble birth?" demanded the same querist.

"I may safely affirm so, madam," replied Quentin. "And are you not," said the younger lady, addressing him in her turn, but with a timorous accent, "the same whom I saw when I was called to wait upon the King at yonder inn?"

Lowering his voice, perhaps from similar feelings of timidity, Quentin answered in the affirmative.

"Then, methinks, my cousin," said the Lady Isabella, addressing the Lady Hameline, "we must be safe under this young gentleman's safeguard; he looks not, at least, like one to whom the execution of a plan of treacherous cruelty upon two helpless women could be with safety entrusted."

"On my honour, madam," said Durward, "by the fame of my house, by the bones of my ancestry, I could not, for France and Scotland laid into one, be guilty of treachery or cruelty towards you!"

"You speak well, young man," said the Lady Hameline;

"but we are accustomed to hear fair speeches from the King of France and his agents. It was by these that the we were induced, when the protection of the Bishop of Liege might have been attained with less risk than now, or when we might have thrown ourselves on that of Wenceslaus of Germany or of Edward of England, to seek refuge in France. And in what did the promises of the King result? In an obscure and shameful concealing of us, under plebeian names, as a sort of prohibited wares, in yonder paltry hostelry, when we, who, as thou knowest, Marthon (addressing her domestic), never put on our headtire save under a canopy, and upon a dais of three degrees, were compelled to attire ourselves standing on the simple floor, as if we had been two milkmaids."

Marthon admitted that her lady spoke a most melancholy truth.

"I would that had been the sorest evil, dear kinswoman," said the Lady Isabelle; "I could gladly have dispensed with state."

"But not with society," said the elder countess; "that, my sweet cousin, was impossible."

"I would have dispensed with all, my dearest kinswoman," answered Isabelle, in a voice which penetrated to the very heart of her young conductor and guard—"with all, for a safe and honourable retirement. I wish not—God knows, I never wished—to occasion war betwixt France and my native Burgundy, or that lives should be lost for such as I am. I only implored permission to retire to the convent of Marmoutier or to any other holy sanctuary."

"You spoke then like a fool, my cousin," answered the elder lady, "and not like a daughter of my noble brother. It is well there is still one alive who hath some of the spirit of the noble house of Croye. How should a high-born lady be known from a sunburnt mildmaid save that spears are broken for the one and only hazel-poles shattered for the other! I tell you, maiden, that while I was in the very earliest bloom, scarcely older than yourself, the famous passage of arms at Haflinghem was held in my honour; the challengers were four, the assailants so many as twelve. It lasted three days, and cost the lives of two adventurous knights, the fracture of one backbone, one collar-bone, three legs and two arms, besides flesh-wounds and bruises beyond the heralds' counting; and thus have the ladies of our house ever been honoured. Ah! had you but half the heart of your noble ancestry, you would find means at some court, where ladies' love and fame in arms are still prized, to maintain a tournament, at which your hand should be the prize, as was that of your great-grandmother of blessed memory at the spear-running of Strasbourg; and thus should you gain the best lance in Europe to maintain the rights of the house of Croye, both against the oppression of Burgundy and the policy of France."

"But, fair kinswoman," answered the younger countess, "I have been told by my old nurse that, although the Rhinegrave was the best lance at the great tournament at Strasbourg, and so won the hand of my respected ancestor, yet the match was no happy one, as he used often to scold, and sometimes even to beat, my great-grandmother of blessed memory."

"And wherefore not?" said the elder countess, in her romantic enthusiasm for the profession of chivalry—"why should those victorious arms, accustomed to deal blows when abroad, be bound to restrain their energies at home? A thousand times rather would I be beaten twice a-day by a husband whose arm was as much feared by others as by me than be the wife of a coward, who dared neither to lift hand to his wife nor to any one else!"

"I should wish you joy of such an active mate, fair aunt," replied Isabelle, "without envying you; for if broken bones be lovely in tourneys, there is nothing less amiable in ladies' bower."

"Nay, but the beating is no necessary consequence of wedding with a knight of fame in arms," said the Lady Hameline; "though it is true that our ancestor of blessed memory, the Rhinegrave Gottfried, was something rough-tempered, and addicted to the use of *Rheinwein*. The very perfect knight is a lamb among ladies and a lion among lances. There was Thibault of Montigni—God be with him!—he was the kindest soul alive, and not only was he never so discourteous as to lift hand against his lady, but, by our good dame, he who beat all enemies without doors found a fair foe who could belabour him within. Well, 'twas his own fault. He was one of the challengers at the passage of Haflinghem, and so well bestirred himself that, if it had pleased Heaven, and your grandfather, there might have been a lady of Montigni who had used his gentle nature more gently."

The Countess Isabelle, who had some reason to dread this passage of Haflinghem, it being a topic upon which her aunt was at all times very diffuse, suffered the conversation to drop; and Quentin, with the natural politeness of one who had been gently nurtured, dreading lest his presence might be a restraint on their conversation, rode forward to join the guide, as if to ask him some questions concerning their route.

Meanwhile, the ladies continued their journey in silence, or in such conversation as is not worth narrating, until day began to break; and as they had then been on horseback for several hours, Quentin, anxious lest they should be fatigued, became impatient to know their distance from the nearest resting-place.

"I will show it you," answered the guide, "in half an hour."

"And then you leave us to other guidance?" continued Quentin.

"Even so, seignior archer," replied the man; "my journeys are always short and straight. When you and others, seignior archer, go by the bow, I always go by the cord."

The moon had by this time long been down, and the lights of dawn were beginning to spread bright and strong in the east, and to gleam on the bosom of a small lake, on the verge of which they had been riding for a short space of time. This lake lay in the midst of a wide plain, scattered over with single trees, groves, and thickets; but which might be yet termed open, so that objects began to be discerned with sufficient accuracy. Quentin cast his eye on the person whom he rode beside, and, under the shadow of a slouched overspreading hat, which resembled the sombrero of a Spanish peasant, he recognised the facetious features of the same Petit-André whose fingers, not long since, had, in concert with those of his lugubrious brother, Trois-Eschelles, been so unpleasantly active about his throat. Impelled by aversion not altogether unmixed with fear (for in his own country the executioner is regarded with almost superstitious horror), which his late narrow escape had not diminished, Durward instinctively moved his horse's head to the right, and pressing him at the same time with the spur, made a demi-volte, which separated him eight feet from his hateful companion.

"Ho, ho, ho, ho!" exclaimed Petit-André; "by our Lady of the Grève, our young soldier remembers us of old. What! comrade, you bear no malice, I trust? Every one wins his bread in this country. No man need be ashamed of having come through my hands, for I will do my work with any that ever tied a living weight to a dead tree. And God hath given me grace to be such a merry fellow withal. Ha! ha! ha! I could tell you such jests I have cracked between the foot of the ladder and the top of the gallows, that, by my halidome, I have been obliged to do my job rather hastily, for fear the fellows should die with laughing, and so shame my mystery!"

As he thus spoke, he edged his horse sideways, to regain the interval which the Scot had left between them, saying at the same time: "Come, seignior archer, let there be no unkindness betwixt us! For my part, I always do my duty without malice, and with a light heart, and I never love a man better than when I have put my scant-of-wind collar about his neck, to dub him knight of the order of St. Patibularius, as the provost's chaplain, the worthy Father Vaconeldiablo, is wont to call the patron saint of the provostry."

"Keep back, thou wretched object!" exclaimed Quentin, as the finisher of the law again sought to approach him closer, "or I shall be tempted to teach you the distance that should be betwixt men of honour and such an outcast."

"La you there, how hot you are!" said the fellow, "Had you said men of *honesty*, there had been some savour of truth in it; but for men of *honour*, good lack, I have to deal with them every day, as nearly and closely as I was about to do business with you. But peace be with you, and keep your company to yourself. I would have bestowed a flagon of Auvernat upon you to wash away every unkindness; but 'tis like you scorn my courtesy. Well. Be as churlish as you list; I never quarrel with my customers—my jerry-come-tumbles, my merry dancers, my little playfellows, as Jacques Butcher says to his lambs—those, in fine, who, like your seigniorship, have H.E.M.P. written on their foreheads. No—no, let them use me as they list, they shall have my good service at last; and yourself shall see, when you next come under Petit-André's hands, that he knows how to forgive an injury."

So saying, and summing up the whole with a provoking wink and such an interjectional *tchick* as men quicken a dull horse with, Petit-André drew off to the other side of the path, and left the youth to digest the taunts he had treated him with as his proud Scottish stomach best might. A strong desire had Quentin to have belaboured him while the staff of his lance could hold together; but he put a restraint on his passion, recollecting that a brawl with such a character could be creditable at no time or place, and that a quarrel of any kind, on the present occasion, would be a breach of duty, and might involve the most perilous consequences. He therefore swallowed his wrath at the ill-timed and professional jokes of Mons. Petit-André, and contented himself with devoutly hoping that they had not reached the ears of his fair charge, on which they could not be supposed to make an impression in favour of himself, as one obnoxious to such sarcasms. But he was speedily aroused from such thoughts by the cry of both the ladies at once: "Look back—look back! For the love of Heaven look to yourself and us; we are pursued!"

Quentin hastily looked back, and saw that two armed men were in fact following them, and riding at such a pace as must soon bring them up with their party. "It can," he said, "be only some of the provostry making their rounds in the forest. Do thou look," he said to Petit-André, "and see what they may be."

Petit-André obeyed; and rolling himself jocosely in the saddle after he had made his observation, replied: "These, fair sir, are neither your comrades nor mine—neither archers nor marshal's-men; for I think they wear helmets, with visors lowered, and gorgets of the same. A plague upon these gorgets, of all other pieces of armour! I have fumbled with them an hour before I could undo the rivets."

"Do you, gracious ladies," said Durward, without attending to Petit-André, "ride forward, not so fast as to raise an opinion of your being in flight, and yet fast enough to avail yourselves of the impediment which I shall presently place between you and these men who follow us."

The Countess Isabelle looked to their guide, and then whispered to her aunt, who spoke to Quentin thus: "We have confidence in your care, fair archer, and will rather abide the risk of whatever may chance in your company than we will go onward with that man, whose mien is, we think, of no good augury."

"Be it as you will, ladies," said the youth. "There are but two who come after us; and though they be knights, as their arms seem to show, they shall, if they have any evil purpose, learn how a Scottish gentleman can do his devoir in the presence and for the defence of such as you. Which of you there," he continued, addressing the guards whom he commanded, "is willing to be my comrade, and to break a lance with these gallants?"

Two of the men obviously faltered in resolution; but the third, Bertrand Guyot, swore "that, *cap de Diou*, were they knights of King Arthur's Round Table, he would try their mettle, for the honour of Gascony."

While he spoke, the two knights—for they seemed of no less rank—came up with the rear of the party, in which Quentin, with his sturdy adherent, had by this time stationed himself. They were fully accoutred in excellent armour of polished steel, without any device by which they could be distinguished.

One of them, as they approached, called out to Quentin: "Sir squire, give place; we come to relieve you of a charge which is above your rank and condition. You will do well to leave these ladies in our care, who are fitter to wait upon them, especially as we know that in yours they are little better than captives."

"In return to your demand, sirs," replied Durward, "know, in the first place, that I am discharging the duty imposed upon me by my present sovereign; and next, that however unworthy I may be, the ladies desire to abide under my protection."

"Out, sirrah!" exclaimed one of the champions; "will you, a wandering beggar, put yourself on terms of resistance against belted knights?"

"They are indeed terms of resistance," said Quentin, "since they oppose your insolent and unlawful aggression; and if there be difference of rank between us, which as yet I know not, your discourtesy has done it away. Draw your sword, or, if you will use the lance, take ground for your career."

While the knights turned their horses and rode back to the distance of about a hundred and fifty yards, Quentin, looking to the ladies, bent low on his saddle-bow, as if desiring their favourable regard, and as they streamed towards him their kerchiefs in token of encouragement, the two assailants had gained the distance necessary for their charge.

Calling to the Gascon to bear himself like a man, Durward put his steed into motion; and the four horsemen met in full career in the midst of the ground which at first separated them. The shock was fatal to the poor Gascon; for his adversary, aiming at his face, which was undefended by a visor, ran him through the eye into the brain, so that he fell dead from his horse.

On the other hand, Quentin, though labouring under the same disadvantage, swayed himself in the saddle so dexterously that the hostile lance, slightly scratching his cheek, passed over his right shoulder; while his own spear, striking his antagonist fair upon the breast, hurled him to the ground. Quentin jumped off, to unhelm his fallen opponent; but the other knight, who had never yet spoken, seeing the fortune of his companion, dismounted still more speedily than Durward, and bestriding his friend, who lay senseless, exclaimed: "In the name of God and St. Martin, mount, good fellow, and get thee gone with thy woman's ware! *Ventre St. Gris*, they have caused mischief enough this morning."

"By your leave, sir knight," said Quentin, who could not

brook the menacing tone in which this advice was given, "I will first see whom I have had to do with, and learn who is to answer for the death of my comrade."

"That shalt thou never live to know or to tell," answered the knight. "Get thee back in peace, good fellow. If we were fools for interrupting your passage, we have had the worst, for thou hast done more evil than the lives of thou and thy whole band could repay. Nay, if thou *wilt* have it (for Quentin now drew his sword and advanced on him), take it with a vengeance!"

So saying, he dealt the Scot such a blow on the helmet as till that moment, though bred where good blows were plenty, he had only read of in romance. It descended like a thunder-bolt, beating down the guard which the young soldier had raised to protect his head, and reaching his helmet of proof, cut it through so far as to touch his hair, but without farther injury; while Durward, dizzy, stunned, and beaten down on one knee, was for an instant at the mercy of the knight, had it pleased him to second his blow. But compassion for Quentin's youth, or admiration of his courage, or a generous love of fair play, made him withhold from taking such advantage; while Durward, collecting himself, sprung up and attacked his antagonist with the energy of one determined to conquer or die, and at the same time with the presence of mind necessary for fighting the quarrel out to the best advantage. Resolved not again to expose himself to such dreadful blows as he had just sustained, he employed the advantage of superior agility, increased by the comparative lightness of his armour, to harass his antagonist, by traversing on all sides, with a suddenness of motion and rapidity of attack against which the knight, in his heavy panoply, found it difficult to defend himself without much fatigue.

It was in vain that this generous antagonist called aloud to Quentin: "That there now remained no cause of fight betwixt them, and that he was loth to be constrained to do him injury." Listening only to the suggestions of a passionate wish to redeem the shame of his temporary defeat, Durward continued to assail him with the rapidity of lightning—now menacing him with the edge, now with the point of his sword; and ever keeping such an eye on the motions of his opponent, of whose superior strength he had had terrible proof, that he was ready to spring backward, or aside, from under the blows of his tremendous weapon.

"Now the devil be with thee for an obstinate and presumptuous fool," muttered the knight, "that cannot be quiet till thou art knocked on the head!" So saying, he changed his mode of fighting, collected himself as if to stand on the defensive, and seemed contented with parrying, instead of returning, the blows which Quentin unceasingly aimed at him, with the internal resolution that, the instant when either loss of breath or any false or careless pass of the young soldier should give an opening, he would put an end to the fight by a single blow. It is likely he might have succeeded in this artful policy, but Fate had ordered it otherwise.

The duel was still at the hottest, when a large party of horse rode up, crying: "Hold, in the King's name!" Both champions stepped back; and Quentin saw with surprise that his captain, Lord Crawford, was at the head of the party who had thus interrupted their combat. There was also Tristan l'Hermite, with two or three of his followers; making, in all, perhaps twenty horse.

CHAPTER XV.

THE GUIDE.

> He was a son of Egypt, as he told me,
> And one descended from those dread magicians,
> Who waged rash war, when Israel dwelt in Goshen,
> With Israel and her Prophet—matching rod
> With his the sons of Levi's—and encountering
> Jehovah's miracles with incantations,
> Till upon Egypt came the avenging angel,
> And those proud sages wept for their first-born,
> As wept the unletter'd peasant.
> *Anonymous.*

THE arrival of Lord Crawford and his guard put an immediate end to the engagement which we endeavoured to describe in the last chapter; and the knight, throwing off his helmet, hastily gave the old lord his sword, saying: "Crawford, I render myself. But hither, and lend me your ear—a word, for God's sake—save the Duke of Orleans!"

"How! what? the Duke of Orleans!" exclaimed the Scottish commander. "How came this, in the name of the foul fiend? It will ruin the callant with the King for ever and a day."

"Ask no questions," said Dunois, for it was no other than he; "it was all my fault. See, he stirs. I came forth but to have a snatch at yonder damsel, and make myself a landed and married man, and see what is come on't. Keep back your canaille; let no man look upon him." So saying, he opened the visor of Orleans, and threw water on his face, which was afforded by the neighbouring lake.

Quentin Durward, meanwhile, stood like one planet-struck, so fast did new adventures pour in upon him. He had now, as the pale features of his first antagonist assured him, borne to the earth the first prince of the blood in France, and had measured swords with her best champion, the celebrated Dunois—both of them achievements honourable in themselves, but whether they might be called good service to the King, or so esteemed by him, was a very different question.

The duke had now recovered his breath, and was able to sit up and give attention to what passed betwixt Dunois and Crawford, while the former pleaded eagerly that there was no occasion to mention in the matter the name of the most noble Orleans, while he was ready to take the whole blame on his own shoulders, and to avouch that the duke had only come thither in friendship to him.

Lord Crawford continued listening, with his eyes fixed on the ground, and from time to time he sighed and shook his head. At length he said, looking up: "Thou knowest, Dunois, that for thy father's sake, as well as thine own, I would full fain do thee a service."

"It is not for myself I demand anything," answered Dunois. "Thou hast my sword, and I am your prisoner; what needs more? But it is for this noble prince, the only hope of France if God should call the Dauphin. He only came hither to do me a favour—in an effort to make my fortune—in a matter which the King had partly encouraged."

"Dunois," replied Crawford, "if another had told me thou hadst brought the noble prince into this jeopardy to serve any purpose of thine own, I had told him it was false. And now that thou dost pretend so thyself, I am hardly believe it is for the sake of speaking the truth."

"Noble Crawford," said Orleans, who had now entirely recovered from his swoon, "you are too like in character to your friend Dunois not to do him justice. It was indeed I that dragged him thither, most unwillingly, upon an enterprise of hare-brained passion, suddenly and rashly undertaken. Look on me all who will," he added, rising up and turning to the soldiery; "I am Louis of Orleans, willing to pay the penalty of my own folly. I trust the King will limit his displeasure to me, as is but just. Meanwhile, as a child of France must not give up his sword to any one—not even to you, brave Crawford—fare thee well, good steel."

So saying, he drew his sword from its scabbard and flung it into the lake. It went through the air like a stream of lightning, and sunk in the flashing waters, which speedily closed over it. All remained standing in irresolution and astonishment, so high was the rank, and so much esteemed was the character of, the culprit; while, at the same time, all were conscious that the consequences of his rash enterprise, considering the views which the King had upon him, were likely to end in his utter ruin.

Dunois was the first who spoke, and it was in the chiding tone of an offended and distrusted friend: "So! your Highness hath judged it fit to cast away your best sword, in the same morning when it was your pleasure to fling away the King's favour and to slight the friendship of Dunois?"

"My dearest kinsman," said the Duke, "when or how was it in my purpose to slight your friendship, by telling the truth when it was due to your safety and my honour?"

"What had you to do with my safety, my most princely cousin, I would pray to know?" answered Dunois, gruffly. "What, in God's name, was it to you if I had a mind to be hanged, or flung into the Loire, or poniarded, or broke on the wheel, or hung up alive in an iron cage, or buried alive in a castle fosse, or disposed of in any other way in which it might please King Louis to get rid of his faithful subject? You need not wink and frown, and point to Tristan l'Hermite; I see the scoundrel as well as you do. But it would not have stood so hard with me. And so much for my safety. And then for your own honour—by the blush of St. Magdalene, I think the honour would have been to have missed this morning's work, or kept it out of sight. Here has your Highness got yourself unhorsed by a wild Scottish boy."

"Tut—tut!" said Lord Crawford; "never shame his Highness for that. It is not the first time a Scottish boy hath broke a good lance. I am glad the youth hath borne him well."

"I will say nothing to the contrary," said Dunois; "yet, had your lordship come something later than you did, there might have been a vacancy in your band of archers."

"Ay—ay," answered Lord Crawford; "I can read your handwriting in that cleft morion. Some one take it from the lad, and give him a bonnet, which, with its steel lining, will keep his head better that that broken loom. And let me tell your lordship, that your own armour of proof is not without some marks of good Scottish handwriting. But, Dunois, I must now request the Duke of Orleans and you to take horse and accompany me, as I have power and commission to convey you to a place different from that which my good-will might assign you."

"May I not speak one word, my Lord of Crawford, to yonder fair ladies?" said the Duke of Orleans.

"Not one syllable," answered Lord Crawford; "I am too much a friend of your Highness to permit such an act of folly." Then addressing Quentin, he added: "You, young man, have done your duty. Go on to obey the charge with which you are entrusted."

"Under favour, my lord," said Tristan, with his usual brutality of manner, "the youth must find another guide. I cannot do without Petit-André when there is so like to be business on hand for him."

"The young man," said Petit-André, now coming forward, "has only to keep the path which lies straight before him, and it will conduct him to a place where he will find the man who is to act as his guide. I would not for a thousand ducats be absent from my chief this day! I have hanged knights and squires many a one, and wealthy echevins, and burgomasters to boot—even counts and marquisses have tasted of my handywork; but, a-humph——" He looked at the duke, as if to intimate that he would have filled up the blank with "a prince of the blood!" "Ho, ho, ho! Petit-André, thou wilt be read of in chronicle!"

"Do you permit your ruffians to hold such language in such a presence?" said Crawford, looking sternly to Tristan.

"Why do you not correct him yourself, my lord?" said Tristan, sullenly.

"Because thy hand is the only one in this company that can beat him without being degraded by such an action."

"Then rule your own men, my lord, and I will be answerable for mine," said the provost-marshal.

Lord Crawford seemed about to give a passionate reply; but, as if he had thought better of it, turned his back short upon Tristan, and requesting the Duke of Orleans and Dunois to ride one on either hand of him, he made a signal of adieu to the ladies, and said to Quentin: "God bless thee, my child; thou hast begun thy service valiantly, though in an unhappy cause." He was about to go off, when Quentin could hear Dunois whisper to Crawford, "Do you carry us to Plessis?"

"No, my unhappy and rash friend," answered Crawford, with a sigh, "to Loches."

"To Loches!" The name of a castle, or rather a prison, yet more dreaded than Plessis itself, fell like a death-toll upon the ear of the young Scotsman. He had heard it described as a place destined to the workings of those secret acts of cruelty with which even Louis shamed to pollute the interior of his own residence. There were in this place of terror dungeons under dungeons, some of them unknown even to the keepers themselves—living graves, to which men were consigned with little hope of farther employment during the rest of their life than to breathe impure air and feed on bread and water. At this formidable castle were also those dreadful places of confinement called "cages," in which the wretched prisoner could neither stand upright nor stretch himself at length—an invention, it is said, of the Cardinal Balue.[1] It is no wonder that the name of this place of horrors, and the consciousness that he had been partly the means of despatching thither two such illustrious victims, struck so much sadness into the heart of the young Scot that he rode for some time with his head dejected, his eyes fixed on the ground, and his heart filled with the most painful reflections.

As he was now again at the head of the little troop, and pursuing the road which had been pointed out to him, the Lady Hameline had an opportunity to say to him:

"Methinks, fair sir, you regret the victory which your gallantry has attained in our behalf?"

There was something in the question which sounded like irony, but Quentin had tact enough to answer simply and with sincerity:

"I can regret nothing that is done in the service of such ladies as you are; but, methinks, had it consisted with your safety, I had rather have fallen by the sword of so good a soldier as Dunois than have been the means of consigning that renowned knight and his unhappy chief, the Duke of Orleans, to yonder fearful dungeons."

"It *was*, then, the Duke of Orleans," said the elder lady, turning to her niece. "I thought so, even at the distance from which we beheld the fray. You see, kinswoman, what we might have been, had this sly and avaricious monarch permitted us to be seen at his court. The first prince of the blood of France, and the valiant Dunois, whose name is known as wide as that of his heroic father! This young gentleman did his devoir bravely and well; but methinks 'tis pity that he did not succumb with honour, since his ill-advised gallantry has stood betwixt us and these princely rescuers."

The Countess Isabelle replied in a firm and almost a dis-

[1] Who himself tenanted one of these dens for more than eleven years.

pleased tone, with an energy, in short, which Quentin had not yet observed her use.

"Madam," she said, "but that I know you jest, I would say your speech is ungrateful to our brave defender, to whom we owe more, perhaps, than you are aware of. Had these gentlemen succeeded so far in their rash enterprise as to have defeated our escort, is it not still evident that, on the arrival of the Royal Guard, we must have shared their captivity? For my own part, I give tears, and will soon bestow masses, on the brave man who has fallen, and I trust," she continued, more timidly, "that he who lives will accept my grateful thanks."

As Quentin turned his face towards her, to return the fitting acknowledgments, she saw the blood which streamed down on one side of his face, and exclaimed, in a tone of deep feeling: "Holy Virgin, he is wounded! he bleeds! Dismount, sir, and let your wound be bound up."

In spite of all that Durward could say of the slightness of his hurt, he was compelled to dismount, and to seat himself on a bank, and unhelmet himself, while the Ladies of Croye, who, according to a fashion not as yet antiquated, pretended to some knowledge of leechcraft, washed the wound, stanched the blood, and bound it with the kerchief of the younger countess, in order to exclude the air, for so their practice prescribed.

In modern times, gallants seldom or never take wounds for ladies' sake, and damsels on their side never meddle with the cure of wounds. Each has a danger the less. That which the men escape will be generally acknowledged; but the peril of dressing such a slight wound as that of Quentin's, which involved nothing formidable or dangerous, was perhaps as real in its way as the risk of encountering it.

We have already said the patient was eminently handsome; and the removal of his helmet, or, more properly, of his morion, had suffered his fair locks to escape in profusion around a countenance in which the hilarity of youth was qualified by a blush of modesty at once and pleasure. And then the feelings of the younger countess, when compelled to hold the kerchief to the wound, while her aunt sought in their baggage for some vulnerary remedy, were mingled at once with a sense of delicacy and embarrassment—a thrill of pity for the patient and of gratitude for his services, which exaggerated, in her eyes, his good mien and handsome features. In short, this incident seemed intended by Fate to complete the mysterious communication in which she had, by many petty and apparently accidental circumstances, established betwixt two persons who, though far different in rank and fortune, strongly resembled each other in youth, beauty, and the romantic tenderness of an affectionate disposition. It was no wonder, therefore, that from this moment the thoughts of the Countess Isabelle, already so familiar to his imagination, should become paramount in Quentin's bosom, nor that, if the maiden's feelings were of a less decided character, at least so far as known to herself, she should think of her younger defender, to whom she had just rendered a service so interesting, with more emotion than of any of the whole band of high-born nobles who had for two years past besieged her with their adoration. Above all, when the thought of Campo-basso, the unworthy favourite of Duke Charles, with his hypocritical mien, his base, treacherous spirit, his wry neck, and his squint, occurred to her, his portrait was more disgustingly hideous than ever, and deeply did she resolve no tyrannny should make her enter into so hateful a union.

In the mean time, whether the good Lady Hameline of Croye understood and admired masculine beauty as much as when she was fifteen years younger (for the good countess was at least thirty-five, if the records of that noble house speak the truth), or whether she thought she had done their young protector less justice than she ought, in the first view which she had taken of his services, it is certain that he began to find favour in her eyes.

"My niece," she said, "has bestowed on you a kerchief for the binding of your wound; I will give you one to grace your gallantry, and to encourage you in your farther progress in chivalry."

So saying, she gave him a richly embroidered kerchief of

blue and silver, and pointing to the housing of her palfrey and the plumes in her riding-cap, desired him to observe that the colours were the same.

The fashion of the time prescribed one absolute mode of receiving such a favour, which Quentin followed accordingly, by tying the napkin round his arm; yet his manner of acknowledgment had more of awkwardness and less of gallantry in it than perhaps it might have had at another time and in another presence; for though the wearing of a lady's favour, given in such a manner, was merely matter of general compliment, he would much rather have preferred the right of displaying on his arm that which bound the wound inflicted by the sword of Dunois.

Meantime, they continued their pilgrimage, Quentin now riding abreast of the ladies, into whose society he seemed to be tacitly adopted. He did not speak much, however, being filled by the silent consciousness of happiness, which is afraid of giving too strong vent to its feelings. The Countess Isabelle spoke still less, so that the conversation was chiefly carried on by the Lady Hameline, who showed no inclination to let it drop; for, to initiate the young archer, as she said, into the principles and practice of chivalry, she detailed to him, at full length, the passage of arms at Haflinghem, where she had distributed the prizes among the victors.

Not much interested, I am sorry to say, in the description of this splendid scene, or in the heraldic bearings of the different Flemish and German knights, which the lady blazoned with pitiless accuracy, Quentin began to entertain some alarm lest he should have passed the place where his guide was to join him—a most serious disaster, and from which, should it really have taken place, the very worst consequences were to be apprehended.

While he hesitated whether it would be better to send back one of his followers to see whether this might not be the case, he heard the blast of a horn, and looking in the direction from which the sound came, beheld a horseman riding very fast towards them. The low size and wild, shaggy, untrained state of the animal reminded Quentin of the mountain breed of horses in his own country; but this was much more finely limbed, and, with the same appearance of hardiness, was more rapid in its movements. The head particularly, which in the Scottish pony is often lumpish and heavy, was small and well placed in the neck of this animal, with thin jaws, full sparkling eyes, and expanded nostrils.

The rider was even more singular in his appearance than the horse which he rode, though that was extremely unlike the horses of France. Although he managed his palfrey with great dexterity, he sat with his feet in broad stirrups, something resembling shovels, so short in the leathers that his knees were wellnigh as high as the pommel of his saddle. His dress was a red turban of small size, in which he wore a sullied plume, secured by a clasp of silver; his tunic, which was shaped like those of the Estradiots—a sort of troops whom the Venetians at that time levied in the provinces on the eastern side of their gulf—was green in colour and tawdrily laced with gold; he wore very wide drawers or trowsers of white, though none of the cleanest, which gathered beneath the knees, and his swarthy legs were quite bare, unless for the complicated laces which bound a pair of sandals on his feet; he had no spurs, the edge of his large stirrups being so sharp as to serve to goad the horse in a very severe manner. In a crimson sash this singular horseman wore a dagger on the right side, and on the left a short crooked Moorish sword; and by a tarnished baldric over the shoulder hung the horn which announced his approach. He had a swarthy and sunburnt visage, with a thin beard, and piercing dark eyes, a well-formed mouth and nose, and other features which might have been pronounced handsome, but for the black elf-locks which hung around his face, and the air of wildness and emaciation, which rather seemed to indicate a savage than a civilised man.

"He also is a Bohemian!" said the ladies to each other. "Holy Mary, will the King again place confidence in these outcasts?"

"I will question the man, if it be your pleasure," said Quentin, "and assure myself of his fidelity as I best may."

Durward, as well as the Ladies of Croye, had recognised in this man's dress and appearance the habit and the manners of those vagrants with whom he had nearly been confounded by the hasty proceedings of Trois-Eschelles and Petit-André, and he, too, entertained very natural apprehensions concerning the risk of reposing trust in one of that vagrant race.

"Art thou come hither to seek us?" was his first question.

The stranger nodded.

"And for what purpose?"

"To guide you to the palace of him of Liege."

"Of the bishop?"

The Bohemian again nodded.

"What token canst thou give me that we should yield credence to thee?"

"Even the old rhyme, and no other," answered the Bohemian:

> "The page slew the boar,
> The peer had the gloire."

"A true token," said Quentin. "Lead on, good fellow; I will speak further with thee presently." Then falling back to the ladies, he said: "I am convinced this man is the guide we are to expect, for he hath brought me a password known, I think, but to the King and me. But I will discourse with him further, and endeavour to ascertain how far he is to be trusted."

CHAPTER XVI.

THE VAGRANT.

> I am as free as Nature first made man,
> Ere the base laws of servitude began,
> When wild in woods the noble savage ran.
> *The Conquest of Granada.*

WHILE Quentin held the brief communication with the ladies necessary to assure them that this extraordinary addition to their party was the guide whom they were to expect on the King's part, he noticed, for he was as alert in observing the motions of the stranger as the Bohemian could be on his part, that the man not only turned his head as far back as he could to peer at them, but that, with a singular sort of agility more resembling that of a monkey than of a man, he had screwed his whole person around on the saddle, so as to sit almost sidelong upon the horse, for the convenience, as it seemed, of watching them more attentively.

Not greatly pleased with this manœuvre, Quentin rode up to the Bohemian, and said to him, as he suddenly assumed his proper position on the horse: "Methinks, friend, you will prove but a blind guide if you look at the tail of your horse rather than his ears."

"And if I were actually blind," answered the Bohemian, "I could not the less guide you through any country in this realm of France or in those adjoining to it."

"Yet you are no Frenchman born," said the Scot.

"I am not," answered the guide.

"What countryman, then, are you?" demanded Quentin.

"I am of no country," answered the guide.

"How! of no country?" repeated the Scot.

"No," answered the Bohemian, "of none. I am a Zingaro, a Bohemian, an Egyptian, or whatever the Europeans, in their different languages, may choose to call our people; but I have no country."

"Are you a Christian?" asked the Scotchman.

The Bohemian shook his head.

"Dog!" said Quentin, for there was little toleration in the spirit of Catholicism in those days, "dost thou worship Mahound?"

"No," was the indifferent and concise answer of the guide, who neither seemed offended or surprised at the young man's violence of manner.

"Are you a pagan, then, or what are you?"

"I have no religion,"[1] answered the Bohemian.

Durward started back; for, though he had heard of Saracens and idolaters, it had never entered into his ideas or belief that any body of men could exist who practised no mode of

[1] See Religion of the Bohemians. Note 26.

worship whatever. He recovered from his astonishment, to ask his guide where he usually dwelt.

"Wherever I chance to be for the time," replied the Bohemian. "I have no home."

"How do you guard your property?"

"Excepting the clothes which I wear and the horse I ride on, I have no property."

"Yet you dress gaily and ride gallantly," said Durward. "What are your means of subsistence?"

"I eat when I am hungry, drink when I am thirsty, and have no other means of subsistence than chance throws in my way," replied the vagabond.

"Under whose laws do you live?"

"I acknowledge obedience to none, but as it suits my pleasure or my necessities," said the Bohemian.

"Who is your leader, and commands you?"

"The father of our tribe, if I choose to obey him," said the guide; "otherwise I have no commander."

"You are then," said the wondering querist, "destitute of all that other men are combined by: you have no law, no leader, no settled means of subsistence, no house or home. You have, may Heaven compassionate you, no country; and, may Heaven enlighten and forgive you, you have no God! What is it that remains to you, deprived of government, domestic happiness, and religion?"

"I have liberty," said the Bohemian. "I crouch to no one—obey no one—respect no one. I go where I will—live as I can—and die when my day comes."

"But you are subject to instant execution, at the pleasure of the judge?"

"Be it so," returned the Bohemian; "I can but die so much the sooner."

"And to imprisonment also," said the Scot; "and where then is your boasted freedom?"

"In my thoughts," said the Bohemian, "which no chains can bind; while yours, even when your limbs are free, remain fettered by your laws and your superstitions, your dreams of local attachment and your fantastic visions of civil policy.

Such as I are free in spirit when our limbs are chained. You are imprisoned in mind, even when your limbs are most at freedom."

"Yet the freedom of your thoughts," said the Scot, "relieves not the pressure of the gyves on your limbs."

"For a brief time that may be endured," answered the vagrant; "and if within that period I cannot extricate myself, and fail of relief from my comrades, I can always die, and death is the most perfect freedom of all."

There was a deep pause of some duration, which Quentin at length broke by resuming his queries.

"Yours is a wandering race, unknown to the nations of Europe. Whence do they derive their origin?"

"I may not tell you," answered the Bohemian.

"When will they relieve this kingdom from their presence, and return to the land from whence they came?" said the Scot.

"When the day of their pilgrimage shall be accomplished," replied his vagrant guide.

"Are you not sprung from those tribes of Israel which were carried into captivity beyond the great river Euphrates?" said Quentin, who had not forgotten the lore which had been taught him at Aberbrothock.

"Had we been so," answered the Bohemian, "we had followed their faith and practised their rites."

"What is thine own name?" said Durward.

"My proper name is only known to my brethren. The men beyond our tents call me Hayraddin Maugrabin, that is, Hayraddin the African Moor."

"Thou speakest too well for one who hath lived always in thy filthy horde," said the Scot.

"I have learned some of the knowledge of this land," said Hayraddin. "When I was a little boy, our tribe was chased by the hunters after human flesh. An arrow went through my mother's head, and she died. I was entangled in the blanket on her shoulders, and was taken by the pursuers. A priest begged me from the provost's archers, and trained me up in Frankish learning for two or three years."

"How came you to part with him?" demanded Durward.

"I stole money from him—even the god which he worshipped," answered Hayraddin, with perfect composure; "he detected me, and beat me; I stabbed him with my knife, fled to the woods, and was again united to my people."

"Wretch!" said Durward, "did you murder your benefactor?"

"What had he to do to burden me with his benefits? The Zingaro boy was no house-bred cur, to dog the heels of his master, and crouch beneath his blows, for scraps of food. He was the imprisoned wolf-whelp, which at the first opportunity broke his chain, rended his master, and returned to his wilderness."

There was another pause, when the young Scot, with a view of still farther investigating the character and purpose of this suspicious guide, asked Hayraddin: "Whether it was not true that his people, amid their ignorance, pretended to a knowledge of futurity, which was not given to the sages, philosophers, and divines of more polished society?"

"We pretend to it," said Hayraddin, "and it is with justice."

"How can it be that so high a gift is bestowed on so abject a race?" said Quentin.

"Can I tell you?" answered Hayraddin. "Yes, I may indeed; but it is when you shall explain to me why the dog can trace the footsteps of a man, while man, the nobler animal, hath not power to trace those of the dog. These powers, which seem to you so wonderful, are instinctive in our race. From the lines on the face and on the hand we can tell the future fate of those who consult us, even as surely as you know from the blossom of the tree in spring what fruit it will bear in the harvest."

"I doubt of your knowledge, and defy you to the proof."

"Defy me not, sir squire," said Hayraddin Maugrabin. "I can tell you that, say what you will of your religion, the goddess whom you worship rides in this company."

"Peace!" said Quentin, in astonishment: "on thy life, not a word farther, but in answer to what I ask thee. Canst thou be faithful?"

"I can; all men can," said the Bohemian.

"But *wilt* thou be faithful?"

"Wouldst thou believe me the more should I swear it?" answered Maugrabin, with a sneer.

"Thy life is in my hand," said the young Scot.

"Strike, and see whether I fear to die," answered the Bohemian.

"Will money render thee a trusty guide?" demanded Durward.

"If I be not such without it, no," replied the heathen.

"Then what will bind thee?" asked the Scot.

"Kindness," replied the Bohemian.

"Shall I swear to show thee such, if thou art true guide to us on this pilgrimage?"

"No," replied Hayraddin, "it were extravagant waste of a commodity so rare. To thee I am bound already."

"How!" exclaimed Durward, more surprised than ever.

"Remember the chestnut-trees on the banks of the Cher. The victim whose body thou didst cut down was my brother, Zamet, the Maugrabin."

"And yet," said Quentin, "I find you in correspondence with those very officers by whom your brother was done to death; for it was one of them who directed me where to meet with you—the same, doubtless, who procured yonder ladies your services as a guide."

"What can we do?" answered Hayraddin, gloomily. "These men deal with us as the sheep-dogs do with the flock: they protect us for a while, drive us hither and thither at their pleasure, and always end by guiding us to the shambles."

Quentin had afterwards occasion to learn that the Bohemian spoke truth in this particular, and that the provost-guard, employed to suppress the vagabond bands by which the kingdom was infested, entertained correspondence among them, and forbore, for a certain time, the exercise of their duty, which always at last ended in conducting their allies to the gallows. This is a sort of political relation between thief and officer, for the profitable exercise of their mutual professions, which has subsisted in all countries, and is by no means unknown to our own.

Durward, parting from the guide, fell back to the rest of the retinue, very little satisfied with the character of Hayraddin, and entertaining little confidence in the professions of gratitude which he had personally made to him. He proceeded to sound the other two men who had been assigned him for attendants, and he was concerned to find them stupid, and as unfit to assist him with counsel as in the encounter they had shown themselves reluctant to use their weapons.

"It is all the better," said Quentin to himself, his spirit rising with the apprehended difficulties of his situation; "that lovely young lady shall owe all to me. What one hand—ay, and one head—can do, methinks I can boldly count upon. I have seen my father's house on fire, and him and my brothers lying dead amongst the flames. I gave not an inch back, but fought it out to the last. Now I am two years older, and have the best and fairest cause to bear me well that ever kindled mettle within a brave man's bosom."

Acting upon this resolution, the attention and activity which Quentin bestowed during the journey had in it something that gave him the appearance of ubiquity. His principal and most favourite post was of course by the side of the ladies, who, sensible of his extreme attention to their safety, began to converse with him in almost the tone of familiar friendship, and appeared to take great pleasure in the naïveté, yet shrewdness, of his conversation. But Quentin did not suffer the fascination of this intercourse to interfere with the vigilant discharge of his duty.

If he was often by the side of the countesses, labouring to describe to the natives of a level country the Grampian Mountains, and, above all, the beauties of Glen Houlakin, he was as often riding with Hayraddin in front of the cavalcade, questioning him about the road and the resting-places, and recording his answers in his mind, to ascertain whether upon cross-examination he could discover anything like meditated treachery. As often again he was in the rear, endeavouring to secure the attachment of the two horsemen, by kind words, gifts, and promises of additional recompense when their task should be accomplished.

In this way they travelled for more than a week, through bye-paths and unfrequented districts, and by circuitous routes, in order to avoid large towns. Nothing remarkable occurred, though they now and then met strolling gangs of Bohemians, who respected them as under the conduct of one of their tribe; straggling soldiers, or perhaps banditti, who deemed their party too strong to be attacked; or parties of the Maré-chaussée, as they would now be termed, whom Louis, who searched the wounds of the land with steel and cautery, employed to suppress the disorderly bands which infested the interior. These last suffered them to pursue their way unmolested, by virtue of a password with which Quentin had been furnished for that purpose by the King himself.

Their resting-places were chiefly the monasteries, most of which were obliged by the rules of their foundation to receive pilgrims, under which character the ladies travelled, with hospitality, and without any troublesome inquiries into their rank and character, which most persons of distinction were desirous of concealing while in the discharge of their vows. The pretence of weariness was usually employed by the Countesses of Croye as an excuse for instantly retiring to rest, and Quentin, as their major-domo, arranged all that was necessary betwixt them and their entertainers with a shrewdness which saved them all trouble, and an alacrity that failed not to excite a corresponding degree of good-will on the part of those who were thus sedulously attended to.

One circumstance gave Quentin peculiar trouble, which was the character and nation of his guide, who, as a heathen and an infidel vagabond, addicted, besides, to occult arts (the badge of all his tribe), was often looked upon as a very improper guest for the holy resting-places at which the company usually halted, and was not in consequence admitted within even the outer circuit of their walls save with extreme reluctance. This was very embarrassing; for, on the one hand, it was necessary to keep in good humour a man who was possessed of the secret of their expedition; and on the other,

Quentin deemed it indispensable to maintain a vigilant though secret watch on Hayraddin's conduct, in order that, as far as might be, he should hold no communication with any one without being observed. This, of course, was impossible if the Bohemian was lodged without the precincts of the convent at which they stopped, and Durward could not help thinking that Hayraddin was desirous of bringing about this latter arrangement, for, instead of keeping himself still and quiet in the quarters allotted to him, his conversation, tricks, and songs were at the same time so entertaining to the novices and younger brethren and so unedifying in the opinion of the seniors of the fraternity, that, in more cases than one, it required all the authority, supported by threats, which Quentin could exert over him to restrain his irreverent and untimeous jocularity, and all the interest he could make with the superiors to prevent the heathen hound from being thrust out of doors. He succeeded, however, by the adroit manner in which he apologised for the acts of indecorum committed by their attendant, and the skill with which he hinted the hope of his being brought to a better sense of principles and behaviour by the neighbourhood of holy relics, consecrated buildings, and, above all, of men dedicated to religion.

But upon the tenth or twelfth day of their journey, after they had entered Flanders and were approaching the town of Namur, all the efforts of Quentin became inadequate to suppress the consequences of the scandal given by his heathen guide. The scene was a Franciscan convent, and of a strict and reformed order, and the prior a man who afterwards died in the odour of sanctity. After rather more than the usual scruples, which were indeed in such a case to be expected, had been surmounted, the obnoxious Bohemian at length obtained quarters in an outhouse inhabited by a lay brother who acted as gardener. The ladies retired to their apartment, as usual, and the prior, who chanced to have some distant alliances and friends in Scotland, and who was fond of hearing foreigners tell of their native countries, invited Quentin, with whose mien and conduct he seemed much pleased, to a slight monastic refection in his own cell. Finding the father a man of intelligence, Quentin did not neglect the opportunity of making himself acquainted with the state of affairs in the country of Liege, of which, during the last two days of their journey, he had heard such reports as made him very apprehensive for the security of his charge during the remainder of their route, nay, even of the bishop's power to protect them when they should be safely conducted to his residence. The replies of the prior were not very consolatory.

He said that "The people of Liege were wealthy burghers who, like Jeshurun of old, had waxed fat and kicked; that they were uplifted in heart because of their wealth and their privileges; that they had divers disputes with the Duke of Burgundy, their liege lord, upon the subject of imposts and immunities; and that they had repeatedly broken out into open mutiny, whereat the Duke was so much incensed, as being a man of a hot and fiery nature, that he had sworn by St. George on the next provocation he would make the city of Liege like to the desolation of Babylon and the downfall of Tyre, a hissing and a reproach to the whole territory of Flanders."

"And he is a prince, by all report, likely to keep such a vow," said Quentin, "so the men of Liege will probably beware how they give him occasion."

"It were to be so hoped," said the prior; "and such are the prayers of the godly in the land, who would not that the blood of the citizens were poured forth like water and that they should perish, even as utter castaways, ere they make their peace with Heaven. Also the good bishop labours night and day to preserve peace, as well becometh a servant of the altar; for it is written in Holy Scripture, *Beati pacifici*. But——" here the good prior stopped with a deep sigh.

Quentin modestly urged the great importance of which it was to the ladies whom he attended to have some assured information respecting the internal state of the country, and what an act of Christian charity it would be if the worthy and reverend father would enlighten them upon that subject.

"It is one," said the prior, "on which no man speaks with willingness; for those who speak evil of the powerful, *etiam in cubiculo*, may find that a winged thing shall carry the matter to his ears. Nevertheless, to render you, who seem an ingenuous youth, and your ladies, who are devout votaresses accomplishing a holy pilgrimage, the little service that is in my power, I will be plain with you."

He then looked cautiously round, and lowered his voice, as if afraid of being overheard.

"The people of Liege," he said, "are privily instigated to their frequent mutinies by men of Belial, who pretend, but, as I hope, falsely, to have commission to that effect from our Most Christian King, whom, however, I hold to deserve that term better than were consistent with his thus disturbing the peace of a neighbouring state. Yet so it is, that his name is freely used by those who uphold and inflame the discontents at Liege. There is, moreover, in the land a nobleman of good descent and fame in warlike affairs, but otherwise, so to speak, *lapis offensionis et petra scandali*—a stumbling-block of offence to the countries of Burgundy and Flanders. His name is William de la Marck."

"Called William with the Beard," said the young Scot, "or the Wild Boar of Ardennes?"

"And rightly so called, my son," said the prior; "because he is as the wild boar of the forest, which treadeth down with his hoofs and rendeth with his tusks. And he hath formed to himself a band of more than a thousand men, all, like himself, contemners of civil and ecclesiastical authority, and holds himself independent of the Duke of Burgundy, and maintains himself and his followers by rapine and wrong, wrought without distinction upon churchmen and laymen. *Imposuit manus in Christos Domini:* he hath stretched forth his hand upon the Anointed of the Lord, regardless of what is written— 'Touch not mine Anointed, and do my prophets no wrong.' Even to our poor house did he send for sums of gold and sums of silver as a ransom for our lives, and those of our brethren; to which we returned a Latin supplication, stating our inability to answer his demand, and exhorting him in the words of the preacher, *Ne moliaris amico tuo malum, cum habet in te fiduciam.* Nevertheless, this Gulielmus Barbatus, this William de la Marck, as completely ignorant of humane letters as of humanity itself, replied, in his ridiculous jargon, '*Si non payatis, brulabo monasterium vestrum.*' " [1]

"Of which rude Latin, however, you, my good father," said the youth, "were at no loss to conceive the meaning?"

"Alas, my son," said the prior, "fear and necessity are shrewd interpreters; and we were obliged to melt down the silver vessels of our altar to satisfy the rapacity of this cruel chief. May Heaven requite it to him sevenfold! *Pereat improbus. Amen—amen, anathema esto!*"

"I marvel," said Quentin, "that the Duke of Burgundy, who is so strong and powerful, doth not bait this boar to purpose, of whose ravages I have already heard so much."

"Alas! my son," said the prior, "the Duke Charles is now at Péronne, assembling his captains of hundreds and his captains of thousands, to make war against France; and thus, while Heaven hath set discord between the hearts of those great princes, the country is misused by such subordinate oppressors. But it is in evil time that the Duke neglects the cure of these internal gangrenes; for this William de la Marck hath of late entertained open communication with Rouslaer and Pavilion, the chiefs of the discontented at Liege, and it is to be feared he will soon stir them up to some desperate enterprise."

"But the Bishop of Liege," said Quentin, "he hath still power enough to subdue this disquieted and turbulent spirit, hath he not, good father? Your answer to this question concerns me much."

"The bishop, my child," replied the prior, "hath the sword of St. Peter as well as the keys. He hath power as a secular prince, and he hath the protection of the mighty house of Burgundy; he hath also spiritual authority as a prelate, and he supports both with a reasonable force of good soldiers and men-at-arms. This William de la Marck was bred in his household, and bound to him by many benefits. But he gave

---

[1] A similar story is told of the Duke of Vendôme, who answered in this sort of macaronic Latin the classical expostulations of a German convent against the imposition of a contribution.

vent, even in the court of the bishop, to his fierce and bloodthirsty temper, and was expelled thence for a homicide, committed on one of the bishop's chief domestics. From thenceforward, being banished from the good prelate's presence, he hath been his constant and unrelenting foe; and now, I grieve to say, he hath girded his loins and strengthened his horn against him."

"You consider, then, the situation of the worthy prelate as being dangerous?" said Quentin, very anxiously.

"Alas! my son," said the good Franciscan, "what or who is there in this weary wilderness whom we may not hold as in danger? But Heaven forefend I should speak of the reverend prelate as one whose peril is imminent. He has much treasure, true counsellors, and brave soldiers; and, moreover, a messenger who passed hither to the eastward yesterday saith that the Duke of Burgundy hath despatched, upon the bishop's request, an hundred men-at-arms to his assistance. This reinforcement, with the retinue belonging to each lance, are enough to deal with William de la Marck, on whose name be sorrow! Amen."

At this crisis their conversation was interrupted by the sacristan, who, in a voice almost inarticulate with anger, accused the Bohemian of having practised the most abominable arts of delusion among the younger brethren. He had added to their nightly meal cups of a heady and intoxicating cordial of ten times the strength of the most powerful wine, under which several of the fraternity had succumbed; and, indeed, although the sacristan had been strong to resist its influence, they might yet see, from his inflamed countenance and thick speech, that even he, the accuser himself, was in some degree affected by this unhallowed potation. Moreover, the Bohemian had sung songs of worldly vanity and impure pleasures; he had derided the cord of St. Francis, made jests of his miracles, and termed his votaries fools and lazy knaves. Lastly, he had practised palmistry, and foretold to the young Father Cherubin that he was beloved by a beautiful lady, who should make him father to a thriving boy.

The father prior listened to these complaints for some time

in silence, as struck with mute horror by their enormous atrocity. When the sacristan had concluded, he rose up, descended to the court of the convent, and ordered the lay brethren, on pain of the worst consequences of spiritual disobedience, to beat Hayraddin out of the sacred precincts with their broom-staves and cart-whips.

This sentence was executed accordingly, in the presence of Quentin Durward, who, however vexed at the occurrence, easily saw that his interference would be of no avail.

The discipline inflicted upon the delinquent, notwithstanding the exhortations of the superior, was more ludicrous than formidable. The Bohemian ran hither and thither through the court, amongst the clamour of voices and noise of blows, some of which reached him not, because purposely misaimed; others, sincerely designed for his person, were eluded by his activity; and the few that fell upon his back and shoulders he took without either complaint or reply. The noise and riot was the greater, that the inexperienced cudgel-players, among whom Hayraddin ran the gauntlet, hit each other more frequently than they did him; till at length, desirous of ending a scene which was more scandalous than edifying, the prior commanded the wicket to be flung open, and the Bohemian, darting through it with the speed of lightning, fled forth into the moonlight.

During this scene, a suspicion which Durward had formerly entertained recurred with additional strength. Hayraddin had, that very morning, promised to him more modest and discreet behaviour than he was wont to exhibit when they rested in a convent on their journey; yet he had broken his engagement, and had been even more offensively obstreperous than usual. Something probably lurked under this; for whatever were the Bohemian's deficiencies, he lacked neither sense nor, when he pleased, self-command; and might it not be probable that he wished to hold some communication, either with his own horde or some one else, from which he was debarred in the course of the day by the vigilance with which he was watched by Quentin, and had recourse to this stratagem in order to get himself turned out of the convent?

No sooner did this suspicion dart once more through Durward's mind than, alert as he always was in his motions, he resolved to follow his cudgelled guide, and observe, secretly if possible, how he disposed of himself. Accordingly, when the Bohemian fled, as already mentioned, out at the gate of the convent, Quentin, hastily explaining to the prior the necessity of keeping sight of his guide, followed in pursuit of him.

CHAPTER XVII.

THE ESPIED SPY.

> What, the rue ranger? and spied spy? Hands off—
> You are for no such rustics.
>   BEN JONSON'S *Tale of Robin Hood.*

WHEN Quentin sallied from the convent, he could mark the precipitate retreat of the Bohemian, whose dark figure was seen in the far moonlight, flying with the speed of a flogged hound quite through the street of the little village, and across the level meadow that lay beyond.

"My friend runs fast," said Quentin to himself; "but he must run faster yet to escape the fleetest foot that ever pressed the heather of Glen Houlakin."

Being fortunately without his cloak and armour, the Scottish mountaineer was at liberty to put forth a speed which was unrivalled in his own glens, and which, notwithstanding the rate at which the Bohemian ran, was likely soon to bring his pursuer up with him. This was not, however, Quentin's object; for he considered it more essential to watch Hayraddin's motions than to interrupt them. He was the rather led to this by the steadiness with which the Bohemian directed his course; and which continuing, even after the impulse of the violent expulsion had subsided, seemed to indicate that his career had some more certain goal for its object than could have suggested itself to a person unexpectedly turned out of good quarters when midnight was approaching, to seek a new place of repose. He never even looked behind him; and consequently Durward was enabled to follow him unobserved. At length the Bohemian having traversed the meadow, and attained the side of a little stream, the banks of which were clothed with alders and willows, Quentin observed that he stood still, and blew a low note on his horn, which was answered by a whistle at some little distance.

"This is a rendezvous," thought Quentin; "but how shall I come near enough to overhear the import of what passes? The sound of my steps, and the rustling of the boughs through which I must force my passage, will betray me, unless I am cautious. I will stalk them, by St. Andrew, as if they were Glen Isla deer; they shall learn that I have not conned woodcraft for nought. Yonder they meet, the two shadows—and two of them there are—odds against me if I am discovered, and if their purpose be unfriendly, as is much to be doubted. And then the Countess Isabelle loses her poor friend! Well, and he were not worthy to be called such, if he were not ready to meet a dozen in her behalf. Have I not crossed swords with Dunois, the best knight in France, and shall I fear a tribe of yonder vagabonds? Pshaw! God and St. Andrew to friend, they will find me both stout and wary."

Thus resolving, and with a degree of caution taught him by his silvan habits, our friend descended into the channel of the little stream, which varied in depth, sometimes scarce covering his shoes, sometimes coming up to his knees, and so crept along, his form concealed by the boughs overhanging the bank, and his steps unheard amid the ripple of the water. (We have ourselves, in the days of yore, thus approached the nest of the wakeful raven.) In this manner, the Scot drew near unperceived, until he distinctly heard the voices of those who were the subject of his observation, though he could not distinguish the words. Being at this time under the drooping branches of a magnificent weeping willow, which almost swept the surface of the water, he caught hold of one of its boughs, by the assistance of which, exerting at once much agility, dexterity, and strength, he raised himself up into the body of the tree, and sat, secure from discovery, among the central branches.

From this situation he could discover that the person with whom Hayraddin was now conversing was one of his own tribe, and, at the same time, he perceived, to his great disappointment, that no approximation could enable him to comprehend their language, which was totally unknown to him. They laughed much; and as Hayraddin made a sign of skipping about, and ended by rubbing his shoulder with his hand, Durward had no doubt that he was relating the story of the bastinading which he had sustained previous to his escape from the convent.

On a sudden, a whistle was again heard in the distance, which was once more answered by a low tone or two of Hayraddin's horn. Presently afterwards, a tall, stout, soldierly-looking man, a strong contrast in point of thewes and sinews to the small and slender-limbed Bohemians, made his appearance. He had a broad baldric over his shoulder, which sustained a sword that hung almost across his person; his hose were much slashed, through which slashes was drawn silk or tiffany of various colours; they were tied by at least five hundred points or strings, made of ribbon, to the tight buff-jacket which he wore, and the right sleeve of which displayed a silver boar's head, the crest of this captain. A very small hat sat jauntily on one side of his head, from which descended a quantity of curled hair, which fell on each side of a broad face, and mingled with as broad a beard, about four inches long. He held a long lance in his hand; and his whole equipment was that of one of the German adventurers, who were known by the name of *lanzknechts*, in English "spearmen," who constituted a formidable part of the infantry of the period. These mercenaries were, of course, a fierce and rapacious soldiery, and having an idle tale current among themselves that a *lanzknecht* was refused admittance into Heaven on account of his vices, and into Hell on the score of his tumultuous, mutinous, and insubordinate disposition, they manfully acted as if they neither sought the one nor eschewed the other.

"*Donner and blitz!*" was his first salutation, in a sort of German-French, which we can only imperfectly imitate, "why have you kept me dancing in attendance dis dree nights?"

"I could not see you sooner, Meinherr," said Hayraddin, very submissively: "there is a young Scot, with as quick an eye as the wild-cat, who watches my least motions. He suspects me already, and, should he find his suspicion confirmed, I were a dead man on the spot, and he would carry back the women into France again."

"*Was henker!*" said the lanzknecht; "we are three—we will attack them to-morrow, and carry the women off without going farther. You said the two valets were cowards; you and your comrade may manage them, and the *Teufel* sall hold me, but I match your Scots wild-cat."

"You will find that foolhardy," said Hayraddin; "for, besides that we ourselves count not much in fighting, this spark hath matched himself with the best knight in France, and come off with honour: I have seen those who saw him press Dunois hard enough."

"*Hagel and sturmwetter!* It is but your cowardice that speaks," said the German soldier.

"I am no more a coward than yourself," said Hayraddin; "but my trade is not fighting. If you keep the appointment where it was laid, it is well; if not, I guide them safely to the bishop's palace, and William de la Marck may easily possess himself of them there, provided he is half as strong as he pretended a week since."

"*Potz tausend!*" said the soldier, "we are as strong and stronger; but we hear of a hundred of the lances of Burgundy —*das ist*, see you, five men to a lance do make five hundreds, and then hold me the devil, they will be fainer to seek for us than we to seek for them; for *der bischoff* hath a goot force on footing—ay, indeed!"

"You must then hold to the ambuscade at the Cross of the Three Kings, or give up the adventure," said the Bohemian.

"*Geb* up—*geb* up the adventure of the rich bride for our noble *hauptmann*. *Teufel!* I will charge through hell first. *Mein* soul, we will be all princes and *hertzogs*, whom they call dukes, and we will hab a snab at the *weinkeller*, and at the mouldy French crowns, and it may be at the pretty garces too, when He with de Beard is weary on them."

"The ambuscade at the Cross of the Three Kings then still holds?" said the Bohemian.

"*Mein Gott*, ay,—you will swear to bring them there; and when they are on their knees before the cross, and down from off their horses, which all men do, except such black heathens as thou, we will make in on them, and they are ours."

"Ay, but I promised this piece of necessary villainy only on one condition," said Hayraddin. "I will not have a hair of the young man's head touched. If you swear this to me, by your Three Dead Men of Cologne, I will swear to you, by the Seven Night Walkers, that I will serve you truly as to the rest. And if you break your oath, the Night Walkers shall wake you seven nights from your sleep, between night and morning, and, on the eighth, they shall strangle and devour you."

"But, *donner and hagel*, what need you be so curious about the life of this boy, who is neither your bloot nor kin?" said the German.

"No matter for that, honest Heinrich; some men have pleasure in cutting throats, some in keeping them whole. So swear to me that you will spare him life and limb, or, by the bright star Aldebaran, this matter shall go no further. Swear, and by the Three Kings, as you call them, of Cologne; I know you care for no other oath."

"*Du bist ein comischer mann*," said the lanzknecht, "I swear——"

"Not yet," said the Bohemian. "Face about, brave lanzknecht, and look to the east, else the kings may not hear you."

The soldier took the oath in the manner prescribed, and then declared that he would be in readiness, observing the place was quite convenient, being scarce five miles from their present leaguer.

"But, were it not making sure work to have a *fähnlein* of riders on the other road, by the left side of the inn, which might trap them if they go that way?"

The Bohemian considered a moment, and then answered:

"No; the appearance of their troops in that direction might alarm the garrison of Namur, and then they would have a doubtful fight, instead of assured success. Besides, they shall travel on the right bank of the Maes, for I can guide them which way I will; for, sharp as this same Scottish mountaineer is, he hath never asked any one's advice save mine upon the direction of their route. Undoubtedly, I was assigned to him by an assured friend, whose word no man mistrusts till they come to know him a little."

"Hark ye, friend Hayraddin," said the soldier, "I would ask you somewhat. You and your *bruder* were, as you say yourself, *gross sternendeuter*, that is, star-lookers and *geister-seers*. Now, what *henker* was it made you not foresee him, your *bruder* Zamet, to be hanged?"

"I will tell you, Heinrich," said Hayraddin; "if I could have known my brother was such a fool as to tell the counsel of King Louis to Duke Charles of Burgundy, I could have foretold his death as sure as I can foretell fair weather in July. Louis hath both ears and hands at the court of Burgundy, and Charles's counsellors love the chink of French gold as well as thou dost the clatter of a wine-pot. But fare thee well, and keep appointment; I must await my early Scot a bow-shot without the gate of the den of the lazy swine yonder, else will he think me about some excursion which bodes no good to the success of his journey."

"Take a draught of comfort first," said the lanzknecht, tendering him a flask; "but I forget, thou art beast enough to drink nothing but water, like a vile vassal of Mahound and Termagund."

"Thou art thyself a vassal of the wine-measure and the flagon," said the Bohemian. "I marvel not that thou art only trusted with the bloodthirsty and violent part of executing what better heads have devised. He must drink no wine who would know the thoughts of others or hide his own. But why preach to thee, who hast a thirst as eternal as a sand-bank in Arabia? Fare thee well. Take my comrade Tuisco with thee: his appearance about the monastery may breed suspicion."

The two worthies parted, after each had again pledged himself to keep the rendezvous at the Cross of the Three Kings.

Quentin Durward watched until they were out of sight, and then descended from his place of concealment, his heart throbbing at the narrow escape which he and his fair charge had made—if, indeed, it could yet be achieved—from a deep-laid plan of villainy. Afraid, on his return to the monastery, of stumbling upon Hayraddin, he made a long detour, at the expense of traversing some very rough ground, and was thus enabled to return to his asylum on a different point from that by which he left it.

On the route, he communed earnestly with himself concerning the safest plan to be pursued. He had formed the resolution, when he first heard Hayraddin avow his treachery, to put him to death so soon as the conference broke up, and his companions were at a sufficient distance; but when he heard the Bohemian express so much interest in saving his own life, he felt it would be ungrateful to execute upon him, in its rigour, the punishment his treachery had deserved. He therefore resolved to spare his life, and even, if possible, still to use his services as a guide, under such precautions as should ensure the security of the precious charge, to the preservation of which his own life was internally devoted.

But whither were they to turn? The Countesses of Croye could neither obtain shelter in Burgundy, from which they had fled, nor in France, from which they had been in a manner expelled. The violence of Duke Charles in the one country was scarcely more to be feared than the cold and tyrannical policy of King Louis in the other. After deep thought, Durward could form no better or safer plan for their security than that, evading the ambuscade, they should take the road to Liege by the left hand of the Maes, and throw themselves, as the ladies originally designed, upon the protection of the excellent bishop. That prelate's will to protect them could not be doubted, and, if reinforced by this Burgundian party of men-at-arms, he might be considered as having the power. At any rate, if the dangers to which he was exposed from the hostility of William de la Marck, and from the troubles in the city of Liege, appeared imminent, he would still be able to protect the unfortunate ladies until they could be despatched to Germany with a suitable escort.

To sum up this reasoning—for when is a mental argument conducted without some reference to selfish considerations?—Quentin imagined that the death or captivity to which King Louis had, in cold blood, consigned him set him at liberty from his engagements to the crown of France; which, therefore, it was his determined purpose to renounce. The Bishop of Liege was likely, he concluded, to need soldiers, and he thought that, by the interposition of his fair friends, who now, especially the elder countess, treated him with much familiarity, he might get some command, and perhaps might have the charge of conducting the Ladies of Croye to some place more safe than the neighbourhood of Liege. And, to conclude, the ladies had talked, although almost in a sort of jest, of raising the countess's own vassals, and, as others did in those stormy times, fortifying her strong castle against all assailants whatever; they had jestingly asked Quentin, whether he would accept the perilous office of their seneschal; and, on his embracing the office with ready glee and devotion, they had, in the same spirit, permitted him to kiss both their hands on that confidential and honourable appointment. Nay, he thought that the hand of the Countess Isabelle, one of the best formed and most beautiful to which true vassal ever did such homage, trembled when his lips rested on it a moment longer than ceremony required, and that some confusion appeared on her cheek and in her eye as she withdrew it. Something might come of all this; and what brave man, at Quentin Durward's age, but would gladly have taken the thoughts which it awakened into the considerations which were to determine his conduct?

This point settled, he had next to consider in what degree he was to use the further guidance of the faithless Bohemian. He had renounced his first thought of killing him in the wood, and if he took another guide and dismissed him alive, it would be sending the traitor to the camp of William de la Marck with intelligence of their motions. He thought of taking the prior into his counsels, and requesting him to detain the Bohemian by force until they should have time to reach the Bishop's castle; but, on reflection, he dared not hazard such a proposition to one who was timid both as an old man and a friar, who held the safety of his convent the most important object of his duty, and who trembled at the mention of the Wild Boar of Ardennes.

At length Durward settled a plan of operation, on which he could the better reckon, as the execution rested entirely upon himself; and, in the cause in which he was engaged, he felt himself capable of everything. With a firm and bold heart, though conscious of the dangers of his situation, Quentin might be compared to one walking under a load, of the weight of which he is conscious, but which yet is not beyond his strength and power of endurance. Just as his plan was determined, he reached the convent.

Upon knocking gently at the gate, a brother, considerately stationed for that purpose by the prior, opened it, and acquainted him that the brethren were to be engaged in the choir till daybreak, praying Heaven to forgive to the community the various scandals which had that evening taken place among them.

The worthy friar offered Quentin permission to attend their devotions; but his clothes were in such a wet condition that the young Scot was obliged to decline the opportunity, and request permission instead to sit by the kitchen fire, in order to his attire being dried before morning, as he was particularly desirous that the Bohemian, when they should next meet, should observe no traces of his having been abroad during the night. The friar not only granted his request, but afforded him his own company, which fell in very happily with the desire which Durward had to obtain information concerning the two routes which he had heard mentioned by the Bohemian in his conversation with the lanzknecht. The friar, entrusted upon many occasions with the business of the convent abroad, was the person in the fraternity best qualified to afford him the information he requested; but observed that, as true pilgrims, it became the duty of the ladies whom Quentin escorted to take the road on the right side of the Maes, by the Cross of the Kings, where the blessed relics of Caspar, Melchior, and Balthasar, as the Catholic Church has named the eastern Magi who came to Bethlehem with their offerings, had rested as they were transported to Cologne, and on which spot they had wrought many miracles.

Quentin replied that the ladies were determined to observe all the holy stations with the utmost punctuality, and would certainly visit that of the Cross either in going to or returning from Cologne, but they had heard reports that the road by the right side of the river was at present rendered unsafe by the soldiers of the ferocious William de la Marck.

"Now may Heaven forbid," said Father Francis, "that the Wild Boar of Ardennes should again make his lair so near us! Nevertheless, the broad Maes will be a good barrier betwixt us, even should it so chance."

"But it will be no barrier between my ladies and the marauder, should we cross the river and travel on the right bank," answered the Scot.

"Heaven will protect its own, young man," said the friar; "for it were hard to think that the kings of yonder blessed city of Cologne, who will not endure that a Jew or infidel should even enter within the walls of their town, could be oblivious enough to permit their worshippers, coming to their shrine as true pilgrims, to be plundered and misused by such a miscreant dog as this Boar of Ardennes, who is worse than a whole desert of Saracen heathens and all the ten tribes of Israel to boot."

Whatever reliance Quentin, as a sincere Catholic, was bound to rest upon the special protection of Melchior, Caspar, and Balthasar, he could not but recollect that, the pilgrim habits of the ladies being assumed out of mere earthly policy, he and his charge could scarcely expect their countenance on the present occasion; and therefore resolved, as far as possible, to avoid placing the ladies in any predicament where miraculous interposition might be necessary; whilst, in the simplicity of his good faith, he himself vowed a pilgrimage to the Three Kings of Cologne in his own proper person, provided the sim-

not an hundred yards from the monastery and the village before Maugrabin joined it, riding as usual on his little active and wild-looking jennet. Their road led them along the side of the same brook where Quentin had overheard the mysterious conference of the preceding evening, and Hayraddin had not long rejoined them ere they passed under the very willow-tree which had afforded Durward the means of concealment when he became an unsuspected hearer of what then passed betwixt that false guide and the lanzknecht.

The recollections which the spot brought back stirred Quentin to enter abruptly into conversation with his guide, whom hitherto he had scarce spoken to.

"Where hast thou found night-quarter, thou profane knave?" said the Scot.

"Your wisdom may guess by looking on my gaberdine," answered the Bohemian, pointing to his dress, which was covered with the seeds of hay.

"A good hay-stack," said Quentin, "is a convenient bed for an astrologer, and a much better than a heathen scoffer at our blessed religion and its ministers ever deserves."

"It suited my Klepper better than me, though," said Hayraddin, patting his horse on the neck, "for he had food and shelter at the same time. The old bald fools turned him loose, as if a wise man's horse could have infected with wit or sagacity a whole convent of asses. Lucky that Klepper knows my whistle, and follows me as truly as a hound, or we had never met again, and you in your turn might have whistled for a guide."

"I have told thee more than once," said Durward, sternly, "to restrain thy ribaldry when thou chancest to be in worthy men's company, a thing which, I believe, hath rarely happened to thee in thy life before now; and I promise thee that, did I hold thee as faithless a guide as I esteem thee a blasphemous and worthless caitiff, my Scottish dirk and thy heathenish heart had ere now been acquainted, although the doing such a deed were as ignoble as the sticking of swine."

"A wild boar is near akin to a sow," said the Bohemian, without flinching from the sharp look with which Quentin regarded him or altering, in the slightest degree, the caustic indifference which he affected in his language; "and many men," he subjoined, "find both pride, pleasure, and profit in sticking them."

Astonished at the man's ready confidence, and uncertain whether he did not know more of his own history and feelings than was pleasant for him to converse upon, Quentin broke off a conversation in which he had gained no advantage over Maugrabin, and fell back to his accustomed post beside the ladies.

We have already observed that a considerable degree of familiarity had begun to establish itself between them. The elder countess treated him, being once well assured of the nobility of his birth, like a favoured equal; and though her niece showed her regard to their protector less freely, yet, under every disadvantage of bashfulness and timidity, Quentin thought he could plainly perceive that his company and conversation were not by any means indifferent to her.

Nothing gives such life and soul to youthful gaiety as the consciousness that it is successfully received; and Quentin had accordingly, during the former period of their journey, amused his fair charge with the liveliness of his conversation, and the songs and tales of his country, the former of which he sung in his native language, while his efforts to render the latter into his foreign and imperfect French gave rise to a hundred little mistakes and errors of speech, as diverting as the narratives themselves. But on this anxious morning he rode beside the Ladies of Croye without any of his usual attempts to amuse them, and they could not help observing his silence as something remarkable.

"Our young companion has seen a wolf," said the Lady Hameline, alluding to an ancient superstition,[1] "and he has lost his tongue in consequence."

"To say I had tracked a fox were nearer the mark," thought Quentin, but gave the reply no utterance.

"Are you well, Seignior Quentin?" said the Countess Isabelle, in a tone of interest at which she herself blushed, while

[1] See Wolf Superstition. Note 27.

she felt that it was something more than the distance between them warranted.

"He hath sat up carousing with the jolly friars," said the Lady Hameline. "The Scots are like the Germans, who spend all their mirth over the *Rheinwein*, and bring only their staggering steps to the dance in the evening, and their aching heads to the ladies' bower in the morning."

"Nay, gentle ladies," said Quentin, "I deserve not your reproach. The good friars were at their devotions almost all night; and for myself, my drink was barely a cup of their thinnest and most ordinary wine."

"It is the badness of his fare that has put him out of humour," said the Countess Isabelle. "Cheer up, Seignior Quentin; and should we ever visit my ancient Castle of Bracquemont together, if I myself should stand your cupbearer and hand it to you, you shall have a generous cup of wine that the like never grew upon the vines of Hochheim or Johannisberg."

"A glass of water, noble lady, from *your* hand——" Thus far did Quentin begin, but his voice trembled; and Isabelle continued, as if she had been insensible of the tenderness of the accentuation upon the personal pronoun.

"The wine was stocked in the deep vaults of Bracquemont by my great-grandfather, the Rhinegrave Godfrey," said the Countess Isabelle.

"Who won the hand of her great-grandmother," interjected the Lady Hameline, interrupting her niece, "by proving himself the best son of chivalry, at the great tournament of Strasbourg. Ten knights were slain in the lists. But those days are over, and no one now thinks of encountering peril for the sake of honour, or to relieve distressed beauty."

To this speech, which was made in the tone in which a modern beauty, whose charms are rather on the wane, may be heard to condemn the rudeness of the present age, Quentin took upon him to reply, "That there was no lack of that chivalry which the Lady Hameline seemed to consider as extinct, and that, were it eclipsed everywhere else, it would still glow in the bosoms of the Scottish gentlemen."

"Hear him!" said the Lady Hameline; "he would have us believe that in his cold and bleak country still lives the noble fire which has decayed in France and Germany! The poor youth is like a Swiss mountaineer, mad with partiality to his native land; he will next tell us of the vines and olives of Scotland."

"No, madam," said Durward; "of the wine and the oil of our mountains I can say little, more than that our swords can compel these rich productions as tribute from our wealthier neighbours. But for the unblemished faith and unfaded honour of Scotland, I must now put to the proof how far you can repose trust in them, however mean the individual who can offer nothing more as a pledge of your safety."

"You speak mysteriously—you know of some pressing and present danger," said the Lady Hameline.

"I have read it in his eye for this hour past!" exclaimed the Lady Isabelle, clasping her hands. "Sacred Virgin, what will become of us?"

"Nothing, I hope, but what you would desire," answered Durward. "And now I am compelled to ask—gentle ladies, can you trust me?"

"Trust you!" answered the Countess Hameline, "certainly. But why the question? Or how far do you ask our confidence?"

"I, on my part," said the Countess Isabelle, "trust you implicitly and without condition. If you can deceive us, Quentin, I will no more look for truth, save in Heaven."

"Gentle lady," replied Durward, highly gratified, "you do me but justice. My object is to alter our route, by proceeding directly by the left bank of the Maes to Liege, instead of crossing at Namur. This differs from the order assigned by King Louis and the instructions given to the guide. But I heard news in the monastery of marauders on the right bank of the Maes, and of the march of Burgundian soldiers to suppress them. Both circumstances alarm me for your safety. Have I your permission so far to deviate from the route of your journey?"

"My ample and full permission," answered the younger lady.

"Cousin," said Lady Hameline, "I believe with you that the youth means us well; but bethink you—we transgress the instructions of King Louis, so positively iterated."

"And why should we regard his instructions?" said the Lady Isabelle. "I am, I thank Heaven for it, no subject of his; and, as a suppliant, he has abused the confidence he induced me to repose in him. I would not dishonour this young gentleman by weighing his word for an instant against the injunctions of yonder crafty and selfish despot."

"Now, may God bless you for that very word, lady," said Quentin, joyously; "and if I deserve not the trust it expresses, tearing with wild horses in this life, and eternal tortures in the next, were e'en too good for my deserts."

So saying, he spurred his horse and rejoined the Bohemian. This worthy seemed of a remarkably passive if not a forgiving, temper. Injury or threat never dwelt, or at least seemed not to dwell, on his recollection; and he entered into the conversation which Durward presently commenced just as if there had been no unkindly word betwixt them in the course of the morning.

"The dog," thought the Scot, "snarls not now, because he intends to clear scores with me at once and for ever, when he can snatch me by the very throat; but we will try for once whether we cannot foil a traitor at his own weapons. Honest Hayraddin," he said, "thou hast travelled with us for ten days, yet hast never shown us a specimen of your skill in fortune-telling; which you are, nevertheless, so fond of practising, that you must needs display your gifts in every convent at which we stop, at the risk of being repaid by a night's lodging under a hay-stack."

"You have never asked me for a specimen of my skill," said the gipsy. "You are like the rest of the world, contented to ridicule those mysteries which they do not understand."

"Give me then a present proof of your skill," said Quentin; and, ungloving his hand, he held it out to the Zingaro.

Hayraddin carefully regarded all the lines which crossed each other on the Scotchman's palm, and noted, with equally scrupulous attention, the little risings or swellings at the roots of the fingers, which were then believed as intimately connected with the disposition, habits, and fortunes of the individual as the organs of the brain are pretended to be in our own time.

"Here is a hand," said Hayraddin, "which speaks of toils endured and dangers encountered. I read in it an early acquaintance with the hilt of the sword; and yet some acquaintance also with the clasps of the mass-book."

"This of my past life you may have learned elsewhere," said Quentin; "tell me something of the future."

"This line from the hill of Venus," said the Bohemian, "not broken off abruptly, but attending and accompanying the line of life, argues a certain and large fortune by marriage, whereby the party shall be raised among the wealthy and the noble by the influence of successful love."

"Such promises you make to all who ask your advice," said Quentin; "they are part of your art."

"What I tell you is as certain," said Hayraddin, "as that you shall in a brief space be menaced with mighty danger; which I infer from this bright blood-red line cutting the table-line transversely, and intimating stroke of sword or other violence, from which you shall only be saved by the attachment of a faithful friend."

"Thyself, ha?" said Quentin, somewhat indignant that the chiromantist should thus practise on his credulity, and endeavour to found a reputation by predicting the consequences of his own treachery.

"My art," replied the Zingaro, "tells me nought that concerns myself."

"In this, then, the seers of my land," said Quentin, "excel your boasted knowledge; for their skill teaches them the dangers by which they are themselves beset. I left not my hills without having felt a portion of the double vision with which their inhabitants are gifted; and I will give thee a proof of it, in exchange for thy specimen of palmistry. Hayraddin, the danger which threatens me lies on the right bank of the river; I will avoid it by travelling to Liege on the left bank."

The guide listened with an apathy which, knowing the circumstances in which Maugrabin stood, Quentin could not by any means comprehend. "If you accomplish your purpose," was the Bohemian's reply, "the dangerous crisis will be transferred from your lot to mine."

"I thought," said Quentin, "that you said but now that you could not presage your own fortune?"

"Not in the manner in which I have but now told you yours," answered Hayraddin; "but it requires little knowledge of Louis of Valois to presage that he will hang your guide because your pleasure was to deviate from the road which he recommended."

"The attaining with safety the purpose of the journey, and ensuring its happy termination," said Quentin, "must atone for a deviation from the exact line of the prescribed route."

"Ay," replied the Bohemian, "if you are sure that the King had in his own eye the same termination of the pilgrimage which he insinuated to you."

"And of what other termination is it possible that he could have been meditating? or why should you suppose he had any purpose in his thought other than was avowed in his direction?" inquired Quentin.

"Simply," replied the Zingaro, "that those who know aught of the Most Christian King are aware that the purpose about which he is most anxious is always that which he is least willing to declare. Let our gracious Louis send twelve embassies, and I will forfeit my neck to the gallows a year before it is due, if in eleven of them there is not something at the bottom of the inkhorn more than the pen has written in the letters of credence."

"I regard not your foul suspicions," answered Quentin; "my duty is plain and peremptory—to convey these ladies in safety to Liege; and I take it on me to think that I best discharge that duty in changing our prescribed route, and keeping the left side of the river Maes. It is likewise the direct road to Liege. By crossing the river, we should lose time and incur fatigue to no purpose. Wherefore should we do so?"

"Only because pilgrims, as they call themselves, destined for Cologne," said Hayraddin, "do not usually descend the

Maes so low as Liege; and that the route of the ladies will be accounted contradictory of their professed destination."

"If we are challenged on that account," said Quentin, "we will say that alarms of the wicked Duke of Gueldres, or of William de la Marck, or of the *écorcheurs* and lanzknechts, on the right side of the river, justify our holding by the left, instead of our intended route."

"As you will, my good seignior," replied the Bohemian. "I am, for my part, equally ready to guide you down the left as down the right side of the Maes. Your excuse to your master you must make out for yourself."

Quentin, although rather surprised, was at the same time pleased with the ready, or at least the unrepugnant, acquiescence of Hayraddin in their change of route, for he needed his assistance as a guide, and yet had feared that the disconcerting of his intended act of treachery would have driven him to extremity. Besides, to expel the Bohemian from their society would have been the ready mode to bring down William de la Marck, with whom he was in correspondence, upon their intended route; whereas, if Hayraddin remained with them, Quentin thought he could manage to prevent the Moor from having any communication with strangers, unless he was himself aware of it.

Abandoning, therefore, all thoughts of their original route, the little party followed that by the left bank of the broad Maes so speedily and successfully that the next day early brought them to the purposed end of their journey. They found that the Bishop of Liege, for the sake of his health, as he himself alleged, but rather, perhaps, to avoid being surprised by the numerous and mutinous population of the city, had established his residence in his beautiful Castle of Schonwaldt, about a mile without Liege.

Just as they approached the castle, they saw the prelate returning in long procession from the neighbouring city, in which he had been officiating at the performance of high mass. He was at the head of a splendid train of religious, civil, and military men, mingled together, or, as the old ballad-maker expresses it—

> With many a cross-bearer before,
> And many a spear behind.

The procession made a noble appearance, as, winding along the verdant banks of the broad Maes, it wheeled into, and was as it were devoured by, the huge Gothic portal of the episcopal residence. But when the party came more near, they found that circumstances around the castle argued a doubt and sense of insecurity, which contradicted that display of pomp and power which they had just witnessed. Strong guards of the bishop's soldiers were heedfully maintained all around the mansion and its immediate vicinity; and the prevailing appearances, in an ecclesiastical residence, seemed to argue a sense of danger in the reverend prelate, who found it necessary thus to surround himself with all the defensive precautions of war. The Ladies of Croye, when announced by Quentin, were reverently ushered into the great hall, where they met with the most cordial reception from the bishop, who met them there at the head of his little court. He would not permit them to kiss his hand, but welcomed them with a salute, which had something in it of gallantry on the part of a prince to fine women, and something also of the holy affection of a pastor to the sisters of his flock.

Louis of Bourbon, the reigning Bishop of Liege, was in truth a generous and kind-hearted prince, whose life had not indeed been always confined, with precise strictness, within the bounds of his clerical profession; but who, notwithstanding, had uniformly maintained the frank and honourable character of the house of Bourbon, from which he was descended.

In later times, as age advanced, the prelate had adopted habits more beseeming a member of the hierarchy than his early reign had exhibited, and was loved among the neighbouring princes as a noble ecclesiastic, generous and magnificent in his ordinary mode of life, though preserving no very ascetic severity of character, and governing with an easy indifference which, amid his wealthy and mutinous subjects, rather encouraged than subdued rebellious purposes.

The bishop was so fast an ally of the Duke of Burgundy, that the latter claimed almost a joint sovereignty in his bishopric, and repaid the good-natured ease with which the prelate admitted claims which he might easily have disputed, by taking his part on all occasions, with the determined and furious zeal which was a part of his character. He used to say: "He considered Liege as his own, the bishop as his brother (indeed they might be accounted such, in consequence of the Duke having married for his first wife the bishop's sister), and that he who annoyed Louis of Bourbon had to do with Charles of Burgundy"—a threat which, considering the character and the power of the prince who used it, would have been powerful with any but the rich and discontented city of Liege, where much wealth had, according to the ancient proverb, made wit waver.

The prelate, as we have said, assured the Ladies of Croye of such intercession as his interest at the court of Burgundy, used to the uttermost, might gain for them, and which, he hoped, might be the more effectual, as Campo-basso, from some late discoveries, stood rather lower than formerly in the Duke's personal favour. He promised them also such protection as it was in his power to afford; but the sigh with which he gave the warrant seemed to allow that his power was more precarious than in words he was willing to admit.

"At every event, my dearest daughters," said the bishop, with an air in which, as in his previous salute, a mixture of spiritual unction qualified the hereditary gallantry of the house of Bourbon, "Heaven forbid I should abandon the lamb to the wicked wolf, or noble ladies to the oppression of faitours. I am a man of peace, though my abode now rings with arms; but be assured I will care for your safety as for my own; and should matters become yet more distracted here, which, with Our Lady's grace, we trust will be rather pacified than inflamed, we will provide for your safe-conduct to Germany; for not even the will of our brother and protector, Charles of Burgundy, shall prevail with us to dispose of you in any respect contrary to your own inclinations. We cannot comply with your request of sending you to a convent; for, alas! such is the influence of the sons of Belial among the inhabitants of Liege, that we know no retreat to which our authority extends, beyond the bounds of our own castle and the protection of our soldiery. But here you are most welcome, and your train shall have all honourable entertainment; especially this youth, whom you recommend so particularly to our countenance, and on whom in especial we bestow our blessing."

Quentin kneeled, as in duty bound, to receive the episcopal benediction.

"For yourselves," proceeded the good prelate, "you shall reside here with my sister Isabelle, a canoness of Triers, and with whom you may dwell in all honour, even under the roof of so gay a bachelor as the Bishop of Liege."

He gallantly conducted the ladies to his sister's apartment, as he concluded the harangue of welcome; and his master of the household, an officer who, having taken deacon's orders, held something between a secular and ecclesiastical character, entertained Quentin with the hospitality which his master enjoined, while the other personages of the retinue of the Ladies of Croye were committed to the inferior departments.

In this arrangement Quentin could not help remarking, that the presence of the Bohemian, so much objected to in country convents, seemed, in the household of this wealthy, and perhaps we might say worldly, prelate, to attract neither objection nor remark.

CHAPTER XIX.

THE CITY.

> Good friends, sweet friends, let me not stir you up
> To any sudden act of mutiny!
> *Julius Cæsar.*

SEPARATED from the Lady Isabelle, whose looks had been for so many days his loadstar, Quentin felt a strange vacancy and chillness of the heart, which he had not yet experienced in any of the vicissitudes to which his life had subjected him. No doubt the cessation of the close and unavoidable intercourse and intimacy betwixt them was the necessary consequence of the countess having obtained a place of settled residence; for, under what pretext could she, had she meditated such an impropriety, have had a gallant young squire such as Quentin in constant attendance upon her?

But the shock of the separation was not the more welcome that it seemed unavoidable, and the proud heart of Quentin swelled at finding he was parted with like an ordinary postilion, or an escort whose duty is discharged; while his eyes sympathised so far as to drop a secret tear or two over the ruins of all those airy castles, so many of which he had employed himself in constructing during their too interesting journey. He made a manly, but at first a vain, effort to throw off this mental dejection; and so, yielding to the feelings he could not suppress, he sat him down in one of the deep recesses formed by a window which lighted the great Gothic hall of Schonwaldt, and there mused upon his hard fortune, which had not assigned him rank or wealth sufficient to prosecute his daring suit.

Quentin tried to dispel the sadness which overhung him by depatching Charlet, one of the valets, with letters to the court of Louis, announcing the arrival of the Ladies of Croye at Liege. At length his natural buoyancy of temper returned, much excited by the title of an old romaunt which had been just printed at Strasbourg, and which lay beside him in the window, the title of which set forth,

> How the squire of lowe degree,
> Loved the king's daughter of Hongarie.[1]

While he was tracing the "letters blake" of the ditty so congenial to his own situation, Quentin was interrupted by a touch on the shoulder, and, looking up, beheld the Bohemian standing by him.

Hayraddin, never a welcome sight, was odious from his late treachery, and Quentin sternly asked him "Why he dared take the freedom to touch a Christian and a gentleman."

"Simply," answered the Bohemian, "because I wished to know if the Christian gentleman had lost his feeling as well as his eyes and ears. I have stood speaking to you these five

[1] See Note 28.

minutes, and you have stared on that scrap of yellow paper as if it were a spell to turn you into a statue and had already wrought half its purpose."

"Well, what dost thou want? Speak, and begone!"

"I want what all men want, though few are satisfied with it," said Hayraddin: "I want my due—my ten crowns of gold for guiding the ladies hither."

"With what face darest thou ask any guerdon beyond my sparing thy worthless life?" said Durward, fiercely; "thou knowest that it was thy purpose to have betrayed them on the road."

"But I did *not* betray them," said Hayraddin; "if I had, I would have asked no guerdon from you or from them, but from him whom their keeping upon the right-hand side of the river might have benefited. The party that I have served is the party who must pay me."

"Thy guerdon perish with thee, then, traitor!" said Quentin, telling out the money. "Get thee to the Boar of Ardennes, or to the devil! but keep hereafter out of my sight, lest I send thee thither before thy time."

"The Boar of Ardennes!" repeated the Bohemian, with a stronger emotion of surprise than his features usually expressed; "it was then no vague guess—no general suspicion which made you insist on changing the road? Can it be—are there really in other lands arts of prophecy more sure than those of our wandering tribes? The willow-tree under which we spoke could tell no tales. But no—no—no—— Dolt that I was! I have it—I have it! The willow by the brook near yonder convent—I saw you look towards it as you passed it, about half a mile from yon hive of drones—that could not indeed speak, but it might hide one who could hear! I will hold my councils in an open plain henceforth: not a bunch of thistles shall be near me for a Scot to shroud amongst. Ha! ha! the Scot hath beat the Zingaro at his own subtle weapons. But know, Quentin Durward, that you have foiled me to the marring of thine own fortune. Yes! the fortune I told thee of, from the lines on thy hand, had been richly accomplished but for thine own obstinacy."

"By St. Andrew," said Quentin, "thy impudence makes me laugh in spite of myself. How or in what should thy successful villainy have been of service to me? I heard, indeed, that you did stipulate to save my life, which condition your worthy allies would speedily have forgotten had we once come to blows; but in what thy betrayal of these ladies could have served me, but by exposing me to death or captivity, is a matter beyond human brains to conjecture."

"No matter thinking of it, then," said Hayraddin, "for I mean still to surprise you with my gratitude. Had you kept back my hire, I should have held that we were quit, and had left you to your own foolish guidance. As it is, I remain your debtor for yonder matter on the banks of the Cher."

"Methinks I have already taken out the payment in cursing and abusing thee," said Quentin.

"Hard words or kind ones," said the Zingaro, "are but wind, which make no weight in the balance. Had you struck me, indeed, instead of threatening——"

"I am likely enough to take out payment in that way, if you provoke me longer."

"I would not advise it," said Zingaro; "such payment, made by a rash hand, might exceed the debt, and unhappily leave a balance on your side, which I am not one to forget or forgive. And now farewell, but not for a long space; I go to bid adieu to the Ladies of Croye."

"Thou!" said Quentin in astonishment—"*thou* be admitted to the presence of the ladies, and here, where they are in a manner recluses under the protection of the bishop's sister, a noble canoness! It is impossible."

"Marthon, however, waits to conduct me to their presence," said the Zingaro, with a sneer; "and I must pray your forgiveness if I leave you something abruptly."

He turned as if to depart, but instantly coming back, said, with a tone of deep and serious emphasis: "I know your hopes; they are daring, yet not vain if I aid them. I know your fears; they should teach prudence, not timidity. Every woman may be won. A count is but a nickname, which will befit Quentin as well as the other nickname of duke befits Charles, or that of king befits Louis."

Ere Durward could reply, the Bohemian had left the hall. Quentin instantly followed; but, better acquainted than the Scot with the passages of the house, Hayraddin kept the advantage which he had gotten; and the pursuer lost sight of him as he descended a small back staircase. Still Durward followed, though without exact consciousness of his own purpose in doing so. The staircase terminated by a door opening into the alley of a garden, in which he again beheld the Zingaro hastening down a pleached walk.

On two sides, the garden was surrounded by the buildings of the castle—a huge old pile, partly castellated and partly resembling an ecclesiastical building; on the other two sides, the inclosure was a high embattled wall. Crossing the alleys of the garden to another part of the building, where a postern-door opened behind a large massive buttress, overgrown with ivy, Hayraddin looked back, and waved his hand in signal of an exulting farewell to his follower, who saw that in effect the postern-door was opened by Marthon, and that the vile Bohemian was admitted into the precincts, as he naturally concluded, of the apartment of the Countesses of Croye. Quentin bit his lips with indignation, and blamed himself severely that he had not made the ladies sensible of the full infamy of Hayraddin's character, and acquainted with his machinations against their safety. The arrogating manner in which the Bohemian had promised to back his suit added to his anger and his disgust; and he felt as if even the hand of the Countess Isabelle would be profaned, were it possible to attain it by such patronage. "But it is all a deception," he said—"a turn of his base juggling artifice. He has procured access to these ladies upon some false pretence, and with some mischievous intention. It is well I have learned where they lodged. I will watch Marthon, and solicit an interview with them, were it but to place them on their guard. It is hard that I must use artifice and brook delay when such as he have admittance openly and without scruple. They shall find, however, that, though I am excluded from their presence, Isabelle's safety is still the chief subject of my vigilance."

While the young lover was thus meditating, an aged gentleman of the bishop's household approached him from the same door by which he had himself entered the garden, and made him aware, though with the greatest civility of manner, that the garden was private, and reserved only for the use of the bishop and guests of the very highest distinction.

Quentin heard him repeat this information twice ere he put the proper construction upon it; and then starting as from a reverie, he bowed and hurried out of the garden, the official person following him all the way, and overwhelming him with formal apologies for the necessary discharge of his duty. Nay, so pertinacious was he in his attempts to remove the offence which he conceived Durward to have taken, that he offered to bestow his own company upon him, to contribute to his entertainment; until Quentin, internally cursing his formal foppery, found no better way of escape than pretending a desire of visiting the neighbouring city, and setting off thither at such a round pace as speedily subdued all desire in the gentleman-usher to accompany him farther than the drawbridge. In a few minutes Quentin was within the walls of the city of Liege, then one of the richest in Flanders, and of course in the world.

Melancholy, even love-melancholy, is not so deeply seated, at least in minds of a manly and elastic character, as the soft enthusiasts who suffer under it are fond of believing. It yields to unexpected and striking impressions upon the senses, to change of place, to such scenes as create new trains of association, and to the influence of the busy hum of mankind. In a few minutes, Quentin's attention was as much engrossed by the variety of objects presented in rapid succession by the busy streets of Liege as if there had neither been a Countess Isabelle nor a Bohemian in the world.

The lofty houses; the stately, though narrow and gloomy, streets; the splendid display of the richest goods and most gorgeous armour in the warehouses and shops around; the walks crowded by busy citizens of every description, passing and repassing with faces of careful importance or eager bustle; the huge wains, which transported to and fro the subjects of exports and import, the former consisting of broadcloths and serge, arms of all kinds, nails and iron-work, while the latter comprehended every article of use or luxury intended either for the consumption of an opulent city or received in barter and destined to be transported elsewhere—all these objects combined to form an engrossing picture of wealth, bustle, and splendour, to which Quentin had been hitherto a stranger. He admired also the various streams and canals drawn from and communicating with the Maes, which, traversing the city in various directions, offered to every quarter the commercial facilities of water-carriage; and he failed not to hear a mass in the venerable old church of St. Lambert, said to have been founded in the 8th century.

It was upon leaving this place of worship that Quentin began to observe that he, who had been hitherto gazing on all around him with the eagerness of unrestrained curiosity, was himself the object of attention to several groups of substantial-looking burghers, who seemed assembled to look upon him as he left the church, and amongst whom arose a buzz and whisper, which spread from one party to another; while the number of gazers continued to augment rapidly, and the eyes of each who added to it were eagerly directed to Quentin, with a stare which expressed much interest and curiosity, mingled with a certain degree of respect.

At length he now formed the centre of a considerable crowd, which yet yielded before him while he continued to move forward; while those who followed or kept pace with him studiously avoided pressing on him or impeding his motions. Yet his situation was too embarrassing to be long endured, without making some attempt to extricate himself, and to obtain some explanation.

Quentin looked around him, and fixing upon a jolly, stout-made, respectable man, whom, by his velvet cloak and gold chain, he concluded to be a burgher of eminence, and perhaps a magistrate, he asked him: "Whether he saw anything particular in his appearance, to attract public attention in a degree so unusual? or whether it was the ordinary custom of the people of Liege thus to throng around strangers who chanced to visit their city?"

"Surely not, good seignior," answered the burgher; "the Liegeois are neither so idly curious as to practise such a custom, nor is there anything in your dress or appearance, saving that which it most welcome to this city, and which our townsmen are both delighted to see and desirous to honour."

"This sounds very polite, worthy sir," said Quentin; "but, by the cross of St. Andrew, I cannot even guess at your meaning."

"Your oath, sir," answered the merchant of Liege, "as well as your accent, convinces me that we are right in our conjecture."

"By my patron St. Quentin!" said Durward, "I am farther off from your meaning than ever."

"There again now," rejoined the Liegeois, looking, as he spoke, most provokingly, yet most civilly, politic and intelligent. "It is surely not for us to see that which you, worthy seignior, deem it proper to conceal. But why swear by St. Quentin, if you would not have me construe your meaning? We know the good Count of St. Paul, who lies there at present, wishes well to our cause."

"On my life," said Quentin, "you are under some delusion: I know nothing of St. Paul."

"Nay, we question you not," said the burgher; "although, hark ye—I say, hark in your ear—my name is Pavillon."

"And what is my business with that, Seignior Pavillon?" said Quentin.

"Nay, nothing; only methinks it might satisfy you that I am trustworthy. Here is my colleague Rouslaer, too."

Rouslaer advanced, a corpulent dignity, whose fair round belly, like a battering-ram, "did shake the press before him," and who, whispering caution to his neighbour, said, in a tone of rebuke: "You forget, good colleague, the place is too open; the seignior will retire to your house or mine, and drink a glass of Rhenish and sugar, and then we shall hear more of our good friend and ally, whom we love with all our honest Flemish hearts."

"I have no news for any of you," said Quentin, impatiently; "I will drink no Rhenish; and I only desire of you, as men of account and respectability, to disperse this idle crowd, and allow a stranger to leave your town as quietly as he came into it."

"Nay, then, sir," said Rouslaer, "since you stand so much on your incognito, and with us, too, who are men of confidence, let me asked you roundly, wherefore wear you that badge of your company if you would remain unknown in Liege?"

"What badge and what order?" said Quentin. "You look like reverend men and grave citizens, yet, on my soul, you are either mad yourselves or desire to drive me so."

"Sapperment!" said the other burgher, "this youth would make St. Lambert swear! Why, who wear bonnets with the St. Andrew's cross and *fleur-de-lys* save the Scottish Archers of King Louis's Guards?"

"And supposing I am an archer of the Scottish Guard, why should you make a wonder of my wearing the badge of my company?" said Quentin, impatiently.

"He has avowed it—he has avowed it!" said Rouslaer and Pavillon, turning to the assembled burghers in attitudes of congratulation, with waving arms, extended palms, and large round faces radiating with glee. "He hath avowed himself an archer of Louis's Guard—of Louis, the guardian of the liberties of Liege!"

A general shout and cry now arose from the multitude, in which were mingled the various sounds of "Long live Louis of France! Long live the Scottish Guard! Long live the valiant archer! Our liberties, our privileges, or death! No imposts! Long live the valiant Boar of Ardennes! Down with Charles of Burgundy! and confusion to Bourbon and his bishopric!"

Half-stunned by the noise, which began anew in one quarter so soon as it ceased in another, rising and falling like the billows of the sea, and augmented by thousands of voices which roared in chorus from distant streets and market-places, Quentin had yet time to form a conjecture concerning the meaning of the tumult, and a plan for regulating his own conduct.

He had forgotten that, after his skirmish with Orleans and Dunois, one of his comrades had, at Lord Crawford's command, replaced the morion, cloven by the sword of the latter, with one of the steel-lined bonnets which formed a part of the proper and well-known equipment of the Scotch Guards. That an individual of this body, which was always kept very close to Louis's person, should have appeared in the streets of a city whose civil discontents had been aggravated by the agents of that king, was naturally enough interpreted by the burghers of Liege into a determination on the part of Louis openly to assist their cause; and the apparition of an individual archer was magnified into a pledge of immediate and active support from Louis—nay, into an assurance that his auxiliary forces were actually entering the town at one or other, though no one could distinctly tell which, of the city gates.

To remove a conviction so generally adopted, Quentin easily saw was impossible—nay, that any attempt to undeceive men so obstinately prepossessed in their belief would be attended with personal risk, which, in this case, he saw little use of incurring. He therefore hastily resolved to temporise, and to get free the best way he could; and this resolution he formed while they were in the act of conducting him to the *stadt-house*, where the notables of the town were fast assembling, in order to hear the tidings which he was presumed to have brought, and to regale him with a splendid banquet.

In spite of all his opposition, which was set down to modesty, he was on every side surrounded by the donors of popularity, the unsavoury tide of which now floated around him. His two burgomaster friends, who were *schoppen* [*schöffen*], or syndics, of the city, had made fast both his arms. Before him, Nikkel Blok, the chief of the butchers' incorporation, hastily summoned from his office in the shambles, brandished his death-doing axe, yet smeared with blood and brains, with a courage and grace which *brantwein* alone could inspire. Behind him came the tall, lean, raw-boned, very drunk, and very patriotic, figure of Claus Hammerlein, president of the mystery of the workers in iron, and followed by at least a thousand unwashed artificers of his class. Weavers, nailers, ropemakers, artisans of every degree and calling, thronged forward to join the procession from every gloomy and narrow street. Escape seemed a desperate and impossible adventure.

In this dilemma, Quentin appealed to Rouslaer, who held one arm, and to Pavillon, who had secured the other, and who were conducting him forward at the head of the ovation of which he had so unexpectedly become the principal object. He hastily acquainted them "with his having thoughtlessly adopted the bonnet of the Scottish Guard, on an accident having occurred to the head-piece in which he had proposed to travel; he regretted that, owing to this circumstance and the sharp wit with which the Liegeois drew the natural inference of his quality and the purpose of his visit, these things had been publicly discovered; and he intimated that, if just now conducted to the *stadt-house*, he might unhappily feel himself under the necessity of communicating to the assembled notables certain matters which he was directed by the King to reserve for the private ears of his excellent gossips, Meinherrs Rouslaer and Pavillon of Liege."

This last hint operated like magic on the two citizens, who were the most distinguished leaders of the insurgent burghers, and were, like all demagogues of their kind, desirous to keep everything within their own management, so far as possible. They therefore hastily agreed that Quentin should leave the town for the time, and return by night to Liege, and converse with them privately in the house of Rouslaer, near the gate opposite to Schonwaldt. Quentin hesitated not to tell them that he was at present residing in the bishop's palace, under pretence of bearing despatches from the French court, although his real errand was, as they had well conjectured, designed to the citizens of Liege; and this tortuous mode of conducting a communication, as well as the character and rank of the person to whom it was supposed to be entrusted, was so consonant to the character of Louis as neither to excite doubt nor surprise.

Almost immediately after this *éclaircissement* was completed, the progress of the multitude brought them opposite of the door of Pavillon's house, in one of the principal streets, but which communicated from behind with the Maes by means of a garden, as well as an extensive manufactory of tan-pits and other conveniences for dressing hides; for the patriotic burgher was a felt-dresser, or currier.

It was natural that Pavillon should desire to do the honours of his dwelling to the supposed envoy of Louis, and a halt before his house excited no surprise on the part of the multitude, who, on the contrary, greeted Meinherr Pavillon with a loud *vivat* as he ushered in his distinguished guest. Quentin speedily laid aside his remarkable bonnet for the cap of a felt-maker, and flung a cloak over his other apparel. Pavillon then furnished him with a passport to pass the gates of the city, and to return by night or day as should suit his convenience; and lastly, committed him to the charge of his daughter, a fair and smiling Flemish lass, with instructions how he was to be disposed of, while he himself hastened back to his colleague to amuse their friends at the *stadt-house* with the best excuses which they could invent for the disappearance of King Louis's envoy. We cannot, as the footman says in the play, recollect the exact nature of the lie which the belwethers told the flock; but no task is so easy as that of imposing upon a multitude whose eager prejudices have more than half done the business, ere the impostor has spoken a word.

The worthy burgess was no sooner gone than his plump daughter, Trudchen, with many a blush and many a wreathed smile, which suited very prettily with lips like cherries, laughing blue eyes, and a skin transparently pure, escorted the handsome stranger through the pleached alleys of the Sieur Pavillon's garden, down to the water-side, and there saw him fairly embarked in a boat, which two stout Flemings, in their trunk-hose, fur caps, and many-buttoned jerkins, had got in readiness with as much haste as their Low-Country nature would permit.

As the pretty Trudchen spoken nothing but German, Quentin—no disparagement to his loyal affection to the Countess of Croye—could only express his thanks by a kiss on those same cherry lips, which was very gallantly bestowed, and accepted with all modest gratitude; for gallants with a form and face like our Scottish Archer were not of every-day occurrence among the *bourgeoisie* of Liege.[1]

While the boat was rowed up the sluggish waters of the Maes, and passed the defences of the town, Quentin had time enough to reflect what account he ought to give of his adventure in Liege, when he returned to the bishop's palace of Schonwaldt; and disdaining alike to betray any person who had reposed confidence in him, although by misapprehension, or to conceal from the hospitable prelate the mutinous state of his capital, he resolved to confine himself to so general an account as might put the bishop upon his guard, while it should point out no individual to his vengeance.

He was landed from the boat within half a mile of the castle, and rewarded his rowers with a guilder, to their great satisfaction. Yet, short as was the space which divided him from Schonwaldt, the castle bell had tolled for dinner, and Quentin found, moreover, that he had approached the castle on a different side from that of the principal entrance, and that to go round would throw his arrival considerably later. He therefore made straight towards the side that was nearest him, as he discerned that it presented an embattled wall, probably that of the little garden already noticed, with a postern opening upon the moat, and a skiff moored by the postern, which might serve, he thought, upon summons, to pass him over. As he approached, in hopes to make his entrance this way, the postern opened, a man came out, and, jumping into the boat, made his way to the farther side of the moat, and then with a long pole pushed the skiff back towards the place where he had embarked. As he came near, Quentin discerned that this person was the Bohemian, who, avoiding him, as was not difficult, held a different path towards Liege, and was presently out of his ken.

Here was new subject for meditation. Had this vagabond heathen been all this while with the Ladies of Croye, and for what purpose should they so far have graced him with their

[1] See Quentin's Adventure at Liege. Note 29.

presence? Tormented with this thought, Durward became doubly determined to seek an explanation with them, for the purpose at once of laying bare the treachery of Hayraddin and announcing to them the perilous state in which their protector, the bishop, was placed by the mutinous state of his town of Liege.

As Quentin thus resolved, he entered the castle by the principal gate, and found that part of the family who assembled for dinner in the great hall, including the bishop's attendant clergy, officers of the household, and strangers below the rank of the very first nobility, were already placed at their meal. A seat at the upper end of the board had, however, been reserved beside the bishop's domestic chaplain, who welcomed the stranger with the old college jest of "*Sero venientibus ossa*," while he took care so to load his plate with dainties as to take away all appearance of that tendency to reality which, in Quentin's country, is said to render a joke either no joke or at best an unpalatable one.[1]

In vindicating himself from the suspicion of ill-breeding, Quentin briefly described the tumult which had been occasioned in the city by his being discovered to belong to the Scottish Archer Guard of Louis, and endeavoured to give a ludicrous turn to the narrative, by saying that he had been with difficulty extricated by a fat burgher of Liege and his pretty daughter.

But the company were too much interested in the story to taste the jest. All operations of the table were suspended while Quentin told his tale; and when he had ceased, there was a solemn pause, which was only broken by the majordomo saying, in a low and melancholy tone, "I would to God that we saw those hundred lances of Burgundy!"

"Why should you think so deeply on it?" said Quentin. "You have many soldiers here, whose trade is arms; and your antagonists are only the rabble of a disorderly city, who will fly before the first flutter of a banner with men-at-arms arrayed beneath it."

"You do not know the men of Liege," said the chaplain, "of whom it may be said that, not even excepting those of

---

[1] "A sooth boord (true joke) is no boord," says the Scot.

Ghent, they are at once the fiercest and the most untameable in Europe. Twice has the Duke of Burgundy chastised them for their repeated revolts against their bishop, and twice hath he suppressed them with much severity, abridged their privileges, taken away their banners, and established rights and claims to himself which were not before competent over a free city of the Empire. Nay, the last time he defeated them with much slaughter near St. Tron, where Liege lost nearly six thousand men, what with the sword, what with those drowned in the flight; and, thereafter, to disable them from farther mutiny, Duke Charles refused to enter at any of the gates which they had surrendered, but, beating to the ground forty cubits breadth of their city wall, marched into Liege as a conqueror, with visor closed and lance in rest, at the head of his chivalry, by the breach which he had made. Nay, well were the Liegeois then assured that, but for the intercession of his father, Duke Philip the Good, this Charles, then called Count of Charalois, would have given their town up to spoil. And yet, with all these fresh recollections, with their breaches unrepaired, and their arsenals scarcely supplied, the sight of an archer's bonnet is sufficient again to stir them to uproar. May God amend all! but I fear there will be bloody work between so fierce a population and so fiery a sovereign; and I would my excellent and kind master had a see of lesser dignity and more safety, for his mitre is lined with thorns instead of ermine. This much I say to you, seignior stranger, to make you aware that, if your affairs detain you not at Schonwaldt, it is a place from which each man of sense should depart as speedily as possible. I apprehend that your ladies are of the same opinion; for one of the grooms who attended them on the route has been sent back by them to the court of France with letters, which, doubtless, are intended to announce their going in search of a safer asylum."

CHAPTER XX.

THE BILLET.

Go to—thou art made, if thou desirest to be so. If not, let me see thee still the fellow of servants, and not fit to touch Fortune's fingers.
Twelfth Night.

When the tables were drawn, the chaplain, who seemed to have taken a sort of attachment to Quentin Durward's society, or who perhaps desired to extract from him farther information concerning the meeting of the morning, led him into a withdrawing-apartment, the windows of which, on one side, projected into the garden; and as he saw his companion's eye gaze rather eagerly upon the spot, he proposed to Quentin to go down and take a view of the curious foreign shrubs with which the bishop had enriched its parterres.

Quentin excused himself, as unwilling to intrude, and therewithal communicated the check which he had received in the morning. The chaplain smiled, and said: "That there was indeed some ancient prohibition respecting the bishop's private garden; but this," he added, with a smile, "was when our reverend father was a princely young prelate of not more than thirty years of age, and when many fair ladies frequented the castle for ghostly consolation. Need there was," he said, with a downcast look, and smile, half simple and half intelligent, "that these ladies, pained in conscience, who were ever lodged in the apartments now occupied by the noble canoness, should have some space for taking the air, secure from the intrusion of the profane. But of late years," he added, "this prohibition, although not formally removed, has fallen entirely out of observance, and remains but as the superstition which lingers in the brain of a superannuated gentleman-usher. If you please," he added, "we will presently descend, and try whether the place be haunted or no."

Nothing could have been more agreeable to Quentin than the prospect of a free entrance into the garden, through means of which, according to a chance which had hitherto attended his passion, he hoped to communicate with, or at least obtain sight of, the object of his affections, from some such turret or balcony-window, or similar "coign of vantage," as at the hostelry of the Fleur-de-Lys, near Plessis, or the Dauphin's Tower, within that castle itself. Isabelle seemed still destined, wherever she made her abode, to be the "lady of the turret."

When Durward descended with his new friend into the garden, the latter seemed a terrestrial philosopher, entirely busied with the things of the earth; while the eyes of Quentin, if they did not seek the heavens, like those of an astrologer, ranged at least all round the windows, balconies, and especially the turrets, which projected on every part from the inner front of the old building, in order to discover that which was to be his cynosure.

While thus employed, the young lover heard with total neglect, if indeed he heard at all, the enumeration of plants, herbs, and shrubs, which his reverend conductor pointed out to him; of which this was choice, because of prime use in medicine; and that more choice, for yielding a rare flavour to pottage; and a third choicest of all, because possessed of no merit but its extreme scarcity. Still it was necessary to preserve some semblance at least of attention; which the youth found so difficult, that he fairly wished at the devil the officious naturalist and the whole vegetable kingdom. He was relieved at length by the striking of a clock, which summoned the chaplain to some official duty.

The reverend man made many unnecessary apologies for leaving his new friend, and concluded by giving him the agreeable assurance, that he might walk in the garden till supper, without much risk of being disturbed.

"It is," said he, "the place where I always study my own homilies, as being most sequestered from the resort of strangers. I am now about to deliver one of them in the chapel, if you please to favour me with your audience. I have been thought to have some gift—but the glory be where it is due!"

Quentin excused himself for this evening, under pretence of a severe headache, which the open air was likely to prove the best cure for; and at length the well-meaning priest left him to himself.

It may be well imagined, that in the curious inspection which he now made, at more leisure, of every window or aperture which looked into the garden, those did not escape which were in the immediate neighbourhood of the small door by which he had seen Marthon admit Hayraddin, as he pretended, to the apartment of the countesses. But nothing stirred or showed itself, which could either confute or confirm the tale which the Bohemian had told, until it was becoming dusky; and Quentin began to be sensible, he scarce knew why, that his sauntering so long in the garden might be subject of displeasure or suspicion.

Just as he had resolved to depart, and was taking what he had destined for his last turn under the windows which had such attraction for him, he heard above him a slight and cautious sound, like that of a cough, as intended to call his attention, and to avoid the observation of others. As he looked up in joyful surprise, a casement opened—a female hand was seen to drop a billet, which fell into a rosemary bush that grew at the foot of the wall. The precaution used in dropping this letter prescribed equal prudence and secrecy in reading it. The garden, surrounded, as we have said, upon two sides by the buildings of the place, was commanded, of course, by the windows of many apartments; but there was a sort of grotto of rock-work, which the chaplain had shown Durward with much complacency. To snatch up the billet, thrust it into his bosom, and hie to this place of secrecy, was the work of a single minute. He there opened the precious scroll, and blessed, at the same time, the memory of the monks of Aberbrothock, whose nurture had rendered him capable of deciphering its contents.

The first line contained the injunction, "Read this in secret,"—and the contents were as follows: "What your eyes have too boldly said mine have perhaps too rashly understood. But unjust persecution makes its victims bold, and it were better to throw myself on the gratitude of one than to remain the object of pursuit to many. Fortune has her throne upon a rock; but brave men fear not to climb. If you dare do aught for one that hazards much, you need but pass into this garden at prime to-morrow, wearing in your cap a blue-and-white feather; but expect no farther communication. Your stars have, they say, destined you for greatness, and disposed you to gratitude. Farewell—be faithful, prompt, and resolute, and doubt not thy fortune." Within this letter was enclosed a ring with a table-diamond, on which were cut, in form of a lozenge, the ancient arms of the house of Croye.

The first feeling of Quentin upon this occasion was unmingled ecstasy—a pride and joy which seemed to raise him to the stars,—a determination to do or die, influenced by which he treated with scorn the thousand obstacles that placed themselves betwixt him and the goal of his wishes.

In this mood of rapture, and unable to endure any interruption which might withdraw his mind, were it but for a moment, from so ecstatic a subject of contemplation, Durward, retiring to the interior of the castle hastily assigned his former pretext of a headache for not joining the household of the bishop at the supper-meal, and, lighting his lamp, betook himself to the chamber which had been assigned him, to read, and read again and again, the precious billet, and to kiss a thousand times the no less precious ring.

But such high-wrought feelings could not remain long in the same ecstatic tone. A thought pressed upon him, though he repelled it as ungrateful—as even blasphemous, that the frankness of the confession implied less delicacy, on the part of her who made it, than was consistent with the high romantic feeling of adoration with which he had hitherto worshipped the Lady Isabelle. No sooner did this ungracious thought intrude itself than he hastened to stifle it, as he would have stifled a hissing and hateful adder that had intruded itself in his couch. Was it for him—him the favoured, on whose account she had stooped from her sphere, to ascribe blame to her for the very act of condescension, without which he dared not have raised his eyes towards her? Did not her very dignity of birth and of condition reverse, in her case, the usual rules which impose silence on the lady until her lover shall have first spoken? To these arguments, which he boldly formed into syllogisms, and avowed to himself, his vanity might possibly suggest one which he cared not to embody even mentally with the same frankness—that the merit of the party beloved might perhaps warrant, on the part of the lady, some little departure from common rules; and, after all, as in the case of Malvolio, there was example for it in chronicle. The squire of low degree, of whom he had just been reading, was, like himself, a gentleman void of land and living, and yet the generous Princess of Hungary bestowed on him, without a scruple, more substantial marks of her affection than the billet he had just received:

> "Welcome," she said, "my swete squyre,
> My heartis roote, my soule's desire;
> I will give thee kisses three,
> And als five hundrid poundis in fee."

And again the same faithful history made the King of Hongrie himself avouch,

> "I have yknown many a page
> Come to be prince by marriage."

So that, upon the whole, Quentin generously and magnanimously reconciled himself to a line of conduct on the countess's part by which he was likely to be so highly benefited.

But this scruple was succeeded by another doubt, harder of digestion. The traitor Hayraddin had been in the apartments of the ladies, for aught Quentin knew, for the space of four hours, and, considering the hints which he had thrown out, of possessing an influence of the most interesting kind over the fortunes of Quentin Durward, what should assure him that this train was not of his laying? and if so, was it not probable that such a dissembling villain had set it on foot to conceal some new plan of treachery—perhaps to seduce Isabelle out of the protection of the worthy bishop? This was a matter to be closely looked into, for Quentin felt a repugnance to this individual proportioned to the unabashed impudence with which he had avowed his profligacy, and could not bring himself to hope, that anything in which he was concerned could ever come to an honourable or happy conclusion.

These various thoughts rolled over Quentin's mind like misty clouds, to dash and obscure the fair landscape which his fancy had at first drawn, and his couch was that night a sleepless one. At the hour of prime, ay, and an hour before it, was he in the castle-garden, where no one now opposed either his entrance or his abode, with a feather of the assigned colour, as distinguished as he could by any means procure in such haste. No notice was taken of his appearance for nearly two hours; at length he heard a few notes of the lute, and presently the lattice opened right above the little postern-door at which Marthon had admitted Hayraddin, and Isabelle, in maidenly beauty, appeared at the opening, greeted him half-kindly, half-shyly, coloured extremely at the deep and significant reverence with which he returned her courtesy, shut the casement and disappeared.

Daylight and champaign could discover no more! The authenticity of the billet was ascertained; it only remained what was to follow, and of this the fair writer had given him no hint. But no immediate danger impended. The countess was in a strong castle, under the protection of a prince, at once respectable for his secular and venerable for his ecclesiastical authority. There was neither immediate room nor occasion for the exulting squire interfering in the adventure; and it was sufficient if he kept himself prompt to execute her commands whenever they should be communicated to him. But Fate purposed to call him into action sooner than he was aware of.

It was the fourth night after his arrival at Schonwaldt, when Quentin had taken measures for sending back on the morrow, to the court of Louis, the remaining groom who had accompanied him on his journey, with letters from himself to his uncle and Lord Crawford, renouncing the service of France, for which the treachery to which he had been exposed by the private instructions of Hayraddin gave him an excuse, both in honour and prudence; and he betook himself to his bed with all the rosy-coloured ideas around him which flutter about the couch of a youth when he loves dearly, and thinks his love as sincerely repaid.

But Quentin's dreams, which at first partook of the nature of those happy influences under which he had fallen asleep, began by degrees to assume a more terrific character.

He walked with the Countess Isabelle beside a smooth and inland lake, such as formed the principal characteristic of his native glen; and he spoke to her of his love, without any consciousness of the impediments which lay between them. She blushed and smiled when she listened, even as he might have expected from the tenor of the letter, which, sleeping or waking, lay nearest to his heart. But the scene suddenly changed from summer to winter, from calm to tempest; the winds and the waves rose with such a contest of surge and whirlwind, as if the demons of the water and of the air had been contending for their roaring empires in rival strife. The rising waters seemed to cut off their advance and their retreat; the increasing tempest, which dashed them against each other, seemed to render their remaining on the spot impossible; and the tumultuous sensations produced by the apparent danger awoke the dreamer.

He awoke; but although the circumstances of the vision had disappeared, and given place to reality, the noise, which had probably suggested them, still continued to sound in his ears.

Quentin's first impulse was to sit erect in bed, and listen with astonishment to sounds, which, if they had announced a tempest, might have shamed the wildest that ever burst down from the Grampians; and again in a minute he became sensible, that the tumult was not excited by the fury of the elements, but by the wrath of men.

He sprung from bed, and looked from the window of his apartment; but it opened into the garden, and on that side all was quiet, though the opening of the casement made him still more sensible, from the shouts which reached his ears, that the outside of the castle was beleaguered and assaulted, and that by a numerous and determined enemy. Hastily collecting his dress and arms, and putting them on with such celerity as darkness and surprise permitted, his attention was solicited by a knocking at the door of his chamber. As Quentin did not immediately answer, the door, which was a slight one, was forced open from without, and the intruder, announced by his peculiar dialect to be the Bohemian, Hayraddin Maugrabin, entered the apartment. A phial, which he held in his hand, touched by a match, produced a dark flash of ruddy fire, by means of which he kindled a lamp, which he took from his bosom.

"The horoscope of your destinies," he said energetically to Durward, without any farther greeting, "now turns upon the determination of a minute."

"Caitiff!" said Quentin, in reply, "there is treachery around us; and where there is treachery, thou *must* have a share in it."

"You are mad," answered Maugrabin, "I never betrayed any one but to gain by it, and wherefore should I betray you, by whose safety I can take more advantage than by your destruction? Hearken for a moment, if it be possible for you, to one note of reason ere it is sounded into your ear by the death-shot of ruin. The Liegeois are up; William de la Marck with his band leads them. Were there means of resistance, their numbers and his fury would overcome them; but there are next to none. If you would save the countess and your own hopes, follow me, in the name of her who sent you a table-diamond, with three leopards engraved on it!"

"Lead the way," said Quentin, hastily. "In that name I dare every danger!"

"As I shall manage it," said the Bohemian, "there is no danger, if you can but withhold your hand from strife which does not concern you; for, after all, what is it to you whether the bishop, as they call him, slaughters his flock, or the flock slaughters the shepherd? Ha! ha! ha! Follow me, but with caution and patience; subdue your own courage, and confide in my prudence; and my debt of thankfulness is paid, and you have a countess for your spouse. Follow me."

"I follow," said Quentin, drawing his sword; "but the moment in which I detect the least sign of treachery, thy head and body are three yards separate!"

Without more conversation, the Bohemian, seeing that Quentin was now fully armed and ready, ran down the stairs before him, and winded hastily through various side-passages, until they gained the little garden. Scarce a light was to be seen on that side, scarce any bustle was to be heard; but no sooner had Quentin entered the open space than the noise on the opposite side of the castle became ten times more stunningly audible, and he could hear the various war-cries of "Liege! Liege! Sanglier! Sanglier!" shouted by the assailants, while the feebler cry of "Our Lady for the Prince Bishop!" was raised in a faint and faltering tone, by those of the prelate's soldiers who had hastened, though surprised and at disadvantage, to the defence of the walls.

But the interest of the fight, notwithstanding the martial character of Quentin Durward, was indifferent to him in comparison of the fate of Isabelle of Croye, which, he had reason to fear, would be a dreadful one, unless rescued from the power of the dissolute and cruel freebooter, who was now, as it seemed, bursting the gates of the castle. He reconciled himself to the aid of the Bohemian, as men in a desperate illness refuse not the remedy prescribed by quacks and mountebanks, and followed across the garden, with the intention of being guided by him until he should discover symptoms of treachery, and then piercing him through the heart, or striking his head from his body. Hayraddin seemed himself conscious that his safety turned on a feather-weight, for he forbore, from the moment they entered the open air, all his wonted gibes and quirks, and seemed to have made a vow to act at once with modesty, courage, and activity.

At the opposite door, which led to the ladies' apartments, upon a low signal made by Hayraddin, appeared two women, muffled in the black silk veils which were then, as now, worn by the women in the Netherlands. Quentin offered his arm to one of them, who clung to it with trembling eagerness, and indeed hung upon him so much that had her weight been greater she must have much impeded their retreat. The Bohemian, who conducted the other female, took the road straight for the postern which opened upon the moat, through the garden-wall, close to which the little skiff was drawn up, by means of which Quentin had formerly observed Hayraddin himself retreating from the castle.

As they crossed, the shouts of storm and successful violence seemed to announce that the castle was in the act of being taken; and so dismal was the sound in Quentin's ears, that he could not help swearing aloud: "But that my blood is irretrievably devoted to the fulfilment of my present duty, I would back to the wall, take faithful part with the hospitable bishop, and silence some of those knaves whose throats are full of mutiny and robbery!"

The lady, whose arm was still folded in his, pressed it lightly as he spoke, as if to make him understand that there was a nearer claim on his chivalry than the defence of Schonwaldt; while the Bohemian exclaimed, loud enough to be heard: "Now, that I call right Christian frenzy, which would turn back to fight, when love and fortune both demand that we should fly. On—on, with all the haste you can make. Horses wait us in yonder thicket of willows."

"There are but two horses," said Quentin, who saw them in the moonlight.

"All that I could procure without exciting suspicion, and enough, besides," replied the Bohemian. "You two must ride for Tongres ere the way becomes unsafe; Marthon will abide with the women of our horde, with whom she is an old acquaintance. Know, she is a daughter of our tribe, and only dwelt among you to serve our purpose as occasion should fall."

"Marthon!" exclaimed the countess, looking at the veiled female with a shriek of surprise; "is not this my kinswoman?"

"Only Marthon," said Hayraddin. "Excuse me that little piece of deceit. I dared not carry off *both* the Ladies of Croye from the Wild Boar of Ardennes."

"Wretch!" said Quentin, emphatically; "but it is not—shall not—be too late: I will back to rescue the Lady Hameline."

"Hameline," whispered the lady, in a disturbed voice, "hangs on thy arm to thank thee for her rescue."

"Ha! what! How is this?" said Quentin, extricating himself from her hold, and with less gentleness than he would at any other time have used towards a female of any rank. "Is the Lady Isabelle then left behind? Farewell—farewell."

As he turned to hasten back to the castle, Hayraddin laid

hold of him. "Nay, hear you—hear you—you run upon your death! What the foul fiend did you wear the colours of the old one for? I will never trust blue and white silk again. But she has almost as large a dower—has jewels and gold—hath pretensions, too, upon the earldom."

While he spoke thus, panting on in broken sentences, the Bohemian struggled to detain Quentin, who at length laid his hand on his dagger, in order to extricate himself.

"Nay if that be the case," said Hayraddin, unloosing his hold, "go, and the devil, if there be one, go along with you!" And, soon as freed from his hold, the Scot shot back to the castle with the speed of the wind.

Hayraddin then turned round to the Countess Hameline, who had sunk down on the ground, between shame, fear, and disappointment.

"Here has been a mistake," he said. "Up, lady, and come with me; I will provide you, ere morning comes, a gallanter husband than this smock-faced boy; and if one will not serve, you shall have twenty."

The Lady Hameline was as violent in her passions as she was vain and weak in her understanding. Like many other persons, she went tolerably well through the ordinary duties of life; but in a crisis like the present she was entirely incapable of doing aught, save pouring forth unavailing lamentations, and accusing Hayraddin of being a thief, a base slave, an impostor, a murderer.

"Call me Zingaro," returned he, composedly, "and you have said all at once."

"Monster! you said the stars had decreed our union, and caused me to write—O wretch that I was!" exclaimed the unhappy lady.

"And so they *had* decreed your union," said Hayraddin, "had both parties been willing; but think you the blessed constellations can make any one wed against his will? I was led into error with your accursed Christian gallantries, and fopperies of ribbons and favours, and the youth prefers veal to beef, I think, that's all. Up and follow me; and take notice, I endure neither weeping nor swooning."

"I will not stir a foot," said the countess, obstinately.

"By the bright welkin, but you shall, though!" exclaimed Hayraddin. "I swear to you, by all that ever fools believed in, that you have to do with one who would care little to strip you naked, bind you to a tree, and leave you to your fortune!"

"Nay," said Marthon, interfering, "by your favour she shall not be misused. I wear a knife as well as you, and can use it. She is a kind woman, though a fool. And, you, madam, rise up and follow us. Here has been a mistake; but it is something to have saved life and limb. There are many in yonder castle would give all the wealth in the world to stand where we do now."

As Marthon spoke, a clamour, in which the shouts of victory were mingled with screams of terror and despair, was wafted to them from the castle of Schonwaldt.

"Hear that, lady!" said Hayraddin, "and be thankful you are not adding your treble pipe to yonder concert. Believe me, I will care for you honestly, and the stars shall keep their words, and find you a good husband."

Like some wild animal, exhausted and subdued by terror and fatigue, the Countess Hameline yielded herself up to the conduct of her guides, and suffered herself to be passively led whichever way they would. Nay, such was the confusion of her spirits and the exhaustion of her strength, that the worthy couple, who half bore, half led her, carried on their discourse in her presence without her even understanding it.

"I ever thought your plan was a folly," said Marthon. "Could you have brought the *young* people together, indeed, we might have had a hold on their gratitude, and a footing in their castle. But what chance of so handsome a youth wedding this old fool?"

"Rizpah," said Hayraddin, "you have borne the name of a Christian, and dwelt in the tents of those besotted people, till thou hast become a partaker in their follies. How could I dream that he would have made scruples about a few years, youth or age, when the advantages of the match were so evident? And thou knowest, there would have been no moving yonder coy wench to be so frank as this coming countess here,

who hangs on our arms as dead a weight as a wool-pack. I
loved the lad too, and would have done him a kindness: to
wed him to this old woman was to make his fortune; to unite
him to Isabelle were to have brought on him De la Marck,
Burgundy, France—every one that challenges an interest in
disposing of her hand. And this silly woman's wealth being
chiefly in gold and jewels, we should have had our share.
But the bow-string has burst and the arrow failed. Away
with her; we will bring her to William with the Beard. By
the time he has gorged himself with wassail, as is his wont,
he will not know an old countess from a young one. Away,
Rizpah; bear a gallant heart. The bright Aldebaran still
influences the destinies of the Children of the Desert!"

CHAPTER XXI.

THE SACK.

The gates of mercy shall be all shut up,
And the flesh'd soldier, rough and hard of heart,
In liberty of bloody hand shall range,
With conscience wide as hell.
Henry V.

THE surprised and affrighted garrison of the castle of Schonwaldt had, nevertheless, for some time made good the defence against the assailants; but the immense crowds which, issuing from the city of Liege, thronged to the assault like bees, distracted their attention and abated their courage.

There was also disaffection at least, if not treachery, among the defenders; for some called out to surrender, and others, deserting their posts, tried to escape from the castle. Many threw themselves from the walls into the moat, and such as escaped drowning flung aside their distinguishing badges, and saved themselves by mingling among the motley crowd of assailants. Some few, indeed, from attachment to the bishop's person, drew around him, and continued to defend the great keep, to which he had fled; and others, doubtful of receiving quarter, or from an impulse of desperate courage, held out other detached bulwarks and towers of the extensive building. But the assailants had got possession of the courts and lower parts of the edifice, and were busy pursuing the vanquished and searching for spoil, while one individual, as if he sought for that death from which all others were flying, endeavoured to force his way into the scene of tumult and horror, under apprehensions still more horrible to his imagination than the realities around were to his sight and senses. Whoever had seen Quentin Durward that fatal night, not knowing the meaning of his conduct, had accounted him a raging madman; whoever had appreciated his motives had ranked him nothing beneath a hero of romance.

Approaching Schonwaldt on the same side from which he had left it, the youth met several fugitives making for the wood, who naturally avoided him as an enemy, because he came in an opposite direction from that which they had adopted. When he came nearer, he could hear, and partly see, men dropping from the garden-wall into the castle fosse, and others who seemed precipitated from the battlements by the assailants. His courage was not staggered, even for an instant. There was not time to look for the boat, even had it been practicable to use it, and it was in vain to approach the postern of the garden, which was crowded with fugitives, who ever and anon, as they were thrust through it by the pressure behind, fell into the moat which they had no means of crossing.

Avoiding that point, Quentin threw himself into the moat, near what was called the little gate of the castle, and where there was a drawbridge, which was still elevated. He avoided with difficulty the fatal grasp of more than one sinking wretch, and, swimming to the drawbridge, caught hold of one of the chains which was hanging down, and, by a great exertion of strength and activity, swayed himself out of the water, and attained the platform from which the bridge was suspended. As with hands and knees he struggled to make good his footing, a lanzknecht, with his bloody sword in his hand, made towards him, and raised his weapon for a blow, which must have been fatal.

"How now, fellow!" said Quentin, in a tone of authority. "Is that the way in which you assist a comrade? Give me your hand."

The soldier in silence, and not without hesitation, reached him his arm, and helped him upon the platform, when without allowing him time for reflection, the Scot continued in the same tone of command: "To the western tower, if you would be rich: the priest's treasury is in the western tower."

These words were echoed on every hand: "To the western tower, the treasure is in the western tower!" And the stragglers who were within hearing the cry, took, like a herd of raging wolves, the direction opposite to that which Quentin, come life, come death, was determined to pursue.

Bearing himself as if he were one, not of the conquered, but of the victors, he made a way into the garden, and pushed across it, with less interruption than he could have expected; for the cry of "To the western tower!" had carried off one body of the assailants, and another was summoned together, by war-cry and trumpet-sound, to assist in repelling a desperate sally, attempted by the defenders of the keep, who had hoped to cut their way out of the castle, bearing the bishop along with them. Quentin, therefore, crossed the garden with an eager step and throbbing heart, commending himself to those Heavenly powers which had protected him through the numberless perils of his life, and bold in his determination to succeed, or leave his life in this desperate undertaking. Ere he reached the garden, three men rushed on him with levelled lances, crying, "Liege—Liege!"

Putting himself in defence, but without striking, he replied, "France—France, friend to Liege!"

"*Vivat France!*" cried the burghers of Liege, and passed on. The same signal proved a talisman to avert the weapons of four or five of La Marck's followers, whom he found straggling in the garden, and who set upon him crying, "Sanglier!"

In a word Quentin began to hope that his character as an emissary of King Louis, the private instigator of the insurgents of Liege, and the secret supporter of William de la Marck, might possibly bear him through the horrors of the night.

On reaching the turret, he shuddered when he found the little side door, through which Marthon and the Countess Hameline had shortly before joined him, was now blockaded with more than one dead body.

Two of them he dragged hastily aside, and was stepping over the third body, in order to enter the portal, when the supposed dead man laid hand on his cloak, and entreated him to stay and assist him to rise. Quentin was about to use rougher methods than struggling to rid himself of this untimely obstruction, when the fallen man continued to exclaim: "I am stifled here, in mine own armour! I am the Syndic Pavillon of Liege! If you are for us, I will enrich you—if you are for the other side, I will protect you; but do not—do not leave me to die the death of a smothered pig!"

In the midst of this scene of blood and confusion, the presence of mind of Quentin suggested to him, that this dignitary might have the means of protecting their retreat. He raised him on his feet, and asked him if he was wounded.

"Not wounded—at least I think not," answered the burgher; "but much out of wind."

"Sit down then on this stone, and recover your breath," said Quentin; "I will return instantly."

"For whom are you?" said the burgher, still detaining him.

"For France—for France," answered Quentin, studying to get away.

"What! my lively young archer?" said the worthy syndic. "Nay, if it has been my fate to find a friend in this fearful night, I will not quit him, I promise you. Go where you will, I follow; and, could I get some of the tight lads of our guildry together, I might be able to help you in turn; but they are all squandered abroad like so many pease. Oh, it is a fearful night!"

During this time, he was dragging himself on after Quentin, who, aware of the importance of securing the countenance of a person of such influence, slackened his pace to assist him, although cursing in his heart the encumbrance that retarded him.

At the top of the stair was an ante-room, with boxes and

trunks, which bore marks of having been rifled, as some of the contents lay on the floor. A lamp, dying in the chimney, shed a feeble beam on a dead or senseless man, who lay across the hearth.

Bounding from Pavillon, like a greyhound from his keeper's leash, and with an effort which almost overthrew him, Quentin sprung through a second and third room, the last of which seemed to be the bedroom of the Ladies of Croye. No living mortal was to be seen in either of them. He called upon the Lady Isabelle's name, at first gently, then more loudly, and then with an accent of despairing emphasis; but no answer was returned. He wrung his hands, tore his hair, and stamped on the earth with deperation. At length, a feeble glimmer of light, which shone through a crevice in the wainscoting of a dark nook in the bedroom, announced some recess or concealment behind the arras. Quentin hasted to examine it. He found there was indeed a concealed door, but it resisted his hurried efforts to open it. Heedless of the personal injury he might sustain, he rushed at the door with his whole force and weight of his body; and such was the impetus of an effort made betwixt hope and despair, that it would have burst much stronger fastenings.

He thus forced his way, almost headlong, into a small oratory, where a female figure, which had been kneeling in agonising supplication before the holy image, now sunk at length on the floor, under the new terrors implied in this approaching tumult. He hastily raised her from the ground, and joy of joys! it was she whom he sought to save—the Countess Isabelle. He pressed her to his bosom—he conjured her to awake—entreated her to be of good cheer—for that she was now under the protection of one who had heart and hand enough to defend her against armies.

"Durward!" she said, as she at length collected herself, "is it indeed you? Then there is some hope left. I thought all living and mortal friends had left me to my fate. Do not again abandon me."

"Never—never!" said Durward. "Whatever shall happen —whatever danger shall approach, may I forfeit the benefits purchased by yonder blessed sign, if I be not the sharer of your fate until it is again a happy one!"

"Very pathetic and touching, truly," said a rough, broken, asthmatic voice behind. "A love affair, I see; and, from my soul, I pity the tender creature, as if she were my own Trudchen."

"You must do more than pity us," said Quentin, turning towards the speaker; "you must assist in protecting us, Meinherr Pavillon. Be assured this lady was put under my especial charge by your ally the King of France; and, if you aid me not to shelter her from every species of offence and violence, your city will lose the favour of Louis of Valois. Above all, she must be guarded from the hands of William de la Marck."

"That will be difficult," said Pavillon, "for these *schelms* of lanzknechts are very devils at rummaging out the wenches; but I'll do my best. We will to the other apartment, and there I will consider. It is but a narrow stair, and you can keep the door with a pike, while I look from the window, and get together some of my brisk boys of the curriers' guildry of Liege, that are as true as the knives they wear in their girdles. But first undo me these clasps; for I have not worn this corslet since the battle of St. Tron,[1] and I am three stone heavier since that time, if there be truth in Dutch beam and scale."

The undoing of the iron inclosure gave great relief to the honest man, who, in putting it on, had more considered his zeal to the cause of Liege than his capacity of bearing arms. It afterwards turned out that, being, as it were, borne forward involuntarily, and hoisted over the walls by his company as they thronged to the assault, the magistrate had been carried here and there, as the tide of attack and defence flowed or ebbed, without the power, latterly, of even uttering a word; until, as the sea casts a log of driftwood ashore in the first creek, he had been ultimately thrown down in the entrance to the Ladies of Croyes' apartments, where the encumbrance of his own armour, with the superincumbent weight of two men slain in the entrance, and who fell above him, might have fixed

See Note 30.

him down long enough, had he not been relieved by Durward.

The same warmth of temper, which rendered Hermann Pavillon a hot-headed and intemperate zealot in politics, had the more desirable consequence of making him, in private, a good-tempered, kind-hearted man, who, if sometimes a little misled by vanity, was always well-meaning and benevolent. He told Quentin to have an especial care of the poor pretty *yungfrau;* and, after this unnecessary exhortation, began to halloo from the window, "Liege—Liege, for the gallant skinners' guild of curriers!"

One or two of his immediate followers collected at the summons, and at the peculiar whistle with which it was accompanied (each of the crafts having such a signal among themselves), and, more joining them, established a guard under the window from which the leader was bawling, and before the postern-door.

Matters seemed now settling into some sort of tranquillity. All opposition had ceased, and the leaders of the different classes of assailants were taking measures to prevent indiscriminate plunder. The great bell was tolled, as summons to a military council, and its iron tongue, communicating to Liege the triumphant possession of Schonwaldt by the insurgents, was answered by all the bells in that city, whose distant and clamorous voices seemed to cry, "Hail to the victors!" It would have been natural, that Meinherr Pavillon should now have sallied from his fastness; but, either in reverent care of those whom he had taken under his protection, or perhaps for the better assurance of his own safety, he contented himself with despatching messenger on messenger, to command his lieutenant, Peterkin Geislaer, to attend him directly.

Peterkin came at length, to his great relief, as being the person upon whom, on all pressing occasions, whether of war, politics, or commerce, Pavillon was most accustomed to repose confidence. He was a stout, squat figure, with a square face and broad black eyebrows, that announced him to be opinionative and disputatious,—an advice-giving countenance, so to speak. He was endued with a buff-jerkin, wore a broad belt and cutlass by his side, and carried a halberd in his hand.

"Peterkin, my dear lieutenant," said his commander, "this has been a glorious day—night, I should say; I trust thou art pleased for once?"

"I am well enough pleased that you are so," said the doughty lieutenant; "though I should not have thought of your celebrating the victory, if you call it one, up in this garret by yourself, when you are wanted in council."

"But *am* I wanted there?" said the syndic.

"Ay, marry are you, to stand up for the rights of Liege, that are in more danger than ever," answered the lieutenant.

"Pshaw, Peterkin," answered his principal, "thou art ever such a frampold grumbler——"

"Grumbler! not I," said Peterkin; "what pleases other people will always please me. Only I wish we have not got King Stork, instead of King Log, like the *fabliau* that the clerk of St. Lambert's used to read us out of Meister Æsop's book."

"I cannot guess your meaning, Peterkin," said the syndic.

"Why, then, I tell you, Master Pavillon, that this Boar, or Bear, is like to make his own den of Schonwaldt, and 'tis probable to turn out as bad a neighbour to our town as ever was the old bishop and worse. Here has he taken the whole conquest in his own hand, and is only doubting whether he should be called prince or bishop; and it is a shame to see how they have mishandled the old man among them."

"I will not permit it, Peterkin," said Pavillon, bustling up; "I disliked the mitre, but not the head that wore it. We are ten to one in the field, Peterkin, and will not permit these courses."

"Ay, ten to one in the field, but only man to man in the castle; besides that Nikkel Blok the butcher, and all the rabble of the suburbs, take part with William de la Marck, partly for *saus* and *braus*, for he had broached all the ale-tubs and wine-casks, and partly for old envy towards us, who are the craftsmen, and have privileges."

"Peter," said Pavillon, "we will go presently to the city. I will stay no longer in Schonwaldt."

"But the bridges of this castle are up, master," said Geislaer; "the gates locked, and guarded by these lanzknechts; and, if we were to try to force our way, these fellows, whose every-day business is war, might make wild work of us, that only fight of a holyday."

"But why has he secured the gates?" said the alarmed burgher; "or what business hath he to make honest men prisoners?"

"I cannot tell—not I," said Peter. "Some noise there is about the Ladies of Croye, who have escaped during the storm of the castle. That first put the Man with the Beard beside himself with anger, and now he's beside himself with drink also."

The burgomaster cast a disconsolate look towards Quentin, and seemed at a loss what to resolve upon. Durward, who had not lost a word of the conversation, which alarmed him very much, saw nevertheless that their only safety depended on his preserving his own presence of mind, and sustaining the courage of Pavillon. He struck boldly into the conversation, as one who had a right to have a voice in the deliberation. "I am ashamed," he said, "Meinherr Pavillon, to observe you hesitate what to do on this occasion. Go boldly to William de la Marck, and demand free leave to quit the castle, you, your lieutenant, your squire, and your daughter. He can have no pretence for keeping you prisoner."

"For me and my lieutenant—that is myself and Peter—good; but who is my squire?"

"I am, for the present," replied the undaunted Scot.

"You!" said the embarrassed burgess; "but are you not the envoy of King Louis of France?"

"True, but my message is to the magistrates of Liege, and only in Liege will I deliver it. Were I to acknowledge my quality before William de la Marck, must I not enter into negotiation with him—ay, and, it is like, be detained by him? You must get me secretly out of the castle in the capacity of your squire."

"Good—my squire. But you spoke of my daughter; my daughter is, I trust, safe in my house in Liege—where I wish her father was, with all my heart and soul."

"This lady," said Durward, "will call you father while we are in this place."

"And for my whole life afterwards," said the countess, throwing herself at the citizen's feet and clasping his knees. "Never shall the day pass in which I will not honour you, love you, and pray for you as a daughter for a father, if you will but aid me in this fearful strait. Oh, be not hard-hearted! think your own daughter may kneel to a stranger, to ask him for life and honour—think of this and give *me* the protection you would wish *her* to receive!"

"In troth," said the good citizen, much moved with her pathetic appeal, "I think, Peter, that this pretty maiden hath a touch of our Trudchen's sweet look,—I thought so from the first; and that this brisk youth here, who is so ready with his advice, is somewhat like Trudchen's bachelor. I wager a groat, Peter, that this is a true-love matter, and it is a sin not to further it."

"It were shame and sin both," said Peter, a good-natured Fleming, notwithstanding all his self-conceit; and as he spoke he wiped his eyes with the sleeve of his jerkin.

"She *shall* be my daughter, then," said Pavillon, "well wrapped up in her black silk veil; and if there are not enough of true-hearted skinners to protect her, being the daughter of their syndic, it were pity they should ever tug leather more. But hark ye, questions must be answered. How if I am asked what should my daughter make here at such an onslaught?"

"What should half the women in Liege make here when they followed us to the castle?" said Peter; "they had no other reason, sure, but that it was just the place in the world that they should *not* have come to. Our *yungfrau* Trudchen has come a little farther than the rest, that is all."

"Admirably spoken," said Quentin: "only be bold, and take this gentleman's good counsel, noble Meinherr Pavillon, and, at no trouble to yourself, you will do the most worthy action since the days of Charlemagne. Here, sweet lady, wrap yourself close in this veil," for many articles of female apparel lay scattered about the apartment; "be but confident, and a few minutes will place you in freedom and safety. Noble sir," he added, addressing Pavillon, "set forward."

"Hold—hold—hold a minute," said Pavillon, "my mind misgives me! This De la Marck is a fury—a perfect boar in his nature as in his name; what if the young lady be one of those of Croye? and what if he discover her, and be addicted to wrath?"

"And if I were one of those unfortunate women," said Isabelle, again attempting to throw herself at his feet, "could you for that reject me in this moment of despair? Oh, that I had been indeed your daughter or the daughter of the poorest burgher!"

"Not so poor—not so poor neither, young lady; we pay as we go," said the citizen.

"Forgive me, noble sir," again began the unfortunate maiden.

"Not noble, nor sir neither," said the syndic; "a plain burgher of Liege, that pays bills of exchange in ready guilders. But that is nothing to the purpose. Well, say you *be* a countess, I will protect you nevertheless."

"You are bound to protect her, were she a duchess," said Peter, "having once passed your word."

"Right, Peter, very right," said the syndic; "it is our old Low Dutch fashion, *ein wort, ein mann;* and now let us to this gear. We must take leave of this William de la Marck; and yet I know not, my mind misgives me when I think of him; and were it a ceremony which could be waived, I have no stomach to go through it."

"Were you not better, since you have a force together, make for the gate and force the guard?" said Quentin.

But with united voice, Pavillon and his adviser exclaimed against the propriety of such an attack upon their ally's soldiers, with some hints concerning its rashness, which satisfied Quentin that it was not a risk to be hazarded with such associates. They resolved, therefore, to repair boldly to the great hall of the castle, where, as they understood, the Wild Boar of Ardennes held his feast, and demand free egress for the syndic of Liege and his company, a request too reasonable, as it seemed, to be denied. Still the good burgomaster groaned when he looked on his companions, and exclaimed to his faithful Peter: "See what it is to have too bold and too tender a heart! Alas! Peterkin, how much have courage and humanity cost me! and how much may I yet have to pay for my virtues before Heaven makes us free of this damned castle of Schonwaldt!"

As they crossed the courts, still strewed with the dying and dead, Quentin, while he supported Isabelle through the scene of horrors, whispered to her courage and comfort, and reminded her that her safety depended entirely on her firmness and presence of mind.

"Not on mine—not on mine," she said "but on yours—on yours only. Oh, if I but escape this fearful night, never shall I forget him who saved me! One favour more only let me implore at your hand, and I conjure you to grant it, by your mother's fame and your father's honour!"

"What is it you can ask that I could refuse?" said Quentin in a whisper.

"Plunge your dagger in my heart," said she, "rather than leave me captive in the hands of these monsters."

Quentin's only answer was a pressure of the young countess's hand, which seemed as if, but for terror, it would have returned the caress. And, leaning on her youthful protector, she entered the fearful hall, preceded by Pavillon and his lieutenant, and followed by a dozen of the *kurschenschaft* [*kürschnerschaft*] or skinner's trade, who attended as a guard of honour on the syndic.

As they approached the hall, the yells of acclamation and bursts of wild laughter, which proceeded from it, seemed rather to announce the revel of festive demons rejoicing after some accomplished triumph over the human race than of mortal beings who had succeeded in a bold design. An emphatic tone of mind, which despair alone could have inspired, supported the assumed courage of the Countess Isabelle; undaunted spirits, which rose with the extremity, maintained that of Durward; while Pavillon and his lieutenant made a virtue of necessity, and faced their fate like bears bound to a stake, which must necessarily stand the dangers of the course.

CHAPTER XXII.

THE REVELLERS.

Cade. Where's Dick, the butcher of Ashford?
Dick. Here, sir.
Cade. They fell before thee like sheep and oxen; and thou behavedst thyself as if thou hadst been in thine own slaughter-house.
King Henry VI., Part II.

THERE could hardly exist a more strange and horrible change than had taken place in the castle-hall of Schonwaldt since Quentin had partaken of the noontide meal there; and it was indeed one which painted, in the extremity of their dreadful features, the miseries of war—more especially when waged by those most relentless of all agents, the mercenary soldiers of a barbarous age—men who, by habit and profession, had become familiarised with all that was cruel and bloody in the art of war, while they were devoid alike of patriotism and of the romantic spirit of chivalry.

Instead of the orderly, decent, and somewhat formal meal, at which civil and ecclesiastical officers had, a few hours before, sat mingled in the same apartment, where a light jest could only be uttered in a whisper, and where, even amid superfluity of feasting and of wine, there reigned a decorum which almost amounted to hypocrisy, there was now such a scene of wild and roaring debauchery as Satan himself, had he taken the chair as founder of the feast, could scarcely have improved.

At the head of the table sat, in the bishop's throne and state, which had been hastily brought thither from his great council-chamber, the redoubted Boar of Ardennes himself, well deserving that dreaded name, in which he affected to delight, and which he did as much as he could think of to deserve. His head was unhelmeted, but he wore the rest of his ponderous and bright armour, which indeed he rarely laid aside. Over his shoulders hung a strong surcoat, made of the dressed skin of a huge wild boar, the hoofs being of solid silver and the tusks of the same. The skin of the head was so arranged that, drawn over the casque when the baron was armed, or over his bare head, in the fashion of a hood, as he often affected when the helmet was laid aside, and as he now wore it, the effect was that of a grinning, ghastly monster; and yet the countenance which it overshadowed scarce required such horrors to improve those which were natural to its ordinary expression.

The upper part of De la Marck's face, as nature had formed it, almost gave the lie to his character; for though his hair, when uncovered, resembled the rude and wild bristles of the hood he had drawn over it, yet an open, high, and manly forehead, broad ruddy cheeks, large, sparkling, light-coloured eyes, and a nose hooked like the beak of the eagle, promised something valiant and generous. But the effect of these more favourable traits was entirely overpowered by his habits of violence and insolence, which, joined to debauchery and intemperance, had stamped upon the features a character inconsistent with the rough gallantry which they would otherwise have exhibited. The former had, from habitual indulgence, swoln the muscles of the cheeks and those around the eyes, in particular the latter; evil practices and habits had dimmed the eyes themselves, reddened the part of them that should have been white, and given the whole face a hideous likeness of the monster which it was the terrible baron's pleasure to resemble. But from an odd sort of contradiction, De la Marck, while he assumed in other respects the appearance of the wild boar, and even seemed pleased with the name, yet endeavoured, by the length and growth of his beard, to conceal the circumstance that had originally procured him that denomination. This was an unusual thickness and projection of the mouth and upper jaw, which, with the huge and projecting side teeth, gave that resemblance to the bestial creation which, joined to the delight which De la Marck had in haunting the forest so called, originally procured for him the name of the Boar of Ardennes. The beard, broad, grisly, and uncombed, neither concealed the natural horrors of the countenance nor dignified its brutal expression.

The soldiers and officers sat around the table, intermixed

with the men of Liege, some of them of the very lowest description; among whom Nikkel Blok, the butcher, placed near De la Marck himself, was distinguished by his tucked-up sleeves, which displayed arms smeared to the elbows with blood, as was the cleaver which lay on the table before him. The soldiers wore, most of them, their beards long and grisly, in imitation of their leader; had their hair plaited and turned upwards, in the manner that might best improve the natural ferocity of their appearance; and intoxicated, as many of them seemed to be, partly with the sense of triumph, and partly with the long libations of wine which they had been quaffing, presented a spectacle at once hideous and disgusting. The language which they held, and the songs which they sung, without even pretending to pay each other the compliment of listening, were so full of license and blasphemy, that Quentin blessed God that the extremity of the noise prevented them from being intelligible to his companion.

It only remains to say, of the better class of burghers who were associated with William de la Marck's soldiers in this fearful revel, that the wan faces and anxious mien of the greater part showed that they either disliked their entertainment or feared their companions; while some of lower education, or a nature more brutal, saw only in the excesses of the soldier a gallant bearing, which they would willingly imitate, and the tone of which they endeavoured to catch so far as was possible, and stimulated themselves to the task by swallowing immense draughts of wine and *schwarzbier*—indulging in a vice which at all times was too common in the Low Countries.

The preparations for the feast had been as disorderly as the quality of the company. The whole of the bishop's plate— nay, even that belonging to the service of the church, for the Boar of Ardennes regarded not the imputation of sacrilege— was mingled with blackjacks, or huge tankards made of leather, and drinking-horns of the most ordinary description.

One circumstance of horror remains to be added and accounted for; and we willingly leave the rest of the scene to the imagination of the reader. Amidst the wild license assumed by the soldiers of De la Marck, one who was excluded from the table—a lanzknecht, remarkable for his courage and for his daring behaviour during the storm of the evening—had impudently snatched up a large silver goblet and carried it off, declaring it should atone for his loss of the share of the feast. The leader laughed till his sides shook at a jest so congenial to the character of the company; but when another, less renowned, it would seem, for audacity in battle, ventured on using the same freedom, De la Marck instantly put a check to a jocular practice which would soon have cleared his table of all the more valuable decorations. "Ho! by the spirit of the thunder!" he exclaimed, "those who dare not be men when they face the enemy must not pretend to be thieves among their friends. What! thou frontless dastard, thou—thou who didst wait for opened gate and lowered bridge, when Conrade Horst forced his way over moat and wall, must *thou* be malapert? Knit him up to the stanchions of the hall-window! He shall beat time with his feet while we drink a cup to his safe passage to the devil."

The doom was scarce sooner pronounced than accomplished; and in a moment the wretch wrestled out his last agonies, suspended from the iron bars. His body still hung there when Quentin and the others entered the hall, and intercepting the pale moonbeam, threw on the castle-floor an uncertain shadow, which dubiously, yet fearfully, intimated the nature of the substance that produced it.

When the syndic Pavillon was announced from mouth to mouth in this tumultuous meeting, he endeavoured to assume, in right of his authority and influence, an air of importance and equality, which a glance at the fearful object at the window, and at the wild scene around him, rendered it very difficult for him to sustain, notwithstanding the exhortations of Peter, who whispered in his ear, with some perturbation, "Up heart, master, or we are but gone men!"

The syndic maintained his dignity, however, as well as he could, in a short address, in which he complimented the company upon the great victory gained by the soldiers of De la Marck and the good citizens of Liege.

"Ay," answered De la Marck, sarcastically, "we have brought down the game at last, quoth my lady's brach to the wolf-hound. But ho! sir burgomaster, you come like Mars, with beauty by your side. Who is this fair one? Unveil—unveil; no woman calls her beauty her own to-night."

"It is my daughter, noble leader," answered Pavillon; "and I am to pray your forgiveness for her wearing a veil. She has a vow for that effect to the Three Blessed Kings."

"I will absolve her of it presently," said De la Marck; "for here, with one stroke of a cleaver, will I consecrate myself Bishop of Liege; and I trust one living bishop is worth three dead kings."

There was a shuddering and murmur among the guests; for the community of Liege, and even some of the rude soldiers, reverenced the Kings of Cologne, as they were commonly called, though they respected nothing else.

"Nay, I mean no treason against their defunct majesties," said De la Marck; "only bishop I am determined to be. A prince both secular and ecclesiastical, having power to bind and loose, will best suit a band of reprobates such as you, to whom no one else would give absolution. But come hither, noble burgomaster, sit beside me, when you shall see me make a vacancy for my own preferment. Bring in our predecessor in the holy seat."

A bustle took place in the hall, while Pavillon, excusing himself from the proffered seat of honour, placed himself near the bottom of the table, his followers keeping close behind him, not unlike a flock of sheep which, when a stranger dog is in presence, may be sometimes seen to assemble in the rear of an old belwether, who is, from office and authority, judged by them to have rather more courage than themselves. Near the spot sat a very handsome lad, a natural son, as was said, of the ferocious De la Marck, and towards whom he sometimes showed affection, and even tenderness. The mother of the boy, a beautiful concubine, had perished by a blow dealt her by the ferocious leader in a fit of drunkenness or jealousy; and her fate had caused her tyrant as much remorse as he was capable of feeling. His attachment to the surviving orphan might be partly owing to these circumstances. Quentin, who had learned this point of the leader's character from the old priest, planted himself as close as he could to the youth in question; determined to make him, in some way or other, either a hostage or a protector, should other means of safety fail them.

While all stood in a kind of suspense, waiting the event of the orders which the tyrant had issued, one of Pavillon's followers whispered Peter: "Did not our master call that wench his daughter? Why, it cannot be our Trudchen. This strapping lass is taller by two inches; and there is a black lock of hair peeps forth yonder from under her veil. By St. Michael of the market-place, you might as well call a black bullock's hide a white heifer's!"

"Hush! hush!" said Peter, with some presence of mind. "What if our master hath a mind to steal a piece of doe-venison out of the bishop's park here without our good dame's knowledge? And is it for thee or me to be a spy on him?"

"That will not I, brother," answered the other, "though I would not have thought of his turning deer-stealer at his years. *Sapperment*—what a shy fairy it is! See how she crouches down on yonder seat, behind folk's backs, to escape the gaze of the Marckers. But hold—hold; what are they about to do with the poor old bishop?"

As he spoke, the Bishop of Liege, Louis of Bourbon, was dragged into the hall of his own palace by the brutal soldiery. The dishevelled state of his hair, beard, and attire bore witness to the ill treatment he had already received; and some of his sacerdotal robes, hastily flung over him, appeared to have been put on in scorn and ridicule of his quality and character. By good fortune, as Quentin was compelled to think it, the Countess Isabelle, whose feelings at seeing her protector in such an extremity might have betrayed her own secret and compromised her safety, was so situated as neither to hear nor see what was about to take place; and Durward sedulously interposed his own person before her, so as to keep her from observing alike, and from observation.

The scene which followed was short and fearful. When

the unhappy prelate was brought before the footstool of the savage leader, although in former life only remarkable for his easy and good-natured temper, he showed in this extremity a sense of his dignity and noble blood, well becoming the high race from which he was descended. His look was composed and undismayed; his gesture, when the rude hands which dragged him forward were unloosed, was noble, and at the same time resigned, somewhat between the bearing of a feudal noble and of a Christian martyr; and so much was even De la Marck himself staggered by the firm demeanour of his prisoner, and recollection of the early benefits he had received from him, that he seemed irresolute, cast down his eyes, and it was not until he had emptied a large goblet of wine, that, resuming his haughty insolence of look and manner, he thus addressed his unfortunate captive: "Louis of Bourbon," said the truculent soldier, drawing hard his breath, clenching his hands, setting his teeth, and using the other mechanical actions to rouse up and sustain his native ferocity of temper, "I sought your friendship, and you rejected mine. What would you now give that it had been otherwise? Nikkel, be ready."

The butcher rose, seized his weapon, and stealing round behind De la Marck's chair, stood with it uplifted in his bare and sinewy arms.

"Look at that man, Louis of Bourbon," said De la Marck again; "what terms wilt thou now offer to escape this dangerous hour?"

The bishop cast a melancholy but unshaken look upon the grisly satellite, who seemed prepared to execute the will of the tyrant, and then he said with firmness: "Hear me, William de la Marck; and good men all, if there be any here who deserve that name, hear the only terms I can offer to this ruffian. William de la Marck, thou hast stirred up to sedition an imperial city, hast assaulted and taken the palace of a prince of the Holy German Empire, slain his people, plundered his goods, maltreated his person; for this thou art liable to the ban of the Empire—hast deserved to be declared outlawed and fugitive, landless and rightless. Thou hast done more than all this. More than mere human laws hast thou broken, more than mere human vengeance hast thou deserved. Thou hast broken into the sanctuary of the Lord, laid violent hands upon a father of the church, defiled the house of God with blood and rapine, like a sacrilegious robber——"

"Hast thou yet done?" said De la Marck, fiercely interrupting him, and stamping with his foot.

"No," answered the prelate, "for I have not yet told thee the terms which you demanded to hear from me."

"Go on," said De la Marck; "and let the terms please me better than the preface, or woe to thy grey head!" And flinging himself back in his seat, he grinded his teeth till the foam flew from his lips, as from the tusks of the savage animal whose name and spoils he wore.

"Such are thy crimes," resumed the bishop, with calm determination; "now hear the terms which, as a merciful prince and a Christian prelate, setting aside all personal offence, forgiving each peculiar injury, I condescend to offer. Fling down thy leading-staff, renounce thy command, unbind thy prisoners, restore thy spoil, distribute what else thou hast of goods to relieve those whom thou hast made orphans and widows, array thyself in sackcloth and ashes, take a palmer's staff in thy hand, and go barefooted on pilgrimage to Rome, and we will ourselves be intercessors for thee with the Imperial Chamber at Ratisbon for thy life, with our Holy Father the Pope for thy miserable soul."

While Louis of Bourbon proposed these terms in a tone as decided as if he still occupied his episcopal throne, and as if the usurper kneeled a suppliant at his feet, the tyrant slowly raised himself in his chair, the amazement with which he was at first filled giving way gradually to rage, until, as the bishop ceased, he looked to Nikkel Blok, and raised his finger, without speaking a word. The ruffian struck, as if he had been doing his office in the common shambles, and the murdered bishop sunk, without a groan, at the foot of his own episcopal throne.[1] The Liegeois, who were not prepared for so horrible a catastrophe, and who had expected to hear the conference end in some terms of accommodation, started up unani-

[1] See Murder of the Bishop of Liege. Note 31.

mously, with cries of execration, mingled with shouts of vengeance.

But William de la Marck, raising his tremendous voice above the tumult, and shaking his clenched hand and extended arm, shouted aloud: "How now, ye porkers of Liege! ye wallowers in the mud of the Maes! do ye dare to mate yourselves with the Wild Boar of Ardennes? Up, ye Boar's brood! (an expression by which he himself and others often designated his soldiers), let these Flemish hogs see your tusks!"

Every one of his followers started up at the command, and mingled as they were among their late allies, prepared too for such a surprisal, each had, in an instant, his next neighbour by the collar, while his right hand brandished a broad dagger that glimmered against lamplight and moonshine. Every arm was uplifted, but no one struck; for the victims were too much surprised for resistance, and it was probably the object of De la Marck only to impose terror on his civic confederates.

But the courage of Quentin Durward, prompt and alert in resolution beyond his years, and stimulated at the moment by all that could add energy to his natural shrewdness and resolution, gave a new turn to the scene. Imitating the action of the followers of De la Marck, he sprung on Carl Eberson, the son of their leader, and mastering him with ease, held his dirk at the boy's throat, while he exclaimed, "Is that your game? then here I play my part."

"Hold! hold!" exclaimed De la Marck, "it is a jest—a jest. Think you I would injure my good friends and allies of the city of Liege? Soldiers, unloose your holds; sit down; take away the carrion (giving the bishop's corpse a thrust with his foot), which hath caused this strife among friends, and let us drown unkindness in a fresh carouse."

All unloosened their holds, and the citizens and soldiers stood gazing on each other, as if they scarce knew whether they were friends or foes.

Quentin Durward took advantage of the moment. "Hear me," he said, "William De la Marck, and you, burghers and citizens of Liege; and do you, young sir, stand still," for the boy Carl was attempting to escape from his gripe, "no harm shall befall you, unless another of these sharp jests shall pass round."

"Who art thou, in the fiend's name," said the astonished De la Marck, "who art come to hold terms and take hostages from us in our own lair—from us, who exact pledges from others, but yield them to no one?"

"I am a servant of King Louis of France," said Quentin boldly; "an archer of the Scottish Guard, as my language and dress may partly tell you. I am here to behold and to report your proceedings; and I see with wonder that they are those of heathens rather than Christians—of madmen rather than men possessed of reason. The hosts of Charles of Burgundy will be instantly in motion against you all; and if you wish assistance from France, you must conduct yourselves in a different manner. For you, men of Liege, I advise your instant return to your own city; and if there is any obstruction offered to your departure, I denounce those by whom it is so offered foes to my master his most gracious Majesty of France."

"France and Liege! France and Liege!" cried the followers of Pavillon, and several other citizens, whose courage began to rise at the bold language held by Quentin.

"France and Liege, and long live the gallant archer! We will live and die with him!"

William de la Marck's eyes sparkled, and he grasped his dagger as if about to launch it at the heart of the audacious speaker; but glancing his eye around, he read something in the looks of his soldiers, which even *he* was obliged to respect. Many of them were Frenchmen, and all of them knew the private support which William had received, both in men and in money, from that kingdom; nay, some of them were rather startled at the violent and sacrilegious action which had been just committed. The name of Charles of Burgundy, a person likely to resent to the utmost the deeds of that night, had an alarming sound, and the extreme impolicy of at once quarrelling with the Liegeois and provoking the monarch of France, made an appalling impression on their minds, confused as their intellects were. De la Marck, in short, saw he would not be supported, even by his own band, in any farther act of immediate violence, and relaxing the terrors of his brow and eye, declared that "he had not the least design against his good friends of Liege, all of whom were at liberty to depart from Schonwaldt at their pleasure, although he had hoped they would revel one night with him, at least, in honour of their victory." He added, with more calmness than he commonly used, that "he would be ready to enter into negotiation concerning the partition of spoil, and the arrangement of measures for their mutual defence, either the next day, or as soon after as they would. Meantime, he trusted that the Scottish gentleman would honour his feast by remaining all night at Schonwaldt."

The young Scot returned his thanks, but said his motions must be determined by those of Pavillon, to whom he was directed particularly to attach himself; but that, unquestionably, he would attend him on his next return to the quarters of the valiant William de la Marck.

"If you depend on my motions," said Pavillon, hastily and aloud, "you are likely to quit Schonwaldt without an instant's delay; and, if you do not come back to Schonwaldt, save in my company, you are not likely to see it again in a hurry."

This last part of the sentence the honest citizen muttered to himself, afraid of the consequences of giving audible vent to feelings which, nevertheless, he was unable altogether to suppress.

"Keep close about me, my brisk *kürschner* lads," he said to his body-guard, "and we will get as fast as we can out of this den of thieves."

Most of the better classes of the Liegeois seemed to entertain similar opinions with the syndic, and there had been scarce so much joy amongst them at the obtaining possession of Schonwaldt, as now seemed to arise from the prospect of getting safe out of it. They were suffered to leave the castle without opposition of any kind; and glad was Quentin when he turned his back on those formidable walls.

For the first time since they had entered that dreadful hall, Quentin ventured to ask the young countess how she did.

"Well—well," she answered, in feverish haste, "excellently well; do not stop to ask a question; let us not lose an instant in words. Let us fly—let us fly!"

She endeavoured to mend her pace as she spoke; but with so little success that she must have fallen from exhaustion had not Durward supported her. With the tenderness of a mother, when she conveys her infant out of danger, the young Scot raised his precious charge in his arms; and, while she encircled his neck with one arm, lost to every other thought save the desire of escaping, he would not have wished one of the risks of the night unencountered, since such had been the conclusion.

The honest burgomaster was, in his turn, supported and dragged forward by his faithful counsellor Peter and another of his clerks; and thus, in breathless haste, they reached the banks of the river, encountering many strolling bands of citizens, who were eager to know the event of the siege, and the truth of certain rumours already afloat, that the conquerors had quarreled among themselves.

Evading their curiosity as they best could, the exertions of Peter and some of his companions at length procured a boat for the use of the company, and with it an opportunity of enjoying some repose, equally welcome to Isabelle, who continued to lie almost motionless in the arms of her preserver, and to the worthy burgomaster, who, after delivering a broken string of thanks to Durward, whose mind was at the time too much occupied to answer him, began a long harangue, which he addressed to Peter, upon his own courage and benevolence, and the dangers to which those virtues had exposed him on this and other occasions.

"Peter—Peter," he said, resuming the complaint of the preceding evening, "if I had not had a bold heart, I would never have stood out against paying the burghers' twentieths, when every other living soul was willing to pay the same. Ay, and then a less stout heart had not seduced me into that other battle of St. Tron, where a Hainault man-at-arms thrust me into a muddy ditch with his lance, which neither heart nor hand that I had could help me out of till the battle was over. Ay, and then, Peter, this very night my courage seduced me, moreover, into too strait a corslet, which would have been the death of me but for the aid of this gallant young gentleman, whose trade is fighting, whereof I wish him heartily joy. And then for my tenderness of heart, Peter, it has made a poor man of me—that is, it would have made a poor man of me if I had not been tolerably well to pass in this wicked world; and Heaven knows what trouble it is like to bring on me yet, with ladies, countesses, and keeping of secrets, which, for aught I know, may cost me half my fortune, and my neck into the bargain!"

Quentin could remain no longer silent, but assured him that, whatever danger or damage he should incur on the part of the young lady now under his protection should be thankfully acknowledged, and, as far as was possible, repaid.

"I thank you, young master squire archer—I thank you," answered the citizen of Liege; "but who was it told you that I desired any repayment at your hand for doing the duty of an honest man? I only regretted that it might cost me so and so; and I hope I may have leave to say so much to my lieutenant, without either grudging my loss or my peril."

Quentin accordingly concluded that his present friend was one of the numerous class of benefactors to others, who take out their reward in grumbling, without meaning more than, by showing their grievances, to exalt a little the idea of the valuable service by which they have incurred them, and therefore prudently remained silent, and suffered the syndic to maunder on to his lieutenant concerning the risk and the loss he had encountered by his zeal for the public good, and his disinterested services to individuals, until they reached his own habitation.

The truth was, that the honest citizen felt that he had lost a little consequence, by suffering the young stranger to take the lead at the crisis which had occurred at the castle-hall of Schonwaldt; and, however delighted with the effect of Durward's interference at the moment, it seemed to him, on reflection, that he had sustained a diminution of importance, for which he endeavoured to obtain compensation, by exaggerating the claims which he had upon the gratitude of his country in general, his friends in particular, and more especially still, on the Countess of Croye and her youthful protector.

But when the boat stopped at the bottom of his garden, and he had got himself assisted on shore by Peter, it seemed as if the touch of his own threshold had at once dissipated those feelings of wounded self-opinion and jealousy, and converted the discontented and obscured demagogue into the honest, kind, hospitable, and friendly host. He called loudly for Trudchen, who presently appeared; for fear and anxiety would permit few within the walls of Liege to sleep during that eventful night. She was charged to pay the utmost attention to the care of the beautiful and half-fainting stranger; and, admiring her personal charms, while she pitied her distress, Gertrude discharged the hospitable duty with the zeal and affection of a sister.

Late as it now was, and fatigued as the syndic appeared, Quentin, on his side, had difficulty to escape a flask of choice and costly wine, as old as the battle of Azincour; and must have submitted to take his share, however unwilling, but for the appearance of the mother of the family, whom Pavillon's loud summons for the keys of the cellar brought forth from her bedroom. She was a jolly little roundabout woman, who had been pretty in her time, but whose principal characteristics for several years had been a red and sharp nose, a shrill voice, and a determination that the syndic, in consideration of the authority which he exercised when abroad, should remain under the rule of due discipline at home.

So soon as she understood the nature of the debate between her husband and his guest, she declared roundly, that the former, instead of having occasion for more wine, had got too much already; and, far from using, in furtherance of his request, any of the huge bunch of keys which hung by a silver chain at her waist, she turned her back on him without ceremony, and ushered Quentin to the neat and pleasant apartment in which he was to spend the night, amid such appliances to rest and comfort as probably he had till that moment been entirely a stranger to; so much did the wealthy Flemings excel, not merely the poor and rude Scots, but the French themselves, in all the conveniences of domestic life.

CHAPTER XXIII.

THE FLIGHT.

>   Now bid me run,
> And I will strive with things impossible—
> Yea, get the better of them.
>
>   Set on your foot;
> And, with a heart new fired, I follow you,
> To do I know not what.
>
>   *Julius Cæsar.*

IN spite of a mixture of joy and fear, doubt, anxiety, and other agitating passions, the exhausting fatigues of the preceding day were powerful enough to throw the young Scot into a deep and profound repose, which lasted until late on the day following; when his worthy host entered the apartment with looks of care on his brow.

He seated himself by his guest's bedside, and began a long and complicated discourse upon the domestic duties of a married life, and especially upon the awful power and right supremacy which it became married men to sustain in all differences of opinion with their wives. Quentin listened with some anxiety. He knew that husbands, like other belligerent powers, were sometimes disposed to sing *Te Deum*, rather to conceal a defeat than to celebrate a victory; and he hastened to probe the matter more closely, " by hoping their arrival had been attended with no inconvenience to the good lady of the household."

"Inconvenience! no," answered the burgomaster. "No woman can be less taken unawares than Mother Mabel—always happy to see her friends—always a clean lodging and a handsome meal ready for them, with God's blessing on bed and board. No woman on earth so hospitable; only 'tis pity her temper is something particular."

"Our residence here is disagreeable to her, in short?" said the Scot, starting out of bed, and beginning to dress himself hastily. "Were I but sure the Lady Isabelle were fit for travel after the horrors of the last night, we would not increase the offence by remaining here an instant longer."

"Nay," said Pavillon, "that is just what the young lady herself said to Mother Mabel; and truly I wish you saw the colour that came to her face as she said it—a milkmaid that has skated five miles to market against the frost-wind is a lily compared to it—I do not wonder Mother Mabel may be a little jealous, poor dear soul."

"Has the Lady Isabelle then left her apartment?" said the youth, continuing his toilette operations with more despatch than before.

"Yes," replied Pavillon; "and she expects your approach with much impatience, to determine which way you shall go, since you are both determined on going. But I trust you will tarry breakfast?"

"Why did you not tell me this sooner?" said Durward impatiently.

"Softly—softly," said the syndic; "I have told it you too soon, I think, if it puts you into such a hasty fluster. Now I have some more matter for your ear, if I saw you had some patience to listen to me."

"Speak it, worthy sir, as soon and as fast as you can; I listen devoutly."

"Well, then," resumed the burgomaster, "I have but one word to say, and that is, that Trudchen, who is as sorry to part with yonder pretty lady as if she had been some sister of hers, wants you to take some other disguise; for there is word in the town that the Ladies of Croye travel the country in pilgrim's dresses, attended by a French life-guardsman of the Scottish Archers; and it is said one of them was brought into Schonwaldt last night by a Bohemian after we had left it; and it was said still farther, that this same Bohemian had assured William de la Marck that you were charged with no message either to him or to the good people of Liege, and that you had stolen away the young countess, and travelled with her as her paramour. And all this news hath come from Schonwaldt this morning; and it had been told to us and the other counsellors, who know not well what to advise; for though our own opinion is that William de la Marck has been a thought too rough both with the bishop and with ourselves, yet there is a great belief that he is a good-natured soul at bottom—that is, when he is sober—and that he is the only leader in the world to command us against the Duke of Burgundy—and, in truth, as matters stand, it is partly my own mind that we must keep fair with him, for we have gone too far to draw back."

"Your daughter advises well," said Quentin Durward, abstaining from reproaches or exhortations, which he saw would be alike unavailing to sway a resolution, which had been adopted by the worthy magistrate in compliance at once with the prejudices of his party and the inclination of his wife; "your daughter counsels well. We must part in disguise, and that instantly. We may, I trust, rely upon you for the necessary secrecy, and for the means of escape?"

"With all my heart—with all my heart," said the honest citizen, who, not much satisfied with the dignity of his own conduct, was eager to find some mode of atonement. "I cannot but remember that I owed you my life last night, both for unclasping that accursed steel doublet, and helping me through the other scrape, which was worse; for yonder Boar and his brood look more like devils than men. So I will be true to you as blade to haft, as our cutlers say, who are the best in the whole world. Nay, now you are ready, come this way; you shall see how far I can trust you."

The syndic led him from the chamber in which he had slept to his own counting-room, in which he transacted his affairs of business; and after bolting the door, and casting a piercing and careful eye around him, he opened a concealed and a vaulted closet behind the tapestry, in which stood more than one iron chest. He proceeded to open one which was full of guilders, and placed it at Quentin's discretion, to take whatever sum he might think necessary for his companion's expenses and his own.

As the money with which Quentin was furnished on leaving Plessis was now nearly expended, he hesitated not to accept the sum of two hundred guilders; and by doing so took a great weight from the mind of Pavillon, who considered the desperate transaction in which he thus voluntarily became the creditor, as an atonement for the breach of hospitality which various considerations in a great measure compelled him to commit.

Having carefully locked his treasure-chamber, the wealthy Fleming next conveyed his guest to the parlour, where, in full possession of her activity of mind and body, though pale from the scenes of the preceding night, he found the countess attired in the fashion of a Flemish maiden of the middling class. No other was present excepting Trudchen, who was sedulously employed in completing the countess's dress, and instructing her how to bear herself. She extended her hand to him, which, when he had reverently kissed, she said to him: "Seignior Quentin, we must leave our friends here, unless I would bring on them a part of the misery which has pursued me ever since my father's death. You must change your dress and go with me, unless you also are tired of befriending a being so unfortunate."

"I!—I tired of being your attendant! To the end of the earth will I guard you! But you—you yourself—are you equal to the task you undertake? Can you, after the terrors of last night——"

"Do not recall them to my memory," answered the countess; "I remember but the confusion of a horrid dream. Has the excellent bishop escaped?"

"I trust he is in freedom," said Quentin, making a sign to Pavillon, who seemed about to enter on the dreadful narrative, to be silent.

"Is it possible for us to rejoin him? Hath he gathered any power?" said the lady.

"His only hopes are in Heaven," said the Scot; "but wherever you wish to go, I stand by your side, a determined guide and guard."

"We will consider," said Isabelle; and after a moment's

pause, she added: "A convent would be my choice, but that I fear it would prove a weak defence against those who pursue me."

"Hem! hem!" said the syndic, "I could not well recommend a convent within the district of Liege; because the Boar of Ardennes, though in the main a brave leader, a trusty confederate, and a well-wisher to our city, has, nevertheless, rough humours, and payeth, on the whole, little regard to cloisters, convents, nunneries, and the like. Men say that there are a score of nuns—that is, such as were nuns—who march always with his company."

"Get yourself in readiness hastily, Seignior Durward," said Isabelle, interrupting its detail, "since to your faith I must needs commit myself."

No sooner had the syndic and Quentin left the room than Isabelle began to ask of Gertrude various questions concerning the roads, and so forth, with such clearness of spirit and pertinence that the latter could not help exclaiming: "Lady, I wonder at you! I have heard of masculine firmness, but yours appears to me more than belongs to humanity."

"Necessity," answered the countess—"necessity, my friend, is the mother of courage, as of invention. No long time since, I might have fainted when I saw a drop of blood shed from a trifling cut; I have since seen life-blood flow around me, I may say, in waves, yet I have retained my senses and my self-possession. Do not think it was an easy task," she added, laying on Gertrude's arm a trembling hand, although she still spoke with a firm voice; "the little world within me is like a garrison besieged by a thousand foes, whom nothing but the most determined resolution can keep from storming it on every hand, and at every moment. Were my situation one whit less perilous than it is—were I not sensible that my only chance to escape a fate more horrible than death is to retain my recollection and self-possession—Gertrude, I would at this moment throw myself into your arms, and relieve my bursting bosom by such a transport of tears and agony of terror as never rushed from a breaking heart!"

"Do not do so, lady!" said the sympathising Fleming;

"take courage, tell your beads, throw yourself on the care of Heaven; and surely, if ever Heaven sent a deliverer to one ready to perish, that bold and adventurous young gentleman must be designed for yours. There is one, too," she added, blushing deeply, "in whom I have some interest. Say nothing to my father; but I have ordered my bachelor, Hans Glover, to wait for you at the eastern gate, and never to see my face more, unless he brings word that he has guided you safe from the territory."

To kiss her tenderly was the only way in which the young countess could express her thanks to the frank and kindhearted city-maiden, who returned the embrace affectionately, and added, with a smile: "Nay, if two maidens and their devoted bachelors cannot succeed in a disguise and an escape, the world is changed from what I am told it wont to be."

A part of this speech again called the colour into the countess's pale cheeks, which was not lessened by Quentin's sudden appearance. He entered completely attired as a Flemish boor of the better class, in the holyday suit of Peter, who expressed his interest in the young Scot by the readiness with which he parted with it for his use; and swore, at the same time, that, were he to be curried and tugged worse than ever was bullock's hide, they should make nothing out of him, to the betraying of the young folks. Two stout horses had been provided by the activity of Mother Mabel, who really desired the countess and her attendant no harm, so that she could make her own house and family clear of the dangers which might attend upon harbouring them. She beheld them mount and go off with great satisfaction, after telling them that they would find their way to the east gate by keeping their eye on Peter, who was to walk in that direction as their guide, but without holding any visible communication with them.

The instant her guests had departed, Mother Mabel took the opportunity to read a long practical lecture to Trudchen upon the folly of reading romances, whereby the flaunting ladies of the court were grown so bold and venturous, that, instead of plying to learn some honest housewifery, they must ride, forsooth, a damsel-erranting through the country, with no better attendant than some idle squire, debauched page, or rakehelly archer from foreign parts, to the great danger of their health, the impoverishing of their substance, and the irreparable prejudice of their reputation.

All this Gertrude heard in silence, and without reply; but, considering her character, it might be doubted whether she derived from it the practical inference which it was her mother's purpose to enforce.

Meantime, the travellers had gained the eastern gate of the city, traversing crowds of people, who were fortunately too much busied in the political events and rumors of the hour to give any attention to a couple who had had so little to render their appearance remarkable. They passed the guards in virtue of a permission obtained for them by Pavillon, but in the name of his colleague Rouslaer, and they took leave of Peter Geislaer with a friendly though brief exchange of good wishes on either side. Immediately afterwards they were joined by a stout young man, riding a good grey horse, who presently made himself known as Hans Glover, the bachelor of Trudchen Pavillon. He was a young fellow with a good Flemish countenance—not, indeed, of the most intellectual cast, but arguing more hilarity and good-humor than wit, and, as the countess could not help thinking, scarce worthy to be bachelor to the generous Trudchen. He seemed, however, fully desirous to second the views which she had formed in their favour; for, saluting them respectfully, he asked of the countess in Flemish, on which road she desired to be conducted.

"Guide me," said she, "towards the nearest town on the frontiers of Brabant."

"You have then settled the end and object of your journey?" said Quentin, approaching his horse to that of Isabelle, and speaking French, which their guide did not understand.

"Surely," replied the young lady; "for, situated as I now am, it must be of no small detriment to me if I were to prolong a journey in my present circumstances, even though the termination should be a rigorous prison."

"A prison!" said Quentin.

"Yes, my friend, a prison; but I will take care that you shall not share it."

"Do not talk—do not think of me," said Quentin. "Saw I you but safe, my own concerns are little worth minding."

"Do not speak so loud," said the Lady Isabelle; "you will surprise our guide—you see he has already rode on before us; for, in truth, the good-natured Fleming, doing as he desired to be done by, had removed from them the constraint of a third person, upon Quentin's first motion towards the lady. "Yes," she continued, when she noticed they were free from observation, "to you, my friend, my protector—why should I be ashamed to call you what Heaven has made you to me?—to you it is my duty to say, that my resolution is taken to return to my native country, and to throw myself on the mercy of the Duke of Burgundy. It was mistaken, though well-meant, advice which induced me ever to withdraw from his protection, and place myself under that of the crafty and false Louis of France."

"And you resolve to become the bride then, of the Count of Campo-basso, the unworthy favourite of Charles?"

Thus spoke Quentin, with a voice in which internal agony struggled with his desire to assume an indifferent tone, like that of the poor condemned criminal, when, affecting a firmness which he is far from feeling, he asks if the death-warrant be arrived.

"No, Durward, no," said the Lady Isabelle, sitting up erect in her saddle, "to that hated condition of Burgundy's power shall not sink a daughter of the house of Croye. Burgundy may seize on my lands and fiefs, he may imprison my person in a convent; but that is the worst I have to expect; and worse than that I will endure ere I give my hand to Campo-basso."

"The worse!" said Quentin; "and what worse can there be than plunder and imprisonment? Oh, think, while you have God's free air around you, and one by your side who will hazard life to conduct you to England, to Germany, even to Scotland, in all of which you shall find generous protectors. Oh, while this is the case, do not resolve so rashly to abandon the means of liberty, the best gift that Heaven gives! Oh, well sung a poet of my own land:

> Ah, freedom is a noble thing;
> Freedom makes man to have liking;
> Freedom the zest to pleasure gives;
> He lives at ease who freely lives.
> Grief, sickness, poortith, want, are all
> Summ'd up within the name of thrall." [1]

She listened with a melancholy smile to her guide's tirade in praise of liberty; and then answered after a moment's pause: "Freedom is for man alone; woman must ever seek a protector, since nature made her incapable to defend herself. And where am I to find one? In that voluptuary Edward of England—in the inebriated Wenceslaus of Germany—in Scotland? Ah, Durward, were I your sister, and could you promise me shelter in some of those mountain-glens which you love to describe, where, for charity, or for the few jewels I have preserved, I might lead an unharassed life, and forget the lot I was born to—could you promise me the protection of some honoured matron of the land—of some baron whose heart was as true as his sword—that were indeed a prospect, for which it were worth the risk of farther censure to wander farther and wider!"

There was a faltering tenderness of voice with which the Countess Isabelle made this admission, that at once filled Quentin with a sensation of joy, and cut him to the very heart. He hesitated a moment ere he made an answer, hastily reviewing in his mind the possibility there might be that he could procure her shelter in Scotland; but the melancholy truth rushed on him, that it would be alike base and cruel to point out to her a course which he had not the most distant power or means to render safe. "Lady," he said at last, "I should act foully against my honour and oath of chivalry did I suffer you to ground any plan upon the thoughts that I have the power in Scotland to afford you other protection than that of the poor arm which is now by your side. I scarce know

---

[1] These noble lines form the commencement of the metrical life of Robert the Bruce, by Barbour, Archdeacon of Aberdeen in the year 1375 (*Laing*).

that my blood flows in the veins of an individual who now lives in my native land. The Knight of Innerquharity stormed our castle at midnight, and cut off all that belonged to my name. Were I again in Scotland, our feudal enemies are numerous and powerful, I single and weak; and even had the king a desire to do me justice, he dared not, for the sake of redressing the wrongs of a poor individual, provoke a chief who rides with five hundred horse."

"Alas!" said the countess, "there is then no corner of the world safe from oppression, since it rages as unrestained amongst those wild hills which afford so few objects to covet, as in our rich and abundant lowlands!"

"It is a sad truth, and I dare not deny it," said the Scot, "that, for little more than the pleasure of revenge and the lust of bloodshed, our hostile clans do the work of executioners on each other; and Ogilvies and the like act the same scenes in Scotland as De la Marck and his robbers do in this country."

"No more of Scotland, then," said Isabelle, with a tone of indifference, either real or affected—"no more of Scotland, which indeed I mentioned but in jest, to see if you really dared recommend to me, as a place of rest, the most distracted kingdom in Europe. It was but a trial of your sincerity, which I rejoice to say may be relied on, even when your partialities are most strongly excited. So, once more, I will think of no other protection than can be afforded by the first honourable baron holding of Duke Charles, to whom I am determined to render myself."

"And why not rather betake yourself to your own estates, and to your own strong castle, as you designed when at Tours?" said Quentin. "Why not call around you the vassals of your father, and make treaty with Burgundy, rather than surrender yourself to him? Surely there must be many a bold heart that would fight in your cause; and I know at least one who would willingly lay down his life to give example."

"Alas!" said the countess, "that scheme, the suggestion of the crafty Louis, and, like all which he ever suggested, designed more for his advantage than for mine, has become impracticable, since it was betrayed to Burgundy by the double traitor Zamet Maugrabin. My kinsman was then imprisoned, and my houses garrisoned. Any attempt of mine would but expose my dependents to the vengeance of Duke Charles; and why should I occasion more bloodshed than has already taken place on so worthless an account? No, I will submit myself to my sovereign as a dutiful vassal, in all which shall leave my personal freedom of choice uninfringed; the rather that I trust my kinswoman, the Countess Hameline, who first counselled, and indeed urged my flight, has already taken this wise and honourable step."

"Your kinswoman!" repeated Quentin, awakened to recollections to which the young countess was a stranger, and which the rapid succession of perilous and stirring events had, as matters of nearer concern, in fact banished from his memory.

"Ay, my aunt, the Countess Hameline of Croye—know you aught of her?" said the Countess Isabelle; "I trust she is now under the protection of the Burgundian banner. You are silent! Know you aught of her?"

The last question, urged in a tone of the most anxious inquiry, obliged Quentin to give some account of what he knew of the countess's fate. He mentioned that he had been summoned to attend her in a flight from Liege, which he had no doubt the Lady Isabelle would be partaker in; he mentioned the discovery that had been made after they had gained the forest; and finally, he told his own return to the castle, and the circumstances in which he found it. But he said nothing of the views with which it was plain the Lady Hameline had left the castle of Schonwaldt, and as little about the floating report of her having fallen into the hands of William de la Marck. Delicacy prevented his even hinting at the one, and regard for the feelings of his companion, at a moment when strength and exertion were most demanded of her, presented him from alluding to the latter, which had, besides, only reached him as a mere rumour.

This tale, though abridged of those important particulars, made a strong impression on the Countess Isabelle, who, after riding some time in silence, said at last, with a tone of cold displeasure: "And so you abandoned my unfortunate relative in a wild forest, at the mercy of a vile Bohemian and a traitorous waiting-woman? Poor kinswoman, thou wert wont to praise this youth's good faith!"

"Had I not done so, madam," said Quentin, not unreasonably offended at the turn thus given to his gallantry, "what had been the fate of one to whose service I was far more devoutly bound? Had I *not* left the Countess Hameline of Croye to the charge of those whom she had herself selected as counsellors and advisers, the Countess Isabelle had been ere now the bride of William de la Marck, the Wild Boar of Ardennes."

"You are right," said the Countess Isabelle, in her usual manner; "and I, who have the advantage of your unhesitating devotion, have done you foul and ungrateful wrong. But oh, my unhappy kinswoman! and the wretch Marthon, who enjoyed so much of her confidence, and deserved it so little—it was she that introduced to my kinswoman the wretched Zamet and Hayraddin Maugrabin, who, by their pretended knowledge in soothsaying and astrology, obtained a great ascendency over her mind; it was she who, strengthening their predictions, encouraged her in—I know not what to call them—delusions concerning matches and lovers, which my kinswoman's age rendered ungraceful and improbable. I doubt not that, from the beginning, we had been surrounded by these snares by Louis of France, in order to determine us to take refuge at his court, or rather to put ourselves into his power; after which rash act on our part, how unkingly, unknightly, ignobly, ungentlemanlike, he hath conducted himself towards us, you, Quentin Durward, can bear witness. But alas! my kinswoman—what think you will be her fate?"

Endeavouring to inspire hopes which he scarce felt, Durward answered that: "The avarice of these people was stronger than any other passion; that Marthon, even when he left them, seemed to act rather as the Lady Hameline's protectress; and, in fine, that it was difficult to conceive any object these wretches could accomplish by the ill usage or murder of the countess, whereas they might be gainers by treating her well, and putting her to ransom."

To lead the Countess Isabelle's thoughts from this melancholy subject, Quentin frankly told her the treachery of the Maugrabin, which he had discovered in the night-quarter near Namur, and which appeared the result of an agreement betwixt the King and William de la Marck. Isabelle shuddered with horror, and then recovering herself, said: "I am ashamed, and I have sinned in permitting myself so far to doubt of the saints' protection, as for an instant to have deemed possible the accomplishment of a scheme so utterly cruel, base, and dishonourable, while there are pitying eyes in Heaven to look down on human miseries. It is not a thing to be thought of with fear or abhorrence, but to be rejected as such a piece of incredible treachery and villainy as it were atheism to believe could ever be successful. But I now see plainly why that hypocritical Marthon often seemed to foster every seed of petty jealousy or discontent betwixt my poor kinswoman and myself, whilst she always mixed with flattery, addressed to the individual who was present, whatever could prejudice her against her absent kinswoman. Yet never did I dream she could have proceeded so far as to have caused my once affectionate kinswoman to have left me behind in the perils of Schonwaldt, while she made her own escape."

"Did the Lady Hameline not mention to you, then," said Quentin, "her intended flight?"

"No," replied the countess, "but she alluded to some communication which Marthon was to make to me. To say truth, my poor kinswoman's head was so turned by the mysterious jargon of the miserable Hayraddin, whom that day she had admitted to a long and secret conference, and she threw out so many strange hints, that—that—in short, I cared not to press on her, when in that humour, for any explanation. Yet it was cruel to leave me behind her."

"I will excuse the Lady Hameline from intending such unkindness," said Quentin; "for such was the agitation of the moment, at the darkness of the hour, that I believe the Lady Hameline as certainly conceived herself accompanied by her niece, as I at the same time, deceived by Marthon's dress and demeanour, supposed I was in the company of both the Ladies of Croye—and of *her* especially," he added, with a low but determined voice, "without whom the wealth of worlds would not have tempted me to leave Schonwaldt."

Isabelle stooped her head forward, and seemed scarce to hear the emphasis with which Quentin had spoken. But she turned her face to him again when he began to speak of the policy of Louis; and it was not difficult for them, by mutual communication, to ascertain that the Bohemian brothers, with their accomplice Marthon, had been the agents of that crafty monarch, although Zamet, the elder of them, with a perfidy peculiar to his race, had attempted to play a double game, and had been punished accordingly. In the same humour of mutual confidence, and forgetting the singularity of their own situation, as well as the perils of the road, the travellers pursued their journey for several hours, only stopping to refresh their horses at a retired *dorff*, or hamlet, to which they were conducted by Hans Glover, who, in all other respects, as well as in leaving them much to their own freedom in conversation, conducted himself like a person of reflection and discretion.

Meantime, the artificial distinction which divided the two lovers, for such we may now term them, seemed dissolved, or removed, by the circumstances in which they were placed; for if the countess boasted the higher rank, and was by birth entitled to a fortune incalculably larger than that of the youth, whose revenue lay in his sword, it was to be considered that, for the present, she was as poor as he, and for her safety, honour, and life exclusively indebted to his presence of mind, valour, and devotion. They *spoke* not indeed of love, for though the young lady, her heart full of gratitude and confidence, might have pardoned such a declaration, yet Quentin, on whose tongue there was laid a check both by natural timidity and by the sentiments of chivalry, would have held it an unworthy abuse of her situation had he said anything which could have the appearance of taking undue advantage of the opportunities which it afforded them. They *spoke* not then of love, but the thoughts of it were on both sides unavoidable; and thus they were placed in that relation to each other in which sentiments of mutual regard are rather understood than announced, and which, with the freedom which it permits, and the uncertainties that attended it, often forms the most delightful hours of human existence, and as frequently leads to those which are darkened by disappointment, fickleness, and all the pains of blighted hope and unrequited attachment.

It was two hours after noon, when the travellers were alarmed by the report of the guide, who, with paleness and horror in his countenance, said that they were pursued by a party of De la Marck's *Schwarzreiters*.[1] These soldiers, or rather banditti, were bands levied in the Lower Circles of Germany, and resembled the lanzknechts in every particular, except that the former acted as light cavalry. To maintain the name of Black Troopers, and to strike additional terror into their enemies, they usually rode on black chargers, and smeared with black ointment their arms and accoutrements, in which operation their hands and faces often had their share. In morals and in ferocity these schwarzreiters emulated their pedestrian brethren the lanzknechts.

On looking back, and discovering along the long level road which they had traversed a cloud of dust advancing, with one or two of the headmost troopers riding furiously in front of it, Quentin addressed his companion: "Dearest Isabelle, I have no weapon left save my sword; but since I cannot fight for you, I will fly with you. Could we gain yonder wood that is before us ere they come up, we may easily find means to escape."

"So be it, my only friend," said Isabelle, pressing her horse to the gallop; "and thou, good fellow," she added, addressing Hans Glover, "get thee off to another road, and do not stay to partake our misfortune and danger."

The honest Fleming shook his head, and I answered her generous exhortation with "*Nein, nein! das geht nicht,*"[1] and continued to attend them, all three riding towards the shelter of the wood as fast as their jaded horses could go, pursued, at

---

[1] See Note 32.   [2] "No, no! that must not be."

the same time, by the schwarzreiters, who increased their pace when they saw them fly. But notwithstanding the fatigue of the horses, still the fugitives, being unarmed, and riding lighter in consequence, had considerably the advantage of the pursuers, and were within about a quarter of a mile of the wood, when a body of men-at-arms, under a knight's pennon, was discovered advancing from the cover, so as to intercept their flight.

"They have bright armour," said Isabelle; "they must be Burgundians. Be they who they will, we must yield to them, rather than to the lawless miscreants who pursue us."

A moment after she exclaimed, looking on the pennon: "I know the cloven heart which it displays! It is the banner of the Count of Crèvecœur, a noble Burgundian; to him I surrender myself."

Quentin Durward sighed; but what other alternative remained? and how happy would he have been but an instant before, to have been certain of the escape of Isabelle, even under worse terms? They soon joined the band of Crèvecœur, and the countess demanded to speak to the leader, who had halted his party till he should reconnoitre the black troopers; and as he gazed on her with doubt and uncertainty, she said: "Noble count, Isabelle of Croye, the daughter of your old companion in arms, Count Reinold of Croye, renders herself, and asks protection from your valour for her and hers."

"Thou shalt have it, fair kinswoman, were it against a host, always excepting my liege Lord of Burgundy. But there is little time to talk of it. These filthy-looking fiends have made a halt, as if they intended to dispute the matter. By St. George of Burgundy, they have the insolence to advance against the Banner of Crèvecœur! What! will not the knaves be ruled? Damian, my lance. Advance banner. Lay your spears in the rest. Crèvecœur to the rescue!"

Crying his war-cry, and followed by his men-at-arms, he galloped rapidly forward to charge the schwarzreiters.

CHAPTER XXIV.

THE SURRENDER.

> Rescue or none, sir knight, I am your captive;
> Deal with me what your nobleness suggests,
> Thinking the chance of war may one day place you
> Where I must now be reckon'd—i' the roll
> Of melancholy prisoners.
>
> *Anonymous.*

The skirmish betwixt the schwarzreiters and the Burgundian men-at-arms lasted scarcely five minutes, so soon were the former put to the rout by the superiority of the latter in armour, weight of horse, and military spirit. In less than the space we have mentioned, the Count of Crèvecœur, wiping his bloody sword upon his horse's mane ere he sheathed it, came back to the verge of the forest, where Isabelle had remained a spectator of the combat. One part of his people followed him, while the other continued to pursue the flying enemy for a little space along the causeway.

"It is shame," said the count, "that the weapons of knights and gentlemen should be soiled by the blood of those brutal swine."

So saying, he returned his weapon to the sheath, and added: "This is a rough welcome to your home, my pretty cousin; but wandering princesses must expect such adventures. And well I came up in time, for, let me assure you, the black troopers respect a countess's coronet as little as a country wench's coif, and I think your retinue is not qualified for much resistance."

"My lord count," said the Lady Isabelle, "without farther preface, let me know if I am a prisoner, and where you are to conduct me."

"You know, you silly child," answered the count, "how I would answer that question, did it rest on my own will. But you and your foolish match-making, marriage-hunting aunt have made such wild use of your wings of late, that I fear you must be contented to fold them up in a cage for a little while. For my part, my duty, and it is a sad one, will be ended when I have conducted you to the court of the Duke, at Péronne; for which purpose I hold it necessary to deliver the command of this reconnoitering party to my nephew, Count Stephen, while I return with you thither, as I think you may need an intercessor. And I hope the young giddy-pate will discharge his duty wisely."

"So please you, fair uncle," said Count Stephen, "if you doubt my capacity to conduct the men-at-arms, even remain with them yourself, and I will be the servant and guard of the Countess Isabelle of Croye."

"No doubt, fair nephew," answered his uncle, "this were a goodly improvement on my scheme; but methinks I like it as well in the way I planned it. Please you, therefore, to take notice, that your business here is not to hunt after and stick these black hogs, for which you seemed but now to have felt an especial vocation, but to collect and bring to me true tidings what is going forward in the country of Liege, concerning which we hear such wild rumours. Let some half score of lances follow me, and the rest remain with my banner under your guidance."

"Yet one moment, cousin of Crèvecœur," said the Countess Isabelle, "and let me, in yielding myself prisoner, stipulate at least for the safety of those who have befriended me in my misfortunes. Permit this good fellow, my trusty guide, to go back unharmed to his native town of Liege."

"My nephew," said Crèvecœur, after looking sharply at Glover's honest breadth of countenance, "shall guard this good fellow, who seems, indeed, to have little harm in him, as far into the territory as he himself advances, and then leave him at liberty."

"Fail not to remember me to the kind Gertrude," said the countess to her guide; and added, taking a string of pearls from under her veil, "Pray her to wear this in remembrance of her unhappy friend."

Honest Glover took the string of pearls, and kissed, with clownish gesture but with sincere kindness, the fair hand which had found such a delicate mode of remunerating his own labours and peril.

"Umph! signs and tokens!" said the count; "any farther bequests to make, my fair cousin? It is time we were on our way."

"Only," said the countess, making an effort to speak, "that you will be pleased to be favourable to this—this young gentleman."

"Umph!" said Crèvecœur, casting the same penetrating glance on Quentin which he had bestowed on Glover, but apparently with a much less satisfactory result, and mimicking, though not offensively, the embarrassment of the countess— "umph! Ay, this is a blade of another temper. And pray, my cousin, what has this—this *very* young gentleman done to deserve such intercession at your hands?"

"He has saved my life and honour," said the countess, reddening with shame and resentment.

Quentin also blushed with indignation, but wisely concluded that to give vent to it might only make matters worse.

"Life and honour! Umph!" said again the Count Crèvecœur; "methinks it would have been as well, my cousin, if you had not put yourself in the way of lying under such obligations to this very young gentleman. But let it pass. The young gentleman may wait on us, if his quality permit, and I will see he has no injury; only I will myself take in future the office of protecting your life and honour, and may perhaps find for him some fitter duty than that of being a squire of the body to damosels errant."

"My lord count," said Durward, unable to keep silence any longer, "lest you should talk of a stranger in slighter terms than you might afterwards think becoming, I take leave to tell you that I am Quentin Durward, an archer of the Scottish Body-Guard, in which, as you well know, none but gentlemen and men of honour are enrolled."

"I thank you for your information, and I kiss your hands, seignior archer," said Crèvecœur, in the same tone of raillery. "Have the goodness to ride with me to the front of the party."

As Quentin moved onward at the command of the count,

who had now the power, if not the right, to dictate his motions, he observed that the Lady Isabelle followed his motions with a look of anxious and timid interest, which amounted almost to tenderness, and the sight of which brought water into his eyes. But he remembered that he had a man's part to sustain before Crèvecœur, who, perhaps, of all the chivalry in France or Burgundy, was the least likely to be moved to anything but laughter by a tale of true-love sorrow. He determined, therefore, not to wait his addressing him, but to open the conversation in a tone which should assert his claim to fair treatment, and to more respect than the count, offended perhaps at finding a person of such inferior note placed so near the confidence of his high-born and wealthy cousin, seemed disposed to entertain for him.

"My Lord Count of Crèvecœur," he said in a temperate but firm tone of voice, "may I request of you, before our interview goes farther, to tell me if I am at liberty, or am to account myself your prisoner?"

"A shrewd question," replied the count, "which, at present, I can only answer by another. Are France and Burgundy, think you, at peace or war with each other?"

"That," replied the Scot, "you, my lord, should certainly know better than I. I have been absent from the court of France, and have heard no news for some time."

"Look you there," said the count; "you see how easy it is to ask questions, but how difficult to answer them. Why, I myself, who have been at Péronne with the Duke for this week and better, cannot resolve this riddle any more than you; and yet, sir squire, upon the solution of that question depends the said point whether you are prisoner or free man; and, for the present, I must hold you as the former. Only, if you have really and honestly been of service to my kinswoman, and if you are candid in your answers to the questions I shall ask, affairs shall stand the better with you."

"The Countess of Croye," said Quentin, "is best judge if I have rendered any service, and to her I refer you on that matter. My answers you will judge yourself of when you ask me your questions."

"Umph! haughty enough," muttered the Count of Crèvecœur, "and very like one that wears a lady's favor in his hat, and thinks he must carry things with a high tone, to honour the precious remnant of silk and tinsel. Well, sir, I trust it will be no abatement of your dignity if you answer me how long you have been about the person of the Lady Isabelle of Croye?"

"Count of Crèvecœur," said Quentin Durward, "if I answer questions which are asked in a tone approaching towards insult, it is only lest injurious inferences should be drawn from my silence respecting one to whom we are both obliged to render justice. I have acted as escort to the Lady Isabelle since she left France to retire into Flanders."

"Ho! ho!" said the count; "and that is to say, since she fled from Plessis-lès-Tours? You, an archer of the Scottish Guard, accompanied her, of course, by the express orders of King Louis?"

However little Quentin thought himself indebted to the King of France, who, in contriving the surprisal of the Countess Isabelle by William de la Marck, had probably calculated on the young Scotchman being slain in her defence, he did not yet conceive himself at liberty to betray any trust which Louis had reposed, or had seemed to repose, in him, and therefore replied to Count Crèvecœur's inference: "That it was sufficient for him to have the authority of his superior officer for what he had done, and he inquired no farther."

"It is quite sufficient," said the count. "We know the King does not permit his officers to send the archers of his Guard to prance like paladins by the bridle-rein of wandering ladies, unless he hath some politic purpose to serve. It will be difficult for King Louis to continue to aver so boldly that he knew not of the Ladies of Croye's having escaped from France, since they were escorted by one of his own life-guard. And whither, sir archer, was your retreat directed?"

"To Liege, my lord," answered the Scot; "where the ladies desired to be placed under the protection of the late bishop."

"The *late* bishop!" exclaimed the Count of Crèvecœur; "is Louis of Bourbon dead? Not a word of his illness had reached the Duke. Of what did he die?"

"He sleeps in a bloody grave, my lord—that is, if his murderers have conferred one on his remains."

"Murdered!" exclaimed Crèvecœur again. "Holy Mother of Heaven! Young man, it is impossible!"

"I saw the deed done with my own eyes, and many an act of horror besides."

"Saw it, and made not in to help the good prelate!" exclaimed the count, "or to raise the castle against his murderers? Know'st thou not, that even to look on such a deed, without resisting it, is profane sacrilege?"

"To be brief, my lord," said Durward, "when this act was done, the castle was stormed by the bloodthirsty William de la Marck, with help of the insurgent Liegeois."

"I am struck with thunder!" said Crèvecœur. "Liege in insurrection! Schonwaldt taken! The bishop murdered! Messenger of sorrow, never did one man unfold such a packet of woes! Speak—knew you of this assault—of this insurrection—of his murder? Speak—thou art one of Louis's trusted archers, and it is he that has aimed this painful arrow. Speak, or I will have thee torn with wild horses!"

"And if I *am* so torn, my lord, there can be nothing rent out of me that may not become a true Scottish gentleman. I knew no more of these villainies than you—was so far from being partaker in them, that I would have withstood them to the uttermost, had my means, in a twentieth degree, equalled my inclination. But what could I do? they were hundreds and I but one. My only care was to rescue the Countess Isabelle, and in that I was happily successful. Yet, had I been near enough when the ruffian deed was so cruelly done on the old man, I had saved his grey hairs, or I had avenged them; and as it was, my abhorrence was spoken loud enough to prevent other horrors."

"I believe thee, youth," said the count; "thou art neither of an age nor nature to be trusted with such bloody work, however well fitted to be the squire of dames. But alas! for the kind and generous prelate, to be murdered on the hearth where he so often entertained the stranger with Christian charity and princely bounty; and that by a wretch—a monster—a portentous growth of blood and cruelty—bred up in the very hall where he has imbrued his hands in his benefactor's blood! But I know not Charles of Burgundy—nay, I should doubt of the justice of Heaven—if vengeance be not as sharp, and sudden, and severe as this villainy has been unexampled in atrocity. And, if no other shall pursue the murderer"—here he paused, grasped his sword, then quitting his bridle, struck both gauntleted hands upon his breast, until his corslet clattered, and finally held them up to Heaven, as he solemnly continued: "I—I, Philip Crèvecœur of Cordès, make a vow to God, St. Lambert, and the Three Kings of Cologne, that small shall be my thought of other earthly concerns till I take full revenge on the murderers of the good Louis of Bourbon, whether I find them in forest or field, in city or in country, in hill or plain, in the king's court or in God's church; and thereto I pledge lands and living, friends and followers, life and honour. So help me God and St. Lambert of Liege, and the Three Kings of Cologne!"

When the Count of Crèvecœur had made his vow, his mind seemed in some sort relieved from the overwhelming grief and astonishment with which he had heard the fatal tragedy that had been acted at Schonwaldt, and he proceeded to question Durward more minutely concerning the particulars of that disastrous affair, which the Scot, nowise desirous to abate the spirit of revenge which the count entertained against William de la Marck, gave him at full length.

"But those blind, unsteady, faithless, fickle beasts, the Liegeois," said the count, "that they should have combined themselves with this inexorable robber and murderer to put to death their lawful prince!"

Durward here informed the enraged Burgundian that the Liegeois, or at least the better class of them, however rashly they had run into the rebellion against their bishop, had no design, so far as appeared to him, to aid in the execrable deed of De la Marck; but, on the contrary, would have prevented it if they had had the means, and were struck with horror when they beheld it.

"Speak not of the faithless, inconstant, plebeian rabble!" said Crèvecœur. "When they took arms against a prince who had no fault save that he was too kind and too good a master for such a set of ungrateful slaves—when they armed against him, and broke into his peaceful house, what could there be in their intention but murder? When they banded themselves with the Wild Boar of Ardennes, the greatest homicide in the marches of Flanders, what else could there be in their purpose *but* murder, which is the very trade he lives by? And again, was it not one of their own vile rabble who did the very deed, by thine own account? I hope to see their canals running blood by the light of their burning houses. Oh, the kind, noble, generous lord whom they have slaughtered! Other vassals have rebelled under the pressure of imposts and penury; but the men of Liege in the fulness of insolence and plenty." He again abandoned the reins of his war-horse and wrung bitterly the hands which his mail-gloves rendered untractable. Quentin easily saw that the grief which he manifested was augmented by the bitter recollection of past intercourse and friendship with the sufferer, and was silent accordingly, respecting feelings which he was unwilling to aggravate, and at the same time felt it impossible to soothe.

But the Count of Crèvecœur returned again and again to the subject—questioned him on every particular of the surprise of Schonwaldt, and the death of the bishop; and then suddenly, as if he had recollected something which had escaped his memory, demanded what had become of the Lady Hameline, and why she was not with her kinswoman. "Not," he added contemptuously, "that I consider her absence as at all a loss to the Countess Isabelle; for, although she was her kinswoman, and upon the whole a well-meaning woman, yet the court of Cocagne never produced such a fantastic fool; and I hold it for certain that her niece, whom I have always observed to be a modest and orderly young woman, was led into the absurd frolic of flying from Burgundy to France by that blundering, romantic, old match-making and match-seeking idiot."

What a speech for a romantic lover to hear! and to hear, too, when it would have been ridiculous in him to attempt what it was impossible for him to achieve—namely, to convince the count, by force of arms, that he did foul wrong to the countess—the peerless in sense as in beauty—in terming her a modest and orderly young woman, qualities which might have been predicated with propriety of the daughter of a sunburnt peasant, who lived by goading the oxen, while her father held the plough. And, then, to suppose her under the domination and supreme guidance of a silly and romantic aunt—the slander should have been repelled down the slanderer's throat. But the open, though severe, physiognomy of the Count of Crèvecœur, the total contempt which he seemed to entertain for those feelings which were uppermost in Quentin's bosom, overawed him; not for fear of the count's fame in arms —that was a risk which would have increased his desire of making out a challenge—but in dread of ridicule, the weapon of all others most feared by enthusiasts of every description, and which, from its predominance over such minds, often checks what is absurd, and fully as often smothers that which is noble.

Under the influence of this fear of becoming an object of scorn rather than resentment, Durward, though with some pain, confined his reply to a confused account of the Lady Hameline having made her escape from Schonwaldt before the attack took place. He could not, indeed, have made his story very distinct without throwing ridicule on the near relation of Isabelle, and perhaps incurring some himself, as having been the object of her preposterous expectations. He added to his embarrassed detail, that he had heard a report, though a vague one, of the Lady Hameline having again fallen into the hands of William de la Marck.

"I trust in St. Lambert that he will marry her," said Crèvecœur; "as, indeed, he is likely enough to do, for the sake of her money-bags; and equally likely to knock her on the head so soon as these are either secured in his own grasp or, at farthest, emptied."

The count then proceeded to ask so many questions concerning the mode in which both ladies had conducted themselves on the journey, the degree of intimacy to which they admitted Quentin himself, and other trying particulars, that, vexed and ashamed and angry, the youth was scarce able to conceal his embarrassment from the keen-sighted soldier and courtier, who seemed suddenly disposed to take leave of him, saying, at the same time: "Umph—I see it is as I conjectured, on one side at least; I trust the other party has kept her senses better. Come, sir squire, spur on and keep the van, while I fall back to discourse with the Lady Isabelle. I think I have learned now so much from you that I can talk to her of these sad passages without hurting her nicety, though I have fretted yours a little. Yet stay, young gallant—one word ere you go. You have had, I imagine, a happy journey through Fairyland—all full of heroic adventure, and high hope, and wild, minstrel-like delusion, like the gardens of *Morgaine la Fée*. Forget it all, young soldier," he added, tapping him on the shoulder. "Remember yonder lady only is the honoured Countess of Croye; forget her as a wandering and adventurous damsel. And her friends—one of them I can answer for—will remember, on their part, only the services you have done her, and forget the unreasonable reward which you have had the boldness to propose to yourself."

Enraged that he had been unable to conceal from the sharp-sighted Crèvecœur feelings which the count seemed to consider as the object of ridicule, Quentin replied indignantly: "My lord count, when I require advice of you, I will ask it; when I demand assistance of you, it will be time enough to grant or refuse it; when I set peculiar value on your opinion of me, it will not be too late to express it."

"Heyday!" said the count; "I have come between Amadis and Oriana, and must expect a challenge to the lists!"

"You speak as if that were an impossibility," said Quentin. "When I broke a lance with the Duke of Orleans, it was against a breast in which flowed better blood than that of Crèvecœur. When I measured swords with Dunois, I engaged a better warrior."

"Now Heaven nourish thy judgment, gentle youth!" said Crèvecœur, still laughing at the chivalrous *inamorato*. "If thou speak'st truth, thou hast had singular luck in this world; and, truly, if it be the pleasure of Providence exposes thee to such trials, without a beard on thy lip, thou wilt be mad with vanity ere thou writest thyself man. Thou canst not move me to anger, though thou mayst to mirth. Believe me, though thou mayst have fought with princes, and played the champion for countesses, by some of those freaks which Fortune will sometimes exhibit, thou art by no means the equal of those of whom thou hast been either the casual opponent or more casual companion. I can allow thee, like a youth who hath listened to romance till he fancied himself a paladin, to form pretty dreams for some time; but thou must not be angry at a well-meaning friend, though he shake thee something roughly by the shoulders to wake thee."

"My Lord of Crèvecœur," said Quentin, "my family——"

"Nay, it was not utterly of family that I spoke," said the count; "but of rank, fortune, high station, and so forth, which place a distance between various degrees and classes of persons. As for birth, all men are descended from Adam and Eve."

"My lord count," repeated Quentin, "my ancestors, the Durwards of Glen Houlakin——"

"Nay," said the count, "if you claim a farther descent for them than from Adam, I have done! Good-even to you."

He reined back his horse, and paused to join the countess, to whom, if possible, his insinuations and advices, however well meant, were still more disagreeable than to Quentin, who, as he rode on, muttered to himself: "Cold-blooded, insolent, overweening coxcomb! Would that the next Scottish archer who has his harquebuss pointed at thee may not let thee off so easily as I did!"

In the evening they reached the town of Charleroi, on the Sambre, where the Count of Crèvecœur had determined to leave the Countess Isabelle, whom the terror and fatigue of yesterday, joined to a flight of fifty miles since morning and the various distressing sensations by which it was accompanied, had made incapable of travelling farther, with safety to her health. The count consigned her, in a state of great exhaustion, to the care of the abbess of the Cistercian convent in Charleroi, a noble lady to whom both the families of Crèvecœur and Croye were related, and in whose prudence and kindness he could repose confidence.

Crèvecœur himself only stopped to recommend the utmost caution to the governor of a small Burgundian garrison who occupied the place, and required him also to mount a guard of honour upon the convent during the residence of the Countess Isabelle of Croye—ostensibly to secure her safety, but perhaps secretly to prevent her attempting to escape. The count only assigned as a cause for the garrison being vigilant some vague rumours which he had heard of disturbances in the bishopric of Liege. But he was determined himself to be the first who should carry the formidable news of the insurrection and the murder of the bishop, in all their horrible reality, to Duke Charles; and for that purpose, having procured fresh horses for himself and suite, he mounted with the resolution of continuing his journey to Péronne without stopping for repose; and informing Quentin Durward that he must attend him, he made, at the same time, a mock apology for parting fair company, but hoped that to so devoted a squire of dames a night's journey by moonshine would be more agreeable than supinely to yield himself to slumber like an ordinary mortal.

Quentin, already sufficiently afflicted by finding that he was to be parted from Isabelle, longed to answer this taunt with an indignant defiance; but aware that the count would only laugh at his anger and despise his challenge, he resolved to wait some future time, when he might have an opportunity of obtaining some amends from this proud lord, who, though for very different reasons, had become nearly as odious to him as the Wild Boar of Ardennes himself. He therefore assented to Crèvecœur's proposal, as to what he had no choice of declining, and they pursued in company, and with all the despatch they could exert, the road between Charleroi and Péronne.

CHAPTER XXV.

THE UNBIDDEN GUEST.

No human quality is so well wove
In warp and woof but there's some flaw in it.
I've known a brave man fly a shepherd's cur,
A wise man so demean him, drivelling idiocy
Had wellnigh been ashamed on't. For your crafty,
Your worldly-wise man, he, above the rest,
Weaves his own snares so fine, he's often caught in them.
Old Play.

QUENTIN, during the earlier part of the night-journey, had to combat with that bitter heartache which is felt when youth parts, and probably for ever, with her he loves. As, pressed by the urgency of the moment and the impatience of Crèvecœur, they hasted on through the rich lowlands of Hainault, under the benign guidance of a rich and lustrous harvest-moon, she shed her yellow influence over rich and deep pastures, woodland, and corn-fields, from which the husbandmen were using her light to withdraw the grain, such was the industry of the Flemings even at that period; she shone on broad, level, and fructifying rivers, where glided the white sail in the service of commerce, uninterrupted by rock or torrent, beside lively [lonely?] quiet villages, whose external decency and cleanliness expressed the ease and comfort of the inhabitants; she gleamed upon the feudal castle of many a gallant baron and knight, with its deep moat, battlemented court, and high belfry, for the chivalry of Hainault was renowned among the nobles of Europe; and her light displayed at a distance, in its broad beam, the gigantic towers of more than one lofty minster.

Yet all this fair variety, however differing from the waste and wilderness of his own land, interrupted not the course of Quentin's regrets and sorrows. He had left his heart behind him, when he departed from Charleroi; and the only reflection which the farther journey inspired was, that every step was carrying him farther from Isabelle. His imagination was taxed to recall every word she had spoken, every look she had directed towards him; and, as happens frequently in such cases, the impression made upon his imagination by the recollection of these particulars was even stronger than the realities themselves had excited.

At length, after the cold hour of midnight was past, in spite alike of love and of sorrow, the extreme fatigue which Quentin had undergone the two preceding days began to have an effect on him, which his habits of exercise of every kind, and his singular alertness and activity of character, as well as the painful nature of the reflections which occupied his thoughts, had hitherto prevented his experiencing. The ideas of his mind began to be so little corrected by the exertions of his senses, worn out and deadened as the latter now were by extremity of fatigue, that the visions which the former drew superseded or perverted the information conveyed by the blunted organs of seeing and hearing; and Durward was only sensible that he was awake by the exertions which, sensible of the peril of his situation, he occasionally made to resist falling into a deep and dead sleep. Every now and then a strong consciousness of the risk of falling from or with his horse roused him to exertion and animation; but ere long his eyes again were dimmed by confused shades of all sorts of mingled colours, the moonlight landscape swam before them, and he was so much overcome with fatigue that the Count of Crèvecœur, observing his condition, was at length compelled to order two of his attendants, one to each rein of Durward's bridle, in order to prevent the risk of his falling from his horse.

When at length they reached the town of Landrecy, the count, in compassion to the youth, who had now been in a great measure without sleep for three nights, allowed himself and his retinue a halt of four hours for rest and refreshment.

Deep and sound were Quentin's slumbers, until they were broken by the sound of the count's trumpet, and the cry of his *fourriers* and harbingers, "*Debout! Debout! Ha! Messires, en route—en route!*" Yet, unwelcomely early as the tones came, they awaked him a different being in strength and spirits from what he had fallen asleep. Confidence in himself and his fortunes returned with his reviving spirits and with the rising sun. He thought of his love no longer as a desperate and fantastic dream, but as a high and invigorating principle, to be cherished in his bosom, although he might never propose to himself, under all the difficulties by which he was beset, to bring it to any prosperous issue. "The pilot," he reflected, "steers his bark by the polar star, although he never expects to become possessor of it; and the thoughts of Isabelle of Croye shall make me a worthy man-at-arms, though I may never see her more. When she hears that a Scottish soldier named Quentin Durward distinguished himself in a well-fought field, or left his body on the breach of a disputed fortress, she will remember the companion of her journey, as one who did all in his power to avert the snares and misfortunes which beset it, and perhaps will honour his memory with a tear, his coffin with a garland."

In this manly mood of bearing his misfortune, Quentin felt himself more able to receive and reply to the jests of the Count of Crèvecœur, who passed several on his alleged effeminacy and incapacity of undergoing fatigue. The young Scot accommodated himself so good-humouredly to the count's raillery, and replied at once so happily and so respectfully, that the change of his tone and manner made obviously a more favourable impression on the count than he had entertained from his prisoner's conduct during the preceding evening, when, rendered irritable by the feelings of his situation, he was alternately moodily silent or fiercely argumentative.

The veteran soldier began at length to take notice of his young companion as a pretty fellow of whom something might be made; and more than hinted to him that, would he but resign his situation in the Archer Guard of France, he would undertake to have him enrolled in the household of the Duke of Burgundy in an honourable condition, and would himself take care of his advancement. And although Quentin, with suitable expressions of gratitude, declined this favour at present, until he should find out how far he had to complain of his original patron, King Louis, he, nevertheless, continued to remain on good terms with the Count of Crèvecœur; and, while his enthusiastic mode of thinking, and his foreign and idiomatical manner of expressing himself, often excited a smile on the grave cheek of the count, that smile had lost all that it had of sarcastic and bitter, and did not exceed the limits of good humour and good manners.

Thus travelling on with much more harmony than on the preceding day, the little party came at last within two miles of the famous and strong town of Péronne, near which the Duke of Burgundy's army lay encamped, ready, as was supposed, to invade France; and in opposition to which Louis XI. had himself assembled a strong force near St. Maxence, for the purpose of bringing to reason his over-powerful vassal.

Péronne,[1] situated upon a deep river, in a flat country, and surrounded by strong bulwarks and profound moats, was accounted in ancient, as in modern, times one of the strongest fortresses in France. The Count of Crèvecœur, his retinue, and his prisoner were approaching the fortress about the third hour after noon; when, riding through the pleasant glades of a large forest, which then covered the approach to the town on the east side, they were met by two men of rank, as appeared from the number of their attendants, dressed in the habits worn in time of peace; and who, to judge from the falcons which they carried on their wrists, and the number of spaniels and greyhounds led by their followers, were engaged in the amusement of hawking. But on perceiving Crèvecœur, with whose appearance and liveries they were sufficiently intimate, they quitted the search which they were making for a heron along the banks of a long canal, and came galloping towards him.

"News—news, Count of Crèvecœur!" they cried both together; "will you give news or take news, or will you barter fairly?"

"I would barter fairly, Messires," said Crèvecœur, after saluting them courteously, "did I conceive you had any news of importance sufficient to make an equivalent for mine."

The two sportsmen smiled on each other; and the elder of the two, a fine baronial figure, with a dark countenance, marked

[1] See Note 33.

with that sort of sadness which some physiognomists ascribe to a melancholy temperament, and some, as the Italian statuary augured of the visage of Charles I., consider as predicting an unhappy death,[1] turning to his companion, said: " Crèvecœur has been in Brabant, the country of commerce, and he has learned all its artifices: he will be too hard for us if we drive a bargain."

"Messires," said Crèvecœur, "the Duke ought in justice to have the first of my wares, as the seigneur takes his toll before open market begins. But tell me, are your news of a sad or a pleasant complexion?"

The person whom he particularly addressed was a lively-looking man, with an eye of great vivacity, which was corrected by an expression of reflection and gravity about the mouth and upper lip—the whole physiognomy marking a man who saw and judged rapidly, but was sage and slow in forming resolutions or in expressing opinions. This was the famous Knight of Hainault, son of Collart, or Nicolas de la Clite, known in history and amongst historians by the venerable name of Philip des Comines,[2] at this time close to the person of Duke Charles the Bold, and one of his most esteemed counsellors. He answered Crèvecœur's question concerning the complexion of the news of which he and his companion, the Baron d'Hymbercourt, were the depositaries. "They were," he said, "like the colours of the rainbow, various in hue, as they might be viewed from different points, and placed against the black cloud or the fair sky. Such a rainbow was never seen in France or Flanders since that of Noah's ark."

"My tidings," replied Crèvecœur, "are altogether like the comet—gloomy, wild, and terrible in themselves, yet to be accounted the forerunners of still greater and more dreadful evils which are to ensue."

"We must open our bales," said Comines to his companion, "or our market will be forestalled by some newcomers, for ours are public news. In one word, Crèvecœur, listen, and wonder—King Louis is at Péronne!"

"What!" said the count, in astonishment; "has the Duke

[1] See D'Hymbercourt. Note 34.   [2] See Note 35.

retreated without a battle? and do you remain here in your dress of peace after the town is besieged by the French, for I cannot suppose it taken?"

"No, surely," said D'Hymbercourt, "the banners of Burgundy have not gone back a foot; and still King Louis is here."

"Then Edward of England must have come over the seas with his bowmen," said Crèvecœur, "and, like his ancestors, gained a second field of Poictiers."

"Not so," said Comines. "Not a French banner has been borne down, not a sail spread from England, where Edward is too much amused among the wives of the citizens of London to think of playing the Black Prince. Hear the extraordinary truth. You know, when you left us, that the conference between the commissioners on the parts of France and Burgundy was broken up, without apparent chance of reconciliation?"

"True; and we dreamt of nothing but war."

"What has followed has been indeed so like a dream," said Comines, "that I almost expect to wake and find it so. Only one day since, the Duke had in council protested so furiously against farther delay, that it was resolved to send a defiance to the King and march forward instantly into France. Toison d'Or, commissioned for the purpose, had put on his official dress, and had his foot in the stirrup to mount his horse, when lo! the French herald Montjoie rode into our camp. We thought of nothing else than that Louis had been beforehand with our defiance; and began to consider how much the Duke would resent the advice which had prevented him from being the first to declare war. But a council being speedily assembled, what was our wonder when the herald informed us that Louis, King of France, was scarce an hour's riding behind, intending to visit Charles Duke of Burgundy with a small retinue, in order that their differences might be settled at a personal interview!"

"You surprise me, Messires," said Crèvecœur; "and yet you surprise me less than you might have expected; for, when I was last at Plessis-lès-Tours, the all-trusted Cardinal Balue, offended with his master, and Burgundian at heart, did hint to me, that he could so work upon Louis's peculiar foibles as to lead him to place himself in such a position with regard to Burgundy that the Duke might have the terms of peace of his own making. But I never suspected that so old a fox as Louis could have been induced to come into the trap of his own accord. What said the Burgundian counsellors?"

"As you may guess," answered D'Hymbercourt; "talked much of faith to be observed and little of advantage to be obtained by such a visit; while it was manifest they thought almost entirely of the last, and were only anxious to find some way to reconcile it with the necessary preservation of appearances."

"And what said the Duke?" continued the Count of Crèvecœur.

"Spoke brief and bold, as usual," replied Comines. "'Which of you was it,' he asked, 'who witnessed the meeting of my cousin Louis and me after the battle of Montl'héry,[1] when I was so thoughtless as to accompany him back within the intrenchments of Paris with half a score of attendants, and so put my person at the King's mercy?' I replied, that most of us had been present, and none could ever forget the alarm which it had been his pleasure to give us. 'Well,' said the Duke, 'you blamed me for my folly, and I confessed to you that I had acted like a giddy-pated boy; and I am aware, too, that, my father of happy memory being then alive, my kinsman, Louis, would have had less advantage by seizing on my person than I might now have by securing his. But, nevertheless, if my royal kinsman comes hither on the present occasion in the same singleness of heart under which I then acted, he shall be royally welcome. If it is meant by this appearance of confidence to circumvent and to blind me till he execute some of his politic schemes, by St. George of Burgundy, let him look to it!' And so, having turned up his mustachios and stamped on the ground, he ordered us all to get on our horses and receive so extraordinary a guest."

"And you met the King accordingly?" replied the Count

* See Note 36.

of Crèvecœur. "Miracles have not ceased! How was he accompanied?"

"As slightly as might be," answered D'Hymbercourt: "only a score or two of the Scottish Guard, and a few knights and gentlemen of his household, among whom his astrologer, Galeotti, made the gayest figure."

"That fellow," said Crèvecœur, "holds some dependence on the Cardinal Balue; I should not be surprised that he has had his share in determining the King to this step of doubtful policy. Any nobility of higher rank?"

"There are Monsieur of Orleans and Dunois," replied Comines.

"I will have a rouse with Dunois," said Crèvecœur, "wag the world as it will. But we heard that both he and the duke had fallen into disgrace, and were in prison?"

"They were both under arrest in the Castle of Loches, that delightful place of retirement for the French nobility," said D'Hymbercourt; "but Louis has released them, in order to bring them with him, perhaps because he cared not to leave Orleans behind. For his other attendants, faith, I think his gossip, the hangman marshal, with two or three of his retinue, and Oliver, his barber, may be the most considerable; and the whole bevy so poorly arrayed that, by my honour, the King resembles most an old usurer going to collect desperate debts, attended by a body of catchpolls."

"And where is he lodged?" said Crèvecœur.

"Nay, that," replied Comines, "is the most marvellous of all. Our duke offered to let the King's Archer Guard have a gate of the town, and a bridge of boats over the Somme, and to have assigned to Louis himself the adjoining house, belonging to a wealthy burgess, Giles Orthen; but, in going thither, the King espied the banners of De Lau and Pencil de Rivière, whom he had banished from France, and scared, as it would seem, with the thought of lodging so near refugees and malcontents of his own making, he craved to be quartered in the Castle of Péronne, and *there* he hath his abode accordingly."

"Why, God ha' mercy!" exclaimed Crèvecœur, "this is

not only venturing into the lion's den, but thrusting his head into his very jaws. Nothing less than the very bottom of the rat-trap would serve the crafty old politician!"

"Nay," said Comines, "D'Hymbercourt hath not told you the speech of Le Glorieux,[1] which, in my mind, was the shrewdest opinion that was given."

"And what said *his* most illustrious wisdom?" asked the count.

"As the Duke," replied Comines, "was hastily ordering some vessels and ornaments of plate and the like, to be prepared as presents for the King and his retinue, by way of welcome on his arrival, 'Trouble not thy small brain about it, my friend Charles,' said Le Glorieux: "I will give thy cousin Louis a nobler and a fitter gift than thou canst, and that is my cap and bells, and my bauble to boot; for, by the mass, he is a greater fool than I am for putting himself in thy power.' 'But if I give him no reason to repent it, sirrah, how then?' said the Duke. 'Then, truly, Charles, thou shalt have cap and bauble thyself, as the greatest fool of the three of us.' I promise you this knavish quip touched the Duke closely. I saw him change colour and bite his lip. And now our news are told, noble Crèvecœur, and what think you they resemble?"

"A mine full-charged with gunpowder," answered Crèvecœur, "to which, I fear, it is my fate to bring the kindled linstock. Your news and mine are like flax and fire, which cannot meet without bursting into flame, or like certain chemical substances which cannot be mingled without an explosion. Friends—gentlemen, ride close by my rein; and when I tell you what has chanced in the bishopric of Liege, I think you will be of opinion that King Louis might as safely have undertaken a pilgrimage to the infernal regions as this ill-timed visit to Péronne."

The two nobles drew up close on either hand of the count, and listened, with half-suppressed exclamations and gestures of the deepest wonder and interest, to his account of the transactions at Liege and Schonwaldt. Quentin was then called

[1] The jester of Charles of Burgundy, of whom more hereafter.

forward, and examined and re-examined on the particulars of the bishop's death, until at length he refused to answer any further interrogatories, not knowing wherefore they were asked, or what use might be made of his replies.

They now reached the rich and level banks of the Somme, and the ancient walls of the little town of Péronne la Pucelle, and the deep green meadows adjourning, now whitened with the numerous tents of the Duke of Burgundy's army, amounting to about fifteen thousand men.

CHAPTER XXVI.

THE INTERVIEW.

> When princes meet, astrologers may mark it
> An ominous conjunction, full of boding,
> Like that of Mars with Saturn.
> *Old Play.*

ONE hardly knows whether to term it a privilege or a penalty annexed to the quality of princes, that, in their intercourse with each other, they are required, by the respect which is due to their own rank and dignity, to regulate their feelings and expressions by a severe etiquette, which precludes all violent and avowed display of passion, and which, but that the whole world are aware that this assumed complaisance is a matter of ceremony, might justly pass for profound dissimulation. It is no less certain, however, that the overstepping of these bounds of ceremonial, for the purpose of giving more direct vent to their angry passions, has the effect of compromising their dignity with the world in general, as was particularly noted when those distinguished rivals, Francis the First and the Emperor Charles, gave each other the lie direct, and were desirous of deciding their differences hand to hand, in single combat.

Charles of Burgundy, the most hasty and impatient, nay, the most imprudent, prince of his time, found himself, nevertheless, fettered within the magic circle which prescribed the most profound deference to Louis, as his suzerain and liege lord, who had deigned to confer upon him, a vassal of the crown, the distinguished honour of a personal visit. Dressed in his ducal mantle, and attended by his great officers and principal knights and nobles, he went in gallant cavalcade to receive Louis XI. His retinue absolutely blazed with gold and silver; for the wealth of the court of England being exhausted by the wars of York and Lancaster, and the expenditure of France limited by the economy of the sovereign, that of Burgundy was for the time the most magnificent in Europe. The *cortège* of Louis, on the contrary, was few in number, and comparatively mean in appearance, and the exterior of the King himself, in a threadbare cloak, with his wonted old high-crowned hat stuck full of images, rendered the contrast yet more striking; and as the Duke, richly attired with the coronet and mantle of state, threw himself from his noble charger, and kneeling on one knee, offered to hold the stirrup while Louis dismounted from his little ambling palfrey, the effect was almost grotesque.

The greeting between the two potentates was, of course, as full of affected kindness and compliment as it was totally devoid of sincerity. But the temper of the Duke rendered it much more difficult for him to preserve the necessary appearances in voice, speech, and demeanour; while in the King every species of simulation and dissimulation seemed so much a part of his nature that those best acquainted with him could not have distinguished what was feigned from what was real.

Perhaps the most accurate illustration, were it not unworthy two such high potentates, would be to suppose the King in the situation of a stranger, perfectly acquainted with the habits and dispositions of the canine race, who, for some purpose of his own, is desirous to make friends with a large and surly mastiff, that holds him in suspicion, and is disposed to worry him on the first symptoms either of diffidence or of umbrage. The mastiff growls internally, erects his bristles, shows his teeth, yet is ashamed to fly upon the intruder, who seems at the same time so kind and so confiding, and therefore the animal endures advances which are far from pacifying him, watching at the same time the slightest opportunity which may justify him in his own eyes for seizing his friend by the throat.

The King was no doubt sensible, from the altered voice, constrained manner, and abrupt gestures of the Duke, that the game he had to play was delicate, and perhaps he more than once repented having ever taken it in hand. But repentance was too late, and all that remained for him was that inimitable dexterity of management which the King understood equally at least with any man that ever lived.

The demeanour which Louis used towards the Duke was such as to resemble the kind overflowing of the heart in a moment of sincere reconciliation with an honoured and tried friend, from whom he had been estranged by temporary circumstances now passed away, and forgotten as soon as removed. The King blamed himself for not having sooner taken the decisive step of convincing his kind and good kinsman, by such a mark of confidence as he was now bestowing, that the angry passages which had occurred betwixt them were nothing in his remembrance when weighed against the kindness which received him when an exile from France, and under the displeasure of the King his father. He spoke of the Good Duke of Burgundy, as Philip the father of Duke Charles was currently called, and remembered a thousand instances of his paternal kindness.

"I think, cousin," he said, "your father made little difference in his affection betwixt you and me; for I remember when by an accident I had bewildered myself in a hunting-party, I found the Good Duke upbraiding you with leaving me in the forest, as if you had been careless of the safety of an elder brother."

The Duke of Burgundy's features were naturally harsh and severe, and when he attempted to smile, in polite acquiescence to the truth of what the King told him, the grimace which he made was truly diabolical.

"Prince of dissemblers," he said in his secret soul, "would that it stood with my honour to remind you *how* you have requited all the benefits of our house!"

"And then," continued the King, "if the ties of consanguinity and gratitude are not sufficient to bind us together, my fair cousin, we have those of spiritual relationship; for I am godfather to your fair daughter Mary, who is as dear to me as one of my own maidens; and when the saints—their holy name be blessed!—sent me a little blossom which withered in the course of three months, it was your princely father who held it at the font, and celebrated the ceremony of baptism with richer and prouder magnificence than Paris itself could have afforded. Never shall I forget the deep, the indelible impression which the generosity of Duke Philip, and yours, my dearest cousin, made upon the half-broken heart of the poor exile!"

"Your Majesty," said the Duke, compelling himself to make some reply, "acknowledged that slight obligation in terms which overpaid all the display which Burgundy could make to show due sense of the honour you had done its sovereign."

"I remember the words you mean, fair cousin," said the King, smiling; "I think they were, that in guerdon of the benefit of that day, I, poor wanderer, had nothing to offer save the persons of myself, of my wife, and of my child. Well, and I think I have indifferently well redeemed my pledge."

"I mean not to dispute what your Majesty is pleased to aver," said the Duke; "but——"

"But you ask," said the King, interrupting him, "how my actions have accorded with my words. Marry thus: the body of my infant child Joachim rests in Burgundian earth; my own person I have this morning placed unreservedly in your power; and for that of my wife—truly, cousin, I think, considering the period of time which has passed, you will scarce insist on my keeping my word in that particular. She was born on the day of the Blessed Annunciation (he crossed himself and muttered an *Ora pro nobis*), some fifty years since; but she is no farther distant than Rheims, and if you insist on my promise being fulfilled to the letter, she shall presently wait your pleasure."

Angry as the Duke of Burgundy was at the barefaced attempt of the King to assume towards him a tone of friendship and intimacy, he could not help laughing at the whimsical reply of that singular monarch, and his laugh was as discordant as the abrupt tones of passion in which he often spoke. Having laughed longer and louder than was at that period, or would now be, thought fitting the time and occasion, he answered in the same tone, bluntly declining the honour of the Queen's company, but stating his willingness to accept that of the King's eldest daughter, whose beauty was celebrated.

"I am happy, fair cousin," said the King, with one of those dubious smiles of which he frequently made use, "that your gracious pleasure has not fixed on my younger daughter Joan. I should otherwise have had spear-breaking between you and my cousin of Orleans; and, had harm come of it, I must on either side have lost a kind friend and affectionate cousin."

"Nay—nay, my royal sovereign," said Duke Charles, "the Duke of Orleans shall have no interruption from me in the path which he has chosen *par amours*. The cause in which I couch my lance against Orleans must be fair and straight."

Louis was far from taking amiss this brutal allusion to the personal deformity of the Princess Joan. On the contrary, he was rather pleased to find that the Duke was content to be amused with broad jests, in which he was himself a proficient, and which, according to the modern phrase, spared much sentimental hypocrisy. Accordingly, he speedily placed their intercourse on such a footing that Charles, though he felt it impossible to play the part of an affectionate and reconciled friend to a monarch whose ill offices he had so often encountered, and whose sincerity on the present occasion he so strongly doubted, yet had no difficulty in acting the hearty landlord towards a facetious guest; and so the want of reciprocity in kinder feelings between them was supplied by the tone of good fellowship which exists between two boon companions—a tone natural to the Duke from the frankness, and it might be added, the grossness, of his character, and to Louis, because, though capable of assuming any mood of social intercourse, that which really suited him best was mingled with grossness of ideas and caustic humour in expression.

Both princes were happily able to preserve, during the period of a banquet at the town-house of Péronne, the same kind of conversation, on which they met as on a neutral ground, and which, as Louis easily perceived, was more available than any other to keep the Duke of Burgundy in that state of composure which seemed necessary to his own safety.

Yet he was alarmed to observe that the Duke had around him several of those French nobles, and those of the highest rank and in situations of great trust and power, whom his own severity or injustice had driven into exile; and it was to secure himself from the possible effects of their resentment and revenge that (as already mentioned) he requested to be lodged in the castle or citadel of Péronne rather than in the town itself.[1] This was readily granted by Duke Charles, with one of those grim smiles of which it was impossible to say whether it meant good or harm to the party whom it concerned.

But when the King, expressing himself with as much delicacy as he could, and in the manner he thought best qualified to lull suspicion asleep, asked whether the Scottish Archers of his Guard might not maintain the custody of the Castle of Péronne during his residence there, in lieu of the gate of the town which the Duke had offered to their care, Charles replied, with his wonted sternness of voice and abruptness of manner, rendered more alarming by his habit, when he spoke, of either turning up his mustachios or handling his sword or dagger, the last of which he used frequently to draw a little way and then return to the sheath[2]—"St. Martin! No, my liege. You are in your vassal's camp and city—so men call me in respect to your Majesty—my castle and town are yours and my men are yours; so it is indifferent whether my men-at-arms or the Scottish Archers guard either the outer gate or defences of castle. No, by St. George! Péronne is a virgin fortress; she shall not lose her reputation by any neglect of

---

[*] See Louis's Suspicious Character. Note 37.

[2] This gesture, very indicative of a fierce character, is also by stage tradition a distinction of Shakespeare's Richard III.

mine. Maidens must be carefully watched, my royal cousin, if we would have them continue to live in good fame."

"Surely, fair cousin, and I altogether agree with you," said the King, "I being in fact more interested in the reputation of the good little town than you are—Péronne being, as you know, fair cousin, one of those upon the same river Somme which, pledged to your father of happy memory for redemption of money, are liable to be redeemed upon repayment. And, to speak truth, coming, like an honest debtor, disposed to clear off my obligations of every kind, I have brought here a few sumpter mules loaded with silver for the redemption— enough to maintain even your princely and royal establishment, fair cousin, for the space of three years."

"I will not receive a penny of it," said the Duke, twirling his mustachios; "the day of redemption is past, my royal cousin; nor was there ever serious purpose that the right should be exercised, the cession of these towns being the sole recompense my father ever received from France when, in a happy hour for your family, he consented to forget the murder of my grandfather, and to exchange the alliance of England for that of your father. St. George! if he had not so acted, your royal self, far from having towns on the Somme, could scarce have kept those beyond the Loire. No; I will not render a stone of them, were I to receive for every stone so rendered its weight in gold. I thank God, and the wisdom and valour of my ancestors, that the revenues of Burgundy, though it be but a duchy, will maintain my state, even when a king is my guest, without obliging me to barter my heritage."

"Well, fair cousin," answered the King, with the same mild and placid manner as before, and unperturbed by the loud tone and violent gestures of the Duke, "I see that you are so good a friend to France that you are unwilling to part with aught that belongs to her. But we shall need some moderator in these affairs when we come to treat of them in council. What say you to St. Paul?"

"Neither St. Paul, nor St. Peter, nor e'er a saint in the calendar," said the Duke of Burgundy, "shall preach me out of the possession of Péronne."

"Nay, but you mistake me," said King Louis, smiling; "I mean Louis de Luxembourg, our trusty constable, the Count of St. Paul. Ah! St. Mary of Embrun! we lack but his head at our conference! the best head in France, and the most useful to the restoration of perfect harmony betwixt us."

"By St. George of Burgundy!" said the Duke, "I marvel to hear your Majesty talk thus of a man false and perjured both to France and Burgundy—one who hath ever endeavoured to fan into a flame our frequent differences, and that with the purposes of giving himself the airs of a mediator. I swear by the order I wear, that his marshes shall not be long a resource for him!"

"Be not so warm, cousin," replied the King, smiling, and speaking under his breath; "when I wished for the constable's *head*, as a means of ending the settlement of our trifling differences, I had no desire for his *body*, which might remain at St. Quentin's with much convenience."

"Ho! ho! I take your meaning, my royal cousin," said Charles, with the same dissonant laugh which some other of the King's coarse pleasantries had extorted, and added, stamping with his heel on the ground, "I allow, in that sense, the head of the constable *might* be useful at Péronne."

These, and other discourses, by which the King mixed hints at serious affairs amid matters of mirth and amusement, did not follow each other consecutively; but were adroitly introduced during the time of the banquet at the *hôtel de ville*, during a subsequent interview in the Duke's own apartments, and, in short, as occasion seemed to render the introduction of such delicate subjects easy and natural.

Indeed, however rashly Louis had placed himself in a risk which the Duke's fiery temper, and the mutual subjects of exasperated enmity which subsisted betwixt them, rendered of doubtful and perilous issue, never pilot on an unknown coast conducted himself with more firmness and prudence. He seemed to sound, with the utmost address and precision, the depths and shallows of his rival's mind and temper, and manifested neither doubt nor fear when the result of his experiments discovered much more of sunken rocks and of dangerous shoals than of safe anchorage.

At length a day closed which must have been a wearisome one to Louis, from the constant exertion, vigilance, precaution, and attention which his situation required, as it was a day of constraint to the Duke, from the necessity of suppressing the violent feelings to which he was in the general habit of giving uncontrolled vent.

No sooner had the latter retired into his own apartment, after he had taken a formal leave of the King for the night, than he gave way to the explosion of passion which he had so long suppressed; and many an oath and abusive epithet, as his jester, Le Glorieux, said, "fell that night upon heads which they were never coined for," his domestics reaping the benefit of that hoard of injurious language which he could not in decency bestow on his royal guest, even in his absence, and which was yet become too great to be altogether suppressed. The jests of the clown had some effect in tranquillising the Duke's angry mood; he laughed loudly, threw the jester a piece of gold, caused himself to be disrobed in tranquillity, swallowed a deep cup of wine and spices, went to bed, and slept soundly.

The *couchée* of King Louis is more worthy of notice than that of Charles; for the violent expression of exasperated and headlong passion, as indeed it belongs more to the brutal than the intelligent part of our nature, has little to interest us in comparison to the deep workings of a vigorous and powerful mind.

Louis was escorted to the lodgings he had chosen in the castle, or citadel, of Péronne by the chamberlains and harbingers of the Duke of Burgundy, and received at the entrance by a strong guard of archers and men-at-arms.

As he descended from his horse to cross the drawbridge, over a moat of unusual width and depth, he looked on the sentinels, and observed to Comines, who accompanied him, with other Burgundian nobles: "They wear St. Andrew's crosses, but not those of my Scottish Archers."

"You will find them as ready to die in your defence, sire," said the Burgundian, whose sagacious ear had detected in the

King's tone of speech a feeling which doubtless Louis would have concealed if he could. "They wear the St. Andrew's cross as the appendage of the collar of the Golden Fleece, my master the Duke of Burgundy's order."

"Do I not know it?" said Louis, showing the collar which he himself wore in compliment to his host. "It is one of the dear bonds of fraternity which exist between my kind brother and myself. We are brothers in chivalry, as in spiritual relationship—cousins by birth, and friends by every tie of kind feeling and good neighbourhood. No farther than the base-court, my noble lords and gentlemen! I can permit your attendance no farther; you have done me enough of grace."

"We were charged by the Duke," said D'Hymbercourt, "to bring your Majesty to your lodging. We trust your Majesty will permit us to obey our master's command."

"In this small matter," said the King, "I trust you will allow my command to outweigh his, even with you his liege subjects. I am something indisposed, my lords—something fatigued. Great pleasure hath its toils as well as great pain. I trust to enjoy your society better to-morrow. And yours too, Seignior Philip of Comines. I am told you are the annalist of the time; we that desire to have a name in history must speak you fair, for men say your pen hath a sharp point, when you will. Good-night, my lords and gentles, to all and each of you."

The lords of Burgundy retired, much pleased with the grace of Louis's manner and the artful distribution of his attentions; and the King was left with only one or two of his own personal followers, under the archway of the base-court of the Castle of Péronne, looking on the huge tower which occupied one of the angles, being in fact the donjon, or principal keep, of the place. This tall, dark, massive building was seen clearly by the same moon which was lighting Quentin Durward betwixt Charleroi and Péronne, which, as the reader is aware, shone with peculiar lustre. The great keep was in form nearly resembling the White Tower in the citadel of London, but still more ancient in its architecture, deriving its date, as was affirmed, from the days of Charlemagne. The walls were of a tremendous thickness, the windows very small, and grated with bars of iron, and the huge clumsy bulk of the building cast a dark and portentous shadow over the whole of the courtyard.

"I am not to be lodged *there!*" the King said, with a shudder that had something in it ominous.

"No," replied the grey-headed seneschal, who attended upon him unbonneted. "God forbid! Your Majesty's apartments are prepared in these lower buildings which are hard by, and in which King John slept two nights before the battle of Poictiers."

"Hum—that is no lucky omen neither," muttered the King; "but what of the tower, my old friend? and why should you desire of Heaven that I may not be there lodged?"

"Nay, my gracious liege," said the seneschal, "I know no evil of the tower at all—only that the sentinels say lights are seen, and strange noises heard, in it at night; and there are reasons why that may be the case, for anciently it was used as a state prison, and there are many tales of deeds which have been done in it."

Louis asked no farther questions; for no man was more bound than he to respect the secrets of a prison-house. At the door of the apartments destined for his use, which, though of later date than the tower, were still both ancient and gloomy, stood a small party of the Scottish Guard, which the Duke, although he declined to concede the point to Louis, had ordered to be introduced, so as to be near the person of their master. The faithful Lord Crawford was at their head.

"Crawford—my honest and faithful Crawford," said the King, "where hast thou been to-day? Are the lords of Burgundy so inhospitable as to neglect one of the bravest and most noble gentlemen that ever trode a court? I saw you not at the banquet."

"I declined it, my liege," said Crawford. "Times are changed with me. The day has been that I could have ventured a carouse with the best man in Burgundy, and that in the juice of his own grape; but a matter of four pints now flusters me, and I think it concerns your Majesty's service to set in this an example to my callants."

"Thou art ever prudent," said the King; "but surely your toil is the less when you have so few men to command? and a time of festivity requires not so severe self-denial on your part as a time of danger."

"If I have few men to command," said Crawford, "I have the more need to keep the knaves in fitting condition; and whether this business be like to end in feasting or fighting, God and your Majesty know better than old John of Crawford."

"You surely do not apprehend any danger?" said the King hastily, yet in a whisper.

"Not I," answered Crawford. "I wish I did; for, as old Earl Tineman[1] used to say, apprehended dangers may be always defended dangers. The word for the night, if your Majesty pleases?"

"Let it be 'Burgundy,' in honour of our host and of a liquor that you love, Crawford."

"I will quarrel with neither duke nor drink so called," said Crawford, "provided always that both be sound. A good night to your Majesty!"

"A good night, my trusty Scot," said the King, and passed on to his apartments.

At the door of his bedroom Le Balafré was placed sentinel. "Follow me hither," said the King as he passed him; and the archer accordingly, like a piece of machinery put in motion by an artist, strode after him into the apartment, and remained there fixed, silent, and motionless, attending the royal command.

"Have you heard from that wandering paladin, your nephew?" said the King; "for he hath been lost to us since, like a young knight who had set out upon his first adventures, he sent us home two prisoners, as the first-fruits of his chivalry."

"My lord, I heard something of that," said Balafré, "and I hope your Majesty will believe that, if he hath acted wrongfully, it was in no shape by my precept or example, since I never was so bold as to unhorse any of your Majesty's most illustrious house, better knowing my own condition, and——"

[1] An Earl of Douglas, so called.

"Be silent on that point," said the King; "your nephew did his duty in the matter."

"There indeed," continued Balafré, "he had the cue from me. 'Quentin,' said I to him, 'whatever comes of it, remember you belong to the Scottish Archer Guard, and do your duty whatever comes on't.'"

"I guessed he had some such exquisite instructor," said Louis; "but it concerns me that you answer my first question. Have you heard of your nephew of late? Stand back, my masters," he added, addressing the gentlemen of his chamber, "for this concerneth no ears but mine."

"Surely, please your Majesty," said Balafré, "I have seen this very evening the groom Charlet, whom my kinsman despatched from Liege, or some castle of the bishop's which is near it, and where he hath lodged the Ladies of Croye in safety."

"Now Our Lady of Heaven be praised for it!" said the King. "Art thou sure of it?—sure of the good news?"

"As sure as I can be of aught," said Le Balafré. "The fellow, I think, hath letters for your Majesty from the Ladies of Croye."

"Haste to get them," said the King. "Give thy harquebuss to one of these knaves—to Oliver—to any one. Now Our Lady of Embrun be praised! and silver shall be the screen that surrounds her high altar!"

Louis, in this fit of gratitude and devotion, doffed, as usual, his hat, selected from the figures with which it was garnished that which represented his favourite image of the Virgin, placed it on a table, and, kneeling down, repeated reverently the vow he had made.

The groom, being the first messenger whom Durward had despatched from Schonwaldt, was now introduced with his letters. They were addressed to the King by the Ladies of Croye, and barely thanked him in very cold terms for his courtesy while at his court, and, something more warmly, for having permitted them to retire, and sent them in safety from his dominions, expressions at which Louis laughed very heartily, instead of resenting them. He then demanded of

Charlet, with obvious interest, whether they had not sustained some alarm or attack upon the road? Charlet, a stupid fellow, and selected for that quality, gave a very confused account of the affray in which his companion, the Gascon, had been killed, but knew of no other. Again Louis demanded of him, minutely and particularly, the route which the party had taken to Liege; and seemed much interested when he was informed, in reply, that they had, upon approaching Namur, kept the more direct road to Liege, upon the right bank of the Maes, instead of the left bank, as recommended in their route. The King then ordered the man a small present and dismissed him, disguising the anxiety he had expressed, as if it only concerned the safety of the Ladies of Croye.

Yet the news, though they inferred the failure of one of his own favourite plans, seemed to imply more internal satisfaction on the King's part than he would have probably indicated in a case of brilliant success. He sighed like one whose breast has been relieved from a heavy burden, muttered his devotional acknowledgments with an air of deep sanctity, raised up his eyes, and hastened to adjust newer and surer schemes of ambition.

With such purpose, Louis ordered the attendance of his astrologer, Martius Galeotti, who appeared with his usual air of assumed dignity, yet not without a shade of uncertainty on his brow, as if he had doubted the King's kind reception. It was, however, favourable, even beyond the warmest which he had ever met with at any former interview. Louis termed him his friend, his father in the sciences, the glass by which a king should look into distant futurity, and concluded by thrusting on his finger a ring of very considerable value. Galeotti, not aware of the circumstances which had thus suddenly raised his character in the estimation of Louis, yet understood his own profession too well to let that ignorance be seen. He received with grave modesty the praises of Louis, which he contended were only due to the nobleness of the science which he practised, a science the rather the more deserving of admiration on account of its working miracles through means of so feeble an agent as himself; and he and the King took leave, for once much satisfied with each other.

On the astrologer's departure, Louis threw himself into a chair, and appearing much exhausted, dismissed the rest of his attendants, excepting Oliver alone, who, creeping around with gentle assiduity and noiseless step, assisted him in the task of preparing for repose.

While he received this assistance, the King, unlike to his wont, was so silent and passive, that his attendant was struck by the unusual change in his deportment. The worst minds have often something of good principle in them: banditti show fidelity to their captain, and sometimes a protected and promoted favourite has felt a gleam of sincere interest in the monarch to whom he owed his greatness. Oliver le Diable, le Mauvais, or by whatever other name he was called expressive of his evil propensities, was, nevertheless, scarcely so completely identified with Satan as not to feel some touch of grateful feeling for his master in this singular condition, when, as it seemed, his fate was deeply interested, and his strength seemed to be exhausted. After for a short time rendering to the King in silence the usual services paid by a servant to his master at the toilet, the attendant was at length tempted to say, with the freedom which his sovereign's indulgence had permitted him in such circumstances: "*Tête-dieu*, sire, you seem as if you had lost a battle; and yet I, who was near your Majesty during this whole day, never knew you fight a field so gallantly.

"A field!" said King Louis, looking up, and assuming his wonted causticity of tone and manner; "*Pasques-dieu*, my friend Oliver, say I have kept the arena in a bull-fight; for a blinder, and more stubborn, untameable, uncontrollable brute, than our cousin of Burgundy, never existed, save in the shape of a Murcian bull, trained for the bull-feasts. Well, let it pass. I dodged him bravely. But, Oliver, rejoice with me that my plans in Flanders have not taken effect, whether as concerning those two rambling Princesses of Croye, or in Liege—you understand me?"

"In faith, I do not, sire," replied Oliver; "it is impossible for me to congratulate your Majesty on the failure of your favourite schemes, unless you tell me some reason for the change in your own wishes and views."

"Nay," answered the King, "there is no change in either, in a general view. But, *Pasques-dieu*, my friend, I have this day learned more of Duke Charles than I before knew. When he was Count de Charolois, in the time of the old Duke Philip and the banished Dauphin of France, we drank, and hunted, and rambled together, and many a wild adventure we have had. And in those days I had a decided advantage over him, like that which a strong spirit naturally assumes over a weak one. But he has since changed—has become a dogged, daring, assuming, disputatious dogmatist, who nourishes an obvious wish to drive matters to extremities, while he thinks he has the game in his own hands. I was compelled to glide as gently away from each offensive topic as if I touched red-hot iron. I did but hint at the possibility of those erratic Countesses of Croye, ere they attained Liege—for thither I frankly confessed that, to the best of my belief, they were gone—falling into the hands of some wild snapper upon the frontiers, and, *Pasques-dieu!* you would have thought I had spoken of sacrilege. It is needless to tell you what he said, and quite enough to say, that I would have held my head's safety very insecure, if, in that moment, accounts had been brought of the success of thy friend, William with the Beard, in his and thy honest scheme of bettering himself by marriage."

"No friend of *mine*, if it please your Majesty," said Oliver; "neither friend nor plan of mine."

"True, Oliver," answered the king; "thy plan had not been to wed, but to shave, such a bridegroom. Well, thou didst wish her as bad a one, when thou didst modestly hint at thyself. However, Oliver, lucky the man who has her not; for hang, draw, and quarter were the most gentle words which my gentle cousin spoke of him who should wed the young countess, his vassal, without his most ducal permission."

"And he is, doubtless, as jealous of any disturbances in the good town of Liege?" asked the favourite.

"As much, or much more so," replied the king, "as your

understanding may easily anticipate; but, ever since I resolved on coming hither, my messengers have been in Liege, to repress, for the present, every movement to insurrection; and my very busy and bustling friends, Rouslaer and Pavilion, have orders to be quiet as a mouse until this happy meeting between my cousin and me is over."

"Judging, then, from your Majesty's account," said Oliver drily, "the utmost to be hoped from this meeting is, that it should not make your condition worse? Surely this is like the crane that thrust her head into the fox's mouth, and was glad to thank her good fortune that it was not bitten off. Yet your Majesty seemed deeply obliged even now to the sage philosopher who encouraged you to play so hopeful a game."

"No game," said the King, sharply, "is to be despaired of until it is lost, and that I have no reason to expect it will be in my own case. On the contrary, if nothing occurs to stir the rage of this vindictive madman, I am sure of victory; and surely, I am not a little obliged to the skill which selected for my agent, as the conductor of the Ladies of Croye, a youth whose horoscope so far corresponded with mine, that he hath saved me from danger, even by the disobedience of my own commands, and taking the route which avoided De la Marck's ambuscade."

"Your Majesty," said Oliver, "may find many agents who will serve you on the terms of acting rather after their own pleasure than your instructions."

"Nay, nay, Oliver," said Louis impatiently, "the heathen poet speaks of *vota diis exaudita malignis*—wishes, that is, which the saints grant to us in their wrath; and such, in the circumstances, would have been the success of William de la Marck's exploit, had it taken place about this time, and while I am in the power of this Duke of Burgundy. And this my own art foresaw—fortified by that of Galeotti; that is, I foresaw not the miscarriage of De la Marck's undertaking, but I foresaw that the expedition of yonder Scottish archer should end happily for me. And such has been the issue, though in a manner different for what I expected; for the stars, though they foretell general results, are yet silent on the means by which such are accomplished, being often the very reverse of what we expect, or even desire. But why talk I of these mysteries to thee, Oliver, who art in so far worse than the very devil, who is thy namesake, since he believes and trembles; whereas thou art an infidel both to religion and to science, and wilt remain so till thine own destiny is accomplished, which, as thy horoscope and physiognomy alike assure me, will be by the intervention of the gallows?"

"And if it indeed shall be so," said Oliver, in a resigned tone of voice, "it will be so ordered, because I was too grateful a servant to hesitate at executing the commands of my royal master."

Louis burst into his usual sardonic laugh. "Thou hast broke thy lance on me fairly, Oliver; and, by Our Lady, thou art right, for I defied thee to it. But, prithee, tell me in sadness, dost thou discover anything in these men's measures towards us, which may argue any suspicion of ill usage?"

"My liege," replied Oliver, "your Majesty and yonder learned philosopher look for augury to the stars and heavenly host; I am an earthly reptile, and consider but the things connected with my vocation. But, methinks, there is a lack of that earnest and precise attention on your Majesty, which men show to a welcome guest of a degree so far above them. The Duke, to-night, pleaded weariness, and saw your Majesty not farther than to the street, leaving to the officers of his household the task of conveying you to your lodgings. The rooms here are hastily and carelessly fitted up: the tapestry is hung up awry; and, in one of the pieces, as you may observe, the figures are reversed and stand on their heads, while the trees grow with their roots uppermost."

"Pshaw! accident, and the effect of hurry," said the King. "When did you ever know me concerned about such trifles as these?"

"Not on their own account are they worth notice," said Oliver; "but as intimating the degree of esteem in which the officers of the Duke's household observe your Grace to be held by him. Believe me, that had his desire seemed sincere that your reception should be in all points marked by scrupulous attention, the zeal of his people would have made minutes do the work of days. And when," he added, pointing to the basin and ewer, "was the furniture of your Majesty's toilet of other substance than silver?"

"Nay," said the King, with a constrained smile, "that last remark upon the shaving utensils, Oliver, is too much in the style of thine own peculiar occupation to be combated by any one. True it is, that when was I only a refugee and an exile, I was served upon gold plate by order of the same Charles, who accounted silver too mean for the Dauphin, though he seems to hold that metal too rich for the King of France. Well, Oliver, we will to bed. Our resolution has been made and executed; there is nothing to be done but to play manfully the game on which we have entered. I know that my cousin of Burgundy, like other wild bulls, shuts his eyes when he begins his career. I have but to watch that moment, like one of the tauridors whom we saw at Burgos, and his impetuosity places him at my mercy."

CHAPTER XXVII.

THE EXPLOSION.

'Tis listening fear, and dumb amazement all,
When to the startled eye the sudden glance
Appears far south, eruptive through the cloud.
THOMSON'S *Summer*.

The preceding chapter, agreeable to its title, was designed as a retrospect, which might enable the reader fully to understand the terms upon which the King of France and the Duke of Burgundy stood together, when the former, moved, partly perhaps by his belief in astrology, which was represented as favourable to the issue of such a measure, and in a great measure doubtless by the conscious superiority of his own powers of mind over those of Charles, had adopted the extraordinary, and upon any other ground altogether inexplicable, resolution of committing his person to the faith of a fierce and exasperated enemy—a resolution also the more rash and unaccountable, as there were various examples in that stormy time to show, that safe-conducts, however solemnly plighted, had proved no assurance for those in whose favour they were conceived; and indeed the murder of the Duke's grandfather, at the bridge of Montereau, in presence of the father of Louis, and at an interview solemnly agreed upon for the establishment of peace and amnesty, was a horrible precedent, should the Duke be disposed to resort to it.

But the temper of Charles, though rough, fierce, headlong and unyielding, was not, unless in the full tide of passion, faithless or ungenerous, faults which usually belong to colder dispositions. He was at no pains to show the King more courtesy than the laws of hospitality positively demanded; but, on the other hand, he evinced no purpose of overleaping their sacred barriers.

On the following morning after the King's arrival, there was a general muster of the troops of the Duke of Burgundy, which were so numerous and so excellently appointed, that, perhaps, he was not sorry to have an opportunity of displaying them before his great rival. Indeed, while he paid the necessary compliment of a vassal to his suzerain, in declaring that these troops were the King's, and not his own, the curl of his upper lip and the proud glance of his eye intimated his consciousness that the words he used were but empty compliment, and that his fine army, at his own unlimited disposal, was as ready to march against Paris as in any other direction. It must have added to Louis's mortification, that he recognised, as forming part of this host, many banners of French nobility, not only of Normandy and Bretagne, but of provinces more immediately subjected to his own authority, who, from various causes of discontent, had joined and made common cause with the Duke of Burgundy.

True to his character, however, Louis seemed to take little notice of these malcontents, while, in fact, he was revolving in his mind the various means by which it might be possible to detach them from the banners of Burgundy and bring them back to his own, and resolved for that purpose, that he would cause those to whom he attached the greatest importance to be secretly sounded by Oliver and other agents.

He himself laboured diligently, but at the same time cautiously, to make interest with the Duke's chief officers and advisers, employing for that purpose the usual means of familiar and frequent notice, adroit flattery, and liberal presents; not as, he represented, to alienate their faithful services from their noble master, but that they might lend their aid in preserving peace betwixt France and Burgundy—an end so excellent in itself, and so obviously tending to the welfare of both countries, and of the reigning princes of either.

The notice of so great and so wise a king was in itself a mighty bribe; promises did much, and direct gifts, which the customs of the time permitted the Burgundian courtiers to accept without scruple, did still more. During a boar hunt in the forest, while the Duke, eager always upon the immediate object, whether business or pleasure, gave himself entirely up to the ardour of the chase, Louis, unrestrained by his presence, sought and found the means of speaking secretly and separately to many of those who were reported to have most interest with Charles, among whom D'Hymbercourt and Comines were not forgotten; nor did he fail to mix up the advances which he made towards those two distinguished persons with praises of the valour and military skill of the first, and of the profound sagacity and literary talents of the future historian of the period.

Such an opportunity of personally conciliating, or, if the reader pleases, corrupting, the ministers of Charles, was perhaps what the King had proposed to himself as a principal object of his visit, even if his art should fail to cajole the Duke himself. The connexion betwixt France and Burgundy was so close, that most of the nobles belonging to the latter country had hopes or actual interests connected with the former, which the favour of Louis could advance or his personal displeasure destroy. Formed for this and every other species of intrigue, liberal to profusion when it was necessary to advance his plans, and skilful in putting the most plausible colour upon his proposals and presents, the King contrived to reconcile the spirit of the proud to their profit, and to hold out to the real or pretended patriot the good of both France and Burgundy as the ostensible motive; whilst the party's own private interest, like the concealed wheel of some machine, worked not the less powerfully that its operations were kept out of sight. For each man he had a suitable bait and a proper mode of presenting it: he poured the guerdon into the sleeve of those who were too proud to extend their hand, and trusted that his bounty, though it descended like the dew without noise and imperceptibly, would not fail to produce, in due season, a plentiful crop of good will at least, perhaps of good offices, to the donor. In fine, although he had been long paving the way by his ministers for an establishment of such an interest in the court of Burgundy as should be advantageous to the interests of France, Louis's own personal exertions, directed doubtless by the information of which he was previously possessed, did more to accomplish that object in a few hours than his agents had effected in years of negotiation.

One man alone the King missed whom he had been particularly desirous of conciliating, and that was the Count de Crèvecœur, whose firmness, during his conduct as envoy at Plessis, far from exciting Louis's resentment, had been viewed as a reason for making him his own if possible. He was not particularly gratified when he learnt that the count, at the head of an hundred lances, was gone towards the frontiers of Brabant to assist the bishop, in case of necessity, against William de la Marck and his discontented subjects; but he consoled himself that the appearance of this force, joined with the directions which he had sent by faithful messengers, would serve to prevent any premature disturbances in that country, the breaking out of which might, he foresaw, render his present situation very precarious.

The court upon this occasion dined in the forest when the hour of noon arrived, as was common in these great hunting parties; an arrangement at this time particularly agreeable to the Duke, desirous as he was to abridge that ceremonious and deferential solemnity with which he was otherwise under the necessity of receiving King Louis. In fact, the King's knowledge of human nature had in one particular misled him on this remarkable occasion. He thought that the Duke would have been inexpressibly flattered to have received such a mark of condescension and confidence from his liege lord; but he forgot that the dependence of this dukedom upon the crown of France was privately the subject of galling mortification to a prince so powerful, so wealthy, and so proud as Charles, whose aim it certainly was to establish an independent kingdom. The presence of the King at the court of the Duke of Burgundy imposed on that prince the necessity of exhibiting himself in the subordinate character of a vassal, and of discharging many rites of feudal observance and deference, which, to one of his haughty disposition, resembled derogation from the character of a sovereign prince, which on all occasions he affected as far as possible to sustain.

But although it was possible to avoid much ceremony by having the dinner upon the green turf, with sound of bugles, broaching of barrels, and all the freedom of a sylvan meal, it was necessary that the evening repast should, even for that very reason, be held with more than usual solemnity.

Previous orders for this purpose had been given, and, upon returning to Péronne, King Louis found a banquet prepared with such a profusion of splendour and magnificence, as became the wealth of his formidable vassal, possessed as he was of almost all the Low Countries, then the richest portion of Europe. At the head of the long board, which groaned under plate of gold and silver, filled to profusion with the most exquisite dainties, sat the Duke, and on his right hand, upon a seat more elevated than his own, was placed his royal guest. Behind him stood on one side the son of the Duke of Gueldres, who officiated as his grand carver, on the other Le Glorieux, his jester, without whom he seldom stirred; for, like most men of his hasty and coarse character, Charles carried to extremity the general taste of that age for court fools and jesters—experiencing that pleasure in their display of eccentricity and mental infirmity which his more acute, but not more benevolent, rival loved better to extract from marking the imperfections of humanity in its nobler specimens, and finding subject for mirth in the "fears of the brave and follies of the wise." And, indeed, if the anecdote related by Brantôme be true, that a court fool, having overheard Louis, in one of his agonies of repentant devotion, confess his accession to the poisoning of his brother, Henry Count of Guyenne, divulged it next day at dinner before the assembled court, that monarch might be supposed rather more than satisfied with the pleasantries of professed jesters for the rest of his life.

But, on the present occasion, Louis neglected not to take notice of the favourite buffoon of the Duke, and to applaud his repartees; which he did the rather that he thought he saw that the folly of Le Glorieux, however grossly it was sometimes displayed, covered more than the usual quantity of shrewd and caustic observation proper to his class.

In fact, Tiel Wetzweiler, called Le Glorieux, was by no means a jester of the common stamp. He was a tall, fine-looking man, excellent at many exercises, which seemed scarce reconcilable with mental imbecility, because it must have required patience and attention to attain them. He usually followed the Duke to the chase and to the fight; and at Mont-l'héry, when Charles was in considerable personal danger, wounded in the throat, and likely to be made prisoner by a French knight who had hold of his horse's rein, Tiel Wetzweiler charged the assailant so forcibly as to overthrow him and disengage his master. Perhaps he was afraid of this being thought too serious a service for a person of his condition, and that it might excite him enemies among those knights and nobles who had left the care of their master's person to the court fool. At any rate, he chose rather to be laughed at than praised for his achievement, and made such gasconading boasts of his exploits in the battle, that most men thought the rescue of Charles was as ideal as the rest of his tale; and it was on this occasion he acquired the title of Le Glorieux (or the boastful), by which he was ever afterwards distinguished.

Le Glorieux was dressed very richly, but with little of the usual distinction of his profession, and that little rather of a symbolical than a very literal character. His head was not shorn; on the contrary, he wore a profusion of long curled hair, which descended from under his cap, and joining with a well-arranged and handsomely trimmed beard, set off features which, but for a wild lightness of eye, might have been termed handsome. A ridge of scarlet velvet, carried across the top of his cap, indicated, rather than positively represented, the professional cock's-comb, which distinguished the headgear of a fool in right of office. His bauble, made of ebony, was crested, as usual, with a fool's head, with ass's ears formed of silver; but so small, and so minutely carved, that, till very closely examined, it might have passed for an official baton of a more solemn character. These were the only badges of his office which his dress exhibited. In other respects, it was such as to match with that of the most courtly nobles. His bonnet displayed a medal of gold; he wore a chain of the same metal around his neck; and the fashion of his rich garments was not much more fantastic than those of young gallants who have their clothes made in the extremity of the existing fashion.

To this personage Charles, and Louis, in imitation of his host, often addressed themselves during the entertainment; and both seemed to manifest, by hearty laughter, their amusement at the answers of Le Glorieux.

"Whose seats be those that are vacant?" said Charles to the jester.

"One of those at least should be mine by right of succession, Charles," replied Le Glorieux.

"Why so, knave?" said Charles.

"Because they belong to the Sieur D'Hymbercourt and Des Comines, who are gone so far to fly their falcons that they have forgot their supper. They who would rather look at a kite on the wing than a pheasant on the board are of kin to the fool, and he should succeed to the stools, as a part of their movable estate."

"That is but a stale jest, my friend Tiel," said the Duke; "but, fools or wise men, here come the defaulters."

As he spoke, Comines and D'Hymbercourt entered the room, and, after having made their reverence to the two princes, assumed in silence the seats which were left vacant for them.

"What ho! sirs," exclaimed the Duke, addressing them, "your sport has been either very good or very bad, to lead you so far and so late. Sir Philip des Comines, you are dejected; hath D'Hymbercourt won so heavy a wager on you? You are a philosopher, and should not grieve at bad fortune. By St. George! D'Hymbercourt looks as sad as thou dost. How now, sirs? Have you found no game? or have you lost your falcons? or has a witch crossed your way? or has the Wild Huntsman[1] met you in the forest? By my honour, you seem as if you were come to a funeral, not a festival."

While the Duke spoke, the eyes of the company were all directed towards D'Hymbercourt and Des Comines; and the embarrassment and dejection of their countenances, neither being of that class of persons to whom such expression of anxious melancholy was natural, became so remarkable, that the mirth and laughter of the company, which the rapid circulation of goblets of excellent wine had raised to a considerable height, was gradually hushed, and, without being able to assign any reason for such a change in their spirits, men spoke in whispers to each other, as on the eve of expecting some strange and important tidings.

"What means this silence, Messires?" said the Duke, elevating his voice, which was naturally harsh. "If you bring these strange looks, and this stranger silence, into festivity, we shall wish you had abode in the marshes seeking for herons, or rather for woodcocks and howlets."

"My gracious lord," said Des Comines, "as we were about to return hither from the forest, we met the Count of Crèvecœur."

"How!" said the Duke; "already returned from Brabant? but he found all well there, doubtless?"

"The count himself will presently give your Grace an account of his news," said D'Hymbercourt, "which we have heard but imperfectly."

"Body of me, where is the count?" said the Duke.

"He changes his dress, to wait upon your Highness," answered D'Hymbercourt.

---

[1] The famous apparition, sometimes called *Le Grand Veneur*. Sully gives some account of this hunting spectre.

"His dress! *Saint-bleau!*" exclaimed the impatient prince, "what care I for his dress? I think you have conspired with him to drive me mad."

"Or rather, to be plain," said Des Comines, "he wishes to communicate these news at a private audience."

"*Teste-dieu!* my lord king," said Charles, "this is ever the way our counsellors serve us. If they have got hold of aught which they consider as important for our ear, they look as grave upon the matter, and are as proud of their burden as an ass of a new pack-saddle. Some one bid Crèvecœur come to us directly! He comes from the frontiers of Liege, and *we*, at least (he laid some emphasis on the pronoun), have no secrets in that quarter which we would shun to have proclaimed before the assembled world."

All perceived that the Duke had drunk so much wine as to increase the native obstinacy of his disposition; and though many would willingly have suggested that the present was neither a time for hearing news, nor for taking counsel, yet all knew the impetuosity of his temper too well to venture on farther interference, and sat in anxious expectation of the tidings which the count might have to communicate.

A brief interval intervened, during which the Duke remained looking eagerly to the door, as if in a transport of impatience, whilst the guests sat with their eyes bent on the table, as if to conceal their curiosity and anxiety. Louis alone maintaining perfect composure, continued his conversation alternately with the grand carver and with the jester.

At length Crèvecœur entered, and was presently saluted by the hurried question of his master: "What news from Liege and Brabant, sir count? The report of your arrival has chased mirth from our table; we hope your actual presence will bring it back to us."

"My liege and master," answered the count, in a firm but melancholy tone, "the news which I bring you are fitter for the council-board than the feasting-table."

"Out with them, man, if they were tidings from Antichrist!" said the Duke; "but I can guess them: the Liegeois are again in mutiny."

"They are, my lord," said Crèvecœur, very gravely.

"Look there, man," said the Duke, "I have hit at once on what you have been so much afraid to mention to me; the harebrained burghers are again in arms. It could not be in better time, for we may at present have the advice of our own suzerain," bowing to King Louis, with eyes which spoke the most bitter, though suppressed, resentment, "to teach us how such mutineers should be dealt with. Hast thou more news in thy packet? Out with them, and then answer for yourself why you went not forward to assist the bishop."

"My lord, the farther tidings are heavy for me to tell, and will be afflicting to you to hear. No aid of mine, or of living chivalry, could have availed the excellent prelate. William de la Marck, united with the insurgent Liegeois, has taken his castle of Schonwaldt, and murdered him in his own hall."

"*Murdered him!*" repeated the Duke, in a deep and low tone, but which nevertheless was heard from the one end of the hall in which they were assembled to the other; "thou hast been imposed upon, Crèvecœur, by some wild report; it is impossible!"

"Alas, my lord!" said the count, "I have it from an eye-witness, an archer of the King of France's Scottish Guard, who was in the hall when the murder was committed by William de la Marck's order."

"And who was doubtless aiding and abetting in the horrible sacrilege!" exclaimed the Duke, starting up and stamping with his foot with such fury, that he dashed in pieces the footstool which was placed before him. "Bar the doors of this hall, gentlemen—secure the windows—let no stranger stir from his seat, upon pain of instant death!" Gentlemen of my chamber, draw your swords." And turning upon Louis, he advanced his own hand slowly and deliberately to the hilt of his weapon; while the King, without either showing fear or assuming a defensive posture, only said:

"These news, fair cousin, have staggered your reason."

"No!" replied the Duke, in a terrible tone, "but they have awakened a just resentment, which I have too long suffered to be stifled by trivial considerations of circumstance and place.

Murderer of thy brother!—rebel against thy parent! tyrant over thy subjects!—treacherous ally!—perjured king!—dishonoured gentleman!—thou art in my power, and I thank God for it."

"Rather thank my folly," said the King; "for when we met on equal terms at Montl'héry, methinks you wished yourself farther from me than we are now."

The Duke still held his hand on the hilt of his sword, but refrained to draw his weapon, or to strike a foe who offered no sort of resistance which could in anywise provoke violence.

Meanwhile, wild and general confusion spread itself through the hall. The doors were now fastened and guarded by order of the Duke; but several of the French nobles, few as they were in number, started from their seats, and prepared for the defence of their sovereign. Louis had spoken not a word either to Orleans or Dunois since they were liberated from restraint at the Castle of Loches, if it could be termed liberation to be dragged in King Louis's train, objects of suspicion evidently rather than of respect and regard; but, nevertheless, the voice of Dunois was first heard above the tumult addressing himself to the Duke of Burgundy. "Sir duke, you have forgotten that you are a vassal of France, and that we, your guests, are Frenchmen. If you lift a hand against our monarch, prepare to sustain the utmost effects of our despair; for, credit me, we shall feast as high with the blood of Burgundy as we have done with its wine. Courage, my Lord of Orleans; and you, gentlemen of France, form yourselves round Dunois, and do as he does!"

It was in that moment when a king might see upon what tempers he could certainly rely. The few independent nobles and knights who attended Louis, most of whom had only received from him frowns or discountenance, unappalled by the display of infinitely superior force, and the certainty of destruction in case they came to blows, hastened to array themselves around Dunois, and, led by him, to press towards the head of the table where the contending princes were seated.

On the contrary, the tools and agents whom Louis had dragged forward out of their fitting and natural places into importance which was not due to them, showed cowardice and cold heart, and, remaining still in their seats, seemed resolved not to provoke their fate by intermeddling, whatever might become of their benefactor.

The first of the more generous party was the venerable Lord Crawford, who, with an agility which no one would have expected at his years, forced his way through all opposition, which was the less violent, as many of the Burgundians, either from a point of honour or a secret inclination to prevent Louis's impending fate, gave way to him, and threw himself boldly between the King and the Duke. He then placed his bonnet, from which his white hair escaped in dishevelled tresses, upon one side of his head; his pale cheek and withered brow coloured, and his aged eye lightened with all the fire of a gallant who is about to dare some desperate action. His cloak was flung over one shoulder, and his action intimated his readiness to wrap it about his left arm, while he unsheathed his sword with his right.

"I have fought for his father and his grandsire," that was all he said, "and, by St. Andrew, end the matter as it will, I will not fail him at this pinch."

What has taken some time to narrate happened, in fact, with the speed of light; for so soon as the Duke assumed his threatening posture, Crawford had thrown himself betwixt him and the object of his vengeance; and the French gentlemen, drawing together as fast as they could, were crowding to the same point.

The Duke of Burgundy still remained with his hand on his sword, and seemed in the act of giving the signal for a general onset, which must necessarily have ended in the massacre of the weaker party, when Crèvecœur rushed forward and exclaimed, in a voice like a trumpet: "My liege Lord of Burgundy, beware what you do! This is *your* hall, you are the King's vassal; do not spill the blood of your guest on your hearth, the blood of your sovereign on the throne you have erected for him, and to which he came under your safeguard. For the sake of your house's honour, do not attempt to revenge one horrid murder by another yet worse!"

"Out of my road, Crèvecœur," answered the Duke, "and let my vengeance pass! Out of my path! The wrath of kings is to be dreaded like that of Heaven."

"Only when, like that of Heaven, it is *just*," answered Crèvecœur firmly. "Let me pray of you, my lord, to rein the violence of your temper, however justly offended. And for you, my lords of France, where resistance is unavailing, let me recommend you to forbear whatever may lead towards bloodshed."

"He is right," said Louis, whose coolness forsook him not in that dreadful moment, and who easily foresaw that if a brawl should commence, more violence would be dared and done in the heat of blood than was likely to be attempted if peace were preserved. "My cousin Orleans—kind Dunois—and you, my trusty Crawford—bring not on ruin and bloodshed by taking offence too hastily. Our cousin the Duke is chafed at the tidings of the death of a near and loving friend, the venerable Bishop of Liege, whose slaughter we lament as he does. Ancient and, unhappily, recent subjects of jealousy lead him to suspect us of having abetted a crime which our bosom abhors. Should our host murder us on this spot— us, his king and his kinsman, under a false impression of our being accessary to this unhappy accident, our fate will be little lightened, but, on the contrary, greatly aggravated, by your stirring. Therefore, stand back, Crawford. Were it my last word, I speak as a king to his officer, and demand obedience. Stand back, and, if it is required, yield up your sword. I command you to do so, and your oath obliges you to obey."

"True—true, my lord," said Crawford, stepping back, and returning to the sheath the blade he had half drawn. "It may be all very true; but, by my honour, if I were at the head of threescore and ten of my brave fellows, instead of being loaded with more than the like number of years, I would try whether I could have some reason out of these fine gallants, with their golden chains and looped-up bonnets, with braw-warld dyes and devices on them."

The Duke stood with his eyes fixed on the ground for a considerable space, and then said, with bitter irony: "Crèvecœur, you say well; and it concerns our honour, that our obligations to this great king, our honoured and loving guest, be not so hastily adjusted, as in our hasty anger we had at first proposed. We will so act, that all Europe shall acknowledge the justice of our proceedings. Gentlemen of France, you must render up your arms to my officers! Your master has broken the truce, and has no title to take farther benefit of it. In compassion, however, to your sentiments of honour, and in respect to the rank which he hath disgraced, and the race from which he hath degenerated, we ask not our cousin Louis's sword."

"Not one of us," said Dunois, "will resign our weapon, or quit this hall, unless we are assured of at least our king's safety, in life and limb."

"Nor will a man of the Scottish Guard," exclaimed Crawford, "lay down his arms, save at the command of the King of France, or his High Constable."

"Brave Dunois," said Louis, "and you, my trusty Crawford, your zeal will do me injury instead of benefit. I trust," he added, with dignity, "in my rightful cause more than in a vain resistance, which would but cost the lives of my best and bravest. Give up your swords; the noble Burgundians who accept such honourable pledges will be more able than you are to protect both you and me. Give up your swords. It is I who command you."

It was thus that, in this dreadful emergency, Louis showed the promptitude of decision and clearness of judgment which alone could have saved his life. He was aware that until actual blows were exchanged he should have the assistance of most of the nobles present to moderate the fury of their prince; but that, were a *mêlée* once commenced, he himself and his few adherents must be instantly murdered. At the same time, his worst enemies confessed that his demeanour had in it nothing either of meanness or cowardice. He shunned to aggravate into frenzy the wrath of the Duke; but he neither deprecated nor seemed to fear it, and continued to look on him with the calm and fixed attention with which a brave man eyes the menacing gestures of a lunatic, whilst conscious that his own steadiness and composure operate as an insensible and powerful check on the rage even of insanity.

Crawford, at the King's command, threw his sword to Crèvecœur, saying: "Take it, and the devil give you joy of it! It is no dishonour to the rightful owner who yields it, for we have had no fair play."

"Hold, gentlemen," said the Duke, in a broken voice, as one whom passion had almost deprived of utterance, "retain your swords; it is sufficient you promise not to use them. And you, Louis of Valois, must regard yourself as my prisoner, until you are cleared of having abetted sacrilege and murder. Have him to the castle. Have him to Earl Herbert's Tower. Let him have six gentlemen of his train to attend him, such as he shall choose. My Lord of Crawford, your guard must leave the castle, and shall be honourably quartered elsewhere. Up with every drawbridge, and down with every portcullis. Let the gates of the town be trebly guarded. Draw the floating-bridge to the right-hand side of the river. Bring round the castle my band of Black Walloons, and treble the sentinels on every post! You, D'Hymbercourt, look that patrols of horse and foot make the round of the town every half hour during the night, and every hour during the next day—if indeed such ward shall be necessary after daybreak, for it is like we may be sudden in this matter. Look to the person of Louis, as you love your life!"

He started from the table in fierce and moody haste, darted a glance of mortal enmity at the King, and rushed out of the apartment.

"Sirs," said the King, looking with dignity around him, "grief for the death of his ally hath made your prince frantic. I trust you know better your duty, as knights and noblemen, than to abet him in his treasonable violence against the person of his liege lord."

At this moment was heard in the streets the sound of drums beating and horns blowing, to call out the soldiery in every direction.

"We are," said Crèvecœur, who acted as the marshal of the Duke's household, "subjects of Burgundy, and must do our duty as such. Our hopes and prayers, and our efforts, will not be wanting to bring about peace and union between your Majesty and our liege lord. Meantime, we must obey his commands. These other lords and knights will be proud to contribute to the convenience of the illustrious Duke of Orleans, of the brave Dunois, and the stout Lord Crawford. I myself must be your Majesty's chamberlain, and bring you to your apartments in other guise than would be my desire, remembering the hospitality of Plessis. You have only to choose your attendants, whom the Duke's commands limit to six."

"Then," said the King, looking around him, and thinking for a moment, "I desire the attendance of Oliver le Dain, of a private of my Life Guard, called Balafré, who may be unarmed if you will, of Tristan l'Hermite, with two of his people, and my right loyal and trusty philosopher, Martius Galeotti."

"Your Majesty's will shall be complied with in all points," said the Count de Crèvecœur. "Galeotti," he added, after a moment's inquiry, "is, I understand, at present supping in some buxom company, but he shall instantly be sent for; the others will obey your Majesty's command upon the instant."

"Forward, then, to the new abode, which the hospitality of our cousin provides for us," said the King. "We know it is strong, and have only to hope it may be in a corresponding degree safe."

"Heard you the choice which King Louis has made of his attendants?" said Le Glorieux to Count Crèvecœur apart, as they followed Louis from the hall.

"Surely, my merry gossip," replied the count. "What hast thou to object to them?"

"Nothing—nothing, only they are a rare election! A panderly barber, a Scottish hired cut-throat, a chief hangman and his two assistants, and a thieving charlatan. I will along with you, Crèvecœur, and take a lesson in the degrees of roguery, from observing your skill in marshalling them. The devil himself could scarce have summoned such a synod, or have been a better president amongst them."

Accordingly, the all-licensed jester, seizing the count's arm familiarly, began to march along with him, while, under a strong guard, yet forgetting no semblance of respect, he conducted the King towards his new apartment.'

CHAPTER XXVIII.

UNCERTAINTY.

> Then happy low, lie down;
> Uneasy lies the head that wears a crown.
> *Henry IV*. Part II.

FORTY men-at-arms, carrying alternately naked swords and blazing torches, served as the escort, or rather the guard, of King Louis, from the town-hall of Péronne to the castle; and as he entered within its darksome and gloomy strength, it seemed as if a voice screamed in his ear that warning which the Florentine has inscribed over the portal of the infernal regions, "Leave all hope behind!"

At that moment, perhaps, some feeling of remorse might have crossed the King's mind, had he thought on the hundreds, nay thousands, whom, without cause, or in light suspicion, he had committed to the abysses of his dungeons, deprived of all hope of liberty, and loathing even the life to which they clung by animal instinct.

The broad glare of the torches outfacing the pale moon, which was more obscured on this than on the former night, and the red smoky light which they dispersed around the ancient buildings, gave a darker shade to that huge donjon, called the Earl Herbert's Tower. It was the same that Louis had viewed with misgiving presentiment on the preceding evening, and of which he was now doomed to become an inhabitant, under the terror of what violence soever the wrathful temper of his overgrown vassal might tempt him to exercise in those secret recesses of despotism.

See Historical Epitome. Note 38.

To aggravate the King's painful feelings, he saw, as he crossed the court-yard, several bodies, over each of which had been hastily flung a military cloak. He was not long of discerning that they were corpses of slain archers of the Scottish Guard, who, having disputed, as the Count Crèvecœur informed him, the command given them to quit the post near the King's apartments, a brawl had ensued between them and the Duke's Walloon body-guards, and before it could be composed by the officers on either side, several lives had been lost.

"My trusty Scots!" said the King, as he looked upon this melancholy spectacle; "had they brought only man to man, all Flanders—ay and Burgundy to boot—had not furnished champions to mate you."

"Yes, an it please your Majesty," said Balafré, who attended close behind the King, "Maistery mows the meadow: few men can fight more than two at once. I myself never care to meet three, unless it be in the way of special duty, when one must not stand to count heads."

"Art thou there, old acquaintance?" said the King, looking behind him; "then I have one true subject with me yet."

"And a faithful minister, whether in your councils, or in his offices about your royal person," whispered Oliver le Dain.

"We are all faithful," said Tristan l'Hermite, gruffly; "for should they put to death your Majesty, there is not one of us whom they would suffer to survive you, even if we would."

"Now, that is what I call good corporal bail for fidelity," said Le Glorieux, who, as already mentioned, with the restlessness proper to an infirm brain, had thrust himself into their company.

Meanwhile, the seneschal, hastily summoned, was turning with laborious effort the ponderous key which opened the reluctant gate of the huge Gothic keep, and was at last fain to call for the assistance of one of Crèvecœur's attendants. When they had succeeded, six men entered with torches, and showed the way through a narrow and winding passage, commanded at different points by shot-holes from vaults and casements constructed behind, and in the thickness of the massive walls. At the end of this passage arose a stair of corresponding rudeness, consisting of huge blocks of stone, roughly dressed with the hammer, and of unequal height. Having mounted this ascent, a strong iron-clenched door admitted them to what had been the great hall of the donjon, lighted but very faintly even during the daytime, for the apertures, diminished in appearance by the excessive thickness of the walls, resembled slits rather than windows, and now, but for the blaze of the torches, almost perfectly dark. Two or three bats, and other birds of evil presage, roused by the unusual glare, flew against the lights and threatened to extinguish them; while the seneschal formally apologised to the King that the state-hall had not been put in order, such was the hurry of the notice sent to him; and adding, that, in truth, the apartments had not been in use for twenty years, and rarely before that time, so far as ever he had heard, since the time of King Charles the Simple.

"King Charles the Simple!" echoed Louis; "I know the history of the tower now. He was here murdered by his treacherous vassal, Herbert, Earl of Vermandois,—so say our annals. I knew there was something concerning the Castle of Péronne which dwelt on my mind, though I could not recall the circumstances. *Here*, then, my predecessor was slain?"

"Not here, not exactly here, and please your Majesty," said the old seneschal, stepping with the eager haste of a cicerone, who shows the curiosities of such a place—"not *here*, but in the side-chamber a little onward, which opens from your Majesty's bedchamber."

He hastily opened a wicket at the upper end of the hall, which led into a bedchamber, small, as is usual in such old buildings, but, even for that reason, rather more comfortable than the waste hall through which they had passed. Some hasty preparations had been here made for the King's accommodation. Arras had been tacked up, a fire lighted in the rusty grate, which had been long unused, and a pallet laid down for those gentlemen who were to pass the night in his chamber, as was then usual.

"We will get beds in the hall for the rest of your attendants," said the garrulous old man; "but we have had such brief notice, if it please your Majesty. And if it please your Majesty to look upon this little wicket behind the arras, it opens into the little old cabinet in the thickness of the wall where Charles was slain, and there is a secret passage from below, which admitted the men who were to deal with him. And your Majesty, whose eyesight I hope is better than mine, may see the blood still on the oak floor, though the thing was done five hundred years ago."

While he thus spoke, he kept fumbling to open the postern of which he spoke, until the King said: "Forbear, old man— forbear but a little while, when thou mayst have a newer tale to tell, and fresher blood to show. My Lord of Crèvecœur, what say you?"

"I can but answer, sire, that these two interior apartments are as much at your Majesty's disposal as those in your own castle at Plessis, and that Crèvecœur, a name never blackened by treachery or assassination, has the guard of the exterior defences of it."

"But the private passage into that closet, of which the old man speaks!" This King Louis said in a low and anxious tone, holding Crèvecœur's arm fast with one hand, and pointing to the wicket door with the other.

"It must be some dream of Mornay's," said Crèvecœur, "or some old and absurd tradition of the place; but we will examine."

He was about to open the closet door, when Louis answered: "No, Crèvecœur, no; your honour is sufficient warrant. But what will your duke do with me, Crèvecœur? He can not hope to keep me long a prisoner; and—in short, give me your opinion, Crèvecœur."

"My lord and sire," said the count, "how the Duke of Burgundy must resent this horrible cruelty on the person of his near relative and ally is for your Majesty to judge; and what right he may have to consider it as instigated by your Majesty's emissaries you only can know. But my master is noble in his disposition, and made incapable, even by the very strength of his passions, of any underhand practices. Whatever he does will be done in the face of day and of the two nations. And I can but add, that it will be the wish of every counsellor around him—excepting perhaps one—that he should behave in this matter with mildness and generosity, as well as justice."

"Ah! Crèvecœur," said Louis, taking his hand as if affected by some painful recollections, "how happy is the prince who has counsellors near him who can guard him against the effects of his own angry passions! Their names will be read in golden letters, when the history of his reign is perused. Noble Crèvecœur, had it been my lot to have such as thou art about *my* person!"

"It had in that case been your Majesty's study to have got rid of them as fast as you could," said Le Glorieux.

"Aha! Sir Wisdom, art thou there?" said Louis, turning round, and instantly changing the pathetic tone in which he had addressed Crèvecœur, and adopting with facility one which had a turn of gaiety in it; "hast *thou* followed us hither?"

"Ay, sire," answered Le Glorieux, "wisdom must follow in motley, where folly leads the way in purple."

"How shall I construe that, Sir Solomon," answered Louis; "wouldst thou change conditions with me?"

"Not I, by my halidome," quoth Le Glorieux, "if you would give me fifty crowns to boot."

"Why, wherefore so? Methinks I could be well enough contented, as princes go, to have thee for my king."

"Ay, sire," replied Le Glorieux; "but the question is, whether, judging of your Majesty's wit from its having lodged you here, I should not have cause to be ashamed of having so dull a fool."

"Peace, sirrah!" said the Count of Crèvecœur; "your tongue runs too fast."

"Let it take its course," said the King; "I know of no such fair subject of raillery as the follies of those who should know better. Here, my sagacious friend, take this purse of gold, and with it the advice, never to be so great a fool as to deem yourself wiser than other people. Prithee, do me so much favour as to inquire after my astrologer, Martius Galeotti, and send him hither to me presently."

"I will, without fail, my liege," answered the jester; "and I wot well I shall find him at Jan Dopplethur's; for philosophers, as well as fools, know where the best wine is sold."

"Let me pray for free entrance for this learned person through your guards, Seignior de Crèvecœur," said Louis.

"For his entrance, unquestionably," answered the count; "but it grieves me to add, that my instructions do not authorise me to permit any one to quit your Majesty's apartments. I wish your Majesty a good night," he subjoined, "and will presently make such arrangements in the outer hall as may put the gentlemen who are to inhabit it more at their ease."

"Give yourself no trouble for them, sir count," replied the King, "they are men accustomed to set hardships at defiance; and, to speak truth, excepting that I wish to see Galeotti, I would desire as little further communication from without this night as may be consistent with your instructions."

"These are, to leave your Majesty," replied Crèvecœur, "undisputed possession of your own apartments. Such are my master's orders."

"Your master, Count Crèvecœur," answered Louis, "whom I may also term mine, is a right gracious master. My dominions," he added, "are somewhat shrunk in compass, now that they have dwindled to an old hall and a bedchamber: but they are still wide enough for all the subjects which I can at present boast of."

The Count of Crèvecœur took his leave; and, shortly after, they could hear the noise of the sentinels moving to their posts, accompanied with the word of command from the officers, and the hasty tread of the guards who were relieved. At length all became still, and the only sound which filled the air was the sluggish murmur of the river Somme, as it glided, deep and muddy, under the walls of the castle.

"Go into the hall, my mates," said Louis to his train; "but do not lie down to sleep. Hold yourselves in readiness, for there is still something to be done to-night, and that of moment."

Oliver and Tristan retired to the hall accordingly, in which Le Balafré and the provost-marshal's two officers had remained when the others entered the bedchamber. They found that those without had thrown fagots enough upon the fire to serve the purpose of light and heat at the same time, and, wrapping themselves in their cloaks, had sat down on the floor, in postures which variously expressed the discomposure and dejection of their minds. Oliver and Tristan saw nothing better to be done than to follow their example; and, never very good friends in the days of their court prosperity, they were both equally reluctant to repose confidence in each other upon this strange and sudden reverse of fortune. So that the whole party sat in silent dejection.

Meanwhile, their master underwent, in the retirement of his secret chamber, agonies that might have atoned for some of those which had been imposed by his command. He paced the room with short and unequal steps, often stood still and clasped his hands together, and gave loose, in short, to agitation, which, in public, he had found himself able to suppress so successfully. At length, pausing, and wringing his hands, he planted himself opposite to the wicket-door, which had been pointed out by old Mornay as leading to the scene of the murder of one of his predecessors, and gradually gave voice to his feelings in a broken soliloquy.

"Charles the Simple—Charles the Simple! What will posterity call the Eleventh Louis, whose blood will probably soon refresh the stains of thine? Louis the Fool—Louis the Driveller—Louis the Infatuated—all are terms too slight to mark the extremity of my idiocy! To think these hot-headed Liegeois, to whom rebellion is as natural as their food, would remain quiet—to dream that the Wild Beast of Ardennes would, for a moment, be interrupted in his career of force and bloodthirsty brutality—to suppose that I could use reason and arguments tc any good purpose with Charles of Burgundy, until I had tried the force of such exhortations with success upon a wild bull! Fool, and double idiot that I was! But the villain Martius shall not escape. He has been at the bottom of this, he and the vile priest, the detestable Balue.[1] If I ever get out of this danger, I will tear from his head the cardinal's cap, though I pull the scalp along with it! But the other traitor is in my hands: I am yet king enough—have yet an empire roomy enough—for the punishment of the quack-salving, word-mongering, star-gazing, lie-coining impostor, who has at once made a prisoner and a dupe of me! The conjunction of the constellations—ay, the conjunction! He must talk nonsense which would scarce gull a thrice-sodden sheep's head, and I must be idiot enough to think I understood him! But we shall see presently what the conjunction hath really boded. But first let me to my devotions."

Above the little door, in memory perhaps of the deed which had been done within, was a rude niche, containing a crucifix cut in stone. Upon this emblem the King fixed his eyes, as if about to kneel, but stopped short, as if he applied to the blessed image the principles of worldly policy, and deemed it rash to approach its presence without having secured the private intercession of some supposed favourite. He therefore turned from the crucifix as unworthy to look upon it, and selecting from the images with which, as often mentioned, his hat was completely garnished, a representation of the Lady of Cléry, knelt down before it, and made the following extraordinary prayer; in which, it is to be observed, the grossness of his superstition induced him, in some degree, to consider the virgin of Cléry as a different person from the Madonna of Embrun, a favourite idol, to whom he often paid his vows.

"Sweet Lady of Cléry," he exclaimed, clasping his hands and beating his breast while he spoke, "blessed Mother of Mercy! thou who art omnipotent with Omnipotence, have compassion with me a sinner! It is true that I have something neglected thee for thy blessed sister of Embrun; but I am a king, my power is great, my wealth boundless; and, were it otherwise, I would double the *gabelle* on my subjects,

---

[1] See Punishment of Balue. Note 39.

"'These news, fair cousin, have staggered your reason.'"

Quentin Durward, Chap. xxvii., p. 388.

rather than not pay my debts to you both. Undo these iron doors—fill up these tremendous moats—lead me, as a mother leads a child, out of this present and pressing danger! If I have given thy sister the county of Boulogne to be held of her for ever, have I no means of showing devotion to thee also? Thou shalt have the broad and rich province of Champagne; and its vineyards shall pour their abundance into thy convent. I had promised the province to my brother Charles; but he, thou knowest, is dead—poisoned by that wicked abbé of St. John d'Angély, whom, if I live, I will punish! I promised this once before, but this time I will keep my word. If I had any knowledge of the crime, believe, dearest patroness, it was because I knew no better method of quieting the discontents of my kingdom. Oh, do not reckon that old debt to my account to-day; but, be as thou hast ever been, kind, benignant, and easy to be entreated! Sweetest Lady, work with thy Child, that He will pardon all past sins, and one—one little deed which I must do this night; nay, it is no *sin*, dearest Lady of Cléry—no sin, but an act of justice privately administered, for the villain is the greatest impostor that ever poured falsehood into a prince's ear, and leans besides to the filthy heresy of the Greeks. He is not deserving of thy protection, leave him to my care; and hold it as good service that I rid the world of him, for the man is a necromancer and wizard, that is not worth thy thought and care—a dog the extinction of whose life ought to be of as little consequence in thine eyes as the treading out a spark that drops from a lamp, or springs from a fire. Think not of this little matter, gentlest, kindest Lady, but only consider how thou canst best aid me in my troubles! and I here bind my royal signet to thy effigy in token that I will keep my word concerning the county of Champagne, and that this shall be the last time I will trouble thee in affairs of blood, knowing thou art so kind, so gentle, and so tender-hearted."

After this extraordinary contract with the object of his adoration, Louis recited, apparently with deep devotion, the seven penitential psalms in Latin, and several aves and prayers especially belonging to the service of the Virgin. He then arose, satisfied that he had secured the intercession of the saint to whom he had prayed, the rather, as he craftily reflected, that most of the sins for which he had requested her mediation on former occasions had been of a different character, and that, therefore, the Lady of Cléry was less likely to consider him as a hardened and habitual shedder of blood, than the other saints whom he had more frequently made confidants of his crimes in that respect.[1]

When he had thus cleared his conscience, or rather whited it over like a sepulchre, the King thrust his head out at the door of the hall, and summoned Le Balafré into his apartment. "My good soldier," he said, "thou hast served me long, and hast had little promotion. We are here in a case where I may either live or die; but I would not willingly die an ungrateful man, or leave, so far as the saints may place it in my power, either a friend or an enemy unrecompensed. Now, I have a friend to be rewarded, that is thyself—an enemy to be punished according to his deserts, and that is the base, treacherous villain, Martius Galeotti, who, by his impostures and specious falsehoods, has trained me hither into the power of my mortal enemy, with as firm a purpose of my destruction as ever butcher had of slaying the beast which he drove to the shambles."

"I will challenge him on that quarrel, since they say he is a fighting blade, though he looks somewhat unwieldy," said Le Balafré. "I doubt not but the Duke of Burgundy is so much a friend to men of the sword, that he will allow us a fair field within some reasonable space; and if your Majesty live so long, and enjoy so much freedom, you shall behold me do battle in your right, and take as proper a vengeance on this philosopher as your heart could desire."

"I commend your bravery and your devotion to my service," said the King. "But this treacherous villain is a stout man-at-arms, and I would not willingly risk thy life, my brave soldier.

"I were no brave soldier, if it please your Majesty," said Balafré, "if I dare not face a better man than he. A fine

[1] See Prayer of Louis XI. Note 40.

thing it would be for me, who can neither read nor write, to be afraid of a fat lurdane, who has done little else all his life!"

"Nevertheless," said the King, "it is not our pleasure so to put thee in venture, Balafré. This traitor comes hither, summoned by our command. We would have thee, so soon as thou canst find occasion, close up with him, and smite him under the fifth rib. Dost thou understand me?"

"Truly I do," answered Le Balafré; "but, if it please your Majesty, this is a matter entirely out of my course of practice. I could not kill you a dog, unless it were in hot assault, or pursuit, or upon defiance given, or such like."

"Why sure *thou* dost not pretend to tenderness of heart?" said the King; "thou who hast been first in storm and siege, and most eager, as men tell me, on the pleasures and advantages which are gained on such occasions by the rough heart and the bloody hand?"

"My lord," answered Le Balafré, "I have neither feared nor spared your enemies, sword in hand. And an assault is a desperate matter, under risks which raise a man's blood so, that, by St. Andrew, it will not settle for an hour or two, which I call a fair license for plundering after a storm. And God pity us poor soldiers, who are first driven mad with danger, and then madder with victory. I have heard of a legion consisting entirely of saints; and methinks it would take them all to pray and intercede for the rest of the army, and for all who wear plumes and corslets, buff-coats and broadswords. But what your Majesty purposes is out of my course of practice, though I will never deny that it has been wide enough. As for the astrologer, if he be a traitor, let him e'en die a traitor's death. I will neither meddle nor make with it. Your Majesty has your provost and two of his marshals-men without, who are more fit for dealing with him than a Scottish gentleman of my family and standing in the service."

"You say well," said the King; "but, at least, it belongs to thy duty to prevent interruption, and to guard the execution of my most just sentence."

"I will do so against all Péronne," said La Balafré. "Your Majesty need not doubt my fealty in that which I can reconcile to my conscience, which, for mine own convenience and the service of your royal Majesty, I can vouch to be a pretty large one—at least, I know I have done some deeds for your Majesty, which I would rather have eaten a handful of my own dagger than I would have done for any else."

"Let that rest," said the King; "and hear you; when Galeotti is admitted, and the door shut on him, do you stand to your weapon, and guard the entrance on the inside of the apartment. Let no one intrude; that is all I require of you. Go hence, and send the provost-marshal to me."

Balafré left the apartment accordingly, and in a minute afterwards Tristan l'Hermite entered from the hall.

"Welcome, gossip," said the King; "what thinkest thou of our situation?"

"As of men sentenced to death," said the provost-marshal, "unless there come a reprieve from the Duke."

"Reprieved or not, he that decoyed us into this snare shall go our *fourrier* to the next world, to take up lodgings for us," said the King, with a grisly and ferocious smile. "Tristan, thou hast done many an act of brave justice: *finis*—I should have said *funis—coronat opus*. Thou must stand by me to the end."

"I will, my liege," said Tristan; "I am but a plain fellow, but I am grateful. I will do my duty within these walls, or elsewhere; and while I live, your Majesty's breath shall pour as potential a note of condemnation, and your sentence be as literally executed, as when you sat on your own throne. They may deal with me the next hour for it if they will, I care not."

"It is even what I expected of thee, my loving gossip," said Louis; "but hast thou good assistance? The traitor is strong and able-bodied, and will doubtless be clamorous for aid. The Scot will do nought but keep the door; and well that he can be brought to that by flattery and humouring. Then Oliver is good for nothing but lying, flattering, and suggesting dangerous counsels; and, *Ventre Saint-dieu!* I think is more like one day to deserve the halter himself than to use it to another. Have you men, think you, and means, to make sharp and sure work?"

"I have Trois-Eschelles and Petit-André with me," said he; "men so expert in their office that out of three men they would hang up one ere his two companions were aware. And we have all resolved to live or die with your Majesty, knowing we shall have as short breath to draw when you are gone as ever fell to the lot of any of our patients. But what is to be our present subject, and it please your Majesty? I love to be sure of my man; for, as your Majesty is pleased sometimes to remind me, I have now and then mistaken the criminal, and slung up in his place an honest labourer, who had given your Majesty no offence."

"Most true," said the other. "Know then, Tristan, that the condemned person is Martius Galeotti. You start, but it is even as I say. The villain has trained us all hither by false and treacherous representations, that he might put us into the hands of the Duke of Burgundy without defence."

"But not without vengeance!" said Tristan; "were it the last act of my life, I would sting him home like an expiring wasp, should I be crushed to pieces on the next instant!"

"I know thy trusty spirit," said the King, "and the pleasure which, like other good men, thou dost find in the discharge of thy duty, since virtue, as the schoolmen say, is its own reward. But away, and prepare the priests, for the victim approaches."

"Would you have it done in your own presence, my gracious liege?" said Tristan.

Louis declined this offer; but charged the provost-marshal to have everything ready for the punctual execution of his commands the moment the astrologer left his apartment; "for," said the King, "I will see the villain once more, just to observe how he bears himself towards the master whom he has led into the toils. I shall love to see the sense of approaching death strike the colour from that ruddy cheek, and dim that eye which laughed as it lied. Oh, that there were but another with him, whose counsels aided his prognostications! But if I survive this—look to your scarlet, my Lord Cardinal! for Rome shall scarce protect you—be it spoken under favour of St. Peter and the blessed Lady of Cléry, who is all over mercy. Why do you tarry? Go get your grooms ready. I expect the villain instantly. I pray to Heaven he take not fear and come not! that were indeed a baulk. Begone, Tristan; thou wert not wont to be so slow when business was to be done."

"On the contrary, an it like your Majesty, you were ever wont to say that I was too fast, and mistook your purpose, and did the job on the wrong subject. Now, please your Majesty to give me a sign, just when you part with Galeotti for the night, whether the business goes on or no. I have known your Majesty once or twice change your mind, and blame me for over-despatch."[1]

"Thou suspicious creature," answered King Louis, "I tell thee I will *not* change my mind. But to silence thy remonstrances, observe, if I say to the knave at parting, 'There is a Heaven above us!' then let the business go on; but if I say, 'Go in peace,' you will understand that my purpose is altered."

"My head is somewhat of the dullest out of my own department," said Tristan l'Hermite. "Stay, let me rehearse. If you bid him depart in peace, I am to have him dealt upon?"

"No, no—idiot, no!" said the King; "in that case you let him pass free. But if I say, '*There is a Heaven above us!*' up with him a yard or two nearer the planets he is so conversant with."

"I wish we may have the means here," said the provost.

"Then *up* with him or *down* with him, it matters not which," answered the King, grimly smiling.

"And the body," said the provost, "how shall we dispose of it?"

"Let me see an instant," said the King; "the windows of the hall are too narrow; but that projecting oriel is wide enough. We will over with him into the Somme, and put a paper on his breast, with the legend, 'Let the justice of the King pass toll-free.' The Duke's officers may seize it for duties if they dare."

The provost-marshal left the apartment of Louis, and sum-

[1] See Louis's Vengeance. Note 41.

moned his two assistants to council in an embrasure in the great hall, where Trois-Eschelles stuck a torch against the wall to give them light. They discoursed in whispers, little noticed by Oliver le Dain, who seemed sunk in dejection, and Le Balafré, who was fast asleep.

"Comrades," said the provost to his executioners, "perhaps you have thought that our vocation was over, or that, at least, we were more likely to be the subjects of the duty of others than to have any more to discharge on our own parts. But courage, my mates! our gracious master has reserved for us one noble cast of our office, and it must be gallantly executed, as by men who would live in history."

"Ay, I guess how it is," said Trois-Eschelles; "our patron is like the old kaisers of Rome, who, when things came to an extremity, or, as we would say, to the ladder-foot with them, were wont to select from their own ministers of justice some experienced person, who might spare their sacred persons from the awkward attempts of a novice or blunderer in our mystery. It was a pretty custom for ethics; but, as a good Catholic, I should make some scruple at laying hands on the Most Christian King."

"Nay, but, brother, you are ever too scrupulous," said Petit-André. "If he issues word and warrant for his own execution, I see not how we can in duty dispute it. He that dwells at Rome must obey the Pope: the marshals-men must do their master's bidding, and he the King's."

"Hush, you knaves!" said the provost-marshal, "there is here no purpose concerning the King's person, but only that of the Greek heretic pagan and Mahomedan wizard, Martius Galeotti."

"Galeotti!" answered Petit-André; "that comes quite natural. I never knew one of these legerdemain fellows, who pass their life, as one may say, in dancing upon a tight-rope, but what they came at length to caper at the end of one— tchick!"

"My only concern is," said Trois-Eschelles, looking upwards, "that the poor creature must die without confession."

"Tush! tush!" said the provost-marshal, in reply, "he is

a rank heretic and necromancer: a whole college of priests could not absolve him from the doom he has deserved. Besides, if he hath a fancy that way, thou hast a gift, Trois-Eschelles, to serve him for ghostly father thyself. But, what is more material, I fear you must use your poniards, my mates; for you have not here the fitting conveniences for the exercise of your profession."

"Now, our Lady of the Isle of Paris forbid," said Trois-Eschelles, "that the King's command should find me destitute of my tools! I always wear around my body St. Francis's cord, doubled four times, with a handsome loop at the further end of it; for I am of the company of St. Francis, and may wear his cowl when I am *in extremis*, I thank God and the good fathers of Saumur."

"And for me," said Petit-André, "I have always in my budget a handy block and sheaf, or a pulley, as they call it, with a strong screw for securing it where I list, in case we should travel where trees are scarce, or high-branched from the ground. I have found it a great convenience."

"That will suit as well," said the provost-marshal; "you have but to screw your pulley into yonder beam above the door, and pass the rope over it. I will keep the fellow in some conversation near the spot until you adjust the noose under his chin, and then——"

"And then we run up the rope," said Petit-Andre, "and, tchick! our astrologer is so far in Heaven that he hath not a foot on earth."

"But these gentlemen," said Trois-Eschelles, looking towards the chimney, "do not these help, and so take a handsel of our vocation?"

"Hem! no," answered the provost; "the barber only contrives mischief, which he leaves other men to execute; and for the Scot, he keeps the door when the deed is a-doing, which he hath not spirit or quickness sufficient to partake in more actively; every one to his trade."

With infinite dexterity, and even a sort of professional delight, which sweetened the sense of their own precarious situation, the worthy executioners of the provost's mandates adapted their rope and pulley for putting in force the sentence which had been uttered against Galeotti by the captive monarch, seeming to rejoice that that last action was to be one so consistent with their past life. Tristan l'Hermite[1] sat eyeing their proceedings with a species of satisfaction; while Oliver paid no attention to them whatever; and Ludovic Lesly, if, awaked by the bustle, he looked upon them at all, considered them as engaged in matters entirely unconnected with his own duty, and for which he was not to be regarded as responsible in one way or other.

CHAPTER XXIX.

RECRIMINATION.

>Thy time is not yet out: the devil thou servest
>Has not as yet deserted thee. He aids
>The friends who drudge for him, as the blind man
>Was aided by the guide, who lent his shoulder
>O'er rough and smooth, until he reach'd the brink
>Of the fell precipice, then hurl'd him downward.
>   *Old Play.*

WHEN obeying the command, or rather the request, of Louis, for he was in circumstances in which, though a monarch, he could only *request* Le Glorieux to go in search of Martius Galeotti, the jester had no trouble in executing his commission, betaking himself at once to the best tavern in Péronne, of which he himself was rather more than an occasional frequenter, being a great admirer of that species of liquor which reduced all other men's brains to a level with his own.

He found, or rather observed, the astrologer in the corner of the public drinking-room—"stove," as it is called in German and Flemish, from its principal furniture—sitting in close colloquy with a female in a singular, and something like a Moorish or Asiatic, garb, who, as Le Glorieux approached Martius, rose as in the act to depart.

[1] See Note 42.

"These," said the stranger, "are news on which you may rely with absolute certainty"; and with that disappeared among the crowd of guests who sat grouped at different tables in the apartment.

"Cousin philosopher," said the jester, presenting himself, "Heaven no sooner relieves one sentinel than it sends another to supply the place. One fool being gone, here I come another, to guide you to the apartments of Louis of France."

"And art thou the messenger?" said Martius, gazing on him with prompt apprehension, and discovering at once the jester's quality, though less intimated, as we have before noticed, than was usual by his external appearance.

"Ay, sir, and like your learning," answered Le Glorieux; "when power sends folly to entreat the approach of wisdom, 'tis a sure sign what foot the patient halts upon."

"How if I refuse to come, when summoned at so late an hour by such a messenger?" said Galeotti.

"In that case we will consult your ease, and carry you," said Le Glorieux. "Here are half a score of stout Burgundian yeomen at the door, with whom he of Crèvecœur has furnished me to that effect. For know that my friend Charles of Burgundy and I have not taken away our kinsman Louis's crown, which he was ass enough to put into our power, but have only filed and clipt it a little; and, though reduced to the size of a spangle, it is still pure gold. In plain terms, he is still paramount over his own people, yourself included, and Most Christian King of the old dining-hall in the Castle of Péronne, to which you, as his liege subject, are presently obliged to repair."

"I attend you, sir," said Martius Galeotti, and accompanied Le Glorieux accordingly, seeing, perhaps, that no evasion was possible.

"Ay, sir," said the fool as they went towards the castle, "you do well; for we treat our kinsman as men use an old famished lion in his cage, and thrust him now and then a calf to mumble, to keep his old jaws in exercise."

"Do you mean," said Martius, "that the King intends me bodily injury?"

"Nay, that you can guess better than I," said the jester; "for though the night be cloudy, I warrant you can see the stars through the mist. I know nothing of the matter, not I; only my mother always told me to go warily near an old rat in a trap, for he was never so much disposed to bite."

The astrologer asked no more questions; and Le Glorieux, according to the custom of those of his class, continued to run on in a wild and disordered strain of sarcasm and folly mingled together, until he delivered the philosopher to the guard at the castle gate of Péronne, where he was passed from warder to warder, and at length admitted within Herbert's Tower.

The hints of the jester had not been lost on Martius Galeotti, and he saw something which seemed to confirm them in the look and manner of Tristan, whose mode of addressing him, as he marshalled him to the King's bedchamber, was lowering, sullen, and ominous. A close observer of what passed on earth, as well as among the heavenly bodies, the pulley and the rope also caught the astrologer's eye; and as the latter was in a state of vibration, he concluded that some one who had been busy adjusting it had been interrupted in the work by his sudden arrival. All this he saw, and summoned together his subtility to evade the impending danger, resolved, should he find that impossible, to defend himself to the last against whomsoever should assail him.

Thus resolved, and with a step and look corresponding to the determination he had taken, Martius presented himself before Louis, alike unabashed at the miscarriage of his predictions, and undismayed at the monarch's anger and its probable consequences.

"Every good planet be gracious to your Majesty!" said Galeotti, with an inclination almost Oriental in manner. "Every evil constellation withhold their influences from my royal master!"

"Methinks," replied the King, "that when you look around this apartment, when you think where it is situated, and how guarded, your wisdom might consider that my propitious stars had proved faithless, and that each evil conjunction had already done its worst. Art thou not ashamed, Martius Galeotti, to see me here and a prisoner, when you recollect by what assurances I was lured hither?"

"And art *thou* not ashamed, my royal sire?" replied the philosopher, "thou whose step in science was so forward, thy apprehension so quick, thy perseverance so unceasing,—art thou not ashamed to turn from the first frown of fortune, like a craven from the first clash of arms? Didst thou propose to become participant of those mysteries which raise men above the passions, the mischances, the pains, the sorrows of life, a state only to be attained by rivalling the firmness of the ancient Stoic; and dost thou shrink from the first pressure of adversity, and forfeit the glorious prize for which thou didst start as a competitor, frightened out of the course, like a scared racer, by shadowy and unreal evils?"

"Shadowy and unreal! frontless as thou art!" exclaimed the King, "is this dungeon unreal? the weapons of the guards of my detested enemy Burgundy, which you may hear clash at the gate, are those shadows? What, traitor, *are* real evils, if imprisonment, dethronement, and danger of life are not so?"

"Ignorance—ignorance, my brother, and prejudice," answered the sage with great firmness, "are the only real evils. Believe me, that kings in the plenitude of power, if immersed in ignorance and prejudice, are less free than sages in a dungeon and loaded with material chains. Towards this true happiness it is mine to guide you; be it yours to attend to my instructions."

"And it is to such philosophical freedom that your lessons would have guided me?" said the King, very bitterly. "I would you had told me at Plessis that the dominion promised me so liberally was an empire over my own passions; that the success of which I was assured related to my progress in philosophy; and that I might become as wise and as learned as a strolling mountebank of Italy! I might surely have attained this mental ascendency at a more moderate price than that of forfeiting the fairest crown in Christendom and becoming tenant of a dungeon in Péronne! Go, sir, and think not to escape condign punishment. *There is a Heaven above us!*"

"I leave you not to your fate," replied Martius, "until I have vindicated, even in your eyes, darkened as they are, that reputation, a brighter gem than the brightest in thy crown, and at which the world shall wonder ages after all the race of Capet are mouldered into oblivion in the charnels of St. Denis."

"Speak on," said Louis; "thine impudence cannot make me change my purposes or my opinion. Yet as I may never again pass judgment as a king, I will not censure thee unheard. Speak, then, though the best thou canst say will be to speak the truth. Confess that I am a dupe, thou an impostor, thy pretended science a dream, and the planets which shine above us as little influential of our destiny as their shadows, when reflected in the river, are capable of altering its course."

"And how know'st thou," answered the astrologer, boldly, "the secret influence of yonder blessed lights? Speak'st thou of their inability to influence waters, when yet thou know'st that even the weakest, the moon herself,—weakest because nearest to this wretched earth of ours,—holds under her domination, not such poor streams as the Somme, but the tides of the mighty ocean itself, which ebb and increase as her disk waxes and wanes, and watch her influence as a slave waits the nod of a sultana? And now, Louis of Valois, answer my parable in turn. Confess, art thou not like the foolish passenger, who becomes wroth with his pilot because he cannot bring the vessel into harbour without experiencing occasionally the adverse force of winds and currents? I could indeed point to thee the probable issue of thine enterprise as prosperous, but it was in the power of Heaven alone to conduct thee thither; and if the path be rough and dangerous, was it in my power to smooth or render it more safe? Where is thy wisdom of yesterday, which taught thee so truly to discern that the ways of destiny are often ruled to our advantage, though in opposition to our wishes?"

"You remind me—you remind me," said the King, hastily, "of one specific falsehood. You foretold yonder Scot should accomplish his enterprise fortunately for my interest and honour; and thou knowest it has so terminated that no more mortal injury could I have received than from the impression which the issue of that affair is like to make on the excited brain of the Mad Bull of Burgundy. This is a direct falsehood. Thou canst plead no evasion here, canst refer to no remote favourable turn of the tide, for which, like an idiot sitting on the bank until the river shall pass away, thou wouldst have me wait contentedly. Here thy craft deceived thee. Thou wert weak enough to make a specific prediction, which has proved directly false."

"Which will prove most firm and true," answered the astrologer, boldly. "I would desire no greater triumph of art over ignorance than that prediction and its accomplishment will afford. I told thee he would be faithful in any honourable commission. Hath he not been so? I told thee he would be scrupulous in aiding any evil enterprise. Hath he not proved so? If you doubt it, go ask the Bohemian, Hayraddin Maugrabin."

The King here coloured deeply with shame and anger.

"I told thee," continued the astrologer, "that the conjunction of planets under which he set forth augured danger to the person; and hath not his path been beset by danger? I told thee that it augured an advantage to the sender, and of that thou wilt soon have the benefit."

"Soon have the benefit!" exclaimed the King; "have I not the result already, in disgrace and imprisonment?"

"No," answered the astrologer, "the end is not as yet; thine own tongue shall ere long confess the benefit which thou hast received, from the manner in which the messenger bore himself in discharging thy commission."

"This is too—too insolent," said the King, "at once to deceive and to insult—— But hence! think not my wrongs shall be unavenged. *There is a Heaven above us!*"

Galeotti turned to depart. "Yet stop," said Louis; "thou bearest thine imposture bravely out. Let me hear your answer to one question, and think ere you speak. Can thy pretended skill ascertain the hour of thine own death?"

"Only by referring to the fate of another," said Galeotti.

"I understand not thine answer," said Louis.

"Know then, O king," said Martius, "that this only I can tell with certainty concerning mine own death, that it shall take place exactly twenty-four hours before that of your Majesty."[1]

"Ha! say'st thou?" said Louis, his countenance again altering. "Hold—hold—go not—wait one moment. Saidst thou, *my* death should follow *thine* so closely?"

"Within the space of twenty-four hours," repeated Galeotti, firmly, "if there be one sparkle of true divination in those bright and mysterious intelligences, which speak, each on their courses, though without a tongue. I wish your Majesty good rest."

"Hold—hold—go not," said the King, taking him by the arm and leading him from the door. "Martius Galeotti, I have been a kind master to thee—enriched thee—made thee my friend—my companion—the instructor of my studies. Be open with me, I entreat you. Is there aught in this art of yours in very deed? Shall this Scot's mission be, in fact, propitious to me? And is the measure of our lives so very—*very* nearly matched? Confess, my good Martius, you speak after the trick of your trade. Confess, I pray you, and you shall have no displeasure at my hand. I am in years—a prisoner—likely to be deprived of a kingdom; to one in my condition truth is worth kingdoms, and it is from thee, dearest Martius, that I must look for this inestimable jewel."

"And I have laid it before your Majesty," said Galeotti, "at the risk that, in brutal passion, you might turn upon me and rend me."

"Who, I, Galeotti?" replied Louis, mildly. "Alas! thou mistakest me! Am I not captive, and should not I be patient, especially since my anger can only show my impotence? Tell me then in sincerity, have you fooled me, or is your science true, and do you truly report it?"

"Your Majesty will forgive me if I reply to you," said Martius Galeotti, "that time only—time and the event—will

[1] See Prediction of Louis XI.'s Death. Note 43.

convince incredulity. It suits ill the place of confidence which I have held at the council-table of the renowned conqueror, Matthias Corvinus of Hungary—nay, in the cabinet of the Emperor himself—to reiterate assurances of that which I have advanced as true. If you will not believe me, I can but refer to the course of events. A day or two days' patience will prove or disprove what I have averred concerning the young Scot; and I will be contented to die on the wheel, and have my limbs broken joint by joint, if your Majesty have not advantage, and that in a most important degree, from the dauntless conduct of that Quentin Durward. But if I were to die under such tortures, it would be well your Majesty should seek a ghostly father; for from the moment my last groan is drawn only twenty-four hours will remain to you for confession and penitence."

Louis continued to keep hold of Galeotti's robe as he led him towards the door, and pronounced as he opened it, in a loud voice: "To-morrow we'll talk more of this. Go in peace, my learned father—*go in peace—go in peace!*"

He repeated these words three times; and, still afraid that the provost-marshal might mistake his purpose, he led the astrologer into the hall, holding fast his robe, as if afraid that he should be torn from him and put to death before his eyes. He did not unloose his grasp until he had not only repeated again and again the gracious phrase, "Go in peace," but even made a private signal to the provost-marshal, to enjoin a suspension of all proceedings against the person of the astrologer.

Thus did the possession of some secret information, joined to audacious courage and readiness of wit, save Galeotti from the most imminent danger; and thus was Louis, the most sagacious as well as the most vindictive amongst the monarchs of the period, cheated of his revenge by the influence of superstition upon a selfish temper, and a mind to which, from the consciousness of many crimes, the fear of death was peculiarly terrible.

He felt, however, considerable mortification at being obliged to relinquish his purposed vengeance; and the disappointment seemed to be shared by his satellites, to whom the execution was to have been committed. Le Balafré alone, perfectly indifferent on the subject, so soon as the countermanding signal was given, left the door at which he had posted himself, and in a few minutes was fast asleep.

The provost-marshal, as the group reclined themselves to repose in the hall after the King retired to his bedchamber, continued to eye the goodly form of the astrologer, with the look of the mastiff watching a joint of meat which the cook had retrieved from his jaws, while his attendants communicated to each other in brief sentences their characteristic sentiments.

"The poor blinded necromancer," whispered Trois-Eschelles, with an air of spiritual unction and commiseration, to his comrade, Petit-André, "hath lost the fairest chance of expiating some of his vile sorceries, by dying through means of the cord of the blessed St. Francis! and I had purpose, indeed, to leave the comfortable noose around his neck, to scare the foul fiend from his unhappy carcass."

"And I," said Petit-André, "have missed the rarest opportunity of knowing how far a weight of seventeen stone will stretch a three-plied cord! It would have been a glorious experiment in our line, and the jolly old boy would have died so easily!"

While this whispered dialogue was going forward, Martius, who had taken the opposite side of the huge stone fireplace, round which the whole group was assembled, regarded them askance and with a look of suspicion. He first put his hand into his vest, and satisfied himself that the handle of a very sharp double-edged poniard, which he always carried about him, was disposed conveniently for his grasp; for, as we have already noticed, he was, though now somewhat unwieldy, a powerful athletic man, and prompt and active at the use of his weapon. Satisfied that this trusty instrument was in readiness, he next took from his bosom a scroll of parchment, inscribed with Greek characters and marked with cabalistic signs, drew together the wood in the fireplace, and made a blaze by which he could distinguish the features and attitude of all who sat or lay around: the heavy and deep slumbers of the Scottish soldier, who lay motionless, with his rough countenance as immovable as if it were cast in bronze; the pale and anxious face of Oliver, who at one time assumed the appearance of slumber, and again opened his eyes and raised his head hastily, as if stung by some internal throe, or awakened by some distant sound; the discontented, savage, bull-dog aspect of the provost, who looked

> Frustrate o his will,
> Not half sufficed, and greedy yet to kill;

while the background was filled up by the ghastly hypocritical countenance of Trois-Eschelles, whose eyes were cast up towards Heaven, as if he was internally saying his devotions; and the grim drollery of Petit-André, who amused himself with mimicking the gestures and wry faces of his comrade before he betook himself to sleep.

Amidst these vulgar and ignoble countenances, nothing could show to greater advantage than the stately form, handsome mien, and commanding features of the astrologer, who might have passed for one of the ancient magi, imprisoned in a den of robbers, and about to invoke a spirit to accomplish his liberation. And, indeed, had he been distinguished by nothing else than the beauty of the graceful and flowing beard which descended over the mysterious roll which he held in his hand, one might have been pardoned for regretting that so noble an appendage had been bestowed on one who put both talents, learning, and the advantages of eloquence, and a majestic person, to the mean purposes of a cheat and an impostor.

Thus passed the night in Count Herbert's Tower, in the Castle of Péronne. When the first light of dawn penetrated the ancient Gothic chamber, the King summoned Oliver to his presence, who found the monarch sitting in his nightgown, and was astonished at the alteration which one night of mortal anxiety had made in his looks. He would have expressed some anxiety on the subject, but the King silenced him by entering into a statement of the various modes by which he had previously endeavoured to form friends at the court of Burgundy, and which Oliver was charged to prosecute so soon as he should be permitted to stir abroad. And never was that wily minister more struck with the clearness of the King's intellect, and his intimate knowledge of all the springs which influence human actions, than he was during that memorable consultation.

About two hours afterwards, Oliver accordingly obtained permission from the Count of Crèvecœur to go out and execute the commissions which his master had entrusted him with; and Louis, sending forth the astrologer, in whom he seemed to have renewed his faith, held with him, in like manner, a long consultation, the issue of which appeared to give him more spirits and confidence than he had at first exhibited; so that he dressed himself, and received the morning compliments of Crèvecœur with a calmness at which the Burgundian lord could not help wondering, the rather that he had already heard that the Duke had passed several hours in a state of mind which seemed to render the King's safety very precarious.

CHAPTER XXX.

UNCERTAINTY

*Our counsels waver like the unsteady bark,
That reels amid the strife of meeting currents.*
Old Play.

IF the night passed by Louis was carefully anxious and agitated, that spent by the Duke of Burgundy, who had at no time the same mastery over his passions, and, indeed, who permitted them almost a free and uncontrolled dominion over his actions, was still more disturbed.

According to the custom of the period, two of his principal and most favoured counsellors, D'Hymbercourt and Des Comines, shared his bedchamber, couches being prepared for them near the bed of the prince. Their attendance was never more necessary than upon this night, when, distracted by sorrow, by passion, by the desire of revenge, and by the sense of honour, which forbade him to exercise it upon Louis in his present condition, the Duke's mind resembled a volcano in eruption, which throws forth all the different contents of the mountain, mingled and molten into one burning mass.

He refused to throw off his clothes, or to make any preparation for sleep; but spent the night in a succession of the most violent bursts of passion. In some paroxysms he talked incessantly to his attendants so thick and so rapidly, that they were really afraid his senses would give way; choosing for his theme the merits and the kindness of heart of the murdered Bishop of Liege, and recalling all the instances of mutual kindness, affection, and confidence which had passed between them, until he had worked himself into such a transport of grief that he threw himself upon his face in the bed and seemed ready to choke with the sobs and tears which he endeavoured to stifle. Then starting from the couch, he gave vent at once to another and more furious mood, and traversed the room hastily, uttering incoherent threats, and still more incoherent oaths of vengeance, while, stamping with his foot, according to his customary action, he invoked St. George, St. Andrew, and whomsoever else he held most holy, to bear witness that he would take bloody vengeance on De la Marck, on the people of Liege, and on *him* who was the author of the whole. These last threats, uttered more obscurely than the others, obviously concerned the person of the King; and at one time the Duke expressed his determination to send for the Duke of Normandy, the brother of the King, and with whom Louis was on the worst terms, in order to compel the captive monarch to surrender either the crown itself, or some of its most valuable rights and appanages.

Another day and night passed in the same stormy and fitful deliberations, or rather rapid transitions of passion; for the Duke scarcely ate or drank, never changed his dress, and, altogether, demeaned himself like one in whom rage might terminate in utter insanity. By degrees he became more composed, and began to hold, from time to time, consultations with his ministers, in which much was proposed, but nothing resolved on. Comines assures us that at one time a courier was mounted in readiness to depart for the purpose of summoning the Duke of Normandy; and in that event the prison of the French monarch would probably have been found, as in similar cases, a brief road to his grave.

At other times, when Charles had exhausted his fury, he sat with his features fixed in stern and rigid immobility, like one who broods over some desperate deed to which he is as yet unable to work up his resolution. And unquestionably it would have needed little more than an insidious hint from any of the counsellors who attended his person, to have pushed the Duke to some very desperate action. But the nobles of Burgundy, from the sacred character attached to the person of a king and a lord paramount, and from a regard to the public faith, as well as that of their Duke, which had been pledged when Louis threw himself into their power, were almost unanimously inclined to recommend moderate measures; and the arguments which D'Hymbercourt and Des Comines had now and then ventured to insinuate during the night were, in the cooler hours of the next morning, advanced and urged by Crèvecœur and others. Possibly their zeal in behalf of the King might not be entirely disinterested. Many, as we have mentioned, had already experienced the bounty of the King; others had either estates or pretensions in France, which placed them a little under his influence; and it is certain that the treasure, which had loaded four mules when the King entered Péronne, became much lighter in the course of these negotiations.

In the course of the third day the Count of Campo-basso brought his Italian wit to assist the counsels of Charles; and well was it for Louis that he had not arrived when the Duke was in his first fury. Immediately on his arrival, a regular meeting of the Duke's counsellors was convened, for considering the measures to be adopted in this singular crisis.

On this occasion Campo-basso gave his opinion couched in the apologue of the traveller, the adder, and the fox; and reminded the Duke of the advice which Reynard gave to the man, that he should crush his mortal enemy, now that chance had placed his fate at his disposal. Des Comines, who saw the Duke's eyes sparkle at a proposal which his own violence of temper had already repeatedly suggested, hastened to state the possibility that Louis might not be, in fact, so directly accessary to the sanguinary action which had been committed at Schonwaldt; that he might be able to clear himself of the imputation laid to his charge, and perhaps to make other atonement for the distractions which his intrigues had occasioned in the Duke's dominions, and those of his allies; and that an act of violence perpetrated on the King was sure to bring both on France and Burgundy a train of the most unhappy consequences, among which not the least to be feared was, that the English might avail themselves of the commotions and civil discord which must needs ensue to repossess themselves of Normandy and Guyenene, and renew those dreadful wars, which had only, and with difficulty, been terminated by the union of both France and Burgundy against the common enemy. Finally, he confessed, that he did not mean to urge the absolute and free dismissal of Louis; but only that the Duke should avail himself no farther of his present condition than merely to establish a fair and equitable treaty between the countries, with such security on the King's part as should make it difficult for him to break his faith, or disturb the internal peace of Burgundy in future. D'Hymbercourt, Crèvecœur, and others signified their reprobation of the violent measures proposed by Campo-basso, and their opinion that in the way of treaty more permanent advantages could be obtained, and in a manner more honourable for Burgundy, than by an action which would stain her with a breach of faith and hospitality.

The Duke listened to these arguments with his looks fixed on the ground, and his brows so knitted together as to bring his bushy eyebrows into one mass. But when Crèvecœur proceeded to say that he did not believe Louis either knew of, or was accessary to, the atrocious act of violence committed at Schonwaldt, Charles raised his head, and darting a fierce look at his counsellor, exclaimed: "Have you too, Crèvecœur, heard the gold of France clink? Methinks it rings in my councils as merrily as ever the bells of St. Denis. Dare any one say that Louis is not the fomenter of these feuds in Flanders?"

"My gracious lord," said Crèvecœur, "my hand has ever been more conversant with steel than with gold; and so far am I from holding that Louis is free from the charge of having caused the disturbances in Flanders, that it is not long since, in the face of his whole court, I charged him with that breach of faith, and offered him defiance in your name. But although his intrigues have been doubtless the original cause of these commotions, I am so far from believing that he authorised the death of the archbishop, that I believe one of his emissaries publicly protested against it; and I could produce the man, were it your Grace's pleasure to see him."

"It *is* our pleasure," said the Duke. "St. George! can you doubt that we desire to act justly? Even in the highest flight of our passion we are known for an upright and a just judge. We will see France ourself; we will ourself charge him with our wrongs, and ourself state to him the reparation which we expect and demand. If he shall be found guiltless of this murder, the atonement for other crimes may be more easy. If he hath been guilty, who shall say that a life of penitence in some retired monastery were not a most deserved and a most merciful doom? Who," he added, kindling as he spoke—"who shall dare to blame a revenge yet more direct and more speedy? Let your witness attend. We will to the castle at the hour before noon. Some articles we will minute down with which he shall comply, or woe on his head! others shall depend upon the proof. Break up the council and dismiss yourselves. I will but change my dress, as this is scarce a fitting trim in which to wait on *my most gracious sovereign.*"

With a deep and bitter emphasis on the last expression, the Duke arose, and strode out of the room.

"Louis's safety, and, what is worse, the honour of Burgundy, depend on a cast of the dice," said D'Hymbercourt to Crèvecœur and to Des Comines. "Haste thee to the castle, Des Comines; thou hast a better filed tongue than either Crèvecœur or I. Explain to Louis what storm is approaching;

he will best know how to pilot himself. I trust this Life Guardsman will say nothing which can aggravate; for who knows what may have been the secret commission with which he was charged?

"The young man," said Crèvecœur, "seems bold, yet prudent and wary far beyond his years. In all which he said to me he was tender of the King's character, as of that of the prince whom he serves. I trust he will be equally so in the Duke's presence. I must go seek him, and also the young Countess of Croye."

"The countess! You told us you had left her at St. Bridget's nunnery?"

"Ay, but I was obliged," said the count, "to send for her express, by the Duke's orders; and she has been brought hither on a litter, as being unable to travel otherwise. She was in a state of the deepest distress, both on account of the uncertainty of the fate of her kinswoman, the Lady Hameline, and the gloom which overhangs her own, guilty as she has been of a feudal delinquency, in withdrawing herself from the protection of her liege lord, Duke Charles, who is not the person in the world most likely to view with indifference what trenches on his seigniorial rights."

The information that the young countess was in the hands of Charles added fresh and more pointed thorns to Louis's reflections. He was conscious that, by explaining the intrigues by which he had induced the Lady Hameline and her to resort to Péronne [Plessis], she might supply that evidence which he had removed by the execution of Zamet Maugrabin; and he knew well how much such proof of his having interfered with the rights of the Duke of Burgundy would furnish both motive and pretext for Charles's availing himself to the uttermost of his present predicament.

Louis discoursed on these matters with great anxiety to the Sieur Des Comines, whose acute and political talents better suited the King's temper than the blunt, martial character of Crèvecœur or the feudal haughtiness of D'Hymbercourt.

"These iron-handed soldiers, my good friend Comines," he said to his future historian, "should never enter a king's cabi, net, but be left with the halberds and partizans in the antechamber. Their hands are indeed made for our use; but the monarch who puts their heads to any better occupation than that of anvils for his enemies' swords and maces ranks with the fool who presented his mistress with a dog-leash for a carcanet. It is with such as thou, Philip, whose eyes are gifted with the quick and keen sense that sees beyond the exterior surface of affairs, that princes should share their council-table, their cabinet—what do I say?—the most secret recesses of their soul."

Des Comines, himself so keen a spirit, was naturally gratified with the approbation of the most sagacious prince in Europe; and he could not so far disguise his internal satisfaction but that Louis was aware he had made some impression on him.

"I would," continued he, "that I had such a servant, or rather that I were worthy to have such a one! I had not then been in this unfortunate situation; which, nevertheless, I should hardly regret, could I but discover any means of securing the services of so experienced a statist."

Des Comines said that all his faculties, such as they were, were at the service of his Most Christian Majesty, saving always his allegiance to his rightful lord, Duke Charles of Burgundy.

"And am I one who would seduce you from that allegiance?" said Louis, pathetically. "Alas! am I not now endangered by having reposed too much confidence in my vassal? and can the cause of feudal good faith be more sacred with any than with me, whose safety depends on an appeal to it? No, Philip des Comines, continue to serve Charles of Burgundy; and you will best serve him by bringing round a fair accommodation with Louis of France. In doing thus you will serve us both, and one, at least, will be grateful. I am told your appointments in this court hardly match those of the Grand Falconer; and thus the services of the wisest counsellor in Europe are put on a level, or rather ranked below, those of a fellow who feeds and physics kites! France has wide lands; her King has much gold. Allow me, my friend, to rectify this scandalous inequality. The means are not distant. Permit me to use them."

The King produced a weighty bag of money; but Des Comines, more delicate in his sentiments than most courtiers of that time, declined the proffer, declaring himself perfectly satisfied with the liberality of his native prince, and assuring Louis that his desire to serve him could not be increased by the acceptance of any such gratuity as he had proposed.

"Singular man!" exclaimed the King; "let me embrace the only courtier of his time at once capable and incorruptible. Wisdom is to be desired more than fine gold; and believe me, I trust in thy kindness, Philip, at this pinch, more than I do in the purchased assistance of many who have received my gifts. I know you will not counsel your master to abuse such an opportunity as fortune, and, to speak plain, Des Comines, as my own folly, has afforded him."

"To *abuse* it, by no means," answered the historian; "but most certainly to *use* it."

"How, and in what degree?" said Louis. "I am not ass enough to expect that I shall escape without some ransom, but let it be a reasonable one; reason I am ever willing to listen to, at Paris or at Plessis, equally as at Péronne."

"Ah, but if it like your Majesty," replied Des Comines, "reason at Paris or Plessis was used to speak in so low and soft a tone of voice, that she could not always gain an audience of your Majesty; at Péronne she borrows the speaking-trumpet of necessity, and her voice becomes lordly and imperative."

"You are figurative," said Louis, unable to restrain an emotion of peevishness; "I am a dull, blunt man, Sir of Comines. I pray you leave your tropes, and come to plain ground. What does your duke expect of me?"

"I am the bearer of no propositions, my lord," said Des Comines; "the Duke will soon explain his own pleasure. But some things occur to me as proposals, for which your Majesty ought to hold yourself prepared; as, for example, the final cession of these towns here upon the Somme."

"I expected so much," said Louis.

"That you should disown the Liegeois and William de la Marck."

"As willingly as I disclaim Hell and Satan," said Louis.

"Ample security will be required, by hostages, or occupation of fortresses, or otherwise, that France shall in future abstain from stirring up rebellion among the Flemings."

"It is something new," answered the King, "that a vassal should demand pledges from his sovereign; but let that pass too."

"A suitable and independent appanage for your illustrious brother, the ally and friend of my master—Normandy or Champagne. The Duke loves your father's house, my liege."

"So well," answered Louis, "that, *mort Dieu!* he's about to make them all kings. Is your budget of hints yet emptied?"

"Not entirely," answered the counsellor: "it will certainly be required that your Majesty shall forbear molesting, as you have done of late, the Duke de Bretagne, and that you will no longer contest the right which he and other grand feudatories have to strike money, to term themselves dukes and princes by the grace of God——"

"In a word, to make so many kings of my vassals. Sir Philip, would you make a fratricide of me? You remember well my brother Charles: he was no sooner Duke of Guyenne than he died. And what will be left to the descendant and representative of Charlemagne, after giving away these rich provinces, save to be smeared with oil at Rheims, and to eat his dinner under a high canopy?"

"We will diminish your Majesty's concern on that score, by giving you a companion in that solitary exaltation," said Philip des Comines. "The Duke of Burgundy, though he claims not at present the title of an independent king, desires nevertheless to be freed in future from the abject marks of subjection required of him to the crown of France; it is his purpose to close his ducal coronet with an imperial arch, and surmount it with a globe, in emblem that his dominions are independent."

"And how dares the Duke of Burgundy, the sworn vassal

of France," exclaimed Louis, starting up and showing an unwonted degree of emotion—"how dares he propose such terms to his sovereign as, by every law of Europe, should infer a forfeiture of his fief?"

"The doom of forfeiture it would in this case be difficult to enforce," answered Des Comines, calmly. "Your Majesty is aware that the strict interpretation of the feudal law is becoming obsolete even in the Empire, and that superior and vassal endeavour to mend their situation in regard to each other as they have power and opportunity. Your Majesty's interferences with the Duke's vassals in Flanders will prove an exculpation of my master's conduct, supposing him to insist that, by enlarging his independence, France should in future be debarred from any pretext of doing so."

"Comines—Comines!" said Louis, arising again and pacing the room in a pensive manner, "this is a dreadful lesson on the text *væ victis!* You cannot mean that the Duke will insist on all these hard conditions?"

"At least I would have your Majesty be in a condition to discuss them all."

"Yet moderation, Des Comines—moderation in success is —no one knows better than you—necessary to its ultimate advantage."

"So please your Majesty, the merit of moderation is, I have observed, most apt to be extolled by the losing party. The winner holds in more esteem the prudence which calls on him not to leave an opportunity unimproved."

"Well, we will consider," replied the King; "but at least thou hast reached the extremity of your duke's unreasonable exaction? There can remain nothing—or if there does, for so thy brow intimates—what is it—what indeed can it be, unless it be my crown, which these previous demands, if granted, will deprive of all its lustre?"

"My lord," said Des Comines, "what remains to be mentioned is a thing partly—indeed, in a great measure—within the Duke's own power, though he means to invite your Majesty's accession to it, for in truth it touches you nearly."

"*Pasques-dieu!*" exclaimed the King impatiently, "what

is it? Speak out, Sir Philip; am I to send him my daughter for a concubine, or what other dishonour is he to put on me?"

"No dishonour, my liege; but your Majesty's cousin, the illustrious Duke of Orleans——"

"Ha!" exclaimed the King; but Des Comines proceeded without heeding the interruption.

"——Having conferred his affections on the young Countess Isabelle de Croye, the Duke expects your Majesty will, on your part, as he on his, yield your assent to the marriage, and unite with him in endowing the right noble couple with such an appanage as, joined to the countess's estates, may form a fit establishment for a child of France."

"Never—never!" said the King, bursting out into that emotion which he had of late suppressed with much difficulty, and striding about in a disordered haste, which formed the strongest contrast to the self-command which he usually exhibited—"never—never! Let them bring scissors and shear my hair like that of the parish fool, whom I have so richly resembled—let them bid the monastery or the grave yawn for me—let them bring red-hot basins to sear my eyes—axe or aconite—whatever they will; but Orleans shall not break his plighted faith to my daughter, or marry another while she lives!"

"Your Majesty," said Des Comines, "ere you set your mind so keenly against what is proposed, will consider your own want of power to prevent it. Every wise man, when he sees a rock giving way, withdraws from the bootless attempt of preventing the fall."

"But a brave man," said Louis, "will at least find his grave beneath it. Des Comines, consider the great loss—the utter destruction, such a marriage will bring upon my kingdom. Recollect, I have but one feeble boy, and this Orleans is the next heir; consider that the church hath consented to his union with Joan, which unites so happily the interests of both branches of my family—think on all this, and think too that this union has been the favourite scheme of my whole life—that I have schemed for it, fought for it, watched for it, prayed for it,—and sinned for it. Philip des Comines, I will not forego it! Think, man—think! pity me in this extremity; thy quick brain can speedily find some substitute for this sacrifice—some ram to be offered up instead of that project which is dear to me as the Patriarch's only son was to him. Philip, pity me! You, at least, should know that to men of judgment and foresight the destruction of the scheme on which they have long dwelt, and for which they have long toiled, is more inexpressibly bitter than the transient grief of ordinary men, whose pursuits are but the gratification of some temporary passion—you, who know how to sympathise with the deeper, the more genuine distress of baffled prudence and disappointed sagacity, will you not feel for me?"

"My lord and king!" replied Des Comines, "I do sympathise with your distress, in so far as duty to my master——"

"Do not mention him!" said Louis, acting, or at least appearing to act, under an irresistible and headlong impulse, which withdrew the usual guard which he maintained over his language. "Charles of Burgundy is unworthy of your attachment. He who can insult and strike his counsellors—he who can distinguish the wisest and most faithful among them by the opprobrious name of Booted Head——!"

The wisdom of Philip des Comines did not prevent his having a high sense of personal consequence; and he was so much struck with the words which the King uttered, as it were, in the career of a passion which overleaped ceremony, that he could only reply by repetition of the words "Booted Head! It is impossible that my master the Duke could have so termed the servant who has been at his side since he could mount a palfrey, and that too before a foreign monarch—it is impossible!"

Louis instantly saw the impression he had made, and avoiding alike a tone of condolence, which might have seemed insulting, and one of sympathy, which might have savoured of affectation, he said, with simplicity, and at the same time with dignity: "My misfortunes make me forget my courtesy, else I had not spoken to you of what it must be unpleasant for you to hear. But you have in reply taxed me with having uttered impossibilities, this touches my honour; yet I must submit to the charge, if I tell you not the circumstances which the Duke, laughing until his eyes ran over, assigned for the origin of that opprobrious name, which I will not offend your ears by repeating. Thus, then, it chanced. You, Sir Philip des Comines, were at a hunting-match with the Duke of Burgundy, your master; and when he alighted after the chase, he required your services in drawing off his boots. Reading in your looks, perhaps, some natural resentment of this disparaging treatment, he ordered you to sit down in turn, and rendered you the same office he had just received from you. But, offended at your understanding him literally, he no sooner plucked one of your boots off than he brutally beat it about your head till the blood flowed, exclaiming against the insolence of a subject who had the presumption to accept of such a service at the hand of his sovereign; and hence he, or his privileged fool Le Glorieux, is in the current habit of distinguishing you by the absurd and ridiculous name of *Tête-botté*, which makes one of the Duke's most ordinary subjects of pleasantry."[1]

While Louis thus spoke, he had the double pleasure of galling to the quick the person whom he addressed—an exercise which it was in his nature to enjoy, even when he had not, as in the present case, the apology that he did so in pure retaliation—and that of observing, that he had at length been able to find a point in Des Comines's character which might lead him gradually from the interests of Burgundy to those of France. But although the deep resentment which the offended courtier entertained against his master induced him at a future period to exchange the service of Charles for that of Louis, yet, at the present moment, he was contented to throw out only some general hints of his friendly inclination towards France, which he well knew the King would understand how to interpret. And indeed it would be unjust to stigmatise the memory of the excellent historian with the desertion of his master on this occasion, although he was certainly now possessed with sentiments much more favourable to Louis than when he entered the apartment.

[2] See Anecdote of the Boots. Note 44.

He constrained himself to laugh at the anecdote which Louis had detailed, and then added: "I did not think so trifling a frolic would have dwelt on the mind of the Duke so long as to make it worth telling again. Some such passage there was of drawing off boots and the like, as your Majesty knows that the Duke is fond of rude play; but it has been much exaggerated in his recollection. Let it pass on."

"Ay, *let* it pass on," said the King; "it is indeed shame it should have detained us a minute. And now, Sir Philip, I hope you are French so far as to afford me your best counsel in these difficult affairs. You have, I am well aware, the clue to the labyrinth, if you would but impart it."

"Your Majesty may command my best advice and service," replied Des Comines, "under reservation always of my duty to my own master."

This was nearly what the courtier had before stated; but he now repeated it in a tone so different, that whereas Louis understood from the former declaration that the reserved duty to Burgundy was the prime thing to be considered, so he now saw clearly that the emphasis was reversed, and that more weight was now given by the speaker to his promise of counsel than to a restriction which seemed interposed for the sake of form and consistency. The King resumed his own seat, and compelled Des Comines to sit by him, listening at the same time to that statesman, as if the words of an oracle sounded in his ears. Des Comines spoke in that low and impressive tone which implies at once great sincerity and some caution, and at the same time so slowly as if he was desirous that the King should weigh and consider each individual word as having its own peculiar and determined meaning. "The things," he said, "which I have suggested for your Majesty's consideration, harsh as they sound in your ear, are but substitutes for still more violent proposals brought forward in the Duke's councils by such as are more hostile to your Majesty. And I need scarce remind your Majesty that the more direct and more violent suggestions find readiest acceptance with our master, who loves brief and dangerous measures better than those that are safe, but at the same time circuitous."

"I remember," said the King, "I have seen him swim a river at the risk of drowning, though there was a bridge to be found for riding two hundred yards round."

"True, sire; and he that weighs not his life against the gratification of a moment of impetuous passion will, on the same impulse, prefer the gratification of his will to the increase of his substantial power."

"Most true," replied the King; "a fool will ever grasp rather at the appearance than the reality of authority. All this I know to be true of Charles of Burgundy. But, my dear friend Des Comines, what do you infer from these premises?"

"Simply this, my lord," answered the Burgundian, "that as your Majesty has seen a skilful angler control a large and heavy fish, and finally draw him to land by a single hair, which fish had broken through a tackle tenfold stronger had the fisher presumed to strain the line on him, instead of giving him head enough for all his wild flourishes, even so your Majesty, by gratifying the Duke in these particulars on which he has pitched his ideas of honour and the gratification of his revenge, may evade many of the other unpalatable propositions at which I have hinted, and which—including, I must state openly to your Majesty, some of those through which France would be most especially weakened—will slide out of his remembrance and attention, and, being referred to subsequent conferences and future discussion, may be altogether eluded."

"I understand you, my good Sir Philip; but to the matter," said the King. "To which of those happy propositions is your duke so much wedded that contradiction will make him unreasonable and untractable?"

"To any or to all of them, if it please your Majesty, on which you may happen to contradict him. This is precisely what your Majesty must avoid; and to take up my former parable, you must needs remain on the watch, ready to give the Duke line enough whenever he shoots away under the impulse of his rage. His fury, already considerably abated, will waste itself if he be unopposed, and you will presently find him become more friendly and more tractable."

"Still," said the King, musing, "there must be some particular demands which lie deeper at my cousin's heart than the other proposals. Were I but aware of these, Sir Philip——"

"Your Majesty may make the lightest of his demands the most important, simply by opposing it," said Des Comines; "nevertheless, my lord, thus far I can say, that every shadow of treaty will be broken off, if your Majesty renounce not William de la Marck and the Liegeois."

"I have already said that I will disown them," said the King, "and well they deserve it at my hand: the villains have commenced their uproar at a moment that might have cost me my life."

"He that fires a train of powder," replied the historian, "must expect a speedy explosion of the mine. But more than mere disavowal of their cause will be expected of your Majesty by Duke Charles; for know, that he will demand your Majesty's assistance to put the insurrection down, and your royal presence to witness the punishment which he destines for the rebels."

"That may scarce consist with our honour, Des Comines," said the King.

"To refuse it will scarcely consist with your Majesty's safety," replied Des Comines. "Charles is determined to show the people of Flanders that no hope, nay, no promise, of assistance from France will save them in their mutinies from the wrath and vengeance of Burgundy."

"But, Sir Philip, I will speak plainly," answered the King. "Could we but procrastinate the matter, might not these rogues of Liege make their own part good against Duke Charles? The knaves are numerous and steady, can they not hold out their town against him?"

"With the help of the thousand archers of France whom your Majesty promised them, they might have done something; but——"

"Whom I promised them!" said the King. "Alas! good Sir Philip! you much wrong me in saying so."

"——But without whom," continued Des Comines, not heeding the interruption, "as your Majesty will not *now* likely find it convenient to supply them, what chance will the burghers have of making good their town, in whose walls the large breaches made by Charles after the battle of St. Tron are still unrepaired; so that the lances of Hainault, Brabant, and Burgundy may advance to the attack twenty men in front?"

"The improvident idiots!" said the King. "If they have thus neglected their own safety, they deserve not my protection. Pass on; I will make no quarrel for their sake."

"The next point, I fear, will sit closer to your Majesty's heart," said Des Comines.

"Ah!" replied the King, "you mean that infernal marriage! I will not consent to the breach of the contract betwixt my daughter Joan and my cousin of Orleans; it would be wresting the sceptre of France from me and my posterity, for that feeble boy the Dauphin is a blighted blossom, which will wither without fruit. This match between Joan and Orleans has been my thought by day, my dream by night. I tell thee, Sir Philip, I cannot give it up! Besides, it is inhuman to require me, with my own hand, to destroy at once my own scheme of policy and the happiness of a pair brought up for each other."

"Are they then so much attached?" said Des Comines.

"One of them at least is," said the King, "and the one for whom I am bound to be most anxious. But you smile, Sir Philip, you are no believer in the force of love."

"Nay," said Des Comines, "if it please you, sire, I am so little an infidel in that particular that I was about to ask whether it would reconcile you in any degree to your acquiescing in the proposed marriage betwixt the Duke of Orleans and Isabelle de Croye, were I to satisfy you that the countess's inclinations are so much fixed on another that it is likely it will never be a match?"

King Louis sighed. "Alas!" he said, "my good and dear friend, from what sepulchre have you drawn such dead man's comfort? *Her* inclination, indeed! Why, to speak truth, supposing that Orleans detested my daughter Joan, yet, but for this ill-ravelled web of mischance, he must needs have married her; so you may conjecture how little chance there is of this damsel being able to refuse him under a similar compulsion, and he a child of France besides. Ah, no, Philip! little fear of her standing obstinate against the suit of such a lover. *Varium et mutabile,* Philip."

"Your Majesty may, in the present instance, undervalue the obstinate courage of this young lady. She comes of a race determinately wilful; and I have picked out of Crèvecœur that she has formed a romantic attachment to a young squire, who, to say the truth, rendered her many services on the road."

"Ha!" said the King, "an archer of my Guards, by name Quentin Durward?"

"The same, as I think," said Des Comines; "he was made prisoner along with the countess, travelling almost alone together."

"Now, Our Lord and Our Lady, and Monseigneur St. Martin, and Monseigneur St. Julian be praised every one of them!" said the King, "and all laud and honour to the learned Galeotti, who read in the stars that this youth's destiny was connected with mine! If the maiden be so attached to him as to make her refractory to the will of Burgundy, this Quentin hath indeed been rarely useful to me."

"I believe, my lord," answered the Burgundian, "according to Crèvecœur's report, that there is some chance of her being sufficiently obstinate; besides, doubtless, the noble Duke himself, notwithstanding what your Majesty was pleased to hint in way of supposition, will not willingly renounce his fair cousin, to whom he has been long engaged.

"Umph!" answered the King. "But you have never seen my daughter Joan. A howlet, man!—an absolute owl, whom I am ashamed of! But let him be only a wise man, and marry her, I will give him leave to be mad *par amours* for the fairest lady in France. And now, Philip, have you given me the full map of your master's mind?"

"I have possessed you, sire, of those particulars on which he is at present most disposed to insist. But your Majesty well knows that the Duke's disposition is like a sweeping torrent, which only passes smoothly forward when its waves encounter no opposition; and what may be presented to chafe him into fury, it is impossible even to guess. Were more distinct evidence of your Majesty's practices—pardon the phrase, where there is so little time for selection—with the Liegeois and William de la Marck to occur unexpectedly, the issue might be terrible. There are strange news from that country: they say La Marck hath married Hameline the elder Countess of Croye."

"That old fool was so mad on marriage that she would have accepted the hand of Satan," said the King; "but that La Marck, beast as he is, should have married her rather more surprises me."

"There is a report also," continued Des Comines, "that an envoy, or herald, on La Marck's part, is approaching Péronne; this is like to drive the Duke frantic with rage. I trust that he has no letters, or the like, to show on your Majesty's part?"

"Letters to a Wild Boar!" answered the King. "No—no, Sir Philip, I was no such fool as to cast pearls before swine. What little intercourse I had with the brute animal was by message, in which I always employed such low-bred slaves and vagabonds that their evidence would not be received in a trial for robbing a hen-roost."

"I can then only further recommend," said Des Comines, taking his leave, "that your Majesty should remain on your guard, be guided by events, and, above all, avoid using any language or argument with the Duke which may better become your dignity than your present condition."

"If my dignity," said the King, "grow troublesome to me, which it seldom doth while there are deeper interests to think of, I have a special remedy for that swelling of the heart. It is but looking into a certain ruinous closet, Sir Philip, and thinking of the death of Charles the Simple; and it cures me as effectually as the cold bath would cool a fever. And now, my friend and monitor, must thou be gone? Well, Sir Philip, the time must come when thou wilt tire reading lessons of state policy to the Bull of Burgundy, who is incapable of comprehending your most simple argument. If Louis of Valois then lives, thou hast a friend in the court of France. I tell thee, my Philip, it would be a blessing to my kingdom should I ever acquire thee, who, with a profound view of subjects of state, hast also a conscience capable of feeling and discerning between right and wrong. So help me, Our Lord and Lady, and Monseigneur St. Martin, Oliver and Balue have hearts as hardened as the nether millstone; and my life is embittered by remorse and penances for the crimes they make me commit. Thou, Sir Philip, possessed of the wisdom of present and past time, canst teach how to become great without ceasing to be virtuous."

"A hard task, and which few have attained," said the historian, "but which is yet within the reach of princes who will strive for it. Meantime, sire, be prepared, for the Duke will presently confer with you."

Louis looked long after Philip when he left the apartment, and at length burst into a bitter laugh. "He spoke of fishing—I have sent him home, a trout properly tickled! And he thinks himself virtuous because he took no bribe, but contented himself with flattery and promises, and the pleasure of avenging an affront to his vanity! Why, he is but so much the poorer for the refusal of the money, not a jot the more honest. He must be mine, though, for he hath the shrewdest head among them. Well, now for nobler game! I am to face this leviathan Charles, who will presently swim hitherward, cleaving the deep before him. I must, like a trembling sailor, throw a tub overboard to amuse him. But I may one day find the chance—of driving a harpoon into his entrails!"[1]

[1] See Philip des Comines. Note 45.

CHAPTER XXXI.

THE INTERVIEW.

Hold fast thy truth, young soldier. Gentle maiden,
Keep you your promise plight; leave age its subtleties,
And grey-hair'd policy its maze of falsehood;
But be you candid as the morning sky,
Ere the high sun sucks vapours up to stain it.
The Trial.

On the perilous and important morning which preceded the meeting of the two princes in the Castle of Péronne, Oliver le Dain did his master the service of an active and skilful agent, making interest for Louis in every quarter, both with presents and promises; so that, when the Duke's anger should blaze forth, all around should be interested to smother, and not to increase, the conflagration. He glided, like night, from tent to tent, from house to house, making himself friends, but not, in the Apostle's sense, with the Mammon of unrighteousness. As was said of another active political agent, "His finger was in every man's palm, his mouth was in every man's ear"; and for various reasons, some of which we have formerly hinted at, he secured the favour of many Burgundian nobles, who either had something to hope or fear from France, or who thought that, were the power of Louis too much reduced, their own duke would be likely to pursue the road to despotic authority, to which his heart naturally inclined him, with a daring and unopposed pace.

Where Oliver suspected his own presence or arguments might be less acceptable, he employed that of other servants of the King; and it was in this manner that he obtained, by the favour of the Count de Crèvecœur, an interview betwixt Lord Crawford, accompanied by Le Balafré, and Quentin Durward, who, since he had arrived at Péronne, had been detained in a sort of honourable confinement. Private affairs were assigned as the cause of requesting this meeting; but it is probable that Crèvecœur, who was afraid that his master might be stirred up in passion to do something dishonourably violent towards Louis, was not sorry to afford an opportunity to Crawford to give some hints to the young archer which might prove useful to his master.

The meeting between the countrymen was cordial, and even affecting.

"Thou art a singular youth," said Crawford, stroking the head of young Durward as a grandsire might do that of this descendant. "Certes, you have had as meikle good fortune as if you had been born with a lucky hood on your head."

"All comes of his gaining an archer's place at such early years," said Le Balafré; "I never was so much talked of, fair nephew, because I was five-and-twenty years old before I was *hors de page*."

"And an ill-looking mountainous monster of a page thou wert, Ludovic," said the old commander, "with a beard like a baker's shool, and a back like old Wallace Wight."

"I fear," said Quentin, with downcast eyes, "I shall enjoy that title to distinction but a short time, since it is my purpose to resign the service of the Archer Guard."

Le Balafré was struck almost mute with astonishment, and Crawford's ancient features gleamed with displeasure. The former at length mustered words enough to say: "Resign!— leave your place in the Scottish Archers! such a thing was never dreamt of. I would not give up my situation, to be made Constable of France."

"Hush! Ludovic," said Crawford; "this youngster knows better how to shape his course with the wind than we of the old world do. His journey hath given him some pretty tales to tell about King Louis; and he is turning Burgundian, that he may make his own little profit by telling them to Duke Charles."

"If I thought so," said Le Balafré, "I would cut his throat with my own hand, were he fifty times my sister's son!"

"But you would first inquire whether I deserve to be so treated, fair kinsman?" answered Quentin. "And you, my lord, know that I am no tale-bearer; nor shall either question or torture draw out of me a word to King Louis's prejudice which may have come to my knowledge while I was in his service. So far my oath of duty keeps me silent. But I will not remain in that service, in which, besides the perils of fair battle with mine enemies, I am to be exposed to the dangers of ambuscade on the part of my friends."

"Nay, if he objects to lying in ambuscade," said the slow-witted Le Balafré, looking sorrowfully at the Lord Crawford, "I am afraid, my lord, that all is over with him! I myself have had thirty bushments break upon me, and truly I think I have laid in ambuscade twice as often myself, it being a favourite practice in our King's mode of making war."

"It is so, indeed, Ludovic," answered Lord Crawford; "nevertheless, hold your peace, for I believe I understand this gear better than you do."

"I wish to Our Lady you may, my lord," answered Ludovic; "but it wounds me to the very midriff to think my sister's son should fear an ambushment."

"Young man," said Crawford, "I partly guess your meaning. You have met foul play on the road where you travelled by the King's command, and you think you have reason to charge him with being the author of it?"

"I have been threatened with foul play in the execution of the King's commission," answered Quentin; "but I have had the good fortune to elude it; whether his Majesty be innocent or guilty in the matter, I leave to God and his own conscience. He fed me when I was a-hungered, received me when I was a wandering stranger; I will never load him in his adversity with accusations which may indeed be unjust, since I heard them only from the vilest mouths."

"My dear boy—my own lad!" said Crawford, taking him in his arms, "ye think like a Scot, every joint of you! Like one that will forget a cause of quarrel with a friend whose back is already at the wall, and remember nothing of him but his kindness."

"Since my Lord Crawford has embraced my nephew," said Ludovic Lesly, "I will embrace him also, though I would have you to know, that to understand the service of an ambushment is as necessary to a soldier as it is to a priest to be able to read his breviary."

"Be hushed, Ludovic," said Crawford; "ye are an ass, my friend, and ken not the blessing Heaven has sent you in this braw callant. And now tell me, Quentin, my man, hath the King any advice of this brave, Christian, and manly resolution of yours: for, poor man, he had need, in his strait, to ken what he has to reckon upon. Had he but brought the whole brigade of Guards with him—but God's will be done! Kens he of your purpose, think you?"

"I really can hardly tell," answered Quentin; "but I assured his learned astrologer, Martius Galeotti, of my resolution to be silent on all that could injure the King with the Duke of Burgundy. The particulars which I suspect I will not—under your favour—communicate even to your lordship; and to the philosopher I was, of course, far less willing to unfold myself."

"Ha—ay!" answered Lord Crawford. "Oliver did indeed tell me that Galeotti prophesied most stoutly concerning the line of conduct you were to hold; and I am truly glad to find he did so on better authority than the stars."

"*He* prophesy!" said Le Balafré, laughing. "The stars never told him that honest Ludovic Lesly used to help yonder wench of his to spend the fair ducats he flings into her lap."

"Hush! Ludovic," said his captain—"hush! thou beast, man! If thou dost not respect my grey hairs, because I have been e'en too much of a *routier* myself, respect the boy's youth and innocence, and let us have no more of such unbecoming daffing."

"Your honour may say your pleasure," answered Ludovic Lesly; "but, by my faith, second-sighted Saunders Souplejaw, the town-souter of Glen Houlakin, was worth Gallotti, or Gallipotty, or whatever ye call him, twice told, for a prophet. He foretold that all my sister's children would die some day; and he foretold it in the very hour that the youngest was born, and that is this lad Quentin, who, no doubt, will one day die, to make up the prophecy—the more's the pity; the whole curney of them is gone but himself. And Saunders foretold to myself one day, that I should be made by marriage, which doubtless will also happen in due time, though it hath not yet come to pass, though how or when, I am hardly guess, as I care not myself for the wedded state, and Quentin is but a lad. Also, Saunders predicted——"

"Nay," said Lord Crawford, "unless the prediction be singularly to the purpose, I must cut you short, my good Ludovic; for both you and I must now leave your nephew, with prayers to Our Lady to strengthen him in the good mind he is in; for this is a case in which a light word might do more mischief than all the Parliament of Paris could mend. My blessing with you, my lad; and be in no hurry to think of leaving our body, for there will be good blows going presently in the eye of day, and no ambuscade."

"And my blessing too, nephew," said Ludovic Lesly; "for, since you have satisfied our most noble captain, I also am satisfied, as in duty bound."

"Stay, my lord," said Quentin, and led Lord Crawford a little apart from his uncle. "I must not forget to mention that there is a person besides in the world, who, having learned from me these circumstances which it is essential to King Louis's safety should at present remain concealed, may not think that the same obligation of secrecy which attaches to me as the King's soldier, and as having been relieved by his bounty, is at all binding on her."

"On *her!*" replied Crawford; "nay, if there be a woman in the secret, the Lord ha' mercy, for we are all on the rocks again!"

"Do not suppose so, my lord," replied Durward, "but use your interest with the Count of Crèvecœur to permit me an interview with the Countess Isabelle of Croye, who is the party possessed of my secret, and I doubt not that can I persuade her to be as silent as I shall unquestionably myself remain concerning whatever may incense the Duke against King Louis."

The old soldier mused for a long time, looked up to the ceiling, then down again upon the floor, then shook his head, and at length said: "There is something in all this which, by my honour, I do not understand. The Countess Isabelle of Croye! an interview with a lady of her birth, blood, and possessions, and thou, a raw Scottish lad, so certain of carrying thy point with her! Thou art either strangely confident, my young friend, or else you have used your time well upon the journey. But, by the cross of St. Andrew! I will move Crèvecœur in thy behalf; and, as he truly fears that Duke Charles may be provoked against the King to the extremity of falling foul, I think it likely he may grant thy request, though, by my honour, it is a comical one."

So saying, and shrugging up his shoulders, the old lord left the apartment, followed by Ludovic Lesly, who, forming his looks on those of his principal, endeavoured, though knowing nothing of the cause of his wonder, to look as mysterious and important as Crawford himself.

In a few minutes Crawford returned, but without his attendant Le Balafré. The old man seemed in singular humour, laughing and chuckling to himself in a manner which strangely distorted his stern and rigid features, and at the same time shaking his head, as at something which he could not help condemning, while he found it irresistibly ludicrous. "My certes, countryman," said he, "but you are not blate: you will never lose fair lady for faint heart! Crèvecœur swallowed your proposal as he would have done a cup of vinegar, and swore to me roundly, by all the saints in Burgundy, that were less than the honour of princes and the peace of kingdoms at stake, you should never see even so much as the print of the Countess Isabelle's foot on the clay. Were it not that he had a dame, and a fair one, I would have thought that he meant to break a lance for the prize himself. Perhaps he thinks of his nephew, the County Stephen. A countess! would no less serve you to be hinting at? But come along; your interview with her must be brief. But I fancy you know how to make the most of little time—ho! ho! ho! By my faith, I can hardly chide thee for the presumption, I have such a good will to laugh at it!"

With a brow like scarlet, at once offended and disconcerted by the blunt inferences of the old soldier, and vexed at beholding in what an absurd light his passion was viewed by every person of experience, Durward followed Lord Crawford in silence to the Ursuline convent, in which the countess was lodged, and in the parlour of which he found the Count de Crèvecœur.

"So, young gallant," said the latter, sternly, "you must see the fair companion of your romantic expedition once more, it seems?"

"Yes, my lord count," answered Quentin, firmly; "and what is more, I must see her alone."

"That shall never be," said the Count de Crèvecœur. "Lord Crawford, I make you judge. This young lady, the daughter of my old friend and companion in arms, the richest heiress in Burgundy, has confessed a sort of a—what was I going to say?—in short, she is a fool, and your man-at-arms here a presumptuous coxcomb. In a word, they shall not meet alone."

"Then will I not speak a single word to the countess in your presence," said Quentin, much delighted. "You have told me much that I did not dare, presumptuous as I may be, even to hope."

"Ay, truly said, my friend," said Crawford. "You have been imprudent in your communications; and, since you refer to me, and there is a good stout grating across the parlour, I would advise you to trust to it, and let them do the worst with their tongues. What, man! the life of a king, and many thousands besides, is not to be weighed with the chance of two young things whillywhawing in ilk other's ears for a minute?"

So saying, he dragged off Crèvecœur, who followed very reluctantly, and cast many angry glances at the young archer as he left the room.

In a moment after the Countess Isabelle entered on the other side of the grate, and no sooner saw Quentin alone in the parlour than she stopped short, and cast her eyes on the ground for the space of half a minute. "Yet why should I be ungrateful," she said, "because others are unjustly suspicious? My friend—my preserver, I may almost say, so much have I been beset by treachery—my only faithful and constant friend!"

As she spoke thus, she extended her hand to him through the grate, nay, suffered him to retain it until he had covered it with kisses, not unmingled with tears. She only said: "Durward, were we ever to meet again, I would not permit this folly."

If it be considered that Quentin had guarded her through so many perils, that he had been, in truth, her only faithful and zealous protector, perhaps my fair readers, even if countesses and heiresses should be of the number, will pardon the derogation.

But the countess extricated her hand at length, and stepping a pace back from the grate, asked Durward, in a very embarrassed tone, what boon he had to ask of her? "For that you have a request to make I have learned from the old Scottish lord, who came here but now with my cousin of Crèvecœur. Let it be but reasonable," she said, "but such as poor Isabelle can grant with duty and honour uninfringed, and you cannot tax my slender powers too highly. But oh! do not speak hastily; do not say," she added, looking around with timidity, "aught that might, if overheard, do prejudice to us both!"

"Fear not, noble lady," said Quentin, sorrowfully; "it is not *here* that I can forget the distance which fate has placed between us, or expose you to the censure of your proud kindred as the object of the most devoted love to one, poorer and less powerful, not perhaps less noble, than themselves. Let that pass like a dream of the night to all but one bosom, where, dream as it is, it will fill up the room of all existing realities."

"Hush—hush!" said Isabelle; "for your own sake, for mine, be silent on such a theme. Tell me rather what it is you have to ask of me."

"Forgiveness to one," replied Quentin, "who, for his own selfish views, hath conducted himself as your enemy."

"I trust I forgive all my enemies," answered Isabelle; "but oh, Durward! through what scenes have your courage and presence of mind protected me! Yonder bloody hall! the good bishop! I knew not till yesterday half the horrors I had unconsciously witnessed."

"Do not think on them," said Quentin, who saw the transient colour which had come to her cheek during their conference fast fading into the most deadly paleness. "Do not look back, but look steadily forward, as they needs must who walk in a perilous road. Hearken to me. King Louis deserves nothing better at your hand, of all others, than to be proclaimed the wily and insidious politician which he really is. But to tax him as the encourager of your flight, still more as the author of a plan to throw you into the hands of De la Marck, will at this moment produce perhaps the King's death or dethronement; and, at all events, the most bloody war between France and Burgundy which the two countries have ever been engaged in."

"These evils shall not arrive for my sake, if they can be prevented," said the Countess Isabelle; "and indeed your slightest request were enough to make me forego my revenge, were that at any time a passion which I deeply cherish. Is it possible I would rather remember King Louis's injuries than your invaluable services? Yet how is this to be? When I am called before my sovereign, the Duke of Burgundy, I must either stand silent or speak the truth. The former would be contumacy; and to a false tale you will not desire me to train my tongue."

"Surely not," said Durward; "but let your evidence concerning Louis be confined to what you yourself positively know to be truth; and when you mention what others have reported, no matter how credibly, let it be as reports only, and beware of pledging your own personal evidence to that which, though you may fully believe, you cannot personally know, to be true. The assembled council of Burgundy cannot refuse to a monarch the justice which in my country is rendered to the meanest person under accusation. They must esteem him innocent until direct and sufficient proofs shall demonstrate his guilt. Now, what does not consist with your own certain knowledge should be proved by other evidence than your report from hearsay."

"I think I understand you," said the Countess Isabelle.

"I will make my meaning plainer," said Quentin; and was

illustrating it accordingly by more than one instance, when the convent-bell tolled.

"That," said the countess, "is a signal that we must part—part for ever! But do not forget me, Durward; I will never forget you; your faithful services——"

She could not speak more, but again extended her hand, which was again pressed to his lips; and I know not how it was that, in endeavouring to withdraw her hand, the countess came so close to the grating that Quentin was encouraged to press the adieu on her lips. The young lady did not chide him; perhaps there was no time, for Crèvecœur and Crawford, who had been from some loophole eye-witnesses, if not ear-witnesses also, of what was passing, rushed into the apartment, the first in a towering passion, the latter laughing and holding the count back.

"To your chamber, young mistress—to your chamber!" exclaimed the count to Isabelle, who, flinging down her veil, retired in all haste, "which should be exchanged for a cell and bread and water. And you, gentle sir, who are so malapert, the time will come when the interests of Kings and Kingdoms may not be connected with such as you are; and you shall then learn the penalty of your audacity in raising your beggarly eyes——"

"Hush—hush! enough said—rein up—rein up," said the old lord; "and you, Quentin, I command you, be silent, and begone to your quarters. There is no such room for so much scorn neither, Sir Count of Crèvecœur, that I must say now he is out of hearing. Quentin Durward is as much a gentleman as the King, only, as the Spaniard says, not so rich. He is as noble as myself, and I am chief of my name. Tush, tush! man, you must not speak to us of penalties."

"My lord—my lord," said Crèvecœur, impatiently, "the insolence of these foreign mercenaries is proverbial, and should receive rather rebuke than encouragement from you, who are their leader."

"My lord count," answered Crawford, "I have ordered my command for these fifty years without advice either from

Frenchman or Burgundian; and I intend to do so, under your favour, so long as I shall continue to hold it."

"Well—well, my lord," said Crèvecœur, "I meant you no disrespect; your nobleness, as well as your age, entitle you to be privileged in your impatience; and for these young people, I am satisfied to overlook the past, since I will take care that they never meet again."

"Do not take that upon your salvation, Crèvecœur," said the old lord, laughing; "mountains, it is said, may meet, and why not mortal creatures that have legs, and life and love to put those legs in motion? Yon kiss, Crèvecœur, came tenderly off; methinks it was ominous."

"You are striving again to disturb my patience," said Crèvecœur, "but I will not give you that advantage over me. Hark! they toll the summons to the castle: an awful meeting, of which God only can foretell the issue."

"This issue I can foretell," said the old Scottish lord, "that if violence is to be offered to the person of the King, few as his friends are, and surrounded by his enemies, he shall neither fall alone nor unavenged; and grieved I am that his own positive orders have prevented my taking measures to prepare for such an issue."

"My Lord of Crawford," said the Burgundian, "to anticipate such evil is the sure way to give occasion to it. Obey the orders of your royal master, and give no pretext for violence by taking hasty offence, and you will find that the day will pass over more smoothly than you now conjecture."

O—Vol. 16

CHAPTER XXXII.

THE INVESTIGATION.

Me rather had, my heart might feel your love,
Than my displeased eye see your courtesy.
Up, cousin, up; your heart is up, I know,
Thus high at least, although your knee—
King Richard II.

AT the first toll of the bell, which was to summon the great nobles of Burgundy together in council, with the very few French peers who could be present on the occasion, Duke Charles, followed by a part of his train, armed with partizans and battle-axes, entered the hall of Herbert's Tower, in the Castle of Péronne. King Louis, who had expected the visit, arose and made two steps towards the Duke, and then remained standing with an air of dignity, which, in spite of the meanness of his dress and the familiarity of his ordinary manners, he knew very well how to assume when he judged it necessary. Upon the present important crisis, the composure of his demeanour had an evident effect upon his rival, who changed the abrupt and hasty step with which he entered the apartment into one more becoming a great vassal entering the presence of his lord paramount. Apparently the Duke had formed the internal resolution to treat Louis, in the outset at least, with the formalities due to his high station; but at the same time it was evident that, in doing so, he put no small constraint upon the fiery impatience of his own disposition, and was scarce able to control the feelings of resentment and the thirst of revenge which boiled in his bosom. Hence, though he compelled himself to use the outward acts, and in some degree the language, of courtesy and reverence, his colour came and went rapidly; his voice was abrupt, hoarse, and broken; his limbs shook, as if impatient of the curb imposed on his motions; he frowned and bit his lip until the blood came; and every look and movement showed that the most passionate prince who ever lived was under the dominion of one of his most violent paroxysms of fury.

The King marked this war of passion with a calm and untroubled eye; for, though he gathered from the Duke's looks a foretaste of the bitterness of death, which he dreaded alike as a mortal and a sinful man, yet he was resolved, like a wary and skilful pilot, neither to suffer himself to be disconcerted by his own fears, nor to abandon the helm, while there was a chance of saving the vessel by adroit pilotage. Therefore, when the Duke, in a hoarse and broken tone, said something of the scarcity of his accommodations, he answered with a smile, that he could not complain, since he had as yet found Herbert's Tower a better residence than it had proved to one of his ancestors.

"They told you the tradition then?" said Charles. "Yes; here he was slain, but it was because he refused to take the cowl, and finish his days in a monastery."

"The more fool he," said Louis, affecting unconcern, "since he gained the torment of being a martyr without the merit of being a saint."

"I come," said the Duke, "to pray your Majesty to attend a high council, at which things of weight are to be deliberated upon concerning the welfare of France and Burgundy. You will presently meet them—that is, if such be your pleasure——"

"Nay, my fair cousin," said the King, "never strain courtesy so far as to entreat what you may so boldly command. To council, since such is your Grace's pleasure. We are somewhat shorn of our train," he added, looking upon the small suite that arranged themselves to attend him; "but you, cousin, must shine out for us both."

Marshalled by Toison d'Or, chief of the heralds of Burgundy, the princes left the Earl Herbert's Tower and entered the castle-yard, which Louis observed was filled with the Duke's body-guard and men-at-arms, splendidly accoutred and drawn up in martial array. Crossing the court, they entered the council-hall, which was in a much more modern part of the building than that of which Louis had been the tenant, and, though in disrepair, had been hastily arranged for the solemnity of a public council. Two chairs of state were erected under the same canopy, that for the King being raised two steps higher than the one which the Duke was to occupy; about twenty of the chief nobility sat, arranged in due order, on either hand of the chair of state; and thus, when both the princes were seated, the person for whose trial, as it might be called, the council was summoned, held the highest place, and appeared to preside in it.

It was perhaps to get rid of this inconsistency, and the scruples which might have been inspired by it, that Duke Charles, having bowed slightly to the royal chair, bluntly opened the sitting with the following words:

"My good vassals and counsellors, it is not unknown to you what disturbances have arisen in our territories, both in our father's time and in our own, from the rebellion of vassals against superiors, and subjects against their princes. And lately we have had the most dreadful proof of the height to which these evils have arrived in our case by the scandalous flight of the Countess Isabelle of Croye, and her aunt the Lady Hameline, to take refuge with a foreign power, thereby renouncing their fealty to us and inferring the forfeiture of their fiefs; and in another more dreadful and deplorable instance, by the sacrilegious and bloody murder of our beloved brother and ally the Bishop of Liege, and the rebellion of that treacherous city, which was but too mildly punished for the last insurrection. We have been informed that these sad events may be traced not merely to the inconstancy and folly of women and the presumption of pampered citizens, but to the agency of foreign power, and the interference of a mighty neighbour, from whom, if good deeds could merit any return in kind, Burgundy could have expected nothing but the most sincere and devoted friendship. If this should prove truth," said the Duke, setting his teeth and pressing his heel against the ground, "what consideration shall withhold us, the means being in our power, from taking such measures as shall effectually, and at the very source, close up the main spring from which these evils have yearly flowed on us?"

The Duke had begun his speech with some calmness, but he elevated his voice at the conclusion; and the last sentence was spoken in a tone which made all the counsellors tremble, and brought a transient fit of paleness across the King's cheek. He instantly recalled his courage, however, and addressed the council in his turn, in a tone evincing so much ease and composure that the Duke, though he seemed desirous to interrupt or stop him, found no decent opportunity to do so.

"Nobles of France and of Burgundy," he said, "knights of the Holy Spirit and of the Golden Fleece, since a king must plead his cause as an accused person, he cannot desire more distinguished judges than the flower of nobleness and muster and pride of chivalry. Our fair cousins of Burgundy hath but darkened the dispute between us in so far as his courtesy has declined to state it in precise terms. I, who have no cause for observing such delicacy, nay, whose condition permits me not to do so, crave leave to speak more precisely. It is to us, my lords—to us, his liege lord, his kinsman, his ally—that unhappy circumstances, perverting our cousin's clear judgment and better nature, have induced him to apply the hateful charges of seducing his vassals from their allegiance, stirring up the people of Liege to revolt, and stimulating the outlawed William de la Marck to commit a most cruel and sacrilegious murder. Nobles of France and Burgundy, I might truly appeal to the circumstances to which I now stand as being in themselves a complete contradiction of such an accusation; for is it to be supposed that, having the sense of a rational being left me, I should have thrown myself unreservedly into the power of the Duke of Burgundy, while I was practising treachery against him such as could not fail to be discovered, and which, being discovered, must place me, as I now stand, in the power of a justly exasperated prince? The folly of one who should seat himself quietly down to repose on a mine, after he had lighted the match which was to cause instant explosion, would have been wisdom compared to mine. I have no doubt that, amongst the perpetrators of those horrible treasons at Schonwaldt, villains have been busy with my name; but am I to be answerable, who have given them no right to use it? If two silly women, disgusted on account of some romantic cause of displeasure, sought refuge at my court, does it follow that they did so by my direction? It will be found, when inquired into, that, since honour and chivalry forbade my sending them back prisoners to the court of Burgundy,—which, I think, gentlemen, no one who wears the collar of these orders would suggest,—that I came as nearly as possible to the same point by placing them in the hands of the venerable father in God, who is now a saint in Heaven." Here Louis seemed much affected, and pressed his kerchief to his eyes. "In the hands, I say, of a member of my own family, and still more closely united with that of Burgundy, whose situation, exalted condition in the church, and, alas! whose numerous virtues qualified him to be the protector of these unhappy wanderers for a little while, and the mediator betwixt them and their liege lord. I say, therefore, the only circumstances which seem, in my brother of Burgundy's hasty view of this subject, to argue unworthy suspicions against me are such as can be explained on the fairest and most honourable motives; and I say, moreover, that no one particle of credible evidence can be brought to support the injurious charges which have induced my brother to alter his friendly looks towards one who came to him in full confidence of friendship, have caused him to turn his festive hall into a court of justice, and his hospitable apartments into a prison."

"My lord—my lord," said Charles, breaking in so soon as the King paused, "for your being here at a time so unluckily coinciding with the execution of your projects, I can only account by supposing that those who make it their trade to impose on others do sometimes egregiously delude themselves. The engineer is sometimes killed by the springing of his own petard. For what is to follow, let it depend on the event of this solemn inquiry. Bring hither the Countess Isabelle of Croye!"

As the young lady was introduced, supported on the one side by the Countess of Crèvecœur, who had her husband's commands to that effect, and on the other by the abbess of the Ursuline convent, Charles exclaimed with his usual harshness of voice and manner: "Soh! sweet princess, you who could scarce find breath to answer us when we last laid our just and reasonable commands on you, yet have had wind enough to run as long a course as ever did hunted doe, what think you of the fair work you have made between two great princes and two mighty countries, that have been like to go to war for your baby face?"

The publicity of the scene and the violence of Charles's manner totally overcame the resolution which Isabelle had formed of throwing herself at the Duke's feet and imploring him into take possession of her estates and permit her to retire into a cloister. She stood motionless like a terrified female in a storm, who hears the thunder roll on every side of her, and apprehends in every fresh peal the bolt which is to strike her dead. The Countess of Crèvecœur, a woman of spirit equal to her birth, and to the beauty which she preserved even in her matronly years, judged it necessary to interfere. "My lord duke," she said, "my fair cousin is under my protection. I know better than your Grace how women should be treated, and we will leave this presence instantly, unless you use a tone and language more suitable to our rank and sex."

The Duke burst out into a laugh. "Crèvecœur," he said, "thy tameness hath made a lordly dame of thy countess; but that is no affair of mine. Give a seat to yonder simple girl, to whom, so far from feeling enmity, I design the highest grace and honour. Sit down, mistress, and tell us at your leisure what fiend possessed you to fly from your native country, and embrace the trade of a damsel adventurous."

With much pain, and not without several interruptions, Isabelle confessed that, being absolutely determined against a match proposed to her by the Duke of Burgundy, she had indulged the hope of obtaining protection of the court of France.

"And under protection of the French monarch," said Charles. "Of that, doubtless, you were well assured?"

"I did indeed so think myself assured," said the Countess Isabelle, "otherwise I had not taken a step so decided." Here Charles looked upon Louis with a smile of inexpressible bitterness, which the King supported with the utmost firmness, except that his lip grew something whiter than it was wont to be. "But my information concerning King Louis's intentions towards us," continued the countess, after a short pause, "was almost entirely derived from my unhappy aunt, the Lady Hameline, and her opinions were formed upon the assertions and insinuations of persons whom I have since discovered to be the vilest traitors and most faithless wretches in the world." She then stated, in brief terms, what she had since come to learn of the treachery of Marthon, and of Hayraddin Maugrabin, and added that "she entertained no doubt that the elder Maugrabin, called Zamet, the original adviser of their flight, was capable of every species of treachery, as well as of assuming the character of an agent of Louis without authority."

There was a pause while the countess had continued her story, which she prosecuted, though very briefly, from the time she left the territories of Burgundy, in company with her aunt, until the storming of Schonwaldt, and her final surrender to the Count of Crèvecœur. All remained mute after she had finished her brief and broken narrative, and the Duke of Burgundy bent his fierce dark eyes on the ground, like one who seeks for a pretext to indulge his passion, but finds none sufficiently plausible to justify himself in his own eyes. "The mole," he said at length, looking upwards, "winds not his dark subterranean path beneath our feet the less certainly, that we, though conscious of his motions, cannot absolutely trace them. Yet I would know of King Louis, wherefore he maintained these ladies at his court, had they not gone thither by his own invitation."

"I did not so entertain them, fair cousin," answered the King. "Out of compassion, indeed, I received them in privacy, but took an early opportunity of placing them under the protection of the late excellent bishop, your own ally, and who was—may God assoil him!—a better judge than I, or any secular prince, how to reconcile the protection due to fugitives with the duty which a king owes to his ally from whose dominions they have fled. I boldly ask this young lady whether my reception of them was cordial or whether it was not, on the contrary, such as made them express regret that they had made my court their place of refuge?"

"So much was it otherwise than cordial," answered the countess, "that it induced me, at least, to doubt how far it was possible that your Majesty should have actually given the invitation of which we had been assured by those who called themselves your agents; since, supposing them to have proceeded only as they were duly authorised, it would have been hard to reconcile your Majesty's conduct with that to be expected from a king, a knight, and a gentleman."

The countess turned her eyes to the King as she spoke, with a look which was probably intended as a reproach, but the breast of Louis was armed against all such artillery. On the contrary, waving slowly his expanded hands, and looking around the circle, he seemed to make a triumphant appeal to all present upon the testimony borne to his innocence in the countess's reply.

Burgundy, meanwhile, cast on him a look which seemed to say that, if in some degree silenced, he was as far as ever from being satisfied, and then said abruptly to the countess: "Methinks, fair mistress, in this account of your wanderings, you have forgot all mention of certain love-passages. So, ho! blushing already? Certain knights of the forest, by whom your quiet was for a time interrupted. Well, that incident hath come to our ear, and something we may presently form out of it. Tell me, King Louis, were it not well, before this vagrant Helen of Troy, or of Croye, set more kings by the ears—were it not well to carve out a fitting match for her?"

King Louis, though conscious what ungrateful proposal was likely to be made next, gave a calm and silent assent to what Charles said; but the countess herself was restored to courage by the very extremity of her situation. She quitted the arm of the Countess of Crèvecœur, on which she had hitherto leaned, came forward timidly, yet with an air of dignity, and, kneeling before the Duke's throne, thus addressed him: "Noble Duke of Burgundy, and my liege lord, I acknowledge my fault in having withdrawn myself from your dominions without your gracious permission, and will most humbly acquiesce in any penalty you are pleased to impose. I place my lands and castles at your rightful disposal, and pray you only of your own bounty, and for the sake of my father's memory, to allow the last of the line of Croye, out of her large estate, such a moderate maintenance as may find her admission into a convent for the remainder of her life."

"What think you, sire, of the young person's petition to us?" said the Duke, addressing Louis.

"As of a holy and humble motion," said the King, "which doubtless comes from that grace which ought not to be resisted or withstood."

"The humble and lowly shall be exalted," said Charles. "Arise, Countess Isabelle; we mean better for you than you have devised for yourself. We mean neither to sequestrate your estates nor to abase your honours, but, on the contrary, will add largely to both."

"Alas! my lord," said the countess, continuing on her knees, "it is even that well-meant goodness which I fear still more than your Grace's displeasure, since it compels me——"

"St. George of Burgundy!" said Duke Charles, "is our will to be thwarted, and our commands disputed, at every turn? Up, I say, minion, and withdraw for the present; when we have time to think of thee, we will so order matters that, *Teste-St.-Gris!* you shall either obey us or do worse."

Notwithstanding this stern answer, the Countess Isabelle remained at his feet, and would probably, by her pertinacity, have driven him to say upon the spot something yet more severe, had not the Countess of Crèvecœur, who better knew that prince's humour, interfered to raise her young friend, and to conduct her from the hall.

Quentin Durward was now summoned to appear, and presented himself before the King and Duke with that freedom, distant alike from bashful reserve and intrusive boldness, which becomes a youth at once well-born and well-nurtured, who gives honour where it is due, but without permitting himself to be dazzled or confused by the presence of those to whom it is to be rendered. His uncle had furnished him with the means of again equipping himself in the arms and dress of an archer of the Scottish Guard, and his complexion, mien, and air suited in an uncommon degree his splendid appearance. His extreme youth, too, prepossessed the counsellors in his favour, the rather that no one could easily believe that the sagacious Louis would have chosen so very young a person to become the confidant of political intrigues; and thus the King enjoyed, in this as in other cases, considerable advantage from his singular choice of agents, both as to age and rank, where such election seemed least likely to be made. At the command of the Duke, sanctioned by that of Louis, Quentin commenced an account of his journey with the Ladies of Croye to the neighbourhood of Liege, premising a statement of King Louis's instructions, which were that he should escort them safely to the castle of the bishop.

"And you obeyed my orders accordingly?" said the King.

"I did, sire," replied the Scot.

"You omit a circumstance," said the Duke. "You were set upon in the forest by two wandering knights."

"It does not become me to remember or to proclaim such an incident," said the youth, blushing ingenuously.

"But it doth not become *me* to forget it," said the Duke of Orleans. "This youth discharged his commission manfully, and maintained his trust in a manner that I shall long remember. Come to my apartment, archer, when this matter is over, and thou shalt find I have not forgot thy brave bearing, while I am glad to see it is equalled by thy modesty."

"And come to mine," said Dunois. "I have a helmet for thee, since I think I owe thee one."

Quentin bowed low to both, and the examination was resumed. At the command of Duke Charles, he produced the written instructions which he had received for the direction of his journey.

"Did you follow these instructions literally, soldier?" said the Duke.

"No, if it please your Grace," replied Quentin. "They directed me, as you may be pleased to observe, to cross the Maes near Namur; whereas I kept the left bank, as being both the nigher and the safer road to Liege."

"And wherefore that alteration?" said the Duke.

"Because I began to suspect the fidelity of my guide,' answered Quentin.

"Now mark the questions I have next to ask thee," said the Duke. "Reply truly to them, and fear nothing from the resentment of any one. But if you palter or double in your answers, I will have thee hung alive in an iron chain from the steeple of the market-house, where thou shalt wish for death for many an hour ere he come to relieve you!"

There was a deep silence ensued. At length, having given the youth time, as he thought, to consider the circumstances in which he was placed, the Duke demanded to know of Durward who his guide was, by whom supplied, and wherefore he had been led to entertain suspicion of him? To the first of these questions Quentin Durward answered by naming Hayraddin Maugrabin, the Bohemian; to the second, that the guide had been recommended by Tristan l'Hermite; and in reply to the third point, he mentioned what had happened in the Franciscan convent, near Namur; how the Bohemian had been expelled from the holy house, and how, jealous of his behaviour, he had dogged him to a rendezvous with one of William de la Marck's lanzknechts, where he overheard them arrange a plan for surprising the ladies who were under his protection.

"Now, hark thee," said the Duke, "and once more remember thy life depends on thy veracity, did these villains mention their having this king's—I mean this very King Louis of France's—authority for their scheme of surprising the escort and carrying away the ladies?"

"If such infamous fellows had said so," replied Quentin, "I know not how I should have believed them, having the word of the King himself to place in opposition to theirs."

Louis, who had listened hitherto with most earnest attention, could not help drawing his breath deeply when he heard Durward's answer, in the manner of one from whose bosom a heavy weight has been at once removed. The Duke again looked disconcerted and moody; and, returning to the charge, questioned Quentin still more closely, whether he did not understand, from these men's private conversation, that the plots which they meditated had King Louis's sanction?"

"I repeat that I heard nothing which could authorise me to say so," answered the young man, who, though internally convinced of the King's accession to the treachery of Hayraddin, yet held it contrary to his allegiance to bring forward his own suspicions on the subject; "and if I *had* heard such men make such an assertion, I again say that I would not have given their testimony weight against the instructions of the King himself."

"Thou art a faithful messenger," said the Duke, with a sneer; "and I venture to say that, in obeying the King's instructions, thou hast disappointed his expectations in a manner that thou mightst have smarted for, but that subsequent events have made thy bull-headed fidelity seem like good service."

"I understand you not, my lord," said Quentin Durward; "all I know is, that my master King Louis sent me to protect these ladies, and that I did so accordingly, to the extent of my ability, both in the journey to Schonwaldt and through the subsequent scenes which took place. I understood the instructions of the King to be honourable, and I executed them honourably; had they been of a different tenor, they would not have suited one of my name or nation."

"*Fier comme un Ecossois,*" said Charles, who, however disappointed at the tenor of Durward's reply, was not unjust enough to blame him for his boldness. "But hark thee, archer, what instructions were those which made thee, as some sad fugitives from Schonwaldt have informed us, parade the streets of Liege, at the head of those mutineers who afterwards cruelly murdered their temporal prince and spiritual father? And what harangue was it which thou didst make after that murder was committed, in which you took upon you, as agent for Louis, to assume authority among the villains who had just perpetrated so great a crime?"

"My lord," said Quentin, "there are many who could testify that I assumed not the character of an envoy of France in the town of Liege, but had it fixed upon me by the obstinate clamours of the people themselves, who refused to give credit to any disclamation which I could make. This I told to those in the service of the bishop when I had made my escape from the city, and recommended their attention to the security of the castle, which might have prevented the calamity and horror of the succeeding night. It is, no doubt, true that I did, in the extremity of danger, avail myself of the influence which my imputed character gave me, to save the Countess Isabelle, to protect my own life, and, so far as I could, to rein in the humour for slaughter, which had already broke out in so dreadful an instance. I repeat, and will maintain it with my body, that I had no commission of any kind from the King of France respecting the people of Liege, far less instructions to instigate them to mutiny; and that, finally, when I did avail myself of that imputed character, it was as if I had snatched up a shield to protect myself in a moment of emergency, and used it, as I should surely have done, for the defence of myself and others, without inquiring whether I had a right to the heraldic emblazonments which it displayed."

"And therein my young companion and prisoner," said Crèvecœur, unable any longer to remain silent, "acted with equal spirit and good sense; and his doing so cannot justly be imputed as blame to King Louis."

There was a murmur of assent among the surrounding nobility which sounded joyfully in the ears of King Louis, whilst it gave no little offence to Charles. He rolled his eyes angrily around; and the sentiments, so generally expressed by so many of his highest vassals and wisest counsellors, would not perhaps have prevented his giving way to his violent and despotic temper, had not Des Comines, who foresaw the danger, prevented it by suddenly announcing a herald from the city of Liege.

"A herald from weavers and nailers?" exclaimed the Duke, "but admit him instantly. By Our Lady, I will learn from this same herald something further of his employer's hopes and projects than this young French-Scottish man-at-arms seems desirous to tell me!"

CHAPTER XXXIII.

THE HERALD.

Ariel. ———Hark! they roar.
Prospero. Let them be hunted soundly.
The Tempest.

THERE was room made in the assembly, and no small curiosity evinced by those present to see the herald whom the insurgent Liegeois had ventured to send to so haughty a prince as the Duke of Burgundy, while in such high indignation against them. For it must be remembered that at this period heralds were only despatched from the sovereign princes to each other upon solemn occasions; and that the inferior nobility employed pursuivants, a lower rank of officers-at-arms. It may be also noticed in passing, that Louis XI., an habitual derider of whatever did not promise real power or substantial advantage, was in especial a professed contemner of heralds and heraldry, "red, blue, and green, with all their trumpery,"[1] to which the pride of his rival Charles, which was of a very different kind, attached no small degree of ceremonious importance.

The herald, who was now introduced into the presence of the monarchs, was dressed in a tabard, or coat, embroidered with the arms of his master, in which the boar's head made a distinguished appearance, in blazonry which, in the opinion of the skilful, was more showy than accurate. The rest of his dress—a dress always sufficiently tawdry—was overcharged with lace, embroidery, and ornament of every kind; and the plume of feathers which he wore was so high, as if intended to sweep the roof of the hall. In short, the usual gaudy splendour of the heraldic attire was caricatured and overdone. The boar's head was not only repeated on every part of his dress, but even his bonnet was formed into that shape, and it was represented with gory tongue and bloody tusks, or, in proper language, "langued and dentated gules"; and there was some-

For a remarkable instance of this, see Disguised Herald. Note 46.

thing in the man's appearance which seemed to imply a mixture of boldness and apprehension, like one who has undertaken a dangerous commission, and is sensible that audacity alone can carry him through it with safety. Something of the same mixture of fear and effrontery was visible in the manner in which he paid his respects, and he showed also a grotesque awkwardness, not usual amongst those who were accustomed to be received in the presence of princes.

"Who art thou, in the devil's name?" was the greeting with which Charles the Bold received this singular envoy.

"I am Rouge Sanglier," answered the herald, "the officer-at-arms of William de la Marck, by the grace of God and the election of the chapter Prince Bishop of Liege——"

"Ha!" exclaimed Charles; but, as if subduing his own passion, he made a sign to him to proceed.

"And, in right of his wife, the Honourable Countess Hameline of Croye, Count of Croye and Lord of Bracquemont."

The utter astonishment of Duke Charles at the extremity of boldness with which these titles were announced in his presence seemed to strike him dumb; and the herald, conceiving, doubtless, that he had made a suitable impression by the annunciation of his character, proceeded to state his errand.

"*Annuncio vobis gaudium magnum,*" he said; "I let you, Charles of Burgundy and Earl of Flanders, to know, in my master's name, that under favour of a dispensation of our Holy Father of Rome, presently expected, and appointing a fitting substitute *ad sacra*, he proposes to exercise at once the office of Prince Bishop, and maintain the rights of Count of Croye."

The Duke of Burgundy, at this and other pauses in the herald's speech, only ejaculated "Ha!" or some similar interjection, without making any answer; and the tone of exclamation was that of one who, though surprised and moved, is willing to hear all that is to be said ere he commits himself by making an answer. To the further astonishment of all who were present he forbore from his usual abrupt and violent gesticulations, remaining with the nail of his thumb pressed against his teeth, which was his favourite attitude when giving attention, and keeping his eyes bent on the ground as if unwilling to betray the passion which might gleam in them.

The envoy, therefore, proceeded boldly and unabashed in the delivery of his message. "In the name, therefore, of the Prince Bishop of Liege and Count of Croye, I am to require of you, Duke Charles, to desist from those pretensions and encroachments which you have made on the free and imperial city of Liege, by connivance with the late Louis of Bourbon, unworthy bishop thereof."

"Ha!" again exclaimed the Duke.

"Also to restore the banners of the community, which you took violently from the town, to the number of six-and-thirty, to rebuild the breaches in their walls, and restore the fortifications which you tyrannically dismantled, and to acknowledge my master, William de la Marck, as Prince Bishop, lawfully elected in a free chapter of canons, of which behold the *procès-verbal*."

"Have you finished?" said the Duke.

"Not yet," replied the envoy: "I am further to require your Grace, on the part of the said right noble and venerable prince, bishop, and count, that you do presently withdraw the garrison from the Castle of Bracquemont, and other places of strength, belonging to the earldom of Croye, which have been placed there, whether in your own most gracious name, or in that of Isabelle, calling herself Countess of Croye, or any other, until it shall be decided by the Imperial Diet whether the fiefs in question shall not pertain to the sister of the late count, my most gracious Lady Hameline, rather than to his daughter, in respect of the *jus emphyteusis*."

"Your master is most learned," replied the Duke.

"Yet," continued the herald, "the noble and venerable prince and count will be disposed, all other disputes betwixt Burgundy and Liege being settled, to fix upon the Lady Isabelle such an appanage as may become her quality."

"He is generous and considerate," said the Duke, in the same tone.

"Now, by a poor fool's conscience," said Le Glorieux apart

to the Count of Crèvecœur, "I would rather be in the worst cow's hide that ever died of the murrain than in that fellow's painted coat! The poor man goes on like drunkards, who only look to the other pot, and not to the score which mine host chalks up behind the lattice."

"Have you yet done?" said the Duke to the herald.

"One word more," answered Rouge Sanglier, "from my noble and venerable lord aforesaid, respecting his worthy and trusty ally, the Most Christian King——"

"Ha!" exclaimed the Duke, starting, and in a fiercer tone than he had yet used; but checking himself, he instantly composed himself again to attention.

"Which Most Christian King's royal person it is rumoured that you, Charles of Burgundy, have placed under restraint, contrary to your duty as a vassal of the crown of France, and to the faith observed among Christian sovereigns; for which reason, my said noble and venerable master, by my mouth, charges you to put his Royal and Most Christian ally forthwith at freedom, or to receive the defiance which I am authorised to pronounce to you."

"Have you yet done?" said the Duke.

"I have," answered the herald, "and await your Grace's answer, trusting it may be such as will save the effusion of Christian blood."

"Now, by St. George of Burgundy——" said the Duke; but ere he could proceed further, Louis arose, and struck in with a tone of so much dignity and authority that Charles could not interrupt him.

"Under your favour, fair cousin of Burgundy," said the King; "we ourselves crave priority of voice in replying to this insolent fellow. Sirrah herald, or whatever thou art, carry back notice to the perjured outlaw and murderer, William de la Marck, that the King of France will be presently before Liege, for the purpose of punishing the sacrilegious murderer of his late beloved kinsman, Louis of Bourbon; and that he proposes to gibbet De la Marck alive, for the insolence of terming himself his ally, and putting his royal name into the mouth of one of his own base messengers."

"Add whatever else on my part," said Charles, "which it may not misbecome a prince to send to a common thief and murderer. And begone! Yet stay. Never herald went from the court of Burgundy without having cause to cry, 'Largesse!' Let him be scourged till the bones are laid bare!"

"Nay, but if it please your Grace," said Crèvecœur and D'Hymbercourt together, "he is a herald, and so far privileged."

"It is you, messires," replied the Duke, "who are such owls as to think that the tabard makes the herald. I see by that fellow's blazoning he is a mere impostor. Let Toison d'Or step forward, and question him in your presence."

In spite of his natural effrontery, the envoy of the Wild Boar of Ardennes now became pale, and that notwithstanding some touches of paint with which he had adorned his countenance. Toison d'Or, the chief herald, as we have elsewhere said, of the Duke, and king-at-arms within his dominions, stepped forward with the solemnity of one who knew what was due to his office, and asked his supposed brother in what college he had studied the science which he professed.

"I was bred a pursuivant at the Heraldic College of Ratisbon," answered Rouge Sanglier, "and received the diploma of *ehrenhold* from that same learned fraternity."

"You could not derive it from a source more worthy," answered Toison d'Or, bowing still lower than he had done before; "and if I presume to confer with you on the mysteries of our sublime science, in obedience to the orders of the most gracious Duke, it is not in hopes of giving, but of receiving, knowledge."

"Go to," said the Duke, impatiently. "Leave off ceremony, and ask him some question that may try his skill."

"It were injustice to ask a disciple of the worthy College of Arms at Ratisbon if he comprehendeth the common terms of blazonry," said Toison d'Or; "but I may, without offence, crave of Rouge Sanglier to say if he is instructed in the more mysterious and secret terms of the science, by which the more learned do emblematically, and as it were parabolically, express to each other what is conveyed to others in the ordinary language, taught in the very accidence as it were of heradry?"

"I understand one sort of blazonry as well as another," answered Rouge Sanglier, boldly; "but it may be we have not the same terms in Germany which you have here in Flanders."

"Alas, that you will say so!" replied Toison d'Or; "our noble science, which is indeed the very banner of nobleness and glory of generosity, being the same in all Christian countries, nay, known and acknowledged even by the Saracens and Moors. I would, therefore, pray of you to describe what coat you will after the celestial fashion, that is, by the planets."

"Blazon it yourself as you will," said Rouge Sanglier; "I will do no such apish tricks upon commandment, as an ape is made to come aloft."

"Show him a coat, and let him blazon it his own way," said the Duke; "and if he fails, I promise him that his back shall be gules, azure, and sable."

"Here," said the herald of Burgundy, taking from his pouch a piece of parchment, "is a scroll, in which certain considerations led me to prick down, after my own poor fashion, an ancient coat. I will pray my brother, if indeed he belong to the honourable College of Arms at Ratisbon, to decipher it in fitting language."

Le Glorieux, who seemed to take great pleasure in this discussion, had by this time bustled himself close up to the two heralds. "I will help thee, good fellow," said he to Rouge Sanglier, as he looked hopelessly upon the scroll. "This, my lords and masters, represents the cat looking out at the dairy-window."

This sally occasioned a laugh, which was something to the advantage of Rouge Sanglier, as it led Toison d'Or, indignant at the misconstruction of his drawing, to explain it as the coat-of-arms assumed by Childebert, King of France, after he had taken prisoner Gondemar, King of Burgundy; representing an ounce, or tiger-cat, the emblem of the captive prince, behind a grating, or, as Toison d'Or technically defined it, "Sable, a musion passant or, oppressed with a trellis gules, cloué of the second."

"By my bauble," said Le Glorieux, "if the cat resemble Burgundy, she has the right side of the grating nowadays."

"True, good fellow," said Louis, laughing, while the rest of the presence, and even Charles himself, seemed disconcerted at so broad a jest—"I owe thee a piece of gold for turning something that looked like sad earnest into the merry game which I trust it will end in."

"Silence, Le Glorieux," said the Duke; "and you, Toison d'Or, who are too learned to be intelligible, stand back; and bring that rascal forward, some of you. Hark ye, villain," he said, in his harshest tone, "do you know the difference between argent and or, except in the shape of coined money?"

"For pity's sake, your Grace, be good unto me! Noble King Louis, speak for me!"

"Speak for thyself," said the Duke. "In a word, art thou herald or not?"

"Only for this occasion!" acknowledged the detected official.

"Now, by St. George!" said the Duke, eyeing Louis askance, "we know no king—no gentleman—save *one*, who would have so prostituted the noble science on which royalty and gentry rest, save that king, who sent to Edward of England a serving man disguised as a herald." [1]

"Such a stratagem," said Louis, laughing or affecting to laugh, "could only be justified at a court where no heralds were at the time, and when the emergency was urgent. But, though it might have passed on the blunt and thick-witted islander, no one with brains a whit better than those of a wild boar would have thought of passing such a trick upon the accomplished court of Burgundy."

"Send him who will," said the Duke, fiercely, "he shall return on their hands in poor case. Here!—drag him to the market-place—slash him with bridle-reins and dog-whips until the tabard hang about him in tatters! Upon the Rouge Sanglier!—ça, ça! Haloo, haloo!"

Four or five large hounds, such as are painted in the hunting-pieces upon which Rubens and Schneiders laboured in

[1] See Note 46.

conjunction, caught the well-known notes with which the Duke concluded, and began to yell and bay as if the boar were just roused from his lair.

"By the rood!" said King Louis, observant to catch the vein of his dangerous cousin, "since the ass has put on the boar's hide, I would set the dogs on him to bait him out of it!"

"Right—right!" exclaimed Duke Charles, the fancy exactly chiming in with his humour at the moment—"it shall be done! Uncouple the hounds! Hyke a Talbot! hyke a Beaumont! We will course him from the door of the castle to the east gate."

"I trust your Grace will treat me as a beast of chase," said the fellow, putting the best face he could upon the matter, "and allow me fair law?"

"Thou art but vermin," said the Duke, "and entitled to no law, by the letter of the book of hunting; nevertheless thou shalt have sixty yards in advance, were it but for the sake of thy unparalleled impudence. Away—away, sirs! we will see this sport." And the council breaking up tumultuously, all hurried, none faster than the two princes, to enjoy the humane pastime which King Louis had suggested.

The Rouge Sanglier showed excellent sport; for, winged with terror, and having half a score of fierce boar-hounds hard at his haunches, encouraged by the blowing of horns and the woodland cheer of the hunters, he flew like the very wind, and had he not been encumbered with his herald's coat (the worst possible habit for a runner), he might fairly have escaped dog-free; he also doubled once or twice in a manner much approved of by the spectators. None of these, nay, not even Charles himself, was so delighted with the sport as King Louis, who, partly from political considerations, and partly as being naturally pleased with the sight of human suffering when ludicrously exhibited, laughed till the tears ran from his eyes, and in his ecstasies of rapture caught hold of the Duke's ermine cloak, as if to support himself; whilst the Duke, no less delighted, flung his arm around the King's shoulder, making thus an exhibition of confidential sympathy and familiarity very much at variance with the terms on which they had so lately stood together.

At length the speed of the pseudo-herald could save him no longer from the fangs of his pursuers: they seized him, pulled him down, and would probably soon have throttled him, had not the Duke called out—"Stave and tail!—stave and tail! Take them off him! He hath shown so good a course that, though he has made no sport at bay, we will not have him despatched."

Several officers accordingly busied themselves in taking off the dogs; and they were soon seen coupling some up, and pursuing others which ran through the streets, shaking in sport and triumph the tattered fragments of painted cloth and embroidery rent from the tabard, which the unfortunate wearer had put on in an unlucky hour.

At this moment, and while the Duke was too much engaged with what passed before him to mind what was said behind him, Oliver le Dain, gliding behind King Louis, whispered into his ear: "It is the Bohemian, Hayraddin Maugrabin. It were not well he should come to speech of the Duke."

"He must die," answered Louis, in the same tone; "dead men tell no tales."

One instant afterwards, Tristan l'Hermite, to whom Oliver had given the hint, stepped forward before the King and the Duke, and said, in his blunt manner: "So please your Majesty and your Grace, this piece of game is mine, and I claim him; he is marked with my stamp: the *fleur-de-lys* is branded on his shoulder, as all men may see. He is a known villain, and hath slain the King's subjects, robbed churches, deflowered virgins, slain deer in the royal parks——"

"Enough—enough," said Duke Charles; "he is my royal cousin's property by many a good title. What will your Majesty do with him?"

"If he is left to my disposal," said the King, "I will at least give him one lesson in the science of heraldry, in which he is so ignorant—only explain to him practically the meaning of a cross *potence*, with a noose dangling proper."

"Not as to be by him borne, but as to bear him. Let him

take the degree under your gossip Tristan; he is a deep professor in such mysteries."

Thus answered the Duke, with a burst of discordant laughter at his own wit, which was so cordially chorussed by Louis that his rival could not help looking kindly at him, while he said:

"Ah, Louis—Louis! would to God thou wert as faithful a monarch as thou art a merry companion! I cannot but think often on the jovial time we used to spend together."

"You may bring it back when you will," said Louis: "I will grant you as fair terms as for very shame's sake you ought to ask in my present condition, without making yourself the fable of Christendom; and I will swear to observe them upon the holy relique which I have ever the grace to bear about my person, being a fragment of the true cross."

Here he took a small golden reliquary, which was suspended from his neck next to his shirt by a chain of the same metal, and having kissed it devoutly, continued:

"Never was false oath sworn on this most sacred relique but it was avenged within the year."

"Yet," said the Duke, "it was the same on which you swore amity to me when you left Burgundy, and shortly after sent the Bastard of Rubempré to murder or kidnap me."

"Nay, gracious cousin, now you are ripping up ancient grievances," said the King; "I promise you that you were deceived in that matter. Moreover, it was not upon *this* relique which I then swore, but upon another fragment of the true cross which I got from the Grand Seignior, weakened in virtue, doubtless, by sojourning with infidels. Besides, did not the war of the 'public good' break out within the year; and was not a Burgundian army encamped at St. Denis, backed by all the great feudatories of France; and was I not obliged to yield up Normandy to my brother? O God, shield us from perjury on such a warrant as this!"

"Well, cousin," answered the Duke, "I do believe thou hadst a lesson to keep faith another time. And now for once, without finesse and doubling, will you make good your promise, and go with me to punish this murdering La Marck and the Liegeois?"

"I will march against them," said Louis, "with the ban and arrière-ban of France, and the oriflamme displayed."

"Nay—nay," said the Duke, "that is more than is needful, or maybe advisable. The presence of your Scottish Guard and two hundred choice lances will serve to show that you are a free agent. A large army might——"

"Make me so in effect, you would say, my fair cousin?" said the King. "Well, you shall dictate the numbers of my attendants."

"And to put this fair cause of mischief out of the way, you will agree to the Countess Isabelle of Croye wedding with the Duke of Orleans?"

"Fair cousin," said the King, "you drive my courtesy to extremity. The duke is the betrothed bridegroom of my daughter Joan. Be generous—yield up this matter, and let us speak rather of the towns on the Somme."

"My council will talk to your Majesty of these," said Charles; "I myself have less at heart the acquisition of territory than the redress of injuries. You have tampered with my vassals, and your royal pleasure must needs dispose of the hand of a ward of Burgundy. Your Majesty must bestow it within the pale of your own royal family, since you have meddled with it; otherwise, our conference breaks off."

"Were I to say I did this willingly," said the King, "no one would believe me; therefore do you, my fair cousin, judge of the extent of my wish to oblige you when I say, most reluctantly, that the parties consenting, and a dispensation from the Pope being obtained, my own objections shall be no bar to this match which you propose."

"All besides can be easily settled by our ministers," said the Duke, "and we are once more cousins and friends."

"May Heaven be praised!" said Louis, "who, holding in His hand the hearts of princes, doth mercifully incline them to peace and clemency, and prevent the effusion of human blood. Oliver," he added apart to that favourite, who ever waited around him like the familiar beside a sorcerer, "hark thee—tell Tristan to be speedy in dealing with yonder runagate Bohemian."

CHAPTER XXXIV.

THE EXECUTION.

I'll take thee to the good green wood,
And make thine own hand choose the tree.
Old Ballad.

"Now God be praised that gave us the power of laughing and making others laugh, and shame to the dull cur who scorns the office of a jester! Here is a joke, and that none of the brightest, though it may pass, since it has amused two princes, which hath gone farther than a thousand reasons of state to prevent a war between France and Burgundy."

Such was the inference of Le Glorieux when, in consequence of the reconciliation of which we gave the particulars in the last chapter, the Burgundian guards were withdrawn from the Castle of Péronne, the abode of the King removed from the ominous Tower of Count Herbert, and, to the great joy both of French and Burgundians, an outward show at least of confidence and friendship seemed so established between Duke Charles and his liege lord. Yet still the latter, though treated with ceremonial observance, was sufficiently aware that he continued to be the object of suspicion, though he prudently affected to overlook it, and appeared to consider himself as entirely at his ease.

Meanwhile, as frequently happens in such cases, whilst the principal parties concerned had so far made up their differences, one of the subaltern agents concerned in their intrigues was bitterly experiencing the truth of the political maxim, that if the great have frequent need of base tools, they make amends to society by abandoning them to their fate so soon as they find them no longer useful.

This was Hayraddin Maugrabin, who, surrendered by the

Duke's officers to the King's provost-marshal, was by him placed in the hands of his two trusty aides-de-camp, Trois-Eschelles and Petit-André, to be despatched without loss of time. One on either side of him, and followed by a few guards and a multitude of rabble—this playing the *allegro*, that the *penseroso*—he was marched off (to use a modern comparison, like Garrick between Tragedy and Comedy) to the neighbouring forest.; where, to save all further trouble and ceremonial of a gibbet and so forth, the disposers of his fate proposed to knit him up to the first sufficient tree.

They were not long in finding an oak, as Petit-André facetiously expressed it, fit to bear such an acorn; and placing the wretched criminal on a bank, under a sufficient guard, they began their extemporaneous preparations for the final catastrophe. At that moment Hayraddin, gazing on the crowd, encountered the eyes of Quentin Durward, who, thinking he recognised the countenance of his faithless guide in that of the detected impostor, had followed with the crowd to witness the execution, and assure himself of the identity.

When the executioners informed him that all was ready, Hayraddin, with much calmness, asked a single boon at their hands.

"Anything, my son, consistent with our office," said Trois-Eschelles.

"That is," said Hayraddin, "anything but my life."

"Even so," said Trois-Eschelles, "and something more; for as you seem resolved to do credit to our mystery, and die like a man, without making wry mouths—why, though our orders are to be prompt, I care not if I indulge you ten minutes longer."

"You are even too generous," said Hayraddin.

"Truly we may be blamed for it," said Petit-André; "but what of that? I could consent almost to give my life for such a jerry-come-tumble, such a smart, tight, firm lad, who proposes to come from aloft with a grace, as an honest fellow should do."

"So that if you want a confessor," said Trois-Eschelles——

"Or a *lire* of wine," said his facetious companion——

"Or a psalm," said Tragedy——

"Or a song," said Comedy——

"Neither, my good, kind, and most expeditious friends," said the Bohemian; "I only pray to speak a few minutes with yonder archer of the Scottish Guard."

The executioners hesitated a moment; but Trois-Eschelles recollecting that Quentin Durward was believed, from various circumstances, to stand high in the favour of their master, King Louis, they resolved to permit the interview.

When Quentin, at their summons, approached the condemned criminal, he could not but be shocked at his appearance, however justly his doom might have been deserved. The remnants of his heraldic finery, rent to tatters by the fangs of the dogs, and the clutches of the bipeds who had rescued him from their fury to lead him to the gallows, gave him at once a ludicrous and a wretched appearance. His face was discoloured with paint, and with some remnants of a fictitious beard, assumed for the purpose of disguise, and there was the paleness of death upon his cheek and upon his lip; yet, strong in passive courage, like most of his tribe, his eye, while it glistened and wandered, as well as the contorted smile of his mouth, seemed to bid defiance to the death he was about to die.

Quentin was struck partly with horror, partly with compassion, as he approached the miserable man, and these feelings probably betrayed themselves in his manner, for Petit-André called out: "Trip it more smartly, jolly archer; this gentleman's leisure cannot wait for you, if you walk as if the pebbles were eggs, and you afraid of breaking them."

"I must speak with him in privacy," said the criminal, despair seeming to croak in his accent as he uttered the words.

"That may hardly consist with our office, my merry leap-the-ladder," said Petit-André; "we know you for a slippery eel of old."

"I am tied with your horse-girths, hand and foot," said the criminal. "You may keep guard around me, though out of earshot; the archer is your own King's servant. And if I give you ten guilders——"

"Laid out in masses, the sum may profit his poor soul," said Trois-Eschelles.

"Laid out in wine or *brantwein*, it will comfort my poor body," responded Petit-André. "So let them be forthcoming, my little crack-rope."

"Pay the blood-hounds their fee," said Hayraddin to Durward; "I was plundered of every stiver when they took me; it shall avail thee much."

Quentin paid the executioners their guerdon, and, like men of promise, they retreated out of hearing—keeping, however, a careful eye on the criminal's motions. After waiting an instant till the unhappy man should speak, as he still remained silent, Quentin at length addressed him: "And to this conclusion thou hast at length arrived?"

"Ay," answered Hayraddin, "it required neither astrologer, nor physiognomist, nor chiromantist, to foretell that I should follow the destiny of my family."

"Brought to this early end by thy long course of crime and treachery!" said the Scot.

"No, by the bright Aldebaran and all his brother twinklers!" answered the Bohemian. "I am brought hither by my folly, in believing that the bloodthirsty cruelty of a Frank could be restrained even by what they themselves profess to hold most sacred. A priest's vestment would have been no safer garb for me than a herald's tabard, however sanctimonious are your professions of devotion and chivalry."

"A detected impostor has no right to claim the immunities of the disguise he had usurped," said Durward.

"Detected!" said the Bohemian. "My jargon was as much to the purpose as yonder old fool of a herald's; but let it pass. As well now as hereafter."

"You abuse time," said Quentin. "If you have aught to tell me, say it quickly, and then take some care of your soul."

"Of my soul!" said the Bohemian, with a hideous laugh. "Think ye a leprosy of twenty years can be cured in an instant? If I have a soul, it hath been in such a course since I was ten years old and more, that it would take me one month to recall all my crimes and another to tell them to the priest;

and were such space granted me, it is five to one I would employ it otherwise."

"Hardened wretch, blaspheme not! Tell me what thou hast to say, and I leave thee to thy fate," said Durward, with mingled pity and horror.

"I have a boon to ask," said Hayraddin, "but first I will buy it of you; for your tribe, with all their professions of charity, give nought for nought."

"I could wellnigh say 'Thy gifts perish with thee,'" answered Quentin, "but that thou art on the very verge of eternity. Ask thy boon; reserve thy bounty, it can do me no good. I remember enough of your good offices of old."

"Why, I loved you," said Hayraddin, "for the matter that chanced on the banks of the Cher; and I would have helped you to a wealthy dame. You wore her scarf, which partly misled me; and indeed I thought that Hameline, with her portable wealth, was more for your market-penny than the other hen-sparrow, with her old roost at Bracquemont, which Charles has clutched, and is likely to keep his claws upon."

"Talk not so idly, unhappy man," said Quentin; "yonder officers become impatient."

"Give them ten guilders for ten minutes more," said the culprit, who, like most in his situation, mixed with his hardihood a desire of procrastinating his fate; "I tell thee it shall avail thee much."

"Use then well the minutes so purchased," said Durward, and easily made a new bargain with the marshals-men.

This done, Hayraddin continued: "Yes, I assure you I meant you well; and Hameline would have proved an easy and convenient spouse. Why, she has reconciled herself even with the Boar of Ardennes, though his mode of wooing was somewhat of the roughest, and lords it yonder in his sty, as if she had fed on mast-husks and acorns all her life."

"Cease this brutal and untimely jesting," said Quentin, "or, once more I tell you, I will leave you to your fate."

"You are right," said Hayraddin, after a moment's pause; "what cannot be postponed must be faced! Well, know then, I came hither in this accursed disguise, moved by a great reward from De la Marck, and hoping a yet mightier one from King Louis, not merely to bear the message of defiance which you may have heard of, but to tell the King an important secret."

"It was a fearful risk," said Durward.

"It was paid for as such, and such it hath proved," answered the Bohemian. "De la Marck attempted before to communicate with Louis by means of Marthon; but she could not, it seems, approach nearer to him than the astrologer, to whom she told all the passages of the journey, and of Schonwaldt; but it is a chance if her tidings ever reach Louis, except in the shape of a prophecy. But hear my secret, which is more important than aught she could tell. William de la Marck has assembled a numerous and strong force within the city of Liege, and augments it daily by means of the old priest's treasures. But he proposes not to hazard a battle with the chivalry of Burgundy, and still less to stand a siege in the dismantled town. This he will do; he will suffer the hot-brained Charles to sit down before the place without opposition, and in the night, make an outfall or sally upon the leaguer with his whole force. Many he will have in French armour, who will cry 'France,' 'St. Louis,' and 'Denis Montjoye,' as if there were a strong body of French auxiliaries in the city. This cannot choose but strike utter confusion among the Burgundians; and if King Louis, with his guards, attendants, and such soldiers as he may have with him, shall second his efforts, the Boar of Ardennes nothing doubts the discomfiture of the whole Burgundian army. There is my secret, and I bequeath it to you. Forward, or prevent the enterprise— sell the intelligence to King Louis or to Duke Charles, I care not. Save or destroy whom thou wilt; for my part, I only grieve that I cannot spring it like a mine, to the destruction of them all!"

"It is indeed an important secret," said Quentin, instantly comprehending how easily the national jealousy might be awakened in a camp consisting partly of French, partly of Burgundians.

"Ay, so it is," answered Hayraddin; "and, now you have

it, you would fain begone, and leave me without granting the boon for which I have paid beforehand."

"Tell me thy request," said Quentin; "I will grant it if it be in my power."

"Nay, it is no mighty demand: it is only in behalf of poor Klepper, my palfrey, the only living thing that may miss me. A due mile south you will find him feeding by a deserted collier's hut; whistle to him thus (he whistled a peculiar note), and call him by his name, Klepper, he will come to you; here is his bridle under my gaberdine—it is lucky the hounds got it not, for he obeys no other. Take him, and make much of him, I do not say for his master's sake, but because I have placed at your disposal the event of a mighty war. He will never fail you at need; night and day, rough and smooth, fair and foul, warm stables and the winter sky, are the same to Klepper; had I cleared the gates of Péronne, and got so far as where I left him, I had not been in this case. Will you be kind to Klepper?"

"I swear to you that I will," answered Quentin, affected by what seemed a trait of tenderness in a character so hardened.

"Then fare thee well!" said the criminal. "Yet stay— stay; I would not willingly die in discourtesy, forgetting a lady's commission. This billet is from the very gracious and extremely silly Lady of the Wild Boar of Ardennes to her black-eyed niece—I see by your look I have chosen a willing messenger. And one word more—I forgot to say, that in the stuffing of my saddle you will find a rich purse of gold pieces, for the sake of which I put my life on the venture which has cost me so dear. Take them, and replace a hundredfold the guilders you have bestowed on these bloody slaves. I make you mine heir."

"I will bestow them in good works, and masses for the benefit of thy soul," said Quentin.

"Name not that word again," said Hayraddin, his countenance assuming a dreadful expression; "there is—there can be—there shall be—no such thing! it is a dream of priestcraft!"

"Unhappy—most unhappy being! Think better! Let me

speed for a priest; these men will delay yet a little longer, I will bribe them to it," said Quentin. "What canst thou expect, dying in such opinions, and impenitent?"

"To be resolved into the elements," said the hardened atheist, pressing his fettered arms against his bosom; my hope, trust, and expectation is, that the mysterious frame of humanity shall melt into the general mass of nature, to be recompounded in the other forms with which she daily supplies those which daily disappear, and return under different forms—the watery particles to streams and showers, the earthly parts to enrich their mother earth, the airy portions to wanton in the breeze, and those of fire to supply the blaze of Aldebaran and his brethren. In this faith have I lived, and I will die in it! Hence! begone! disturb me no farther! I have spoken the last word that mortal ears shall listen to!"

Deeply impressed with the horrors of his condition, Quentin Durward yet saw that it was vain to hope to awaken him to a sense of his fearful state. He bid him, therefore, farewell; to which the criminal only replied by a short and sullen nod, as one who, plunged in reverie, bids adieu to company which distracts his thoughts. He bent his course towards the forest, and easily found where Klepper was feeding. The creature came at his call, but was for some time unwilling to be caught, snuffling and starting when the stranger approached him. At length, however, Quentin's general acquaintance with the habits of the animal, and perhaps some particular knowledge of those of Klepper, which he had often admired while Hayraddin and he travelled together, enabled him to take possession of the Bohemian's dying bequest. Long ere he returned to Péronne, the Bohemian had gone where the vanity of his dreadful creed was to be put to the final issue—a fearful experience for one who had neither expressed remorse for the past nor apprehension for the future!

CHAPTER XXXV.

A PRIZE FOR HONOUR.

'Tis brave for beauty when the best blade wins her.
The Count Palatine.

WHEN Quentin Durward reached Péronne, a council was sitting, in the issue of which he was interested more deeply than he could have apprehended, and which, though held by persons of a rank with whom one of his could scarce be supposed to have community of interest, had nevertheless the most extraordinary influence on his fortunes.

King Louis, who, after the interlude of De la Marck's envoy, had omitted no opportunity to cultivate the returning interest which that circumstance had given him in the Duke's opinion, had been engaged in consulting him, or, it might be almost said, receiving his opinion, upon the number and quality of the troops, by whom, as auxiliary to the Duke of Burgundy, he was to be attended in their joint expedition against Liege. He plainly saw the wish of Charles was to call into his camp such Frenchmen as, from their small number and high quality, might be considered rather as hostages than as auxiliaries; but, observant of Crèvecœur's [Des Comines'] advice, he assented as readily to whatever the Duke proposed as if it had arisen from the free impulse of his own mind.

The King failed not, however, to indemnify himself for his complaisance by the indulgence of his vindictive temper against Balue, whose counsels had led him to repose such exuberant trust in the Duke of Burgundy. Tristan, who bore the summons for moving up his auxiliary forces, had the farther commission to carry the cardinal to the Castle of Loches, and there shut him up in one of those iron cages which he himself is said to have invented.

"Let him make proof of his own devices," said the King; "he is a man of holy church—we may not shed his blood; but, *Pasques-dieu!* his bishopric, for ten years to come, shall have an impregnable frontier to make up for its small extent! And see the troops are brought up instantly."

Perhaps, by this prompt acquiescence, Louis hoped to evade the more unpleasing condition with which the Duke had clogged their reconciliation. But if he so hoped, he greatly mistook the temper of his cousin; for never man lived more tenacious of his purpose than Charles of Burgundy, and least of all was he willing to relax any stipulation which he had made in resentment, or revenge, of a supposed injury.

No sooner were the necessary expresses despatched to summon up the forces who were selected to act as auxiliaries than Louis was called upon by his host to give public consent to the espousals of the Duke of Orleans and Isabelle of Croye. The King complied with a heavy sigh, and presently after urged a slight expostulation, founded upon the necessity of observing the wishes of the duke himself.

"These have not been neglected," said the Duke of Burgundy: "Crèvecœur hath communicated with Monsieur d'Orleans, and finds him—strange to say—so dead to the honour of wedding a royal bride, that he acceded to the proposal of marrying the Countess of Croye as the kindest proposal which father could have made to him."

"He is the more ungracious and thankless," said Louis; "but the whole shall be as you, my cousin, will, if you can bring it about with consent of the parties themselves."

"Fear not that," said the Duke; and accordingly, not many minutes after the affair had been proposed the Duke of Orleans and the Countess of Croye, the latter attended, as on the preceding occasion, by the Countess of Crèvecœur and the abbess of the Ursulines, were summoned to the presence of the princes, and heard from the mouth of Charles of Burgundy, unobjected to by that of Louis, who sat in silent and moody consciousness of diminished consequence, that the union of their hands was designed by the wisdom of both princes, to confirm the perpetual alliance which in future should take place betwixt France and Burgundy.

The Duke of Orleans had much difficulty in suppressing the joy which he felt upon the proposal, and which delicacy rendered improper in the presence of Louis; and it required his habitual awe of that monarch to enable him to rein in his delight, so much as merely to reply, "that his duty compelled him to place his choice at the disposal of his sovereign."

"Fair cousin of Orleans," said Louis, with sullen gravity, "since I must speak on so unpleasant an occasion, it is needless for me to remind you that my sense of your merits had led me to propose for you a match into my family. But, since my cousin of Burgundy thinks that the disposing of your hand otherwise is the surest pledge of amity between his dominions and mine, I love both too well not to sacrifice to them my own hopes and wishes."

The Duke of Orleans threw himself on his knees, and kissed, —and, for once, with sincerity of attachment,—the hand which the King, with averted countenance, extended to him. In fact he, as well as most present, saw, in the unwilling acquiescence of this accomplished dissembler, who, even with that very purpose, had suffered his reluctance to be visible, a king relinquishing his favourite project, and subjugating his paternal feelings to the necessities of state and interest of his country. Even Burgundy was moved, and Orleans' heart smote him for the joy which he involuntarily felt on being freed from his engagement with the Princess Joan. If he had known how deeply the King was cursing him in his soul, and what thoughts of future revenge he was agitating, it is probable his own delicacy on the occasion would not have been so much hurt.

Charles next turned to the young countess, and bluntly announced the proposed match to her, as a matter which neither admitted delay nor hesitation; adding, at the same time, that it was but a too favourable consequence of her intractability on a former occasion.

"My Lord Duke and Sovereign," said Isabelle, summoning up all her courage, "I observe your Grace's commands, and submit to them."

"Enough, enough," said the Duke, interrupting her, "we will arrange the rest. Your Majesty," he continued, addresssing Louis, "hath had a boar's hunt in the morning; what say you to rousing a wolf in the afternoon?"

The young countess saw the necessity of decision. "Your Grace mistakes my meaning," she said, speaking, though timidly, yet loudly and decidedly enough to compel the Duke's attention, which, from some consciousness, he would otherwise have willingly denied to her. "My submission," she said, "only respected those lands and estates which your Grace's ancestors gave to mine, and which I resign to the house of Burgundy if my sovereign thinks my disobedience in this matter renders me unworthy to hold them."

"Ha! St. George!" said the Duke, stamping furiously on the ground, "does the fool know in what presence she is, and to whom she speaks?"

"My lord," she replied, still undismayed, "I am before my suzerain, and, I trust, a just one. If you deprive me of my lands, you take away all that your ancestors' generosity gave, and you break the only bonds which attach us together. You gave not this poor and persecuted form, still less the spirit which animates me. And these it is my purpose to dedicate to Heaven in the convent of the Ursulines, under the guidance of this holy mother abbess."

The rage and astonishment of the Duke can hardly be conceived, unless we could estimate the surprise of a falcon against whom a dove should ruffle its pinions in defiance. "Will the holy mother receive you without an appanage?" he said, in a voice of scorn.

"If she doth her convent, in the first instance, so much wrong," said the Lady Isabelle, "I trust there is charity enough among the noble friends of my house to make up some support for the orphan of Croye."

"It is false!" said the Duke; "it is a base pretext to cover some secret and unworthy passion. My Lord of Orleans, she shall be yours, if I drag her to the altar with my own hands!"

The Countess of Crèvecœur, a high-spirited woman, and confident in her husband's merits and his favour with the Duke, could keep silent no longer. "My lord," she said, "your passions transport you into language utterly unworthy. The hand of no gentlewoman can be disposed of by force."

"And it is no part of the duty of a Christian prince," added the abbess, "to thwart the wishes of a pious soul, who, broken with the cares and persecutions of the world, is desirous to become the bride of Heaven."

"Neither can my cousin of Orleans," said Dunois, "with honour accept a proposal to which the lady has thus publicly stated her objections."

"If I were permitted," said Orleans, on whose facile mind Isabelle's beauty had made a deep impression, "some time to endeavour to place my pretensions before the countess in a more favourable light——"

"My lord," said Isabelle, whose firmness was now fully supported by the encouragement which she received from all around, "it were to no purpose: my mind is made up to decline this alliance, though far above my deserts."

"Nor have I time," said the Duke, "to wait till these whimsies are changed with the next change of the moon. Monseigneur d'Orleans, she shall learn within this hour that obedience becomes matter of necessity."

"Not in my behalf, sire," answered the prince, who felt that he could not, with any show of honour, avail himself of the Duke's obstinate disposition; "to have been once openly and positively refused is enough for a son of France. He cannot prosecute his addresses farther."

The Duke darted one furious glance at Orleans, another at Louis; and reading in the countenance of the latter, in spite of his utmost efforts to suppress his feelings, a look of secret triumph, he became outrageous.

"Write," he said to the secretary, "our doom of forfeiture and imprisonment against this disobedient and insolent minion. She shall to the *zuchthaus*, to the penitentiary, to herd with those whose lives have rendered them her rivals in effrontery!"

There was a general murmur.

"My lord Duke," said the Count of Crèvecœur, taking the word for the rest, "this must be better thought on. We, your faithful vassals, cannot suffer such a dishonour to the nobility and chivalry of Burgundy. If the countess hath done amiss, let her be punished, but in the manner that becomes her rank and ours, who stand connected with her house by blood and alliance."

The Duke paused a moment, and looked full at his counsellor with the stare of a bull which, when compelled by the neatherd from the road which he wishes to go, deliberates with himself whether to obey or to rush on his driver and toss him into the air.

Prudence, however, prevailed over fury; he saw the sentiment was general in his council, was afraid of the advantages which Louis might derive from seeing dissension among his vassals; and probably, for he was rather of a coarse and violent than of a malignant temper, felt ashamed of his own dishonourable proposal.

"You are right," he said, "Crèvecœur, and I spoke hastily. Her fate shall be determined according to the rules of chivalry. Her flight to Liege hath given the signal for the bishop's murder. He that best avenges that deed, and brings us the head of the Wild Boar of Ardennes, shall claim her hand of us; and if she denies his right, we can at least grant him her fiefs, leaving it to his generosity to allow her what means he will to retire into a convent."

"Nay!" said the countess, "think I am the daughter of Count Reinold—of your father's old, valiant, and faithful servant. Would you hold me out as a prize to the best sword-player?"

"Your ancestress," said the Duke, "was won at a tourney; you shall be fought for in real *mêlée*. Only thus far, for Count Reinold's sake, the successful prizer shall be a gentleman, of unimpeached birth and unstained bearings; but, be he such, and the poorest who ever drew the strap of a sword-belt through the tongue of a buckle, he shall have at least the proffer of your hand. I swear it, by St. George, by my ducal crown, and by the order that I wear! Ha! messires," he added, turning to the nobles present, "this is at least, I think, in conformity with the rules of chivalry?"

Isabelle's remonstrances were drowned in a general and

jubilant assent, above which was heard the voice of old Lord Crawford, regretting the weight of years that prevented his striking for so fair a prize. The Duke was gratified by the general applause, and his temper began to flow more smoothly, like that of a swollen river when it hath subsided within its natural boundaries.

"Are we, to whom fate has given dames already," said Crèvecœur, "to be bystanders at this fair game? It does not consist with my honour to be so, for I have myself a vow to be paid at the expense of that tusked and bristled brute, De la Marck."

"Strike boldly in, Crèvecœur," said the Duke; "win her, and since thou canst not wear her thyself, bestow her where thou wilt—on Count Stephen, your nephew, if you list."

"Gramercy, my lord!" said Crèvecœur, "I will do my best in the battle; and, should I be fortunate enough to be foremost, Stephen shall try his eloquence against that of the lady abbess."

"I trust," said Dunois, "that the chivalry of France are not excluded from this fair contest?"

"Heaven forbid! brave Dunois," answered the Duke, "were it but for the sake of seeing you do your uttermost. But," he added, "though there be no fault in the Lady Isabelle wedding a Frenchman, it will be necessary that the Count of Croye must become a subject of Burgundy."

"Enough, enough," said Dunois, "my bar sinister may never be surmounted by the coronet of Croye: I will live and die French. But yet, though I should lose the lands, I will strike a blow for the lady."

Le Balafré dared not speak aloud in such a presence, but he muttered to himself: "Now, Saunders Souplejaw, hold thine own! Thou always saidst the fortune of our house was to be won by marriage, and never had you such a chance to keep your word with us."

"No one thinks of me," said Le Glorieux, "who am sure to carry off the prize from all of you."

"Right, my sapient friend," said Louis; "when a woman is in the case, the greatest fool is ever the first in favour."

While the princes and their nobles thus jested over her fate, the abbess and the Countess of Crèvecœur endeavoured in vain to console Isabelle, who had withdrawn with them from the council-presence. The former assured her, that the Holy Virgin would frown on every attempt to withdraw a true votaress from the shrine of Saint Ursula; while the Countess of Crèvecœur whispered more temporal consolation, that no true knight, who might succeed in the emprize proposed, would avail himself, against her inclinations, of the Duke's award; and that perhaps the successful competitor might prove one who should find such favour in her eyes as to reconcile her to obedience. Love, like despair, catches at straws; and, faint and vague as was the hope which this insinuation conveyed, the tears of the Countess Isabelle flowed more placidly while she dwelt upon it.[1]

CHAPTER XXXVI.

THE SALLY.

> The wretch condemn'd with life to part
>   Still, still on hope relies,
> And every pang that rends the heart
>   Bids expectation rise.
>
> Hope, like the glimmering taper's light,
>   Adorns and cheers the way,
> And still the darker grows the night,
>   Emits a brighter ray.
>
> GOLDSMITH.

FEW days had passed ere Louis had received, with a smile of gratified vengeance, the intelligence that his favourite and his counsellor, the Cardinal Balue, was groaning within a cage of iron, so disposed as scarce to permit him to enjoy repose in any posture except when recumbent; and of which, be it said in passing, he remained the unpitied tenant for nearly twelve years. The auxiliary forces which the Duke had required Louis to bring up had also appeared; and he comforted himself that their numbers were sufficient to protect his person

[1] See Prize of Honour. Note 47.

against violence, although too limited to cope, had such been his purpose, with the large army of Burgundy. He saw himself also at liberty, when time should suit, to resume his project of marriage between his daughter and the Duke of Orleans; and, although he was sensible to the indignity of serving with his noblest peers under the banners of his own vassal, and against the people whose cause he had abetted, he did not allow these circumstances to embarrass him in the mean time, trusting that a future day would bring him amends. "For chance," said he to his trusty Oliver, "may indeed gain one hit, but it is patience and wisdom which win the game at last."

With such sentiments, upon a beautiful day in the latter end of harvest, the King mounted his horse; and indifferent that he was looked upon rather as a part of the pageant of a victor than in the light of an independent sovereign surrounded by his guards and his chivalry, King Louis sallied from under the Gothic gateway of Péronne to join the Burgundian army, which commenced at the same time its march against Liege.

Most of the ladies of distinction who were in the place attended, dressed in their best array, upon the battlements and defences of the gate, to see the gallant show of the warriors setting forth on the expedition. Thither had the Countess Crèvecœur brought the Countess Isabelle. The latter attended very reluctantly; but the peremptory order of Charles had been, that she who was to bestow the palm in the tourney, should be visible to the knights who were about to enter the lists.

As they thronged out from under the arch, many a pennon and shield was to be seen, graced with fresh devices, expressive of the bearer's devoted resolution to become a competitor for a prize so fair. Here a charger was painted starting for the goal, there an arrow aimed at a mark; one knight bore a bleeding heart, indicative of his passion, another a skull and a coronet of laurels, showing his determination to win or die. Many others there were; and some so cunningly intricate and obscure, that they might have defied the most ingenious interpreter. Each knight, too, it may be presumed, put his courser to his mettle, and assumed his most gallant seat in the saddle, as he passed for a moment under the view of the fair bevy of dames and damsels, who encouraged their valour by their smiles, and the waving of kerchiefs and of veils. The Archer Guard, selected almost at will from the flower of the Scottish nation, drew general applause, from the gallantry and splendour of their appearance.

And there was one among these strangers who ventured on a demonstration of acquaintance with the Lady Isabelle which had not been attempted even by the most noble of the French nobility. It was Quentin Durward, who, as he passed the ladies in his rank, presented to the Countess of Croye, on the point of his lance, the letter of her aunt.

"Now, by my honour," said the Count of Crèvecœur, "that is over insolent in an unworthy adventurer!"

"Do not call him so, Crèvecœur," said Dunois; "I have good reason to bear testimony to his gallantry, and in behalf of that lady, too."

"You make words of nothing," said Isabelle, blushing with shame, and partly with resentment; "it is a letter from my unfortunate aunt: she writes cheerfully, though her situation must be dreadful."

"Let us hear—let us hear what says the Boar's bride," said Crèvecœur.

The Countess Isabelle read the letter, in which her aunt seemed determined to make the best of a bad bargain, and to console herself for the haste and indecorum of her nuptials by the happiness of being wedded to one of the bravest men of the age, who had just acquired a princedom by his valour. She implored her niece not to judge of her William, as she called him, by the report of others, but to wait till she knew him personally. He had his faults, perhaps, but they were such as belonged to characters whom she had ever venerated. William was rather addicted to wine, but so was the gallant Sir Godfrey, her grandsire; he was something hasty and sanguinary in his temper, such had been her brother, Reinold of blessed memory; he was blunt in speech, few Germans were otherwise; and a little wilful and peremptory, but she believed all men loved to rule. More there was to the same purpose; and the whole concluded with the hope and request that Isabelle would, by means of the bearer, endeavour her escape from the tyrant of Burgundy, and come to her loving kinswoman's court of Liege,, where any little differences concerning their mutual rights of succession to the earldom might be adjusted by Isabelle's marrying Carl Eberson—a bridegroom younger indeed than his bride, but that, as she (the Lady Hameline) might perhaps say from experience, was an inequality more easy to be endured than Isabelle could be aware of.[1]

Here the Countess Isabelle stopped; the abbess observing, with a prim aspect, that she had read quite enough concerning such worldly vanities, and the Count of Crèvecœur breaking out: "Aroint thee, deceitful witch! Why, this device smells rank as the toasted cheese in a rat-trap. Now fie, and double fie, upon the old decoy-duck!"

The Countess of Crèvecœur gravely rebuked her husband for his violence. "The Lady Hameline," she said, "must have been deceived by De la Marck with a show of courtesy."

"He show courtesy!" said the count; "I acquit him of all such dissimulation. You may as well expect courtesy from a literal wild boar; you may as well try to lay leaf-gold on old rusty gibbet-irons. No—idiot as she is, she is not quite goose enough to fall in love with the fox who has snapped her, and that in his very den. But you women are all alike—fair words carry it; and, I dare say, here is my pretty cousin impatient to join her aunt in this fool's paradise, and marry the Boar-Pig."

"So far from being capable of such folly," said Isabelle, "I am doubly desirous of vengeance on the murderers of the excellent bishop, because it will, at the same time, free my aunt from the villain's power."

"Ah! there indeed spoke the voice of Croye!" exclaimed the count; and no more was said concerning the letter.

But while Isabelle read her aunt's epistle to her friends, it must be observed that she did not think it necessary to recite

[1] See Bride of De la Marck. Note 48.

a certain *postscript*, in which the Countess Hameline, ladylike, gave an account of her occupations, and informed her niece that she had laid aside for the present a surcoat which she was working for her husband, bearing the arms of Croye and La Marck in conjugal fashion, parted per pale, because her William had determined, for purposes of policy, in the first action to have others dressed in his coat-armour, and himself to assume the arms of Orleans, with a bar sinister— in other words, those of Dunois. There was also a slip of paper in another hand, the content of which the countess did not think it necessary to mention, being simply these words: "If you hear not of me soon, and that by the trumpet of Fame, conclude me dead, but not unworthy."

A thought, thither repelled as wildly incredible, now glanced with double keenness through Isabelle's soul. As female wit seldom fails in the contrivance of means, she so ordered it, that ere the troops were fully on march, Quentin Durward received from an unknown hand the billet of Lady Hameline, marked with three crosses opposite to the postscript, and having these words subjoined: "He who feared not the arms of Orleans when on the breast of their gallant owner cannot dread them when displayed on that of a tyrant and murderer." A thousand thousand times was this intimation kissed and pressed to the bosom of the young Scot! for it marshalled him on the path where both honour and love held out the reward, and possessed him with a secret unknown to others, by which to distinguish him whose death could alone give life to his hopes, and which he prudently resolved to lock up in his own bosom.

But Durward saw the necessity of acting otherwise respecting the information communicated by Hayraddin, since the proposed sally of De la Marck, unless heedfully guarded against, might prove the destruction of the besieging army; so difficult was it, in the tumultuous warfare of those days, to recover from a nocturnal surprise. After pondering on the matter, he formed the additional resolution, that he would not communicate the intelligence save personally, and to both the princes while together; perhaps because he felt that, to mention so well-contrived and hopeful a scheme to Louis whilst in private might be too strong a temptation to the wavering probity of that monarch, and lead him to assist rather than repel the intended sally. He determined, therefore, to watch for an opportunity of revealing the secret whilst Louis and Charles were met, which, as they were not particularly fond of the constraint imposed by each other's society, was not likely soon to occur.

Meanwhile the march continued, and the confederates soon entered the territories of Liege. Here the Burgundian soldiers, at least a part of them, composed of those bands who had acquired the title of *écorcheurs*, or flayers, showed by the usage which they gave the inhabitants, under pretext of avenging the bishop's death, that they well deserved that honourable title; while their conduct greatly prejudiced the cause of Charles—the aggrieved inhabitants, who might otherwise have been passive in the quarrel, assuming arms in self-defence, harassing his march, by cutting off small parties, and falling back before the main body upon the city itself, thus augmenting the numbers and desperation of those who had resolved to defend it. The French, few in number, and those the choice soldiers of the country, kept, according to the King's orders, close by their respective standards, and observed the strictest discipline; a contrast which increased the suspicions of Charles, who could not help remarking that the troops of Louis demeaned themselves as if they were rather friends to the Liegeois than allies of Burgundy.

At length, without experiencing any serious opposition, the army arrived in the rich valley of the Maes, and before the large and populous city of Liege. The Castle of Schonwaldt they found had been totally destroyed, and learned that William de la Marck, whose only talents were of a military cast, had withdrawn his whole forces into the city, and was determined to avoid the encounter of the chivalry of France and Burgundy in the open field. But the invaders were not long of experiencing the danger which must always exist in attacking a large town, however open, if the inhabitants are disposed to defend it desperately.

A part of the Burgundian vanguard, conceiving that, from the dismantled and breached state of the walls, they had nothing to do but to march into Liege at their ease, entered one of the suburbs with the shouts of "Burgundy—Burgundy! Kill—kill! All is ours! Remember Louis of Bourbon!" But as they marched in disorder through the narrow streets, and were partly dispersed for the purpose of pillage, a large body of the inhabitants issued suddenly from the town, fell furiously upon them, and made considerable slaughter. De la Marck even availed himself of the breaches in the walls, which permitted the defenders to issue out at different points, and, by taking separate routes into the contested suburb, to attack, in the front, flank, and rear, at once, the assailants, who, stunned by the furious, unexpected, and multiplied nature of the resistance offered, could hardly stand to their arms. The evening, which began to close, added to their confusion.

When this news was brought to Duke Charles, he was furious with rage, which was not much appeased by the offer of King Louis, to send the French men-at-arms into the suburbs, to rescue and bring off the Burgundian vanguard. Rejecting this offer briefly, he would have put himself at the head of his own guards, to extricate those engaged in the incautious advance; but D'Hymbercourt and Crèvecœur entreated him to leave the service to them, and marching into the scene of action at two points, with more order and proper arrangement for mutual support, these two celebrated captains succeeded in repulsing the Liegeois and in extricating the vanguard, who lost, besides prisoners, no fewer than eight hundred men, of whom about a hundred were men-at-arms. The prisoners, however, were not numerous, most of them having been rescued by D'Hymbercourt, who now proceeded to occupy the contested suburb, and to place guards opposite to the town, from which it was divided by an open space or esplanade of five or six hundred yards, left free of buildings for the purposes of defence. There was no moat betwixt the suburb and town, the ground being rocky in that place. A gate fronted the suburb, from which sallies might be easily made; and the wall was pierced by two or three of those breaches which Duke

Charles had caused to be made after the battle of Saint Tron, and which had been hastily repaired with mere barricades of timber. D'Hymbercourt turned two culverins on the gate, and placed two others opposite to the principal breach, to repel any sally from the city, and then returned to the Burgundian army, which he found in great disorder.

In fact, the main body and rear of the numerous army of the Duke had continued to advance while the broken and repulsed vanguard was in the act of retreating; and they had come into collision with each other, to the great confusion of both. The necessary absence of D'Hymbercourt, who discharged all the duties of *maréchal du camp*, or, as we should now say, of quartermaster-general, augmented the disorder; and to complete the whole, the night sunk down dark as a wolf's mouth: there fell a thick and heavy rain, and the ground on which the beleaguering army must needs take up their position was muddy and intersected with many canals. It is scarce possible to form an idea of the confusion which prevailed in the Burgundian army, where leaders were separated from their soldiers and soldiers from their standards and officers. Every one, from the highest to the lowest, was seeking shelter and accommodation where he could individually find it; while the wearied and wounded, who had been engaged in the battle, were calling in vain for shelter and refreshment, and while those who knew nothing of the disaster were pressing on to have their share in the sack of the place, which they had no doubt was proceeding merrily.

When D'Hymbercourt returned he had a task to perform of incredible difficulty, and embittered by the reproaches of his master, who made no allowance for the still more necessary duty in which he had been engaged, until the temper of the gallant soldier began to give way under the Duke's unreasonable reproaches. "I went hence to restore some order in the van," he said, "and left the main body under your Grace's own guidance; and now, on my return, I can neither find that we have front, flank, nor rear, so utter is the confusion."

"We are the more like a barrel of herrings," answered Le

Glorieux, "which is the most natural resemblance for a Flemish army."

The jester's speech made the Duke laugh, and perhaps prevented a farther prosecution of the altercation betwixt him and his general.

By dint of great exertion, a small *lusthaus*, or country villa, of some wealthy citizen of Liege was secured and cleared of other occupants for the accommodation of the Duke and his immediate attendants; and the authority of D'Hymbercourt and Crèvecœur at length established a guard in the vicinity, of about forty men-at-arms, who lighted a very large fire, made with the timber of the outhouses, which they pulled down for the purpose.

A little to the left of this villa, and betwixt it and the suburb, which, as we have said, was opposite to the city gate, and occupied by the Burgundian vanguard, lay another pleasure-house, surrounded by a garden and courtyard, and having two or three small inclosures or fields in the rear of it. In this the King of France established his own headquarters. He did not himself pretend to be a soldier, further than a natural indifference to danger and much sagacity qualified him to be called such; but he was always careful to employ the most skilful in that profession, and reposed in them the confidence they merited. Louis and his immediate attendants occupied this second villa; a part of his Scottish Guard were placed in the court, where there were outhouses and sheds to shelter them from the weather; the rest were stationed in the garden. The remainder of the French men-at-arms were quartered closely together and in good order, with alarm-posts stationed, in case of their having to sustain an attack.

Dunois and Crawford, assisted by several old officers and soldiers, amongst whom Le Balafré was conspicuous for his diligence, contrived, by breaking down walls, making openings through hedges, filling up ditches, and the like, to facilitate the communication of the troops with each other, and the orderly combination of the whole in case of necessity.

Meanwhile, the King judged it proper to go without farther ceremony to the quarters of the Duke of Burgundy, to ascertain what was to be the order of proceeding and what co-operation was expected from him. His presence occasioned a sort of council of war to be held, of which Charles might not otherwise have dreamed.

It was then that Quentin Durward prayed earnestly to be admitted, as having something of importance to deliver to the two princes. This was obtained without much difficulty, and great was the astonishment of Louis when he heard him calmly and distinctly relate the purpose of William de la Marck to make a sally upon the camp of the besiegers under the dress and banners of the French. Louis would probably have been much better pleased to have had such important news communicated in private; but as the whole story had been publicly told in presence of the Duke of Burgundy, he only observed, "that, whether true or false, such a report concerned them most materially."

"Not a whit—not a whit!" said the Duke, carelessly. "Had there been such a purpose as this young man announces, it had not been communicated to me by an archer of the Scottish Guard."

"However that may be," answered Louis, "I pray you, fair cousin, you and your captains, to attend, that to prevent the unpleasing consequences of such an attack, should it be made unexpectedly, I will cause my soldiers to wear white scarfs over their armour. Dunois, see it given out on the instant— that is," he added, "if our brother and general approves of it."

"I see no objections," replied the Duke, "if the chivalry of France are willing to run the risk of having the name of Knights of the Smock-sleeve bestowed on them in future."

"It would be a right well adapted title, friend Charles," said Le Glorieux, "considering that a woman is the reward of the most valiant."

"Well spoken, sagacity," said Louis. "Cousin, good-night, I will go arm me. By the way, what if I win the countess with mine own hand?"

"Your Majesty," said the Duke, in an altered tone of voice, "must then become a true Fleming."

"I cannot," answered Louis, in a tone of the most sincere confidence, "be more so than I am already, could I but bring you, my dear cousin, to believe it."

The Duke only replied by wishing the King good-night, in a tone resembling the snort of a shy horse, starting from the caress of the rider when he is about to mount, and is soothing him to stand still.

"I could pardon all his duplicity," said the Duke to Crèvecœur, "but cannot forgive his supposing me capable of the gross folly of being duped by his professions."

Louis, too, had his confidences with Oliver le Dain when he returned to his own quarters. "This Scot," he said, "is such a mixture of shrewdness and simplicity, that I know not what to make of him. *Pasques-dieu!* think of his unpardonable folly in bringing out honest De la Marck's plan of a sally before the face of Burgundy, Crèvecœur, and all of them, instead of rounding it in my ear, and giving me at least the choice of abetting or defeating it!"

"It is better as it is, sire," said Oliver; "there are many in your present train who would scruple to assail Burgundy undefied, or to ally themselves with De la Marck."

"Thou art right, Oliver. Such fools there are in the world, and we have no time to reconcile their scruples by a little dose of self-interest. We must be true men, Oliver, and good allies of Burgundy, for this night at least; time may give us a chance of a better game. Go, tell no man to unarm himself; and let them shoot, in case of necessity, as sharply on those who cry 'France' and 'St. Denis' as if they cried 'Hell' and 'Satan.' I will myself sleep in my armour. Let Crawford place Quentin Durward on the extreme point of our line of sentinels, next to the city. Let him e'en have the first benefit of the sally which he has announced to us; if his luck bear him out, it is the better for him. But take an especial care of Martius Galeotti, and see he remain in the rear, in a place of the most absolute safety; he is even but too venturous, and like a fool, would be both swordsman and philosopher. See to these things, Oliver, and good-night. Our Lady of Cléry, and Monseigneur St. Martin of Tours, be gracious to my slumbers!"[1]

CHAPTER XXXVIII.

THE SALLY.

> He look'd, and saw what numbers numberless
> The city-gates out-pour'd.
> *Paradise Regained.*

A DEAD silence soon reigned over that great host which lay in leaguer before Liege. For a long time the cries of the soldiers repeating their signals, and seeking to join their several banners, sounded like the howling of bewildered dogs seeking their masters. But at length, overcome with weariness by the fatigues of the day, the dispersed soldiers crowded under such shelter as they could meet with, and those who could find none sunk down through very fatigue under walls, hedges, and such temporary protection, there to wait for morning—a morning which some of them were never to behold. A dead sleep fell on almost all, excepting those who kept a faint and weary watch by the lodgings of the King and the Duke. The dangers and hopes of the morrow—even the schemes of glory which many of the young nobility had founded upon the splendid prize held out to him who should avenge the murdered Bishop of Liege—glided from their recollection as they lay stupified with fatigue and sleep. But not so with Quentin Durward. The knowledge that he alone was possessed of the means of distinguishing La Marck in the contest—the recollection by whom that information had been communicated, and the fair augury which might be drawn from her conveying it to him—the thought that his fortune had brought him to a most perilous and doubtful crisis indeed, but one where there was still, at least, a chance of his coming off triumphant, banished every desire to sleep, and strung his nerves with vigour, which defied fatigue.

[1] See Attack upon Liege. Note 49.

Posted, by the King's express order, on the extreme point between the French quarters and the town, a good way to the right of the suburb which we have mentioned, he sharpened his eye to penetrate the mass which lay before him, and excited his ears to catch the slightest sound which might annouce any commotion in the beleaguered city. But its huge clocks had successively knelled three hours after midnight, and all continued still and silent as the grave.

At length, and just when Quentin began to think the attack would be deferred till daybreak, and joyfully recollected that there would be then light enough to descry the bar sinister across the fleur-de-lys of Orleans, he thought he heard in the city a humming murmur, like that of disturbed bees mustering for the defence of their hives. He listened; the noise continued, but it was of a character so undistinguished by any peculiar or precise sound, that it might be the murmur of a wind rising among the boughs of a distant grove, or perhaps some stream swollen by the late rain, which was discharging itself into the sluggish Maes with more than usual clamour. Quentin was prevented by these considerations from instantly giving the alarm, which, if done carelessly, would have been a heavy offence.

But when the noise rose louder, and seemed pouring at the same time towards his own post, and towards the suburb, he deemed it his duty to fall back as silently as possible, and call his uncle, who commanded the small body of archers destined to his support. All were on their feet in a moment, and with as little noise possible. In less than a second, Lord Crawford was at their head, and, despatching an archer to alarm the King and his household, drew back his little party to some distance behind their watch-fire, that they might not be seen by its light. The rushing sound, which had approached them more nearly, seemed suddenly to have ceased; but they still heard distinctly the more distant heavy tread of a large body of men approaching the suburb.

"The lazy Burgundians are asleep on their post," whispered Crawford; "make for the suburb, Cunningham, and awaken the stupid oxen."

"Keep well to the rear as you go," said Durward; "if ever I heard the tread of mortal men, there is a strong body interposed between us and the suburb."

"Well said, Quentin, my dainty callant," said Crawford; "thou art a soldier beyond thy years. They only make halt till the others come forward. I would I had some knowledge where they are!"

"I will creep forward, my lord," said Quentin, "and endeavour to bring you information."

"Do so, my bonny chield; thou hast sharp ears and eyes, and good will; but take heed, I would not lose thee for two and a plack."

Quentin, with his harquebuss ready prepared, stole forward, through ground which he had reconnoitred carefully in the twilight of the preceding evening, until he was not only certain that he was in the neighbourhood of a very large body of men, who were standing fast betwixt the King's quarters and the suburbs, but also that there was a detached party of smaller numbers in advance, and very close to him. They seemed to whisper together, as if uncertain what to do next. At last, the steps of two or three *enfans perdus*, detached from that smaller party, approached him so near as twice a pike's length. Seeing it impossible to retreat undiscovered, Quentin called out aloud: "*Qui vive?*" and was answered by "*Vive Li—Li—ege—c'est à dire,*" added he who spoke, correcting himself, "*Vive la France!*" Quentin instantly fired his harquebuss; a man groaned and fell, and he himself, under the instant but vague discharge of a number of pieces, the fire of which ran in a disorderly manner along the column, and showed it to be very numerous, hastened back to the main guard.

"Admirably done, my brave boy!" said Crawford. "Now, callants, draw in within the courtyard; they are too many to mell with in the open field."

They drew within the courtyard and garden accordingly, where they found all in great order, and the King prepared to mount his horse.

"Whither away, sire?" said Crawford; "you are safest here with your own people."

"Not so," said Louis; "I must instantly to the Duke. He must be convinced of our good faith at this critical moment, or we shall have both Liegeois and Burgundians upon us at once." And springing on his horse, he bade Dunois command the French troops without the house, and Crawford the Archer Guard and other household troops to defend the *lusthaus* and its inclosures. He commanded them to bring up two sakers and as many falconets (pieces of cannon for the field), which had been left about half a mile in the rear; and, in the mean time, to make good their posts, by but no means to advance, whatever success they might obtain; and having given these orders, he rode off, with a small escort, to the Duke's quarters.

The delay which permitted these arrangements to be carried fully into effect was owing to Quentin's having fortunately shot the proprietor of the house, who acted as guide to the column which was designed to attack it, and whose attack, had it been made instantly, might have had a chance of being successful.

Durward, who, by the King's order, attended him to the Duke's, found the latter in a state of choleric distemperature, which almost prevented his discharging the duties of a general, which were never more necessary; for, besides the noise of a close and furious combat which had now taken place in the suburb, upon the left of their whole army—besides the attack upon the King's quarters, which was fiercely maintained in the centre—a third column of Liegeois, of even superior numbers, had filed out from a more distant breach, and, marching by lanes, vineyards, and passes known to themselves, had fallen upon the right flank of the Burgundian army, who, alarmed at their war-cries of "*Vive la France!*" and "*Denis Montjoye!*" which mingled with those of "*Liege*" and "*Rouge Sanglier*," and at the idea thus inspired, of treachery on the part of the French confederates, made a very desultory and imperfect resistance; while the Duke, foaming, and swearing, and cursing his liege lord and all that belonged to him, called out to shoot with bow and gun on all that was French, whether black or white—alluding to the sleeves with which Louis's soldiers had designated themselves.

The arrival of the King, attended only by Le Balafré and Quentin, and half a score of archers, restored confidence between France and Burgundy. D'Hymbercourt, Crèvecœur, and others of the Burgundian leaders, whose names were then the praise and dread of war, rushed devotedly into the conflict; and, while some commanders hastened to bring up more distant troops, to whom the panic had not extended, others threw themselves into the tumult, reanimated the instinct of discipline, and while the Duke toiled in the front, shouting, hacking, and hewing, like an ordinary man-at-arms, brought their men by degrees into array, and dismayed the assailants by the use of their artillery. The conduct of Louis, on the other hand, was that of a calm, collected, sagacious leader, who neither sought nor avoided danger, but showed so much self-possession and sagacity that the Burgundian leaders readily obeyed the orders which he issued.

The scene was now become in the utmost degree animated and horrible. On the left the suburb, after a fierce contest, had been set on fire, and a wide and dreadful conflagration did not prevent the burning ruins from being still disputed. On the centre, the French troops, though pressed by immense odds, kept up so close and constant a fire that the little pleasure-house shone bright with the glancing flashes, as if surrounded with a martyr's crown of flames. On the left, the battle swayed backwards and forwards with varied success, as fresh reinforcements poured out of the town, or were brought forward from the rear of the Burgundian host; and the strife continued with unremitting fury for three mortal hours, which at length brought the dawn, so much desired by the besiegers. The enemy, at this period, seemed to be slackening their efforts upon the right and in the centre, and several discharges of cannon were heard from the *lusthaus*.

"Go," said the King, to Le Balafré and Quentin, the instant his ear had caught the sound; "they have got up the sakers and falconets; the pleasure-house is safe, blessed by the Holy Virgin! Tell Dunois to move this way, but rather nearer the walls of Liege, with all our men-at-arms, excepting what he may leave for the defence of the house, and cut in between those thick-headed Liegeois on the right and the city, from which they are supplied with recruits."

The uncle and nephew galloped off to Dunois and Crawford, who, tired of their defensive war, joyfully obeyed the summons, and filing out at the head of a gallant body of about two hundred French gentlemen, besides squires, and the greater part of the archers and their followers, marched across the field, trampling down the wounded, till they gained the flank of the large body of Liegeois, by whom the right of the Burgundians had been so fiercely assailed. The increasing daylight discovered that the enemy were continuing to pour out from the city, either for the purpose of continuing the battle on that point, or of bringing safely off the forces who were already engaged.

"By Heaven!" said old Crawford to Dunois, "were I not certain it is *thou* that art riding by my side, I would say I saw thee among yonder banditti and burghers, marshalling and arraying them with thy mace—only, if yon be thou, thou art bigger than thou art wont to be. Art thou sure yonder armed leader is not thy wraith, thy double-man, as these Flemings call it?"

"My wraith!" said Dunois; "I know not what you mean. But yonder is a caitiff with my bearings displayed on crest and shield, whom I will presently punish for his insolence."

"In the name of all that is noble, my lord, leave the vengeance to me!" said Quentin.

"To *thee* indeed, young man!" said Dunois; "that is a modest request. No—these things brook no substitution." Then turning on his saddle, he called out to those around him: "Gentlemen of France, form your line, level your lances! Let the rising sunbeams shine through the battalions of yonder swine of Liege and hogs of Ardennes, that masquerade in our ancient coats."

The men-at-arms answered with a loud shout of "A Dunois—a Dunois! Long live the bold Bastard! Orleans to the rescue!" And, with their leader in the centre, they charged at full gallop. They encountered no timid enemy. The large body which they charged consisted, excepting some mounted officers, entirely of infantry, who, setting the butt of their lances against their feet, the front rank kneeling, the second stooping, and those behind presenting their spears over their heads, offered such resistance to the rapid charge of the men-at-arms as the hedgehog presents to his enemy. Few were able to make way through that iron wall; but of those few was Dunois, who, giving spur to his horse, and making the noble animal leap more than twelve feet at a bound, fairly broke his way into the middle of the phalanx, and made towards the object of his animosity. What was his surprise to find Quentin still by his side, and fighting in the same front with himself—youth, desperate courage, and the determination to do or die having still kept the youth abreast with the best knight in Europe, for such was Dunois reported, and truly reported, at the period.

Their spears were soon broken; but the lanzknechts were unable to withstand the blows of their long heavy swords; while the horses and riders, armed in complete steel, sustained little injury from their lances. Still Dunois and Durward were contending with rival efforts to burst forward to the spot where he who had usurped the armorial bearings of Dunois was doing the duty of a good and valiant leader, when Dunois, observing the boar's head and tusks, the usual bearing of William de la Marck, in another part of the conflict, called out to Quentin: "Thou art worthy to avenge the arms of Orleans! I leave thee the task. Balafré, support your nephew; but let none dare to interfere with Duncis's boar-hunt."

That Quentin Durward joyfully acquiesced in this division of labour cannot be doubted, and each pressed forward upon his separate object, followed, and defended from behind, by such men-at-arms as were able to keep up with them.

But at this moment the column which De la Marck had proposed to support, when his own course was arrested by the charge of Dunois, had lost all the advantages they had gained during the night; while the Burgundians, with returning day, had begun to show the qualities which belong to superior discipline. The great mass of Liegeois were compelled to retreat, and at length to fly; and, falling back on those who were engaged with the French men-at-arms, the whole became a confused tide of fighters, fliers, and pursuers, which rolled itself towards the city walls, and at last was poured into the ample and undefended breach through which the Leigeois had sallied.

Quentin made more than human exertions to overtake the special object of his pursuit, who was still in his sight, striving, by voice and example, to renew the battle, and bravely supported by a chosen party of lanzknechts. Le Balafré and several of his comrades attached themselves to Quentin, much marvelling at the extraordinary gallantry displayed by so young a soldier. On the very brink of the breach De la Marck—for it was himself—succeeded in effecting a momentary stand, and repelling some of the most forward of the pursuers. He had a mace of iron in his hand, before which everything seemed to go down, and was so much covered with blood that it was almost impossible to discern those bearings on his shield which had so much incensed Dunois.

Quentin now found little difficulty in singling him out; for the commanding situation of which he had possessed himself, and the use he made of his terrible mace, caused many of the assailants to seek safer points of attack than that where so desperate a defender presented himself. But Quentin, to whom the importance attached to victory over this formidable antagonist was better known, sprung from his horse at the bottom of the breach, and letting the noble animal, the gift of the Duke of Orleans, run loose through the tumult, ascended the ruins to measure swords with the Boar of Ardennes. The latter, as if he had seen his intention, turned towards Durward with mace uplifted; and they were on the point of encounter when a dreadful shout of triumph, of tumult, and of despair announced that the besiegers were entering the city at another point, and in the rear of those who defended the breach. Assembling around him, by voice and bugle, the desperate partners of his desperate fortune, De la Marck, at those appalling sounds, abandoned the breach, and endeavoured to effect his retreat towards a part of the city from which he might escape to the other side of the Maes. His immediate followers formed a deep body of well-disciplined men, who, never having given quarter, were resolved now not to ask it, and who, in that hour of despair, threw themselves into such firm order that their front occupied the whole breadth of the street through which they slowly retired, making head from time to time, and checking the pursuers, many of whom began to seek a safer occupation by breaking into the houses for plunder. It is therefore probable that De la Marck might have effected his escape, his disguise concealing him from those who promised themselves to win honour and grandeur upon his head, but for the stanch pursuit of Quentin, his uncle Le Balafré, and some of his comrades. At every pause which was made by the lanzknechts a furious combat took place betwixt them and the archers, and in every *mêlée* Quentin sought De la Marck; but the latter, whose present object was to retreat, seemed to evade the young Scot's purpose of bringing him to single combat. The confusion was general in every direction. The shrieks and cries of women, the yelling of the terrified inhabitants, now subjected to the extremity of military license, sounded horribly shrill amid the shouts of battle, like the voice of misery and despair contending with that of fury and violence, which should be heard farthest and loudest.

It was just when De la Marck, retiring through this infernal scene, had passed the door of a small chapel of peculiar sanctity, that the shouts of "France—France! Burgundy—Burgundy!" apprized him that a part of the besiegers were entering the farther end of the street, which was a narrow one, and that his retreat was cut off. "Conrade," he said, "take all the men with you. Charge yonder fellows roundly, and break through if you can; with me it is over. I am man enough, now that I am brought to bay, to send some of these vagabond Scots to hell before me."

His lieutenant obeyed, and, with most of the few lanzknechts who remained alive, hurried to the farther end of the street, for the purpose of charging those Burgundians who were advancing, and so forcing their way so as to escape.

About six of De la Marck's best men remained to perish with their master, and fronted the archers, who were not many more in number. "Sanglier! Sanglier! Hola! gentlemen of Scotland," said the ruffian but undaunted chief, waving his mace, "who longs to gain a coronet—who strikes at the Boar of Ardennes? You, young man, have, methinks, a hankering; but you must win ere you wear it."

Quentin heard but imperfectly the words, which were partly lost in the hollow helmet; but the action could not be mistaken, and he had but time to bid his uncle and comrades, as they were gentlemen, to stand back, when De la Marck sprung upon him with a bound like a tiger, aiming at the same time a blow with his mace, so as to make his hand and foot keep time together, and giving his stroke full advantage of the descent of his leap; but, light of foot and quick of eye, Quentin leaped aside, and disappointed an aim which would have been fatal had it taken effect.

They then closed, like the wolf and the wolf-dog, their comrades on either side remaining inactive spectators, for Le Balafré roared out for fair play, adding, "that he would venture his nephew on him, were he as wight as Wallace."

Neither was the experienced soldier's confidence unjustified; for, although the blows of the despairing robber fell like those of the hammer on the anvil, yet the quick motions and dexterous swordsmanship of the young archer enabled him to escape and to requite them with the point of his less noisy though more fatal weapon; and that so often and so effectually, that the huge strength of his antagonist began to give way to fatigue, while the ground on which he stood became a puddle of blood. Yet, still unabated in courage and ire, the Wild Boar of Ardennes fought on with as much mental energy as at first, and Quentin's victory seemed dubious and distant, when a female voice behind him called him by his name, ejaculating, "Help—help! for the sake of the blessed Virgin!"

He turned his head, and with a single glance beheld Gertrude Pavillon, her mantle stripped from her shoulders, dragged forcibly along by a French soldier, one of several, who, breaking into the chapel close by, had seized, as their prey, on the terrified females who had taken refuge there.

"Wait for me but one moment," exclaimed Quentin to De la Marck, and sprung to extricate his benefactress from a situation of which he conjectured all the dangers.

"I wait no man's pleasure," said De la Marck, flourishing his mace, and beginning to retreat, glad, no doubt, of being free of so formidable an assailant.

"You shall wait mine, though, by your leave," said Balafré; "I will not have my nephew baulked." So saying, he instantly assaulted De la Marck with his two-handed sword.

Quentin found, in the mean while, that the rescue of Gertrude was a task more difficult than could be finished in one moment. Her captor, supported by his comrades, refused to relinquish his prize; and while Durward, aided by one or two of his countrymen, endeavoured to compel him to do so, the former beheld the chance which Fortune had so kindly afforded him for fortune and happiness glide out of his reach; so that, when he stood at length in the street with the liberated Gertrude, there was no one near them. Totally forgetting the defenceless situation of his companion, he was about to spring away in pursuit of the Boar of Ardennes, as the greyhound tracks the deer, when, clinging to him in her despair, she exclaimed: "For the sake of your mother's honour, leave me not here! As you are a gentleman, protect me to my father's house, which once sheltered you and the Lady Isabelle. For her sake leave me not."

Her call was agonising, but it was irresistible; and bidding a mental adieu, with unutterable bitterness of feeling, to all the gay hope which had stimulated his exertion, carried him through that bloody day, and which at one moment seemed to approach consummation, Quentin, like an unwilling spirit who obeys a talisman which he cannot resist, protected Gertrude to Pavillon's house, and arrived in time to defend that and the syndic himself against the fury of the licentious soldiery.

Meantime, the King and the Duke of Burgundy entered the city on horseback, and through one of the breaches. They were both in complete armour, but the latter, covered with blood from the plume to the spur, drove his steed furiously up the breach, which Louis surmounted with the stately pace of one who leads a procession. They despatched orders to stop the sack of the city, which had already commenced, and to assemble their scattered troops. The princes themselves proceeded towards the great church, both for the protection of many of the distinguished inhabitants, who had taken refuge there, and in order to hold a sort of military council after they had heard high mass.

Busied like other officers of his rank in collecting those under his command, Lord Crawford, at the turning of one of the streets which leads to the Maes, met Le Balafré sauntering composedly towards the river, holding in his hand, by the gory locks, a human head, with as much indifference as a fowler carries a game-pouch.

"How now, Ludovic!" said his commander; "what are you doing with that carrion?"

"It is all that is left of a bit of work which my nephew shaped out, and nearly finished, and I put the last hand to," said Le Balafré—"a good fellow that I despatched yonder, and who prayed me to throw his head into the Maes. Men have queer fancies when old Small Back[1] is gripping them; but Small Back must lead down the dance with us all in our time."

"And you are going to throw that head into the Maes?" said Crawford, looking more attentively on the ghastly memorial of mortality.

"Ay, truly am I," said Ludovic Lesly. "If you refuse a dying man his boon, you are likely to be haunted by his ghost, and I love to sleep sound at nights."

"You must take your chance of the ghaist, man," said Crawford; "for, by my soul, there is more lies on that dead pow than you think for. Come along with me—not a word more—come along with me."

"Nay, for that matter," said Le Balafré, "I made him no promise; for, in truth, I had off his head before the tongue had well done wagging; and as I feared him not living, by

[1] A cant expression in Scotland for death, usually delineated as a skeleton.

St. Martin of Tours, I fear him as little when he is dead. Besides, my little gossip, the merry friar of St. Martin's will lend me a pot of holy water."

When high mass had been said in the cathedral church of Liege, and the terrified town was restored to some moderate degree of order, Louis and Charles, with their peers around, proceeded to hear the claims of those who had any to make for services performed during the battle. Those which respected the county of Croye and its fair mistress were first received, and, to the disappointment of sundry claimants who had thought themselves sure of the rich prize, there seemed doubt and mystery to involve their several pretensions. Crèvecœur showed a boar's hide such as De la Marck usually wore; Dunois produced a cloven shield, with his armorial bearings; and there were others who claimed the merit of having despatched the murderer of the bishop, producing similar tokens—the rich reward fixed on De la Marck's head having brought death to all who were armed in his resemblance.

There was much noise and contest among the competitors, and Charles, internally regretting the rash promise which had placed the hand and wealth of his fair vassal on such a hazard, was in hopes he might find means of evading all these conflicting claims, when Crawford pressed forward into the circle, dragging Le Balafré after him, who, awkward and bashful, followed like an unwilling mastiff towed on in a leash, as his leader exclaimed: "Away with your hoofs and hides, and painted iron! No one, save he who slew the Boar, can show the tusks!"

So saying, he flung on the floor the bloody head, easily known as that of De la Marck by the singular conformation of the jaws, which in reality had a certain resemblance to those of the animal whose name he bore, and which was instantly recognised by all who had seen him.[1]

"Crawford," said Louis, while Charles sat silent, in gloomy and displeased surprise, "I trust it is one of my faithful Scots who has won this prize?"

[1] See Anachronisms. Note 50.

"It is Ludovic Lesly, sire, whom we call Le Balafré," replied the old soldier.

"But is he noble," said the Duke—"is he of gentle blood? Otherwise our promise is void."

"He is a cross ungainly piece of wood enough," said Crawford, looking at the tall, awkward, embarrassed figure of the archer; "but I will warrant him a branch of the tree of Rothes for all that, and they have been as noble as any house in France or Burgundy, ever since it is told of their founder that,

> Between the less-lee [1] and the mair
> He slew the knight, and left him there."

"There is then no help for it," said the Duke, "and the fairest and richest heiress in Burgundy must be the wife of a rude mercenary soldier like this, or die secluded in a convent—and she the only child of our faithful Reginald [Reinold] de Croye! I have been too rash."

And a cloud settled on his brow, to the surprise of his peers, who seldom saw him evince the slightest token of regret for the necessary consequences of an adopted resolution.

"Hold but an instant," said the Lord Crawford, "it may be better than your Grace conjectures. Hear but what this cavalier has to say. Speak out, man, and a murrain to thee," he added, apart to Le Balafré.

But that blunt soldier, though he could make a shift to express himself intelligibly enough to King Louis, to whose familiarity he was habituated, yet found himself incapable of enunciating his resolution before so splendid an assembly as that in presence of which he then stood; and after having turned his shoulder to the princes, and preluded with a hoarse chuckling laugh, and two or three tremendous contortions of countenance, he was only able to pronounce the words, "Saunders Souplejaw?"—and then stuck fast.

"May it please your Majesty and your Grace," said Crawford, "I must speak for my countryman and old comrade. You shall understand that he has had it prophesied to him by a seer in his own land, that the fortune of his house is to be

[1] See Descent of the Leslies.   Note 51.

made by marriage; but as he is, like myself, something the worse for the wear,—loves the wine-house better than a lady's summer-parlour, and, in short, having some barrack tastes and likings which would make greatness in his own person rather an encumbrance to him, he hath acted by my advice, and resigns the pretensions acquired by the fate of slaying William de la Marck to him by whom the Wild Boar was actually brought to bay, who is his maternal nephew."

"I will vouch for that youth's services and prudence," said King Louis, overjoyed to see that fate had thrown so gallant a prize to one over whom he had some influence. "Without his prudence and vigilance we had been ruined. It was he who made us aware of the night-sally."

"I then," said Charles, "owe him some reparation for doubting his veracity."

"And I can attest his gallantry as a man-at-arms," said Dunois.

"But," interrupted Crèvecœur, "though the uncle be a Scottish *gentillâtre*, that makes not the nephew necessarily so."

"He is of the house Durward," said Crawford; "descended from that Allan Durward who was High Steward of Scotland."

"Nay, if it be young Durward," said Crèvecœur, "I say no more. Fortune has declared herself on his side too plainly for me to struggle farther with her humoursome ladyship; but it is strange, from lord to horseboy, how wonderfully these Scots stick by each other."

"Highlanders, shoulder to shoulder!" answered Lord Crawford, laughing at the mortification of the proud Burgundian. "We have yet to inquire," said Charles, thoughtfully, "what the fair lady's sentiments may be towards this fortunate adventurer."

"By the mass!" said Crèvecœur, "I have but too much reason to believe your Grace will find her more amenable to authority than on former occasions. But why should I grudge this youth his preferment, since, after all, it is sense, firmness, and gallantry which have put him in **possession of WEATH, RANK, and BEAUTY?**"

I HAD already sent these sheets to the press, concluding, as
I thought, with a moral of excellent tendency for the encouragement of all fair-haired, blue-eyed, long-legged, stout-hearted emigrants from my native country who might be willing in stirring times to take up the gallant profession of cavalieros of fortune. But a friendly monitor, one of those who like the lump of sugar which is found at the bottom of a tea-cup as well as the flavour of the souchong itself, has entered a bitter remonstrance, and insists that I should give a precise and particular account of the espousals of the young heir of Glenhoulakin and the lovely Flemish countess, and tell what tournaments were held, and how many lances were broken, upon so interesting an occasion; nor withhold from the curious reader the number of sturdy boys who inherited the valour of Quentin Durward, and of bright damsels in whom were renewed the charms of Isabelle de Croye. I replied in course of post, that times were changed, and public weddings were entirely out of fashion. In days, traces of which I myself can remember, not only were the "fifteen friends" of the happy pair invited to witness their union, but the bridal minstrelsy still continued, as in the *Ancient Mariner*, to "nod their heads" till morning shone on them. The sack-posset was eaten in the nuptial chamber, the stocking was thrown and the bride's garter was struggled for in presence of the happy couple whom Hymen had made one flesh. The authors of the period were laudably accurate in following its fashions. They spared you not a blush of the bride, not a rapturous glance of the bridegroom, not a diamond in her hair, not a button on his embroidered waistcoat; until at length, with Astræa, "they fairly put their characters to bed." But how little does this agree with the modest privacy which induces our modern brides—sweet bashful darlings!—to steal from pomp and plate, and admiration and flattery, and, like honest Shenstone,

Seek for freedom at an inn!

To these, unquestionably, an exposure of the circumstances

of publicity with which a bridal in the 15th century was always celebrated must appear in the highest degree disgusting. Isabelle de Croye would be ranked in their estimation far below the maid who milks and does the meanest chares; for even she, were it in the church-porch, would reject the hand of her journeyman shoemaker should he propose "*faire des noces,*" as it is called on Parisian signs, instead of going down on the top of the long coach to spend the honeymoon *incognito* at Deptford or Greenwich. I will not, therefore, tell more of this matter, but will steal away from the wedding as Ariosto from that of Angelica, leaving it to whom it may please to add farther particulars, after the fashion of their own imagination.

> Some better bard shall sing, in feudal state
> How Braquemont's Castle op'd its Gothic gate,
> When on the wand'ring Scot its lovely heir
> Bestow'd her beauty and an earldom fair.[1]

---

[1] E come a ritornare in sua contrada
Trovasse e buon naviglio e miglior tempo,
E dell' India a Medor desse lo scettro
Forse altri cantera con miglior plettro.
  Orlando Furioso, Canto xxx. Stanza 16.

NOTES TO QUENTIN DURWARD.

NOTE 1.—PRICE ON THE PICTURESQUE, p. 24.

SEE Price's *Essay on the Picturesque*, in many passages ; but I would particularise the beautiful and highly poetical account which he gives of his own feelings on destroying, at the dictate of an improver, an ancient sequestrated garden, with its yew hedges, ornamented iron gates, and secluded wilderness.

NOTE 2.—HUGHES'S ITINERARY, p. 32.

This Journal, or *Itinerary*, with etchings by the author, was published at London, 1822, 8vo, and was followed by a volume in folio [4to], entitled *Views in the South of France, chiefly on the Rhone*, engraved by W. B. Cooke, etc., from drawings by P. De Wint, after original sketches by John Hughes, Lond. 1825.

Mr. Lockhart, in his *Life of Scott*, has, by some oversight, connected the late Mr. Skene's name with *Quentin Durward* instead of with *Anne of Geierstein*. There is good authority for correcting this (*Laing*).

NOTE 3.—EDITION OF CENT NOUVELLES, p. 45.

This *editio princeps*, which, when in good preservation, is much sought after by connoisseurs, is entitled, *Les Cent Nouvelles Nouvelles, contenant Cent Histoires Nouveaux, qui sont moult plaisans à raconter en toutes bonnes compagnies par manière de joyeuxeté. Paris, Antoine Verard. Sans date d'année d'impression; in-folio gotique.* See De Bure.

NOTE 4.—ST. HUBERT, p. 16.

Every vocation had, in the middle ages, its protecting saint. The chase, with its fortunes and its hazards, the business of so many and the amusement of all, was placed under the direction of St. Hubert. This silvan saint was the son of Bertrand Duke of Acquitaine, and, while in the secular state, was a courtier of King Pepin. He was passionately fond of the chase, and used to neglect attendance on divine worship for this amusement. While he was once engaged in this pastime, a stag appeared before him, having a crucifix bound betwixt its horns, and he heard a voice which menaced him with eternal punishment if he did not repent of his sins. He retired from the world and took orders, his wife having also retreated into the cloister, Hubert afterwards became Bishop of Maestricht and Liege; and from his zeal in destroying remnants of idolatry is called the Apostle of Ardennes and of Brabant. Those who were descended of his race were supposed to possess the power of curing persons bitten by mad dogs.

Note 5.—Covin Tree, p. 66.

The large tree in front of a Scottish castle was sometimes called so. It is difficult to trace the derivation; but at that distance from the castle the laird received guests of rank, and thither he convoyed them on their departure.

Note 6.—Duke of Gueldres, p. 72.

This was Adolphus, son of Arnold and of Catherine de Bourbon. The present story has little to do with him, though one of the most atrocious characters of his time. He made war against his father; in which unnatural strife he made the old man prisoner, and used him with the most brutal violence, proceeding, it is said, even to the length of striking him with his hand. Arnold, in resentment of this usage, disinherited the unprincipled wretch, and sold to Charles of Burgundy whatever rights he ever had over the duchy of Gueldres and earldom of Zutphen. Mary of Burgundy, daughter of Charles, restored these possessions to the unnatural Adolphus, who was slain in 1477.

Note 7.—Constable St. Paul, p. 73.

This part of Louis XI.'s reign was much embarrassed by the intrigues of the Constable St. Paul, who affected independence, and carried on intrigues with England, France, and Burgundy at the same time. According to the usual fate of such versatile politicians, the Constable ended by drawing upon himself the animosity of all the powerful neighbours whom he had in their turn amused and deceived. He was delivered up by the Duke of Burgundy to the King of France, tried, and hastily executed for treason, 1475.

Note 8.—Bishop and Stephens, p. 84.

Sir Henry R. Bishop, the popular composer, and sometime professor of music in Edinburgh University, died in 1855. Miss Catherine Stephens was a delightful vocalist, who performed at the principal concerts and musical festivals about the time this was written. In 1838 she became Countess of Essex by her marriage with George, the fifth earl (*Laing*).

Note 9.—Use of Stilts, p. 89.

The crutches or stilts which in Scotland are used to pass rivers. They are employed by the peasantry of the country near Bourdeaux to traverse those deserts of loose sand called Landes.

NOTES.

NOTE 10.—"BETTER KIND FREMIT," ETC., p. 101.

"Better kind strangers than estranged kindred." The motto is engraved on a dirk belonging to a person who had but too much reason to choose such a device. It was left by him to my father, and is connected with a strange course of adventures, which may one day be told. The weapon is now in my possession.

NOTE 11.—SKENE DHU, p. 103.

Black knife; a species of knife without clasp or hinge, formerly much used by the Highlanders, who seldomed travelled without such an ugly weapon, though it is now rarely used.

NOTE 12.—GIPSIES OR BOHEMIANS, p. 105.

In a former volume (*Guy Mannering*) of this edition of the Waverley Novels, the reader will find some remarks on the gipsies as they are found in Scotland. But it is well known that this extraordinary variety of the human race exists in nearly the same primitive state, speaking the same language, in almost all the kingdoms of Europe, and conforming in certain respects to the manners of the people around them, but yet remaining separated from them by certain material distinctions, in which they correspond with each other, and thus maintain their pretensions to be considered as a distinct race. Their first appearance in Europe took place in the beginning of the 15th century, when various bands of this singular people appeared in the different countries of Europe. They claimed an Egyptian descent, and their features attested that they were of Eastern origin. The account given by these singular people was, that it was appointed to them, as a penance, to travel for a certain number of years. This apology was probably selected as being most congenial to the superstitions of the countries which they visited. Their appearance, however, and manners strongly contradicted the allegation that they travelled from any religious motive.

Their dress and accoutrements were at once showy and squalid; those who acted as captains and leaders of any horde, and such always appeared as their commanders, were arrayed in dresses of the most showy colours, such as scarlet or light green, were well mounted, assumed the title of dukes and counts, and affected considerable consequence. The rest of the tribe were most miserable in their diet and apparel, fed without hesitation on animals which had died of disease, and were clad in filthy and scanty rags, which hardly sufficed for the ordinary purposes of common decency. Their complexion was positively Eastern, approaching to that of the Hindoos.

Their manners were as depraved as their appearance was poor and beggarly. The men were in general thieves, and the women of the most abandoned character. The few arts which they studied with success were of a slight and idle, though ingenious, description. They practised working in iron, but never upon any great scale. Many were good sportsmen, good musicians, and masters, in a word, of all those trivial arts the practice of which is little better than mere idleness. But their ingenuity never ascended into industry. Two or three other peculiarities seem to have distinguished them in all countries. Their pretensions to read fortunes, by palmistry and by astrology, acquired them sometimes respect, but oftener drew them under suspicion as sorcerers; and lastly, the universal accusation that they augmented their horde by stealing children subjected them to doubt and execration. From this it happened that the pretension set up by these wanderers of being pilgrims in the act of penance, although it was at first admitted, and in many instances obtained them protection from the governments of the countries through which they travelled, was afterwards totally disbelieved, and they were considered as incorrigible rogues and vagrants; they incurred almost everywhere sentence of banishment, and, where suffered to remain, were rather objects of persecution than of protection from the law.

There is a curious and accurate account of their arrival in France in the journal of a doctor of theology, which is preserved and published by the learned Pasquier [*Les Recherches de la France*, iv. chap. xix. 1723]. The following is an extract:—"On August 27th, 1427, came to Paris twelve penitents, *penaciers* (penance doers), as they called themselves, viz. a duke, an earl, and ten men, all on horseback, and calling themselves good Christians. They were of Lower Egypt, and gave out that, not long before, the Christians had subdued their country, and obliged them to embrace Christianity on pain of being put to death. Those who were baptized were great lords in their own country, and had a king and queen there. Soon after their conversion, the Saracens overran the country, and obliged them to renounce Christianity. When the Emperor of Germany, the King of Poland, and other Christian princes heard of this, they fell upon them, and obliged the whole of them, both great and small, to quit the country and go to the Pope at Rome, who enjoined them seven years' penance to wander the world, without lying in a bed.

"They had been wandering five years when they came to Paris first; the principal people, and soon after the commonalty, about 100 or 120, reduced (according to their own account) from 1000 or 1200, when they went from home, the rest being dead, with their king and queen. They were lodged by the police at some distance from the city, at Chapel St. Denis.

"Nearly all of them had their ears bored, and wore two silver rings in each, which they said were esteemed ornaments in their country. The men were black, their hair curled; the women remarkably black, their only clothes a large old duffle garment, tied over the shoulders with a cloth or cord, and under it a miserable rocket. In short, they were the most poor miserable creatures that had ever been seen in France; and notwithstanding their poverty, there were among them women who, by looking into people's hands, told their fortunes, and what was worse, they picked people's pockets of their money, and got it into their own, by telling these things through airy magic, *et cætera*."

Notwithstanding the ingenious account of themselves rendered by these gipsies, the Bishop of Paris ordered a friar, called Le Petit Jacobin, to preach a sermon, excommunicating all the men and women who had had recourse to these Bohemians on the subject of the future, and shown their hands for that purpose. They departed from Paris for Pontoise in the month of September.

Pasquier remarks upon this singular journal, that, however the story of a penance savours of a trick, these people wandered up and down France, under the eye, and with the knowledge, of the magistrates, for more than a hundred years; and it was not till 1561 that a sentence of banishment was passed against them in that kingdom.

The arrival of the Egyptians, as these singular people were called, in various parts of Europe corresponds with the period in which Timur or Tamerlane invaded Hindostan, affording its natives the choice between the Koran and death. There can be little doubt that these wanderers consisted originally of the Hindostanee tribes, who, displaced, and flying from the sabres of the Mohammedans, undertook this species of wandering life, without well knowing whither they were going. It is natural to suppose the band, as it now exists, is much mingled with Europeans; but most of these have been brought up from childhood among them, and learned all their practices.

It is strong evidence of this, that when they are in closest contact with the ordinary peasants around them, they still keep their language a mystery. There is little doubt, however, that it is a dialect of the Hindostanee, from the specimens produced by Grellmann, Hoyland, and others, who have written on the subject. But the Author has, besides their authority, personal occasion to know that an individual, out of mere curiosity, and availing himself with patience and assiduity of such opportunities as offered, has made himself capable of conversing with any gipsy whom he meets, or can, like the royal Hal, drink with any tinker in his own language. The astonishment excited among these vagrants on finding a stranger participant of their mystery occasions very ludicrous scenes. It is to be hoped this gentleman will publish the knowledge he possesses on so singular a topic.

There are prudential reasons for postponing this disclosure at present; for although much more reconciled to society since they have been less the objects of legal persecution, the gipsies are a ferocious and vindictive people.

But, notwithstanding this is certainly the case, I cannot but add, from my own observation of nearly fifty years, that the manners of these vagrant tribes are much ameliorated, that I have known individuals amongst them who have united themselves to civilized society, and maintain respectable characters, and that great alteration has been wrought in their cleanliness and general mode of life.

NOTE 13.—PETIT-ANDRÉ, p. 110.

One of these two persons, I learned from the *Chronique de Jean de Troyes*, but too late too avail myself of the information, might with more accuracy have been called Petit-Jean than Petit-André. This was actually the name of the son of Henry de Cousin, master executioner of the High Court of Justice. The Constable St. Paul was executed by him with such dexterity that the head, when struck off, struck the ground at the same time with the body. This was in 1475.

The History of Louis XI., King of France, attributed to Jean de Troyes, forms a supplement to the *Memoirs* of Philip de Comines. It was originally published under the title of *The Chronicle of the very Christian and very Victorious Louis of Valois*, etc., 1460 to 1483; but was afterwards vulgarly called *La Chronique Scandaleuse*.

A convenient edition of the translation of *Comines* and this supplement forms two volumes of Bohn's series of French Memoirs (*Laing*).

Note 14.—Quarrels of Scottish Archers, p. 121.

Such disputes between the Scots Guards and the other constituted authorities of the ordinary military corps often occurred. In 1474, two [three] Scotsmen had been concerned in robbing John Pensart, a fishmonger, of a large sum of money. They were accordingly apprehended by Philip du Four, provost, with some of his followers. But ere they could lodge one of them, called Mortimer, in the prison of the Chastellet, they were attacked by two archers of the King's Scottish Guard, who rescued the prisoner. See *Chronique de Jean de Troyes*, at the said year, 1474.

Note 15.—Scottish Auxiliaries, p. 123.

In both these battles, the Scottish auxiliaries of France, under Stewart Earl of Buchan, were distinguished. At Beaugé they were victorious, killing the Duke of Clarence, Henry V.'s brother, and cutting off his army. At Vernoil they were defeated and nearly extirpated.

Note 16.—Oliver Dain, p. 134.

Oliver's name, or nickname, was Le Diable, which was bestowed on him by public hatred, in exchange for Le Daim, or Le Dain. He was originally the King's barber, but afterwards a favourite counsellor.

Note 17.—Card-Playing, p. 142.

Dr. Dryasdust here remarks that cards, said to have been invented in a preceding reign, for the amusement of Charles V. [VI.] during the intervals of his mental disorder, seem speedily to have become common among the courtiers, since they already furnished Louis XI. with a metaphor. The same proverb was quoted by Durandarte, in the enchanted cave of Montesinos. The alleged origin of the invention of cards produced one of the shrewdest replies I have ever heard given in evidence. It was made by the late Dr. Gregory of Edinburgh to a counsel of great eminence at the Scottish bar. The Doctor's testimony went to prove the insanity of the party whose mental capacity was the point at issue. On a cross-interrogation, he admitted that the person in question played admirably at whist. "And do you seriously say, doctor," said the learned counsel, "that a person having a superior capacity for a game so difficult, and which requires in a pre-eminent degree memory, judgment, and combination, can be at the same time deranged in his understanding?" "I am no card-player," said the doctor, with great address, "but I have read in history that cards were invented for the amusement of an insane king." The consequences of this reply were decisive.

Note 18.—Order of Golden Fleece, p. 143.

The military order of the Golden Fleece was instituted by Philip the Good, Duke of Burgundy, in the year 1429, the King of Spain being grandmaster of the order, as Duke of Burgundy. The number of knights were limited to thirty-one (*Laing*).

NOTES.

NOTE 19.—LOUIS AND HIS DAUGHTER, p. 153.

Here the King touches on the very purpose for which he pressed on the match with such tyrannic severity, which was, that, as the Princess's personal deformity admitted little chance of its being fruitful, the branch of Orleans, which was next in succession to the crown, might be, by the want of heirs, weakened or extinguished. In a letter to the Compte de Dammartin, Louis, speaking of his daughter's match, says, "Qu'ils n'auroient pas beaucoup d'embarras à nourrir les enfans que naitroient de leur union; mais cependant elle aura lieu, quelque chose qu'on en puisse dire."—Wraxall's *History of France*, vol. i. p. 143, note.

NOTE 20.—BALUE'S HORSEMANSHIP, p. 155.

A friendly, though unknown, correspondent has pointed out to me that I have been mistaken in alleging that the cardinal was a bad rider. If so, I owe his memory an apology; for there are few men who, until my latter days, have loved that exercise better than myself. But the cardinal may have been an indifferent horseman, though he wished to be looked upon as equal to the dangers of the chase. He was a man of assumption and ostentation, as he showed at the siege of Paris in 1465, where, contrary to the custom and usage of war, he mounted guard during the night with an unusual sound of clarions, trumpets, and other instruments. In imputing to the cardinal a want of skill in horsemanship, I recollected his adventure in Paris when attacked by assassins, on which occasion his mule, being scared by the crowd, ran away with the rider, and taking its course to a monastery, to the abbot of which he formerly belonged, was the means of saving his master's life.—See Jean de Troyes's *Chronicle*.

NOTE 21.—LOUIS XI. AND CHARLEMAGNE, p. 166.

Charlemagne, I suppose on account of his unsparing rigour to the Saxons and other heathens, was accounted a saint during the dark ages; and Louis XI., as one of his successors, honoured his shrine with peculiar observance.

NOTE 22.—MURDER OF DOUGLAS, p. 171.

The Princess Margaret, eldest daughter of King James the First, when only eleven years of age, was married to Louis, Dauphin of France, at the age of twelve, on the 6th of July 1436. It proved an unfortunate marriage, and the accomplished princess (her husband not succeeding till 1461 to the throne of France) died without issue, August 1445, in her twenty-third year, it is said of a broken heart. The allusion in the text is to the fate of James Earl of Douglas, who, upon the faith of a safe-conduct, after several acts of rebellion, visited James the Second in the Castle of Stirling. The king, irritated by some personal affront, but quite unpremeditated, drew his dagger and stabbed Douglas, who received his mortal wound from Sir Patrick Grey, one of the king's attendants (who had previously vowed revenge against the proud earl), on the 22d February 1452 (*Laing*).

Note 23.—Louis's Humour, p. 176.

The nature of Louis XI.'s coarse humour may be guessed at by those who have perused the *Cent Nouvelles Nouvelles*, which are grosser than most similar collections of the age.

The work is dedicated by its anonymous author to the Dauphin of France, afterwards Louis XI. It was first printed at Paris in 1486 by Antoine Verard, and, according to Brunet, afterwards passed through ten editions (*Laing*).

Note 24.—Galeotti, p. 204.

Martius Galeotti was a native of Narni, in Umbria. He was secretary to Matthias Corvinus, King of Hungary, and tutor to his son, John Corvinus, While at his court, he composed a work, *De Jocose Dictis et Factis Regis Matthiæ Corvini*. He left Hungary in 1477, and was made prisoner at Venice on a charge of having propagated heterodox opinions in a treatise entitled, *De Homine Interiore et Corpore ejus*. He was obliged to recant some of these doctrines, and might have suffered seriously but for the protection of Sextus IV., then Pope, who had been one of his scholars. He went to France, attached himself to Louis XI., and died in his service.

Note 25. Invention of Printing, p. 206.

The invention of printing was really first practised at Mayence, on the Rhine. While the first book issued from that press bears the date 1457, the first from Frankfort is dated 1507 (*Laing*). [This ignores the claims made on behalf of Coster of Haarlem.]

Note 26.—Religion of the Bohemians, p. 236.

It was a remarkable feature of the character of these wanderers that they did not, like the Jews, whom they otherwise resembled in some particulars, possess or profess any particular religion, whether in form or principle. They readily conformed, as far as might be required, with the religion of any country in which they happened to sojourn, nor did they ever practise it more than was demanded of them. It is certain that in India they embraced neither the tenets of the religion of Bramah nor of Mohamet. They have hence been considered as belonging to the outcast East Indian tribes of Nuts or Parias. Their want of religion is supplied by a good deal of superstition. Such of their ritual as can be discovered, for example that belonging to marriage, is savage in the extreme, and resembles the customs of the Hottentots more than of any civilised people. They adopt various observances, picked up from the religion of the country in which they live. It is, or rather was, the custom of the tribes on the Borders of England and Scotland to attribute success to those journeys which are commenced by passing through the parish church; and they usually try to obtain permission from the beadle to do so when the church is empty, for the performance of divine service is not considered as essential to the omen. They are, therefore, totally devoid of any effectual sense of religion; and the higher or more instructed class may be considered as

NOTES.

acknowledging no deity save those of Epicurus, and such is described as being the faith, or no faith, of Hayraddin Maugrabin.

I may here take notice that nothing is more disagreeable to this indolent and voluptuous people than being forced to follow any regular profession. When Paris was garrisoned by the Allied troops in the year 1815, the Author was walking with a British officer near a post held by the Prussian troops. He happened at the time to smoke a cigar, and was about, while passing the sentinel, to take it out of his mouth, in compliance with a general regulation to that effect, when, greatly to the astonishment of the passengers, the soldier addressed them in these words: "*Rauchen sie immerfort; verdammt sey der Preussische Dienst!*" that is, "Smoke away; may the Prussian service be d—d!" Upon looking closely at the man, he seemed plainly to be a *zigeuner*, or gipsy, who took this method of expressing his detestation of the duty imposed on him. When the risk he ran by doing so is considered, it will be found to argue a deep degree of dislike which could make him commit himself so unwarily. If had been overheard by a sergeant or corporal, the *prügel* would have been the slightest instrument of punishment employed.

Note 27.—Wolf Superstition, p. 262.

> Vox quoque Mœrim
> Jam fugit ipsa; lupi Mœrim videre priores.
> Virgilii *Écloga*, ix.

The commentators add, in explanation of this passage, the opinion of Pliny: "The being beheld by a wolf in Italy is accounted noxious, and is supposed to take away the speech of a man, if these animals behold him ere he sees them."

Note 28.—The Squire of Lowe Degree, p. 272.

There are two written black-letter editions of this old English poem or tale, but only one perfect copy is known, from which it was reprinted by Ritson, in his *Ancient National Romances*, 1802; and since, more accurately, in Mr. Hazlitt's collected *Remains of Early Popular Poetry of England*, 1866 (*Laing*).

Note 29.—Quentin's Adventure at Liege, p. 283.

The adventure of Quentin at Liege may be thought overstrained, yet it is extraordinary what slight circumstances will influence the public mind in a moment of doubt and uncertainty. Most readers must remember that, when the Dutch were on the point of rising against the French yoke, their zeal for liberation received a strong impulse from the landing of a person in a British volunteer uniform, whose presence, though that of a private individual, was received as a guarantee of succours from England.

Note 30.—Battle of St. Tron, p. 303.

Fought by the insurgents of Liege against the Duke of Burgundy, Charles the Bold, when Count of Charolais, in which the people of Liege were defeated with great slaughter.

Note 31.—Murder of the Bishop of Liege, p. 317.

In assigning the present date to the murder of the Bishop of Liege, Louis de Bourbon, history has been violated. It is true that the bishop was made prisoner by the insurgents of that city. It is also true that the report of the insurrection came to Charles with a rumour that the bishop was slain, which excited his indignation against Louis, who was then in his power. But these things happened in 1467, and the bishop's murder did not take place till 1482. In the months of August and September of that year, William de la Marck, called the Wild Boar of Ardennes, entered into a conspiracy with the discontented citizens of Liege against their bishop, Louis of Bourbon, being aided with considerable sums of money by the King of France. By this means, and the assistance of many murderers and banditti, who thronged to him as to a leader befitting them, De la Marck assembled a body of troops, whom he dressed in scarlet as a uniform, with a boar's head on the left sleeve. With this little army he approached the city of Liege. Upon this the citizens, who were engaged in the conspiracy, came to their bishop, and, offering to stand by him to the death, exhorted him to march out against these robbers. The bishop, therefore, put himself at the head of a few troops of his own, trusting to the assistance of the people of Liege. But so soon as they came in sight of the enemy, the citizens, as before agreed, fled from the bishop's banner, and he was left with his own handful of adherents. At this moment De la Marck charged at the head of his banditti with the expected success. The bishop was brought before the profligate knight, who first cut him over the face, then murdered him with his own hand, and caused his body to be exposed naked in the great square of Liege before St. Lambert's cathedral.

Such is the actual narrative of a tragedy which struck with horror the people of the time. The murder of the bishop has been fifteen years antedated in the text, for reasons which the reader of romances will easily appreciate.

Note 32.—Schwarzreiters, p. 338.

Fynes Morrison describes this species of soldiery as follows: "He that at this day looks upon their *schwartz reytern* (that is, black horsemen) must confess that, to make their horses and boots shine, they make themselves as black as collyers. These horsemen wear black clothes, and poor though they be, yet spend no small time in brushing them. The most of them have black horses, which, while they painfully dress, and (as I said) delight to have their boots and shoes shine with blacking stuff, their hands and faces become black, and thereof they have their foresaid name. Yea I have heard Germans say that they do thus make themselves black to seem more terrible to their enemies."—*Itinerary*, edition 1617 [Part III.], p. 165.

Note 33.—Péronne, p. 355.

Indeed, though lying on an exposed and warlike frontier, it was never taken by an enemy, but preserved the proud name of Péronne la Pucelle, until the Duke of Wellington, a great destroyer of that sort of reputation, took the place in the memorable advance upon Paris in 1815.

NOTE 34.—D'HYMBERCOURT, p. 356.

D'Hymbercourt, or Imbercourt, was put to death by the inhabitants of Ghent with the Chancellor of Burgundy in the year 1477. Mary of Burgundy, daughter of Charles the Bold, appeared in mourning in the market-place, and with tears besought the life of her servants from her insurgent subjects, but in vain.

NOTE 35.—PHILIP DES COMINES, p. 356.

Philip des Comines was described in the former editions of this work as a little man, fitted rather for counsel than action. This was a description made at a venture, to vary the military portraits with which the age and work abound. Sleidan the historian, upon the authority of Matthieu d'Arves, who knew Philip des Comines, and had served in his household, says he was a man of tall stature and a noble presence. The learned Monsieur Petitot, editor of the edition of *Memoirs relative to the History of France*, a work of great value, intimates that Philip des Comines made a figure at the games of chivalry and pageants exhibited on the wedding of Charles of Burgundy with Margaret of England in 1468. See the *Chronicle* of Jean de Troyes, in Petitot's edition of the *Mémoires Relatifs à l'Histoire de France* [first series], vol. xiii. p. 375, note. I have looked into Olivier de la Marche, who, in lib. ii. chapter iv. of his *Memoirs*, gives an ample account of these "fierce vanities," containing as many miscellaneous articles as the reticule of the old merchant of *Peter Schlemihl*, who bought shadows, and carried with him in his bag whatever any one could wish or demand in return. There are in that splendid description knights, dames, pages, and archers, good store besides of castles, fiery dragons, and dromedaries; there are leopards riding upon lions; there are rocks, orchards, fountains, spears broken and whole, and the twelve labours of Hercules. In such a brilliant medley I had some trouble in finding Philip des Comines. He is the first named, however, of a gallant band of assailants, knights, and noblemen, to the number of twenty, who, with the Prince of Orange as their leader, encountered, in a general tourney, with a party of the same number under the profligate Adolf of Cleves, who acted as challenger, by the romantic title of *Arbre d'Or*. The encounter, though with arms of courtesy, was very fierce, and separated by main force, not without difficulty. Philip des Comines has, therefore, a title to be accounted *tam Marte quam Mercurio*, though, when we consider the obscurity which has settled on the rest of this *troupe dorée*, we are at no loss to estimate the most valuable of his qualifications. [Compare also Note 45, p. 448.]

NOTE 36.—MEETING OF LOUIS AND CHARLES AFTER THE BATTLE OF MONTL'HÉRY, p. 358.

After the battle of Montl'héry, in 1465, Charles, then Compte de Charolais, had an interview with Louis under the walls of Paris, each at the head of a small party. The two princes dismounted and walked together, so deeply engaged in discussing the business of their meeting, that Charles forgot the peculiarity of his situation; and when Louis turned back towards the town of Paris, from which he came, the Count of Charolais kept him company so far as to pass the line of outworks with which Paris was surrounded, and enter a field-work which communicated with the town by a trench. At this period he had only five or six persons in company with him. His escort caught an alarm for his safety, and his principal followers rode forward from where he had left them, remembering that his grandfather had been assassinated at Montereau in a similar parley, on 10th September 1419. To their great joy the count returned uninjured, accompanied with a guard belonging to Louis. The Burgundians taxed him with rashness in no measured terms. "Say no more of it," said Charles; "I acknowledge the extent of my folly, but I was not aware what I was doing till I entered the redoubt."—*Mémoires de Philippe des Comines*, chap. xiii.

Louis was much praised for his good faith on this occasion; and it was natural that the duke should call it to recollection when his enemy so unexpectedly put himself in his power by his visit to Péronne.

NOTE 37.—LOUIS'S SUSPICIOUS CHARACTER, p. 366.

The arrival of three brothers, princes of the house of Savoy, of Monseigneur de Lau, whom the King had long detained in prison, of Sire Poncet de Rivière, and the Seigneur d'Urfé—who, by the way, as [ancester of] a romance writer of a peculiar turn, might have been happily enough introduced into the present work, but the fate of the Euphuist was a warning to the Author—all of these nobles bearing the emblems of Burgundy, the cross, namely, of St. Andrew, inspired Louis with so much suspicion that he very impolitically demanded to be lodged in the old castle of Péronne, and thus rendered himself an absolute captive.—See Comines's *Memoirs for the Year* 1468.

NOTE 38.—HISTORICAL EPITOME, p. 395.

The historical facts attending this celebrated interview are expounded and enlarged upon in chapter xxvii. Agents sent by Louis had tempted the people of Liege to rebel against their superior, Duke Charles, and persecute and murder their bishop. But Louis was not prepared for their acting with such promptitude. They flew to arms with the temerity of a fickle rabble, took the bishop prisoner, menaced and insulted him, and tore to pieces one or two of his canons. This news was sent to the Duke of Burgundy at the moment when Louis had so unguardedly placed himself in his power; and the consequence was, that Charles placed guards on the Castle of Péronne, and, deeply resenting the treachery of the King of France in exciting sedition in his dominions, while he pretended the most intimate friendship, he deliberated whether he should not put Louis to death.

Three days Louis was detained in this very precarious situation; and it was only his profuse liberality amongst Charles's favourites and courtiers which finally ensured him from death or deposition. Comines, who was the Duke of Burgundy's chamberlain at the time and slept in his apartment, says Charles neither undressed nor slept, but flung himself from time to time on the bed, and at other times wildly traversed the apartment.

It was long before his violent temper became in any degree tractable. At length he only agreed to give Louis his liberty on condition of his accompanying him in person against, and employing his troops in subduing, the mutineers whom his intrigues had instigated to arms.

This was a bitter and degrading alternative. But Louis, seeing no other mode of compounding for the effects of his rashness, not only submitted to this discreditable condition, but swore to it upon a crucifix said to have belonged to Charlemagne. These particulars are from Comines. There is a succinct epitome of them in Sir Nathaniel Wraxall's *History of France*, vol. i.

Note 39.—Punishment of Balue, p. 402.

Louis kept his promise of vengeance against Cardinal La Balue, whom he always blamed as having betrayed him to Burgundy. After he had returned to his own kingdom, he caused his late favourite to be immured in one of the iron cages at Loches. These were constructed with horrible ingenuity, so that a person of ordinary size could neither stand up at his full height or lie lengthwise in them. Some ascribe this horrid device to Balue himself. At any rate, he was confined in one of these dens for eleven years, nor did Louis permit him to be liberated till his last illness.

Note 40.—Prayer of Louis XI., p. 403.

While I perused these passages in the old manuscript chronicle, I could not help feeling astonished that an intellect acute as that of Louis XI. certainly was could so delude itself by a sort of superstition of which one would think the stupidest savages incapable; but the terms of the King's prayer, on a similar occasion, as preserved by Brantôme, are of a tenor fully as extraordinary. It is that which, being overheard by a fool or jester, was by him made public, and let in light on an act of fratricide which might never have been suspected. The way in which the story is narrated by the corrupted courtier, who could jest with all that is criminal as well as with all that is profligate, is worthy the reader's notice; for such actions are seldom done where there are not men with hearts of the nether millstone, capable and willing to make them matters of laughter.

Among the numerous good tricks of dissimulation, feints, and finesses, of gallantry which the good King (Louis XI.) did in his time, he put to death his brother, the Duke de Guyenne, at the moment when the Duke least thought of such a thing, and while the King was making the greatest show of love to him during his life, and of affection for him at his death, managing the whole concern with so much art that it would never have been known had not the King taken into his own service a fool who had belonged to his deceased brother. But it chanced that Louis, being engaged in his devout prayers and orisons at the high altar of Our Lady of Cléry, whom he called his good patroness, and no person nigh except this fool, who, without his knowledge, was within earshot, he thus gave vent to his pious homilies:

"Ah, my good Lady, my gentle mistress, my only friend, in whom alone I have resource, I pray you to supplicate God in my behalf, and to be my advocate with Him that He may pardon me the death of my brother, whom I caused to be poisoned by that wicked abbot of St. John. I confess my guilt to thee as to my good patroness and mistress. But then what could I do? he was perpetually causing disorder in my kingdom. Cause me then to be pardoned, my good Lady, and I know what a reward I will give thee."

This singular confession did not escape the jester, who upbraided the King with the fratricide in the face of the whole company at dinner, which Louis was fain to let pass without observation, in case of increasing the slander.

NOTE 41.—LOUIS'S VENGEANCE, p. 408.

Varillas, in a history of Louis XI., observes, that his provost-marshal was often so precipitate in execution as to slay another person instead of him whom the King had indicated. This always occasioned a double execution, for the wrath or revenge of Louis was never satisfied with a vicarious punishment.

NOTE 42.—TRISTAN L'HERMITE, p. 411.

The Author has endeavoured to give to the odious Tristan l'Hermite a species of dogged and brutal fidelity to Louis similar to the attachment of a bull-dog to its master. With all the atrocity of his execrable character, he was certainly a man of courage, and was, in his youth, made knight on the breach of Fronsac, with a great number of other young nobles, by the honour-giving hand of the elder Dunois, the celebrated hero of Charles V. [VII.]'s reign.

NOTE 43.—PREDICTION OF LOUIS XI.'S DEATH, p. 417.

The death of Martius Galeotti was in some way connected with Louis XI. The astrologer was at Lyons, and hearing that the King was approaching the city, got on horseback in order to meet him. As he threw himself hastily from his horse to pay his respects to the King, he fell with a violence which, joined to his extreme corpulence, was the cause of his death in 1478.

But the acute and ready-witted expedient to escape instant death had no reference to the history of this philosopher. The same, or nearly the same, story is told of Tiberius, who demanded of a soothsayer, Thrasyllus, if he knew the day of his own death, and received for answer, "It would take place just three days before that of the Emperor." On this reply, instead of being thrown over the rocks into the sea, as had been the tyrant's first intention, he was taken great care of for the rest of his life.—*Taciti Annal.*, lib. vi. cap. 20-22.

The circumstances in which Louis XI. received a similar reply from an astrologer are as follows: The soothsayer in question had presaged that a female favourite, to whom the King was very much attached, should die in a week. As he proved a true prophet, the King was as much incensed as if the astrologer could have prevented the evil he predicted. He sent for the philosopher, and had a party stationed to assassinate him as he retired from the royal presence. Being asked by the King concerning his own fortunes, he confessed that he perceived signs of imminent danger. Being farther questioned concerning the day of his own death, he was shrewd enough to answer with composure, that it would be exactly three days before that of his Majesty. There was, of course, care taken that he should escape his destined fate; and he was ever after much protected by the King, as a man of real science, and intimately connected with the royal destinies.

Although almost all the historians of Louis represent him as a dupe to the common but splendid imposture of judicial astrology, yet his credulity could not be deep-rooted, if the following anecdote, reported by Bayle, be correct.

Upon one occasion, Louis, intending to hunt, and doubtful of the weather, inquired of an astrologer near his person whether it would be fair. The sage, having recourse to his astrolabe, answered with confidence in the affirmative. At the entrance of the forest the royal cortège was met by a charcoalman, who expressed to some menials of the train his surprise that the King should have thought of hunting in a day which threatened tempest. The collier's prediction proved true. The King and his court were driven from their sport well drenched; and Louis having heard what the collier had said, ordered the man before him. "How were you more accurate in foretelling the weather, my friend," said he, "than this learned man?" "I am an ignorant man, sire," answered the collier, "was never at school, and cannot read or write. But I have an astrologer of my own, who shall foretell weather with any of them. It is, with reverence, the ass who carries my charcoal, who always, when bad weather is approaching, points forward his ears, walks more slowly than usual, and tries to rub himself against walls; and it was from these signs that I foretold yesterday's storm." The King burst into a fit of laughing, dismissed the astrological biped, and assigned the collier a small pension to maintain the quadruped, swearing he would never in future trust to any other astrologer than the charcoalman's ass.

But if there is any truth in this story, the credulity of Louis was not of a nature to be removed by the failure there mentioned. He is said to have believed in the prediction of Angelo Cattho, his physician, and the friend of Comines, who foretold the death of Charles of Burgundy in the very time and hour when it took place at the battle of Morat [Nancy]. Upon this assurance, Louis vowed a silver screen to the shrine of St. Martin, which he afterwards fulfilled at the expense of one hundred thousand francs. It is well known, besides, that he was the abject and devoted slave of his physicians. Coctier, or Cothier, one of their number, besides the retaining fee of ten thousand crowns, extorted from his royal patient great sums in lands and money, and in addition to all, the bishopric of Amiens for his nephew. He maintained over Louis unbounded influence, by using to him the most disrespectful harshness and insolence. "I know," he said to the suffering King, "that one morning you will turn me adrift like so many others. But, by Heaven, you had better beware, for you will not live eight days after you have done so!" It is unnecessary to dwell longer on the fears and superstitions of a prince whom the wretched love of life induced to submit to such indignities.

NOTE 44.—ANECDOTE OF THE BOOTS, p. 433.

The story is told more bluntly, and less probably, in the French memoirs of the period, which affirm that Comines, out of a presumption inconsistent with his excellent good sense, had asked of Charles of Burgundy to draw off his boots, without having been treated with any previous familiarity to lead to such a freedom. I have endeavoured to give the anecdote a turn more consistent with the sense and prudence of the great author concerned.

NOTE 45.—PHILIP DES COMINES, p. 440.

There is little doubt that, during the interesting scene at Péronne, Philip des Comines first learned intimately to know the great powers of mind of Louis XI., by which he was so much dazzled that it is impossible, in reading his *Memoirs*, not to be sensible that he was blinded by them to the more odious shades of his character. He entertained from this time forward a partiality to France. The historian passed into France about 1472, and rose high in the good graces of Louis XI. He afterwards became the proprietor of the lordship of Argenton and others, a title which was given him by anticipation in the earliest editions of this work. He did not obtain it till he was in the French service. After the death of Louis, Philip des Comines fell under the suspicion of the daughter of Louis, called our Lady of Beaujeu, as too zealous a partizan of the rival house of Orleans. The historian himself was imprisoned for eight months in one of the iron cages he so forcibly described. It was there that he regretted the fate of a court life. "I have ventured on the great ocean," he said, in his affliction, "and the waves have devoured me." He was subjected to a trial, and exiled from court for some years by the Parliament of Paris, being found guilty of holding intercourse with disaffected persons. He survived this cloud, however, and was afterwards employed by Charles VIII. in one or two important missions, where talents were required. Louis XII. also transferred his favour to the historian, but did not employ him. He died at his Castle of Argenton in 1509, and was regretted as one of the most profound statesmen, and certainly the best historian, of his age. In a poem to his memory by the poet Ronsard, he received the distinguished praise that he was the first to show the lustre which valour and noble blood derived from being united with learning. [Compare also Note 35, p. 529.]

NOTE 46.—DISGUISED HERALD, p. 465.

The heralds of the middle ages, like the *feciales* of the Romans, were invested with a character which was held almost sacred. To strike a herald was a crime which inferred a capital punishment; and to counterfeit the character of such an august official was a degree of treason towards those men who were accounted the depositaries of the secrets of monarchs and the honour of nobles. Yet a prince so unscrupulous as Louis XI. did not hesitate to practise such an imposition, when he wished to enter into communication with Edward IV. of England.

Exercising that knowledge of mankind for which he was so eminent, he selected, as an agent fit for his purpose, a simple valet. This man, whose address had been known to him, he disguised as a herald, with all the insignia of his office, and sent him in that capacity to open a communication with the English army. Two things are remarkable in this transaction. First, that the stratagem, though of so fraudulent a nature, does not seem to have been necessarily called for, since all that King Louis could gain by it would be, that he did not commit himself by sending a more responsible messenger. The other circumstance worthy of notice is, that Comines, though he mentions the affair at great length, is so pleased with the King's shrewdness in selecting, and dexterity at indoctrinating, his pseudo-herald that he forgets all remark on the impudence and fraud of the imposition, as well as the great risk of discovery; from both which circumstances we are led to the conclusion, that the solemn character which the heralds endeavoured to arrogate to themselves had already begun to lose regard among statesmen and men of the great world.

Even Ferne, zealous enough for the dignity of the herald, seems to impute this intrusion on their rights in some degree to necessity.

"I have heard some," he says, "but with shame enough, allow of the action of Louis the Eleventh, King of France, who had so unknightly a regard both of his own honour and also of armes, that he had seldom about his court any officer-at armes. And therefore, at such time as King Edward the Fourth, King of England, had entered France with hostile power, and lay before the town of St. Quentin, the same French king, for want of a herald to carry his mind to the English king, was constrained to subordinate a vadelict, or common 'serving-man, with a trumpet-banner, having a hole made through the middest for this preposterous herauld to put his head through, and to cast it over his shoulders instead of a better coat-armour of France. And thus came this hastily arrayed courier as a counterfeit officer-at-armes, with instructions from his sovereign's mouth to offer peace to our king. 'Well,' replies Torquatus, the other interlocutor in the dialogue, 'that fault was never yet to be found in any of our English kings, nor ever shall be, I hope.'"—*Blazon of Gentrie*, 1586, pp. 161, 162.

In this curious book, the author, besides some assertions in favour of coat-armour, too nearly approaching blasphemy to be quoted, informs us that the Apostles were gentlemen of blood, and many of them descended from that worthy conqueror, Judas Maccabæus ; but through the course of time and persecution of wars, poverty oppressed the kindred, and they were constrained to servile works. So were the four doctors and fathers of the church (Ambrose, Augustine, Heirome, and Gregorie) gentlemen both of blood and arms (p. 98). The Author's copy of this rare tract (memorial of a hopeful young friend, now no more)exhibits a curious sally of the national and professional irritability of a Scottish herald.

This person appears to have been named Thomas Drysdale, Islay Herald, who purchased the volume in 1619, and seems to have perused it with patience and profit till he came to the following passage in Ferne, which enters into the distinction between sovereign and feudatory crowns. "There is also a king, and he a homager, or fædatorie to the estate and majestie of another king, as to his superior lord, as that of Scotland to our English empire." This assertion set on fire the Scottish blood of Islay Herald, who, forgetting the book had been printed nearly forty years before, and that the author was probably dead, writes on the margin in great wrath, and in a half-text hand : " He is a traitor and lyar in his throat, and I offer him the combat, that says Scotland's kings were ever feudatorie to England."

Note 47.—Prize of Honour, p. 491.

The perilling the hand of an heiress upon the event of a battle was not so likely to take place in the 14th century as when the laws of chivalry were in more general observance. Yet it was not unlikely to occur to so absolute a prince as Duke Charles, in circumstances like those supposed.

Note 48.—Bride of De la Marck, p. 494.

It is almost unnecessary to add, that the marriage of William de la Marck with the Lady Hameline is as apocryphal as the lady herself. The real bride of the Wild Boar of Ardennes was Joan D'Arschel, Baroness of Schoonhoven.

Note 49.—Attack upon Liege, p. 502.

The Duke of Burgundy, full of resentment for the usage which the bishop had received from the people of Liege (whose death, as already noticed did not take place for some years after), and knowing that the walls of the town had not been repaired since they were breached by himself after the battle of St. Tron, advanced recklessly to their chastisement. His commanders shared his presumptuous confidence; for the advanced guard of his army, under the Maréchal of Burgundy and Seigneur D'Hymbercourt, rushed upon one of the suburbs, without waiting for the rest of their army, which, commanded by the Duke in person, remained about seven or eight leagues in the rear. The night was closing, and, as the Burgundian troops observed no discipline, they were exposed to a sudden attack from a party of citizens commanded by Jean de Vilde, who, assaulting them in front and rear, threw them into great disorder, and killed more than eight hundred men, of whom one hundred were men-at-arms.

When Charles and the King of France came up, they took up their quarters in two villas situated near to the wall of the city. In the two or three days which followed, Louis was distinguished for the quiet and regulated composure with which he pressed the siege, and provided for defence in case of sallies; while the Duke of Burgundy, no way deficient in courage, and who showed the rashness and want of order which was his principal characteristic, seemed also extremely suspicious that the King would desert him and join with the Liegeois.

They lay before the town for five or six days, and at length fixed the 30th of October 1468 for a general storm. The citizens, who had probably information of their intent, resolved to prevent their purpose, and determined on anticipating it by a desperate sally through the breaches in their walls. They placed at their head six hundred of the men of the little territory of Franchemont, belonging to the bishopric of Liege, and reckoned the most valiant of their troops. They burst out of the town on a sudden, surprised the Duke of Burgundy's quarters ere his guards could put on their armour, which they had laid off to enjoy some repose before the assault. The King of France's lodgings were also attacked and endangered. A great confusion ensued, augmented incalculably by the mutual jealousy and suspicions of the French and Burgundians. The people of Liege were, however, unable to maintain their hardy enterprise, when the men-at-arms of the King and Duke began to recover from their confusion, and were finally forced to retire within their walls, after narrowly missing the chance of surprising both King Louis and the Duke of Burgundy, the most powerful princes of their time. At daybreak the storm took place, as had been originally intended, and the citizens, disheartened and fatigued by the nocturnal sally, did not make so much resistance as was expected. Liege was taken and miserably pillaged, without regard to sex or age, things sacred or things profane. These particulars are fully related by Comines in his *Memoirs*, liv. ii. chaps. 11, 12, 13, and do not differ much from the account of the same events in chapters xxxv. and xxxvi.

Note 50.—Anachronisms, p. 514.

We have already noticed the anachronism respecting the crimes of this atrocious baron; and it is scarce necessary to repeat, that if he in reality murdered the Bishop of Liege in 1482, the Count of La Marck could not be slain in the defence of Liege four[teen] years earlier. In fact, the Wild Boar of Ardennes, as he was usually termed, was of high birth, being the third son of John I., Count of La Marck and Aremberg, and ancestor of the branch called Barons of Lumain. He did not escape the punishment due to his atrocity, though it did not take place at the time, or in the manner, narrated in the text. Maximilian, Emperor of Austria, caused him to be arrested at Utrecht, where he was beheaded in the year 1485 three years after the Bishop of Liege's death.

Note 51.—Descent of the Leslies, p. 515.

An old rhyme, by which the Leslies vindicate their descent from an ancient hero, who is said to have slain a gigantic Hungarian champion, and to have formed a proper name for himself by a play of words upon the place where he fought his adversary.

GLOSSARY

OF

WORDS, PHRASES, AND ALLUSIONS.

ABERBROTHOCK, now called Arbroath, a town in Forfarshire
ABONNÉ, was, subscribed
ABOULCASEM, of Basra, noted for his generosity and magnificence. *See* Weber, *Tales of the East*, vol. ii. p. 308
ABYE, to pay the penalty for
AD SACRA, for holy things
AGNES SOREL, or SOREAU, mistress of Charles VII. of France, who is said to have prompted the patriotic efforts of that king against the English in the 15th century
AIGUILETTES, tagged points
ALDEBARAN, the name given to a star of the first magnitude in the constellation Taurus (Bull), one of the four "royal stars" of the ancient Egyptians
ALLEGRO, joy, mirth. *Compare* Milton's *L'Allegro*
AMADIS AND ORIANA, the hero and heroine of the romance of chivalry entitled *Amadis of Gaul*
ANGELICA, the heroine of Ariosto's *Orlando Furioso*, who falls in love with the obscure squire Medoro
ANGELO, HENRY, celebrated riding and fencing master at the beginning of the 19th century. *See* his *Reminiscences* (2 vols. 1828-30)
ANGUS, the old name of Forfarshire
ANNUNCIO VOBIS GAUDIUM MAGNUM, I announce to you tidings of great joy
ARBRE D'OR, golden tree
AROINT, avaunt, begone
ASSIETTÉE, plateful
ASTRÆA, the English dramatist, Aphra Behn (1640-89), whose plays are too frequently coarse and indelicate
ASTUCIOUS, astute, crafty
AUBERGE, inn
AUGHT, possession
AUTANT DE PERDU, so much lost
AUVERNAT, red wine of Orleans
"AUXERRE EST LA BOISSON DES ROIS," Auxerre (wine) is the drink of kings
AZINCOUR, Agincourt, fought in 1415

BACK-FRIEND, a backer, friend to fall back upon
BADAUD, gazer, gossip
BAILEY, a space between two circuits or walls of defence in a castle
BAN AND ARRIÈRE-BAN, the entire feudal force
BANDE NOIRE, a company of speculators who bought up the large estates of the old noble families of France, then demolished the châteaux and sold the land in small parcels
BARBOUR, Scotch poet (14th century), author of a long poem on the exploits of Robert Bruce
BASTARD OF RUBEMPRÉ, a nephew of the Count of Croy, who was accused of being an agent of Louis XI. employed to carry off (1464) the Count of Charolais (Charles of Burgundy)
BAVAROISE, tea sweetened with vegetable syrup (capillaire)
BAYES. *See The Rehearsal*, Act. iv. sc. 1

BEATI PACIFICI, Blessed are the peaceful

BEATI QUI IN DOMINO MORIUNTUR, Blessed are the dead that die in the Lord

BENEDICITE, blessing, returning of thanks

BIFTECK DE MOUTON, beefsteak of mutton

BLACK WALLOONS. The Walloons, descendants of the Gallic Belgæ, live in the Ardennes and on both sides of the Franco-Belgian frontier. Black was no doubt the colour of the uniform worn by Charles of Burgundy's Walloons soldiers

BLATE, bashful

BOTTRINE, small leather flask

BOUILLI, boiled meat

BRACH, hound that hunts by scent

BRAEMAN, one who lives on the southern slope of the Grampians

BRAG, to challenge, proudly defy

BRANTWEIN, brandy

BRAW-WARLD, showy, gaudy

BROGUE, a Highlander's shoe of undressed hide

BROWST, brewage, beverage brewed

BRUDER, brother

BUCHAN. JOHN STUART, EARL OF, commanded the Scottish auxiliaries in France in the reign of Charles VII.; he was a son of Regent Albany, and grandson of Robert II. of Scotland

BUSHMENT, or AMBUSHMENT, an ambush

CABARET, wine-shop, tavern

CALLANT, boy, stripling; BRAW CALLANT, a fine fellow

CALTHROP, or CALTROP, a spiked iron ball; gin, trap

CANAILLE, rascal mob

CAP DE DIOU, God's head—a Gascon oath

CARCANET, necklace, chain of jewels

CARTE, menu, bill of fare

CASERNE, barracks

CATCHPOLL, a warrant-officer who arrests for debt

CATHAY, China

CENSÉ, reputed

CERNEAU, the half kernel of an unripe walnut

CHAM (of Tartary), khan, *i. e.* chief ruler of the Tartars in Muscovy

CHAPEAU À PLUMES, hat with feathers, plumed hat

CHAPEAU BRAS, three-cornered hat with a low crown

CHARES, household work

CHASSE-CAFÉ, more correctly POUSSE-CAFÉ, a small glass of brandy or liqueur taken after coffee

CHÂTEAU MARGOUT, or MARGAUX, claret of the very first brand

CHÂTEAU OF SULLY, called Sully, on the left bank of the Loire (modern dept. Loiret), where the great minister of Henry IV. wrote his *Mémoires*

CHIELD, fellow

CHIROMANTIST, one who tells fortunes by palmistry or the hand

CHOUSE, cheat, swindle

CINQ FRANCS, five francs (the bottle)

CLÉRY, about 10 miles below Orleans on the Loire; Louis XI. was buried there

COCAGNE, an imaginary country, where good living and idleness are the chief objects or pursuits of the inhabitants

COCKERED, pampered, brought up indulgently

COLIN MAILLARD, blindman's buff

COMBUST, astrological term for a planet that is too near the sun

COMFITURE, preparation of preserved fruit, confection

COMING (COUNTESS), inclined to make advances, forward, eager

CONDÉ, LOUIS JOSEPH DE BOURBON, PRINCE OF, French general in the Seven Years' War, and the military chief of the *émigrés* on the Rhine, after the fall of the Bastille

CORBIE, raven

CÔTELETTE À LA MAINTENON, mutton cutlets served with parsley, mushrooms, and brown sauce

COUCHÉE, a levee held just before retiring to sleep

CRAIG, neck

CROIX DE ST. LOUIS, the decoration of a military order founded by Louis XIV. in 1693, for distinguished service by Roman Catholic officers, was a gold eight-armed cross bearing on one side the effigy of St. Louis of France, and on the other side a flaming sword passed through a laurel crown

CULLION, poltroon

CURNEY, small number

DAFFING, loose talk
DARIOLE, a pastry cake containing cream
DAS IST, that is, *i.e.*
DEAS, dais
DEBOUT, etc. (p. 353), Arise—arise, gentlemen; its time to be going!
DE BURE, G. F., a celebrated French bibliographer of the 18th century
DEMI-SOLDE, half-pay
DENIS MONTJOYE, the old war-cry of the French
DER BISCHOFF, or BISCHOF, the bishop
DODDERED, covered with twining parasites, such as mistletoe
DOGBERRY. The allusion is to *Much Ado About Nothing*, Act. iv. sc. 2
DOLLY, a cook who gave her name to Dolly's Tavern in Paternoster Row, London; her portrait was painted by Gainsborough
DONNER AND BLITZ, thunder and lightning! a German oath; **DONNER AND HAGEL**, thunder and hail!
DORFF, or DORF, a village
DOUGLAS, ARCHIBALD, FOURTH EARL OF, entered the service of France and was made Duke of Touraine, in 1423
DU BIST EIN COMISCHER MAN, you are a funny fellow
DUFFLE, a coarse woollen cloth with a thick nap
DU GUESCLIN, BERTRAND, Constable of France, her greatest soldier during the 14th century
DURINDARTE, should be **DURINDANA, or DURANDANA**, the sword of Orlando (Roland) in the *Orlando Furioso*
DYES, gewgaws, paltry ornaments

EBLIS, in Mohammedan mythology, the chief of the fallen angels
EBRO'S TEMPER. The allusion is doubtless to the celebrated weapons of Toledo, although that town is on the Tagus, not the Ebro
ÉCHEVIN, sheriff, municipal magistrate
ÉCLAIRCISSEMENT, explanation
ÉCOSSE, EN AVANT, Scotland, (step) forward
EHRENHOLD, German for "herald"
EIN WORT, EIN MANN, a man of his word
EMBRUN, OUR LADY OF, a figure of the Virgin much worshipped by Louis XI., preserved in a church at Embrun, in Dauphiné (modern dept. Hautes Alpes)
ENFANS PERDUS, the forlorn hope
EPHEMERIDES, an astronomical almanac
ESCALIER DÉROBÉ, private staircase
ÉTANG, pond, lake
ETHNIC, pagan
ETIAM IN CUBICULO, even in the bed-chamber
EUPHUIST, Sir Piercie Shafton in *The Monastery*

FABLIAU, fable, moral tale
FACTIONNAIRE, sentry
FÄHNLEIN, troop
FAIRE DES NOCES. The Paris innkeeper's notice runs *salle à faire des noces*, "a hall for wedding festivities."
FAITOUR, traitor, rascal
FASTE, ostentation
FECIALES, or FETIALES, a college of priests who watched over the sanctity of treaties
FERME ORNÉE, a model farm
FIER COMME UN ÉCOSSAIS, proud as a Scotchman
FINIS—I SHOULD HAVE SAID, etc. (p. 406), Finis, I should have said the rope (*funis*), is the end of the work (book)
FLEUR-DE-LYS, lilies, the royal arms of France
FLORENTIN (p. 395), Dante, in *Inferno*, iii. 9
FLORIO. The Italian-English dictionary of John Florio, entitled *A World of Words* (1598), is doubtless what is alluded to (p. 26)
FOSSA CUM FURCA, the right of life and death exercised by a feudal noble over his dependants—of hanging the males and drowning the females
FOURRIERS AND HARBINGERS, both officers whose duty it was to procure and make all arrangements for the lodgings of people of high rank; **FOURRIER**, avant-courier, messenger sent on in advance
FRAMPOLD, unruly, peevish
FREE COMPANIES, mercenary troops owning no master except their own captains, who sold their services to whomsoever paid them best

FREMIT, strangers; cold, indifferent

GABELLE, tax on salt
GARCE, a young girl, now a dishonourable appellation
GARÇON PERRUQUIER, hair-dresser
GAUNTOIS AND LIEGEOIS, people of Ghent (or Gand) and Liege,
GEAR, business, affair, thing owned; GEAR, LET US TO THIS, set we about the matter in hand
GEB (UP), give (up)
GEISTER-SEERS, or GEISTER-SEHER, seers of ghosts
GENS DE LETTRES, etc. (p. 26), literary men, whom you call Sir Scott, I believe
GENTILLÂTRE, country squire, poor gentleman
GHAIST, ghost
GOTTFRIED, Godfrey
GRANDE CHÈRE, good living
GRAND SEIGNIOR, the sultan of the Ottoman Turks
G--VE, OUR LADY OF. In the Place le Gréve, Paris, criminals were executed
GROSS STERNENDEUTER, clever interpreters of the stars
GUILDER, a Dutch florin=1s. 8d.
GUILDRY, a guild, the members of a guild
GUINGUETTE, a place of refreshment, tea-garden, outside Paris
GUT GETROFFEN, well hit

HAGEL AND STURMWETTER, hail and stormy weather! a German oath
HANAP, a large drinking-cup
HANDSEL, earnest-money
HANGUISSE, or ANGUS, an old name for the Scottish county of Forfar
HAUPTMANN, captain, leader
HAUT-DE-CHAUSSES À CANON, knee-breeches ornamented with canons or indented ornamental rolls
HERMETICAL PHILOSOPHY, a system ascribed to Hermes Trismegistus, *i.e.* the god Thoth, the traditional author of Egyptian culture
HERZOG, duke
HOCHHEIM, a celebrated Rhenish vintage
HÔPITAL DES FOUS, lunatic asylum
HORS DE PAGE, finished serving one's apprenticeship as a page
HÔTEL DE VILLE, town-hall
HYKE A TALBOT, a hunter's cry to his dog, occurs in Dame Berners, *Boke of Hawking and Hunting* (1486)

IMPAYABLE, excellent
INAMORATO, lover
IN COMMENDAM, in trust, along with

JABOT, frill
JACQUES BONHOMME, equivalent to our Hodge, a generic name for the French peasant
JAIZA, or JAICE, formerly the capital of Bosnia, was captured after a long siege by Matthias Corvinus in 1463, and vainly stormed during three days by the sultan, Mahomet II., in 1464
JANUS PANNONIUS, or JEAN DE CISNIGE, Hungarian poet of the 15th century
JARDIN ANGLOIS, an English garden, the characteristic of which, as distinguished from a stiff, regularly-arranged French garden, is the appearance of untrammelled nature it exhibits.
JAZERAN, or JASERAN, a flexible shirt of linked mail
JEAN QUI PLEURE, Weeping John; JEAN QUI RIT, Laughing John
JERRY-COME-TUMBLE, acrobat, tumbler
JESHURUN, the chosen of Israel. *See* Deut. xxxii. 15
JOHANNISBERG, the most valuable of Rhenish wines
JOUR MAIGRE, fast day
JOYOUS SCIENCE, BRETHREN OF, minstrels
JUS EMPHYTEUSIS, the law whereby one person acquires a perpetual right to the use of land that belongs to another person

KAISAR, or KAISER, emperor
KING OF CASTILE, probably Philip III. of Spain, whose death was caused partly through his sitting too near to a brazier, and the punctilious etiquette of his attendants in refusing to move it until the proper functionary came
KLEPPER, hack, nag
KNIGHT WITHOUT FEAR AND REPROACH, Chevalier Bayard (1476-1524)
KURSCHENSCHAFT, intended for KÜRSCHNERSCHAFT, the trade asso-

GLOSSARY. 543

ciation of the furriers and skinners (*compare* p. 320); but this being an unusual compound, perhaps BURSCHENSCHAFT, corporation, association, was intended

LA GUERRE EST MA PATRIE, etc. (p. 5), The battlefield is my fatherland; my armour my home; my life a perpetual warfare

LANDES, low flat deserts of loose sand bordering on the Bay of Biscay, in the south of France

LANZKNECHTS, or LANZKNECHTE, also LANDSKNECHTE, mercenary foot-soldiers, armed with pikes and swords, first organized by the Emperor Maximilian I. in 1487

LAPIS OFFENSIONIS, etc. (p. 245), a stone of offence and a stumbling-block

LARGESSE, a present, the herald's cry when soliciting gratuities after the performance of some public function

LEAGUER, a permanent fortified camp; LIE LEAGUER, take up permanent quarters

"LEAVE ALL HOPE BEHIND," from Dante's *Inferno*, iii. 9

LEGION OF SAINTS, or THEBAN LEGION, were all massacred in the persecution of the Emperor Maximin, about the year 286

LIARD, small French coin, current after the 14th century=¼d silver penny English

LINEA VITÆ, in palmistry, the line of life, the principal on the hand

LIRE, should doubtless be LITRE=a little less than a quart

LOCHES, on the Indre, some twenty-five miles southeast of Tours

LOOM, article, headpiece

LOON, fellow

LORETTO, on the Adriatic coast of Italy, 15 miles from Ancona, where is preserved the reputed house in which the Virgin Mary lived at Nazareth—a celebrated shrine

LOWER CIRCLES, or provinces in Lower (North) Germany, the principal of which were Westphalia and Saxony

LUCIO, in Shakespeare's *Measure for Measure*, Act. v. sc. 1

LURDANE, blockhead

LUSTHAUS, country villa

MACARONIC LATIN, a modern language used with Latin inflections and construction

MACHIAVEL, or MACHIAVELLI, NICCOLO DI BERNARDO DEI, a Florentine statesman of the 16th century, who taught that rulers may commit every treacherous and unlawful act in the interests of strong government

MAHOMET'S COFFIN, according to Mohammedan tradition, is suspended in mid-air between two magnets

MAHOUND, a contemptuous name given to a devil, meant to represent Mahomet, in the mediæval mystery-plays

MAIGRE, thin, applied to soup made without meat

MAÎTRE DE CUISINE, head cook; MAÎTRE D'HÔTEL, steward

MALVOLIO. *See* Shakespeare's *Twelfth Night*, Act. ii. sc. 5

MARÉCHAUSSÉE, police horse-patrol

MARMOUTIER, THE ABBEY OF, in the environs of Tours, founded by St. Martin of Tours (4th century), and one of the most influential and powerful in France in the Middle Ages

MATELOT, or MATELOTE, a rich fish stew with wine sauce flavoured with onions and herbs

MEIKLE, much

MEIN, my; MEIN GOTT, my God! MEINHERR, sir

MEISTER (ÆSOP), master, a title of honour given by Germans to an approved master in his art or craft

MELL, to interfere, meddle

MELPOMENE, in ancient Greek mythology, the Muse of Tragedy

MELUSINA, in old French folklore was every Saturday transformed from a woman into a serpent from the waist downwards

MÉTAIRIE, farmhouse

MIEUX VAULT BON REPAS QUE BEL HABIT, a good meal is better than a fine coat

MILADI LAC, *The Lady of the Lake*, Scott's poem

MINSTREL, THE (p. 94), or BLIND HARRY, author of a long poem descriptive of the exploits of Wallace (about 1460)

MINTING, aiming

MOLIÈRE'S COMEDY, *L'Amour Médecin. See* Act. 1. sc. 1, the persons being, however, a dealer in tapestry and a goldsmith
MORE MEO, in my own way
MORGAINE LA FÉE, pupil of Merlin the Magician, and half-sister of King Arthur
MUMBLE, to chew gently with the gums
MURCIAN BULL, one bred in Murcia, a province in the southeast of Spain
MUSION, the wildcat, term of heraldry

NE MOLIARIS AMICO, etc. (p. 245), Devise not evil against thy neighbour, seeing he dwelleth securely by thee
NOM DE GUERRE, nick-name
NOSTRADAMUS, or MICHEL DE NOTREDAME, famous French astrologer (16th century)
ORA PRO NOBIS, pray for us—a religious supplication.
ORDONNANCE, COMPANIES OF, independent companies, not enrolled among the ordinary regiments
ORIANA. *See* Amadis and Oriana
ORLANDO, the Italian form of Roland

PAR AMOURS, by illicit love, in matters of love
PASQUES-DIEU, the favorite oath of Louis XI.
PASQUIER, ÉTIENNE, a French magistrate and historian (1529-1615), who wrote *Lettres* (1723) and other works
PÂTÉ DE PÉRIGORD, pasties of partridges with truffles
PAULUS JOVIUS, or PAOLO GIOVIO, an Italian historian of the 16th century, lived at the Pope's court, and wrote, amongst other works, *Elogia Doctorum Virorum* (Venice, 1546)
PAUVRES REVENANTS, poor ghosts
PAYSAGE, landscape
PAYSANNE, country girl
PENSEROSO, sadness, melancholy. *Compare* Milton's *Il Penseroso*
PEREAT IMPROBUS, etc. (p. 246), Let the wicked perish, Amen! and let him be anathema
PER PALE, divided vertically
PETER SCHLEMIHL, the hero of a tale by the German poet Adelbert von Chamisso (1781-1838)
PETITE POINTE D'AIL, slight flavour of garlic
PETIT PLAT, little dish
PIGAULT LE BRUN, Charles A. G. Pigault de l'Épinoy, known as Pigault-Lebrun, a popular French novelist (1753-1835)
PILLEUR, plunderer
PIRN, the bobbin of a spinning-wheel; ILL-WINDED PIRNS TO RAVEL OUT, knotty difficulties to solve or adjust
PISTOL EATING THE LEEK. *See* Shakespeare's *Henry V.*, Act v. sc. 1
PLACK, an old Scotch copper coin = ⅓d penny, English
PLEACHED, with branches interwoven
PLEXITIUM, a chase, woodlands inclosed for game
POLK, or PULK, a squadron, troop of Cossacks
POORTITH, poverty
POST TOT PROMISSA, after so many promises
POTAGE, (formerly) vegetables; POTAGER, kitchen garden
POTENCE, gallows
POTZ TAUSEND, the deuce
POUR PASSER LE TEMPS, to pass away the time
POW, head
PRÉVENANCE, kind attention, obliging kindness
PRÜGEL, cudgel, stick
PUBLIC GOOD, WAR OF, grew out of a league formed by the great feudatory princes of France against Louis XI.
PUCELLE, virgin

QUI VIVE? Who goes there?

REGALE, treat, entertainment
RHEIMS. *See* Smeared with oil, etc.
RHEINWEIN, Rhenish wine
RHINEGRAVE, the title of the feudal lord of the *gau* or county of the Rhine
RIFACIMENTO, restoration, repairing
ROCHET, or ROCKET, a short cloak worn formerly by both men and women; in Pasquier's passage the original French signifies "petticoat." *Compare* p. 522
ROMAN COMIQUE, PLAYER IN, a famous novel (1651-57), by Paul Scarron

GLOSSARY.

ROMAUNT, a poetical romance of chivalry

ROUSE, a bumper

ROUTIER, an experienced man; VIEUX ROUTIER, an old stager

RUBEMPRÉ, BASTARD OF. *See* Bastard of Rubempré

RUNLET, a barrel (of spirits) holding 18½ gallons

ST. BARTHOLOMEW, was flayed alive

ST. DENIS, 4 miles north of Paris; the abbey-church there was long the burial-place of the sovereigns of France

ST. FRANCIS'S CORD, the founder of the monastic order of Franciscans, dressed in a coarse woollen tunic, girt about with a hempen cord

ST. GATIEN, the cathedral of Tours

ST. JOHN (JEAN) D'ANGÉLY, about 16 miles southeast from La Rochelle. Jean Favre, abbot of St. Jean d'Angély, was popularly believed to have poisoned (1472), at Louis XI.'s instigation, that king's brother, Charles Duke of Berri and of Guyenne

ST. JUDE, 28th October

ST. LAMBERT, patron saint of Liege

ST. LAMBERT'S, the old cathedral of Liege, demolished by the French Revolutionists in 1794, and altogether removed in 1808

ST. MARTIN, bishop of Tours, died just before the year 400

ST. PATIBULARIUS, derived from Latin *patibulum*, a fork-shaped gibbet

ST. PERPETUUS, third successor of St. Martin of Tours, erected over that bishop's bones the church of St. Martin, consecrated in 472

ST. TRON, more correctly ST. TROND, about 20 miles north-west of Liege

SAINTS, LEGION OF. *See* Legion of saints

SAKER, a small gun formerly used in sieges

SANCTE HUBERTE, etc. (p. 209), St. Hubert, St. Julian, St. Martin, St. Rosalia, all ye saints who hear me, pray for me a sinner

SANCTE JULIANE, etc. (p. 199), Holy Julian, listen to our prayers. Pray—pray for us

SANGLIER, wild boar

SANTON, a Mohammedan prophet or saint

SAUMUR, GOOD FATHERS OF, belonging to the ancient abbey of St. Laurent in Saumur, which dates back to the 11th century

SAUS AND BRAUS, revelry in good things. *In Saus und Braus leben* = to live at heck and manger

SCHAKOS, or SHAKO, a military head-dress, a tall cylindrical hat, with a shield in the front of it

SCHEIK EBN HALI, or ALI BEN ABEN-RAGEL, an Arab astrologer of the 11th century

SCHELM, rogue, scoundrel

SCHNEIDERS, or SNYDERS, FRANS, Flemish painter (1579-1657)

SCHOPPEN, meant for SCHÖFFEN, alderman, municipal magistrates. *Schoppen* means pint-measures

SCHWARZBIER, black beer

SCHWARZREITERS, or SCHWARZREITER, black horsemen, black troopers

SCOTCHED (SNAKE), slightly wounded

SERO VENIENTIBUS OSSA, the bones are for late comers

SHEERLY, thoroughly, quite

SHENSTONE, WILLIAM, English poet and landscape-gardener. The line "Seek for freedom at an inn," etc. (p. 517), is adapted from the verses headed *Written at an Inn at Henley*

SHOOL, shovel

"SHOWING THE CODE," etc. (p. 29), altered from *As You Like It*, Act. iv. sc. 3

SIGILLUM CONFESSIONIS, the seal of confession

SI NON PAYATIS, etc. (p. 246), If you do not pay, I will burn your monastery

SKAITH, hurt, harm

SMEARED WITH OIL (p. 429). The coronation of the French kings usually took place at Rheims

SMOCK-FACED, effeminate-looking, pale-faced

SNAPPED, snatched up, stolen

SOUTER, cobbler

SPREAGH, cattle carried of in a raiding expedition

STADT-HOUSE, or STADT-HAUS, the town-house, town-hall

STATIST, politician, statesman

STAVE AND TAIL, to strike the bear with a staff, and pull off the dogs by the tail, to separate them

STOUP, a flagon, deep narrow vessel for holding liquids

STRAICK, a measure of capacity=two bushels; the quantity of malt generally used for one brewing
SULLY, MAXIMILIEN DE BÉTHUNE, DUKE OF, author of *Mémoires des Sages et Royales Economies d'Estat de Henri le Grand* (1634-62)
SYNDIC, a magistrate, administrative officer

TABATIÈRE, snuff-box
TABOURET, stool
TAM MARTE QUAM MERCURIO, as distinguished for arms as for diplomacy
TASKER, labourer
TAURIDOR, bull-fighter
TENDER, to cherish, value, esteem
TERMAGUND, or TERMAGAUNT, an Oriental devil introduced into the mediæval mystery plays. *Compare* Mahound
TESTE-ST-GRIS, probably meant for "By the head of Christ"
TÊTE-BLEAU, or TÊTE-BLEU, TÊTE-DIEU, God's head—an oath
TEUFEL, the devil
THEBAIS, DESERTS OF, in the neighbourhood of Thebes on the Nile
"THE SMALL RARE VOLUME," etc. (p. 39), from Dr. John Ferriar's *Bibliomania, an Epistle to Richard Heber, Esq.* (1809)
TIFFANY, a kind of thin silk, gauze
TOCQUE, a small bonnet or low cap with narrow brim
TO-NAME, nickname, honourary descriptive title
TRIERS, or TRIER, Treves, in the Palatinate
TROUPE DORÉE, choice company, *élite*
TRUDCHEN, an affectionate diminutive of Gertrude

TWO AND A PLACK, two Scotch pennies and a plack=½d. English

UN HOMME COMME IL FAUT, a perfect gentleman

VACONELDIABLO, doubtless for *Baco el Diablo*, Bacchus (wine) the Devil
VÆ VICTIS, woe to the vanquished
VARIUM ET MUTABILE, fickle and changeable (are women)
VENTRE ST. GRIS, an oath presumed to be translatable as "the body of St. Christ"
VIEUX ROUTIER. *See* Routier
VIN ORDINAIRE, the wine in common use
VIVE BOURGOGNE, long live Burgundy!
VOLÉE, flight
VOTA DIIS EXAUDITA MALIGNIS, vows listened to by unfriendly-disposed deities

WALLACE WIGHT, Wallace the strong—a favourite designation of Scotland's great hero
WALLOONS. *See* Black Walloons
WAS HENKER, WHAT HENKER, what the deuce!
WEINKELLER, wine-cellar
WENCESLAUS, was emperor of Germany from 1378 to 1400. The reigning emperor at the time of this romance was Frederick IV. (1440-93)
WHILLYWHAWING, talking in an intimate way like lovers

YUNGFRAU, or JUNGFRAU, maiden, young woman

ZUCHTHAUS, prison

INDEX.

"AH! County Guy, the hour is nigh," 85
"Ah, freedom is a noble thing," 332
Anachronisms, 514, 537
Archers, Scottish, 86; quarrels of, 121, 524; banquet of, 123
Ardennes, Boar of. *See* Marck, William de la
Arnot, Scottish Archer, 126
Astrologer. *See* Galeotti
Author, his Introduction, 16

BALAFRÈ, Le, 65, 87; interview with his nephew, 88; contrasts Charles of Burgundy with Louis XI., 94; astonished at his nephew's fortune, 164; questioned by Louis XI., 372; refuses to kill Galeotti, 405; his honest stupidity, 442; carrying La Marck's head, 513; resigns his claims to Quentin, 516
Balue, Cardinal, 133; sent after Crèvecœur, 148; his horsemanship, 155, 525; intrigues with Crèvecœur, 158; dines with Louis XI., 173; his punishment, 402, 531
"Better kind fremit," etc., 101, 521
Bishop, Sir H. R., 84, 520
Blok, Nikkel, 305, 312; kills the bishop, 317
Bohemian, Bohemians. *See* Hayraddin, Marthon, Zamet, and Gipsies
Bonhomme, Jacques, 118
Boots, anecdote of, 433, 533
Brantôme, quoted, 531
Burgundy, Duke of. *See* Charles the Bold

CAMPO-BASSO, 423
Card-playing, 142, 524
Cent Nouvelles Nouvelles, 45, 519
Chaplain, Bishop of Liege's, 284
Charlemagne, Louis XI. and, 166, 525
Charles the Bold, meetings with Louis XI., 358, 529; rough reception of Comines and D'Hymbercourt, 386; his violent temper, 388, 421; holds a grand council, 453; reception of the herald, 466; thwarted by Isabelle, 487; offers her as a prize of war, 489; before Liege, 496
Charles the Simple, murder of, 397
Charlet, sent back with letters, 272; delivers them, 373
Chivalry, time of Louis XI., 7, 9, 42
Cologne, Three Kings of, 258
Comines, Philip des, meets Crèvecœur, 355; account of, 356, 529, 534; brings disagreeable news, 386; interview with Louis XI., 426; anecdote of Booted Head, 433, 533
"County Guy," song, 85
Covin tree, 66, 520
Crawford, Lord, 120; at the banquet, 124; arrests Orleans and Dunois, 226; prepares to defend Louis XI., 390; interview with Quentin, 442; recognises La Marck's head, 513
Crèvecœur, Count of, 142; defies Louis XI., 147; intrigues with Balue, 158; dines with Louis, 173; meets Quentin and Isabelle, 339; questions Quentin, 344; his vow of vengeance, 346; conversation with Des Comines and D'Hymbercourt, 355; announces the tidings from Liege, 387; conducts Louis XI to the town, 395; opposes Quentin's meeting with Isabelle, 446
Crèvecœur, Countess of, 457, 487
Croye, Lady Hameline, 181; questions Quentin, 216; her note to him, 288; escape from Schonwaldt, 294; letter to Isabelle, 493
Croye, Lady Isabelle, at the inn, 74; song of "County Guy," 85; reason of her journey, 125; demanded by Crèvecœur, 145; in

R—Vol. 16

the gallery, 181; attentions from Orleans, 186; Louis XI.'s conspiracy against her, 196; journeys to Liege, 214; dresses Quentin's wound, 231; her trust in him, 264; rescued by him, 302; sheltered in Pavillon's House, 323; thanks Trudchen, 328; flight from Liege, 329; falls in with Crèvecœur, 339; interview with Quentin, 447; before the grand council, 456; refuses to wed Orleans, 487; offered as a prize of war, 489, 536; gets her aunt's letter, 493; sends intelligence to Quentin, 495

Cunningham, Scottish Archer, 111, 117, 124

DAIN, Oliver, 134, 524; summons Quentin, 163; in consultation with Louis XI., 191, 375; makes friends for him, 441

Dibdin, Dr., at Château de Hautlieu, 36

Dorothy, Aunt, marriage of, 19

Douglas, Earl of, murder of, 171, 525

Dunois, Count of, 131; reports Crèvecœur's arrival, 139; assails Quentin, 224; taken into custody, 226; his courage before Liege, 507

Durward, Quentin, 49; arrives at the Cher, 51; converses with Louis XI., 54, 63; at breakfast, 70; first glimpse of Isabelle, 74; questions the host, 81; hears the lute, 84; interview with Le Balafré, 88; reflections, 99; inquires for Maître Pierre, 101; cuts down the Bohemian, 103; condemned to death, 106; rescued, 111; enrolled in the Scottish Archers, 121; in the presence-chamber, 130; apology from Tristan, 135; rescues Louis XI., 160; summoned before him, 163; in Roland's Gallery, 166; made sentinel, 172, 178; sees Isabelle, 180; allows Orleans to pass, 185; reprimanded, 190; interview with Galeotti, 204; escorts the Ladies of Croye, 214; attacked by Dunois and Orleans, 223; his wound dressed by Isabelle, 231; questions Hayraddin, 235; discovers his treachery, 249; has his fortune told, 265; pays Hayraddin, 273; bidden leave the garden, 276; scene with the people of Liege, 277, 527; receives Lady Hameline's note, 288; roused by Hayraddin, 293; rescues Lady Hameline, 294; returns for Isabelle, 299; saves Pavillon, 301; finds Isabelle, 302; seizes Carl Eberson, 318; sheltered in Pavillon's house, 323; flight from Liege, 330; falls in with Crèvecœur, 339; questioned by him, 343; his descent ridiculed, 350; his report to Lord Crawford, 442; interview with Isabelle, 447; before the Burgundian council, 460; at Hayraddin's execution, 478; secures Klepper, 483; gives Isabelle the note, 493; reports La Marck's stratagem, 500; on outpost duty, 502; seeks to encounter La Marck, 509; saves Trudchen, 512

EBERSON, Carl, 314; seized by Quentin, 318

Europe, time of Louis XI., 14

Evil, principle of, in literature, 8

FÉNELON, his description of Louis XI., 13

Ferne, *Blazon of Gentrie*, quoted 535

Feudal superior, rights of, 15

Fleur de Lys, inn, 68; host of, 80

France, style of living in, 18; time of Louis XI., 41

GALEOTTI, Martius, interview with Louis XI., 205, 526; despises his reward, 211; summoned before him, 412; predicts his death, 417, 532

Gascon, the, 214, 223

Geislaer, Peterkin, 304

Gipsies, threaten Quentin, 104; attacked by soldiers, 106; in France, 105, 521; religion of, 236, 526

Glorieux, Le, 360; description of, 384; jests on Louis, 399; fetches Galeotti, 412

Glover, Hans, 330, 341

Goethe, *Faust*, 8

Golden Fleece, order of, 143, 524

Gregory, Dr., 524

Gueldres, Duke of, 72, 520

Guthrie, Scottish Archer, 118, 126

HAFLINGHEM, passage of arms at, 217

Hautlieu, Marquis of, 21; his château, 23; on English literature, 29; on Sully's château, 30; Au-

INDEX.

thor's dinner with, 33; his library, 36

Hayraddin Maugrabin, 234; questioned by Quentin, 235; his tricks on the monks, 243; his plot, 250; tells Quentin's fortune, 265; claims his hire, 273; awakens Quentin, 293; disguised as a herald, 465; chased by dogs, 472; his execution, 477; imparts a secret to Quentin, 481

Herald, disguised, 11, 534. *See also* Hayraddin Maugrabin

Hughes, *Itinerary of Provence*, 32, 519

Hymbercourt, Baron d', 356, 529; brings disagreeable news, 386

INTRODUCTION, Author's, 7, 16

JACQUELINE. See Croye, Isabelle de

Joan, Princess, her marriage with Orleans, 132, 138, 153, 525; description of, 137; in Roland's Gallery, 180

KLEPPER, Hayraddin's pony, 261, 483

LA JEUNESSE, Marquis de Hautlieu's factotum, 33

Lanzknecht, 251

Leslies, feud with the Ogilvies, 90; descent of, 515, 537

Lesly, Ludovic. See Balafré, Le

Liege, people of, 245; town, 276; scene in, 277; siege of, 502, 536

Liege, Bishop of, 268; murder of, 317

Lindesay, Scottish Archer, 118, 125

Loches, Castle of, 229

Louis XI., character of, 7, 42; watches Quentin's approach, 51; his personal appearance, 53; converses with Quentin, 54, 63; gives him a breakfast, 70; waited on by Countess Isabelle, 74; holds court, 136; reception of Crèvecœur, 142; sends Balue after him, 148; teazes Balue, 152; policy regarding Princess Joan, 153, 525; at the boarhunt, 158; rescued by Quentin, 160; and Charlemagne, 166, 525; posts Quentin as sentinel, 172; entertains Crèvecœur and Balue, 173; his humour, 176, 526; reprimands Quentin, 190; in consultation with Oliver le Dain, 191, 375; his superstition, 199, 533; interview with Galeotti, 204; meets Charles at Péronne, 362; his suspicious character, 366, 530; his lodging at Péronne, 369; inquires about Quentin, 372; methods of corruption, 381; at the banquet, 383; put in the tower, 395, 530; reflections on Charles the Simple's end, 401; prayer to the Lady of Cléry, 402, 531; sounds Le Balafré, 404; condemns Galeotti to death, 407; his love of vengeance, 408, 532; interview with Galeotti, 413; conversation with Comines, 426; his speech before the Burgundian council, 455; before Liege, 499

MADELON, of Château Hautlieu, 25

Marck, William de la, 310; causes the bishop to be killed, 317; his bride, 493, 536; in battle, 509; death of, 513

Margaret, Princess of Scotland, 525

Marthon, the Bohemian, 295

Mephistophiles, 8

Mercenary troops, 42, 251, 338, 528

Montl'héry, 358, 529

Morrison, Fynes, quoted, 528

OGILVIES, feud with the Leslies, 90

Oliver le Dain. See Dain, Oliver le

Oriflamme, French national flag, 125

Orleans, Duke of, 131; relations to Princess Joan, 132, 138, 153; fear of Louis XI., 139; enters Roland's Gallery, 185; attempts to carry off Isabelle, 222; taken into custody, 226; proposed alliance with Isabelle, 485

PAVILLON, the syndic, 277; rescued by Quentin, 301; takes Isabelle under his protection, 307; his lament to Geislaer, 323; shelters Isabelle and Quentin, 323; gives money to Quentin, 326

Pavillon, Mabel, 323; lectures Trudchen, 329

Pavillon, Trudchen, 282; thanked by Isabelle, 329; saved by Quentin, 512

Péronne, 355, 528; Earl Herbert's Tower, 395

Petit André, the humorous hangman, 109; acts as guide, 219; prepares for Galeotti, 410; hangs Hayraddin, 477; note on, 523

Picturesque, Price on, 24, 519

Pierre, Maître. See Louis XI.

Plessis-lès-Tours, Castle of, 49, 61
Printing, invention of, 206, 526
Prior, Franciscan, 243
Prize of honour, 491, 536

Quentin Durward, the novel, 7

RIZPAH. *See* Marthon
Rouge Sanglier. *See* Hayraddin
Rouslaer, of Liege, 278

ST. HUBERT, 59, 519
St. Paul, Constable, 73, 520
St. Quentin, 73
Schonwaldt, Castle of, 269; garden, 275; assault on, 292, 298; revel in, 310
Schwarzreiters, 338, 528
Scottish Archers. *See* Archers, Scottish
Scottish auxiliaries, in France, 123, 524. *See also* Archers, Scottish
Seneschal of Péronne Castle, 396
Skene dhu, 103, 521
Sorel, Agnes, 10
Squire of Lowe Degree, 272, 527

Stephens, Miss, 84, 520
Stilts, use of, 89, 520
Sully, Duke of, 30

TOISON D'OR, Burgundian herald, 147; questions Rouge Sanglier, 469
Tristan l'Hermite, 51; condemns Quentin to death, 106; worsted by the Scottish Archers, 114; apologises to Quentin, 135; takes charge of Dunois and Orleans, 229; prepares to execute Galeotti, 410; the historical person, 532
Trois-Eschelles, the lugubrious hangman, 109; at Péronne, 410; hangs Hayraddin, 177
Troyes, Jean de, his *Chronicle*, 191, 523
Trudchen. *See* Pavillon, Trudchen

WETZWEILER, Tiel. *See* Glorieux, Le

ZAMET MAUGRABIN, 103

END OF QUENTIN DURWARD.